Judicial review proceedings

a practitioner's guide

Jonathan Manning was called to the Bar in 1989 and joined Arden Chambers as a founder member in 1993. He specialises in public law and human rights, local government and housing law. He is co-author of *Local Government Constitutional and Administrative Law* (2nd edn, 2008, Sweet & Maxwell), *A Guide to the Greater London Authority* (2000, Sweet & Maxwell), and *Blackstone's Guide to the Anti-social Behaviour Act 2003* (2004, OUP). He regularly lectures on judicial review.

Sarah Salmon is a barrister at Arden Chambers. After graduating from university, she obtained an LLM in Public Law at University College London focusing on administrative law, judicial review and human rights. Sarah practises in local government, housing and landlord and tenant law, with a particular emphasis on anti-social behaviour, education, and the public law aspects of housing law. Sarah is an assistant editor of the *Encyclopaedia of Housing Law* (Sweet & Maxwell) and has written for *Journal of Housing Law*, *New Law Journal* and *Solicitors Journal*.

Robert Brown was called to the Bar in 2008 after working in the civil service, local government and the charity sector. During that time he gained experience of bringing and defending judicial review claims. He joined Arden Chambers in 2010 and specialises in public law and housing. Robert is an editor of the *Housing Law Reports* and co-authored the *Current Law* annotations on the Localism Act 2011 and the Local Government Finance Act 2012.

Available as an ebook at www.lag.org.uk/ebooks

The purpose of the Legal Action Group is to promote equal access to justice for all members of society who are socially, economically or otherwise disadvantaged. To this end, it seeks to improve law and practice, the administration of justice and legal services.

Judicial review proceedings

a practitioner's guide

THIRD EDITION

Jonathan Manning, Sarah Salmon and Robert Brown

 Legal Action Group
2013

This edition published in Great Britain 2013
by LAG Education and Service Trust Limited
242 Pentonville Road, London N1 9UN
www.lag.org.uk

British Library Cataloguing in Publication Data
a CIP catalogue record for this book is available from the British Library.

This book has been produced using Forest Stewardship Council (FSC) certified paper. The wood used to produce FSC certified products with a 'Mixed Sources' label comes from FSC certified well-managed forests, controlled sources and/or recycled material.

Print ISBN   978 1 903307 79 3
ebook ISBN   978 1 908407 16 0

Typeset by Regent Typesetting, London
Printed in Great Britain by Hobbs the Printers, Totton, Hampshire

For Guy and Edward

Preface

In the preface to the second edition of this book, I reflected (some might say self-indulgently) that the increase in its girth in the nine years since the first edition mirrored the development of my own physique. By way of a strange parallel, the nine years since the second edition saw the birth of my two children; now I also have the delight of two co-authors for this third edition. Without wishing to get too introspective, their addition to my judicial review family has improved the quality of my life and of this edition in equally large measure.

The legal developments which we have sought to reflect in the third edition have in some ways been more subtle than those which came about prior to the last edition. Then, for example, we had the Human Rights Act 1998, the new CPR Part 54 procedural regime and the birth of the domestic proportionality jurisdiction to deal with. This time around, the main changes have been either in the way that these concepts and provisions have evolved or in areas of substantive law which we have once again sought to summarise in the subject chapters in the middle of the book. The creation of a judicial review jurisdiction in the Upper Tribunal is an interesting development; the changes to legal aid (as we can now call it again) an increasingly depressing one, of which we have been unable to take full account, as the latest proposals, including the removal of legal aid for the permission stage of judicial review proceedings, were only announced after we had delivered the manuscript (in a cynical move by the Secretary of State). That particular proposal, if implemented, is likely to have a profound impact on the ability of judicial review to hold public bodies to account.

Despite these changes and developments, however, the essential aim of this book has remained the same: to provide a comprehensive introduction to the law and practice of judicial review and to explain both in as straightforward a manner as we are able. I hope that we have been able to achieve that aim.

The law is stated as at 1 March 2013, although we have taken account of subsequent developments where possible.

Jonathan Manning
Arden Chambers
London

June 2013

Acknowledgments

We must first express our debt of gratitude to our publisher at LAG, Esther Pilger, for persevering with us to publication of this edition. The level of our indebtedness greatly exceeds even that which precipitated the global economic crisis. We are also very grateful to everyone else at LAG who worked on this edition with their customary efficiency, patience, good humour and helpfulness.

We should also like to express our thanks, once again, to Andrew Arden QC for his continuing support and practical help, both in relation to this edition and generally over the last 23 (Jonathan), 6 (Sarah) and 4 (Robert) years respectively. It was he who introduced the first edition of this work to LAG back in 1994.

Sam Madge-Wyld updated and wrote the first draft of chapter 8, (Judicial review and immigration and asylum law), and we are extremely grateful to him for doing so, not least because his knowledge and experience of that area of work has been of immense benefit to us.

On a personal note, we should all like to thank our families for their patient support, although regrettably, on this occasion, none of us managed to evade any particularly onerous domestic obligations involving subterranean renovations (so far as we are aware).[1]

There are many other people who have given their time, help and support, and still more who have refrained from telling us just how annoyed they are with us, and to all of them we offer our sincere thanks.

---

1   See second edition, Acknowledgements, p ix.

Contents

Table of cases

Table of statutes

Table of statutory instruments

Table of European legislation

Abbreviations

ADR	alternative dispute resolution
AJA	Access to Justice Act
CA	Children Act
DPA	Data Protection Act
EA	Equality Act
ECJ	Court of Justice of the European Union
ECJ	European Court of Justice
ECtHR	European Court of Human Rights
EEA	European Economic Area
FOIA	Freedom of Information Act
FTT	First-tier Tribunal
GLC	Greater London Council
HESC	Health, Education and Social Care Chamber
HRA	Human Rights Act
ICO	Information Commissioner's Office
IPCC	Independent Police Complaints Commission
IRP	Independent Review Panel
LAA	Legal Aid Agency
LASPOA	Legal Aid, Sentencing and Punishment of Offenders Act
LEA	local education authority
LSC	Legal Services Commission
MEP	member of the European Parliament
NIAA	Nationality, Immigration and Asylum Act
NPPF	National Planning Policy Framework
OIA	Office of the Independent Adjudicator for Higher Education
PACE	Police and Criminal Evidence Act 1984
PAT	Police Appeals Tribunal
PCO	protective costs order
PSED	Public Sector Equality Duty
RSC	Rules of the Supreme Court
SCA	Senior Courts Act
SENDIST	Special Educational Needs and Disability Tribunal
SENT	Special Educational Needs Tribunal
SSFA	School Standards and Framework Act
TCEA	Tribunals, Courts and Enforcement Act
TCPA	Town and Country Planning Act
TEU	Treaty of European Union
TFEU	Treaty on the Functioning of the European Union
UT	Upper Tribunal

CHAPTER 1

Sources of law

Introduction

1.1 There are three main legal sources that feed into the law of judicial review. The first is common law – judicial review is a common law remedy. The second and third sources derive from Europe: European Union law and human rights law. In this chapter, each will be briefly examined.

Common law

1.2 The power of the High Court to entertain challenges to the decisions of government and other public bodies has been developed by the courts themselves. The provisions of the Senior Courts Act 1981[1] and rules of court do not create the jurisdiction, but merely regulate it in essentially procedural terms.

1.3 Indeed, the courts have consistently rejected parliamentary attempts to limit or remove its supervisory jurisdiction. An example of this has been the attitude of the courts to ouster, finality and 'no certiorari' clauses.[2]

1.4 The courts have, however, accepted constitutional limits to their powers: Acts of Parliament are not susceptible to review, nor are certain exercises of royal prerogative.[3] In addition, where Parliament has provided a different form of remedy, such as a statutory right of appeal, the courts have been willing to accept that judicial review will generally not be available.[4]

---

1 Formerly the Supreme Court Act 1981, its name was amended by the Constitutional Reform Act 2005, presumably to avoid confusion once the new Supreme Court took over the judicial role formerly undertaken by the Appellate Committee of the House of Lords.

2 See, eg, *Anisminic Ltd v Foreign Compensation Commission* [1969] 2 AC 147, HL; *R v Medical Appeal Tribunal ex p Gilmore* [1957] 1 QB 574, CA. See paras 7.69–7.80 below.

3 These were, in traditional terms, entirely 'forbidden areas' as to which the court could not assert jurisdiction (see paras 2.55–2.65 below). The extent of such areas is now considerably more open to question, especially where matters of EU law and/or Convention rights under the HRA 1998 are also in play.

4 See generally, on alternative remedies, paras 7.15–7.30. The existence of a right of appeal does not always rule out judicial review, however: see, eg, *Ellis & Sons Fourth Amalgamated Properties v Southern Rent Assessment Panel* (1984) 14 HLR 48, QBD, in which the court held that judicial review was a preferable remedy to the statutory right of appeal, and see now also *R (Cart) v Upper Tribunal* [2011] UKSC 28, [2012] 1 AC 663 as to the relationship between the right of appeal to the Upper Tribunal and judicial review.

European Union and human rights law

1.5 Public law in England and Wales is no longer comprehensible without an understanding of the principles and effect of European Union law and European human rights law, which engage with domestic law at a number of points and on different levels. The majority of these engagements are discussed elsewhere in (and throughout) this book as part of the treatment of the substantive topics to which they relate. The starting-point of this explanation of the interaction between domestic law and law from Europe is, however, to be found in the following sections of this chapter. The next section contains a basic outline of the institutions and principles of EU law. The final section introduces European human rights law and the Human Rights Act 1998.

European Union law

Institutions of the European Union

The Council of the European Union

1.6 The Council of the European Union comprises representatives from each member state, who must be authorised to 'commit' the government of that state.[5] Usually, the minister responsible for the particular matter under discussion will be the state's representative. The Council meets whenever convened by the President of the Council, whether of his own motion or at the request of either a member state or of the Commission.[6] Each member state holds the presidency of the council for six months, during which time its representative will arrange, set the agenda for and chair meetings, and may well initiate policies in areas of concern to the state in question or to the Council as a whole.

1.7 The Council's functions are set out in article 16 of the Treaty of the European Union and articles 290 and 291 of the Treaty on the Functioning of the European Union. Most important among these is to decide whether legislative proposals from the Commission (see para 1.10 below) will become law. Such decisions are taken by vote, requiring either unanimity or a qualified or simple majority depending upon the provisions of the treaty article governing the

5 Treaty of European Union (TEU) art 16.
6 Treaty on the Functioning of the European Union (TFEU) art 237.

subject-matter in question. The Council may ask the Commission to formulate proposals for legislation that it considers desirable for the attainment of common objectives.[7] It may also delegate to the Commission power to pass further regulations on any particular matter, although this may be subject to the condition that such regulations are acceptable to a committee (or committees) comprised of representatives of the member states, to ensure that such regulations accord with the Council's own wishes.

1.8   The Council has additional powers relating to the police and judiciary in criminal matters.[8]

The European Council

1.9   The European Council consists of the member states' heads of government, together with the President of the Commission, assisted by the members' foreign ministers and other Commission officials. It must meet at least twice a year under the chairmanship of the member whose state currently holds the presidency of the Council, and must submit a report to the European Parliament after each such meeting, and an annual report on the progress achieved by the Union. Its role is to provide the Union with 'the necessary impetus for its development' and to 'define the general political directions and priorities thereof'.[9]

The Commission

1.10   The most important aspect of the Commission's role is the initiation of legislation, upon which the Council of the European Union acts, and the shaping of general policy strategies for the EU as a whole. The Commission also exercises powers, delegated from the Council of the EU, to make subordinate legislation in the form of regulations.[10] Its main administrative function is to oversee the implementation of legislation by the member states to ensure that the rules are commonly and uniformly applied. The Commission also plays an important role in the formulation of the EU's budget and in external relations.

---

7   TFEU art 241.
8   TEU art 82.
9   TEU art 15.
10 TFEU art 289.

1.11   The Commission is comprised of 27 commissioners[11] who must be persons 'whose independence is beyond doubt' and who 'shall neither seek nor take instructions from any government or other institution, body, office or entity'.[12] Until 31 October 2014, the Commission will consist of one commissioner for each member state. From 1 November 2014, the number of commissioners will be equivalent to two-thirds of the number of member states. Commissioners will then be chosen from among the member states on the basis of strictly equal rotation between them. Commissioners are nominated by national governments, each member state being entitled to either one or two commissioners, subject to a vote of approval by the European Parliament. The President of the Commission is nominated by the European Council for election by the European Parliament by a majority of its component members. Appointment to membership of the Commission requires the common accord of the Council and the President-Elect.[13]

1.12   There is also an extensive Commission bureaucracy, organised into directorates general, each covering one of the major fields of activity and headed by a director general. Under the director general are several directors who run the various directorates within the directorate general.

The European Parliament

1.13   The Parliament is an autonomous body, currently comprising 736 members of the European Parliament (MEPs), who are directly elected representatives of each member state, elected according to the national electoral procedures of the state in question.[14] The distribution of seats broadly reflects the distribution of population across the Union. Members are elected for a term of five years, and sit in political rather than national groupings. The Parliament determines its own methods of operation and adopts its own rules of procedure.[15] It elects its own President together with 14 vice-presidents for two-and-a-half-year terms, who form the Bureau of Parliament.

1.14   The Parliament has no power to initiate legislation, but does have various roles in the legislative process. In some cases, it must be

---

11 The number may be altered by the Council, acting unanimously: TEU art 17.

12 TEU art 17.

13 TEU art 17.

14 The Lisbon Treaty allows for 751 MEPs, but it had not come into force when elections for the Parliament were most recently held.

15 TFEU art 232.

consulted before legislation can be adopted, and a failure to wait for its opinion can result in the measure being annulled,[16] although the Council is not obliged to act in accordance with its opinion. In other cases, the Council can only adopt the legislative measure if the Parliament has approved it or failed to take a decision within three months. Alternatively, the Parliament can reject or propose amendments to the proposal by absolute majority. If the measure is rejected, it can only be adopted by unanimous vote of the Council. If it is amended, the Commission must re-examine it, in the light of the amendments, and the Council may then adopt or further amend the Commission's amendments by unanimity, and adopt the measure by qualified majority. In yet other cases, the Parliament has an effective right of veto if it votes by an absolute majority to reject the measure. If it proposes amendments, these must be re-examined by the Commission and the Council, in a manner similar to that described above.

The Court of Justice of the European Union

1.15   The Court of Justice of the European Union[17] currently consists of 27 judges, assisted by eight advocates general. They are appointed by agreement of the member states for a term of six years. Attached to the ECJ is the General Court,[18] which has jurisdiction to hear and determine certain classes of action (subject to appeal on a point of law to the ECJ). The General Court also consists of 27 judges. It has no advocates general, but the members of the General Court may be called upon to perform the task of an advocate general.[19]

1.16   Currently, the General Court has power to hear all actions brought by 'non-privileged' parties, ie parties other than member states or Community institutions, as well as staff disputes within those institutions and appeals against some Commission decisions.[20] Although the ECJ has general competence to give preliminary rulings, the General Court may, in specific cases, also be entrusted with that responsibility by the ECJ Statute.

1.17   The ECJ is the final court of appeal of the EU. Its most important function is to 'ensure that in the interpretation and application of

---

16 See, eg, *European Parliament v Council (Generalised Tariff Preferences)* [1995] ECR I–643.

17 Commonly referred to as the European Court of Justice (ECJ).

18 Formerly known as the Court of First Instance.

19 Statute of the Court of Justice of the European Union (ECJ Statute), art 49.

20 See TFEU art 256.

[the EC Treaty], the law is observed'.[21] The court has used this provision to extend its jurisdiction over bodies not expressly subject to it (such as the European Parliament) and over functions beyond those referred to in the EC Treaty. It also now has power to impose pecuniary penalties against member states that have failed to comply with previous judgments against them or failed to fulfil their obligations to notify measures transposing a directive.[22]

The Court of Auditors

1.18 The Court of Auditors has the status of the 'fifth Community institution', since the enactment of the Treaty of the EU.[23] Its principal role is to scrutinise the finances of the EU and ensure sound financial management. It also assists the Parliament and the Council in the control of the implementation of the budget.

Types of EU legislation

1.19 There are three main types of legislative instrument: regulations, decisions and directives. Articles 288–292 of the Treaty on the Functioning of the European Union provide that:

> In order to carry out their task and in accordance with the provisions of this Treaty, the European Parliament acting jointly with the Council, the Council and the Commission shall make regulations and issue directives, take decisions, make recommendations or deliver opinions.

> A regulation shall have general application. It shall be binding in its entirety and directly applicable in all member states.

> A directive shall be binding, as to the result to be achieved, upon each Member State to which it is addressed, but shall leave to the national authorities the choice of form and methods.

> A decision shall be binding in its entirety upon those to whom it is addressed.

> Recommendations and opinions shall have no binding force.

---

21 TEU art 19. For the court's jurisdiction generally, see TFEU arts 258–279.
22 TFEU art 260. The ECJ has held that penalties may take the form of both a penalty payment (a fine at a daily rate) and a lump sum: Case C-304/02 *Commission v France* [2005] ECR I-6263, [2005] CMLR 13.
23 TEU art 13. Its role is set out in TFEU arts 285–287.

Regulations

1.20   In most instances, the Treaty does not specify the form in which legislation is to be made. Regulations are the form of legislation most akin to national primary or subordinate legislation. They apply to all member states and are directly applicable.

1.21   The term 'directly applicable' has two meanings. First, regulations take effect as part of the member states' national legal systems without the need for any national legislation to incorporate them. Indeed, national legislation purporting to enact them would be contrary to EU law, as it would 'jeopardise the simultaneous and uniform application in the whole of the Community',[24] and may 'affect the jurisdiction of the court to pronounce on any question involving the interpretation of Community law ... which means that no procedure is permissible whereby the Community nature of a legal rule is concealed from those subject to it'.[25]

1.22   Secondly, the term has been interpreted by the ECJ as meaning that regulations create rights that individuals can enforce through their own national courts.[26]

1.23   The ECJ will decide whether what purports to be a regulation is in fact a regulation in substance. If it is not, it will take effect as a decision.

Decisions

1.24   Decisions may be addressed to member states or to companies (for instance in competition cases), but they are binding in their entirety upon their addressees, taking effect when notified to them. The Council may delegate to the Commission the power to take decisions that the Council itself could take.[27]

Directives

1.25   Directives do not necessarily bind all member states; only those to whom they are addressed. While they are binding as to the result to be achieved, they leave it to the individual state to determine the form and method of implementation. The ECJ has held, however, that like regulations, directives have direct effect enabling individuals to rely on them in actions against the state (though not necessarily

24 *Commission v Italy* Case 39/72 [1973] ECR 101.
25 *Variola v Amministrazione delle Finanze* Case 34/73 [1973] ECR 981.
26 See paras 1.35–1.47 below.
27 TFEU art 290.

in other types of action).[28] A state may be liable in damages for failing to implement a directive, even if it was not directly effective at the time.[29]

Recommendations and opinions

1.26 The fact that these measures have no binding force does not prevent a member state from seeking a ruling from the ECJ as to their validity or interpretation.[30]

Effect of EU law

Interpretation

1.27 Significant areas of UK law enforced by the UK courts now come into play directly from Europe.[31] In this context, it is appropriate to draw attention to the different approach taken under European law – and, importantly, also by UK courts when considering either primary or secondary legislation intended to implement European directives[32] – from that traditionally taken under domestic law. When considering European provisions, a predominantly purposive, or teleological, interpretation is to be applied, designed to give effect to the spirit rather than the letter of the provision, even filling in gaps as they may appear.[33]

1.28 It may be that, with the advance of the purposive approach to construction in English law, the distinction between the approaches may gradually erode but, *Pepper v Hart*[34] notwithstanding, there can be

---

28 See, *eg*, *Van Duyn v Home Office* [1974] ECR 1337.

29 *Francovich v Italy* Case C-6/90; *Bonifaci v Italy* Case C-9/90 [1991] ECR I-5357, [1993] 2 CMLR 66.

30 See, eg, *Grimaldi v Fonds des Maladies Professionelles* Case C-322/88 [1989] ECR 4407.

31 Some of the best known, outside the commercial arena, arise in the context of employment, social security and consumer law.

32 *Litster v Forth Dry Dock Engineering Co Ltd* [1990] 1 AC 546, HL.

33 *HP Bulmer Ltd v J Bollinger SA* [1974] Ch 41, CA; *R v Henn* [1981] AC 850, HL.

34 [1993] AC 593, HL, and subsequent cases, eg, *Sidhu v British Airways plc* [1997] AC 430, HL. In *Pepper v Hart*, the House of Lords accepted for the first time, on strict conditions, it would be permissible for the court, construing the meaning of a statutory provision, to have regard to statements that were made during parliamentary debates, reported in *Hansard*. The conditions are (a) that the statutory provision in question is ambiguous or obscure (which means more than that the parties disagree as to its meaning); (b) that the statement referred to was made by the sponsor of the Bill; and (c) that the statement is sufficiently clear.

no doubt that, at present, the starting points are different: in English law, the court starts with the wording, resorting to additional material – whether or not including *Hansard* – where necessary to seek an alternative interpretation; in European law, and when implementing it, the court will start with the purpose or intention and apply the wording accordingly.

Supremacy of Community law

1.29 The European Communities Act 1972 gives Community law primacy over national law.[35] The courts are required to interpret national law in accordance with EU legislation, whether that legislation was enacted before or after the national legislation.[36] Community law must also be given primacy over any incompatible domestic legislation.[37]

1.30 This does not mean, however, that courts are required to disapply domestic legislation that is incompatible with rights arising under the European Convention on Human Rights, notwithstanding the reference to the Convention (on which see paras 1.50–1.55 below) in the EU Treaty.[38]

1.31 It is for national courts to determine how to protect an individual whose rights under EU law have been infringed.[39] While the ECJ does not require national courts to create new remedies for the enforcement of EU rights which would not be available under national law,[40] nevertheless rights derived from EU law must be protected with remedies no less favourable than those applicable to analogous rights

---

35 Section 2(1) concerning existing law and s2(4) on subsequent law. See also *Macarthys Ltd v Smith* [1979] 3 All ER 325, CA at 328, and [1981] QB 180, ECJ and CA; *R v Secretary of State for Transport ex p Factortame (No 1)* [1990] 2 AC 85, HL.

36 *Marleasing SA v La Comercial Internacional de Alimentacion SA* [1990] ECR I-4135, ECJ (considered at para 1.45 below).

37 *Costa v ENEL* [1964] ECR 585; *Administrazione delle Finanze dello Stato v Simmenthal SpA* [1978] ECR 629, ECJ; *A v Chief Constable of West Yorkshire* [2004] UKHL 21.

38 TEU, art 6. Case C-571/10 *Kamberaj v Istituto per l'Edilizia sociale della Provincia autonoma di Bolzano*. The powers under the Human Rights Act 1998 to interpret and strike down domestic legislation are considered at paras 1.75–1.94 below.

39 *Rewe-Zentralfinanz eG and Rewe-Zentral AG v Landwirtschaftskammerfur das Saarland Case* 33/76 [1976] ECR 1989, ECJ].

40 *Rewe-Handelsgesellschaft Nord mbH v Hauptzollamt Kiel Case* 158/80 [1981] ECR 1805.

arising under domestic law.[41] The penalties imposed by member states for breach of European provisions must, however, be proportionate.[42] The ECJ has also held that if the right to seek judicial review is to be an effective remedy, it will generally be required that reasons are given for decisions curtailing or denying EU rights, and that a person seeking to defend the EU right must be able to do so under the 'best possible conditions.'[43]

1.32　　A certain tension has arisen, however, between the principle that member states need not create new remedies ('national autonomy'), and the principle that EU rights must be given effective protection ('effectiveness'). In *R v Secretary of State for Transport ex p Factortame Ltd (No 2)*,[44] the ECJ held that any provision of a national legal system, and any legislative, administrative or judicial practice which impaired the effectiveness of EU law by withholding from the national courts the power to do everything necessary to set aside national legislative provisions, which might prevent, even temporarily, EU rules from having full force and effect are incompatible with the requirements of the EU Treaty. This was as much the case where the rule prevented the grant of relief in any given circumstances, including interim relief. Accordingly, 'a court which in those circumstances would grant interim relief, if it were not for a rule of national law, is obliged to set aside that rule'. It appears, therefore, that the principle of 'effectiveness' must take precedence over the principle of national autonomy.

1.33　　In addition, in *Francovich*,[45] the ECJ held that each member state must make provision to permit claims for compensation against the state for breach of EU law. The court gave very little guidance concerning the circumstances in which such a remedy must be available, and such guidance as it did give related only to the non- or mis-implementation of directives: that the directive should entail the grant of rights to individuals; that it should be possible to identify the content of those rights from the provisions of the directive; and that there must be a causal link between the breach of the state's

---

41　It is because of this that a Community right will be brought into the public law forum and will be enforceable by public law remedies by way of judicial review. See *Burgoin SA v Minister of Agriculture, Fisheries and Food* [1986] QB 716, CA.

42　*Sagulo, Brenca and Bakhouche* Case 8/77 [1977] ECR 1495.

43　*UNECTEF v Heylens* Case 222/84 [1987] ECR 4097 at para 15.

44　[1991] 1 AC 603, ECJ and HL.

45　*Francovich v Italy* Case C-6/90; *Bonifaci v Italy* Case C-9/90 [1991] ECR I–5357.

obligation and the harm suffered.[46] The court has since added a further condition that the breach must be sufficiently serious.[47]

1.34 The UK courts have demonstrated a willingness to apply directly effective provisions directly, even if this involves setting aside an inconsistent Act of Parliament, as in *R v Secretary of State for Transport ex p Factortame Ltd (No 2)* where the House of Lords spelt out that the operation of a statute may be suspended pending the resolution of a European challenge.[48] Judicial review of an inconsistent Act is also, now, possible.[49] In the case of non-directly effective provisions, the courts have shown themselves willing to apply domestic legislation in conformity with them, even where this is not in accordance with the *prima facie* meaning of the words used.[50]

Direct effect

1.35 This doctrine applies to treaty provisions, regulations and certain directives. It was first enunciated by the ECJ in the case of *Van Gend en Loos*.[51] In that case, which related to the imposition of import duties on goods imported from Germany to the Netherlands, the applicant appealed against payment of the duty, contending that it was in contravention of article 12 of the EC Treaty (now TFEU art 30). The national court referred to the ECJ the question whether that article had direct application, in the sense that nationals of a state could use it as the basis of a claim to rights which the court must protect. The ECJ held that the European Community (as it was then known) constituted a new system of international law:[52]

> ... for the benefit of which states have limited their sovereign rights, albeit within limited fields, and the subjects of which comprise not only member states but also their nationals. Independently of the legislation of member states, Community law therefore not only imposes obligations on individuals but is also intended to confer upon them rights which become part of their legal heritage. These rights arise

---

46 See also *Spencer v Secretary of State for Work and Pensions* [2008] EWCA Civ 750.
47 *Brasserie du Pecheur SA v Germany* Case C-46/93; *R v Secretary of State for Transport ex p Factortame Ltd and others* (No 3) C-48/93 [1996] ECR I–1029.
48 [1991] 1 AC 603, ECJ and HL.
49 *Equal Opportunities Commission v Secretary of State for Employment* [1995] 1 AC 1, HL.
50 See, eg, *Webb v EMO Air Cargo (UK) Ltd* [1993] 1 WLR 49, HL; *Pickstone v Freemans* [1989] 1 AC 66, HL.
51 *NV Algemene Transporten Expeditie Onderneming van Gend en Loos v Nederlandse Administratie der Belastingen* Case 26/62 [1963] ECR 1.
52 [1963] ECR 1 at [12].

not only where they are expressly granted by the Treaty, but also by reason of obligations which the Treaty imposes in a clearly defined way upon individuals as well as upon the member states and upon the institutions of the Community.

1.36 The conditions for direct effect, set out by the ECJ in *Van Gend en Loos*, were that the provision laid down a clear and unconditional prohibition, which was a negative obligation, not qualified by any reservation on the part of states and not requiring any legislative intervention by them.[53] The fact that the subjects of the obligation under article 12[54] were the member states themselves did not imply that their nationals could not benefit from the obligation.

1.37 The ECJ has extended this principle in subsequent cases. In *Reyners v Belgium*,[55] for example, it stated that the principles of freedom of movement and establishment by self-employed workers, and of non-discrimination were directly effective, even though the Community legislation implementing the relevant articles of the EC Treaty[56] had not yet been adopted. The rule of equal treatment with nationals was one of the fundamental legal provisions of the Community. It required the achievement of a precise result, made easier by implementing measures but not dependent upon them. The directives provided for by the EC Treaty were superfluous with regard to implementing the rule on nationality, as the treaty provisions had direct effect.[57]

1.38 The principle of direct effect also applies to regulations.[58]

1.39 The ECJ has held that decisions, which apply only to their addressees, could be directly effective, notwithstanding that no reference is made in the EC Treaty to 'direct applicability' in respect of them. In *Franz Grad v Finanzamt Traunstein*,[59] the ECJ held that:[60]

> Particularly in cases where, for example, the Community authorities by means of a decision have imposed an obligation upon a member

53 [1963] ECR 1 at [13].
54 Now TFEU art 30.
55 Case 2/74 [1974] ECR 631.
56 Now TFEU arts 49, 50 and 53.
57 See also *Defrenne v Societe Anonyme Belge de Navigation Aerienne* Case 43/75 [1976] ECR 455, in which the court held that the core principle of equal pay for equal work was directly effective, in a case where it was conceded that the female applicant, an air stewardess, was doing the same work as her male colleagues.
58 *Commission v Italy* Case 39/72 [1973] ECR 101; *Variola v Amministrazione delle Finanze* Case 34/73 [1973] ECR 981.
59 Case 9/70 [1970] ECR 825.
60 [1970] ECR 825 at [5].

state or all the member states to act in a certain way, the effectiveness ... of such a measure would be weakened if the nationals of that state could not invoke it in the courts and the national courts could not take it into consideration as part of Community law. Although the effects of a decision may not be identical with those of a provision contained in a regulation, this difference does not exclude the possibility that the end result, namely the right of the individual to invoke the measure before the courts, may be the same as that of a directly applicable provision of a regulation.

1.40   The obligation imposed by the decision was sufficiently unconditional, clear and precise to be capable of having direct effect.

1.41   Directives always require implementation by the individual member states, since they are binding as to their result, but allow the national state to determine the form and method of achieving that result.[61] This has not prevented the ECJ from ruling that directives are capable of having direct effect, depending upon whether the nature, general scheme and wording of the provision in question are capable of having direct effects on the relations between member states and individuals. Moreover, article 267[62] – which enables national courts to refer to the ECJ questions concerning the validity and interpretation of all acts of the Community institutions, without distinction – implies that these acts may be invoked by individuals in the national courts.[63]

1.42   In a subsequent case, the ECJ emphasised that a member state should not be able to rely, as against individuals, on its own failure to implement the measures required by a directive within the prescribed period.[64]

It follows that a national court requested by a person who has complied with the provisions of a directive not to apply a national provision incompatible with the directive not incorporated into the internal legal order of a defaulting member state, must uphold that request if the obligation in question is unconditional and sufficiently precise.

1.43   It was only once the prescribed period for implementation of the directive had expired, however, and in the event of default, that the directive could have direct effect. Until then, the member state remained 'free in the field'.[65]

61   See para 1.19 above.
62   Formerly EC Treaty art 234.
63   *Van Duyn v Home Office* Case 41/74 [1974] ECR 1337.
64   *Pubblico Ministero v Tullio Ratti* Case 148/78 [1979] ECR 1629.
65   [1979] ECR 1629.

1.44 **Limits to the doctrine of direct effect** In order to have direct effect, the provision of the directive must be sufficiently clear, precise and unconditional. If there is any discretion left to the member state with regard to the particular provision, that provision will not be sufficiently precise and unconditional. In *Francovich*,[66] the court had to determine whether Directive 80/987 on the protection of employees in the event of their employers' insolvency was sufficiently precise. Member states were required to set up guarantee institutions to protect employees' rights, but Italy had not done so within the stipulated time limit. The court held that the relevant provisions of the directive, which stated 'member states shall lay down detailed rules for the organisation, financing and operation of the guarantee institutions ...' were not sufficiently precise. Member states enjoyed a wide discretion with regard to the organisation, the functioning and the financing of guarantee institutions. While the beneficiaries and the content of the guarantee could be determined, the provisions did not identify the institutions liable under the guarantee.

1.45 In *Marshall v Southampton and South-West Hampshire AHA (Teaching)*,[67] the ECJ held that the binding nature of a directive only existed in relation to 'each member state to which it is addressed'. It followed that a directive may not of itself impose obligations on an individual and that a provision of a directive may not be relied upon as against such a person, but only in an action against the state. The Court of Appeal, however, held that the plaintiff could rely on the directive in her claim against the health authority, on the basis that the authority was an emanation, or organ, of the state.[68]

1.46 **Organs of the state** The impact of the *Marshall* decision – that directly effective provisions could only be relied on in actions against the state – has been somewhat lessened by the broad definition of 'state', which the ECJ has adopted for the purpose of the enforcement of directives. It has been held that the 'state' will include 'all organs of the administration, including decentralised authorities such as municipalities'.[69] This is because directives are binding upon all the authorities of the member state.

1.47 For this purpose, then, local authorities and various other bodies are treated as organs of the state, themselves required to apply the provisions of directly effective but unimplemented Community law

---

66 *Francovich v Italy* Case C-6/90; *Bonifaci v Italy* Case C-9/90 [1991] ECR I–5357.
67 Case 152/84 [1986] QB 401, [1986] 1 CMLR 688.
68 [1986] 1 CMLR 688, CA.
69 *Fratelli Costanzo SpA v Comune di Milano* Case 103/88 [1989] ECR 1839.

in preference to inconsistent provisions of national law. In *Foster v British Gas plc*,[70] it was held that:

> ... a body, whatever its legal form, which has been made responsible, pursuant to a measure adopted by the state, for providing a public service under the control of the state and has for that purpose special powers beyond those which result from the normal rules applicable in relations between individuals, is included in any event among the bodies against which the provisions of a directive capable of having direct effect may be relied upon.

Indirect effect

1.48   Even where directives cannot have direct effect, national law must be read and interpreted in the light of them and in such a way as to conform to their provisions. The ECJ held this to be the position even in a case between two private individuals, ie where there was no organ of the state that could be held responsible for non-implementation of the directive.[71]

European public law doctrines

1.49   The doctrine of proportionality is one of a number of European law doctrines[72] for determining the legality of administrative action. It is still only now in the infancy of its incorporation into English law jurisprudence, and, currently, at any rate, only where fundamental rights are at stake.[73] So far as the European courts are concerned, it involves a closer level of scrutiny than the traditional tests available to the court in judicial review and has the potential, therefore, to facilitate a more interventionist approach. That has not always been the way in which the UK courts have approached the doctrine in domestic cases.[74] A full discussion of the principles of the European public law doctrines can be found elsewhere in this book.[75]

---

70   Case 188/89 [1990] ECR I–3313, [1991] 1 QB 405, [1990] 2 CMLR 833.

71   *Marleasing SA v La Comercial Internacionale de Alimentacion SA* Case C-106/89 [1990] ECR I–4135, [1992] 1 CMLR 305.

72   Including that of the margin of appreciation.

73   See *R (Alconbury Ltd) v Secretary of State for the Environment, Transport and the Regions* [2001] UKHL 23, [2003] 2 AC 295, per Lord Slynn at [51]; *R (Daly) v Secretary of State for the Home Department* [2001] UKHL 26, [2001] 2 AC 532, per Lord Cooke at [32]; *Association of British Civilian Internees – Far Eastern Region v Secretary of State for Defence* [2003] EWCA Civ 473, [2003] QB 1397, per Dyson LJ at [34].

74   See, eg, *Manchester CC v Pinnock* [2010] UKSC 45, [2011] 2 AC 104.

75   See paras 1.56–1.64 below in the context of European human rights law, and paras 6.18–6.37 in the context of the approach of the UK courts since enactment of the Human Rights Act 1998.

European human rights law

European Court of Human Rights jurisprudence

Interpretation of Convention rights

1.50   The European Court of Human Rights (ECtHR) distinguishes between two kinds of complaint: those where what is alleged is an 'interference' with a right (ie a positive, detrimental act of interference); and those where it is claimed that positive action is required in order to guarantee the right. In either case, it is necessary, first, to establish on the true construction of the European Convention on Human Rights (the Convention), whether the right relied on is even capable of protecting the applicant from the conduct complained of.

1.51   For this purpose, the court utilises a number of different methods of construction: such as taking the ordinary meaning of the words used in the provisions;[76] or subjecting the Convention to a grammatical analysis, which involves comparing the English and French versions of the text;[77] considering the importance of the provision in the context of the whole Convention and attempting to ascertain the meaning of the provision in question by analysing its position in the Convention.[78]

1.52   Use may be made of the background papers, or *travaux preparatoires*, of the Convention,[79] but not if the meaning of the words used in the Convention is sufficiently clear and in keeping with the purpose of the Convention.[80] Their use may also be limited if the court is employing an 'evolutive' or purposive approach.

Purposive approach to construction

1.53   Most important among these methods of construction is the purposive approach.[81] The court will construe the Convention by considering its aim, which is the protection of individual rights:[82]

> In interpreting the Convention, regard must be had to its special character as a treaty for the collective enforcement of human rights and

---

76 *Johnston v Ireland* (1986) A-112; (1987) 9 EHRR 203.
77 *Lawless v Ireland* (1961) A-3; *Brogan v United Kingdom* (1988) A-145-B.
78 *Klass v Germany* (1978) A-28.
79 *Johnston v Ireland* (1986) A-112; (1987) 9 EHRR 203; *Glasenapp v Federal Republic of Germany* (1986) A-104.
80 *Lawless v Ireland* (1961) A-3.
81 See paras 1.27–1.28 above, in relation to the ECJ approach.
82 *Soering v United Kingdom* (1989) 11 EHRR 439 at [87].

fundamental freedoms ... Thus the object and purpose of the Convention as an instrument for the protection of individual human beings require that its provisions be interpreted and applied so as to make its safeguards practical and effective ... In addition, any interpretation of the rights and freedoms guaranteed has to be consistent with 'the general spirit of the Convention, an instrument designed to maintain and promote the ideals and values of a democratic society.

1.54 The ECtHR has emphasised, in a number of decisions,[83] that the Convention is a living document, and that interpretation of its meaning must be considered in the light of prevailing conditions at the time of the alleged breach, rather that at the date of the drafting of the Convention. Having said that, the court cannot, by means of such an evolutive approach, derive from the Convention and its protocols a right that was not present at the outset.[84]

1.55 If the Convention right relied on is not, on its true construction, capable of protecting the applicant from the conduct complained of, that is plainly an end of the matter. If it is so capable, the court then looks to see whether that conduct did, in fact, violate the right relied on. The approach of the ECtHR to these questions involves a number of other legal concepts, and is of particular relevance in the context of the responsibilities of public authorities.

European public law doctrines[85]

1.56 **Margin of appreciation** National authorities are accorded a 'margin of appreciation' in the manner in which they guarantee the Convention rights of their citizens. The wider the variations between the practices of different signatory states, the wider this margin of appreciation is likely to be. Thus, in *Johnston*[86] the court held, in respect of the applicant's claim that under article 8 of the Convention, he had a right to be able to obtain a divorce, that:[87]

> ... the notion of 'respect' is not clear-cut: having regard to the diversity of the practices followed and the situations obtaining in the contracting states, the notion's requirements will vary considerably from case

---

83 For example, *Marckx v Belgium* (1979) A-31; *Johnston v Ireland* (1986) A-112. On this point see generally Baroness Hale, 'Common law and Convention law: the limits to interpretation', EHRLR 2011, 534–543.

84 See, eg, *Johnston v Ireland* (1986) A-112; (1987) 9 EHRR 203.

85 This is considered elsewhere at paras 6.18–6.37, in the context of the application of the doctrine by the UK courts since the enactment of the HRA 1998.

86 *Johnston v Ireland* (1986) A-112; (1987) 9 EHRR 203.

87 (1986) A-112 at para 55(c).

to case. Accordingly, this is an area in which the contracting parties enjoy a wide margin of appreciation in determining the steps to be taken to ensure compliance with the Convention with due regard to the needs and resources of the community and of individuals ....

1.57 **Balance** The language of the court's reference to the 'needs and resources of the community and of individuals' is in terms of a balance. The court has emphasised the balancing exercise to be undertaken: '... regard must be had to the fair balance that has to be struck between the general interest of the community and the interests of the individual, the search for which balance is inherent in the whole of the Convention.'[88]

1.58 This balancing exercise may even fall to be undertaken in cases where the Convention does not itself allow for limitations or restrictions on rights. In *Soering v United Kingdom*,[89] it was alleged that the UK was in breach of article 3 of the Convention (which – as the court emphasised – makes provision for no exceptions or derogations) by deciding to extradite the applicant to the United States where he was to be tried for capital murder in Virginia. The applicant thus ran the risk of exposure to the 'death row phenomenon', which was alleged to be inhuman and/or degrading treatment and/or punishment.

1.59 The ECtHR held that, in interpreting and applying the notions of inhuman or degrading treatment or punishment, one of the factors to be taken into account – indeed inherent in the whole of the Convention – was:[90]

> ... [a] search for a fair balance between the demands of the general interest of the community and the requirements of the protection of the individual's fundamental rights. As movement about the world becomes easier and crime takes on a larger international dimension, it is increasingly in the interest of all nations that suspected offenders who flee abroad should be brought to justice. Conversely, the establishment of safe havens for fugitives would not only result in danger for the state obliged to harbour the protected person but also tend to undermine the foundations of extradition.

1.60 **Proportionality** Consideration of proportionality may take a number of forms, and arise in a number of different contexts relating both to the interference itself, and/or to any number of subsidiary

---

88 See, in other contexts, among others, *James v United Kingdom* (1986) 1986 A-98 at [50], and *Sporrong and Lönnroth v Sweden* (1982) A-52 at [69]; *Rees v United Kingdom* (1986) A-106 at [37].

89 (1989) 11 EHRR 439.

90 (1989) 11 EHRR 439 at [89].

questions that the ECtHR is required to answer in order to arrive at a conclusion.[91]

1.61   A challenge, for example, by a lawyer to the Belgian legal professional requirement to undertake pro bono work for clients who could not afford to pay, on the basis that this amounted to forced or compulsory labour in contravention of article 4 of the Convention, failed, in part because the court did not consider the burden imposed by this requirement to be disproportionate. The amount of time the applicant was required to spend on pro bono work allowed sufficient time for the performance of his paid work.[92]

1.62   In *Gaskin v United Kingdom*,[93] it was alleged that the UK was, by article 8 of the Convention, under a positive obligation to allow the applicant access to personal records concerning his having been taken into care. The court held that the UK system of allowing access to such records with the consent of the contributor was in principle 'compatible with the obligation under article 8, taking into account the State's margin of appreciation'.

1.63   Such a system must, however, also secure the right of access where a contributor was not available to consent or withheld that consent improperly: 'Such a system is only in conformity with the principle of proportionality if it provides that an independent authority finally decides whether access has to be granted in cases where a contributor fails to answer or withholds consent.'[94]

1.64   Accordingly, a breach of the Convention was established.

Domestic jurisprudence

Pre-Human Rights Act 1998

1.65   In a series of cases in the 1970s, the Court of Appeal came close to giving effect to the Convention in domestic law, even though (subsequently) this approach was renounced. In *R v Secretary of State for the Home Department ex p Phansopkar*,[95] Lord Scarman held that it was

---

91 See, eg, *Soering v United Kingdom* (1989) 11 EHRR 439 at [104] and [110] where proportionality was considered in a number of different contexts.

92 *Van der Mussele v Belgium* (1983) A-70 at [39].

93 (1989) A-160.

94 *Gaskin v United Kingdom* (1989) A-160 at [49].

95 [1976] QB 606, CA.

the duty of public authorities administering the law, as well as the courts, to have regard to the Convention:[96]

> It may, of course, happen under our law that the basic rights to justice undeferred and to respect for family and private life have to yield to the express requirements of a statute. But in my judgment it is the duty of the courts, so long as they do not defy or disregard clear unequivocal provision, to construe statutes in a manner which promotes, not endangers, those rights. Problems of ambiguity or omission, if they arise under the language of an Act, should be resolved so as to give effect to, or at the very least so as not to derogate from the rights recognised by Magna Carta and the European Convention.

1.66   There followed a period of retrenchment by the courts, most famously in *R v Secretary of State for the Home Department ex p Brind*[97] in which the House of Lords confirmed that the Convention was no part of English law, and so a failure to act in accordance with it would not give rise to a ground for judicial review. While the presumption that Parliament intended to legislate in conformity with it might be resorted to in order to resolve an ambiguity or uncertainty in a statutory provision, there was no presumption that the Secretary of State's discretion must be exercised in accordance with it.[98]

1.67   An alternative view, which found favour in *Brind* in the Court of Appeal,[99] and to some extent in *Porter v Magill* in the Divisional Court,[100] was that the protections afforded to the individual by the common law were coterminous with those afforded by the Convention.[101] Moreover, in *R v Ministry of Defence ex p Smith*[102] it was held

96 [1976] QB 606 at 626F–G. See also *R v Secretary of State for the Home Department ex p Bhajan Singh* [1976] QB 198, CA, at 207F, in which Lord Denning MR stated that both immigration officers and the secretary of state should take account of the principles set out in the Convention when carrying out their duties, since they were under a public law duty to act fairly and the Convention was a statement of the principles of fair dealing.

97 [1991] 1 AC 696, HL.

98 [1991] 1 AC 696, per Lord Bridge at 748; per Lord Ackner at 760–2. See also *Derbyshire CC v Times Newspapers Ltd* [1994] AC 534, HL, per Lord Keith of Kinkel at 550–1.

99 *R v Secretary of State for the Home Department ex p Brind* [1991] 1 AC 696, HL, per Lord Donaldson MR at 717E.

100 (1998) 30 HLR 997, DC, where the court held that there was no distinction which could be drawn between the rights conferred by article 6 of the Convention (see paras 6.151–6.175 below) and those conferred by the common law. See now the decision of the House of Lords at [2001] UKHL 67, [2002] AC 357.

101 Although the ECtHR certainly did not share this view in *Smith and Grady v United Kingdom* (1999) 29 EHRR 493.

102 [1996] QB 517, CA.

by the Court of Appeal that Convention could be used as an aid to the construction of the common law as well as statute.

Human Rights Act 1998

1.68   The Human Rights Act (HRA) 1998 is the vehicle for introducing Convention rights into domestic law. The Act does not incorporate the Convention; instead, it includes the majority (but not all) of the Convention rights in its Schedule 1, and provides that public authorities may not act incompatibly with them, and that the courts must construe legislation compatibly with them if it is possible to do so.

1.69   While the HRA 1998 does not require challenges to the conduct of public authorities to be brought by way of judicial review, this is nevertheless the most appropriate method of challenge in many cases, not least because the claimant is likely to be seeking one or more domestic public law remedies that are available only on judicial review, and is likely also to wish to raise other public law grounds of challenge. This does not preclude a claimant from bringing a claim under the HRA in any court,[103] or a defendant from raising an alleged breach of a Convention right as a defence to proceedings.[104]

Acting compatibly

1.70   Section 6(1) of HRA 1998 renders it unlawful for a public authority to act in a way that is incompatible with any of the Convention rights contained in Schedule 1. 'Acting' includes a failure to act.[105] The definition of 'public authority', for these purposes and more generally is considered elsewhere.[106]

1.71   The general prohibition on acting incompatibly with Convention rights is subject to two defences, provided by HRA 1998 s6(2). The language used to create these defences is as follows:

> (2) Subsection (1) does not apply to an act if –
> > (a) as a result of one or more provisions of primary legislation, the authority could not have acted differently; or
> > (b) in the case of one or more provisions of, or made under, primary legislation which cannot be read or given effect in a way which is compatible with the Convention rights, the authority was acting so as to give effect to or enforce those provisions.

---

103 HRA 1998 s7(1), CPR r7.11. The only exception relates to claims in respect of judicial acts which must be brought in the High Court: *ibid.*

104 *Manchester CC v Pinnock* [2010] UKSC 45, [2011] 2 AC 104.

105 HRA 1998 s6(6).

106 See paras 2.80–2.103.

1.72 The purpose of section 6(2) is to preserve the sovereignty of Parliament.[107]

1.73 The House of Lords explained the difference between section 6(2)(a) and section 6(2)(b) in *R (Hooper) v Secretary of State for Work and Pensions*.[108] Lord Hoffmann said that section 6(2)(a) applied where a public authority could not have acted differently. Section 6(2)(b) had a different purpose; it assumes that the public authority could have acted differently, but liability is excluded if it was giving effect to a statutory provision that could not be read as Convention-compliant.[109]

1.74 In *Doherty v Birmingham City Council*[110] a majority of the House of Lords held that section 6(2)(b) protects a decision by an authority whether or not to exercise a discretion that is available to them under statutory provisions, but whether this approach can withstand the discussion in *Manchester CC v Pinnock*,[111] is to be doubted. In particular, the Supreme Court, in *Pinnock*, approved the following observation of Lord Mance, who was not part of the majority on this issue in *Doherty*:[112]

> Accordingly, a local authority which fails to take into account Convention values when deciding whether or not to give any and if so what length of notice to quit cannot, in my opinion, be said to be acting so as to give effect to or enforce statutory provisions which are incompatible with the Convention rights.

---

107 See *R (Hooper) v Secretary of State for Work and Pensions* [2005] UKHL 29, [2005] 1 WLR 1681, per Lord Hoffmann at [51]. In an early decision on s6(2)(b), *R (Bono) v Harlow DC*, [2002] EWHC 423 (Admin), [2002] 1 WLR 2475, it was held that it would only save an act carried out under the requirements of subordinate legislation if the subordinate legislation itself could not have been framed in terms which would have complied with the Convention because of incompatible primary legislation. Even at the time, this seemed unlikely to be correct as it would render it impossible for public authorities to act lawfully – they could comply with the subordinate legislation and breach s6(1), or comply with s6(1) and breach the subordinate legislation.

108 [2005] UKHL 29, [2005] 1 WLR 1681.

109 *Hooper*, [48]–[49]. Although Lord Nicholls and Lord Scott thought that it was not necessary to decide which of section 6(2)(a) or section 6(2)(b) applied as the difference on the facts of that case was immaterial.

110 [2008] UKHL 57, [2009] 1 AC 367.

111 [2010] UKSC 45, [2011] 2 AC 104, especially at [93]–[103].

112 *Doherty* (above), per Lord Mance at [153], approved in *Pinnock* at [103].

Reading legislation compatibly

1.75 The courts are obliged to read and give effect to primary and subordinate legislation so far as they can in a way that is compatible with the Convention rights.[113] In the leading case on the interpretative obligation imposed by this provision, *Ghaidan v Godin-Mendoza*,[114] the House of Lords held that it may require legislation to be given a different meaning so as to make it compatible with Convention rights, even if the meaning of the legislation would otherwise be clear when construed according to the ordinary principles of interpretation.

1.76 Lord Nicholls said that section 3 enables a court to modify the meaning and effect of primary and secondary legislation, which may require the addition or subtraction of words so as to change the meaning of the legislation, bounded only by what is 'possible'.[115] Lord Nicholls did not explain exactly what he meant by 'possible', but he added the following partial explanation:[116]

> Parliament, however, cannot have intended that in the discharge of this extended interpretative function the courts should adopt a meaning inconsistent with a fundamental feature of legislation. That would be to cross the constitutional boundary section 3 seeks to demarcate and preserve. Parliament has retained the right to enact legislation in terms which are not Convention-compliant. The meaning imported by application of section 3 must be compatible with the underlying thrust of the legislation being construed. Words implied must, in the phrase of my noble and learned friend, Lord Rodger of Earlsferry, 'go with the grain of the legislation'. Nor can Parliament have intended that section 3 should require courts to make decisions for which they are not equipped. There may be several ways of making a provision Convention-compliant, and the choice may involve issues calling for legislative deliberation.

1.77 Thus, the issue for the court is whether reading whatever words into the legislation may be necessary to render it Convention-compliant can be accomplished while leaving the essential principles and scope

---

113 HRA 1998 s3.
114 [2004] UKHL 30, [2004] 2 AC 557.
115 *Ghaidan v Godin-Mendoza* [2004] UKHL 30, [2004] 2 AC 557, per Lord Nicholls at [32].
116 At [33].

of the legislation intact. The nature of the court's function under section 3 is one of interpretation, not legislation.[117]

1.78   An illustration of the limits on what a court may appropriately do under section 3 can be found in *Hounslow LBC v Powell*.[118] In that case, the Supreme Court refused to read section 89 of the Housing Act 1980 as allowing a court to postpone execution of a possession order, where the occupier had no security of tenure, for longer than six weeks, where section 89 explicitly prohibited courts from granting more than six weeks' postponement.

1.79   If it is not possible to read and give effect to legislation in a way that is compatible with Convention rights, the validity of the legislation is not affected, but the court may make a declaration of incompatibility in appropriate circumstances.[119]

1.80   The court has no power to strike down incompatible primary legislation, only to declare it to be incompatible. Such a declaration, if made, does not affect the validity or continued enforceability of the legislation. Nor does it affect the rights of the parties to the claim in which the declaration is made (or, therefore, to any other person). In the case of subordinate legislation, the courts may strike it down unless the primary legislation under which it was made prevents the removal of the incompatibility. In the latter case, again, a declaration of incompatibility is all that is available.[120]

1.81   A declaration of incompatibility is a measure of last resort, which must be avoided unless it is plainly impossible to do so.[121]

1.82   Likewise, a declaration of incompatibility should not normally be made where the public authority concerned is not, on the facts,

---

117 *Ghaidan v Godin-Mendoza* [2004] UKHL 30, [2004] 2 AC 557, per Lord Rodgers at [122], where his Lordship continued 'Of course, the greater the extent of the proposed implication, the greater the need to make sure that the court is not going beyond the scheme of the legislation and embarking upon amendment. Nevertheless, what matters is not the number of words but their effect.'

118 [2011] UKSC 8, [2011] 2 AC 186.

119 HRA 1998 ss3 and 4.

120 HRA 1998 s4, and see *R (Bono) v Harlow DC* [2002] EWHC 423 (Admin), [2002] 1 WLR 2475.

121 *R v A (No 2)* [2001] UKHL 25, [2002] 1 AC 45, per Lord Steyn at [44]; *R (Nasseri) v Secretary of State for the Home Department* [2009] UKHL 23, [2010] 1 AC 1, per Lord Hoffmann at [18]. In *Hounslow LBC v Powell* [2011] UKSC 8, [2011] 2 AC 186, the Supreme Court refused to apply s3 to interpret s89 of the Housing Act 1980 (noted at para 1.78 above) and held that there was no need to make a declaration of incompatibility either as there was no evidence before the court that the maximum period provided for by s89 was insufficient.

acting in a way that is incompatible with a Convention right. While
it is possible that the court might consider it convenient to make a
declaration of incompatibility even though the public authority had
not been acting so as to infringe Convention rights, it will be a rare
case in which the court will do so.[122]

1.83   Where there is no realistic possibility that any remedial action
that could be taken if a declaration of incompatibility was granted
would benefit the party seeking the declaration, it has been held that
it is doubtful in the extreme that a court would exercise its discretion
in favour of that party.[123]

1.84   The courts have made 27 declarations of incompatibility, eight of
which were overturned on appeal.[124] Of the 19 declarations of incompatibility that have become final, 11 were remedied by subsequent
primary legislation; three were remedied by a remedial order;[125] four
related to provisions which had already been amended at the time of
the declaration; and one is still subject to Government consideration
as to how to remedy the incompatibility.[126]

Interpreting Convention rights

1.85   In approaching their tasks under the HRA 1998 the courts are obliged
to have regard to the jurisprudence of the ECtHR.[127] They are not,

---

122 *R (Nasseri) v Secretary of State for the Home Department* [2009] UKHL 23, [2010]
    1 AC 1, per Lord Hoffmann at [18]–[19].

123 *Lancashire CC v Taylor* [2005] EWCA Civ 284, [2005] 1 WLR 2668. In any event
    the claimant in that case was not a 'victim' for the purposes of HRA 1998 s7
    (see paras 4.33–4.38 below), having not been affected by the alleged breach.

124 As at 31 July 2012: Ministry of Justice *Responding to human rights judgments:
    Report to the Joint Committee on Human Rights on the Government response to
    human rights judgments 2011–12* (Cm 8432, 2012).

125 HRA 1998 s10.

126 *Smith v Scott* [2007] CSIH 9, [2007] SC 345, where a declaration of
    incompatibility was made in relation to section 3 of the Representation of the
    People Act 1983, which removes the electoral franchise from prisoners. The
    issue has been the subject of a number of decisions of the ECtHR and much
    media and parliamentary debate.

127 HRA 1998 s2(1). Account must be taken of any judgment, decision,
    declaration or advisory opinion of the court, any opinion of the Commission
    in a report adopted under article 31 of the Convention, and decision of the
    Commission in connection with article 26 or article 27(2) of the Convention,
    and any decision of the Committee of Ministers taken under article 46 of the
    Convention.

however, bound by it or obliged to adopt or follow it even on the construction or effect of Convention rights. As Laws LJ has stated:[128]

> But I should say that I think it important to have in mind that the court's task under the HRA, in this context as in many others, is not simply to add on the Strasbourg learning to the corpus of English law, as if it were a compulsory adjunct taken from an alien source, but to develop a municipal law of human rights by the incremental method of the common law, case by case, taking account of the Strasbourg jurisprudence as HRA section 2 enjoins us to do.

1.86 In *Pinnock*,[129] the Supreme Court said:

> This court is not bound to follow every decision of the European court. Not only would it be impractical to do so: it would sometimes be inappropriate, as it would destroy the ability of the court to engage in the constructive dialogue with the European court which is of value to the development of Convention law: see e g *R v Horncastle* [2010] 2 AC 373. Of course, we should usually follow a clear and constant line of decisions by the European court: *R (Ullah) v Special Adjudicator* [2004] 2 AC 323. But we are not actually bound to do so or (in theory, at least) to follow a decision of the Grand Chamber. As Lord Mance pointed out in *Doherty v Birmingham City Council* [2009] AC 367, para 126, section 2 of the 1998 Act requires our courts to take into account European court decisions, not necessarily to follow them. Where, however, there is a clear and constant line of decisions whose effect is not inconsistent with some fundamental substantive or procedural aspect of our law, and whose reasoning does not appear to overlook or misunderstand some argument or point of principle, we consider that it would be wrong for this court not to follow that line.

1.87 The reference to following the clear and constant jurisprudence of the ECtHR was first made by Lord Slynn in *R (Alconbury) v Secretary of State for the Environment, Transport and the Regions*.[130] Moreover, in *R (RJM) v Secretary of State for Work and Pensions*, the House of Lords held that it would require 'the most exceptional circumstances' for domestic courts not to follow a reasoned decision of the Grand Chamber.[131]

---

128 *Runa Begum v Tower Hamlets LBC* [2002] EWCA Civ 239, [2002] 1 WLR 2491, per Laws LJ at [17]. (The House of Lords decision on appeal is at [2003] UKHL 5, [2003] 2 AC 430).

129 Above, per Lord Neuberger at [48].

130 [2001] UKHL 23, [2003] 2 AC 295.

131 [2008] UKHL 63, [2009] 1 AC 311.

1.88   In *R (Ullah) v Special Adjudicator*,[132] Lord Bingham explained that
this requirement to follow decisions of the ECtHR reflected:

> the fact that the Convention is an international instrument, the cor-
> rect interpretation of which can be authoritatively expounded only by
> the Strasbourg court. From this it follows that a national court subject
> to a duty such as that imposed by section 2 should not without strong
> reason dilute or weaken the effect of the Strasbourg case law. It is
> indeed unlawful under section 6 of the 1998 Act for a public author-
> ity, including a court, to act in a way which is incompatible with a
> Convention right. It is of course open to member states to provide
> for rights more generous than those guaranteed by the Convention,
> but such provision should not be the product of interpretation of the
> Convention by national courts, since the meaning of the Conven-
> tion should be uniform throughout the states party to it. The duty of
> national courts is to keep pace with the Strasbourg jurisprudence as it
> evolves over time: no more, but certainly no less.

1.89   The House of Lords came to reconsider this point in *R (Al-Skeini)
v Secretary of State for Defence*.[133] Lord Brown suggested that the last
sentence of the passage from Lord Bingham set out in the last paragraph '... could as well have ended: "no less, but certainly no more"'[134]
although the correctness of Lord Brown's dictum has subsequently
been questioned by other justices of the Supreme Court.[135]

1.90   In *R v Horncastle*,[136] the Supreme Court did decline to follow the
decisions of the ECtHR in relation to the use of hearsay evidence in
criminal trials. Lord Phillips said this:[137]

> The requirement to 'take into account' the Strasbourg jurisprudence
> will normally result in this Court applying principles that are clearly
> established by the Strasbourg Court. There will, however, be rare occa-
> sions where this court has concerns as to whether a decision of the
> Strasbourg Court sufficiently appreciates or accommodates particular
> aspects of our domestic process. In such circumstances it is open to
> this court to decline to follow the Strasbourg decision, giving reasons
> for adopting this course. This is likely to give the Strasbourg Court
> the opportunity to reconsider the particular aspect of the decision that
> is in issue, so that there takes place what may prove to be a valuable
> dialogue between this court and the Strasbourg Court.

132 [2004] UKHL 26, [2004] 2 AC 323 at [20].
133 [2007] UKHL 26, [2008] 1 AC 153.
134 At [106].
135 *British Broadcasting Corporation v Sugar (No 2)* [2012] UKSC 4, [2012] 1 WLR
     439, per Lord Wilson at [59] and Lord Mance at [113].
136 *R v Horncastle* [2009] UKSC 14, [2010] 2 AC 373.
137 At [11].

The courts' response to the Human Rights Act 1998

1.91   The courts' response to and treatment of the HRA 1998 has been mixed. On the one hand, and looked at as a whole, the body of substantive rights and protections conferred by UK law in relation to the specific matters addressed by the European Convention do not look very different 12 years after the 1998 Act came into force than they did before its enactment.[138] The courts have in general not applied the Act to expand the content of rights available to people in their dealings with public authorities.

1.92   By contrast, the courts' response to the HRA 1998 in terms of its effect on the process of judicial review itself, including the kinds of issues that the court may review, the degree of judicial scrutiny that should be applied on that review and the principles that govern the application of that scrutiny, has, at least at times, suggested that a quiet revolution may occur. The courts have asserted, at least where 'fundamental rights' are at stake, a considerably more interventionist model of judicial review (based on the doctrine of proportionality) and an objective assessment by the court of the positive justification for the decision under challenge that has to be offered by the defendant. Even the possibility of a 'full-merits' review, ie review of the facts, has become accepted in some contexts.[139]

1.93   In one case, the Court of Appeal even suggested dispensing with the doctrine of *Wednesbury*[140] unreasonableness altogether, whether or not any human rights issues were at stake, in favour of the more precise and sophisticated model of judicial review offered by proportionality.[141] In another,[142] one member of the House of Lords suggested that *Wednesbury* was an 'unfortunately retrogressive

---

138 The previous edition of this book, at para 1.73, made the same point only three years after the 1998 Act had come into force. While the subsequent nine years have led to further developments, the general proposition still holds true.

139 See, in particular, *R v Secretary of State for the Home Department ex p Mahmood* [2001] 1 WLR 840, CA; *R (Daly) v Secretary of State for the Home Department* [2001] UKHL 26, [2001] 2 AC 532; *R (Wilkinson) v Broadmoor Special Hospital Authority* [2001] EWCA Civ 1545, [2002] 1 WLR 419.

140 *Associated Provincial Picture Houses v Wednesbury Corporation* [1948] 1 KB 223, CA.

141 *Association of British Civilian Internees – Far Eastern Region v Secretary of State for Defence* [2003] EWCA Civ 473, [2003] QB 1397 at [34]. The Court of Appeal recognised that only the House of Lords could abolish the *Wednesbury* doctrine (but refused leave to appeal to the House of Lords).

142 *R (Daly) v Secretary of State for the Home Department* [2001] UKHL 26, [2001] 2 AC 532.

decision',[143] and another suggested that a proper proportionality approach would entitle the court to decide what factors were relevant and what weight should be given to each one.[144]

1.94   Yet in the following decade the courts have resisted the urge to adopt proportionality as a free-standing ground of review, or as a replacement for *Wednesbury* in cases that do not involve human rights or even in some cases that do.[145]

1.95   The detail of the courts' response to the HRA 1998, in so far as it has affected judicial review, is described elsewhere throughout this book, in relation to each of the substantive public law concepts and issues that are considered in the following chapters. It should certainly not be thought that UK law and Strasbourg law are now in any sense identical in relation to these issues. Perhaps the most striking aspect of the courts' response to the HRA 1998 has been the lack of any uniform response, and, following an initial burst of enthusiasm, the cautious and incremental approach that has been adopted, especially by the House of Lords and Supreme Court.

---

143 Per Lord Cooke of Thorndon at [32].
144 Per Lord Steyn at [27]–[28].
145 See eg *Runa Begum v Tower Hamlets LBC* [2003] UKHL 5, [2003] 2 AC 430.

Bodies amenable to judicial review

Bodies amenable to review

2.1   In general terms, there are three types of body whose decisions may be challenged by way of judicial review:

- inferior courts;
- tribunals; and
- other bodies performing public acts and duties, including local authorities.

2.2   Broadly, the same categories of body are public authorities for the purposes of the HRA 1998,[1] with the significant difference that superior as well as inferior courts are included within the definition.

Inferior courts

2.3   These are the county courts, magistrates' courts, coroners' courts and, in some circumstances, the Crown Court.

County courts

2.4   The High Court has long asserted a supervisory jurisdiction to control the county court,[2] even where Parliament had, on the face of it, sought to oust such jurisdiction.[3]

2.5   In *R (Sivasubramaniam) v Wandsworth County Court*,[4] the Court of Appeal considered again the principles applicable to the availability of judicial review in respect of decisions of the county court.

2.6   The appellant had brought judicial review proceedings against two decisions of a circuit judge:

---

1   Human Rights Act 1998 s6. The definition of 'public authority' under this section is discussed at paras 2.80–2.103 below.

2   *R v HHJ Sir Shirley Worthington-Evans ex p Madan* [1959] 2 QB 145, DC; *R v Keighley County Court ex p Home Insulation Ltd* [1989] COD 174; *R v HHJ Sir Donald Hurst ex p Smith* [1960] 2 QB 133, QBD; *R v Wandsworth County Court ex p Munn* (1994) 26 HLR 697, QBD; *Re Racal Communications Ltd* [1981] AC 374, HL.

3   See, eg, County Courts Act 1959 s107.

4   [2002] EWCA Civ 1738, [2003] 1 WLR 475.

- a refusal of permission to appeal against a decision of a district judge, from which refusal there could be no further appeal;[5] and
- a refusal to set aside an award made by the district judge in arbitration proceedings that had been concluded some years previously.

2.7   Permission to apply for judicial review was refused, and the claimant appealed to the Court of Appeal.[6]

2.8   On the appeal, the Lord Chancellor was permitted to intervene to contend that either:

- the CPR Pt 52 procedure impliedly ousted the court's supervisory jurisdiction; or that
- in any event, judicial review should be refused on principle by the court, because Parliament had legislated so that the right of litigants to challenge a judicial decision is limited to the CPR Pt 52 appellate procedure (which includes the unavailability of any right of appeal against a refusal of permission to appeal).[7] It would be contrary to this clear legislative policy if its circumvention were permitted by entertaining judicial review applications in respect of refusals of permission to appeal.

2.9   The Court of Appeal dismissed both of the appellant's appeals. In relation to the refusal to set aside the arbitration award, the appellant had had an alternative remedy, by way of a right of appeal under CPR Pt 52, which he ought to have utilised. The general rule that judicial review of a discretionary decision would not be permitted if there was an alternative remedy would only be departed from if the alternative remedy would be less satisfactory than judicial review. Usually, however, a right of appeal would be more convenient and judicial review would be refused, save in exceptional cases (an example of which the Court of Appeal could not envisage).[8]

2.10   In the situation where permission to appeal had been refused, the Court of Appeal rejected the argument that Access to Justice Act (AJA) 1999 s54(4) had impliedly ousted the court's power to entertain judicial review proceedings in an appropriate case. There was a clear line

---

5   Access to Justice Act 1999 and CPR r52.5. Section 54(4) of the 1999 Act provides that no appeal may be made against a decision of a court to grant or refuse permission to appeal. See also sections 54(1), (3) and 56(1); the Access to Justice Act 1999 (Destination of Appeals) Order 2000 SI No 1071 (in force from 2 May 2000); and CPR rr52.3 and 52.13.

6   CPR r54.15. See further chapter 13 below.

7   That is, by Access to Justice Act 1999 s54.

8   *Sivasubramaniam* [2002] EWCA Civ 1738, [2003] 1 WLR 475, per Lord Phillips of Worth Matravers MR at [47]–[48].

of authority that only the clearest words could have effect to oust certioriari,[9] which left no room for implied ouster. It was, nevertheless, contrary to principle for litigants to be able to circumvent the legislative policy of the AJA 1999 by the use of judicial review proceedings. Parliament, while not having ousted the court's jurisdiction, had not contemplated the spate of applications of this sort, and it was disproportionate and inappropriate for Administrative Court judges to be required to deal with such matters where one judge, on an application for permission to appeal, had already reviewed the decision complained of and found there to be no grounds for appeal.

2.11   Accordingly, judges should summarily refuse permission to apply for judicial review in such cases in the exercise of their discretion, because the CPR Pt 52 procedure was proportionate and sensible, and all issues regarding the legality of the decision sought to be appealed could be raised on an application for permission to appeal. The same reasoning would apply to any judicial review claim in respect of a grant of permission to appeal, should such a claim be brought.[10]

2.12   Judicial review would only be available in exceptional circumstances, such as in the rare case where the challenge to the decision was founded on a claim of old-style jurisdictional error (ie where the error arose outside – rather than from – the reasons given for refusing permission to appeal, the judge having stepped outside of or misunderstood his powers) or where a procedural irregularity had occurred of a kind that constituted a denial of the claimant's right to a fair hearing.[11]

2.13   In *R (Strickson) v Preston County Court*,[12] the Court of Appeal explained further the circumstances in which judicial review would be available against a decision of the circuit judge to refuse permission to appeal. Laws LJ held that the case would need to be truly exceptional, and that a defect much more fundamental than an error of law would need to be established:[13]

> How should such a defect be described in principle? I think a distinction may be drawn between a case where the judge simply gets it wrong, even extremely wrong (and wrong on the law, or the facts, or

---

9   See, eg, *R v Medical Appeal Tribunal ex p Gilmore* [1957] 1 QB 574, per Denning LJ at 585. Certiorari is now known as a quashing order, see paras 5.1–5.2 below.

10   *Sivasubramaniam* at [53]–[55].

11   *Sivasubramaniam* at [56].

12   [2007] EWCA Civ 1132.

13   [2007] EWCA Civ 1132 at [32]. See further para 7.20 below.

both) and a case where, as I would venture to put it, the judicial process itself has been frustrated or corrupted. This, I think, marks the truly exceptional case. It will or may include the case of pre-*Anisminic* jurisdictional error, where the court embarks upon an enquiry which it lacks all power to deal with, or fails altogether to enquire or adjudicate upon a matter which it was its unequivocal duty to address. It would include substantial denial of the right to a fair hearing, and it may include cases where the lower court has indeed acted 'in complete disregard of its duties' (*Gregory*), and cases where the court has declined to go into a point of law in a particular area which, against a background of conflicting decisions of a lower tribunal, the public interest obviously requires to be decided (*Sinclair*). The *Sinclair* type of case is perhaps a sub-class of the *Gregory* case. Both, in any event, may be less hard-edged than the pure pre- *Anisminic* jurisdictional error case. The courts will have to be vigilant to see that only truly exceptional cases – where there has indeed, as I have put it, been a frustration or corruption of the very judicial process – are allowed to proceed to judicial review in cases where further appeal rights are barred by section 54(4).

2.14 An example of a truly exceptional case (in which a refusal of permission to appeal was quashed) arose in *R (Sharing) v Preston County Court*.[14] Wilkie J held 'with very great hesitation and regret'[15] that the case satisfied Laws LJ's test in *Strickson*, on the basis that he had:[16]

> ... been forced, by reading the transcript of the [permission to appeal] hearing, to conclude that [the circuit judge] did act in such a way that a fair-minded and independent bystander would conclude that he had finally and firmly made up his mind from the outset of the application that he was going to refuse it, that he was going to refuse to admit the fresh evidence ..., and that his repeated interruptions of the claimant's counsel and the way in which he focused on the way in which the district judge had decided the case, was the clearest possible evidence of that apparent bias.

2.15 In *R (Cart) v Upper Tribunal*,[17] the Supreme Court considered *Sivasibramanium* in relation to whether judicial review may be sought of a refusal of permission to appeal by the Upper Tribunal in relation to a decision by a First-tier Tribunal. The court declined to apply the same test, holding that it would be preferable to apply, by analogy, the test for bringing a second appeal under CPR r52.13.[18] Whether

14 [2012] EWHC 515 (Admin).
15 At [44].
16 At [44].
17 [2011] UKSC 28, [2012] 1 AC 663.
18 See the discussion at paras 2.50–2.51 below.

this reopens the question of the appropriate test for judicial review in relation to county court refusals of permission to appeal is unclear. The Supreme Court, while pointing out some of the disadvantages of an 'exceptional circumstances' approach, did not doubt the correctness of *Sivasubramanium* in relation to county court cases, holding, rather, that the approach should not be imported into the tribunal system.[19]

2.16   In relation to other decisions of the county court, judicial review may, on occasion, be a more appropriate remedy than appeal, although it would seem to follow from the reasoning in *Sivasubramaniam* that the appellate route should generally be used where it is available. Significant breaches of the principles of natural justice, or cases where the court simply had no jurisdiction to make the decision in question, may be examples of where it would be appropriate to seek judicial review, instead of appealing, a county court decision.

Magistrates' courts

2.17   In the magistrates' court, the position is, in principle at least, analogous to that in *Sivasubramaniam*, in that the right to appeal against magistrates' decisions will constitute an alternative remedy which generally speaking ought to be used. The analogy, however, is not exact and judicial review of the magistrates is far more common and widely accepted than of the county court. In particular, the appellate regime has not been the subject of procedural changes equivalent to those in relation to civil appeals that was the foundation for the *Sivasubramaniam* decision.[20] Nor does the aspect of *Sivasubramaniam* concerning challenges to refusals of permission to appeal apply, because there is generally no requirement of permission to appeal in criminal cases.[21] Where the essence of the challenge is not to the substance of the court's decision but to the manner in which it was reached, judicial review is a proper procedure to use.[22] In other cases, a variety of factors may justify the use of judicial review rather than

---

19   See, in particular, on this point, the Opinion of Baroness Hale at [41]–[44].

20   Although the Criminal Procedure Rules 2005–2012 have codified and amended criminal procedure in a manner which draws clear parallels with the CPR, the position concerning appeals has not changed substantively.

21   Senior Courts Act 1981 s18; Access to Justice Act 1999 s54(2); and Criminal Procedure Rules Pt 63.

22   See, eg, *R v Bristol Magistrate' Court ex p Rowles* [1994] COD 137, DC; but see also *R v Folkestone Magistrates' Court ex p Bradley* [1994] COD 138.

case stated, including urgency (ie the ability to seek urgent, including interim, relief, which is not available on an appeal by way of case stated).

2.18   Moreover, where a court has been asked to state a case and has refused on the basis that the application is 'frivolous', judicial review has long been accepted as permissible, and continues to be used without objection.[23] In cases involving the magistrates' court's civil jurisdiction, judicial review may have a broader role to play, in the light of the decision of Roch J in *R v Chesterfield Justices ex p Kovacs*,[24] that the power of a magistrates court in civil proceedings to state an interlocutory case was discretionary, not – as in final criminal decisions – mandatory (subject to frivolity), and should be exercised sparingly and only in exceptional circumstances.

2.19   In recent years, however, the courts have imposed a stricter requirement that rights of appeal should be used, where they are available, even if they are less convenient. In *R (Clark-Darby) v Highbury Magistrates' Court*,[25] on a challenge by way of judicial review to the making of a council tax liability order, on the basis that the claimant that had not received notice of the hearing and so had not been able to put her defence, the court held that it was bound by previous authority[26] to hold that the use of judicial review was permissible, but that where points of 'pure' law were concerned, as distinct from breaches of natural justice, the appropriate route and that primarily intended by Parliament for the correction of errors of law would be an appeal by way of case stated to the Divisional Court.[27]

2.20   In *R (Brighton and Hove CC) v Brighton and Hove Justices*,[28] the court held that the appropriate procedure for challenging a magistrates' court's decision to set aside a liability order was by way of case stated, but that there was a discretion to permit such a challenge to proceed by way of judicial review. Stanley Burnton J held that, as neither the defendant nor the interested party had filed an acknowledgment of service or challenged the use of the judicial review procedure

23 See, eg, *R (Newham LBC) v Stratford Magistrates' Court* [2012] EWHC 325 (Admin).

24 [1992] 2 All ER 325, QBD, at 333 f–h.

25 [2001] EWHC 959 (Admin), [2002] RVR 35.

26 *R v Hereford Magistrates' Court ex p Rowlands* [1998] QB 110, QBD.

27 See also *Falmouth and Truro Port Health Authority v South West Water* [2001] QB 445, CA, in relation to the use of judicial review instead of a statutory right of appeal to the magistrates' court, as to which see also chapter 7 below.

28 [2004] EWHC 1800 (Admin), [2005] ACD 38. See also *R (Newham LBC) v Stratford Magistrates' Court* [2008] EWHC 125 (Admin), (2009) 172 JP 30; and *R (Sangha) v Stratford Magistrates' Court* [2008] EWHC 2979 (Admin).

until the interested party sought to do so after permission had been granted and after the defendant had agreed to a consent order, there had been no prejudice caused to any party by the claimant's use of the wrong procedure and the claim should therefore be allowed to proceed by way of judicial review.[29]

2.21   It has been held that the High Court is not concerned with a miscarriage of justice arising on the evidence, and that quashing, mandatory or prohibiting orders should only be made if:

- the court has failed properly to exercise its jurisdiction;
- some error of law appears on the face of the record; or
- there has been a breach of the principles of natural justice, etc.[30]

Quashing orders[31]

2.22   So long as the justices have not exceeded their powers, a quashing order cannot be sought to challenge the exercise of their discretion as to, for example, how much weight to give a piece of evidence, or whether or not to acquit following a trial on the merits.[32] If, however, there has been an error in procedure, such as where an order has been made or sentence passed that is not authorised by law, or where there has been an invalid committal for sentence, then quashing orders can be used effectively. In *R v Hendon Justices ex p Director of Public Prosecutions*,[33] it was held that a quashing order would lie to quash an acquittal where the information had been dismissed for want of prosecution, due to the late attendance at court of the prosecutor, ie without a trial on the merits.[34]

2.23   Moreover, if the High Court considers that a convicted person's sentence was in excess of the magistrates' jurisdiction, it may substitute the proper sentence that the lower court did have power to impose. It appears that a sentence that is so harsh and oppressive

---

29 [2004] EWHC 1800 (Admin) at [25].

30 For example, *R v Bristol Magistrates' Court ex p Rowles* [1994] COD 137, DC; but see also *R v Folkestone Magistrates' Court ex p Bradley* [1994] COD 138. See also *Re Racal Communications* [1981] AC 374, HL, per Lord Diplock at 383.

31 For a more detailed consideration of the remedies available in judicial review proceedings, see chapter 5 below.

32 *R v Dorking Justices ex p Harrington* [1984] AC 743, HL.

33 [1994] QB 167, DC.

34 See also *R v Stipendiary Magistrates ex p Director of Serious Fraud Office* [1994] COD 509, DC, where it was held that judicial review was appropriate where the magistrates' decision contained serious errors of law on its face. It was not necessary to state a case.

that no reasonable tribunal could have passed it may be regarded as having been passed in excess of jurisdiction.[35] A defendant should, however, appeal against sentence to the Crown Court before seeking permission to apply for judicial review.[36]

Mandatory orders

2.24 A mandatory order requires a judge, or justices, to do an act relating to the duties of their office. It will not be granted where some form of appeal exists that would be equally effective. Such an order will only be appropriate where there has been a wrongful refusal of jurisdiction, rather than an error in the exercise of that jurisdiction.[37] It will, therefore, not be appropriate where, for instance, there has been a refusal to receive admissible evidence or to allow a line of cross-examination. In such a situation, the justices, although perhaps acting wrongly, are not acting outside their jurisdiction.

2.25 A mandatory order may, however, be sought, for example in relation to a decision to refuse to grant public funding for extraneous reasons or a refusal to consider each case on its merits. In *R v Brown*,[38] magistrates who refused to try an information on the basis that other persons ought also to have been charged were compelled by a mandatory order to do so.

Prohibiting orders

2.26 These will only be appropriate where the proceedings to be reviewed are not yet concluded and so there is a possibility of correcting the alleged defect. A classic example is where there has been inordinate delay in bringing a matter to trial and the justices have ordered that the trial go ahead, failing to consider who caused the delay and whether the defendant has been prejudiced by it.[39]

---

35 *R v St Albans' Crown Court ex p Cinnamond* [1981] QB 480, DC.
36 *R v Battle Justices ex p Shepherd* (1983) 5 Cr App R (S) 124, DC. See generally chapter 7 below.
37 See *Re Racal Communications* [1981] AC 374, HL and *R (Sivasubramaniam) v Wandsworth County Court* [2002] EWCA Civ 1738, [2003] 1 WLR 475.
38 (1857) 7 E&B 757.
39 *R v West London Stipendiary Magistrate ex p Anderson* (1984) 148 JP 683, QBD.

Crown Courts

2.27　The Crown Court, which is not an inferior court, is susceptible to judicial review except in matters relating to trial on indictment.[40] In the main, Crown Court decisions taken in the exercise of its appellate jurisdiction from the magistrates' court, or on a committal for sentence, will be reviewable. In *R v Wolverhampton Crown Court ex p Crofts*,[41] the prosecution successfully applied for judicial review of a decision by the Crown Court to allow an appeal from the magistrates, where the evidence on which the appeal had been allowed had been shown to the Crown Court to be false.

2.28　In *R v Harrow Crown Court ex p Dave*,[42] however, the court took the view that decisions of the Crown Court exercising its appellate jurisdiction should not be challenged by way of judicial review when it is clear from the decision that the issue could be resolved on an appeal by way of case stated.[43] In fact, in *ex p Dave* itself, the court quashed the decision in question, and held that when sitting in an appellate capacity, the court must give sufficient reasons to demonstrate that it had identified the main issues in contention in the case and how it had resolved each of them.

2.29　In *R v Inner London Crown Court ex p Bentham*,[44] a local authority admitted the offence of statutory nuisance, on a prosecution brought by one of its tenants.[45] The magistrates made a nuisance order requiring the carrying out of specified works. The authority appealed to the Crown Court against the order. The Crown Court refused an application for legal aid by the prosecutor (ie the tenant – the victim of the nuisance). The basis for the refusal was that she did not fall within the relevant provisions of the Legal Aid Act 1974, as she was not a person resisting an appeal by a person convicted or sentenced by the magistrates. The applicant successfully applied to quash that decision, as the Crown Court had erred in law in its interpretation of the Act.

2.30　In *R (Oldham MBC) v Manchester Crown Court*,[46] the Divisional Court quashed a decision to allow an appeal against the imposition

40　Senior Courts Act 1981 s29(3).
41　[1983] 1 WLR 204, QBD.
42　[1994] 1 WLR 98, DC.
43　[1994] 1 WLR 98 at 107E.
44　[1989] 1 WLR 408, CA.
45　The prosecution was brought under the Public Health Act 1936, now Environmental Protection Act 1990 s82.
46　[2005] EWHC 930 (Admin).

of an anti-social behaviour order, where the respondent authority had asked for an adjournment of the appeal in order to obtain more information. The Crown Court bench had retired to consider the application for an adjournment, but had then reconvened and simply allowed the appeal. In the judicial review proceedings brought by the authority, the judge held that the Crown Court had been wrong to act as it had; although the application for an adjournment had been rightly dismissed, that did not mean that the appeal should automatically have been allowed.

2.31   Where a Crown Court gives inadequate reasons for dismissing an appeal, it seems that the appellant can seek judicial review of that decision without having to ask the Crown Court for further reasons.[47]

Matters relating to trial on indictment

2.32   The general exclusion of judicial review in respect of matters relating to trial on indictment has been given a relatively narrow construction by the courts.[48]

2.33   In *Re Smalley*,[49] the House of Lords, while declining to prescribe in the abstract any precise test as to those issues that would and those that would not relate to trial on indictment, offered a 'helpful pointer' to the legislative purposes behind the provision, namely to exclude review 'of any decision affecting the conduct of a trial on indictment, whether given in the course of the trial or by way of pre-trial directions'.[50]

2.34   A further helpful pointer was offered by Lord Browne-Wilkinson in *R v Manchester Crown Court ex p Director of Public Prosecutions*,[51] where he said:[52]

> It may ... be a helpful further pointer ... to ask the question 'Is the decision sought to be reviewed one arising in the issue between the Crown and the defendant formulated by the indictment (including the costs of such issue)?' If the answer is 'Yes', then to permit the decision to be challenged by judicial review may lead to delay in the

---

47 *R (Aitchison) v Sheffield Crown Court* [2012] EWHC 2844 (Admin), cf the procedure in civil courts where further reasons should be requested: *English v Emery Reimbold & Strick Ltd* [2002] EWCA Civ 605, [2002] 1 WLR 2409.

48 See especially *Re Smalley* [1985] AC 622, HL and *Re Sampson* [1987] 1 WLR 194, HL.

49 [1985] AC 622, HL.

50 [1985] AC 622, per Lord Bridge of Harwich at 642F.

51 [1993] 1 WLR 1524, [1993] 4 All ER 928, HL.

52 [1993] 4 All ER 928 at 933J–934A.

trial: the matter is therefore probably excluded from review by the section. If the answer is 'No', the decision of the Crown Court is truly collateral to the indictment of the defendant and judicial review of that decision will not delay his trial: therefore it may well not be excluded by the section.

2.35 In *R v Maidstone Crown Court ex p Harrow LBC*,[53] the Divisional Court held that the provisions of the Senior Courts Act (SCA) 1981 s29(3) did not bite where the Crown Court had acted entirely without jurisdiction. In that case, the defendant had pleaded not guilty by way of insanity. The judge had neither held a trial of that issue before the jury, nor had the defendant been convicted of the offence. The judge nevertheless, without jurisdiction, imposed an order requiring the defendant to be supervised by the local authority's social services department for two years. There was no right of appeal, the defendant not having been convicted.

2.36 The Divisional Court held that, in such a case, it was entitled to accept jurisdiction notwithstanding that the order that had been made was unarguably a matter relating to trial on indictment, which would not ordinarily be amenable to judicial review. Where the foundation of the judicial review application was absence of jurisdiction, as distinct from a challenge to the quality of a decision that was within jurisdiction, the court would not decline jurisdiction just because of SCA 1981 s29(3). The court enjoyed a supervisory jurisdiction over all Crown Court decisions save where the Crown Court exercised its jurisdiction relating to trial on indictment; Parliament cannot have intended, however, in enacting SCA 1981 s29(3), that decisions wholly outside the Crown Court's jurisdiction, which were also unappealable, would remain effective and uncorrected.[54]

2.37 The exclusion of judicial review provided by SCA 1981 s29(3) has been held to be compatible with a defendant's human rights under the HRA 1998. In *R (Shields) v Liverpool Crown Court*,[55] the Divisional Court held that a defendant's right to appeal against conviction provided an effective remedy for the purposes of article 6 (right to a fair trial). There was no requirement under the European Convention on Human Rights that a remedy must be provided at an earlier stage. Accordingly, there was no right to seek judicial review of the judge's

53 [2000] QB 719, DC.
54 See also *R (Kenneally) v Snaresbrook Crown Court* [2001] EWHC 968 (Admin), [2002] QB 1169, DC.
55 [2001] EWHC 90 (Admin), [2001] ACD 325, DC.

refusal to extend legal aid to enable the defendant to instruct Queen's Counsel.

2.38   The court reached the same conclusion in *R v Canterbury Crown Court ex p Regentford Ltd*,[56] holding that SCA 1981 s29(3) precluded an acquitted defendant challenging by judicial review the judge's refusal to make a costs order in its favour, and that although there was no right of appeal against that decision, the exclusion of judicial review was not incompatible with any Convention right, as there was no Convention right to have decisions reviewed by judicial review.[57]

2.39   The following types of order have been held be excluded from challenge by judicial review, pursuant to the SCA 1981 s29(3) exclusion:

- an order relating to the composition of a jury;[58]
- an order that certain counts on an indictment be stayed on the ground of delay;[59]
- an order quashing an indictment on the basis that the charges it contained fell outside the Crown Court's jurisdiction;[60]
- an order that an acquitted, legally-aided defendant contribute to the costs of his own defence;[61]
- orders concerning costs in general;[62]
- a decision not to hold a trial of the issue whether the defendant was fit to plead;[63]

---

56 [2001] HRLR 18, DC.
57 The court considered, however, that the failure of English law to provide any remedy, may well conflict with article 13 of the European Convention on Human Rights and therefore the UK's treaty obligations, although article 13 was not included in Schedule 1 to the HRA 1998. Cf also *R v Maidstone Crown Court ex p Harrow LBC* [2000] QB 719, DC, referred to at para 2.35 above.
58 *R v Sheffield Crown Court ex p Brownlow* [1980] QB 530, CA.
59 *Re Ashton* [1994] AC 9, HL.
60 *R v Crown Court at Manchester ex p Director of Public Prosecutions* [1993] 1 WLR 1524, HL.
61 *Re Sampson* [1987] 1 WLR 194, HL.
62 *ex p Meredith* [1973] 1 WLR 435, DC; *R v Cardiff Crown Court ex p Jones* [1974] QB 113, DC (doubted in *Re Smalley* [1985] AC 622, HL); *R v Smith (Martin)* [1975] QB 531, CA. See also *R v Canterbury Crown Court ex p Regentford Ltd* [2001] HRLR 18, DC. Note that the ECtHR has held that there was a breach of article 6 where a judge's refused to grant a costs order to a defendant who was acquitted due to a prosecution witness not attending: *Hussain v UK* (2006) 43 EHRR 22.
63 *R v Crown Court at Bradford ex p Bottomley* [1994] COD 422, DC. The court held that 'nothing could be plainer' than that the question related to trial on indictment.

- the imposition of a mandatory life sentence;[64]
- a decision not to impose a compensation order following the making of a confiscation order;[65]
- a refusal to lift a stay of proceedings against the applicant;[66]
- a decision not to impose reporting restrictions in relation to the conviction of a minor;[67]
- a decision that documents were relevant and not covered by public interest immunity and so ought to be disclosed to the defence;[68]
- a decision not to dismiss a charge as an abuse of process.[69]

2.40   In contrast, the following issues have been held to be amenable to judicial review:

- an order forfeiting the recognisance of a surety;[70]
- a decision to refuse bail;[71]
- an order dismissing charges before arraignment on the ground of insufficient evidence for a jury to convict;[72]
- a decision concerning the listing of a trial which may affect its validity;[73]
- a costs order made against the Crown after an acquittal;[74]

---

64 *R v Daniella Lichniak* in the Court of Appeal [2001] QB 296 (affirmed by the House of Lords: [2002] UKHL 47, [2003] 1 AC 903).

65 *R (Faithfull) v Crown Court at Ipswich* [2007] EWHC 2763 (Admin), [2008] 1 WLR 1636.

66 *R v Plymouth Crown Court ex p Withey* (1999) 11 October, unreported; *R v Central Criminal Court ex p Raymond* [1986] 1 WLR 710.

67 Under Children and Young Persons Act 1933 s39. *R v Winchester Crown Court ex p B (A Minor)* [1999] 1 WLR 788, DC.

68 *R (Customs and Excise Comrs) v Leicester Crown Court* [2001] EWHC 33 (Admin), (2001) *Times* 23 February.

69 *R (Snelgrove) v Woolwich Crown Court* [2004] EWHC 2172 (Admin), [2005] 1 WLR 3223.

70 *Re Smalley* [1985] AC 622, HL.

71 *R (O) v Harrow Crown Court* [2003] EWHC 868 (Admin), [2003] 1 WLR 2756.

72 *R v Central Criminal Court ex p Director of the Serious Fraud Office* [1993] 1 WLR 949, DC, although the jurisdiction should only be exercised in extremely limited circumstances. See also *R v Crown Court at Snaresbrook ex p Director of the Serious Fraud Office* (1998) 95(44) LSG 35, (1998) 42 SJLB 263. The *Central Criminal Court* case was strongly doubted in *R (Snelgrove) v Woolwich Crown Court* [2004] EWHC 2172 (Admin), [2005] 1 WLR 3223.

73 *R v Southwark Crown Court ex p Comrs for Customs and Excise* [1993] 1 WLR 764, DC (but see comments in *Re Ashton* [1994] AC 9, HL).

74 *R v Wood Green Crown Court ex p Director of Public Prosecutions* [1993] 1 WLR 723, DC. The correctness of this decision was, however, doubted in *Hunter v Newcastle Crown Court* [2013] EWHC 191 (Admin), [2013] 2 Costs LR 348, DC and may therefore no longer be good law.

- an order purporting to control proceedings which were continuing in the magistrates' court;[75]
- an order that a bail application be held in private.[76]

2.41 It can be seen from these examples that the Crown is frequently the claimant in such cases, presumably because its rights to appeal are much more limited than are those of defendants.

2.42 Where SCA 1981 s29(3) precludes the grant of one of the prerogative orders, the court has no jurisdiction to grant a declaration.[77]

Ultra vires as a defence to criminal proceedings[78]

2.43 Public law challenges may also be used as a shield. An individual, for example, charged with an offence of contravening subordinate legislation or a decision of a public body, or acting without a relevant licence, may wish to raise as a defence to those proceedings the invalidity of the measure or decision that he is charged with contravening.

2.44 In *Boddington v British Transport Police*,[79] the defendant was convicted of a charge of smoking in a railway carriage where smoking was prohibited, contrary to a railway byelaw.[80] He sought to defend himself on the basis that the relevant byelaw was ultra vires and void, but was not permitted to do so. The House of Lords held that a defendant to a criminal charge was normally entitled as a matter of right to raise such a defence, absent a clear parliamentary intention to the contrary. The presumption, moreover, that a legislative measure was valid until a court ruled otherwise did not affect the principle that once a court decided it to be ultra vires, it was void from the start and would be treated as never having had any legal effect.[81]

2.45 There are some situations in which the *Boddington* principle will not apply, as whether a court has jurisdiction to rule on a defence

---

75 *R (Customs and Excise Comrs) v Canterbury Crown Court* [2002] EWHC 2584 (Admin), [2003] Crim LR 195, DC.

76 *R (Malik) v Central Criminal Court* [2006] EWHC 1539 (Admin), [2007] 1 WLR 2455.

77 *R v Chelmsford Crown Court ex p Chief Constable of Essex* [1994] 1 WLR 359, DC. See also *R (Faithfull) v Crown Court at Ipswich* [2007] EWHC 2763 (Admin), [2008] 1 WLR 1636.

78 See, in general, chapter 3 below.

79 [1999] 2 AC 143, HL.

80 Contrary to byelaw 20 of the British Railways Board's Byelaws 1965, made under the authority of Transport Act 1962 s67(1).

81 [1999] 2 AC 143, per Lord Irvine of Lairg LC at 155B–D. See further at paras 7.37–7.51 below.

based on arguments of the invalidity of subordinate legislation or of an administrative act under the statute will depend on an examination of the particular statutory context. The courts may still hold that Parliament has legislated to preclude such challenges being made by way of defence, in the interest, for example, of promoting certainty about the legitimacy of administrative acts on which the public may have to rely.[82] This appears particularly likely where the acts sought to be challenged by way of defence were administrative acts that were aimed specifically at the defendant who had enjoyed had ample opportunity under the scheme to challenge those acts.[83]

Election courts

2.46　Under the Representation of the People Act 1983, proceedings challenging a parliamentary election must be commenced by a parliamentary election petition and tried by an election court, which has the same powers, jurisdiction and authority as the High Court. Nonetheless, a parliamentary election court is an inferior tribunal the actions of which can be the subject of judicial review; the scope of which review is not confined to excesses of jurisdiction in the narrow sense, but extends to correcting errors of law. Ordinarily, however, a party's failure to utilise the statutory procedure[84] for stating a special case for the opinion of the High Court, in relation to an issue of law arising during the hearing of an election petition, would afford very strong reasons for the High Court to decline as a matter of discretion to exercise its judicial review jurisdiction.[85]

Tribunals

2.47　It has been established for many years that the decisions of all types of tribunal are reviewable in respect of any error of law.[86] The modern tribunal system, however, as legislated for by the Tribunals, Courts

---

82　*Boddington* (above), per Lord Irvine of Lairg LC at 160 C–D. Examples of such schemes, given in *Boddington* itself, were *R v Wicks* [1998] AC 92, HL (planning legislation) and *Quietlynn Ltd v Plymouth City Council* [1988] QB 114 (sex shop licensing legislation): see *Boddington* at 160D–161H.

83　*Boddington* (above) at 161G–H.

84　Representation of the People Act 1983 s146.

85　*R (Woolas) v Parliamentary Election Court* [2010] EWHC 3169 (Admin), [2012] QB 1.

86　See *Anisminic Ltd v Foreign Compensation Commission* [1969] 2 AC 147, HL.

and Enforcement Act 2007 provides for a system of First-tier Tribunals and Upper Tribunals, significantly reducing the role of judicial review. It is not proposed to set out here any detailed provisions relating to the availability of, or interrelationship between, statutory appeals and judicial review in the context of tribunal decisions, nor on the conduct of or procedure concerning statutory appeals.[87] What follows is by way of an outline of the role that judicial review still plays in relation to tribunals.

2.48   The Upper Tribunals have an appellate jurisdiction over the First-tier Tribunals. There is a right to appeal, with permission, from a decision of an Upper Tribunal to the Court of Appeal,[88] except in the case of 'excluded decisions'.[89]

2.49   One such excluded decision is any decision of the Upper Tribunal on any application for permission to appeal.[90] Therefore, if permission to appeal is refused by both the First-tier Tribunal and the Upper Tribunal, the would-be appellant has not further route of appeal.

2.50   The Supreme Court held in *R (Cart) v Upper Tribunal*,[91] that there was nothing in the Tribunals, Courts and Enforcement Act 2007 that excluded judicial review of such decisions of the Upper Tribunal. In order, however, to ensure that the limited resources of the courts were not overstretched, permission for judicial review should only granted where the criteria for a second appeal were met.[92] In other

87 For further information on these matters see Jacobs *Tribunal Practice and Procedure* (LAG, 2nd edn, 2011). See also Lady Hale's account of the tribunal system in *R (Cart) v Upper Tribunal* [2011] UKSC 28, [2012] 1 AC 663 at [11]–[29]. Laws LJ's detailed description of the history and structure of the tribunal system and the jurisdiction of judicial review in the Court of Appeal in *R (Cart) v Upper Tribunal* [2009] EWHC 3052 (Admin), [2011] QB 120 remains of great value, although his conclusions were rejected by the Supreme Court.

88 Tribunals, Courts and Enforcement Act 2007 s13(1)-(4).

89 Tribunals, Courts and Enforcement Act, 2007 s13(1)

90 Tribunals, Courts and Enforcement Act 2007 s13(8)(c). The other excluded decisions are decisions of an Upper Tribunal: (a) on an appeal under s28(4) or (6), Data Protection Act 1998 (appeals against national security certificate), (b) on an appeal under s60(1) or (4), Freedom of Information Act 2000 (appeals against national security certificate), (c) under s10, 2007 Act (i) to review, or not to review, an earlier decision of the tribunal, (ii) to take no action, or not to take any particular action, in the light of a review of an earlier decision of the tribunal, or (iii) to set aside an earlier decision of the tribunal, (d) that is set aside under s10, 2007 Act (including a decision set aside after proceedings on an appeal have begun), or (e) that is of a description specified in an order made by the Lord Chancellor: ibid s13(8), (9).

91 [2011] UKSC 28, [2012] 1 AC 663. See, to the same effect in Scotland, *Eba v Advocate General for Scotland* [2011] UKSC 29, [2012] 1 AC 710.

92 Contained in CPR 52.13. See further paras 7.75–7.79 below.

words, the court would only entertain an application for judicial review if it raised an important point of principle or practice or there was some other compelling reason for the court to hear it.[93]

2.51 Interestingly, the Supreme Court in *Cart* considered at some length the approach in *Sivasubramanium*,[94] but rejected it in favour of the second appeals approach. The court[95] held that the problem with an exceptional circumstances approach is that it restricts the scope of judicial review in a way that creates its own problems and does not target arguable errors of law of general importance.[96] On the other hand, applying the second appeal criteria offered the following advantages:

- it ensured that errors on important points of principle or practice would not become fossilised within the Upper Tribunal system, including, perhaps, where although the law was clear the Tribunal had been systematically misapplying it;[97]
- the 'some other compelling reason' limb of the test would enable the court to examine an arguable error of law in a decision of the First-tier Tribunal that may not in itself raise an important point of principle or practice, but that cried out for consideration by the court if the Upper Tribunal refused to do so. Compelling reasons could include cases where it was strongly arguable that (a) the individual had suffered a wholly exceptional collapse of fair procedure or (b) there had been an error of law that had caused truly drastic consequences.

---

93 See CPR r52.13.
94 *R (Sivasubramaniam) v Wandsworth County Court* [2002] EWCA Civ 1738, [2003] 1 WLR 475. See the discussion paras 2.5–2.12 above.
95 See particularly the Opinions of Baroness Hale at [39]–[44], [52]–[57], Lord Phillips at [87]–[94] and Lord Dyson at [128]–[131]. The other members of the court agreed.
96 *Cart* (above), per Baroness Hale JSC at [39]–[44] and [52]–[57]; Lord Dyson at [128]–[131].
97 A situation in which the Court of Appeal considered a second appeal to be permissible in *Cramp v Hastings BC* [2005] EWCA Civ 1005, [2005] 4 All ER 1014, [2005] HLR 48.

Other bodies performing public acts and duties

2.52　This last category is somewhat nebulous, but the modern trend has been to expand the range of bodies whose decisions fall within the scope of the Administrative Court. Moreover, with the increasing influence of European law principles, even those certainties that used to exist are no longer so clearly correct.

The Crown

2.53　The traditional position is that the Crown itself is not amenable to the prerogative orders,[98] although its servants are. This is, however, no longer a safe assumption. Where a challenge to a statute is based on an overriding provision of European law,[99] the operation of the statute may, and in some circumstances must, be suspended pending the resolution of the challenge, and the offending provisions of the Act can be held invalid.[100] Where the provision of an Act of Parliament is incompatible with Convention rights granted by the HRA 1998, the courts cannot quash the offending provision, but can only declare it incompatible, which does not affect its continued operation, nor the rights of anyone under it.[101]

2.54　A declaration has always been available against the Crown. In terms of interim relief, a stay may be granted pending the outcome of the application for review, and/or an injunction.[102] The Court of Appeal has also held that a stay may be ordered not only of judicial proceedings but also of decisions of the Secretary of State and the process by which such decisions have been reached; the term 'stay' is simply the public law description of what; in private law, is called an injunction, as in judicial review proceedings the claimant and the decision-maker are not in any true sense opposing parties.[103] For the

---

98　See chapter 5 below.

99　See paras 1.29–1.34 above.

100　*R v Secretary of State for Transport ex p Factortame (No 2)* [1991] 1 AC 603, ECJ and HL, especially per Lord Bridge of Harwich at 658–9, see also *Equal Opportunities Commission v Secretary of State for Employment* [1995] 1 AC 1, HL.

101　Human Rights Act 1998 s4.

102　*Re M* [1994] AC 377, HL; see also, in a European context, *R v Secretary of State for Transport ex p Factortame (No 2)* [1991] 1 AC 603, ECJ and HL, which was overruled in part, ie in relation to domestic (non-EC) disputes, by *Re M* [1994] AC 377, HL.

103　*R v Secretary of State for Education ex p Avon CC* [1991] 1 QB 558, CA, per Glidewell LJ.

principles upon which the court will decide whether to grant a stay, see chapter 5 below.

Prerogative powers[104]

2.55 Traditionally, the courts would not review the exercise of prerogative powers. In *Council of Civil Service Unions v Minister of State for the Civil Service*,[105] however, the House of Lords held that the exercise of such powers was reviewable, so long as the subject-matter of the power was justiciable. The courts would not, for example, review the exercise of treaty-making powers, honours, mercy, etc, because these were not matters suitable to be ruled on by a court.

2.56 The number and type of such powers that the courts will now regard as justiciable may be increasing. For instance, in *R v Secretary of State for the Home Department ex p Bentley*,[106] where the Secretary of State had refused to grant a pardon, the court held that the prerogative power of mercy was amenable to review in an appropriate case, and requested the minister to reconsider the matter, while declining to make any order on the judicial review application itself.

2.57 The court considered, in *R (Campaign for Nuclear Disarmament) v Prime Minister*,[107] the question of justiciability and the extent of so-called 'forbidden areas' within which exercises of the prerogative will not be reviewable. The claimant sought an advisory declaration that UN Security Council Resolution 1441 did not authorise military action to be taken against Iraq and that any such action without the obtaining of a second UN resolution would be unlawful as a matter of international law.

2.58 A three-judge Administrative Court held that it had no jurisdiction to entertain the claim. The court would not make a declaration on the meaning of an international instrument that had no domestic existence having not been incorporated into UK law, and where no determination fell to be made regarding the rights of people in the UK that would require that instrument to be construed by the

---

104 See also paras 3.72–3.73 below.

105 [1985] AC 374, HL.

106 [1994] QB 349, DC. See also *R v Secretary of State for Foreign and Commonwealth Affairs ex p Everett* [1989] 1 QB 811, CA, where the court entertained a challenge to (but upheld) the policy of the secretary of state to refuse a passport to a person in respect of whom there was an outstanding arrest warrant, especially per Taylor LJ at 820; *R v Secretary of State for Foreign and Commonwealth Affairs ex p Rees-Mogg* [1994] QB 552, QBD.

107 [2002] EWHC 2777 (Admin), [2003] ACD 36.

court.[108] In any event, the subject-matter of the claim was not justiciable as it involved matters of international relations, defence and national security and so should not be determined by a court.

2.59 The court also accepted the defendant's contention that it would be damaging to the public interest for the court even to consider the issue, as that would oblige the defendant to bind itself to a particular position that would harm the public interest in that it would weaken the government's international negotiating position and harm its international relations.[109] A question would not be justiciable where any determination by the court would damage the public interest in areas of international relations, national security or defence.[110]

2.60 In any event, the court would not act to make advisory declarations unless there was a good reason to do so, which was not the case here.[111] The issues, however, were so obviously important that permission to apply would be granted but the substantive claim dismissed.

2.61 By contrast, in *R (Abbasi) v Secretary of State for Foreign and Commonwealth Affairs*,[112] the Court of Appeal was prepared to entertain an application for judicial review, seeking an order to require the Foreign Secretary to intervene with the US authorities in relation to the continued administrative detention of the claimant, a British citizen, at Camp Delta in Guantanamo Bay, Cuba.

2.62 The court held that where fundamental human rights of British citizens were at stake, the courts would be prepared to review the actions of a foreign sovereign state. The claimant had been and continued to be detained arbitrarily, and indefinitely, with no opportunity to challenge the legitimacy of that detention before any court or tribunal. While this treatment was objectionable, however, the court

---

108 [2002] EWHC 2777 (Admin), per Simon Brown LJ at [36]–[40]. See also *R v Lyons* [2002] UKHL 44, [2003] 1 AC 976, in which it was held that the English courts have no jurisdiction to interpret or apply international treaties, as they do not form part of English law. In that case, the House of Lords applied this principle to refuse to quash convictions entered prior to the coming into force of the HRA 1998 on the ground that the ECtHR had held that they had not enjoyed a fair trial for the purposes of article 6 of the European Convention on Human Rights.

109 A proposition the court regarded as self-evident: per Simon Brown LJ at [41]–[42].

110 *R (Campaign for Nuclear Disarmament) v Prime Minister* [2002] EWHC 2777 (Admin), [2003] ACD 36, per Simon Brown LJ at [41]–[45]; per Richards J at [55]–[60].

111 [2002] EWHC 2777 (Admin) at [46].

112 [2002] EWCA Civ 1598, [2003] UKHRR 76.

could provide no direct remedy. The claimant was outside the jurisdiction of the UK for the purposes of his Convention rights, given that there was no act by any UK body which had caused his current situation, nor which had violated any of his rights. Nor did the UK authorities have any control over his detention.

2.63 Having said this, the Court of Appeal refused to accept the Secretary of State's contention that judicial review was excluded in relation to his refusal to lend diplomatic assistance to a British citizen whose human rights were violated by the conduct of the foreign state, merely because the decision involved an exercise of prerogative power. The question was not whether the source of Foreign Office power was prerogative, but whether the subject-matter of the claim was justiciable.

2.64 There was a legitimate expectation that the authorities would properly consider a request for such assistance. The decision whether or not to accede to such a request would be reviewable if it were irrational or contrary to that legitimate expectation. The court was therefore entitled to investigate whether such a request had properly been considered. If it had, but the defendant refused the request for assistance, the court could not properly entertain a challenge to that refusal, as that decision involved issues of foreign policy that were matters for governmental decision. For the court to seek to determine such matters would involve entering the 'forbidden areas' of non-justiciable discretion. In the circumstances of the case, the request for assistance had been properly considered and it would be inappropriate to order the Secretary of State to express a view as to the legality of the claimant's detention or to make any specific representations to the United States government, as to do so would plainly have an impact on the conduct of foreign policy at a particularly delicate time.[113]

2.65 In R (Al-Haq) v Secretary of State for Foreign and Commonwealth Affairs,[114] the Divisional Court held that it had no jurisdiction to hear an application for permission to apply for judicial review by a non-governmental human rights organisation that sought declarations that the government of the United Kingdom had breached its international obligations in respect of Israel. The court repeated that the controlling factor in considering whether a particular exercise of prerogative power was susceptible to judicial review was not its source but its subject matter. The conduct of foreign affairs was exclusively

---

113 [2002] EWCA Civ 1598, per Lord Phillips of Worth Matravers MR at [106]–[107].

114 [2009] EWHC 1910 (Admin), [2009] ACD 76. See also para 3.74 below.

a matter for the Executive and it would take an exceptional case for the court to intervene in cases involving considerations of foreign policy.[115]

Other decisions

2.66 A person or body exercising powers delegated by prerogative power may also be susceptible to review. Moreover, it seems that an administrative recommendation to a minister may be susceptible to review.[116] In *Tower Hamlets LBC v Secretary of State for the Environment*,[117] a declaration was granted to the effect that two paragraphs of the Secretary of State's Homelessness Code of Guidance were wrong in law. The Secretary of State did not argue, in the Court of Appeal, that the nature of the code rendered judicial review inappropriate, which the court referred to as a 'correct and responsible position'.[118] The activities of the Parliamentary Ombudsman are, it appears, also amenable to review, although the court will not readily be persuaded to interfere with the exercise of his discretion.[119]

Other bodies

2.67 A non-statutory body whose authority derives solely from contract, such as an employer's disciplinary tribunal, falls outside the scope of review.[120]

2.68 In recent years, however, the courts have shifted the emphasis from the traditional test based solely on the source of the body's powers to one founded on both the source and also the nature of the

---

115 See also *R (Hassan) v Secretary of State for Trade and Industry* [2007] EWHC 2630 (Admin), [2008] ACD 10, appealed to the Court of Appeal on a different point and reported as [2008] EWCA Civ 1312, [2009] 3 All ER 539; *R (Khan) v Secretary of State for Foreign and Commonwealth Affairs* [2012] EWHC 3728 (Admin).

116 *R v Secretary of State for Transport ex p APH Road Safety Ltd* [1993] COD 240, QBD; but see *R v Secretary of State for the Home Department ex p Westminster Press Ltd* [1992] COD 303, DC, where it was held that a government circular to police chiefs concerning information to be given to the media was not reviewable.

117 [1993] QB 632, CA.

118 [1993] QB 632, per Stuart-Smith LJ at 644.

119 *R v Parliamentary Commissioner for Administration ex p Dyer* [1994] 1 WLR 621, DC.

120 See *R v British Broadcasting Corporation ex p Lavelle* [1983] 1 WLR 23, QBD; *R v East Berkshire Health Authority ex p Walsh* [1985] QB 152, CA; compare *R v Secretary of State for the Home Department ex p Benwell* [1985] QB 554, QBD.

functions performed or powers exercised by the body.[121] Accordingly, non-statutory bodies set up to undertake public functions have been held to fall within the scope of review, so long as their powers are not derived exclusively from contract.

2.69   In *R v Panel on Takeovers and Mergers ex p Datafin*,[122] the Court of Appeal held that the source of power and functions performed were both relevant factors, to be given different weight in different circumstances:

> In all the reports it is possible to find enumerations of factors giving rise to the [supervisory] jurisdiction, but it is a fatal error to regard the presence of all those factors as essential or as being exclusive of other factors. Possibly the only essential elements are what can be described as a public element, which can take many different forms, and the exclusion from the jurisdiction of bodies whose sole source of power is a consensual submission to its jurisdiction.[123]

2.70   It seems, then, that in broad terms, a body is amenable to judicial review if, on consideration of the source and nature of its powers, it has an essential public law element or 'nexus'. Without falling into the fatal error referred to above, it may be said that a body may have such a public law element where, for example, the elements suggested in *Datafin* itself can be identified:

- it performs or operates in the public domain as an integral part of a regulatory system which performs public law duties;
- it is non-statutory by government decision but is established 'under the authority of government';[124]
- it is supported by a periphery of statutory powers and penalties;
- it is embraced by government and performs functions that government would otherwise perform;
- it is under a duty in exercising what amount to public powers to act judicially; and/or
- the source of its power does not derive exclusively from a consensual submission to its jurisdiction.[125]

---

121 See, eg, *Council of Civil Service Unions v Minister of State for the Civil Service* [1985] AC 374, HL.

122 [1987] QB 815, CA.

123 [1987] QB 815, per Sir John Donaldson MR at 838E.

124 [1987] QB 815, per Lloyd LJ at 849D.

125 [1987] QB 815 at 849D. See also *R v Insurance Ombudsman ex p Aegon Life Insurance Ltd* [1994] COD 426: the Insurance Ombudsman's decisions were not reviewable; his jurisdiction was purely contractual. Whether this case would be decided in the same way today is not entirely clear. The Financial Services Ombudsman, who has replaced him (with a broader jurisdiction) has been the subject of judicial review.

2.71 It does not follow from this that a public body's decision will inevitably fall outside the scope of the remedy if it involves an employment, or other, contractual relationship. The essential question is that of the existence of a public law nexus in the issue that has been raised.[126] If one is to be found, such as the use of a contractual power for an improper purpose,[127] then, especially if no remedy is available in private law,[128] it is likely that judicial review will still be available.

2.72 In *McLaughlin v Governor of the Cayman Islands*,[129] for example, Lord Bingham said:[130]

> It is a settled principle of law that if a public authority purports to dismiss the holder of a public office in excess of its powers, or in breach of natural justice, or unlawfully (categories which overlap), the dismissal is, as between the public authority and the office-holder, null, void and without legal effect, at any rate once a court of competent jurisdiction so declares or orders. Thus the office-holder remains in office, entitled to the remuneration attaching to such office, so long as he remains ready, willing and able to render the service required of him, until his tenure of office is lawfully brought to an end by resignation or lawful dismissal.[131]

2.73 Likewise, in *R (Shoesmith) v Ofsted*,[132] a former local authority Director of Children's Services, which was a statutory office under the Children Act 2004, successfully sought judicial review of the procedure operated by the Secretary of State and the local authority in removing her from her role and subsequently dismissing her, on the basis of breaches of the requirements of procedural fairness. The claimant's post had been created, required and defined by and under statute. It

---

126 See further paras 3.13–3.23 below.

127 In *R v Liverpool CC ex p Ferguson* (1985) *Times* 20 November, DC, a decision to dismiss school teachers was a direct consequence of a decision to set an unlawful rate, which meant that it was not properly or legitimately taken in the furtherance of the authority's duty as an education authority. See also, eg, *Roberts v Hopwood* [1925] AC 578, HL.

128 *R v Hammersmith and Fulham LBC ex p National Association of Local Government Officers* [1991] COD 397, DC, where it was considered that there would be no remedy in the industrial tribunal.

129 [2007] UKPC 50, [2007] 1 WLR 2839.

130 At [14].

131 See also *Ridge v Baldwin* [1964] AC 40, HL.

132 [2011] EWCA Civ 642, [2011] PTSR 1459.

enjoyed sufficient statutory underpinning to entitle the officer-holder to seek judicial review of her dismissal.[133]

2.74   Since *Datafin*, it has been held that state school governors are susceptible to review,[134] as is a district valuer,[135] the Parliamentary and Local Government Ombudsmen,[136] the National Health Service,[137] a hospital ethics committee,[138] an electricity board,[139] the police,[140] a code of practice committee,[141] the General Dental Council,[142] and registrars of births, deaths and marriages.[143]

2.75   Conversely, those bodies held to be outside the scope of review include the Insurance Ombudsman,[144] the Jockey Club,[145] the Football Association,[146] the Chief Rabbi,[147] the Independent Broadcasting

---

133 *Shoesmith*, above, per Maurice Kay LJ at [89]–[91]. See also eg *R (Lock) v Leicester CC* [2012] EWHC 2058 (Admin) in which a dismissed local authority chief executive, who had also been its head of paid service sought to quash her dismissal. The judgment does not consider the availability of judicial review. See also *Mattu v University Hospitals of Coventry and Warwickshire NHS Trust* [2012] EWCA Civ 641, [2012] 4 All ER 359, [2013] ICR 270, in which the Court of Appeal considered whether article 6, Schedule 1 of the HRA 1998 was engaged by the dismissal of a doctor.

134 And governors of a city technology college: *R v Governors of Haberdashers' Aske's College Trust ex p T* [1995] ELR 350; but not independent school governors: *R v Fernhill Manor School ex p A* [1994] ELR 67.

135 *R v Kidderminster District Valuer ex p Powell* (1992) 4 Admin LR 193.

136 *R v Parliamentary Commissioner for Administration ex p Dyer* [1994] 1 WLR 621; *R v Local Commissioner for Administration for the South, etc, ex p Eastleigh BC* [1988] QB 855.

137 *Re Walker's Application* (1987) Times 25 November 25.

138 *R v Ethical Committee of St Mary's Hospital (Manchester) ex p Harriott* [1988] 1 Federal Law Reports 512 (FC), an Australian case.

139 *R v Midlands Electricity Board ex p Busby* (1987) Times 28 October.

140 *R v Commissioner of Police for the Metropolis ex p P* (1996) 8 Admin LR 6.

141 *R v Code of Practice Committee of British Pharmaceutical Society ex p Professional Counselling Aids Ltd* [1991] COD 228, QBD.

142 *Lynch v General Dental Council* [2003] EWHC 2987 (Admin), [2004] 1 All ER 1159.

143 *R v Registrar of Births, Deaths and Marriages ex p Minhas* [1977] QB 1.

144 Whose jurisdiction is purely contractual (by agreement between insurance companies): *R v Insurance Ombudsman ex p Aegon Life Insurance Ltd* [1994] CLC 88, [1994] COD 426.

145 *R v Disciplinary Committee of the Jockey Club ex p Aga Khan* [1993] 1 WLR 909, CA; *R v Jockey Club ex p RAM Racecourses Ltd* [1993] 2 All ER 225, DC; *R v Disciplinary Committee of Jockey Club ex p Massingberd-Mundy* [1993] 2 All ER 207, DC.

146 *R v Football Association Ltd ex p Football League Ltd* [1993] 2 All ER 833, QBD.

147 *R v Chief Rabbi of the United Hebrew Congregation of Great Britain and the Commonwealth ex p Wachmann* [1992] 1 WLR 1036, QBD.

Authority,[148] and the Medical Defence Union.[149] As stated above, a non-statutory body whose authority derives solely from contract, such as an employer's disciplinary tribunal, falls outside the scope of review.[150]

2.76　　Neither of the *Datafin* propositions (ie 'essential public law element' and 'no consensual submission to jurisdiction') has ever been the subject of significant discussion in the House of Lords or Supreme Court. *Datafin* was applied almost *sub silentio* by the Privy Council in *Mohit v DPP of Mauritius*,[151] and by the House of Lords in *YL v Birmingham CC*.[152] Of course, the process of adopting a hybrid 'functions-based' and 'source of power' test, in place of considering source of powers alone, was started by the House of Lords in *Council of Civil Service Unions*.[153] It is unthinkable, particularly in this age of contracting out ever larger numbers of 'governmental' functions, that the courts will revert to the former approach.

2.77　　The *Datafin* approach does create uncertainties about which bodies are and which are not susceptible to review. The examples given above[154] – of bodies not so susceptible – are explicable on the basis of function as much as by reference to the nature of the body. Moreover, as has been seen in relation to the analogous question arising under the HRA 1998,[155] the reasons given by the courts for their

148　Acting under its articles of association: *R v Independent Broadcasting Authority ex p Rank Organisation plc* (1986) *Times* 14 March.

149　[2006] EWHC 1948 (Admin), [2006] ACD 102.

150　See, eg, *R v British Broadcasting Corporation ex p Lavelle* [1983] 1 WLR 23; *R v East Berkshire Health Authority ex p Walsh* [1985] QB 152, CA; compare *R v Secretary of State for the Home Department ex p Benwell* [1985] QB 554.

151　[2006] UKPC 20, [2006] 1 WLR 3343. In that case, Lord Bingham referred, at [20], only to *Datafin* for the proposition that a power is reviewable if its source is statutory; it is a little surprising that by 2006, it was thought to cite authority for such a proposition.

152　[2007] UKHL 27, [2008] 1 AC 95. The issue in *YL* related to the question of whether a private body was performing a public function for the purposes of section 6(3)(b) of the HRA 1998, rather than to the domestic classification of a body, but the issues are so closely related that the House of Lords would inevitably had said so had they considered the *Datafin* to be incorrect. In the event, only Lord Mance commented at all on the central principles established by the case (at [101]–[102]), expressing neither approval nor disapproval.

153　*Council of Civil Service Unions v Minister of State for the Civil Service* [1985] AC 374, HL.

154　Para 2.75.

155　Section 6(3)(b) provides that a public authority includes any person certain of whose functions are functions of a public nature.

conclusions in different cases cannot be reconciled entirely with each other.[156]

2.78 In *R v Derbyshire CC ex p Noble*,[157] however, Woolf LJ stated that 'the courts have, over the years, by decisions in individual cases, indicated the approximate divide' between bodies which are amenable to review and those which are not. In *R v Legal Aid Board ex p Donn & Co (a firm)*,[158] Ognall J took the view that the 'answer must ... fall to be decided as one of overall impression, and one of degree. There can be no universal test'.

2.79 In *R (Weaver) v London & Quadrant Housing Trust Ltd*,[159] the Divisional Court held that a body which was a public authority for the purposes of the HRA 1998 would also be amenable to judicial review on a conventional basis (a point not challenged on appeal).

'Public authorities' in human rights cases – the analogous issue

2.80 The HRA 1998 defines a 'public authority' as including: (a) a court or tribunal, and (b) any person with functions of a public nature.[160] In relation to a particular act, however, a body will not be a public authority for the purposes of the Act by virtue only of (b) above if the nature of the act is private.[161] It can be seen that all courts fall within this definition, whether or not they are inferior.[162]

2.81 In judicial review cases involving human rights issues, the range of bodies whose decisions may be open to challenge could have been held to be significantly wider than in cases which have no human rights element. Indeed, on the wording of the Act itself, it seems to have been open to the courts to adopt a purely functions-based test.

2.82 In *Poplar HARCA v Donoghue*,[163] the Court of Appeal was faced with the issue whether a registered social landlord, now termed a private registered provider of social housing (PRP)[164] was a public

---

156 See paras 2.80–2.103 below.

157 [1990] ICR 808, CA, at 814.

158 [1996] 3 All ER 1, QBD, at 11.

159 [2008] EWHC 1377 (Admin), [2009] 1 All ER 17, appealed to the Court of Appeal, but not on this point [2009] EWCA Civ 587, [2010] 1 WLR 363.

160 HRA 1998 s6(3).

161 HRA 1998 s6(5).

162 See paras 2.3–2.46 above.

163 [2001] EWCA Civ 595, [2002] QB 48.

164 Now termed a private registered provider of social housing: Housing and Regeneration Act 2008, Pt 2, Ch.3.

authority, for the purpose of challenging a decision it had made to seek a possession order in respect of a property it had let under an assured tenancy, on the mandatory ground available under the Housing Act 1988.[165] The court held that while HRA 1998 s6 required a generous interpretation, it was clearly inspired by the approach adopted by the courts in judicial review proceedings following *Datafin*.[166]

2.83 The Court of Appeal observed that the fact that a body performs functions that a public body would otherwise be obliged to perform cannot necessarily render the function a public function. Public bodies can use private bodies to perform their functions without the nature of the function thereby inevitably being considered public so as to turn the private body into a public authority for the purposes of HRA 1998 s6. Otherwise, every bed and breakfast hotel which provided temporary accommodation for homeless persons would be obliged to comply with the HRA 1998.[167]

2.84 In holding, nonetheless, that the PRP was a public authority, the court took account of the following features:

- in transferring its housing stock to the PRP, the local authority had not transferred its primary duties. The PRP was simply the means by which the local authority performed those duties;
- the act of providing accommodation is not, without more, a public function for the purposes of HRA 1998 s6, irrespective of the section of society for whom that accommodation is provided;
- the fact that a body does not conduct its activities for profit, but is motivated in doing so by its perception of the public interest, does not point to the body being a public authority;
- what can make an act that would otherwise be private into a public act is a 'feature or combination of features which impose a public character or stamp on that act'.[168] Statutory control over the act can at least help to mark it as public, as can the extent of control over it exercised by another public authority. The mere fact of supervision by a regulatory body does not render the acts done public acts, but the more closely the acts in question are enmeshed with the activities of a public body, the more likely those acts are to be public. This was analogous to the position in judicial review where a regulator may be deemed public but supervise the private activities of those it regulates;

165 Housing Act 1988 Sch 2, ground 8.
166 [2001] EWCA Civ 595, per Lord Woolf CJ at [58].
167 [2001] EWCA Civ 595.
168 [2001] EWCA Civ 595, per Lord Woolf at [65].

- the closeness of the relationship between the PRP and the local authority: the local authority had created the PRP for the purpose of taking a stock transfer; five of the PRP's board members were councillors of the local authority; the PRP was subject to the guidance of the local authority in its acts towards the tenants;[169]
- at the time of the stock transfer, the tenant was a tenant of the local authority and it was intended that she would be treated no better and no worse after the transfer than if she had remained a tenant of the local authority. The PRP therefore stood in relation to her in very much the position that had previously been occupied by the local authority.[170]

2.85 The court emphasised that, in addition to taking account of these factors, it was desirable to step back and look at the situation as a whole. Lord Woolf CJ said:[171]

> As is the position on applications for judicial review, there is no clear demarcation line which can be drawn between public and private bodies and functions. In a borderline case, such as this, the decision is very much one of fact and degree. Taking into account all the circumstances, we have come to the conclusion that while the activities of housing associations need not involve the performance of public functions, in this case, in providing accommodation for the defendant and then seeking possession, the role of Poplar is so closely assimilated to that of Tower Hamlets that it was performing public and not private functions ... We emphasise that this does not mean that all of Poplar's functions are public.

2.86 In *R (Heather) v Leonard Cheshire Foundation*,[172] the Court of Appeal reached the opposite conclusion where a challenge was brought by a resident of a residential home, placed there pursuant to the local authority's obligations under National Assistance Act 1948 s21, to the defendant's decision to close it.

2.87 The defendant was manifestly not performing public functions. While the degree of public funding for an otherwise private body can be relevant to the question of whether or not the functions performed were public in nature, this was not the case here. There was no distinction other than the funding of the activities in question, between what was happening to those residents who were privately funded

---

169 This kind of factor was subsequently held not to be relevant to the question of whether a hybrid body was a functional public authority: *R (Weaver) v London & Quadrant Housing Trust* [2009] EWCA Civ 587, [2010] 1 WLR 363.

170 [2001] EWCA Civ 595 at [65].

171 [2001] EWCA Civ 595 at [66].

172 [2002] EWCA Civ 366, [2002] 2 All ER 936.

to reside in the home and those who were being funded by the local authority. Nor was there any other evidence of any public flavour to the defendant or its functions. The defendant was not standing in the shoes of the local authority: the National Assistance Act 1948 authorised the actions of the local authority but did not give the defendant any powers; nor were any other statutory powers being performed by the defendant when performing functions for the residents.[173]

2.88   The situation might have been different if the local authority could divest itself of its article 8 Convention obligations by contracting out its duties under the National Assistance Act 1948. In such a case, the court would have a responsibility to approach the interpretation of HRA 1998 s6(3), in relation to the definition of 'public authority', to ensure that the residents' article 8 rights were protected. That was not the case, however. The local authority remained under an article 8 obligation to the residents, who also enjoyed contractual rights against the defendant.[174]

2.89   In *R (A) v Partnerships in Care Ltd*,[175] a patient detained in a private psychiatric hospital under Mental Health Act 1983 s3(1), sought judicial review of the hospital managers' decision to change the focus of her specialist ward from the care and treatment of people with personality disorders to the care and treatment of mentally ill people. The claimant alleged that this caused her no longer to receive the treatment she required. The hospital contended that changing the focus of the ward did not amount to a public function that could render them a public body amenable to judicial review or a public authority for the purposes of the HRA 1998.

2.90   Keith J held that the hospital was amenable to judicial review and a public authority. Although not part of the National Health Service, it was registered as a mental nursing home under Registered Homes Act 1984 Pt 2. The Nursing Homes and Mental Nursing Homes Regulations 1984,[176] moreover, applied to it, so that the Secretary of State acting through the relevant health authority was accorded a measure of control and supervision over the hospital. More importantly, the regulations imposed obligations directly on the hospital, in particular those of providing adequate professional staff and adequate

---

173 *R (Heather) v Leonard Cheshire Foundation* [2002] EWCA Civ 366, per Lord Woolf CJ at [35].

174 [2002] EWCA Civ 366 at [33].

175 [2002] EWHC 529 (Admin), [2002] 1 WLR 2610.

176 SI No 1578, repealed, along with the Registered Homes Act 1984, by the Care Standards Act 2000.

treatment facilities.[177] The Mental Health Act 1983, in addition, laid down a comprehensive statutory regime governing the admission and treatment of detained patients and, indeed, provided for their compulsory detention.[178]

2.91   Given these important statutory functions, which were devolved to the managers of the hospital itself and the specific statutory underpinning of their decisions concerning the facilities and staff to be provided, given also the public interest in the care and treatment of the hospital's patients so as not to prolong their detention by reason of their not receiving the necessary care and treatment, the managers' decision did have a public flavour and the managers were a functional public authority.[179]

2.92   The nature of the test in relation to hybrid bodies, or functional public authorities as those bodies who exercise some public and some private functions have come to be called, under HRA 1998 s6, can be seen from these cases, to be similar to the approach in *Datafin*. The courts have continued to regard the source of the powers as a critical part of the test whether the body is a public authority in relation to a particular activity.[180]

2.93   In *Aston Cantlow and Wilmcote with Billesley Parochial Church Council v Wallbank*,[181] the House of Lords concluded that a church council's decision to require a lay rector pay for chancel repairs did not amount to the discharge of a function of a public nature within the meaning of HRA 1998 s6(3)(b). Lord Nicholls of Birkenhead suggested that 'public function' in this context should be given generous interpretation so as to further the statutory aim of protecting human rights, and observed that there could be no universal test of what is a public function:

> ... given the diverse nature of governmental functions and the variety of means by which these functions are discharged today. Factors to be taken into account include the extent to which in carrying out the relevant function the body is publicly funded, or is exercising statutory powers, or is taking the place of central government or local authorities, or is providing a public service.

---

177 Regulation 12(1).

178 *R (A) v Partnerships in Care Ltd* [2002] EWHC 529 (Admin), per Keith J at [16]–[17].

179 [2002] EWHC 529 (Admin) at [24]–[25].

180 See also *Hampshire County Court v Graham Beer (t/a Hammer Trout Farm)* [2003] EWCA Civ 1056, [2004] 1 WLR 233.

181 [2003] UKHL 37, [2004] 1 AC 546.

2.94   The House of Lords considered the issue of functional public authorities again in *YL v Birmingham City Council*.[182] The local authority had made arrangements, under section 26 of the National Assistance Act 1948, to accommodate the appellant in a nursing home owned and run by a private company providing care and accommodation. By a bare majority the House of Lords held that the company was not acting as public authority for the purposes of section 6(3)(b) in providing accommodation under that arrangement.[183]

2.95   The majority in *YL* considered that the following factors were insufficient to render the provision of residential accommodation to the appellant by the company, under the arrangement with the authority, a function of a public nature:

- the existence of a detailed statutory scheme for regulation of care homes;
- the benefit to the public of provision of care and accommodation for the elderly and infirm;
- the particular vulnerability of the elderly and infirm;
- the fact that care and accommodation is provided pursuant to a statutory duty on local authorities to arrange for its provision;
- the funding of care and accommodation by local authorities;
- local authorities' power to provide care and accommodation in their own care homes; and
- the policy contention that a person with Convention rights against a public authority within the 1998 Act should not lose them because that authority contract out their functions.

2.96   Instead, the following factors when taken together established, in the opinion of the majority, that the company was not acting as a public authority for the purposes of section 6(3)(b):

- the activities of the company in providing care and accommodation to a resident were not susceptible to judicial review;
- a resident would not be treated by the ECtHR as having rights under the European Convention against the company, although he would retain such rights against the authority;
- the company's functions with regard to the provision of care and accommodation would not be regarded as functions of government;

---

182 [2007] UKHL 27, [2008] 1 AC 95.

183 The decision was effectively reversed by section 145 of the Health and Social Care Act 2008, although that does not affect the reasoning of the House of Lords.

- a company managing care homes has no special statutory or other powers in relation to those to whom it provides care and accommodation;
- neither the company nor any aspect of its operation, as opposed to the cost of the care and accommodation provided to the resident, was funded by the authority; and,
- the rights and liabilities between the company and the resident arose under a private contract.

2.97   The majority in *YL* took the view that the Court of Appeal in *Donoghue* had placed too much emphasis on the close historical links between the landlord and the authority in deciding that it was exercising a function of a public nature. Instead, the court should have concentrated on the nature of the function of providing social housing.[184]

2.98   In *R (Weaver) v London & Quadrant Housing Trust*,[185] the Court of Appeal was again required to consider which acts of a private body would render it a functional public authority for the purposes of section 5(3)(b) of the HRA 1998.

2.99   *Weaver* was another case concerning a PRP. A majority of the Court of Appeal held that when considered cumulatively, the following factors established that in providing social housing the housing association was exercising a public function for the purposes of section 6(3)(b):

- the Housing Corporation[186] provided the PRP with substantial public subsidy that enabled it to achieve its objectives;
- the PRP's freedom to allocate its properties was severely circumscribed by nomination agreements made with local housing authorities under a statutory duty to co-operate;[187] this factor was reinforced by the fact that the association had taken a transfer of local authority housing stock;[188]
- the provision of subsidised housing, as opposed to the provision of housing per se, was a governmental function and not a commercial activity; as one of the larger providers of social housing, the PRP made a valuable contribution to achieving the government's objective of providing subsidised housing;

---

184 [2007] UKHL 27, per Baroness Hale at [61]. See also Lord Mance at [105].
185 [2009] EWCA Civ 587, [2010] 1 WLR 363.
186 Now the Homes and Communities Agency: Housing and Regeneration Act 2008, Pt 1.
187 Housing Act 1996 s170.
188 This appears remarkably close to one of the factors that the House of Lords in *YL* considered irrelevant: see para 2.95 above.

- the PRP was acting in the public interest and had charitable objectives; and,
- the Housing Corporation's regulation of the PRP was not
designed simply to render its activities more transparent nor to
ensure proper standards of performance in the public interest;
rather, regulation of matters such as levels of rent and eviction
were designed to ensure that government objectives with respect
to a vulnerable group in society were achieved and that low-cost
housing was effectively provided to those in need of it.

2.100   In the view of the majority, because the provision of social housing
by the association was a public function, it followed that acts that
were necessarily involved in the regulation of that function must also
be public acts.

2.101   The grant of a tenancy and its subsequent termination were part
and parcel of determining who should be allowed to take advantage
of a public benefit. It followed that the act of the PRP in attempting
to terminate the claimant's tenancy was not a private act for the purposes of section 6(5).[189]

2.102   Permission to appeal against the Court of Appeal's decision in
Weaver was refused, although the Supreme Court's reasons for doing
so leave open the possibility that permission will be granted in a different case: 'The point is clearly one for the Supreme Court but this
is not a suitable case on its facts. If a suitable case can be identified consideration should be given to applying for leap-frog to the
Supreme Court.'

2.103   Thus it seems that the courts have not finished with this issue;
nor could they realistically believe that they had done so, particularly while they decline to do much more to set out the principles on
which such decisions will fall to be made than to enunciate conclusions limited to the specific factual situation of the particular case. It
may be thought that more could be expected of the senior judiciary.

Emanation or organ of the state

2.104   In this context, it may be recalled[190] that similar issues arise in relation to the question of whom should be considered an 'emanation

---

189 Rix LJ in the minority would have held that the decision of the association to
terminate a tenancy was not the exercise of a function of a public nature, but
was a private act arising out of the contract between the parties.
190 See paras 1.45–1.47 above.

of the state', for the purposes of Community law and, in particular, directly effective provisions of Community legislation. The European Court of Justice (ECJ), holding that the (then nationalised) gas utility, British Gas, was an emanation of the state,[191] posed a similar, yet significantly different, test to that in *Datafin* and *Poplar*:[192]

> ... a body, whatever its legal form, which has been made responsible, pursuant to a measure adopted by the state, for providing a public service under the control of the state and has for that purpose special powers beyond those which result from the normal rules applicable in relations between individuals, is included in any event among the bodies against which the provisions of a directive capable of having direct effect may be relied upon.[193]

---

191 *Foster v British Gas* [1990] ECR I–3313, [1991] 1 QB 405 at 427G–H.

192 *R v Panel on Takeovers and Mergers ex p Datafin* [1987] QB 815, CA; *Poplar HARCA v Donoghue* [2001] EWCA Civ 595, [2001] QB 48.

193 See also, eg, *Byrne v Motor Insurers' Bureau* [2007] EWHC 1268 (QB), [2008] 2 WLR 234; *Farrell v Whitty* [2007] ECR I-3067, [2007] 2 CMLR 46; *Dominguez v Centre Informatique du Centre Ouest Atlantique* [2012] 2 CMLR 14.

CHAPTER 3

Reviewable decisions

Public and private law

3.1   As has already been seen, judicial review is concerned, primarily, with the improper exercise of public powers and duties. It is, therefore, only decisions or actions in a public law context that may be subject to review (and not even all of those[1]). This is so even though the body that took the decision may be classified as a public or a private body. The discussion of the *Datafin*,[2] *YL*[3] and *Weaver*[4] cases in the previous chapter[5] indicates the potentially complex interrelationship between the true classification of the act and the nature and form of the body that performed it.

3.2   Whether a body is a judicially reviewable public body or a HRA public authority[6] will be affected by both its own form and structure and the nature of the acts it performs. We know that only public law decisions of public bodies/authorities are challengeable, but the nature of the body will affect whether the act under challenge is properly classified as a public or a private act, while the classification of the act as public or private may well determine whether the body is a public authority.[7]

3.3   Until it is accepted that in many cases it may be impossible to disentangle the two issues, the process undertaken by the courts may appear to be quite circular: the classification of the act (particularly under the HRA 1998) determines the status of the body as a public authority (or not), but the nature of the body informs the classification of the act. These issues have been discussed elsewhere.[8]

3.4   In other cases, where there is no dispute that the decision-maker is a public body, such as central government or a local authority, it will still be necessary to analyse the nature of the decision or act to decide whether it is properly classified as existing in public or private law, given that for judicial review to be the appropriate form of

---

1   See paras 3.69–3.76 below.

2   *R v Panel on Takeovers and Mergers ex p Datafin* [1987] QB 815, CA.

3   *YL v Birmingham CC* [2007] UKHL 27, [2008] 1 AC 95.

4   *R (Weaver) v London & Quadrant Housing Trust* [2009] EWCA Civ 587, [2010] 1 WLR 363.

5   See paras 2.69–2.79 above.

6   Human Rights Act 1998 s6(3)(b).

7   See, in particular, *R (Weaver) v London & Quadrant Housing Trust* [2009] EWCA Civ 587, [2010] 1 WLR 363.

8   See paras 2.82–2.103 and see also *R (Weaver) v London & Quadrant Housing Trust* [2009] EWCA Civ 587, [2010] 1 WLR 363 and the discussion at paras 3.59–3.67 below.

challenge, it is necessary that the decision or act exists in public law. Public bodies perform private law acts all the time in respect of which they can sue and be sued in private law proceedings: breaches of contract and covenants in leases and tenancy agreements, nuisance and negligence, employment of staff, personal injury, etc.

3.5   The importance of the correct identification of an act or decision as existing in public or private law has been considerable, not least because the potential consequences of misidentification and therefore challenge by the wrong procedure were, under the old rules,[9] severe. A private law action would be liable to be struck out as an abuse of the process of the court if brought to challenge an act that the court considered to be a public law act. Judicial review would likewise be refused to challenge a private law matter except in very limited circumstances where the court was able to permit the claim to proceed as a private law action.[10]

3.6   The consequences of such mistakes may no longer be so significant.[11] CPR r54.20 confers on the court a comprehensive power to transfer cases out of or into the Administrative Court. The courts, in addition, unhappy for years about the amount of time and public money frequently devoted to debates concerning the form of proceedings rather than dealing with the substantive dispute,[12] took the opportunity afforded by the introduction of the CPR to attempt to bring such arid procedural disputes to an end, and to promote a new, more flexible approach under which the rules would accommodate justifiable errors of procedure without resort to the draconian remedy of strike out,[13] and the courts would be far less amenable to deciding cases on procedural grounds rather than on the legal merits of the challenge.

3.7   In spite of this welcome and sensible development, the distinction between public law rights and duties and those that exist in private

9   Rules of the Supreme Court (RSC) Ord 53.

10 See RSC Ord 53 r9(5). See also, eg, *R v BBC ex p Lavelle* [1983] 1 WLR 23, QBD.

11 But they may be: see *Trim v North Dorset District Council* [2010] EWCA Civ 1446, [2011] 1 WLR 1901, where a powerful Court of Appeal (Laws, Carnwath and Patten LJJ) struck out a private law challenge to a planning notice on the basis that it was a matter of pure public law and could only be challenged by way of judicial review.

12 *Roy v Kensington and Chelsea Family Practitioner Committee* [1992] 1 AC 624, HL, per Lord Lowry at 651; *Trustees of the Dennis Rye Pension Fund v Sheffield CC* [1998] 1 WLR 840, CA.

13 See, eg, *Clark v University of Lincolnshire and Humberside* [2000] 1 WLR 1988, CA; *R (Heather) v Leonard Cheshire Foundation* [2002] EWCA Civ 366, [2002] 2 All ER 936.

law is still important. In domestic law, there is no right to damages for breach of a public law obligation.[14] Moreover, the quashing of a decision may be more advantageous to the applicant than any available private law remedy.[15] The classification of the act will also be likely to determine what, if any, remedy under the HRA 1998 will be available; the procedure and time limits for, as well as the remedies available in relation to public and/or private law matters are of course significantly different. Leniency by the courts in relation to use of the incorrect procedure is less likely where the error is one that ought not to have been made or where the party has made a deliberate decision with the aim of obtaining a tactical advantage.[16]

3.8   It must also be said that reconciling the different decisions of the courts in relation to what are and what are not public law functions is not an entirely easy task. This topic is discussed in more detail below.

Classification of acts and decisions

O'Reilly v Mackman and the general rule

3.9   When considering the classification of decisions as matters of public or private law, two points should be kept in mind. First, it is difficult, in English law, to draw bright-line distinctions between public and private law rights, as its jurisprudence never formally evolved distinctions of that kind until the House of Lords created (without analysing) them in *O'Reilly v Mackman*.[17] Secondly, it does not automatically follow from the classification of a duty, power or right as existing solely in the realm of public law that issues concerning the exercise of that power, duty or right must be litigated in judicial review proceedings rather than an ordinary private law claim (such as if they are linked to a private law right, if they arise by way of defence to such a claim, or

---

14   See, eg, *R v Northavon DC ex p Palmer* (1995) 27 HLR 576, CA, and *O'Rourke v Camden LBC* [1998] AC 188, HL, where claims for damages for alleged breaches of the duties owed to homeless persons under the Housing Act 1985 Pt 3 (now Housing Act 1996 Pt 7) were dismissed on the basis that such duties existed in public law only. See also Law Commission *Administrative Redress: Public Bodies and the Citizen* (Law Com No 322, 2010), which argued for the availability of damages as an additional remedy in judicial review claims.

15   Eg in the employment context, the quashing of a dismissal is more advantageous than any order which the Employment Tribunal could make.

16   *Clark v University of Lincolnshire and Humberside* [2000] 1 WLR 1988.

17   [1983] 2 AC 237 (see further below).

if Convention rights are at stake; these matters are discussed further below).

3.10   In *O'Reilly*, the House of Lords held that, as a 'general rule', it was contrary to public policy and an abuse of the process of the court to permit a dissatisfied applicant to proceed by way of an ordinary action (ie in modern procedural parlance, a CPR Pt 7 claim) and avoid the judicial review procedure,[18] when the substance of the complaint was founded in public law. This was because to allow the circumvention of judicial review procedure would enable an applicant to evade the provisions of the rules of court governing such claims,[19] which are designed to afford safeguards for public authorities against groundless and unmeritorious applications, in the interests of good administration. Those safeguards, in particular, were the following four matters which remain important under the current, CPR Pt 54, procedural regime:

- the requirement for permission;[20]
- the strict time limits for making applications;[21]
- the need for sworn evidence[22] making full and frank disclosure of all relevant facts;[23] and,
- the court's discretionary control over both disclosure and cross-examination.[24]

3.11   Accordingly, the House of Lords in *O'Reilly* held that the courts would insist on challenges being brought by way of judicial review and would strike out any other action.

3.12   While the principle is easy enough to state, the subsequent history of litigation on these issues, most of which involved applications to strike out applications which were alleged to have been brought using the wrong procedure, and many of which ended up in the House of Lords on that issue, demonstrates the difficulty of its application in practice. Almost immediately after *O'Reilly*, problems began to arise, particularly in cases involving combinations of public and private

---

18 Then to be found in RSC Ord 53, now CPR Pt 54.

19 Then, RSC Ord 53; now CPR Pt 54.

20 Senior Courts Act 1981 s31(3); CPR r54.4. See paras 18.135–18.137 below.

21 Senior Courts Act 1981 s31(6); CPR r54.5. See paras 18.19–18.69 below.

22 Now a pleaded statement of facts verified by a statement of truth: CPR rr54.6 and 22.1; PD 54A para 5.6.

23 See paras 18.115–18.127 below.

24 *O'Reilly v Mackman* [1983] 2 AC 237 at 280G–281D and 284B. See also *Cocks v Thanet DC* [1983] 2 AC 286, HL, per Lord Bridge of Harwich at 294E–H. As to these procedural requirements, see paras 20.44–20.49 below.

law rights, or in which there was more than one possible analysis of the position. This often occurred where contractual obligations were superimposed upon those imposed by statute. More recently, the courts have had to deal with almost the same issues in the context of HRA claims.[25]

Applying *O'Reilly*: public or private?

3.13   In *Cocks v Thanet District Council*,[26] decided on the same day as *O'Reilly*, the distinction between public and private law rights was considered again by the House of Lords. Lord Bridge held that the general rule expounded in *O'Reilly* applied where it was necessary, as a condition precedent to the enforcement of a statutory private law right, to impugn an authority's public law decision. He referred to a 'dichotomy' between the 'decision-making' and 'executive' functions of an authority. The former involved the exercise of discretionary powers invested in the authority by Parliament and which are for the authority to exercise rather than for the court. Those functions could only exist in public law. The latter functions were no more than the implementation of the public law decision and could be enforced by private action.[27] Thus, the decision whether an applicant fulfilled the statutory conditions to entitle him to housing were a matter of public law. The actual obligation to house a qualifying applicant would be a matter of private law, however, enforceable by an action for injunction and damages. The decision challenged fell within the 'decision-making' category.

3.14   In *O'Rourke v Camden LBC*,[28] the House of Lords disapproved this approach, rejecting the classifications of 'decision-making' or 'executive' as a basis for the distinction between duties that do, and those that do not, give rise to a private law right of action. Such a distinction would give rise to the anomaly that an authority that accepts that a duty is owed but that discharges it inadequately would be liable in damages, while an authority that perversely refuses to accept that they are under any duty at all would not be so liable.[29] That would be contrary to principle.

25 See paras 2.80–2.103 above.

26 [1983] 2 AC 286, HL.

27 *Cocks v Thanet DC* [1983] 2 AC 286, HL, per Lord Bridge at 292D–293B; *Mohram Ali v Tower Hamlets LBC* [1993] QB 407, CA, per Nolan LJ at 413G–414B.

28 [1998] AC 188, HL.

29 [1998] AC 188 at 196G.

3.15 The House of Lords held that the question whether any private law duty exists depends, rather, on whether on a correct construction of the statute such a duty has been intended by Parliament. This is the same test as applied by the courts to the related question whether there has been a breach of statutory duty that gives rise to a private law claim for damages.[30]

3.16 Accordingly, where the existence of a duty is dependent upon 'a good deal of judgment' on the part of the authority, and the authority enjoy a wide discretion about the discharge of any duty that does arise, it is unlikely that Parliament will have intended errors of judgment to give rise to a private law right of action for breach of statutory duty, and so the duty will exist in public law.[31] Where the duty arises under a comprehensive statutory scheme that also contains a detailed, self-contained and exhaustive procedure for enforcing the duties of the authority, this is likewise indicative of a Parliamentary intention not to create a private law right of action.

3.17 This modified approach may or may not be preferable to that enunciated in *Cocks*, but it is open to doubt whether it has changed the landscape very much. After all, the factors that lead to the conclusion whether Parliament intended there to be a private right of action are very similar to those that had previously informed the conclusion whether function fell on the decision-making or executive side of the line. The main difference is that on the *O'Rourke* approach, it is not appropriate to split functions into their component elements in order to analyse their nature. The matter is to be considered in the round.

3.18 The Court of Appeal considered the distinction between a public authority's public and private acts in *R (Supportways Community Services Ltd) v Hampshire CC*.[32] A local authority entered into an agreement with a service provider for the provision of supported housing.[33] The agreement provided that the authority was required to conduct periodic reviews of the housing scheme. Following one such review, it decided not to renew the agreement. The service provider challenged the decision by way of judicial review and was successful

---

30 For, still, the leading authority on the principles applicable to the question whether a statutory duty is owed, see *X (Minors) v Bedfordshire CC* [1995] 2 AC 633, HL. See also *Stovin v Wise* [1996] AC 923, HL; *Phelps v Hillingdon LBC* [2001] 2 AC 619, HL; and *Gorringe v Calderdale MBC* [2004] UKHL 15, [2004] 1 WLR 1057.

31 *O'Rourke v Camden LBC* [1998] AC 188, HL, per Lord Hoffmann at 194B–E.

32 [2006] EWCA Civ 1035, [2006] BLGR 836.

33 Under the *Supporting People* regime.

at first instance, where the authority was ordered to carried out a further review.[34]

3.19   The authority appealed successfully to the Court of Appeal. There was no public law basis for ordering a further review of a private law arrangement. The mere fact that the party alleged to be in breach of contract is a public body does not turn a private law claim into a public law matter, nor does it entitle a party (in the absence of exceptional circumstances) to a public law remedy.

3.20   In another case, *R (Gamesa Energy UK Ltd) v National Assembly for Wales*,[35] the High Court made the same point. The claimant energy company applied, unsuccessfully, for judicial review of a tendering process undertaken in a procurement exercise. The application was refused; Gibbs J noted that the distinction between decisions with a sufficient public law flavour and those without was not always an easy one to make but considered that the challenge was really a commercial dispute between the parties.[36]

3.21   Employment disputes give rise to particular issues. Most employment disputes involving public authorities are not suitable for judicial review proceedings, as they are only about the employees contractual rights.[37] There is, however, a category of cases in which judicial review has been held to be available.

3.22   A public servant who is the holder of a public office, especially where he can only be dismissed from that office for cause, such as a chief constable,[38] or a probationary police constable,[39] are entitled to a procedure in accordance with the principles of natural justice, which they may enforce by way of judicial review. So to could a prison officer (who technically also held the office of constable and who has

---

34   [2005] EWHC 3101 (Admin), (2006) 9 CCLR 227.

35   [2006] EWHC 2167 (Admin).

36   See also, in the context of employment law, the cases on statutory 'office-holders' such as police officers and directors of children's services, who are entitled to bring judicial review claims to challenge breaches of procedural fairness in the process by which they were dismissed, and other employees who are not, see paras 2.71–2.73 and 3.22–3.23 below.

37   See, eg, *R v BBC ex p Lavelle* [1983] 1 WLR 23, QBD; *R v East Berkshire Health Authority ex p Walsh* [1985] QB 152, CA; *McClaren v Home Office* [1990] ICR 824, CA; *Wandsworth LBC v A* [2000] 1 WLR 1246, CA.

38   *Ridge v Baldwin* [1964] AC 40, HL.

39   *R v Chief Constable of North Wales ex p Evans* [1982] 1 WLR 1155, HL.

no contract of employment and no private law rights).[40] In *McLaughlin v Governor of the Cayman Islands*,[41] Lord Bingham said:[42]

> It is a settled principle of law that if a public authority purports to dismiss the holder of a public office in excess of its powers, or in breach of natural justice, or unlawfully (categories which overlap), the dismissal is, as between the public authority and the office-holder, null, void and without legal effect, at any rate once a court of competent jurisdiction so declares or orders. Thus the office-holder remains in office, entitled to the remuneration attaching to such office, so long as he remains ready, willing and able to render the service required of him, until his tenure of office is lawfully brought to an end by resignation or lawful dismissal.

3.23   So where a director of children's services, who held a post created, required and defined by statute, was summarily dismissed, she was permitted to challenge her dismissal by way of judicial review notwithstanding that she had an alternative remedy available in the Employment Tribunal.[43] The public law remedy was much more advantageous to her both financially, given the low level of compensation that a tribunal could award, and in reputational terms. Even though the judicial review court would not order her reinstatement, or even quash the dismissal, a declaration that her dismissal had been unlawful, coupled with a remission to the Administrative Court to consider the appropriate level of compensation (whether on a *McLaughlin* or some more limited basis), would be appropriate.[44]

Applying *O'Reilly*: exceptions

3.24   In *O'Reilly*, Lord Diplock recognised that there may be exceptions to the mandatory use of the judicial review procedure, particularly where the legality of a public law decision arose as a collateral issue in a claim for infringement of a private law right.[45] He also accepted that it may be permissible for the parties to proceed (by consent) by way of private action rather than judicial review,[46] and that whether

---

40 *R v Secretary of State for the Home Department ex p Benwell* [1985] QB 554, QBD.
41 [2007] UKPC 50, [2007] 1 WLR 2839.
42 At [14].
43 *R (Shoesmith) v Ofsted* [2011] EWCA CIV 642, [2011] PTSR 1459.
44 Per Maurice Kay LJ at [98]–[99] and [128]–[132].
45 *O'Reilly v Mackman* [1983] 2 AC 237 at 285F.
46 *O'Reilly v Mackman* [1983] 2 AC 237 and see, eg, *Gillick v West Norfolk and Wisbech Area Health Authority and the Department of Health and Social Security* [1986] AC 112, HL.

or not further exceptions should be made must be decided on a case-by-case basis. These matters have been considered extensively by the courts, in a series of cases from which the following principles have emerged.[47]

3.25   The first class of exception permitted by the courts arises where the public law element of the claim is merely peripheral; in such cases that element may not be sufficient to justify proceeding by way of judicial review.[48] Moreover, if the public and private law elements are inextricably linked, then it appears that matters can proceed either way. In *An Bord Bainne Co-operative Ltd (Irish Dairy Board) v Milk Marketing Board*,[49] Sir John Donaldson MR allowed a private action to continue on the basis that although the matter could be said to be one of public law, private rights were involved and it could cause injustice to require the use of the public law procedure.

3.26   Throughout the 1990s, the courts became increasingly frustrated at the large quantity of satellite litigation spawned by the decision in *O'Reilly*, as public bodies frequently applied to strike out private law proceedings taken against them, such litigation often reaching the Court of Appeal and House of Lords. In one case, *Roy v Kensington and Chelsea Family Practitioner Committee*,[50] the House of Lords considered whether *O'Reilly* had ever laid down a rule applicable to all cases or whether it only applied to those in which there were no private rights also at stake.

3.27   In the event, the House of Lords declined to decide between the two approaches, but Lord Lowry, with whom the rest of the House agreed, said that he much preferred the second of these approaches:[51]

> ... which is both traditionally orthodox and consistent with the *Pyx Granite* principle [1960] AC 260, 286, as applied in *Davy v Spelthorne Borough Council* [1984] AC 262, 274 and in *Wandsworth London Borough Council v Winder* [1985] AC 461, 510. It would also, if adopted, have the practical merit of getting rid of a procedural minefield.

---

47 See especially *Cocks v Thanet DC* [1983] 2 AC 286, HL; *Wandsworth LBC v Winder* [1985] AC 461, HL; *Mohram Ali v Tower Hamlets LBC* [1993] QB 407, CA; *Tower Hamlets LBC v Abdi* (1992) 25 HLR 80, (1992) 91 LGR 300, CA; *Hackney LBC v Lambourne* (1992) 25 HLR 172, CA; *O'Rourke v Camden LBC* [1998] AC 188, HL; *Trustees of the Dennis Rye Pension Fund v Sheffield CC* [1998] 1 WLR 840, CA. See also *R v Northavon DC ex p Palmer* (1995) 27 HLR 576, CA.

48 See *Davy v Spelthorne BC* [1984] AC 262, HL.

49 [1984] 2 CMLR 584, (1984) 128 Sol Jo 417, CA.

50 [1992] 1 AC 624, HL.

51 [1992] 1 AC 624 at 653.

3.28 Even adopting the other approach, however, for the purposes of the appeal, Lord Lowry considered that there were many indications in favour of a liberal attitude towards the exceptions to the rule contemplated but not spelt out by Lord Diplock. He concluded:[52]

> In conclusion, my Lords, it seems to me that, unless the procedure adopted by the moving party is ill-suited to dispose of the question at issue, there is much to be said in favour of the proposition that a court having jurisdiction ought to let a case be heard rather than entertain a debate concerning the form of the proceedings.

3.29 The courts have built on this approach in subsequent cases. In *Trustees of the Dennis Rye Pension Fund v Sheffield City Council*,[53] the Court of Appeal held that the statutory code for the approval of housing grants[54] entitled a person to payment of the grant once he had complied with statutory conditions for payment, and that there was no reason why he could not bring a private law action to recover the amount of the unpaid grant as an ordinary debt.

3.30 In the course of his judgment, Lord Woolf MR suggested the following guidance.[55]

• Where it is not clear whether judicial review or an ordinary private action is appropriate, it is safer to apply for judicial review because there could then be no question of any abuse of process by seeking to avoid the protection it offered to public bodies. In most cases, it should not be necessary for procedural reasons to become involved in 'arid arguments' about whether the issues are correctly treated as involving public or private law or both (though it may be necessary to consider this for reasons of substantive law). If judicial review is used when it should not be, the court can safeguard its resources by directing either that the case should proceed as if begun by private action, or else that it should be heard by a non-Administrative Court judge.

• If a case is brought by an ordinary private law action and an application is made to strike it out on the basis that it should have been brought by way of judicial review, the court should ask itself, if the correct procedure is not clear, whether permission would have

52 [1992] 1 AC 624 at 651.
53 [1998] 1 WLR 840, CA.
54 Then, Housing Grants, Construction and Regeneration Act 1993 Pt 1.
55 [1998] 1 WLR 840, per Lord Woolf MR at 848E–849B. See also *Mercury Communications Ltd v Director General of Telecommunications* [1996] 1 WLR 48, HL, per Lord Slynn of Hadley at 57.

been granted if the judicial review procedure had been used.[56] If so, that would indicate that the avoidance of the protections conferred by the judicial review procedure has done no harm. The court should consider, in addition, which procedure would be the most appropriate to try the case. If an ordinary action is equally or more appropriate than a judicial review claim, that would be a further indication that the case should not be struck out.

- Where it is not clear whether proceedings have been properly brought by ordinary action, it should be remembered that, by consultation with the Administrative Court Office, the case could be transferred to the Administrative Court as an alternative to being struck out.

3.31   This topic was revisited by Lord Woolf MR in the Court of Appeal in the case of *Clark v University of Lincoln and Humberside.*[57] Lord Woolf felt free to reconsider Lord Diplock's guidance in *O'Reilly* in the light of the new Civil Procedure Rules, even though CPR Pt 54 was not yet in force. He highlighted the importance of these procedural changes and in particular the enhanced control that the court would exercise in relation to all proceedings, not just those brought by way of judicial review. The intention of the CPR was to harmonise procedures as far as possible and avoid barren procedural disputes.[58]

3.32   In particular, he said, if ordinary actions under CPR Pt 7 or Pt 8 were brought raising public law issues, they would now be subject to the provisions of CPR Pt 24, which enabled the court to give a summary judgment on a claim or an issue, whether of its own motion or on application, where it considered the claimant to have no real prospect of success. Accordingly, the distinction between judicial review proceedings and ordinary actions was now limited – in judicial review claims, the claimant requiring permission needed to establish a real prospect of success; in ordinary actions, the defendant making a CPR Pt 24 application needed to establish that the claimant had no real prospect of success.[59]

3.33   The courts would today be flexible in their approach to abuse of process arguments, in the light of the changes brought about by the

---

56 See *Jones v Powys Local Health Board* [2008] EWHC 2562 (Admin), (2009) 12 CCLR 68, where a claim was struck out as an abuse of process, apparently on the basis that permission would not have been granted (no issue being taken about delay).

57 [2000] 1 WLR 1988, CA.

58 *Clark v University of Lincolnshire and Humberside* [2000] 1 WLR 1988, per Lord Woolf MR at [37].

59 [2000] 1 WLR 1988 at [27]–[28].

CPR. Those changes include a requirement that parties must act reasonably both before and after they have commenced proceedings. They are under an obligation to assist the court to further the overriding objective, which includes ensuring that cases are dealt with expeditiously and fairly. They should not allow the choice of procedure to achieve procedural advantages.[60]

3.34   Moreover, even outside judicial review cases, the courts were now entitled to consider whether delay in commencing proceedings within the limitation period was such as to render those proceedings abusive. In cases where judicial review would usually be the appropriate procedure, the court would be entitled to consider whether there has been unjustified delay in commencing the proceedings. The court could also consider the nature of the claim. Delay in bringing proceedings for a discretionary remedy has always been a factor that could be taken into account. If the claim would affect the public generally, the court would adopt a stricter approach than if only the immediate parties were affected. Where a claim was brought in contract where it could more appropriately have been brought by way of judicial review, the court would not strike it out solely because of the procedure adopted but would consider whether in all the circumstances, including delay, there had been an abuse of the CPR. This was the same approach as would be adopted on an application under CPR Pt 24.[61]

3.35   Lord Woolf concluded that since *O'Reilly*, the emphasis had changed:[62]

> What is likely to be important ... will not be whether the right procedure has been adopted but whether the protection provided by Order 53[63] has been flouted in circumstances which are inconsistent with the proceedings being able to be conducted justly in accordance with the general principles contained in Part 1.[64] Those principles are now central to determining what is due process.

3.36   In *R (Heather) v Leonard Cheshire Foundation*,[65] the Court of Appeal (Lord Woolf CJ) having concluded that the defendant was not a public authority for the purposes of HRA 1998 s6, because it had not been exercising a public function in deciding to close a residential

---

60 [2000] 1 WLR 1988 at [33]–[34].

61 [2000] 1 WLR 1988 at [35]–[38].

62 *Clark v University of Lincolnshire and Humberside* [2000] 1 WLR 1988, per Lord Woolf MR at [39].

63 Now CPR Pt 54.

64 Ie of the CPR.

65 [2002] EWCA Civ 366, [2002] 2 All ER 936.

care home which it operated, turned to deal with a contention that the defendant had raised, namely that proceedings ought not to have been brought by way of judicial review.

3.37   Lord Woolf was clearly unimpressed by the raising of the issue, describing it as '... an echo of the old demarcation disputes as to when judicial review was or was not appropriate under Order 53. CPR Part 54 is intended to avoid any such disputes which are wholly unproductive.'[66]

3.38   Once again, he again emphasised the scope for using the judicial review procedure:[67]

> In a case such as the present where a bona fide contention is being advanced (although incorrect) that LCF [Leonard Cheshire Foundation] was performing a public function, that is an appropriate issue to be brought to the court by way of judicial review.

3.39   Lord Woolf also emphasised the flexibility of the CPR:[68]

> We wish to make clear that the CPR provides a framework which is sufficiently flexible to enable all the issues between the parties to be determined. Issues if any as to the private law rights of the claimants have not been determined. A decision had to be reached as to what happened to these proceedings. In view of the decisions of [the judge below] and this Court the claimants have no public law rights ... In view of a possibility of a misunderstanding as to the scope of judicial review we draw attention to this and the powers of transfer under Part 54.

Applying *O'Reilly*: end of the road for abuse of process?

3.40   In the light of the decisions set out above, the scope for disputes on the correct forum for a claim is likely to be significantly reduced, but it is clear that it has not disappeared entirely.[69] In *Trim v North Dorset DC*,[70] for example, the Court of Appeal struck out a private law claim for a declaration that a failure to comply with a planning notice was lawful as the notice had been served out of time. Carnwath LJ held[71] that the exclusivity principle established by *O'Reilly* was,

---

66   [2002] EWCA Civ 366, per Lord Woolf CJ at [38].

67   [2002] EWCA Civ 366 at [38].

68   [2002] EWCA Civ 366 at [39].

69   See, eg, *Jones v Powys Local Health Board* [2008] EWHC 2562 (Admin), (2009) 12 CCLR 68 and *Swann v Attorney General of the Turks and Caicos Islands* [2009] UKPC 22.

70   [2010] EWCA Civ 1446, [2011] 1 WLR 1901.

71   At [26].

... directly applicable in the present case. The service of a breach of condition notice is a purely public law act. There is strong public interest in its validity, if in issue, being established promptly, both because of its significance to the planning of the area, and because it turns what was merely unlawful into criminal conduct. It is an archetypal example of the public action which Lord Diplock would have had in mind. It does not come within any other categories ... requiring a more flexible approach.

3.41 Revisiting some of the issues concerning the protection for public authorities, he continued:[72]

> Once a ... notice is served, the person responsible has a choice if he wishes to regularise his planning position. He may seek judicial review promptly to challenge the validity of the notice, or he may apply to the authority under section 73 to discharge the condition. If he does neither, he must accept the consequent uncertainty affecting his property ...
>
> ... the existence of unresolved factual issues is not itself a reason for avoiding judicial review. The strict time limits for judicial review reinforce the case for procedural exclusivity; they are not a reason for relaxing it.

3.42 In addition, the substantive importance of the distinction between public and private law rights, referred to by Lord Woolf in *Dennis Rye*,[73] will still have certain procedural consequences, particularly where what is at stake is not a mixture of public and private law rights and obligations, but one or the other. It seems, for example, that a private law action claiming damages for breach of what, on analysis, is a public law obligation (leaving aside human rights cases)[74] will still be abusive because it is hopeless.

3.43 Accordingly, it is still necessary to keep in mind the principles enunciated in the cases referred to above on abuse of process.

Applying *O'Reilly*: defending private law proceedings

3.44 Where a person is defending a private action against a public body, it is permissible to raise a public law defence and/or counterclaim in those proceedings without seeking an adjournment to apply for judicial review. In *Wandsworth LBC v Winder*,[75] the House of Lords permitted a secure local authority tenant to defend the authority's

72 At [36]–[37].
73 See paras 3.29–3.30 above.
74 On damages for which, see paras 5.23–5.41 below.
75 [1985] AC 461, HL.

possession proceedings based on rent arrears, on the basis that the only rent unpaid related to an unlawful and perverse rent increase. If the defence were made out, the tenant would have established a defence on the merits: that he had not been liable to pay the sum claimed and so there were no rent arrears, and no ground for possession could be established. The tenant, furthermore, had not chosen the forum of the proceedings, and it would be a strange use of language to describe his behaviour as abusive.[76]

3.45   A line of authority developed, beginning the late 1980s,[77] that *Winder* would only apply where the public law defence raised could be linked to a private law merits defence, as had been the case on the facts of *Winder* itself. According to these authorities, a defendant seeking to raise a defence that amounted to no more than a public law challenge (such as a challenge to the legality of the decision to institute the proceedings) would not be able to raise those arguments as a defence, but must instead seek an adjournment of the private action to enable an application for judicial review to be made, or, if already made, to be resolved. For an adjournment to be obtained, there would need to be a real possibility that permission for judicial review would be granted.[78]

3.46   Accordingly, in numerous cases, the courts held that a defence to private law proceedings was not properly relied on, where the only ground of defence was alleged to be the illegality of the decision to bring the proceedings.[79]

3.47   That limitation on the *Winder* principle has now, however, probably been overtaken by the jurisprudence which led, eventually, to

---

76 Per Lord Fraser at 509E. See also *Leeds CC v Spencer* [2000] BLGR 68, where the Court of Appeal approved the circuit judge's decision that the defendant could defend debt proceedings by arguing the illegality of the claimant authority's statutory notice requiring the defendant to take steps, the defendant's failure to comply with which had led to the claimant taking the steps itself and claiming the cost of so doing from the defendant.

77 *Avon CC v Buscott* [1988] 1 All ER 841, CA. See also *West Glamorgan CC v Rafferty* [1987] 1 WLR 457.

78 See also, *Manchester CC v Cochrane* [1999] 1 WLR 809, CA.

79 See, eg, *Mohram Ali v Tower Hamlets LBC* [1993] QB 407, CA; *Tower Hamlets LBC v Abdi* (1992) 25 HLR 80; (1992) 91 LGR 300, CA; *Hackney LBC v Lambourne* (1992) 25 HLR 172, CA; *Waverley DC v Hilden* [1988] 1 WLR 246, ChD. See also *Manchester CC v Cochrane* [1999] 1 WLR 809, CA where the defendant introductory tenants could not raise a defence to the possession proceedings against them based on an allegedly procedurally defective review which the local authority had carried out, when the governing legislation (Housing Act 1996 Pt 5 ch 1) was held not to permit the county court to entertain any such defence.

an acceptance by the Supreme Court that article 8 of the European Convention on Human Rights could afford a defence to a possession claim even if there was no defence in domestic law.[80] Most of the cases referred to above have not been doubted or overruled, but the law seems now to have moved in a different direction, especially where Convention rights are at stake.

3.48   In *Kay v Lambeth LBC*,[81] Lord Hope (with whom the majority of the House of Lords agreed) said:[82]

> ... if the requirements of the law have been established and the right to possession is unqualified, the only situations in which it would be open to the court to refrain from proceeding to summary judgment and making the possession order are these: ... (b) if the defendant wishes to challenge the decision of a public authority to recover possession as an improper exercise of their powers at common law on the ground that it was a decision which no reasonable person would consider justifiable, he should be permitted to do this provided again that the point is seriously arguable.

3.49   Lord Hope's '(b)', which became known as 'gateway (b)',[83] is inconsistent with the proposition that a *Winder* defence required a public law defence that was linked to a private law defence on the merits, because the whole point of *Kay* and the other article 8 cases that came before the higher courts was that the occupiers had, as a matter of law, no private law defence at all.

3.50   In *Taylor v Central Bedfordshire Council*,[84] the Court of Appeal held that a challenge to the rationality of a public authority's decision to recover possession of a property could be brought in relation both to the initial decision to commence such proceedings and to any subsequent decision to continue them. This was confirmed in *Manchester CC v Pinnock*,[85] subject to the proposition that:[86] '... it would almost always require a marked change of circumstances following a ... decision to approve the proceedings, before an attempt could properly be

---

80 *Manchester CC v Pinnock* [2010] UKSC 45, [2011] 2 AC 104; and *Hounslow LBC v Powell* [2011] UKSC 8, [2011] 2 AC 186.

81 [2006] UKHL 10, [2006] 2 AC 465.

82 *Kay* at [110].

83 Gateway (a) related to the circumstances in which an article 8 defence could be raised, and was departed from in *Manchester CC v Pinnock* [2010] UKSC 45, [2011] 2 AC 104.

84 [2009] EWCA Civ 613, [2010] 1 WLR 446.

85 [2010] UKSC 45, [2011] 2 AC 140.

86 Per Lord Neuberger at [72].

made to judicially review the continuance of proceedings which were initially justified.'

3.51   It is less clear what should be the effect of a successful argument that the decision to issue the proceedings was unlawful. In *Waverley BC v Hilden*,[87] Scott J held that proceedings issued without the authority having considered the statutory criterion, or perversely, or in reliance on a decision that was 'for any reason void', would not be a nullity, as the authority had statutory power to bring the proceedings, derived from section 222 of the Local Government Act 1972, and the action was on foot albeit that the authority was – until a proper decision had been reached – an 'incompetent' claimant. Accordingly it was open to the authority to ratify the decision to issue the claim.[88]

3.52   It is easier to see how such ratification may operate if a decision to issue proceedings is quashed in judicial review proceedings, leaving the private law proceedings in being but without what Scott J described as a competent claimant. If, however, the challenge to the proceedings is raised by way of defence, what option does the county court have other than to dismiss the claim?

3.53   In *Croydon LBC v Barber*,[89] the authority sought to recover possession of the vulnerable occupier's accommodation without having regard to their relevant policy or dealing properly, in accordance with that policy, with the occupier's mental health issues, including the expert evidence that there was a risk to his life should he be evicted. The Court of Appeal held that the decision to recover possession was *Wednesbury* unreasonable and set aside the possession order and dismissed the possession claim.

3.54   Conversely, in *Barnsley MBC v Norton*,[90] the authority had failed to take any account of the occupier's daughter's disability when deciding to recover possession of their accommodation, and had also failed to have regard to its public sector equality duty.[91] The Court of Appeal declined to set aside the possession order, in part on the basis that the authority's duties to the daughter were continuing and could still be performed (albeit not in the current accommodation). Lloyd LJ said:[92]

---

87   [1988] 1 WLR 246, ChD.
88   At 256 D–H.
89   [2010] EWCA Civ 51, [2010] HLR 26.
90   [2011] EWCA Civ 834, [2012] PTSR 56.
91   Equality Act 2010 s149.
92   [2011] EWCA Civ 834, [2012] PTSR 56 at [36]–[37].

If the Council's failure ... had been challenged by an application for judicial review rather than by way of a defence to the possession claim, it would have been open to the Administrative Court to conclude that, despite a proven past breach, the Council's decisions already taken should not be set aside, if the court considered that the Council could now be relied on to exercise its relevant future functions properly, with (of course) the sanction – if it were not to do so – of further proceedings ...

By analogy, given that a breach of a public law duty is relied on by way of defence in the present case, it seems to me that it is open to the court in this situation to take the view that, if the decision would not have been set aside on an application for judicial review, it should not provide a basis for a defence to the proceedings for possession ....

Applying *O'Reilly*: defending criminal proceedings

3.55   It is now clear that a person charged with a criminal offence may generally raise, as a defence to the prosecution, the invalidity, whether procedural or substantive, of the measure pursuant to which the prosecution was brought. In *Boddington v British Transport Police*,[93] the House of Lords held that there was no proper basis for the distinction that the cases had previously drawn between procedural invalidity (which could form the basis of the defence) and substantive invalidity (which could not).[94] Accordingly, in *Boddington*, the defendant had been entitled to defend himself in a prosecution for smoking on a train in breach of a railway byelaw, by contending that the byelaw was invalid and a nullity, although on the merits, the defence failed.

3.56   This general right does not apply, however, where the particular statutory scheme that created the offence is construed as requiring any challenge to the validity of the measure by other means. In *Boddington*, itself, Lord Irvine held that, as with so much in judicial review, there will be circumstances in which a court has no jurisdiction to rule on a defence based on arguments of invalidity, whether of subordinate legislation or of an administrative act under the statute. In each case, this will depend on an examination of the particular statutory context to see whether Parliament has legislated to preclude such challenges being made by way of defence, in the interest, for example, of promoting certainty about the legitimacy

---

93   [2000] 2 AC 143, HL.
94   See, eg, *Bugg v DPP* [1993] QB 473.

of administrative acts on which the public may have to rely.[95] This appears particularly likely where the acts sought to be challenged by way of defence were administrative acts that were aimed specifically at the defendant who had enjoyed ample opportunity under the scheme to challenge those acts.[96]

3.57   Thus, on a prosecution for an alleged breach of an anti-social behaviour order,[97] the alleged invalidity of the order cannot be relied upon as a defence; any issue as to the validity of the order should be raised by way of an appeal against the imposition of the order or a claim for judicial review.[98]

Express indication of appropriate forum

3.58   Some statutes give an express indication of the most appropriate forum for litigation. For instance, under Housing Act 1985 s110, any question arising under Part 4 of the Act (relating to public sector security of tenure) may be determined by the county court. This clear indication that such matters are more appropriately litigated in the county court, and not by way of judicial review proceedings, is reinforced by a costs penalty provision in section 110(3). This states that if proceedings are brought in the High Court which, by virtue of the section, could have been brought in the county court, the person bringing them shall not be entitled to recover any costs. Identical provisions also appear in Housing Act 1996 ss138(3) and 143N(4).

Human Rights Act 1998 – acts of public authorities

3.59   The significance of the definition of 'public authority' in section 6 of the HRA 1998 has already been discussed,[99] but it is important to recall that in relation to so-called 'hybrid' or 'functional' authorities, a two-stage approach must be adopted. First, is the body one certain of whose *functions* are functions of a public nature?[100] Secondly, in

---

95 *Boddington* (above), per Lord Irvine of Lairg LC at 160 C–D. Examples of such schemes, given in *Boddington* itself, were *R v Wicks* [1998] AC 92, HL (planning legislation) and *Quietlynn Ltd v Plymouth City Council* [1988] QB 114 (sex shop licensing legislation): see *Boddington* at 160D–161H.

96 *Boddington* (above) at 161G–H.

97 Crime and Disorder Act 1998 Pt 1.

98 *DPP v T* [2006] EWHC 728 (Admin), [2007] 1 WLR 209.

99 See the discussion at paras 2.80–2.103 above.

100 HRA 1998 s6(3)(b).

relation to a particular *act* of that body, is the nature of the act public or private?[101]

3.60 Lord Neuberger considered the distinction between functions and acts in *YL v Birmingham CC*.[102]

> In my view, both as a matter of ordinary language and on a fair reading of the section, there is a difference between 'functions', the word used in section 6(3)(b), and 'act[s]', the word used in section 6(2) and (5) and defined in section 6(6). The former has a more conceptual, and perhaps less specific, meaning than the latter. A number of different acts can be involved in the performance of a single function.[103]

3.61 In *YL*, the House of Lords was considering the functions and acts of a privately owned and operated care home, providing accommodation for self-funding residents but also for those placed there by a local authority in pursuance of its statutory functions.[104] It held that the care home was not exercising functions of a public nature within the meaning of section 6(3)(b) of the HRA 1998, but only contractual functions arising from the agreement to provide the accommodation. There was a clear distinction between the local authority that had a statutory duty to arrange care and accommodation and the private company providing the service with which the authority contracted on a commercial basis in order to fulfil its duty. The provision, as distinct from the arrangement, of care and accommodation was not an inherently governmental function. Indeed, the company providing the accommodation did so for commercial gain.[105]

3.62 In *R (Weaver) v London & Quadrant Housing Trust*,[106] the Court of Appeal considered whether the decision of a housing association to terminate a tenancy was an act of a public nature that could render the association a public authority for the purposes of the HRA 1998 (and thus also for judicial review purposes).

3.63 It was conceded that London & Quadrant was a hybrid authority (ie that some of its activities would be of a public nature, while others would not – HRA 1998 s6(3)). The critical question, therefore, in deciding whether the tenant's human rights were engaged was whether the specific act in question, ie the act of terminating the ten-

---

101 HRA 1998 s6(5).

102 [2007] UKHL 27, [2008] 1 AC 95.

103 *YL v Birmingham CC* [2007] UKHL 27, [2008] 1 AC 95, per Lord Neuberger at [130].

104 National Assistance Act 1948 s 21.

105 The result has now been reversed by statute, though this does not affect the reasoning of the House of Lords: s145 of the Health and Social Care Act 2008.

106 [2009] EWCA Civ 587, [2010] 1 WLR 363.

ancy, was a private or a public act. This issue required consideration of the context in which the act took place, taking account both of the source of the powers in play and their nature.

3.64   Elias LJ commented[107] that the distinction between functions and acts was not straightforward, echoing Lord Neuberger in *YL*, and said:

> ... once it is determined that the body concerned is a hybrid authority – in other words that it exercises functions at least some of which are of a public nature – the only relevant question is whether the act in issue is a private act. Even if the particular act under consideration is connected in some way with the exercise of a public function, it may nonetheless be a private one. Not all acts concerned with carrying out a public function will be public acts. Conversely, it is also logically possible for an act not to be a private act notwithstanding that the function with which it is most closely connected is a private function, although it is difficult to envisage such a case. Such situations are likely to be extremely rare.[108]

3.65   The majority of the court[109] decided that as provision of social housing by the association was a public function, it followed that acts that were necessarily involved in the regulation of that function must be public acts. A number of features brought the act of terminating a tenancy of social housing within the purview of the HRA 1998:[110]

(i) the association's function of allocating and managing housing, taking into account the extent to which it was:
     (a) publicly funded;
     (b) exercising statutory powers;
     (c) taking the place of central or local government; and
     (d) providing a public service;
(ii) the association had significant reliance on public finance and, although not directly taking the place of local authority provision, it operated in very close harmony with local government. Moreover, the provision of subsidised housing was a governmental function and London & Quadrant was providing a public service;
(iii) the association was a charity and acted in the public interest, which, therefore, placed it outside the traditional area of private commercial activity. Government had sought to achieve its

---

107 *Weaver* at [29].
108 *Weaver* at [28].
109 Lord Collins of Mapesbury and Elias LJ.
110 Per Elias LJ at [67]–[72].

objectives concerning the housing of a vulnerable group by regulating the activities of registered social landlords.[111]

3.66 These factors, taken together, established a sufficiently public flavour to the activities of the landlord to bring it, in respect of its provision of social housing, within the ambit of public law. The act of terminating a tenancy was so inextricably linked with the provision of social housing, that if that provision amounted to the exercise of a public function, then acts necessarily involved in the regulation of that function must also be public acts. If an act were necessarily private in nature on the basis that it concerned the exercise of private law rights, then the protection which Parliament intended to afford in respect of hybrid authorities would be considerably undermined. The identification of a body as a hybrid authority would be of only limited value if contractual acts were always to be considered private acts falling within section 6(5) of the 1998 Act.[112]

3.67 It may be a little difficult, conceptually, to see the difference between *YL* and *Weaver*. Each case, after all, concerned the termination of a right to occupy residential accommodation. Indeed, in the latter case, Rix LJ, who dissented, considered the statutory underpinning in *YL* to be stronger than that in *Weaver*.[113] The majority in the Court of Appeal took the view, however, that the need to focus on the specific act of the body in question did not entail considering that act divorced from the broad context of the role and function of the body acting, its place within the statutory and policy superstructure of provision for those requiring assistance in obtaining housing, and even the impact on the HRA 1998 of holding that the act in question was private in nature. In some ways, the approach of the Court of Appeal in *Weaver*, placing such emphasis on the nature of the association and its role in delivering Parliament's scheme for the less well-off in society, and less on the nature of the act in itself, represents an alignment of the court's approach to human rights cases with the *Datafin* approach to the analogous issue in domestic judicial review.

---

111 Now, private registered providers of social housing: Housing and Regeneration Act 2008 Pt 2.
112 Per Elias LJ at [72], [76]–[79]. Rix LJ, who dissented, reached exactly that conclusion: ie that the decision to terminate the claimant's tenancy was a private act arising out of the contract between her and the housing association.
113 *Weaver* at [149]–[153].

Summary

3.68   It can be seen, then, that notwithstanding the courts' reluctance to become embroiled in purely tactical use of procedural provisions, it remains essential to be aware of the distinctions discussed above. If there is genuine doubt, when acting for a claimant, about the appropriate way to proceed, it should be remembered that in genuinely difficult cases, the courts have demonstrated their unwillingness to permit technical arguments over the proper form of an action to result in the striking out of an otherwise meritorious and responsibly brought case.[114] The court has the power to transfer cases into and out of the Administrative Court.[115]

Non-reviewable public law decisions

Target duties

3.69   There is an important class of powers and duties that, although existing in public law, are not enforceable at the suit of an individual. They have become known as 'target' duties, meaning that they set a target for the authority to aim at, mere failure to achieve which will not ordinarily entitle an individual to seek judicial review.[116] The duty is owed to society as a whole or a specific section of it. Parliament has not intended to confer specific rights upon which an individual may rely.[117] There is 'a fundamental difference in public law between a duty to provide benefits or services for a particular individual and a general or target duty that is owed to a whole population.'[118]

3.70   In *R v Inner London Education Authority ex p Ali*,[119] the Divisional Court held that the authority's obligation to secure that there were sufficient schools available in their area for providing primary and

---

114   See the discussion at paras 3.24–3.39 above.

115   See CPR Pt 30; r54.20 and see *R (Heather) v Leonard Cheshire Foundation* [2002] EWCA Civ 366, [2002] 2 All ER 396.

116   Such duties have also been referred to, in the context of a tort claim, as 'exhortatory': *Kent v Griffiths (No 3)* [2001] QB 36, per Lord Woolf MR at [40].

117   *R (G) v Barnet LBC* [2003] UKHL 57, [2004] 2 AC 208, upholding [2001] EWCA Civ 1624, [2002] HLR 13.

118   *R (Ahmad) v Newham LBC* [2009] UKHL 14, [2009] 3 All ER 755, per Baroness Hale at [13].

119   (1990) 2 Admin LR 822, QBD.

secondary education was a target duty.[120] Woolf LJ stated[121] that a 'degree of elasticity' was built into the duty. While a number of standards must be achieved by the authority, 'the setting of those standards is, in the first instance, for the local education authority alone to determine so long as those standards are not outside the tolerance provided by the section'. Likewise, in *R (G) v Barnet LBC*,[122] the House of Lords confirmed that the obligation of a local authority under Children Act 1989 s17(1)[123] was only a target duty.[124]

3.71   This does not necessarily take the decision-maker outside the scope of judicial review altogether, if the decision can be shown to have been taken in contravention of the established principles of public law, such as the obligation to take account of all relevant matters, ignore the irrelevant, not to fetter a discretion, not to act perversely, etc. There is, nevertheless, no specific duty enforceable at the suit of the individual.

Prerogative functions

3.72   Another area of uncertainty concerns the ability of the courts to review certain acts of government, regardless of their public law nature, particularly in the field of foreign affairs. This is because, as Lord Roskill explained in *Council of Civil Service Unions v Minister for the Civil Service*:[125]

> Prerogative powers such as those relating to the making of treaties, the defence of the realm, the prerogative of mercy, the grant of honours, the dissolution of Parliament and the appointment of ministers as well as others are not, I think susceptible to judicial review because their nature and subject matter are such as not to be amenable to the

---

120 Education Act 1944 s8.

121 (1990) 2 Admin LR 822 at 828D.

122 [2003] UKHL 57, [2004] 2 AC 208. See specifically Lord Hope of Craighead at [85]–[91]; Lord Millett at [107]–[109] and Lord Scott of Foscote [113]–[119] and [135]. See also Lord Nicholls of Birkenhead, dissenting in part, at [25]–[30], with whom Lord Steyn agreed, at [64].

123 To safeguard and promote the welfare of children in their area who are in need and, so far as consistent with that duty, to promote the upbringing of children by their families by providing a range and level of services appropriate to those children's needs.

124 See also, eg, *R v Islington LBC ex p Rixon* [1997] ELR 66, (1998) 1 CCLR 119, QBD; *R v Bath Mental Healthcare NHS Trust ex p Beck* (2000) 3 CCLR 5, QBD; *R v Kensington and Chelsea RLBC ex p Kujtim* [1999] 4 All ER 161, (2000) 32 HLR 579, CA; *R (R) v Children and Family Court Advisory and Support Service (CAFCASS)* [2012] EWCA Civ 853, [2012] 2 FLR 1432.

125 [1985] AC 374, HL, at 418B–C.

judicial process. The courts are not the place wherein to determine whether a treaty should be concluded or the armed forces disposed in a particular manner or Parliament dissolved on one date rather than another.

3.73 For a discussion of more recent cases on this topic, see paras 2.57–2.65.

Other decisions

3.74 A decision that has no effect on individual rights in the UK may not engage public law principles or a right to seek a remedy from the courts.[126]

3.75 In some circumstances, it has been held that review can only be sought of a decision that has already been taken; a belief that a certain decision will be taken is insufficient.[127] In others, however, the absence of a decision has not been an obstacle to judicial review.[128] Plainly, if an order is sought to prevent a decision from being taken, seeking a prohibiting order, the fact that the decision has not already been taken will not prevent the court from acting, should it be satisfied that the public body in question is proposing to act unlawfully. It would be contrary to the nature of the order for the claimant to await the outcome of the process that it is sought to stop.[129]

3.76 Some interim decisions may be challengeable in their own right,[130] even though the claimant is entitled to wait until the conclusion of the proceedings.[131] Others, however, may not be challenged: the claimant

---

126 See, eg, *R (Campaign for Nuclear Disarmament) v Prime Minister* [2002] EWHC 2777 (Admin), [2003] ACD 36; *R (A) v Chief Constable of C* [2001] 1 WLR 461, QBD; *R (Southall) v Secretary of State of Foreign and Commonwealth Affairs* [2003] EWCA Civ 1002, [2003] ACD 321. See also *R (Al-Haq) v Secretary of State for Foreign and Commonwealth Affairs* [2009] EWHC 1910 (Admin), [2009] ACD 76.

127 See, eg, *R v Leicestershire Education Authority ex p Cannon* [1991] COD 120, DC. See also *R v Secretary of State for the Home Department ex p Wynne* [1993] 1 WLR 115.

128 See, eg, *R v Secretary of State for Employment ex p Equal Opportunities Commission* [1995] 1 AC 1, HL; *R v Secretary of State for Transport ex p LB Richmond-upon-Thames (No 3)* [1995] Env LR 409, QBD; *R v Secretary of State for the Home Department ex p Tower Hamlets LBC* [1993] QB 632, CA.

129 See chapter 2 above and chapter 5 below.

130 See, eg, the consideration of this issue in *R (Burkett) v Hammersmith and Fulham LBC* [2002] UKHL 23, [2002] 1 WLR 1593, per Lord Steyn at [42].

131 Although it has been held in the context of challenges to procurement and tender processes that where a challenge is brought to published criteria the impugned decision is taken when the criteria are published, not when

may only bring a challenge after the conclusion of the proceedings, or process, in which it was taken. An example of this class of case is where, for example, a formal decision-making process exists, which Parliament intended to be used in its entirety prior to judicial review being sought.[132]

Alternative remedies

3.77   There is a conceptual distinction, though a good deal of overlap in practice, between decisions which may not be challenged by way of judicial review and those in respect of which there is simply another more appropriate alternative remedy that the courts will require claimants to utilise. In practical terms, the two are so closely related that the concepts may become blurred such that the distinction is without a difference.

3.78   In *Re C (Adoption: Religious Observance)*,[133] Wilson J held that judicial review was wholly inappropriate to challenge a local authority's decisions concerning a child where care proceedings were already underway and could be resolved within those proceedings.

3.79   Similarly, in *R (X and Y) v Gloucestershire CC*,[134] the parents of an unborn baby were refused an injunction to restrain the local authority from bringing emergency protection proceedings in relation to the baby. Munby J held that judicial review proceedings to restrain the issue of proceedings could only be appropriate in exceptional circumstances, such as: where the court would have no jurisdiction to hear those other proceedings; or they would be vexatious or otherwise an

they are applied, the cases either predated or did not consider *R (Burkett) v Hammersmith and Fulham LBC* [2002] UKHL 23, [2002] 1 WLR 1593, and so their authority may be in doubt. See, eg, *Jobsin Co UK Plc (t/a Internet Recruitment Solutions) v Department of Health* [2001] EWCA Civ 1241, [2002] 1 CMLR 44; *Hereward & Foster LLP v Legal Services Commission* [2010] EWHC 3370 (Admin), [2011] Eu LR 524.

132   See, eg, *R (DR) v Head Teacher of St George's Catholic School* [2002] EWCA Civ 1822, [2003] BLGR 371, where the court refused relief on judicial review, on the basis that it was inappropriate to have brought the claim challenging a decision to exclude a child from school, confirmed at the first stage of the statutory appeals process, because Parliament intended the remaining stages of that 'tailor-made' process to be exhausted. See also, eg, *R v Association of Futures Brokers and Dealers Ltd ex p Mordens Ltd* [1991] COD 40, QBD.

133   [2002] 1 FLR 1119, QBD. See also *Re L (Care Proceedings: Human Rights Claims)* [2003] EWHC 665 (Fam), [2003] 2 FLR 160, per Munby J at [36], where he applied the same principle to the raising of human rights challenges in judicial review proceedings rather than in the existing care proceedings.

134   [2003] EWHC 850 (Admin), [2003] 2 FLR 171.

abuse of process; or a party to existing proceedings would be severely prejudiced by the issue of further proceedings. In addition, judicial review should not be used where another equally effective remedy is available; it is a blunt and unsatisfactory tool to deal with such sensitive and difficult matters as care and similar cases; and it would be intolerable if the court should deny a child the protection it urgently needed because it felt inhibited from taking steps that may impinge on the judicial review claim.

Powers and duties

3.80   Reviewable decisions or actions will be taken pursuant either to a duty imposed on the decision-maker in question or a power conferred upon her or him. Most of the cases in this area of the law concern the exercise by bodies of discretionary powers, or of duties that include some discretionary elements: where statute imposes a straightforward duty on a body, a private law right to the discharge of that duty may well be conferred upon the intended beneficiaries of the duty, giving rise to a private action for an injunction and/or damages for breach of statutory duty.[135]

3.81   Accordingly, judicial review is more frequently concerned with two kinds of duty, each of which involves elements of discretion or judgment to be exercised by the body discharging the duty. The first type is where the duty only arises if certain subjective criteria are satisfied (eg '... if it appears to the authority that ... then the authority shall ...'). The second is where the duty itself contains subjective elements (eg the duty to secure that 'suitable' accommodation becomes available).[136]

3.82   Such duties may be treated in the same way as pure discretions (eg '... if the authority is satisfied that ... it may ...')[137] in so far as review is sought of the discretionary element(s) of the duty – for instance, the 'suitability' of the accommodation offered. The same factors – relevant and irrelevant considerations, motives, fettering of discretion, etc – will need to be considered, whether the decision is taken pursuant to a power or a duty.[138] In addition, where a public

---

135 See *X (Minors) v Bedfordshire CC* [1995] 2 AC 633, HL.
136 Housing Act 1996 ss193(2) and 206.
137 See, as an example, Housing Act 1996 s198(1).
138 See chapter 6 – Grounds on which review may be sought.

authority has a power, it will be under a duty to consider whether or not to exercise it.

3.83 If review is sought of a failure to comply with the duty at all, one basis of review, leaving aside bad faith, would generally be that the authority had misdirected itself in law or, in other words, applied the wrong test. This may occur, for instance, if an authority were to decide that notwithstanding the fact that an applicant satisfied all the criteria for the provision of a particular benefit, the authority still did not intend to provide it.

3.84 It is important to note, and can be seen by studying any Act that creates public law duties and powers, that in so far as the discretionary elements are concerned, some decisions require a higher degree of certainty than others on the part of the decision-maker regarding whether the criteria for the making of the decision are fulfilled. Some powers may be exercisable 'if it appears to the authority', others 'if the authority is satisfied',[139] yet others 'if the authority has reason to believe'.

3.85 It is now clear that no power, however subjectively worded, is unfettered, unreviewable or exercisable unreasonably.[140] Nevertheless, it will be easier to show that a decision-maker could not have had 'reason to believe' that certain facts were so on the evidence before her or him, than that the same facts could not have 'appeared' to be so to the same decision-maker.[141]

---

139 The modern formulation of this test is, apparently, 'if the authority thinks'.

140 See, eg *R v Chief Constable of North Wales ex p Evans* [1982] 1 WLR 1155, HL; *R v Tower Hamlets LBC ex p Chetnik Developments* [1988] AC 858, HL.

141 For grounds for review and the effect of subjective wording, see paras 6.6–6.7, especially *Padfield v Minister of Agriculture, Fisheries and Food* [1968] AC 997, HL; *Secretary of State for Education and Science v Tameside BC* [1977] AC 1014, HL, and the dissenting speech of Lord Atkin in *Liversidge v Anderson* [1942] AC 206, HL.

CHAPTER 4

Parties

4.1   There are three potential parties to judicial review proceedings:
- the claimant;
- the defendant; and
- any interested party or intervener.

The claimant – sufficient interest

4.2   The claimant must be someone with 'sufficient interest' in the matter to which the application relates.[1] This is commonly referred to as *locus standi* or 'standing'.

4.3   What constitutes a sufficient interest is a matter of mixed fact and law. In *R v Inland Revenue Commissioners ex p National Federation of Self-Employed and Small Businesses Ltd (NFSSB)*,[2] the House of Lords held that the issue is relevant both at the permission stage and on the substantive hearing. A different test, however, is to be applied at each.

- On a permission application, standing is merely a 'threshold' question for the court, designed only to turn away hopeless or meddlesome applications and prevent abuse by busybodies, cranks and other mischief-makers.[3] A ruling at this stage in favour of the claimant is, however, only provisional and may be revised on further consideration by the court hearing the full application.
- The test at the full hearing is whether the claimant can show a strong enough case on the merits, judged in relation to his or her own concern with the subject-matter of the application. This is because the merits of the case and the standing of the claimant are inextricably linked.

4.4   It is wrong, therefore, to treat the question of standing as a preliminary issue: it cannot be considered in the abstract or as an isolated point but must be taken together with the legal and factual context. The statutory test is, after all, whether the claimant has a sufficient interest in the matter to which the application relates.[4]

---

1   Senior Courts Act 1981 s31(3).

2   [1982] AC 617, HL

3   See also *R (Ewing) v Office of the Deputy Prime Minister* [2005] EWCA Civ 1583, [2006] 1 WLR 1260 at [37]–[39] for the interaction with Senior Courts Act 1981 s42, in relation to vexatious litigants.

4   [1982] AC 617, especially per Lord Wilberforce at 630C–E; Lord Diplock at 643G–644B; Lord Scarman at 653G.

4.5   This point was considered further in *AXA General Insurance v HM Advocate*.[5] Lord Reed observed that as a public authority can violate the rule of law without necessarily infringing the rights of any individual, a rights-based approach to standing would be incompatible with the court's role in preserving the rule of law, which requires more than the protection of private rights. Thus the correct approach to standing must be based, not on the concept of rights, but on that of interests.[6]

> A requirement that the applicant demonstrate an interest in the matter complained of will not however operate satisfactorily if it is applied in the same way in all contexts. In some contexts, it is appropriate to require an applicant for judicial review to demonstrate that he has a particular interest in the matter complained of: the type of interest which is relevant, and therefore required in order to have standing, will depend upon the particular context. In other situations, such as where the excess or misuse of power affects the public generally, insistence upon a particular interest could prevent the matter being brought before the court, and that in turn might disable the court from performing its function to protect the rule of law. I say 'might', because the protection of the rule of law does not require that every allegation of unlawful conduct by a public authority must be examined by a court ... Even in a context of that kind, there must be considerations which lead the court to treat the applicant as having an interest which is sufficient to justify his bringing the application before the court. What is to be regarded as sufficient interest to justify a particular applicant's bringing a particular application before the court, and thus as conferring standing, depends therefore upon the context, and in particular upon what will best serve the purposes of judicial review in that context.

4.6   Standing cannot be conferred by the consent of the parties – it goes to the heart of the court's jurisdiction and is for the court to consider.[7]

Examples

4.7   In most cases, it will be clear whether or not a person has sufficient interest to bring an application. A person who is directly affected by a decision will almost always have standing, but the same is not necessarily true where the person affected is a member of his family.

---

5   [2011] UKSC 46, [2012] 1 AC 868. See also *Walton v Scottish Ministers* [2012] UKSC 44, [2013] PTSR 51.

6   At [169]–[170].

7   *R v Secretary of State for Social Services ex p Child Poverty Action Group* [1990] 2 QB 540, CA.

An applicant did not have sufficient standing to challenge a decision of the Serious Fraud Office relating to his wife.[8] Nor were parents entitled to challenge the refusal of an army board of inquiry to disclose to them its report relating to the death of their son.[9]

4.8   In *Feakins v Secretary of State for Environment, Food and Rural Affairs*,[10] the court held that where a claimant did not have a sufficient private interest to support a claim to standing, the courts should not accord them standing just because their claim raised an issue of public interest. It was difficult to conceive of circumstances in which the court would accord a claimant standing if they had no private law interest and were acting out of ill-will or some other improper purpose, even if there was a public interest in testing the lawfulness of the decision under challenge. The facts in *Feakins* did not, however, demonstrate that the claimant's purpose in making the application was improper; it was held that he did have standing.

4.9   In *R (Davies) v Secretary of State for Environment, Food and Rural Affairs*,[11] the court struck out a claim as an abuse of the process of the court where the named claimant was purporting to pursue the claim on behalf of a company that had been moribund since the 1850s.

4.10   In a housing law context, standing was accorded to landlords in *R v Manchester City Council ex p Baragrove Properties Ltd*,[12] to challenge housing benefit decisions that had been made in respect of their tenants. The local authority had decided to treat the benefit applicants as not liable to make payments in respect of their tenancies, and therefore as not entitled to any benefit.[13] The standing decision was based on the fact that the claimant's own conduct was central to the authority's decision: the authority's view had been that the claimant was deliberately seeking tenants who were eligible for benefit in order to charge high rents that would be paid by housing benefit.

8 *R v Director of the Serious Fraud Office ex p Johnson (Malcolm Keith)* [1993] COD 58, QBD.
9 *R v Secretary of State for Defence ex p Sancto* (1993) 5 Admin LR 673, QBD.
10 [2003] EWCA Civ 1546, [2004] 1 WLR 1761.
11 [2002] EWHC 2762 (Admin), [2003] ACD 34.
12 (1991) 23 HLR 337, QBD.
13 Under Housing Benefit (General) Regulations 1987 SI No 1971 reg 7(b), now Housing Benefit Regulations 2006 SI No 213, reg 9(1)(l).

A more appropriate challenger?

4.11   The availability of another, more appropriate, party to bring a challenge may influence the decision as to whether or not a claimant should be accorded standing. In *Durayappah v Fernando*,[14] the House of Lords remarked that if the person principally affected by a decision chose to take no action to challenge it, there seemed no reason why anybody else should be permitted to do so.[15]

4.12   In *R (Bulger) v Secretary of State for the Home Department*,[16] the court refused standing to the father of a murdered child to apply for judicial review of a decision of the Lord Chief Justice to reduce the tariffs of the sentences being served by the children who had committed the murder. Since the Crown or a defendant would be able to challenge the decision, it was unnecessary and undesirable for a third party to seek to intervene. The Lord Chief Justice's invitation to the claimant to make representations to him did not confer standing on the claimant to challenge the tariff.

4.13   In *R (Hammerton) v London Underground Ltd*[17] it was held that the absence of a better-placed challenger was not an essential prerequisite of standing, although it was a relevant factor.

Education cases

4.14   In education cases, such as those relating to refusals of admission or school closure or reorganisation, there has been judicial consideration of whether the parent or the child (or both) would have standing to bring a challenge. In the context of school admissions cases, it has been held that while the child may well have a sufficient interest to mount a challenge, nevertheless the parent(s) should usually be named as the claimant(s) as the only reason for bringing a challenge in the name of the child would usually be to obtain public funding for the challenge and to protect the parents in costs should the challenge fail. This was an abuse and a device and reason for refusing permission to apply for judicial review.[18]

---

14 [1967] 2 AC 337, HL.

15 See also *R v Bow County Court ex p Pelling (No 1)* [1999] 1 WLR 1807.

16 [2001] EWHC 119 (Admin), [2001] 3 All ER 449, QBD.

17 [2002] EWHC 2307 (Admin).

18 *R v Richmond LBC Appeal Committee ex p JC* [2001] BLGR 146, [2001] ELR 13, CA, and *B v Head Teacher of Alperton Community School* [2001] EWHC 229 (Admin), [2002] BLGR 132.

4.15   In relation to school closure, however, the position appears to be somewhat different. In *R (WB) and KA v Leeds School Organisation Committee*,[19] Scott Baker J held that issue was relevant not to standing but to abuse and therefore the court's discretion. Both parents and children had a sufficient interest to bring judicial review proceedings in school closure or reorganisation cases, and while in many cases it may be the parents who had the real interest and while it may be an abuse of process to name the child as the claimant for the purposes of obtaining funding and protection against a possible costs order, clear evidence would be needed to establish such an abuse. The school admissions cases, referred to above, were distinguished on the basis that the appellate regime under consideration in those cases made it clear that the right of appeal was that of the parent and not the child. There was no indication that the court's decisions in those cases were intended for any wider application.[20]

Capacity

4.16   At one time it was thought that, in addition to standing, the claimant must have capacity (on ordinary civil law principles) to bring litigation;[21] the issue to be determined at the permission stage.[22] More recently, the courts appear to have relaxed this requirement somewhat. In a number of cases, unincorporated associations have brought challenges successfully.[23]

4.17   In *R v Traffic Commissioner for the North Western Traffic Area ex p 'Brake'*,[24] the court suggested that there may be no requirement for capacity in public law claims, which were different from private actions. In a claim concerning breach of a private right, such a right had to be shown to exist and this could only be so if the claimant was a legal person who could enjoy such a right. In public law claims, however, the focus was on the decision of the public body. The dispute, at

19 [2002] EWHC 1927 (Admin), [2003] ELR 67.

20 [2002] EWHC 1927 (Admin) at [32]–[37].

21 *R v Darlington BC ex p Association of Darlington Taxi Owners* [1994] COD 424, QBD (unincorporated association lacked capacity).

22 *R v Darlington BC ex p Association of Darlington Taxi Owners* [1994] COD 424, QBD.

23 See, eg, *R v Gloucestershire CC ex p Barry* [1996] 4 All ER 421, (1997–98) 1 CCLR 40, CA, where in one of two conjoined appeals the Royal Association for Disability and Rehabilitation was substituted for the original claimant following her death; *R v Liverpool CC ex p Baby Products Association* (2000) 2 LGLR 689, [2000] BLGR 171, QBD.

24 [1996] COD 248.

least technically, was between the Crown and the public body[25] and the issue was whether the act challenged was unlawful, and whether the claimant could show a sufficient interest to bring the challenge. It was not in every case that a claimant would have to show, therefore, that a right of his or hers had been infringed, but rather that the illegality of the public body's act had in some way affected her or him.[26]

4.18 In *R v Ministry of Agriculture, Fisheries and Food ex p British Pig Industry Support Group*,[27] it was held that there was no reason in principle why an unincorporated association should not be entitled to bring judicial review proceedings, so long as proper provision was made for the defendant to be protected in costs. It may not be possible to make an order of security for costs against a party who was not a corporate body[28] and, if that were so, it may be that the court ought, as a condition of the grant of permission, to require that a legal person be joined as a party for the purpose of ensuring that an effective costs order can be made where appropriate should the defendant succeed.

Public interest challenges

4.19 Public interest challenges have been described as having the 'essential characteristics' that they raise issues of general importance in circumstances where the challenger has no private interest in the outcome of the case.[29] In *NFSSB*,[30] Lord Diplock expressed the view that traditional tests of standing may be too restrictive in such cases:[31]

> It would, in my view, be a grave lacuna in our system of public law if a pressure group ... or even a single public-spirited taxpayer were prevented by outdated technical rules of *locus standi* from bringing the matter to the attention of the court to vindicate the rule of law and get the unlawful conduct stopped ... It is not ... a sufficient answer to say that judicial review of the actions of officers or departments of central government is unnecessary because they are accountable to Parliament for the way in which they carry out their functions. They are

---

25 But see, on this point, *R (Ben-Abdelaziz) v Haringey LBC* [2001] EWCA Civ 803, [2001] 1 WLR 1485.

26 Cf the comments of Lord Reed in *AXA General Insurance v HM Advocate* [2011] UKSC 46, [2012] 1 AC 868, referred to at para 4.5 above.

27 [2000] Eu LR 724, [2001] ACD 3, QBD.

28 See CPR r25.13(2)(c).

29 *R v Lord Chancellor ex p Child Poverty Action Group* [1999] 1 WLR 347, QBD.

30 *R v Inland Revenue Commissioners ex p NFSSB* [1982] AC 617, HL.

31 At 644E.

accountable to Parliament for what they do so far as regards efficiency and policy, and of that Parliament is the only judge; they are accountable to a court of justice for the lawfulness of what they do, and of that the court is the only judge.

4.20 The courts have, in recent times, adopted a liberal approach to standing in such cases.[32] Mere busybodies will not have sufficient interest,[33] although clearly there is some room for difference of opinion on where the line may properly be drawn between busybodies and the 'public-spirited' people of whom Lord Diplock spoke with approval in NFSSB.[34] In R v Her Majesty's Treasury ex p Smedley,[35] a claimant in his capacity of elector and taxpayer was permitted to challenge (albeit unsuccessfully) the government's undertaking to pay by Order in Council its contribution of £121 million to the European Community. In R v Secretary of State for Foreign and Commonwealth Affairs ex p Rees-Mogg,[36] the claimant's long-standing and 'sincere interest in constitutional affairs' was held to be a sufficient basis for according him standing to challenge the implementation of the Maastricht treaty (although the claimant was also a taxpayer).

4.21 An even more liberal example can be seen in R (Hassan) v Secretary of State for Trade and Industry.[37] The claimant was a Palestinian who lived in a village near Bethlehem. He made a living by cultivating olives and almonds. In 2005, the Israeli Defence Force (IDF) destroyed his trees and fenced off his land, preventing him from returning. He contended that the IDF had used military machinery and equipment which had been sold to it by UK companies and sought judicial review of the decision of the Secretary of State to grant the relevant export licences.

---

32 The decision of Schiemann J in R v Secretary of State for the Environment ex p Rose Theatre Trust Company [1990] 1 QB 504, QBD has not been followed. In that case, he held that a person could not obtain sufficient interest simply by writing to the decision-maker and receiving a reply. Nor would a group of individuals each without sufficient interest in a matter acquire a sufficient interest simply by forming themselves into a group or company, purporting to have such an interest, used as their 'campaign's vehicle'; see 521C–E.

33 See, eg, R v Monopolies and Mergers Commission ex p Argyll Group plc [1986] 1 WLR 763, CA.

34 For example, R v Legal Aid Board ex p Bateman [1992] 1 WLR 711, CA, where standing was accorded to a 'responsible' person.

35 [1985] QB 657, CA.

36 [1994] QB 552, QBD.

37 [2007] EWHC 2630 (Admin), [2008] ACD 10, appealed to the Court of Appeal on a different point and reported as [2008] EWCA Civ 1311, [2009] 3 All ER 539.

4.22 The judge at first instance considered whether or not the claimant could be said to have sufficient interest so as to bring the application. In concluding that he did, it was significant that he was a Palestinian living in the occupied territories and was therefore affected by Israel's attempts to contain attacks against its citizens and so (albeit indirectly) also affected by any trade in military equipment to Israel. The judge also took into account the fact that it was unclear who would have sufficient interest if not the claimant, holding that the law should be applied sufficiently flexibly to ensure that the legality of decisions taken by public authorities could be scrutinised.[38]

4.23 Pressure and public interest groups also appear to have the requisite standing in suitable cases (and see above[39] in relation to the requirement or otherwise for legal capacity). The Child Poverty Action Group has been held to have standing in an application to challenge the manner in which the Secretary of State was administering the law to the alleged detriment of claimants of benefits.[40]

4.24 The standing of interest groups was considered in more detail in *R v HM Inspectorate of Pollution and Ministry of Agriculture, Fisheries and Food ex p Greenpeace Ltd*.[41] Otton J held that the claimant pressure group did have sufficient interest to challenge the decision of the inspectorate to vary authorisations granted to British Nuclear Fuels Ltd to discharge certain forms of radioactive waste from Sellafield, to permit the testing of a Thermal Oxide Reprocessing Plant.

4.25 The question of standing was, he held, primarily one of discretion and it was appropriate to take into account, in considering the matter, the nature of Greenpeace and the extent of its interest in the issues raised in the application, the remedy it sought to achieve and the nature of the relief sought. Considering these matters, the judge noted the level of support Greenpeace enjoyed worldwide, its consultative status with several United Nations bodies and the fact that it was a respectable and responsible body with a genuine concern for the environment and a bona fide interest in BNFL's activities at Sellafield and the discharge of radioactive waste. In particular, he had

38 Cf the comments of Lord Reed in *AXA General Insurance v HM Advocate* [2011] UKSC 46, [2012] 1 AC 868, referred to at para 4.5 above.

39 At paras 4.16–4.18.

40 *R v Secretary of State for Social Services ex p CPAG* (1984) *Times* 16 August, QBD. CPAG has subsequently brought a number of judicial review challenges against decisions of the Secretary of State for Social Services and the Secretary of State for Work and Pensions, most recently at [2010] UKSC 54, [2011] 2 AC 15, [2011] EWHC 2616 (Admin), [2011] Eq LR 1233; and [2012] EWHC 2579 (Admin), [2012] ACD 190.

41 [1994] 4 All ER 329, QBD (see also, on appeal [1994] 1 WLR 570, CA).

regard to the fact that 2,500 of the body's UK supporters came from the Cumbria region and it would be to ignore the blindingly obvious for the court to disregard the concern and perception of danger to their health and safety from any additional radioactive discharge, which such people inevitably felt. In addition, Greenpeace had been treated as one of the consultees during the consultation process and had been invited to comment on the Inspectorate's letter, in which it had stated it was 'minded to vary' BNFL's existing authorisations.

4.26   Moreover, if Greenpeace were denied standing, those it represented might not have an effective way of bringing these issues before the court. It was unlikely that an individual neighbour or employee of BNFL would command the expertise that was at the disposal of Greenpeace, and so a less well-informed challenge might be mounted that would stretch, unnecessarily, the court's resources and would not afford the court the assistance it required to do justice between the parties. In addition, if an individual applicant was legally aided, the respondents would have no effective remedy in costs.

4.27   As to relief, while the House of Lords had held in *NFSSB*[42] that the seeking of an order of mandamus (a mandatory order) may be a reason to decline jurisdiction, here certiorari (a quashing order) was sought, and the injunction that was claimed, in the event that the decision were quashed, would still be in the discretion of the court.[43] It was not to be assumed, however, that Greenpeace or any other interest group would automatically possess standing in any application for judicial review. The matter must be decided on the facts of each individual case as a matter of discretion.

4.28   Conversely, however, in *R (Al-Haq) v Secretary of State for Foreign and Commonwealth Affairs*,[44] standing was denied to a non-governmental organisation based in the West Bank, which sought an order compelling the Secretary of State, *inter alia*, to denounce publicly Israel's military activities in Lebanon; suspend all exports of military equipment to Israel; and suspend all other assistance to Israel.

4.29   The court held that Al-Haq did not have standing to bring the application. Not only was the organisation not claiming any substantive right for itself, but it was for a UK national (or pressure group) to challenge UK foreign policy, not a foreign NGO. If that were not so,

---

42 *R v Inland Revenue Commissioners ex p NFSSB* [1982] AC 617, HL.

43 On the relevance of standing to the remedy, if any, which the court grants, see also *Walton v Scottish Ministers* [2012] UKSC 44, [2013] PTSR 51.

44 [2009] EWHC 1910 (Admin), [2009] ACD 76.

then any foreign party could seek to use the courts to bring about a change in government policy.

4.30 Parties should not assume, therefore, that standing will necessarily be accorded merely because of the importance of the subject-matter of the challenge. While that is a relevant factor, the court's discretion is still to be exercised on a much broader basis.

Control of public interest challenges

4.31 While the courts have generally adopted a liberal approach to standing in relation to challenges brought by public interest groups,[45] it has nonetheless been suggested that they will require strict compliance with the rules in such cases. Although they are now accepted and are, indeed, a 'greatly valued dimension of the judicial review jurisdiction' they are open to potential abuse, meaning that delay will be tolerated less readily.[46] This should not, however, be seen as creating too high a hurdle, nor as encouraging premature applications.

4.32 In *R v Secretary of State for Trade and Industry ex p Greenpeace*,[47] the court could not envisage many cases where on the same facts a public interest challenge would be refused because of delay where a private claimant would be permitted to proceed.

Standing in Human Rights Act 1998 cases

4.33 In human rights cases, there is a different test for standing. The European Convention on Human Rights[48] and the HRA 1998[49] frame the test in terms that the person seeking review must be a 'victim' of the act or decision complained of.

4.34 A 'victim' for the purposes of article 34 can be a natural or legal person.[50]

---

45 See, eg, *R v Secretary of State for Foreign and Commonwealth Affairs ex p World Development Movement* [1995] 1 WLR 386, DC, where the claimant was successful in challenging aid for the building of the Pergau Dam; *R v Secretary of State for the Environment ex p Kirkstall Valley Campaign Ltd* [1996] 3 All ER 304, QBD.

46 *R v Secretary of State for Trade and Industry ex p Greenpeace Ltd* [1998] Env LR 415, QBD, per Laws J at 425.

47 [2000] 2 CMLR 94, [2000] Env LR 221, QBD.

48 Article 34.

49 Human Rights Act 1998 s7(1).

50 *AXA General Insurance v HM Advocate* [2011] UKSC 46, [2012] 1 AC 868.

4.35   The jurisprudence of the Strasbourg Court has been relatively elastic as to who may properly be considered a 'victim' – article 34 does not define the term – though it is clear that there must be some connection between the claimant and the injury or violation complained of. In other words, the claimant must show he or she has been, or that there is a reasonable likelihood that he or she will be, directly affected in some way. In *Cullen v Chief Constable of the Royal Ulster Constabulary*,[51] Lord Millett noted that a person could qualify as a victim, in accordance with Strasbourg case-law, even if the alleged breach of her or his rights had caused no damage.[52]

4.36   In *Lancashire CC v Taylor*,[53] it was held that the HRA 1998 s7 made it clear that members of the public were not intended to be able to use the HRA to challenge legislation that they considered to be incompatible with the Convention but by which they were not adversely affected. Such people would not be considered 'victims'.

4.37   The Convention makes no provision for applications taking the form of a 'popular action',[54] and the HRA defines 'victim' in terms of its meaning under the Convention.[55] Thus, although in other respects the Strasbourg jurisprudence is merely something to which due regard must be paid,[56] in relation to the definition of 'victim' Convention law will be decisive. It is unlikely in the extreme that a pressure group will be able to assert that it is a victim for the purposes of the HRA 1998 even though it may well represent victims. Accordingly, in relation to issues arising under that Act, there would seem to be no alternative to the old approach in judicial review proceedings of selecting a 'test claimant'.[57] The pressure group itself, however, may well be able to appear as an interested party.[58]

4.38   The position is somewhat different where a claim is brought on behalf of a victim, eg by a parent on behalf of a child. In those circumstances an application for judicial review may be made by the parent, although it is generally preferable for the child to be joined as a party.[59]

---

51   [2003] UKHL 39, [2003] 1 WLR 1763.
52   [2003] UKHL 39, [2003] 1 WLR 1763 at [81].
53   [2005] EWCA Civ 284, [2005] 1 WLR 2668.
54   European Convention art 34.
55   Human Rights Act 1998 s7(7).
56   Human Rights Act 1998 s2(1).
57   For example, *R v HM Treasury ex p Smedley* [1985] QB 657, CA.
58   See paras 4.44–4.47 below. See also para 21.31 below.
59   *Re E (A Child)* [2008] UKHL 66; [2009] 1 AC 536 at [42]. See also the education cases on standing referred to at paras 4.14–4.15 above.

The position of the Crown

4.39 In *R (Ben-Abdelaziz) v Haringey LBC*,[60] the Court of Appeal held that the position of the Crown in judicial review proceedings (given that it is listed as a party in every claim) was best described as 'nominal'. In reality, the claim was a contest between the claimant, who brought and pursued it, and the defendant; the proceedings were not brought by the Crown or at the Crown's instigation.[61] The requirement for permission could not be construed as having any effect on this position.[62]

The defendant

4.40 The defendant must be an inferior court, a tribunal or some other public body. It must, in addition, have been acting in a public law rather than a private law capacity in relation to the act or decision under challenge.[63]

Claimant and defendant

4.41 On occasion, public bodies, especially local authorities, have sought judicial review of decisions they themselves have taken. While, conceptually, this would seem to pose difficulties, the courts have generally adopted a relaxed attitude, especially where the alternative to such actions is even less attractive, such as permitting clearly unlawful conduct to continue in circumstances where there is no other available mode of challenge and/or no other claimant likely to come forward.

4.42 In *R v Birmingham City Council and Fitzpatrick ex p Birmingham City Council*,[64] the court permitted the authority to challenge a

---

60 [2001] EWCA Civ 803, [2001] 1 WLR 1485.
61 But see the court's comments in *ex p 'Brake'*, para 4.17 above.
62 This may seem rather a strange matter for the court to be asked to determine in the 21st century. In fact, it concerned rather an ingenious attempt to circumvent the provisions of HRA 1998 s22(4) to enable a claimant to claim compensation for an act that was completed prior to the Act coming into force, by arguing that the judicial review proceedings they had brought were proceedings brought by a public authority (the Crown).
63 See chapter 2 above, regarding identifying a public body amenable to review, and chapter 3 above, on reviewable decisions.
64 (1992) 24 HLR 279, QBD.

decision of its own housing benefit review board, in circumstances where the board's decision – that the housing benefit applicant was entitled to benefit – clearly contravened the Housing Benefit Regulations and was unlawful. Similarly, the leader of an authority has been entitled to seek judicial review of a decision of his authority's planning committee on the ground of bias/fraud,[65] and the adoption of a new constitution by an authority has been quashed on the application of the authority's chief executive where a procedural error had the effect that, by statute, all of the authority's elected members had ceased to be members of the authority.[66]

4.43   Claims of this kind should normally be brought, formally, on the application of the authority's leader or chief executive.[67]

Third parties

4.44   Interested third parties have a right to be served with the application and appear on the hearing of the application.[68] In certain circumstances, such as in a human rights case where a declaration of incompatibility is to be sought, the Crown must be served as an interested third party. It will usually be for the claimant to give informal notice to the Crown, and for the court to decide whether the making of a declaration is sufficiently likely to render formal notice necessary.[69]

4.45   Any person, even if not served, may apply to the court to file evidence and/or to make representations at the hearing of the judicial review claim as an intervener.[70] Such an application should be made by letter to the Administrative Court Office, setting out who the applicant is and why and in what form he or she wishes to participate in the proceedings. If a protective costs order[71] is sought, the letter should also set out the type of, and grounds for, the order sought.

---

65   *R v Bassetlaw DC ex p Oxby* [1998] PCLR 283, CA. See also *R v Port Talbot BC ex p Jones* (1988) 20 HLR 265 (and CA transcript 9 November 1988) where the leader of the authority successfully challenged an allocation of housing to one of its councilors, not made in accordance with the authority's allocation policy. See also *R v Macclesfield BC ex p Duddy* [2001] JHL D16.

66   *R (Meredith) v Merthyr Tydfil County Borough Council* [2002] EWHC 634 (Admin).

67   See *Oxby* above,

68   CPR rr54.7 and 54.17. See further paras 18.128 and 21.31 below.

69   *Poplar HARCA v Donoghue* [2001] EWCA Civ 595, [2002] QB 48, [2001] 4 All ER 604, (2001) 33 HLR 823.

70   CPR r54.17.

71   See paras 18.171–18.184 below.

Applications of this type must be made at the earliest reasonable opportunity as it will usually be essential not to delay the hearing of the claim.[72] Where all parties consent, the court may deal with such an application without a hearing.[73] The court may give permission on conditions and may also give case management directions.[74]

4.46   These provisions are considerably wider than their equivalents under the old procedural regime.[75] Before the introduction of CPR Pt 54, however, interested third parties frequently participated. There was no general right for a third party to be heard on appeal, even if he or she had taken part at first instance,[76] though this did not preclude the appellate court in its discretion from allowing such a person to be heard. Whether the court would take the same approach under the CPR is not clear, but in *Thurrock BC v Secretary of State for the Environment, Transport and the Regions,*[77] Brooke LJ cautioned against the use of old authorities on procedural issues, holding that, as the CPR created a new procedural code, such authorities may be of little use and could even be positively misleading.

4.47   Parties who wish to intervene in a case should take note of the words of caution of Lord Hoffmann in *Re E (A Child):*[78]

> ... In recent years the House has frequently been assisted by the submissions of statutory bodies and non-governmental organisations on questions of general public importance. Leave is given to such bodies to intervene and make submissions, usually in writing but sometimes orally from the bar, in the expectation that their fund of knowledge or particular point of view will enable them to provide the House with a more rounded picture than it would otherwise obtain. The House is grateful to such bodies for their help.
>
> An intervention is however of no assistance if it merely repeats points which the appellant or respondent has already made. An intervener will have had sight of their printed cases and, if it has nothing to add, should not add anything. It is not the role of an intervener to be an additional counsel for one of the parties. This is particularly important in the case of an oral intervention. I am bound to say that in this

---

72 CPR PD 54 paras 13.3–13.5.
73 CPR PD 54 para 13.1.
74 CPR PD 54 para 13.2.
75 RSC Ord 53 r9(1).
76 *R v Licensing Authority ex p Smith Kline & French Laboratories Ltd* [1990] 1 AC 64, HL.
77 [2001] CP Rep 55, [2001] 1 PLR 94 at [23].
78 [2008] UKHL 66, [2009] 1 AC 536 at [2]–[3]. Lord Hoffmann's observations were made in the particular context of interveners in the House of Lords, but there is no reason to think that they do not apply equally at other levels.

appeal the oral submissions on behalf of the NIHRC only repeated in rather more emphatic terms the points which had already been quite adequately argued by counsel for the appellant. In future, I hope that interveners will avoid unnecessarily taking up the time of the House in this way.

CHAPTER 5

Remedies available in judicial review

continued

5.1 The following remedies may be available in judicial review proceedings:

- a quashing order (formerly known as an order of certiorari);[1]
- a mandatory order (formerly known as an order of mandamus);[2]
- a prohibiting order (formerly known as an order of prohibition);[3]
- a declaration;[4]
- an injunction;[5]
- damages;[6]
- restitution.[7]

5.2 The first three of the remedies were known as the 'prerogative' orders, as they derive from the prerogative writs of the same names, which were traditionally used by the common law courts to control the use and abuse of powers.[8] In accordance with the philosophy of the Civil Procedure Rules, to modernise legal language including, among other things, avoiding the use of Latin terms, they became referred to in the CPR by their new names. Section 29 of the Senior Courts Act (SCA) 1981 has now been amended to reflect that approach and accordingly any reference in any statutory provision to certiorari, mandamus or prohibition should now be read as a reference to a quashing order, a mandatory order, or a prohibiting order.[9]

5.3 In addition to those remedies listed above, the court has certain ancillary powers, and it is possible to apply for interim relief (see below). It should be remembered that the grant of a remedy is

1 CPR r54.2(c).
2 CPR r54.2(a).
3 CPR r54.2(b).
4 CPR r54.3(1)(a).
5 Senior Courts Act 1981 ss30, 31(2) and CPR r54.2(d); r54.3(b).
6 Senior Courts Act 1981 s31(4) and CPR r54.3(2).
7 Senior Courts Act 1981 s31(4) and CPR r54.3(2).
8 Senior Courts Act 1981 s29, especially sub-ss (1), (1A) and (5). The history of these remedies is beyond the scope of this book. The interested reader should refer to S A de Smith 'The Prerogative Writs' (1951) 11 CLJ 40; S A de Smith *Judicial Review of Administrative Action* (Stevens & Sons, 3rd edn, 1973) 507–19; L Jaffe and E Henderson 'Judicial Review and the Rule of Law: Historical Origins' (1956) 72 LQR 345.
9 SCA 1981 s29(5).

discretionary, even if the court is satisfied that the decision under challenge was reached improperly.[10]

The quashing order[11]

5.4 As its new name states, a quashing order results in the quashing of the decision or order under challenge. In some cases, the court may remit the matter back and direct that the body or tribunal reach a conclusion in accordance with the court's findings.[12] In others, the court may take the decision itself.[13] More usually, however, the court will simply quash the decision and leave it to the decision-maker to reconsider the matter.

5.5 It follows from the nature of this remedy, and indeed of judicial review as a whole, that although a claimant may succeed in obtaining a quashing order, this does not necessarily mean that he will succeed in obtaining a different or more favourable decision when the matter is reconsidered. It may well be that once the matter is considered in accordance with the law, the decision-maker can quite lawfully reach the same decision on the merits once again.

5.6 Where a quashing order is sought, a stay or injunction is likely to be available, in principle, as an interim measure, pending the full hearing.[14]

The mandatory order[15]

5.7 A mandatory order is an order requiring the performance of a specified act or duty. A claimant will not usually be entitled to claim a mandatory order requiring the defendant to do the substantive act or to reach the substantive decision, which the claimant desires (ie to decide in the claimant's favour on the merits).

---

10 Traditionally, the discretionary nature of relief was reflected in judicial review terminology – 'relief' was 'sought' not 'claimed'. This use of language has been continued in the judicial review claim form (N461) section 6 ('sought'), but not in CPR r54.6(1)(c) ('claiming'). See further below, as to the discretionary nature of relief, paras 7.1–7.36.

11 See also paras 2.22–2.23 above.

12 See para 5.43 below.

13 See para 5.44 below.

14 See paras 5.65–5.71 below.

15 See also paras 2.24–2.25 above.

5.8 Unless:

- there exists an absolute duty, as distinct from a mere discretion or a duty arising only upon the defendant being satisfied regarding certain facts; or
- the defendant has already decided in the claimant's favour all the issues necessary to impose a duty to do that which the claimant seeks; or
- only two decisions were possible and, of those two, the one made by the defendant has been held to be perverse by the court, leaving only one lawful option available,

it will not be possible to seek a mandatory order requiring the body to act in accordance with the claimant's wishes. All that may be sought is an order with the effect of requiring that the defendant reconsider the application, this time in accordance with the law, and without making the errors (or any others) that led to the first decision being quashed.

5.9 In most cases, the courts are reluctant to grant mandatory orders, as it is generally presumed (with good cause) that if the court has ruled a decision to be unlawful, the defendant will comply with – and give effect to – that ruling by reconsidering the matter without the need for a specific order. Accordingly, it is often advisable for an applicant to seek a declaration in addition or in the alternative (see paras 5.12–5.17 below).

The prohibiting order

5.10 A prohibiting order prevents the decision-maker concerned from acting or continuing to act in excess of jurisdiction. As with mandatory orders, however, the court may well consider that it is sufficient to grant a declaration in terms that the proposed action is in excess of the decision-maker's jurisdiction, or otherwise improper, unless the claimant can demonstrate that declaratory relief would not suffice and that a prohibiting order is actually necessary on the facts.

5.11 A stay or injunction is available as an interim measure.

Declaration and injunction

5.12 A declaration is not a prerogative order, nor is it a remedy in the same sense as the other orders discussed in this chapter. It does not quash anything nor require anyone to do or refrain from doing anything, but is simply a determination by the court of the respective rights and obligations of the parties (or in some circumstances of the error into which the decision-maker has fallen).[16] In judicial review proceedings, the court, in its discretion, frequently grants declarations instead of mandatory relief, on the basis that public bodies comply with decisions of the court without the necessity of a mandatory order, or on the basis that it would be inappropriate to quash the decision in all the circumstances.[17]

5.13   By CPR r54.3, the Part 54 procedure may, but need not, be used for judicial review claims where all that is sought is a declaration and/or an injunction. There is one exception: an application for an injunction that seeks to restrain a person from acting in any office in which he or she is not entitled to act, must be made in Part 54 proceedings.[18]

5.14   A declaration or injunction will only be granted where one of the prerogative writs could have been granted,[19] although this does not prevent a claimant from seeking such remedies instead of a prerogative order. Indeed, where a declaration of unlawful conduct is necessary in order to facilitate a claim for damages, the court will generally be willing to allow a claim to proceed, even where no substantive relief is required.[20]

5.15   A declaration or injunction may be granted where the court considers it just and convenient to do so, taking account of the matters in respect of which relief is sought, the nature of the persons and/or bodies against whom relief is sought and to all the circumstances of the case.[21] In some circumstances, however, declaratory relief will not be appropriate. In *R (Campaign for Nuclear Disarmament) v Prime*

---

16 See, eg, *R v Secretary of State for Social Security ex p Association of Metropolitan Authorities* (1992) 25 HLR 131, QBD.

17 See paras 7.32–7.33 below.

18 SCA 1981 s30 and CPR r54.2(d).

19 *R v Inland Revenue Commissioners ex p National Federation of Self-Employed and Small Businesses* [1982] AC 617, HL, per Lord Scarman at 648; cited in *Davy v Spelthorne DC* [1984] AC 262, HL, per Lord Wilberforce at 278D; see also *R v Chelmsford Crown Court ex p Chief Constable of Essex* [1994] 1 WLR 359, DC, and SCA 1981 s31(2).

20 See, eg, *R v Northavon DC ex p Palmer* (1993) 25 HLR 674, QBD. On the hearing of the damages claim (1994) 26 HLR 572, QBD, the court held that the matters complained of gave rise to no right to damages. As to the right to claim damages, see further paras 5.18–5.22 below. See also: *O'Rourke v Camden LBC* [1998] AC 188, HL; *O'Rourke v United Kingdom* (2001) 26 June, unreported, and *R (Morris) v Newham LBC* [2002] EWHC 1262 (Admin). But compare *R v Blandford Justices ex p Pamment* [1990] 1 WLR 1490, CA.

21 SCA 1981 s31(2).

Minister,[22] for example, the court declined to grant an advisory declaration as to whether UN resolution 1441 authorised military action to be taken against Iraq, on the basis that it was not appropriate for the court to grant declarations on the meaning of international instruments that had no existence in UK law, and where no rights of any UK citizen were affected by it.

5.16 Similarly, in *R (Southall) v Secretary of State for Foreign and Commonwealth Affairs*,[23] the Court of Appeal refused permission to appeal a refusal of permission to apply for judicial review where the claimant sought a declaration that the government must hold a referendum or general election prior to approving any European constitution. The court held that the declarations sought were inappropriately vague and that the case was unarguable, but that in any event, as a matter of discretion the court would refuse a declaration where there was no draft treaty in existence to which all the relevant governments had consented and so it was impossible to evaluate what domestic constitutional effect the implementation of such a treaty would have.

5.17 Declaratory relief will not be granted where it would not serve any useful purpose, such as where mistakes had been made some years before the hearing, not as the result of any systemic administrative failure but due instead to individual muddles and misunderstandings that had already been acknowledged by the decision-maker.[24]

Damages not involving claims under the Human Rights Act 1998

5.18 A judicial review claim may include a claim for damages but may not seek damages alone.[25] An award of damages is discretionary, and the court may only make one, other than in human rights cases that are considered separately below, if it is satisfied that if the claim had been brought as a private law action, begun at the same time as the judicial review claim, the claimant could or would have been awarded damages. In other words, a damages claim may only be included in order to bring a valid private law claim for damages in the same proceedings as the public law challenge.

---

22 [2002] EWHC 2777 (Admin), [2013] ACD 36.
23 [2003] EWCA Civ 1002, [2003] ACD 321.
24 *R (Bernard) v Secretary of State for the Home Department* [2005] EWHC 452 (Admin); [2006] 1 Prison LR 180 (delay in holding Parole Board hearings).
25 CPR r54.3(2).

5.19   The court enjoys no wider jurisdiction to award damages to a claimant than it would have if a damages claim came before it in the usual way; nor does a claimant have any cause of action for damages in respect of a breach of a public law duty.[26] In numerous cases, the court has refused a claim for damages on the ground that the duty breached existed only in public law and so gave rise to no private law right to damages.[27]

5.20   Under the old procedural rules, any loss and damage claimed had to be fully particularised,[28] and although there is no specific equivalent provision contained in CPR Pt 54, it is advisable that any claimant wishing to include a claim for damages should give as much information in the claim form concerning the grounds for and amount of the claim as he would if bringing a CPR Pt 7 claim.

5.21   In practice, if a claim for judicial review has been successful, a course frequently taken by the court is to order, at the conclusion of the substantive hearing, that the damages claim proceed as if commenced by private action and stand adjourned, sometimes to the Queen's Bench Division and sometimes even to the county court, for an assessment of damages hearing. Given the difficulty of adjudicating on factual disputes in the Administrative Court, it is unusual for the judicial review court to hear the damages claim, or to assess the quantum, itself.[29]

5.22   In 2010, the Law Commission put forward proposals for reforming the law in this area, arguing that damages should be available as an additional remedy in judicial review claims. It stopped developing these proposals, however, following responses to its consultation exercise.[30]

---

26   SCA 1981 s31(4), and see *Calveley v Chief Constable of Merseyside Police* [1989] QB 136, CA.
27   See the cases referred to at note 20 above.
28   RSC Ord 53 r7(2) applying RSC Ord 18 r12.
29   See, eg, *R v Lambeth LBC ex p Campbell* (1994) 26 HLR 618, and the cases noted at note 20 above.
30   Law Commission *Administrative Redress: Public Bodies and the Citizen* (Law Com No 322, 2010). Many of the ombudsmen schemes have power to award compensation for maladministration causing injustice regardless of whether the maladministration found concerned public or private law matters. Some schemes are only available, however, where litigation is not in prospect: see eg Local Government Act 1974, Pt 3.

Damages in human rights cases

5.23 Damages for any unlawful act, or proposed act, by a public authority, may only be awarded by a court that has power to award damages or order the payment of compensation in civil proceedings.[31] The court's jurisdiction to award damages is confined by the requirements of HRA 1998 s8(3), which provides that:

> (3) No award of damages is to be made unless, taking account of all the circumstances of the case, including –
>> (a) any other relief or remedy granted, or order made, in relation to the act in question (by that or any other court), and
>> (b) the consequences of any decision (of that or any other court) in respect of that act,
>
> the court is satisfied that the award is necessary to afford just satisfaction to the person in whose favour it is made.

5.24 In *Cullen v Chief Constable of the Royal Ulster Constabulary*,[32] Lord Millett stated that the significance of the limitation applied by this provision should not be overlooked.

> It means that Parliament has contemplated that there would be cases where breach of a Convention right did not automatically give rise to an award of damages, and this is inconsistent with the notion that such an award is necessary to vindicate the right.

The most obvious example of such a case was where no damage had been suffered.[33]

5.25 In determining whether to make an award and, if so, in what amount, the court is also obliged to take account of the principles applied by the ECtHR in relation to compensation awards under article 41 of the Convention.[34] The European Court has adopted a somewhat cautious approach to the issue of damages, both in terms of the circumstances in which it will make an award and of the amount of any award it does make. Financial compensation tends only to be awarded where it is impossible to reverse all the consequences of the breach of the Convention right in question, ie where the claimant cannot be put back in the position in which he or she ought to have been had the breach not occurred.

---

31 HRA 1998 s8(2).
32 [2003] UKHL 39, [2003] 1 WLR 1736.
33 [2003] UKHL 39 at [84]. The comments of Lord Millett on this subject were strictly speaking obiter dicta, as the alleged wrong had been committed prior to the coming into force of the HRA 1998.
34 HRA 1998 s8(4).

5.26   The decisions of the European Court in this context, however, are frequently inconsistent and contradictory, which has left the field clearer for the domestic courts to derive their own principles for awarding damages, given that taking account of the ECtHR's principles takes the matter no further. This is so particularly in relation to the availability of damages to compensate non-pecuniary loss.[35]

5.27   In *Cullen*,[36] Lord Millett noted that it was difficult to discern any consistent principles from the jurisprudence of the European Court, but that where a claimant cannot establish either pecuniary or non-pecuniary loss, the decision of the court that the conduct complained of constitutes a breach of a Convention right will generally be considered to be sufficient just satisfaction. Given the court's power to make appropriate declarations there was little reason for making an award of nominal damages, which would be both inconsistent with the principles applied by the European Court and unnecessary. To make such an award would probably also be inconsistent with HRA 1998 s8(3).[37]

5.28   It follows from the above that the court will only have power to award damages for breaches of Convention rights if the combination of other remedies that the claimant has been awarded in legal proceedings, and/or other action taken by any court, is insufficient to compensate the claimant properly in respect of the breach. Damages are therefore very much a secondary remedy.

5.29   Notwithstanding the above, damages in the context of breach of Convention rights may extend a claimant's right to be compensated further than would be permissible on ordinary common law principles. In particular, the availability of damages for breach of Convention rights may well extend their ambit into areas of public authorities' activity that might traditionally have been regarded as existing in public law only and so conferring no right to compensation.[38]

5.30   It must be remembered, however, that the position, in judicial review proceedings, remains governed by SCA 1981 s31(4), which provides that damages can only be claimed in judicial review

---

35 See, in particular, *R (KB) v Mental Health Review Tribunal (Damages)* [2003] EWHC 193 (Admin), [2004] QB 936, per Stanley Burnton J at [33]–[41], and the European cases there cited.

36 *Cullen v Chief Constable of the Royal Ulster Constabulary* [2003] UKHL 39, [2003] 1 WLR 39. See also *R (KB) v Mental Health Review Tribunal* [2003] EWHC 193 (Admin) at [41].

37 *Cullen v Chief Constable of the Royal Ulster Constabulary* [2003] UKHL 39, per Lord Millett at [78]–[83].

38 But see *R (Ben-Abdelaziz) v Haringey LBC* [2001] EWCA Civ 803, [2001] 1 WLR 1485.

proceedings if they would have been awarded in a private law action brought by the claimant at the time of commencing the judicial review claim.[39]

Principles of awarding damages

5.31   In *R (KB) v Mental Health Review Tribunal (Damages)*,[40] Stanley Burnton J described the object of an award of damages as 'to provide compensation for injury: no more, no less'.[41] It was not the function of such awards to mark the court's disapproval of the conduct complained of nor to compel future compliance with Convention rights. Even though there may be a discernible tendency on the part of the ECtHR to make larger awards in cases in which it disapproved of the conduct in question or where there had been repeated breaches, this was not expressly reflected in any principle applied by the court.[42] HRA 1998 s9(3) expressly prohibits an award of non-compensatory damages in relation to a judicial act done in good faith. Accordingly, exemplary damages would not be available[43] (although aggravated damages may be). Nor were damages for loss of a chance, as such an award would be contrary to the principles applied by the European Court.[44]

5.32   In claims for distress and inconvenience, damages would not be available for every feeling of frustration or distress, particularly given that domestic law did not usually recognise such losses as free-standing heads of damage, and the court should be reluctant to create anomalies between damages recoverable for breach of Convention rights and those for other civil wrongs. Thus, while full account must be taken of the claimant's state of health, including his or her mental health, damages under this head would only be available if the frustration and distress was significant and of such intensity that it would justify an award of compensation for non-pecuniary damage.[45]

---

39 See paras 5.18–5.22 above and see *R (Ben-Abdelaziz) v Haringey LBC* [2001] EWCA Civ 803, [2001] 1 WLR 1485.
40 [2003] EWHC 193 (Admin), [2004] QB 936.
41 [2003] EWHC 193 (Admin) at [50].
42 [2003] EWHC 193 (Admin) at [50].
43 As *KB* was a claim for damages against a tribunal: [2003] EWHC 193 (Admin) at [60].
44 [2003] EWHC 193 (Admin) at [64].
45 [2003] EWHC 193 (Admin) at [71]–[73].

5.33   In *Anufrijeva v Southwark LBC*,[46] Lord Woolf CJ stressed the importance of keeping human rights damages awards within modest bounds. The case concerned allegations by asylum-seekers that, due to maladministration, they had not received the benefits to which they were entitled. Lord Woolf observed that public resources were limited and the paying of substantial awards of damages would deplete the resources available to the public for primary care.

5.34   The following procedures should therefore be applied where a claim was made for damages under the HRA 1998:

- the court should look critically at any HRA damages claim in respect of alleged maladministration unless it was brought by way of judicial review;
- even if judicial review was not possible, such as where damages only were claimed, claims should still be brought in the Administrative Court as ordinary claims;
- before permission was granted, the claimant should be required to explain why it was not more appropriate to use an internal complaints procedure or make a complaint to the relevant ombudsman;
- if there was a legitimate claim for other relief, the permission decision in respect of the damages claim should possibly be adjourned, or that claim stayed until the claimant had made appropriate use of alternative dispute resolution (ADR);
- where the court must hear such a claim, decisions should be made in a summary manner, the hearing should be limited to half a day save in exceptional circumstances, and the citing of more than three authorities would need to be justified.[47]

Measure of damages

5.35   In *R (Bernard) v Enfield LBC*,[48] decided shortly after the coming into force of the HRA 1998, a local authority's unexplained failure to make arrangements, under National Assistance Act 1948 s21, for the provision of suitably adapted accommodation for a disabled claimant or to act in accordance with its social services department's recommendations in this regard, was held to breach the claimant's article 8

---

46 [2003] EWCA Civ 1406, [2004] QB 1124.
47 *Anufrijeva* at [81].
48 [2002] EWHC 2282 (Admin), [2003] HLR 27.

Convention rights. She had been obliged to remain in unsatisfactory (because unadapted) living conditions and the authority's

> failure to enable the claimant to live as normal a family life as possible showed a singular lack of respect for her private and family life and condemned her to living in conditions which made it virtually impossible to have any meaningful private or family life.[49]

Damages were awarded because a refusal to do so would not have afforded the claimant just satisfaction and would have been 'unjust'.[50]

5.36   As to the measure of damages, the judge saw no reason why the award should not be comparable with an award for tortious conduct, even though there was no comparable tort. He therefore chose to assess damages by reference to Local Government Ombudsmen awards on the basis that the breaches of duty amounted to an extreme example of maladministration. Damages of £10,000 were awarded.[51]

5.37   In *R (KB) v Mental Health Review Tribunal (Damages)*,[52] the claimants successfully contended that repeated adjournments in their applications to the Mental Health Review Tribunal were unjustified and breached the right to a speedy hearing under article 5(4) of the Convention. They claimed damages for distress, deprivation of liberty, damage to mental health and loss of the chance of earlier discharge. On the measure of damages, the court adopted a similar approach to *Bernard*, feeling free to depart from ECtHR decisions (which laid down only very general principles) in order to award adequate, but not excessive, damages in UK terms.[53] There was no basis for awarding less under the HRA 1998 'just satisfaction' jurisdiction than would have been awarded for a comparable tort.[54]

5.38   The correctness of this kind of approach must now be doubted, since the House of Lords held in *R (Greenfield) v Secretary of State for the Home Department*,[55] albeit an article 6 case, that awards of damages under section 8 of the HRA 1998 are not appropriately assessed by reference to tortious awards in domestic courts. This was for three main reasons:[56]

---

49 [2002] EWHC 2282 (Admin), per Sullivan J at [34].
50 [2002] EWHC 2282 (Admin) at [42].
51 [2002] EWHC 2282 (Admin) at [60].
52 [2003] EWHC 193 (Admin), [2004] QB 936.
53 [2003] EWHC 193 (Admin) at [47].
54 [2003] EWHC 193 (Admin) at [74].
55 [2005] UKHL 14, [2005] 1 WLR 673.
56 [2005] UKHL 14, [2005] 1 WLR 673, per Lord Bingham at [19].

... First, the 1998 Act is not a tort statute. Its objects are different and broader. Even in a case where a finding of violation is not judged to afford the applicant just satisfaction, such a finding will be an important part of his remedy and an important vindication of the right he has asserted. ... Secondly, the purpose of incorporating the Convention in domestic law through the 1998 Act was not to give victims better remedies at home than they could recover in Strasbourg but to give them the same remedies without the delay and expense of resort to Strasbourg. ... Thirdly, section 8(4) requires a domestic court to take into account the principles applied by the European court under article 41 not only in determining whether to award damages but also in determining the amount of an award. There could be no clearer indication that courts in this country should look to Strasbourg and not to domestic precedents. ... The court routinely describes its awards as equitable, which I take to mean that they are not precisely calculated but are judged by the court to be fair in the individual case. Judges in England and Wales must also make a similar judgment in the case before them. They are not inflexibly bound by Strasbourg awards in what may be different cases. But they should not aim to be significantly more or less generous than the court might be expected to be, in a case where it was willing to make an award at all.

5.39   That a finding of violation may constitute, at least, some part of the just satisfaction was relied upon by the Court of Appeal in *R (Faulkner) v Secretary of State for Justice*, [57] when setting the appropriate level of damages for a breach of article 5.[58] Indeed, in *R (Degainis) v Secretary of State for Justice*,[59] the fact that the Secretary of State had admitted a breach of article 5 and apologised for it constituted just satisfaction where the breach had not extended the time that the claimant had spent in custody.

5.40   Similarly damages were not available for a breach of article 5 where a prisoner had only been seeking transfer to open conditions rather than release.[60] Although, as a matter of principle, damages would not

---

57 [2011] EWCA Civ 349, [2011] HRLR 23. The point does not appear to have been argued before the Supreme Court: [2013] UKSC 23.

58 The Court awarded £10,000 for 10 months' loss of a prisoner's conditional liberty by reason of the Secretary of State's delays in providing material to the Parole Board who would probably have approved the prisoner's release had the material been provided timeously. The court disavowed any suggestion that it had applied a multiplier to a monthly sum. After a detailed review of the ECtHR authorities, the Supreme Court reduced the award to £6,500: [2013] UKSC 23.

59 [2010] EWHC 137 (Admin), [2010] ACD 46.

60 *R (Biggin) v Secretary of State for Justice* [2009] EWHC 1704 (Admin), [2010] 1 Prison LR 269.

always be inappropriate in such circumstances, the seriousness of the claimant's offence meant that damages were not necessary.[61]

5.41 In *Rabone v Pennine Care NHS Foundation Trust*,[62] damages awards of £5,000 were made to both parents of a voluntary psychiatric patient who committed suicide after a home visit had been authorised by hospital staff, despite it being known that she was suicidal. The Supreme Court held that this was a bad breach of article 2, which merited an award well above the lower end of the range.

Damages in EU cases

5.42 Damages may be awarded against public bodies for breaches of EU law.[63] In certain cases damages may also be awarded against the Attorney-General for errors made by domestic courts in applying EU laws.[64]

Remission back to decision-maker

5.43 Where the court quashes a decision, it may also remit the matter back to the decision-maker, with a direction to reconsider it in accordance with the findings and judgment of the court.[65] This power is not commonly exercised, and would not seem appropriate in cases where there are disputes on the facts and evidence or where the complaint concerns a procedural flaw in the decision. In such cases, the decision-maker would generally be expected to reconsider the decision from the beginning. It may be appropriate, however, where the decision-maker has been guilty of an error of law, or where there is a formal reason for remission, for example where the decision-maker was a court or tribunal that, having made the decision, no longer has jurisdiction over the matter.

---

61 See also *R (Downing) v Parole Board* [2008] EWHC 3198 (Admin), [2009] Prison LR 327.

62 [2012] UKSC 2, [2012] 2 AC 72.

63 See *Francovich v Italy* Case C-6/90; *Bonifaci v Italy* Case C-9/90 [1991] ECR I–5357; *Brasserie du Pecheur SA v Germany* Case C-46/93 [1996] QB 404; and para 1.33 above. See also *Spencer v Secretary of State for Work and Pensions* [2008] EWCA Civ 750, [2009] QB 358; *Poole v HM Treasury* [2007] EWCA Civ 1021, [2008] 1 All ER (Comm) 1132; and *R (Negassi) v Secretary of State for the Home Department* [2011] EWHC 386 (Admin), [2011] 2 CMLR 36.

64 *Cooper v Attorney General* [2010] EWCA Civ 464, [2011] QB 976.

65 Senior Courts Act 1981 s31(5)(a) ('findings'); CPR r54.19(2)(a) ('judgment').

Retention of the decision

5.44 On quashing a decision, the court may substitute its own decision for the decision in question, so far as any enactment permits.[66] Until 5 April 2008, CPR r54.19(3) limited the power to circumstances in which the court considered there to be 'no purpose to be served' in remitting the matter back to the decision-maker,[67] although no such restriction appears in section 31(5)(b) of the SCA 1981.

5.45 It seems unlikely that the new, less restricted, formulation of this power is intended to – or can – make any major change to the general constitutional position that, on quashing a decision, the court will normally leave it to the decision-maker to take it afresh. It is, after all, one of the hallmarks of a public law function that the statutory designate of that function is entitled to exercise it, and is usually in a far better position to exercise it than the court would be.[68] If, on the other hand, the only lawful conclusion that the authority could reach is the one contended for by the claimant, whether because on the court's findings, there is only one lawful course available, or because while in principle there are a number of possible decisions open to the authority the facts are so likely to admit of only one outcome that the authority should not be afforded another opportunity to reconsider the matter, the court may decide to take the decision itself.[69]

Proceedings to continue as if begun by private action

5.46 The court now has broad powers to order that a judicial review claim should continue as if it had not been brought using the CPR Pt 54 procedure. If it does so, it may give directions about the future

---

66 Senior Courts Act 1981 s31(5)(b); CPR r54.19(2)(b).

67 CPR r54.19(3). It continued '[w]here a statutory power is given to a tribunal, person or other body it may be the case that the court cannot take the decision itself'.

68 See, eg, *R (Ahmad) v Newham LBC* [2009] UKHL 14, [2009] PTSR 632, per Baroness Hale at [15]–[16], [22], per Lord Neuberger at [46]–[48], [62]; See also *Ali (Mohram) v Tower Hamlets LBC* [1993] QB 407, CA, especially per Nolan LJ at 413G–414B.

69 See, eg, *Slater v Lewisham LBC* [2006] EWCA Civ 394, [2006] HLR 37; *Ekwuru v Westminster CC* [2003] EWCA Civ 1293, [2004] HLR 14 at [22]–[30].

management of the claim.[70] This replaces the considerably more circumscribed powers available under the old rules.[71]

5.47　　One of the situations in which the court is likely to exercise its powers is where damages are claimed. The court may, having granted the application, order that the action continue as if begun by private law action, and then adjourn the assessment of damages to the master or even transfer it to the county court.[72] There were conflicting judicial statements under the old rules as to whether, if the judicial review application was misconceived but the claim for damages arguable, the court would exercise its power or refuse the claim,[73] but in the light of comments by the then Lord Chief Justice regarding the flexibility of the CPR to permit claims to be heard in the most effective manner and to avoid the old technical procedural disputes, it seems likely that if the claim is, in all the circumstances, appropriate to be heard, the court will make the necessary orders to permit this to happen.[74]

5.48　　It was held to be inappropriate under the old rules, and presumably would remain so, for a defendant who had filed no evidence to apply for an order that a claim should proceed as if begun by private law action in order to seek to gain a further opportunity to defend the claim.[75]

5.49　　In *R v Blandford Justices ex p Pamment*,[76] the Court of Appeal considered a case where damages were claimed in an application for judicial review of a criminal matter. The court indicated that in criminal causes, given that there was no right of appeal from the Divisional Court to the Court of Appeal, the best course where the actual judicial review application had become academic, in that its sole or main purpose was to facilitate a damages claim (as in *Pamment* itself), would be for the Divisional Court to decline, as a matter of discretion, to deal with the application for judicial review, and to allow the damages claim to proceed as if commenced by private law

---

70　CPR r54.20.

71　RSC Ord 53 r9(4)–(5).

72　See, for example, *R v Sandwell MBC ex p Thomas* (1992) 22 December, unreported, where the latter course was taken.

73　See *Calveley v Chief Constable of Merseyside Police* [1989] QB 136, CA; compare *R v Secretary of State for the Home Department ex p Dew* [1987] 1 WLR 881, QBD.

74　See *R (Heather) v Leonard Cheshire Foundation* [2002] EWCA Civ 366, [2002] 2 All ER 936; *Clark v University of Lincolnshire and Humberside* [2000] 1 WLR 1988, CA.

75　*R v Reading Justices, Chief Constable of Avon and Somerset ex p South West Meat Ltd* [1992] COD 224, DC.

76　[1990] 1 WLR 1490, CA.

claim. In that way the claim for damages could be heard without any pre-judgment as to the legitimacy of the order challenged and there would be a clear route to the Court of Appeal (Civil Division).[77]

Power to vary sentence

5.50   In criminal cases, where judicial review is claimed to challenge a sentence which the sentencing court had no power to pass, the court may vary the sentence itself. It does this by substituting a sentence that the court under challenge would have had power to pass, rather than granting a quashing order to quash the sentence.[78] This applies only to sentences passed by the magistrates' court or by the Crown Court on committal for sentence or on appeal from the magistrates.[79] There is no power to review sentences passed on indictment.[80] This is a matter for the Court of Appeal (Criminal Division).

Dismissal of application

5.51   The application may, of course, also be dismissed. It is for the claimant to prove his or her case to the ordinary civil standard of proof,[81] save in rare situations such as illegal entrant cases. Where the Home Secretary asserts that a person is an illegal entrant, it is for him to prove the facts relied on by the immigration officer as justifying that conclusion.[82]

Suspending operation of judgment

5.52   In *HM Treasury v Ahmed*,[83] the Supreme Court was invited to suspend the operation of its judgment, declaring provisions in secondary

---

77 [1990] 1 WLR 1490 at 1496D. Compare *R v Northavon DC ex p Palmer* (1993) 25 HLR 674, QBD. Whether or not damages may be available in a criminal context is another matter: see, eg, *Olotu v Home Office* [1997] 1 WLR 328, CA.

78 SCA 1981 s43(1).

79 SCA 1981 s43(1).

80 SCA 1981 s29(3).

81 There is only one civil standard of proof: the balance of probabilities, which does not vary with the severity of the issues under consideration: *Re B (Children) (Care Proceedings: Standard of Proof)* [2008] UKHL 35, [2009] 1 AC 11 at [13].

82 *Khawaja v Secretary of State for the Home Department* [1984] AC 74, HL.

83 [2010] UKSC 5, [2010] 2 AC 534

legislation ultra vires and quashing them, because of the effect that the operation of the judgment would otherwise have on third parties. The court, by a majority of six to one, declined to accept that invitation. Suspending the operation of the judgment would not affect the decision that the statutory instruments were unlawful. Nor should the court lend itself to a procedure that was designed to obfuscate the effect of its judgment.[84]

Interim relief

5.53 An application may be made for an interim order at any stage in proceedings, although it is usual to do so at the permission stage. On, or even before, the grant of permission,[85] the court has power to grant interim remedies in accordance with CPR Pt 23. In practice, the most important types of application are likely to be for an interim injunction, for disclosure, or for cross-examination.[86]

Injunction

5.54 Temporary injunctions may be granted at any stage, even after judgment. Traditionally, an interim injunction was not available against the Crown.[87] If, however, it has acted contrary to EU law, the Crown is susceptible to this remedy. This is because if injunctive relief is necessary to ensure the full effectiveness of EU law, a national rule preventing such a remedy (such as Crown Proceedings Act 1947 s21(2)) must not be applied.[88] In *Re M*,[89] the House of Lords held that as, historically, prerogative orders had been made against the Crown and its officers, Crown Proceedings Act 1947 s21 did not prevent injunctions issuing against ministers and other officers of the Crown in similar circumstances.

---

84 [2010] UKSC 5, per Lord Phillips at [8]. Lord Hope in the minority would have suspended operation of the judgment for a short period. See also *R (T) v Chief Constable of Greater Manchester* [2013] EWCA Civ 25, [2013] 1 Cr App R 27, [2013] HRLR 14, per Lord Dyson MR at [83].

85 *Re M* [1994] 1 AC 377, HL.

86 For the procedure to apply for interim relief, see paras 18.93–18.94 below.

87 Crown Proceedings Act 1947 s21(2).

88 See para 1.32 above.

89 [1994] 1 AC 377, HL.

5.55   The courts also have jurisdiction to grant interim injunctions against ministers and other officers of the Crown,[90] although this power should only be exercised in limited circumstances.

5.56   As with other interim injunctions, the principles set out in *American Cyanamid Company v Ethicon Ltd*[91] will apply, although the courts have modified the considerations to some extent. In *R v Secretary of State for Transport ex p Factortame (No 2)*,[92] Lord Goff of Chievely stated that where a judicial review claim involves a public authority seeking to enforce the law, damages would not usually be an adequate remedy for either party. Accordingly, in considering the balance of convenience, the court must also take account of the interests of the public in general to whom the authority owes duties. In such a case, the claimant is not required to show a strong *prima facie* case that the law which the authority seeks to enforce is invalid. The matter is one for the discretion of the court. The court should not restrain the authority from enforcing the law, however, unless satisfied that the challenge to its validity is sufficiently firmly based to justify that exceptional course being taken.[93] In general, it seems that it will be more difficult to establish that the balance of convenience favours the granting of an injunction.[94]

5.57   Where a mandatory injunction is sought, it was generally considered necessary to demonstrate an additional matter, namely a strong *prima facie* case.[95] Whether that approach survives the decision of the Privy Council in *National Commercial Bank Jamaica Ltd v Olint Corpn Ltd*[96] is unclear. In *Olint* Lord Hoffmann described as 'barren' arguments over whether an injunction should be classified as prohibitive or mandatory; what mattered was what the practical consequences of an injunction would be.[97]

5.58   The court had, in any case, not always applied the strong *prima facie* case. In *R v Cardiff City Council ex p Barry*,[98] a lower test and, arguably, a more practical line was suggested by the court, which it continued to follow at least in homelessness cases until most

90   SCA 1981 s31(2).
91   [1975] AC 396, HL.
92   [1991] 1 AC 603, ECJ and HL.
93   [1991] 1 AC 603 at 674.
94   See *Smith v Inner London Education Authority* [1978] 1 All ER 411, CA.
95   See *R v Kensington and Chelsea RLBC ex p Hammell* [1989] QB 518, CA.
96   [2009] UKPC 16, [2009] 1 WLR 1405.
97   [2009] UKPC 16 at [20].
98   (1989) 22 HLR 261, CA.

such cases were removed from the judicial review jurisdiction.[99] In *Barry*, the court held that where permission is granted, an injunction requiring the authority to provide temporary accommodation (or at least allow the applicant to remain in the currently provided temporary accommodation) would generally follow, unless, for example, the defendant was prepared to agree to that course without such an order being made. In *R (Casey) v Restormel BC*,[100] it was held to be appropriate to continue a mandatory injunction, which had been granted on a without notice basis, when permission was granted.

5.59   In *Leeds Unique Education Ltd (t/a Leeds Professional College) v Secretary of State for the Home Department*,[101] interim relief was granted when the claimants were granted permission to challenge the decisions of the Secretary of State to revoke sponsorship licences, which enabled the claimants to issue visa letters for students to gain entry clearance to the United Kingdom.[102] One of the factors taken into account by Nicol J was that the pressures on Administrative Court listing were such that the substantive applications for judicial review were unlikely to be heard in the immediate future.

5.60   Interim relief was also granted in *R (Medical Justice) v Secretary of State for the Home Department*.[103] Cranston J held that there was a strong public interest in permitting a public authority to continue to apply its policy when it was supposedly acting in the public interest, but that the weight to be attached to that wider public interest turned in part on the juridical basis of the policy. The weight to be given to interests varied if the basis was not contained in primary legislation. Where the policy under challenge was not contained in a statutory instrument, had not been laid before Parliament and did not seem to have been subject to satisfactory consultation before it had been promulgated, the appropriate balance of convenience lay in favour of granting interim relief.

99 By the Housing Act 1996 s204 which created a right of appeal on a point of law to the county court in respect of most decisions taken in homelessness cases (such decisions being listed at Housing Act 1996 s202).
100 [2007] EWHC 2554 (Admin), [2008] ACD 1.
101 [2010] EWHC 1030 (Admin).
102 As to which see paras 8.10–8.11 below.
103 [2010] EWHC 1425 (Admin), [2010] ACD 70.

Undertaking in damages

5.61   Cross-undertakings in damages may be required, although this requirement is applied less strictly than in private law cases.[104] If acting for a defendant, it must be remembered to request such an undertaking, if appropriate, and for what it may be worth, as such matters are frequently overlooked. Courts will not normally require such an undertaking from publicly funded claimants, although as explained by Lord Walker in *Belize Alliance of Conservation Non-Governmental Organisations v Department of the Environment of Belize (Practice Note)*,[105] that is not automatically the case:

> ... when the court is asked to grant an interim injunction in a public law case, it should approach the matter on the lines indicated by the House of Lords in *American Cyanamid Co v Ethicon Ltd* [1975] AC 396 , but with modifications appropriate to the public law element of the case. The public law element is one of the possible 'special factors' referred to by Lord Diplock in that case ... Another special factor might be if the grant or refusal of interim relief were likely to be, in practical terms, decisive of the whole case ...

> In some public law cases, ... the issue is a straightforward dispute between a public or quasi-public body ... and citizens to whom the services are being provided. In such a case an injunction may be granted to the citizen, without any undertaking in damages, if justice requires that course. ...

> ... (because the range of public law cases is so wide) the court has a wide discretion to take the course which seems most likely to produce a just result (or to put the matter less ambitiously, to minimise the risk of an unjust result). ... The court is never exempted from the duty to do its best, on interlocutory applications with far-reaching financial implications, to minimise the risk of injustice. ... But there may be cases where the risk of serious and uncompensated detriment to the defendant cannot be ignored. The rich plaintiff may find, if ultimately unsuccessful, that he has to pay out a very large sum as the price of having obtained an injunction which (with hindsight) ought not to have been granted to him. ...

5.62   If interim relief is sought, after the substantive application has been dismissed, pending appeal, it will be necessary to show that the appeal has good prospects of success.

---

104 *Belize Alliance of Conservation Non-Governmental Organisations v Department of the Environment of Belize (Practice Note)* [2003] UKPC 63, [2003] 1 WLR 2839.

105 [2003] UKPC 63 at [35], [37], [39].

Declaration

5.63   In *Re M*,[106] Lord Woolf said that, that in order to avoid having to grant interim injunctions against officers of the Crown, there could be advantages in the courts being able to grant interim declarations.[107]

5.64   Under CPR r25.1(1), the courts do now have the power to grant an interim declaration. The power appears to have been used sparingly. Tomlinson J remarked in *Amalgamated Metal Trading Ltd v City of London Police Financial Investigation Unit* [108] that the circumstances in which it might be appropriate to resort to the new jurisdiction remained to be worked out.

Stay

5.65   Where permission is granted, the court has power to grant a stay of proceedings to which the claim relates.[109] The court has power to order a stay, not only of judicial proceedings, but also of decisions of ministers and of the process by which such decisions were reached.[110] It is a precondition of the exercise of this power, however, that permission is granted.[111]

5.66   The case of *R v HM Inspectorate of Pollution, Ministry of Agriculture, Fisheries and Food ex p Greenpeace Ltd*[112] is illustrative of the principles to be applied when considering a stay, particularly where the applicant is an interest group. On granting permission to apply for judicial review, Brooke J considered an application for an interim stay to prevent the commissioning of the THORP plant at Sellafield, pending the full hearing of the claimant's challenge. The defendant and British Nuclear Fuels Ltd (BNFL) submitted that very considerable losses would be suffered if a stay was granted, amounting to £2 million per week. The claimant had current assets of just under

---

106 [1994] 1 AC 377, HL.

107 [1994] 1 AC 377 at 423A.

108 [2003] EWHC 703 (Comm), [2003] 1 WLR 2711 at [10]. An application for an interim declaration was refused in that case. See also *R (Mayer Parry Recycling Ltd) v Environment Agency (Interim Relief)* [2001] CP Rep 63, [2001] Env LR 35, QBD.

109 CPR r54.10(2).

110 *R v Secretary of State for Education and Science ex p Avon CC (No 2)* [1991] 1 QB 558, CA.

111 CPR r54.10, and see *R (H) v Ashworth Hospital Authority* [2002] EWCA Civ 923, [2003] 1 WLR 127, per Dyson LJ at [47].

112 [1994] COD 56, QBD; see paras 4.24–4.26 above, for the report of the substantive hearing.

£1 million and liabilities of £1.2 million. A further difficulty was that BNFL, against whom the stay was sought, was not a party to the application.

5.67   The judge undertook the conventional *American Cyanamid* balancing exercise,[113] stating that it was a difficult balancing exercise to perform. He took into account the fact that the claimant would still have to establish at the full hearing that it had standing to bring the application (although the courts were more and more willing these days to entertain applications by such bodies). The judge was also considerably influenced by the likely financial loss to BNFL and the claimant's likely inability to pay for it. The Inspectorate's view, moreover, was that the effect of the planned testing of the plant would be minimal, although that was plainly not the claimant's view. Should the claimant succeed at the full hearing, BNFL would have to bear the cost of decommissioning the plant. Accordingly, a stay was refused. An appeal against that decision was dismissed.[114]

5.68   In *Scotia Pharmaceuticals International Ltd v Secretary of State for Health and Norgine Ltd (No 2)*[115] the court considered the principles upon which a stay should be granted in the context of what was essentially a commercial dispute. Application was made by Norgine to discharge a stay that had been imposed on the grant to it of a product licence. The stay had been granted at the application of Scotia, pending a reference of the litigation between them to the ECJ. The court held that the principles applicable to challenges to primary or secondary legislation were inappropriate to a trade dispute and that it should ask only whether there was a serious question to be tried. Having decided that there was, the well-known *American Cyanamid* principles[116] were applicable, and the application to remove the stay dismissed.

5.69   In *R (H) v Ashworth Hospital Authority*,[117] the Court of Appeal held that the court had power to order a stay of a Mental Health Review Tribunal decision to discharge a compulsorily detained patient, even

---

113 *American Cyanamid Company v Ethicon Ltd* [1975] AC 396, HL.

114 [1994] 1 WLR 570, CA.

115 [1994] COD 241, DC.

116 *American Cyanamid Company v Ethicon Ltd* [1975] AC 396, HL. An injunction will be granted to preserve the status quo where there is doubt whether damages would provide an adequate remedy.

117 Joined with *R (Ashworth Hospital Authority) v Mental Health Review Tribunal for West Midlands and North West Region* [2002] EWCA Civ 923, [2003] 1 WLR 127.

where that decision had already been fully implemented.[118] That power should only be used, however, if there was a strong and not merely an arguable case that the tribunal's decision had been unlawful, together with cogent evidence that the patient posed a risk to her or himself or to others and/or was dangerous. Where a stay is ordered, it is essential that the validity of the tribunal's decision should be determined by the court with the greatest possible speed.[119]

5.70   The court may order a stay on directions given for a misconduct hearing, but where that would have the practical consequence of effectively deciding the substantive judicial review claim (because it would not be possible to convene a substantive hearing before the misconduct hearing was due to take place) the court should subject the claim to stronger scrutiny than would otherwise be the case.[120]

5.71   On judicial review of a magistrates' court's refusal to stay a criminal prosecution as an abuse of process, the court's powers will be strictly limited. This is, however, a different aspect of the stay jurisdiction, not related to interim relief.[121]

Disclosure

5.72   The ability of claimants to obtain disclosure of documents containing personal information about themselves is now wider and more comprehensive than was previously the case, given the rights conferred by the Freedom of Information Act 2001 and Data Protection Act 1998 s7.[122]

5.73   Other than as stated above, however, disclosure is not obtainable as of right in judicial review proceedings, but only at the discretion of the court. Generally, the courts have restricted the circumstances in which disclosure will be ordered. In *O'Reilly v Mackman*,[123] Lord Diplock stated that neither disclosure nor cross-examination would usually be ordered except to the extent that justice in the individual case required it. In *R v Inland Revenue Commissioners ex p National*

118 In *H*, the patient had been discharged but had remained in hospital as a voluntary patient having nowhere else to go.

119 [2002] EWCA Civ 923, per Dyson LJ at [47].

120 *R (Bonnard) v Sharpling* [2012] EWHC 3384 (Admin). Despite the 'stronger scrutiny', a stay was granted.

121 See, eg, *R v Barry Magistrates' Court ex p Malpas* [1998] COD 90, DC applying *R v Willesden Justices ex p Clemmings* (1988) 87 Cr App R 280.

122 See paras 14.4–14.41 below.

123 [1983] 2 AC 237 at 282–3.

Federation of Self-Employed and Small Businesses,[124] Lord Scarman stated that for disclosure to be ordered, first, there must be evidence revealing reasonable grounds for believing that there has been a breach of a public law duty and, second, disclosure should be strictly limited to documents relevant to the issue arising from the affidavits.

5.74   The court will not allow an application for disclosure to be used to fill gaps in the claimant's evidence, or that amounts to a 'fishing expedition'.[125] The Court of Appeal has held that it would be improper to allow disclosure of documents to permit the claimant who seeks to go behind the defendant's evidence to ascertain whether it is correct, unless there is some material outside the evidence that suggests that in some material respect it is inaccurate, misleading or in a material respect incomplete.[126] Nor will the court permit an application for disclosure to see, in effect, whether disclosure has been properly given. That is not the function of disclosure and is impermissible.[127]

5.75   It has also been held, on the other hand, that the grant of permission may, in an appropriate case, raise a sufficient inference of irrationality for there to be room for an order for production of a relevant document.[128] In *R v Governor of Pentonville Prison ex p Herbage (No 2)*,[129] it was held that disclosure will be ordered where necessary to advance the justice of the case and/or for the fair disposal of the matter. If an application for judicial review is bound to fail, disclosure should not be ordered.

5.76   It has been suggested that the position concerning disclosure may not be so strict in human rights cases, or under the CPR, Pt 31 of which applies to judicial review, as to all other kinds of civil proceedings.[130]

---

124 [1982] AC 617 at 654. See also, generally, para 4.3.

125 See *R v Inland Revenue Commissioners ex p Taylor (No 1)* [1989] 1 All ER 906, CA.

126 *R v Secretary of State for the Environment ex p Islington LBC and London Lesbian and Gay Centre* [1992] COD 67, CA. See also *R v Secretary of State for Education ex p J* [1993] COD 146, QBD, and *R v Arts Council of England ex p Women's Playhouse Trust* [1998] COD 175.

127 *R v Secretary of State for Transport ex p Factortame Ltd* (1997) 9 Admin LR 591, [1997] COD 432, DC, referring to *Berkeley Administration Inc v McClelland* [1990] FSR 381.

128 *R v Secretary of State for Transport ex p APH Road Safety Ltd (No 1)* [1993] COD 150, QBD.

129 [1987] QB 1077, CA.

130 See *R v Ministry of Defence ex p Smith* [1996] QB 517, CA, per Henry LJ at 543. See also *R (S) v Plymouth City Council* [2002] EWCA Civ 388, [2002] 1 WLR 2583.

5.77 The Supreme Court considered disclosure in a human rights context in *Tweed v Parades Commission for Northern Ireland*.[131] The Court concluded that where the central issue in an application for judicial review was the proportionality of the defendant's actions, disclosure would be ordered more readily. Disclosure should still, however, be limited to the issues for which it was required in the interests of justice.

5.78 It was also suggested in *Tweed*, albeit probably *obiter*, that it was desirable to apply a more flexible and less prescriptive principle than had previously been the case, by which the need for disclosure would be judged in accordance with the requirements of the particular case, taking into account all the facts and circumstances.[132]

Oral evidence and cross-examination

5.79 The courts have been similarly restrictive in defining the circumstances in which they will permit the cross-examination of witnesses and oral evidence generally. Lord Diplock in *O'Reilly v Mackman*[133] stated that although the grant of leave to cross-examine is governed by the same principles as apply in any action begun by originating summons,[134] and should be permitted whenever the justice of the case requires, it would be rare that the issues arising on judicial review would call for cross-examination. The reason for this is that the decision-maker's factual findings are not generally open to review by the court.[135] To allow cross-examination, Lord Diplock said, '... presents the court with a temptation, not always easily resisted, to substitute its own view of the facts for that of the decision-making body upon whom the exclusive jurisdiction to determine facts has been conferred by Parliament ...'.

5.80 Allegations of breach of natural justice or of procedural unfairness are, he said, in general, exceptions to this.

5.81 In *R v Reigate Justices ex p Curl*,[136] the court held that it would not generally hear oral evidence of what had occurred in an inferior court, even where a breach of natural justice was alleged, as this

---

131 [2006] UKHL 53, [2007] 1 AC 650.
132 [2006] UKHL 53, per Lord Carswell at [32].
133 [1983] 2 AC 237, HL at 282G.
134 The nearest CPR equivalent of which is the Part 8 claim.
135 This may not apply in *Edwards v Bairstow* [1956] AC 14 type situations (see chapter 6).
136 [1991] COD 66, DC.

would involve the magistrates in attending the High Court to justify the decisions they took during the hearing before them.

Oral evidence and cross-examination in fundamental rights cases

5.82 The courts are, however, more willing to permit cross-examination in cases involving fundamental rights, and even to decide the facts where it is necessary to do so.

5.83 In *R (Wilkinson) v Broadmoor Special Hospital Authority*,[137] the claimant, detained in hospital under Mental Health Act 1983 s3, sought to challenge by way of judicial review the decision of the defendant to administer anti-psychotic drugs to him without his consent. On the grant of permission, he applied for an order that the doctors who had approved the treatment should attend the substantive hearing to be cross-examined as to their belief that the claimant was not mentally capable of refusing consent to the treatment.

5.84 On appeal from the judge's refusal of such an order, the Court of Appeal held that, since the HRA 1998 was in force, the court could, where a claimant's fundamental human rights were at stake, decide for itself an issue of fact, namely, in that case, whether the claimant was capable of giving (and so also withholding) consent to the medical treatment which the defendant wished to carry out. The court could carry out a full merits review if appropriate, and for that purpose order the attendance of doctors to be cross-examined at the full hearing.

5.85 While a majority of a differently constituted Court of Appeal rejected the suggestion that *Wilkinson* was authority for the proposition that the court could, on judicial review, undertake a review of the facts where Parliament had decided that a particular body – not the court – should be the decision-maker of fact,[138] a third court, in

---

137 [2001] EWCA Civ 1545, [2002] 1 WLR 419. See also *S v Airedale NHS Trust* [2002] EWHC 1780 (Admin), [2003] Lloyd's Rep Med 21 (an appeal against the outcome of the decision was allowed by the Court of Appeal, where it was heard with *R (Munjaz) v Mersey Care NHS Trust* [2003] EWCA Civ 1036, [2004] QB 395. *Munjaz* was, in turn, overturned by the House of Lords: [2005] UKHL 58, [2006] 2 AC 148. It seems that the factual challenges were not in issue on the appeals).

138 *Adan v Tower Hamlets LBC* [2001] EWCA Civ 1919, [2002] 1 WLR 2120.

R (Mullen) v Secretary of State for the Home Department,[139] observed that *Wilkinson* 'amply demonstrates' that the court on judicial review can and will, if necessary, assess relevant facts for itself, even to the extent of ordering cross-examination of witnesses.

5.86   In *R (PG) v Ealing LBC*,[140] Munby J held that *Wilkinson* plainly indicates that there will be judicial review cases in which cross-examination is not only appropriate, but essential, and that there will be cases in which the intensity of the review demanded by a challenge based on an alleged breach of Convention rights, will require cross-examination to be ordered so that the court complies with its own obligations under the Convention.

5.87   *Wilkinson* was relied upon by the Supreme Court to overrule practical objections to the court being asked, on an application for judicial review, to determine as a fact the age of an asylum-seeker.[141] Cross-examination has consequently been allowed in such cases.[142]

5.88   Notwithstanding *Wilkinson* and the approval of that case in the asylum-seeker age cases, eg *R (A) v Croydon LBC*,[143] recourse to cross-examination is still very much the exception. The overwhelming bulk of judicial review cases would continue to be determined without oral evidence.[144]

Expedition or abridgement of time for evidence

5.89   A potentially important interim remedy for claimants is an order for an expedited hearing and/or the abridgement of time for the service of the defendant's detailed grounds of defence and evidence. This will be particularly relevant where an application for an interim

---

139 [2002] EWHC 230 (Admin), [2002] 1 WLR 1857. In fact, Simon Brown LJ gave the leading judgment in both *Wilkinson* and *Mullen*. Hale LJ, who gave a concurring judgment in *Wilkinson* dissented in *Adan*. The decision of the Divisional Court in *Mullen* was reversed by the Court of Appeal ([2002] EWCA Civ 1882, [2003] QB 993), and then reinstated by the House of Lords ([2004] UKHL 18, [2005] 1 AC 1), but this point was not in issue on appeal.

140 [2002] EWHC 250 (Admin), [2002] ACD 48.

141 *R (A) v Croydon LBC* [2009] UKSC 8, [2009] 1 WLR 2557, per Baroness Hale at [33]. The issue was whether the claimants were children and so entitled to support and accommodation from the defendant's children's services department or whether they were adults and so only entitled to the less beneficial asylum support provided for adults by the Secretary of State and the National Asylum Support Service.

142 See, eg, *R (Z) v Croydon LBC* [2011] EWCA Civ 59, [2011] PTSR 747; *R (CJ) v Cardiff CC* [2011] EWCA Civ 1590, [2012] PTSR 1235.

143 [2009] UKSC 8, [2009] 1 WLR 2557.

144 [2002] EWHC 250 (Admin) at [30].

injunction cannot be made or has been refused, as current waiting times in the Administrative Court for a full hearing, following the grant of permission, can be many months.[145] As part of its 'case for change' for reform of judicial review, the Government stated that:[146]

> in 2011, it took on average 11 weeks for a decision on permission to be taken on the papers, and a further 21 weeks if the matter went to an oral renewal. Overall, it took around 10 months on average for a Judicial Review to reach a conclusion.

Bail

5.90   The High Court has a fairly wide power, arising from its inherent jurisdiction, to grant bail. This power arises on the adjournment of a permission application as well as on the grant of permission itself, although not where permission is refused. The Court of Appeal has power to grant bail on an appeal against a refusal of permission, and a refusal by the single judge to grant bail may itself be appealed to the Court of Appeal.[147] CPR Sch 1, RSC 79 r9[148] governs the procedure for making bail applications in criminal cases to the High Court.

5.91   In immigration cases, the court's approach appears to be slightly different.[149] Where a person is detained pending a decision about whether to grant him or her leave to enter the UK, the immigration adjudicator has jurisdiction to grant bail, on terms if appropriate, and an application should be made by that route rather than to the High Court. Where a person is detained pending removal from the UK, the Home Secretary can grant temporary admission, but cannot attach terms to it. In such cases, if the Home Secretary refuses to do so and opposes bail, the courts will not grant bail unless it can be shown that, in refusing temporary admission, the Home Secretary has erred in principle, or that decision is unreasonable in the *Wednesbury* sense.[150] Where the Home Secretary has refused temporary

---

145   See, eg, *Practice Statement (Admin Ct: Administration of Justice)* [2002] 1 WLR 810; *letter from Her Majesty's Courts Service 'Overview of current position in the Administrative Court'* (available at www.publiclawproject.org.uk/documents/ AdCrt-PositionJuly08.pdf).

146   Ministry of Justice *Judicial Review: proposals for reform* (CP25/2012), p11.

147   See *R v Secretary of State for the Home Department ex p Turkoglu* [1988] QB 398.

148   Retained in force at CPR Sch 1.

149   *Re Vilvarajah's application for bail* (1987) *Times* 31 October, CA.

150   *Associated Provincial Picture Houses v Wednesbury Corporation* [1948] 1 KB 223, CA.

admission but would not oppose bail on terms, the court would usually grant conditional bail.

Remedies against third parties

5.92   In *R v HM Inspectorate of Pollution ex p Greenpeace Ltd (No 1)*,[151] the Court of Appeal confirmed the decision of Brooke J[152] that where a stay was sought that would affect a third party whom it was not sought to make a party to the action, the correct approach was still to follow the usual principles applied when an interim injunction was sought against another party.

5.93   In *R (Prokopp) v London Underground Ltd*,[153] the claimant sought to prevent the first defendant from undertaking demolition works in connection with a proposed extension of one of its railway lines. He sought judicial review against them, and against the two relevant local authorities, whose decisions not to take enforcement action against the railway company he challenged on the basis that the railway company did not have planning permission for the demolition. (The permission that had been granted had expired because, due to a mistake in its implementation rendering that implementation unlawful, it had not been lawfully implemented within the requisite five-year period.) The claimant obtained an interim injunction against the railway company prohibiting them from commencing work, notwithstanding concerns about his standing as a private individual to seek to enforce breaches of planning control in circumstances where the authorities charged with doing so had decided not to take action.

5.94   The court held that it could be appropriate to grant interim relief to a private individual against a developer, to prevent the taking of irrevocable steps that the claimant contended to be unlawful but that were not being enforced by the local planning authority. In such a case, while the claim would initially be brought against the developer, the local authority must be added as a defendant and the claim would proceed against the authority with the developer taking part as an interested party. A private individual could not, however, obtain a permanent injunction in a public law claim, which would, in effect, amount to the enforcement action that was the responsibility of the

151 [1994] 1 WLR 570, CA.
152 Discussed at paras 5.66–5.67 above.
153 [2003] EWHC 960 (Admin), [2003] 19 EG 119 (CS). Hackney LBC and Tower Hamlets LBC were the second and third defendants.

local authority and that carried with it procedural safeguards for the developer such as a right of appeal.

5.95   The Court of Appeal reversed the judge's decision on other grounds, and did not comment on these issues.[154]

Habeas corpus ad subjiciendum

5.96   Examination of this related remedy is beyond the scope of this book.[155] It is a prerogative remedy, whereby the detention of the individual pursuant to administrative orders may be supervised by the court. If granted, the writ requires the release of the applicant from detention.

5.97   The use of this remedy is significantly less important now than it was in former years, as it now appears to be treated simply as a branch of judicial review.[156] The same legal principles apply to habeas corpus as to judicial review, although it is not a discretionary remedy.[157] The remedy is now used predominantly in immigration and mental health cases.

5.98   Applications are governed by CPR Sch 1, RSC r54, which together with its Practice Direction,[158] sets out the procedure to be adopted. In essence, the rules have retained the old procedure, forms and practice directions applicable to the making of such applications prior to 26 April 1999.[159]

---

154 [2003] EWCA Civ 961, [2004] Env LR 8.

155 A detailed analysis of habeas corpus can be found in *Rahmatullah v Secretary of State for Foreign and Commonwealth Affairs* [2012] UKSC 48, [2012] 3 WLR 1087.

156 Although entitlement to habeas corpus is not coterminous with the right to judicial review: *Rahmatullah v Secretary of State for Foreign and Commonwealth Affairs* [2012] UKSC 48, [2012] 3 WLR 1087.

157 See *R v Secretary of State for the Home Department ex p Khawaja* [1984] AC 74, HL and *Rahmatullah v Secretary of State for Foreign and Commonwealth Affairs* [2012] UKSC 48, [2012] 3 WLR 1087.

158 RSC PD 54.

159 RSC PD 54, in particular at paras 2.2, 3.1, 4.1 and 7.1.

CHAPTER 6

Grounds on which review may be sought

Vires

6.1   The term 'ultra vires' is frequently used in judicial review, usually to describe a decision taken, or a policy adopted, by a public body that was outside the powers of that body. The concept of vires, meaning jurisdiction or power, is the central concept of administrative law.[1] A decision-maker with statutory powers has, of definition, only those powers that Parliament has conferred, and may only act 'within the four corners of' those powers.[2] Any act done or decision made outside, or in excess of, such powers will be ultra vires. Ultra vires acts are often described as void, although this description is not entirely accurate as, unless and until quashed, such an act or decision may well have legal effects.[3]

6.2   To give a basic example, if a body with power to decide to build roads, were to decide to build a railway line, that decision would be ultra vires: there would be no power in the body in question to make it.[4] In this sense, the question of whether or not an act or decision is ultra vires may simply be a matter of construing the power in question, contained in the empowering legislation, and ascertaining whether or not it authorised the act or decision under challenge.

6.3   Likewise, a local authority's practice of holding prayers as part of the formal business of full council meetings was recently held to be unlawful on the basis that there was no statutory power permitting the practice.[5] (Local authorities in England, but not in Wales, have now been given a general power of competence, which provides that a 'local authority has power to do anything that individuals generally may do'.)[6]

---

1   See, eg, *Boddington v British Transport Police* [1999] 2 AC 143, HL, per Lord Steyn at 171F–G (citing with approval a passage in Wade and Forsyth *Administrative Law* (OUP, 7th edn), p41).

2   See, for example, *Associated Provincial Picture Houses Ltd v Wednesbury Corporation* [1948] 1 KB 223, CA, per Lord Greene MR at 233–4.

3   Regarding the difficult question of the status of ultra vires decisions, see paras 7.37–7.51 below.

4   See, for example, the unsuccessful challenge in *Westminster Corporation v London and North Western Railway Co* [1905] AC 426, HL, para 6.90 below.

5   *R (National Secular Society) v Bideford Town Council* [2012] EWHC 175 (Admin), [2012] 2 All ER 1175. The claimant's argument that the practice amounted to religious discrimination whether under the Equality Act 2006 (now Equality Act 2010) or HRA 1998 failed.

6   Localism Act 2011 s1(1). The implementation of section 1 was brought forward as a response to the decision in *R (National Secular Society) v Bideford Town Council* [2012] EWHC 175 (Admin), noted above. Welsh local authorities have a 'well-being' power under Local Government Act 2000 s2. As to the extent

6.4   Vires has, however, been given a broader meaning in the context of judicial review. In *Anisminic v Foreign Compensation Commission*,[7] the House of Lords held that no tribunal has jurisdiction to make any error of law.

> Lack of jurisdiction may arise in various ways ... [W]hile engaged on a proper inquiry, the tribunal may depart from the rules of natural justice; or it may ask itself the wrong questions; or it may take into account matters which it was not directed to take into account. Thereby it would step outside its jurisdiction. It would turn its inquiry to something not directed by Parliament and fail to make the inquiry which Parliament did direct. Any of these things would cause its purported decisions to be a nullity ...

6.5   In this way, all errors of law may be errors that can be said to render the resulting decision ultra vires. In the example given above, if the body determined to build a road but, in reaching that decision, took account of an irrelevant consideration, or failed to consider something relevant, the resultant decision could be termed ultra vires: the body only has power to make a lawful decision to build a road. It has no more power to reach a decision to build a road taking the wrong factors into account than it does to decide to build a railway. In *R v Hull University Visitor ex p Page*,[8] Lord Browne-Wilkinson said: 'If the decision-maker exercises his powers outside the jurisdiction conferred, in a manner which is procedurally irregular or is *Wednesbury* unreasonable, he is acting ultra vires his powers and therefore unlawfully.'

6.6   For this reason, each of the potential grounds for review set out below may be considered to involve aspects of the principles of vires and ultra vires.

Ultra vires and the basis of challenge

6.7   A reviewable decision may arise from the exercise of, or failure to exercise, a public law power or duty. The fact that such a power or duty may well be worded in subjective terms (such as 'if it appears to the authority'; 'if the Secretary of State considers'; 'if the tribunal

and limitations of that power, see in *R (J) v Enfield London Borough Council* [2002] EWHC 432 (Admin), [2002] HLR 38; *R (Theophilus) v Lewisham London Borough Council* [2002] EWHC 1371 (Admin), [2002] 3 All ER 851; and *Brent London Borough Council v Risk Management Partners Ltd* [2009] EWCA Civ 490, [2010] PTSR 349 (section 2 of the 2000 Act was not in issue before the Supreme Court: [2011] UKSC 7, [2011] 2 AC 34).

7   [1969] 2 AC 147, HL, per Lord Pearce at 195.
8   [1993] AC 682 at 701.

has reason to believe') does not exclude the remedy of judicial review. Public law powers may only validly be used in accordance with the administrative law principles described in this chapter. The concepts of discretion unfettered by the rule of law and of unreviewable administrative action have always been firmly rejected by the courts as anathema to a constitutional system of government based on the rule of law. The relevant questions are, therefore, not whether a decision is reviewable at all, but about the scope and intensity of that review (or, to put it another way, the breadth of the discretion conferred), the answers to which will depend on the intention of Parliament, the context, and the importance of the rights at stake.[9]

6.8   While, therefore, the decision-maker's judgment will not itself be impugned by the courts so long as it is made in accordance with the principles of administrative law, this is simply another way of stating the proposition that the court will not substitute its own view for that of the decision-maker. It does not exclude the court's supervision of the way in which the decision was reached.[10]

6.9   The classic statement of the grounds for judicial review remains that of Lord Greene MR in *Associated Provincial Picture Houses Ltd v Wednesbury Corporation*,[11] despite some recent judicial criticism that it constitutes an overly restrictive approach.[12] Lord Greene said:[13]

> Bad faith and dishonesty stand by themselves. A decision-maker must also direct himself properly in law ... I will summarise once again the principle applicable. The court is entitled to investigate the action of the local authority with a view to seeing whether they have

9   See, eg, *R v Tower Hamlets LBC ex p Chetnik Developments Ltd* [1988] AC 858, HL, especially per Lord Bridge of Harwich at 872A–873G, citing with approval Wade *Administrative Law* (5th edn, 1982), pp355–356. See also *Secretary of State for Education and Science v Tameside MBC* [1977] AC 1014, HL, and, eg, *R (Daly) v Secretary of State for the Home Department* [2001] UKHL 26, [2001] 2 AC 532, per Lord Steyn at [27]; *R (Mahmood) v Secretary of State for the Home Department* [2001] 1 WLR 840, CA. Always interesting is the dissenting speech of Lord Atkin in *Liversidge v Anderson* [1942] AC 206, HL.

10   See *Secretary of State for Education and Science v Tameside MBC* [1977] AC 1014, HL. See also, eg, *Mercury Communications Ltd v Director General of Telecommunications* [1996] 1 WLR 48, HL, per Lord Slynn of Hadley at 58G–H.

11   [1948] 1 KB 223, CA.

12   See *R (Daly) v Secretary of State for the Home Department* [2001] UKHL 26, [2001] 2 AC 532, per Lord Cooke of Thorndon at [32], in which he described *Wednesbury* as an 'unfortunately retrogressive decision in English administrative law' a description of the case that may have surprised lawyers at the time (and subsequently); *R (Association of British Civilian Internees (Far East Region)) v Secretary of State for Defence* [2003] EWCA Civ 473, [2003] QB 1397, per Lord Phillips of Worth Matravers at [34]–[35].

13   [1948] KB 223 at 233–4.

taken into account matters which they ought not to take into account, or, conversely, have refused to take into account or neglected to take into account matters which they ought to take into account. Once that question is answered in favour of the local authority, it may still be possible to say that although the local authority have kept within the four corners of the matters which they ought to consider, they have nevertheless come to a conclusion so unreasonable that no reasonable authority could ever have come to it.

6.10 In *Council of Civil Service Unions v Minister of State for the Civil Service* (*CCSU*),[14] Lord Diplock reformulated the grounds for seeking review under three heads:

(a) illegality;
(b) irrationality; and
(c) procedural impropriety.

By 'illegality', I mean that the decision-maker must understand correctly the law that regulates his decision-making power and must give effect to it ... By 'irrationality', I mean what can by now be succinctly referred to as '*Wednesbury* unreasonableness' ... I have described the third head as 'procedural impropriety' rather than a failure to observe the basic rules of natural justice or failure to act with procedural fairness ... This is because susceptibility to judicial review under this head covers also failure by an administrative tribunal to observe procedural rules that are expressly laid down in the legislative instrument by which its jurisdiction is conferred, even where such failure does not involve any denial of natural justice.[15]

6.11 It has not been entirely clear, however, where the lines fall to be drawn between these three categories. Clearly irrationality can be equated with *Wednesbury* unreasonableness, and was by Lord Bridge of Harwich in *R v Secretary of State for the Environment ex p Hammersmith and Fulham LBC*.[16] *Wednesbury*, however, also classified as 'unreasonable' misdirections of law and having regard to irrelevant matters, which *CCSU* and *Hammersmith and Fulham* classified as 'illegality'. Procedural irregularities could, in one sense, themselves be classified within 'illegality' given that to fall into procedural error is, in terms of *Anisminic*,[17] to commit an error of law.

---

14 [1985] AC 374, HL.
15 [1985] AC 374 at 410.
16 [1991] 1 AC 521, HL, at 597F.
17 *Anisminic v Foreign Compensation Commission* [1969] 2 AC 147, HL. See also, on this point, *Begum (Nipa) v Tower Hamlets LBC* [2000] 1 WLR 306, CA.

6.12   In *Leeds CC v Spencer*[18] Brooke LJ stated:

... it seems to me that to speak of '*Wednesbury* unreasonableness' and link this phrase exclusively with perversity or with a decision which defies logic tends to muddy the waters. ... the council was bound to take into account all relevant considerations, and if it failed to do so, the cases show that it could be castigated for acting unreasonably in the *Wednesbury* sense. In terms of strict legal analysis it would be abusing the power given to it by Parliament by failing to take into account all the matters it should have taken into account, and its act would be ultra vires.

6.13   The extent to which, in practical terms, the correct classification of a ground for review as falling within one or other(s) of the *CCSU* categories matters is, perhaps, open to doubt. While, in *Boddington*,[19] Lord Steyn spoke of categorisation as an 'indispensible tool in the search for rationality and coherence in law', it was recognised by Lord Greene MR in *Wednesbury* itself that the different grounds tend to 'run into each other' and are not hermetically sealed one from the other.[20]

6.14   Thus, while the traditional grounds of intervention fall broadly within certain categories, such grounds and categories are, at best, really only examples of the reasons for the court's intervention in different cases. They are by no means rigid, self-contained, or mutually exclusive. It may well be possible to characterise an error made by a decision-maker as unlawful for a number of reasons, and on several 'grounds'.

Fundamental rights cases

Common law 'anxious scrutiny'

6.15   Even before the coming into force of the HRA 1998, the judicial review courts had begun to develop the principles of review enshrined by *Wednesbury* and *CCSU*, as they applied in cases where human rights were at stake. In *R v Ministry of Defence ex p Smith*,[21] where a challenge

---

18 [2000] BLGR 68, CA, at 75.
19 *Boddington v British Transport Police* [1999] 2 AC 143, HL at 170F. This was in the different context of whether it was possible to draw a rational distinction between the 'substantive' and 'procedural' invalidity of a byelaw.
20 See also, eg, *Wheeler v Leicester CC* [1985] AC 1054, HL, per Lord Roskill at 1078B–C; *R v Secretary of State for the Environment ex p Nottinghamshire CC* [1986] AC 240, HL, per Lord Scarman at 249D–E; *R v Panel on Take-overs and Mergers ex p Guinness plc* [1990] 1 QB 146, CA, per Lord Donaldson MR at 160A–C; *Boddington v British Transport Police* [1999] 2 AC 143, per Lord Steyn at 170E.
21 [1996] QB 517, CA.

was brought to the Secretary of State's policy of not permitting gay men and lesbians to serve in the armed forces, the Court of Appeal held that it was not appropriate to adopt a strict *Wednesbury* approach to reviewing the Secretary of State's policy. Instead, the conventional *Wednesbury* approach must be adapted to a human rights context. The court would give 'anxious scrutiny' to the policy under challenge (this has also been referred to as a 'super-*Wednesbury*' approach).[22]

6.16   The effect of this approach was to require the Secretary of State to show an important competing public interest which he could reasonably judge sufficient to justify the policy. The court would only strike the policy down if satisfied that this justification was perverse. The more substantial the interference with human rights, the more that would be required by way of justification before the court would be satisfied that the decision was within the range of reasonable decisions open to the Secretary of State.[23]

6.17   Likewise, in *R (Mahmood) v Secretary of State for the Home Department*,[24] Laws LJ held that the appropriate intensity of review in a case involving fundamental rights was greater than that which would be applied on a conventional *Wednesbury* basis, and emphasised the objective basis of the approach to be adopted. Where a fundamental right was engaged, the court would 'insist that that fact be respected by the decision-maker, who would accordingly be required to demonstrate either that his proposed action did not in truth interfere with the right, or, if it did, that there existed considerations which may reasonably be accepted as amounting to a substantial objective justification for the interference'.[25] The intensity of review in a public law case would depend on the subject-matter at hand and so, in particular, any interference with a fundamental right would require a substantial objective justification. This approach and that of conventional *Wednesbury* were not, however, sealed hermetically one from the other. There was 'rather, what may be called a sliding scale of review; the graver the impact of the decision in question upon the individual affected by it, the more substantial the justification that will be required'.[26]

22 See *Vilvarajah v United Kingdom* (1991) 14 EHRR 248, ECHR.
23 See the slightly different formulations of the approach of Simon Brown LJ at 540F and Sir Thomas Bingham MR at 554E–G. Henry LJ agreed with the Master of the Rolls (at 563A).
24 [2001] 1 WLR 840, CA.
25 [2001] 1 WLR 840 at [16].
26 [2001] 1 WLR 840 at [18]–[19]. See also the judgment of Lord Phillips of Worth Matravers MR at [37]. The case of *R v Lord Saville of Newdigate ex p A* [2000] 1 WLR 1855, CA, per Lord Woolf MR at [37] is also instructive.

'Anxious scrutiny' and proportionality

6.18   Since the coming into force of the HRA 1998, the courts have developed this approach further. The HRA 1998 itself obliges the court to have regard to the jurisprudence of the ECtHR,[27] and this has rapidly led to the development of a more intensive approach to review, founded on the principles set out in such cases as *Mahmood* but now in conjunction with the European concept of proportionality, which has become the benchmark test of intervention where fundamental rights are in play, in place of the *Wednesbury* test.

6.19   The relationship, or perhaps the difference, between the traditional *Wednesbury* test and that derived from Europe, and founded on proportionality, was explained by Laws J, in *R v Ministry of Agriculture, Fisheries and Food ex p First City Trading Limited*,[28] in the following way.

> By our domestic law, if a public decision-maker were to treat apparently identical cases differently there would no doubt be a *prima facie Wednesbury* case against him, since on the face of it such an approach bears the hall-mark of irrationality. To that extent the rule is akin to the European principle. The Court would look for an explanation of the difference; but the justification offered would in the ordinary way only be rejected on grounds of perversity. That, I think, marks the divide. The Community rule requires the decision-maker to demonstrate a substantive justification for a discriminatory decision ... In case after case ... the Court of Justice has proceeded on the footing that the facts must be examined by the reviewing court and a view reached as to whether the decision taken measures up to the substantive standards which it has set ...
>
> The difference between *Wednesbury* and European review is that in the former case the legal limits lie further back. I think there are two factors. First, the limits of domestic review are not, as the law presently stands, constrained by the doctrine of proportionality. Secondly, at least as regards a requirement such as that of objective justification in an equal-treatment case, the European rule requires the decision-maker to provide a fully-reasoned case. It is not enough merely to set out the problem, and assert that within his discretion the Minister chose this or that solution, constrained only by the requirement that his decision must have been one which a reasonable Minister might make. Rather the Court will test the solution arrived at, and pass it only if substantial factual considerations are put forward in its

---

27   HRA 1998 s2(1).

28   [1997] 1 CMLR 250, QBD, at 278–9. This analysis was approved by the Court of Appeal in *R v Secretary of State for Health ex p Eastside Cheese Co* [1999] 3 CMLR 123, CA.

justification: considerations which are relevant, reasonable and proportionate to the aim in view. But as I understand the jurisprudence the Court is not concerned to agree or disagree with the decision: that would be to travel beyond the boundaries of proper judicial authority, and usurp the primary decision-maker's function. Thus *Wednesbury* and European review are different models – one looser, one tighter – of the same juridical concept, which is the imposition of compulsory standards on decision-makers so as to secure the repudiation of arbitrary power.

6.20   In *R (Daly) v Secretary of State for the Home Department,*[29] Lord Steyn described the application of the principle of proportionality in terms of a three-stage test.[30] The court should ask itself:

> ... whether (i) the legislative object is sufficiently important to justify limiting a fundamental right; (ii) the measures designed to meet the legislative imperative are rationally connected to it; and (iii) the means used to impair the right or freedom are no more than is necessary to accomplish the objective.

6.21   Lord Steyn recognised the overlap between the traditional grounds of review and the approach of proportionality. Most cases would be decided in the same way whichever approach was adopted. He did, however, refer to three concrete differences between proportionality and *Wednesbury*: first, proportionality may require the reviewing court to assess for itself the appropriateness of the balance between competing interests that the decision-maker has struck and not merely consider whether that balance is within the range of rational or reasonable decisions. Secondly, proportionality may require the attention of the court to be directed to the relative weight attached to the various relevant interests and considerations. Thirdly, even the heightened scrutiny test developed in *Smith*[31] would not necessarily be appropriate to the protection of human rights.[32] The ECtHR in the same case had concluded that the threshold of the test for irrationality applied by the Court of Appeal had been set so high that it effectively excluded any consideration of whether the policy under challenge met a pressing social need or was proportionate to the aims pursued.

29 [2001] UKHL 26, [2001] 2 AC 532 at [27].

30 First propounded by the Privy Council in *de Freitas v Permanent Secretary of Ministry of Agriculture, Fisheries, Lands and Housing* [1999] 1 AC 69, per Lord Clyde at 80.

31 *R v Ministry of Defence ex p Smith* [1996] QB 517, CA.

32 A point repeated in *E v Chief Constable of the Royal Ulster Constabulary* [2008] UKHL 66, [2009] 1 AC 536.

6.22   This did not mean that there had been a shift from the court's supervisory role to a full review of the merits of the decision. It was, however, important that human rights cases be analysed in the correct way. *Mahmood* had been correct to emphasise that the appropriate intensity of review would depend on the subject matter of the case in hand, even in cases involving Convention rights. 'In law context is everything.'[33]

6.23   In *Southampton Port Health Authority v Seahawk Marine Foods Ltd*,[34] the Court of Appeal expressed considerable doubt as to whether it would be wise for the court to attempt the lines of enquiry suggested by Lord Steyn in *Daly* (in particular as concerned assessing the balance struck by the decision-maker and the relative weight he or she had accorded to relevant factors)[35] in cases involving technical or professional decision-making without the benefit of evidence regarding usual practices and the practicability of the suggested alternatives. While in some cases, the court may be able to rely on common sense and its own understanding of government and administration, this would be difficult in cases involving decision-making on technical issues.[36]

6.24   Lord Steyn's opinion in *Daly* was described as 'justly-celebrated' by Lord Bingham in *Huang v Secretary of State for the Home Department*.[37] Lord Bingham added a further element to Lord Steyn's three-stage test:[38] 'the need to balance the interests of society with those of individuals and groups'.[39]

6.25   The question that the court must decide is not whether a public authority have properly considered whether a claimant's rights

---

33   *R (Mahmood) v Secretary of State for the Home Department* [2001] 1 WLR 840, CA at [27]–[28].

34   [2002] EWCA Civ 54, [2002] ACD 35.

35   Above at paras 6.20–6.21.

36   For further applications of the proportionality test at the highest judicial level, see *Tweed v Parades Commission for Northern Ireland* [2006] UKHL 53, [2007] 1 AC 650; *R (Countryside Alliance) v Attorney General* [2007] UKHL 52, [2008] 1 AC 719; *Zalewska v Department for Social Development* [2008] UKHL 67, [2008] 1 WLR 2602; *R (RJM) v Secretary of State for Work and Pensions* [2008] UKHL 63, [2009] 1 AC 311; *Norris v Government of the United States of America (No 2)* [2010] UKSC 9, [2010] 2 AC 487; *R (Quila) v Secretary of State for the Home Department* [2011] UKSC 45, [2012] 1 AC 621; *AXA General Inusrance Ltd v HM Advocate* [2011] UKSC 46, [2012] 1 AC 868. Also interesting are the judgments in *R (Sinclair Collis Ltd) v Secretary of State for Health* [2011] EWCA Civ 437, [2012] QB 394 (and see also *Sinclair Collis Ltd v Lord Advocate* [2012] CSIH 80).

37   [2007] UKHL 11, [2007] 2 AC 167 at [13].

38   See para 6.20 above.

39   [2007] UKHL 11 at [19].

under the Convention would be violated but whether there had actually been a violation of those rights.[40]

6.26   Where an authority's decision does not amount to a disproportionate restriction on Convention rights, the authority's failure to refer specifically to those rights does not vitiate the decision.[41] As Lord Bingham explained in *R (SB) v Denbigh High School*:[42] '... what matters in any case is the practical outcome, not the quality of the decision-making process that led to it.'[43]

6.27   It follows that the decision on proportionality is ultimately one for the court.[44] The views of the decision-maker may still carry some weight, as Baroness Hale stated in *R (Quila) v Secretary of State for the Home Department*:[45]

> Of course, where delicate and difficult judgments are involved ..., this court will treat with appropriate respect the views taken by those whose primary responsibility it is to make the judgments in question. But those views cannot be decisive. Ultimately, it is for the court to decide whether or not the Convention rights have been breached.[46]

6.28   Having said this, it can be misleading to consider such statements of principle in the abstract, shorn of their context. Whatever the theoretical position, the fact remains, whether because of the nature of the right in issue, or because of the procedural safeguards already enshrined in domestic law, that there are some Convention rights in respect of which the courts will accept the lawful conclusions of the decision-maker save in highly exceptional cases,[47] while in others, a much more interventionist approach is adopted.[48]

---

40 *Belfast CC v Miss Behavin' Ltd* [2007] UKHL 19, [2007] 1 WLR 1420.
41 *Belfast CC v Miss Behavin' Ltd* [2007] UKHL 19, [2007] 1 WLR 1420.
42 [2006] UKHL 15, [2007] 1 AC 100.
43 [2006] UKHL 15 at [31].
44 *Mayor of London v Hall* [2010] EWCA Civ 817, [2011] 1 WLR 504, per Lord Neuberger MR at [43], relying on *R (SB) v Denbigh High School* [2006] UKHL 15, [2007] 1 AC 100, and *Belfast CC v Miss Behavin' Ltd* [2007] UKHL 19, [2007] 1 WLR 1420. See also *E v Chief Constable of the Royal Ulster Constabulary* [2008] UKHL 66, [2009] 1 AC 536, per Lord Carswell at [54].
45 [2011] UKSC 45, [2012] 1 AC 621.
46 [2011] UKSC 45 at [61].
47 See *Manchester CC v Pinnock* [2010] UKSC 45, [2011] 2 AC 104; *Hounslow LBC v Powell* [2011] UKSC 8, [2011] 2 AC 186; *Corby BC v Scott* [2012] EWCA Civ 276, [2013] PTSR 141; *Birmingham CC v Lloyd* [2012] EWCA Civ 969, [2012] HLR 44.
48 Eg *Huang v Secretary of State for the Home Department* [2007] UKHL 11, [2007] 2 AC 167 at [15]–[16], [19]–[20].

Wednesbury, proportionality and the margin of appreciation

6.29   The *Wednesbury* test affords the decision-maker a very wide margin of appreciation – any decision may validly be taken so long as no error is made and a reasonable decision-maker could have taken it. In *R v Secretary of State for the Home Department ex p Farrakhan*,[49] the Court of Appeal held that such a margin was far too wide to accommodate the requirements of the Convention. In deciding whether a restriction on a Convention right was permissible, the doctrine of proportionality must therefore be applied. The breadth of the margin of appreciation accorded the decision was flexible – it would vary according to the rights in play and the facts of the case. The *Wednesbury* approach, on the other hand, was not flexible. In applying the principles of proportionality, however, it was essential to recognise and give proper respect to the margin of appreciation to which the decision-maker is entitled; only by doing so could the court avoid substituting its own decision for the decision under challenge. On the facts of that case, a very wide margin of appreciation should be accorded.

Two tests?

6.30   In *Mahmood*, Laws LJ referred to a sliding scale of review, the intensity of which would increase with the gravity of the subject-matter. This does not, however, entirely dispense with the difficulty that in cases where no Convention right is engaged, conventional *Wednesbury* would still appear to be the test properly applied by the courts, whereas in a Convention case, a more intense version of review, founded on the doctrine of proportionality, is likely to be undertaken by the court. While it can be argued that this is as it should be – the more serious the case, the more anxious should be the scrutiny applied to the decision under challenge – there are three difficulties with such an argument.

6.31   First, it is only persuasive if it can be demonstrated that the rights at stake in all cases involving Convention rights are more grave, or fundamental, than those at stake in every case which does not. This is not necessarily the case. The engagement of Convention rights in individual cases is not, after all, solely a function of the importance of what is at stake for the claimant.[50] Secondly, it is a little unconvincing

49   [2002] EWCA Civ 606, [2002] QB 1391.
50   See *Runa Begum v Tower Hamlets LBC* [2003] UKHL 5, [2003] 2 AC 430, per Lord Bingham at [49]–[50]: '49. ... When one is dealing with a welfare scheme which, in the particular case, does not engage human rights (does not, for

that the availability of the doctrine of proportionality to test the legality of a decision should depend exclusively on whether or not a Convention right is at stake. That this is so results from the fact that the court historically set its face against entertaining proportionality as a distinct head of challenge or means of testing a decision.[51] It is therefore only available to the court where the HRA 1998, which requires the court to have regard to European jurisprudence, is in play. Thirdly, it is unsatisfactory that the court should be developing and called upon to apply two increasingly distinct and divergent bodies of public law to cases brought before it under the same procedure, seeking the same remedies in respect of the same kind of (ie public law) decision.

6.32   As to the first difficulty mentioned in the last paragraph, it is by no means clear that all cases involving a Convention right concern more significant rights than all those that do not. This is frequently because the availability of a human rights argument does not depend on the importance of the right at stake but on whether the HRA 1998 can be said to have added anything to the protection of a particular right afforded by common law or statute. In many cases, the courts have held that a particular Convention right is in issue, or engaged,[52] but that any infringement has been lawful for reasons unrelated to the importance of the right itself, but related instead to such matters as the respect which the courts must have for the will of Parliament as expressed in legislation.[53] Such decisions prevent reliance on the European Convention in future cases involving the same right, but does not affect the importance of the right itself.[54]

example, require consideration of article 8) then the intensity of review must depend upon what one considers to be most consistent with the statutory scheme. ... 17 years ago Lord Brightman, speaking for a unanimous Appellate Committee in *R v Hillingdon London Borough Council ex p Puhlhofer* [1986] AC 484, 518, made it clear that their Lordships contemplated a fairly low level of judicial interventionism ... 50. All that we are concerned with in this appeal is the requirements of article 6, which I do not think mandates a more intensive approach to judicial review of questions of fact. ... It seems to me sufficient to say that in the case of the normal Part VII decision, engaging no human rights other than article 6, conventional judicial review ... is sufficient.'

51 See, eg, *R v Secretary of State for the Home Department ex p Brind* [1991] 1 AC 696, HL.

52 But see the mild judicial disapproval of the term 'engaged' and the suggestion that 'applicable' is the more appropriate term: *Harrow LBC v Qazi* [2003] UKHL 43, [2004] 1 AC 983, per Lord Hope at [47].

53 See, eg, *Poplar Housing and Regeneration Community Association Ltd v Donoghue* [2001] EWCA Civ 595, [2002] QB 48; *Begum (Runa) v Tower Hamlets LBC* [2003] UKHL 5, [2003] 2 AC 430.

54 See the comments of Lord Bingham in *Runa Begum*, note 50 above.

6.33   If this is correct, then the above justifications do not provide an entirely sound basis for distinguishing between when the correct approach is that of conventional *Wednesbury* and when it is likely to require proportionality or some form of enhanced scrutiny.

6.34   The problem of two tests was considered by Lord Slynn of Hadley in *R (Alconbury) v Secretary of State for the Environment, Transport and the Regions*.[55] He said:

> I consider that even without reference to the HRA the time has come to recognise that this principle is part of English administrative law, not only when judges are dealing with Community acts but also when they are dealing with acts subject to domestic law. Trying to keep the *Wednesbury* principle and proportionality in separate compartments seems to me to be unnecessary and confusing.

6.35   In *Daly*, Lord Cooke of Thorndon went further, suggesting that:[56]

> ... the day will come when it will be more widely recognised that *Associated Provincial Picture Houses Ltd v Wednesbury Corporation* [1948] 1 KB 223 was an unfortunately retrogressive decision in English administrative law, insofar as it suggested that there are degrees of unreasonableness and that only a very extreme degree can bring an administrative decision within the legitimate scope of judicial invalidation. The depth of judicial review and the deference due to administrative discretion vary with the subject matter. It may well be, however, that the law can never be satisfied in any administrative field merely by a finding that the decision under review is not capricious or absurd.

6.36   In *R (Association of British Civilian Internees (Far East Region)) v Secretary of State for Defence*,[57] the Court of Appeal again considered the issue, and concluded that the time had come for the *Wednesbury* approach to be dispensed with (while recognising that only the House of Lords could 'perform its burial rites'),[58] though for rather different reasons than those put forward by Lord Cooke of Thorndon

---

55 [2001] UKHL 23, [2003] 2 AC 295 at [51].
56 [2001] UKHL 26, [2001] 2 AC 532 at [32].
57 [2003] EWCA Civ 473, [2003] QB 1397, per Lord Phillips of Worth Matravers at [34]–[35].
58 If that time ever comes, there may be some mourning – Lord Walker remarked in *R (ProLife Alliance) v BBC* [2003] UKHL 23, [2004] 1 AC 185 at [144], that the '*Wednesbury* test ..., for all its defects, had the advantage of simplicity, and it might be thought unsatisfactory that it must now be replaced (when human rights are in play) by a much more complex and contextually sensitive approach'.

in *Daly*.[59] In the view of Lord Phillips MR, while the criteria of proportionality were more precise and sophisticated, the strictness of the *Wednesbury* test had been relaxed in recent years so that it was, in any event, moving closer to proportionality, so much so that in some cases it was not possible to see daylight between the two tests.[60]

6.37   In *Somerville v Scottish Ministers*,[61] the House of Lords left open the possibility that proportionality could be an independent ground of review, as it was not necessary to decide the issue in order to determine the case (because Convention rights were engaged).

Abuse of power: a doctrine of reconciliation

6.38   There has been some suggestion that a general doctrine of abuse of power may now be assuming centre stage as an all-embracing rationale for the general principles of administrative law. In *R v Department for Education and Employment ex p Begbie*,[62] Laws LJ stated that abuse of power 'has become, or is fast becoming, the root concept which governs and conditions our general principles of public law'.[63] He described it as the rationale for the *Wednesbury* and *Padfield*[64] doctrines, for illegality as a ground of challenge, and for the requirements of proportionality, procedural fairness and legitimate expectation.

6.39   Similarly, in *R v North and East Devon Health Authority ex p Coughlan*,[65] Lord Woolf MR stated, in the context of legitimate expectations:

> We would prefer to regard the *Wednesbury* categories themselves as the major instances (not necessarily the sole ones ...) of how public power may be misused. Once it is recognised that conduct which is an abuse of power is contrary to law its existence must be for the court to determine.[66]

---

59 *R (Daly) v Secretary of State for the Home Department* [2001] UKHL 26, [2001] 2 AC 523.

60 But see *R (H) v A City Council* [2011] EWCA Civ 403, [2011] BLGR 590 at [41] and [43] on the difference that still exists between the two tests and criticism of the judge at first instance for equiperating the two.

61 [2007] UKHL 44, [2007] 1 WLR 2734.

62 [2000] 1 WLR 1115, CA at 1129.

63 See also *R (Nadarajah) v Secretary of State for the Home Department* [2005] EWCA Civ 1363; (2005) *Times* 14 December, at para 6.41 below.

64 *Padfield v Ministry of Agriculture, Fisheries and Food* [1968] AC 997, HL.

65 [2001] QB 213, CA.

66 [2001] QB 213 at [81].

6.40 Likewise, in *R (Zeqiri) v Secretary of State for the Home Department*,[67] the House of Lords referred to the denial of a legitimate expectation as but one form of the more general concept of abuse of power.

6.41 Laws LJ returned to the theme in *R (Nadarajah) v Secretary of State for the Home Department*,[68] where he said:

> Principle is not in my judgment supplied by the call to arms of abuse of power. Abuse of power is a name for any act of a public authority that is not legally justified. It is a useful name, for it catches the moral impetus of the rule of law. ... But it goes no distance to tell you, case by case, what is lawful and what is not. I accept, of course, that there is no formula which tells you that; if there were, the law would be nothing but a checklist. Legal principle lies between the overarching rubric of abuse of power and the concrete imperatives of a rule-book.[69]

Grounds

6.42 Be all of that as it may, and in spite of certain uncertainties in this area of public law, it is still possible to discuss the general grounds for review in much the same terms, or at least under much the same rubric, as in the first two editions of this book, and that is still the approach taken below. The different grounds listed below have been set out under Lord Diplock's three headings in *CCSU*, as further explained by *Hammersmith and Fulham LBC v Secretary State for the Environment*,[70] and *Leeds CC v Spencer*.[71]

Illegality

Misdirection of law

6.43 A decision-maker must only act within the confines of the powers that have been conferred on her or him.[72] The decision-maker must

---

67 [2002] UKHL 3, [2002] Imm AR 296.
68 [2005] EWCA Civ 1363; (2005) *Times* 14 December.
69 [2005] EWCA Civ 1363 at [67].
70 [1991] 1 AC 521 at 597.
71 [2000] BLGR 68 at 75.
72 See, eg, *R (Bancoult) v Secretary of State for the Foreign and Commonwealth Office* [2001] QB 1067, DC. The Divisional Court's decision was overruled in a subsequent claim brought by the same claimant, but not on this point: *R (Bancoult) v Secretary of State for Foreign and Commonwealth Affairs* [2008] UKHL 61, [2009] 1 AC 453. See also *Wednesbury* [1948] 1 KB 223, CA; *Anisminic v Foreign Compensation Commission* [1969] AC 426, HL; and *Council of Civil Service Unions v Minister of State for the Civil Service* [1985] AC 374, HL.

also direct himself properly in law, ie understand and apply the law correctly. Thus, a decision based on a misunderstanding or misapplication of the law will not have been reached lawfully or properly.[73]

Decision not in accordance with the facts

No fundamental rights at stake

6.44 A decision must be reached on the basis of the facts of the matter in question. A decision totally at variance with the facts or for which there is no factual basis cannot be sustained. Prior to the coming into force of the HRA 1998, the courts were at pains to point out that judicial review is concerned with errors of law and not errors of fact. Thus, where no fundamental rights are at stake, to proceed (or succeed) on this basis it will be necessary to establish:

(i) that the fact in question affected the jurisdiction of the decision-maker (ie it was a jurisdictional or precedent fact); or

(ii) if not jurisdictional, that –[74]

    (a) the decision made proceeded on an incorrect understanding of the facts, or

    (b) there was no evidence to support the finding of fact made, or

    (c) the decision-maker took no account of them, in the sense of simply applying a pre-ordained policy, regardless of the merits,[75] or

    (d) in finding the facts, the decision-maker failed to take account of relevant matters or took account of irrelevancies, or

    (e) the finding of fact was perverse or irrational, or

    (f) the decision-maker made a mistake of established fact.[76]

6.45 In *Sagnata Investments Ltd v Norwich Corporation*,[77] a local authority resolved not to permit amusement arcades in Norwich. The appellant was refused a licence and appealed. Phillimore LJ said:[78]

> ... the Council had not exercised any form of discretion. They had simply dismissed the application after going through the necessary

---

73 See *Wednesbury* (above); *Re Islam* [1983] 1 AC 688, HL. See also *Mercury Communications Ltd v Director General of Telecommunications* [1996] 1 WLR 48, HL.

74 See, eg, *Edwards v Bairstow* [1956] AC 14, HL; *Begum v Tower Hamlets LBC* [2003] UKHL 5, [2003] 2 AC 430.

75 See also 'Fettering of discretion' at paras 6.104–6.109 below.

76 See *E v Secretary of State for the Home Department* [2004] EWCA Civ 49, [2004] QB 1044.

77 [1971] 2 QB 614, CA.

78 [1971] 2 QB 614 at 639.

motions without regard to its individual merits or demerits ... the council's committee had failed to keep an open mind and had applied their policy without regard to the facts of the individual case.

6.46 In *Secretary of State for Education and Science v Tameside MBC*,[79] Lord Wilberforce said:[80]

> If a judgment requires, before it can be made, the existence of some facts, then, although the evaluation of those facts is for the Secretary of State alone, the court must enquire whether those facts exist, and have been taken into account, whether the judgment has been made on a proper self direction as to those facts, whether the judgment has not been made on other facts which ought not to have been taken into account. If these requirements are not met, then the exercise of judgment, however *bona fide* it may be, becomes capable of challenge: see *Secretary of State for Employment v Associated Society of Locomotive Engineers and Firemen (No 2)* [1972] 2 QB 455, per Lord Denning MR at 493.

6.47 He continued:[81]

> ... if [the Secretary of State] had exercised his judgment on the basis of the factual situation in which this newly elected authority were placed – with a policy approved by their electorate, and massively supported by the parents – there was no ground, however much he might disagree with the new policy ... on which he could find that the authority were acting or proposing to act unreasonably.

6.48 See also *Hemns v Wheeler*, in which Tucker LJ said:[82]

> It is for the county court judge to find the facts and to draw the inferences from those facts, but ... it is always a question of law, which will warrant the interference of this court, whether there was any evidence to support his findings of fact and whether the inferences he has drawn are possible inferences from the facts as found.

6.49 **Jurisdictional errors and precedent facts** Where the decision-maker has wrongly decided a question of fact (or of law, or a mixed question) either to deprive himself of, or confer upon himself, jurisdiction, the court can review the issue of jurisdictional fact or law. In such cases, the court does not approach the matter on the basis set out above, ie by asking whether the decision-maker approached the question correctly, but will decide the jurisdictional question for itself.

---

79 *Secretary of State for Education and Science v Tameside MBC* [1977] AC 1014, HL.
80 [1977] AC 1014 at 1047D–F.
81 [1977] AC 1014 at 1052.
82 [1948] 2 KB 61, CA, per Tucker LJ at 65–6.

6.50   This may arise, for example, where a particular status is under consideration. An example of this is *R v Secretary of State for the Environment ex p Davies*.[83] By Town and Country Planning Act 1990 s174, only a person with an interest in land has a right of appeal against an enforcement notice. The applicant was a traveller who claimed to have such an interest by virtue of being in adverse possession of the land in question and purported to appeal against the service of an enforcement notice upon her by the local authority. The Secretary of State decided that she had no interest in the land and that therefore he had no jurisdiction to hear the appeal. The Court of Appeal held that it had power to determine the matter for itself. The Secretary of State had conceded for the purposes of the appeal that a person in adverse possession could have an interest in land. On the facts, however, the court held that the applicant was not in adverse possession.[84]

6.51   It is not entirely clear what evidence the court will consider in such matters. In *R v Secretary of State for the Home Department ex p Khawaja*,[85] the House of Lords took the view that the court could take into account any evidence before it, whether or not it had been before the Secretary of State.[86] In *R v Secretary of State for the Environment ex p Powis*,[87] the Court of Appeal likewise held that where the jurisdiction of the minister depended on a question of fact, the court could entertain additional evidence for the purpose of determining the jurisdictional fact for itself. In *Davies*,[88] however, the court held

---

83 (1990) 61 P&CR 487, CA. On the issue of adverse possession, *Davies* was held to have been wrongly decided by the House of Lords in *JA Pye (Oxford) Ltd v Graham* [2002] UKHL 30, [2003] 1 AC 419. It was not overruled on the issue of precedent fact, however.

84 Although it has now been overruled on this point (see note 83 above). See also *R v Secretary of State for the Home Department ex p Khawaja*, where the question was whether or not a person was an 'illegal entrant'.

85 [1984] AC 74, HL. In *R v Dyfed CC ex p S (Minors)* [1995] ELR 98, the Court of Appeal doubted whether the *Khawaja* principle was of application outside liberty of the subject cases, but the Supreme Court decision in *R (A) v Croydon LBC* [2009] UKSC 8, [2009] 1 WLR 2557, relying on *Khawaja*, seems to answer this doubt (see para 6.53 below).

86 See especially Lord Wilberforce at 105, Lord Scarman at 110, and Lord Bridge at 125. See also *R v Secretary of State for the Home Department ex p Hussain* [1978] 1 WLR 700, CA.

87 [1981] 1 WLR 584, CA.

88 (1990) 61 P&CR 487, CA.

that it must consider the matter solely on the basis of the evidence before the minister.[89]

6.52   The *Davies* approach seems doubtful – it would be wholly unsatisfactory if the question of a decision-maker's jurisdiction were to depend on whether the right evidence happened to have been put before him, rather than on all the evidence available to the court; a person's jurisdiction ought to be determined by what the facts are rather than by how they may have appeared at some earlier stage of the process.

6.53   In *R (A) v Croydon LBC*,[90] the Supreme Court considered a local authority's duties under Children Act 1989, which turned on whether a person was a child in need. The Supreme Court held that whether a person was a child, ie under the age of 18, was a question of precedent fact and that if there was a dispute the courts would have to determine the person's age on the evidence.[91] Whether that person was 'in need' was, however, for the local authority to decide, subject to the control of the courts on the ordinary principles of judicial review.[92] These were different kinds of question: whether a child was 'in need', permitted a number of different value judgments to be made, but whether a person is a 'child', admitted of a right and a wrong answer.[93]

6.54   So far as the court is concerned to determine the age of a person, it can do so following cross-examination of that person (and others who have assessed their age).[94] It follows that the *Davies* approach does not apply, at least in age assessment cases and appears to have been ignored in other cases. It is probably an aberration and incorrect.

6.55   Other precedent facts include whether or not a councillor has been disqualified,[95] whether a measure qualifies as state aid under the

---

89   There is no reference to *Khawaja* [1984] AC 74, HL or *Powis* [1981] 1 WLR 584, CA in the judgments of the court.

90   [2009] UKSC 8, [2009] 1 WLR 2557.

91   Per Baroness Hale at [26]–[33]. See also *R (Z) v Croydon LBC* [2011] EWCA Civ 59, [2011] PTSR 747; *R (CJ) v Cardiff CC* [2011] EWCA Civ 1590, [2012] PTSR 1235. Such claims will now be heard in the Upper Tribunal (Immigration and Asylum Chamber), see paras 8.41–8.45 below.

92   [2009] UKSC 8.

93   [2009] UKSC 8, per Baroness Hale at [26]–[27].

94   See, eg, *R (Z) v Croydon LBC* [2011] EWCA Civ 59, [2011] PTSR 747, [2011] HLR 22; *R (CJ) v Cardiff CC* [2011] EWCA Civ 1590, [2012] PTSR 1235.

95   *R v Islington LBC ex p Camp* [2004] BLGR 58, QBD.

EC Treaty,[96] whether a person's detention was 'pending removal',[97] whether, in a planning context, information qualified as information relating to the environment,[98] whether a person was a deposed native chief, and thus subject to a power to be removed from an area.[99]

6.56   The following have been held not to be jurisdictional facts: whether an asylum-seeker is a refugee,[100] whether a traveller is a gipsy,[101] whether a person has the requisite mental capacity necessary to be treated as a homeless applicant,[102] whether a fresh asylum application had been made.[103]

6.57   **Mistake of established fact** The existence of mistake of established fact as a ground for judicial review was recognised by the Court of Appeal in *E v Secretary of State for the Home Department*, a case concerning asylum appeals.[104] Carnwath LJ, giving the judgment of the Court of Appeal said:[105]

> In our view, the time has now come to accept that a mistake of fact giving rise to unfairness is a separate head of challenge in an appeal on a point of law, at least in those statutory contexts where the parties share an interest in co-operating to achieve the correct result. Asylum law is undoubtedly such an area. Without seeking to lay down a precise code, the ordinary requirements for a finding of unfairness are ... First, there must have been a mistake as to an existing fact, including a mistake as to the availability of evidence on a particular matter. Secondly, the fact or evidence must have been 'established', in the sense that it was uncontentious and objectively verifiable. Thirdly, the appellant (or his advisers) must not been have been responsible for the mistake. Fourthly, the mistake must have played a material (not necessarily decisive) part in the tribunal's reasoning.[106]

---

96   *R v Commissioners of Customs and Excise ex p Lunn Poly Ltd* [1999] 1 CMLR 1357, [1999] EuLR 653.

97   *Tan Te Lam v Superintendent of Tai A Chau Detention Centre* [1997] AC 97.

98   *R v Secretary of State for the Environment, Transport and the Regions ex p Alliance Against the Birmingham Northern Relief Road (No 1)* [1999] Env LR 447.

99   *Eshugbayi Eleko v Officer Administering the Government of Nigeria* [1931] AC 662, PC.

100 *Bugdaycay v Secretary of State for the Home Department* [1987] AC 514, HL.

101 *R v South Hams DC ex p Gibb* [1995] QB 158, CA.

102 *R v Oldham MBC ex p Garlick* [1993] AC 509, HL.

103 *R v Secretary of State for the Home Department ex p Onibiyo* [1996] QB 768, CA; *R v Secretary of State for the Home Department ex p Cakabay (No 2)* [1999] Imm AR 176.

104 [2004] EWCA Civ 49, [2004] QB 1044.

105 At [66].

106 [2004] EWCA Civ 49 at [66].

6.58   Thus facts that involve a decision-maker reaching a conclusion based on an evaluation of the evidence will not be challengeable on this basis. The requirement for the fact in question to be 'established' means that this is a somewhat limited ground for challenge.

Fundamental rights cases

6.59   Where fundamental rights are at stake, a rather more interventionist approach to disputes of fact may be appropriate. In *R v Criminal Injuries Compensation Board ex p A*,[107] Lord Slynn of Hadley accepted that the court had jurisdiction to quash the decision of the Board on the ground of a material error of fact, although he did not decide the case on that basis. In *R (Alconbury Developments Ltd) v Secretary of State for the Environment, Transport and the Regions*,[108] Lord Slynn again referred to the potential ability of a judicial review court to review material errors of fact, which ability strengthened the argument that judicial review was an adequate remedy for the purposes of article 6 of the European Convention.

6.60   In *R (Wilkinson) v Broadmoor Special Hospital Authority*,[109] the claimant, who was detained under the Mental Health Act 1983, challenged the defendant's decision that he should be compulsorily treated with anti-psychotic medication (on the basis that his mental state was not such that he could validly withhold his consent). The claimant claimed interim relief in the form of an order that the doctors who had made the decision be ordered to attend court for cross-examination. The judge at first instance refused to make such an order, but the Court of Appeal allowed the claimant's appeal.

6.61   Simon Brown LJ, with whom the other members of the court agreed, stated that since the coming into force of the HRA 1998, the provisions of article 6 of the Convention required that where fundamental rights were at stake the court not only had power to, but 'must now inevitably reach its own view' on the disputed issues of fact: namely, whether the claimant was capable of consenting or refusing consent to the proposed treatment and whether the administration of the treatment would itself be contrary to the claimant's Convention rights.[110] The claimant could have litigated his claim by other means which would necessarily have entailed the adducing of oral

---

107   [1999] 2 AC 330, HL, at 344F–345C.
108   [2001] UKHL 23, [2003] 2 AC 295 at [53]–[54].
109   [2001] EWCA Civ 1545, [2002] 1 WLR 419. See generally the analysis in the judgment of Simon Brown LJ at [24]–[36], with which Brooke LJ and Hale LJ agreed.
110   [2001] EWCA Civ 1545 at [26].

evidence – such as an action in tort against the hospital authority for assault, or a claim under the HRA 1998 itself, for breach of Convention rights. The court would accordingly order the attendance of the doctors for cross-examination and conduct a 'full merits' review of the propriety of the treatment proposed.[111]

6.62   The *Wilkinson* decision was considered in *Adan v Newham LBC*.[112] In that case, it was argued that on an appeal on a point of law (applying judicial review principles), the court, in the exercise of its supervisory jurisdiction, could reverse a 'material error of fact' if it considered that the fact which had been found was 'wrong'. The majority of the Court of Appeal[113] rejected this argument which was contrary to 'very powerful judicial statements throughout the common law world'.[114] The court held that it was

> quite clear ... that a court of supervisory jurisdiction does not, without more, have the power to substitute its own view of the primary facts for the view reasonably adopted by the body to whom the fact-finding power has been entrusted.[115]

6.63   Simon Brown LJ returned to this topic as a member of the Divisional Court in *R (Mullen) v Secretary of State for the Home Department*.[116] In that case, there was no dispute of fact at all, just a question of whether, on the true construction of Criminal Justice Act 1988 s133 (compensation for victims of miscarriages of justice) the claimant was entitled to compensation in circumstances where his conviction had been set aside by the Court of Appeal, notwithstanding that the finding of guilt was not challenged, on the basis that his trial constituted an abuse of process due to his having been illegally returned to the United Kingdom from Zimbabwe.

6.64   The court rejected an argument that judicial review was not an adequate remedy for the purposes of article 6 of the Convention, not only because there was no issue of fact involved but on a broader basis. The court could well envisage a case in which a factual dispute may arise, which would raise the issue of the appropriate intensity of review on a judicial review application:[117]

---

111 [2001] EWCA Civ 1545 at para [36].
112 [2001] EWCA Civ 1916, [2002] 1 WLR 2120, CA.
113 The majority included Brooke LJ who had been a member of the Court of Appeal in *Wilkinson*. The dissenting judge was Hale LJ who had also been a member of the *Wilkinson* Court of Appeal.
114 [2001] EWCA Civ 1916, per Brooke LJ at [36].
115 [2001] EWCA Civ 1916 at [41].
116 [2002] EWHC 230 (Admin), [2002] 1 WLR 1857.
117 [2002] EWHC 230 (Admin), per Simon Brown LJ at [30].

As the recent Court of Appeal decision in *R (Wilkinson) v Broad-moor Special Hospital Authority* ... amply demonstrates, the Court on judicial review can and will if necessary assess any relevant facts for itself even to the extent of ordering the attendance of witnesses for cross-examination.

6.65 The decision of the Divisional Court was reversed on appeal to the Court of Appeal,[118] but subsequently reinstated by the House of Lords,[119] by which time the issues had become matters of statutory construction and review of discretion.

6.66 The position, then, as to the extent of the judicial review court's power to entertain factual challenges in fundamental rights cases seems relatively clear. In *S v Airedale NHS Trust*,[120] oral expert evidence was given in a challenge to a decision to seclude a patient in a non-secure hospital. In *R (PG) v Ealing LBC*,[121] Munby J, while confirming the power of the Administrative Court to hear oral evidence, stated that *Wilkinson* plainly indicated that there would be judicial review cases in which cross-examination will be appropriate, or even essential, and cases in which compliance by the court with the Convention would demand cross-examination as part of a more intense review. Recourse to such powers would, nevertheless, be very much the exception, and the overwhelming bulk of judicial review cases would continue to be determined without oral evidence.

6.67 This has been confirmed in general terms by the House of Lords in *Begum v Tower Hamlets LBC*,[122] although neither *Wilkinson* nor *Mullen* was referred to in the speeches in that case. The judicial committee confirmed, nonetheless, that on an appeal to the county court on a point of law, in a homelessness case, where only article 6 of the Convention was in issue (ie no other Convention rights were at stake), no more intensive approach to judicial review of questions of fact was mandated, and the conventional bases of intervention in factual issues (ie no evidence to support a finding of fact, perverse finding or finding made having regard to irrelevant factors or having

---

118 [2002] EWCA Civ 1882, [2003] QB 993.
119 [2004] UKHL 18, [2005] 1 AC 1.
120 [2002] EWHC 1780 (Admin), [2003] Lloyd's Rep Med 21 (an appeal against the outcome of the decision was allowed by the Court of Appeal, where it was heard with *R (Munjaz) v Mersey Care NHS Trust* [2003] EWCA Civ 1036, [2004] QB 395. *Munjaz* was, in turn, overturned by the House of Lords: [2005] UKHL 58, [2006] 2 AC 148. It seems that the factual challenges were not in issue on the appeals). See also *R (N) v M* [2002] EWHC 1911 (Admin), [2003] ACD 17.
121 Also reported as *R (G) v Ealing LBC (No 2)* [2002] EWHC 250 (Admin), [2002] ACD 48.
122 [2003] UKHL 5, [2003] 2 AC 430.

no regard to relevant ones) would generally be sufficient.[123] The court could not substitute its own findings of fact for those of the decision-making authority if there was evidence to support them. Questions regarding the weight to be given to a particular piece of evidence and on the credibility of witnesses was a matter for the decision-making authority and not for the court.[124]

Relevant and irrelevant considerations

6.68   A decision-maker must take into account all relevant considerations before making its decision and must ignore the irrelevant.[125] Which factors are relevant and which irrelevant will, of course, depend on the facts of the individual case.

6.69   While generally, the weight to be given to a relevant consideration is a matter for the decision-maker, with which the court will not interfere, it may sometimes be unlawful for a decision-maker to pay too much regard to a relevant consideration. In *R v Winchester CC ex p Ashton*,[126] for example, Purchas LJ held that:

> Parliament could never have intended [the prevailing housing circumstances in the local authority's area][127] to be more than something to which a local authority may have regard and I do not think Mr Stephenson would submit that it is or should be the overall determining factor. It is something that must be weighed carefully in the balance with the other factors upon which the decision under Housing Act 1996 s60(1) is reached.

6.70   Similarly, in *South Oxfordshire DC v Secretary of State for the Environment*,[128] Woolf J held that while the planning history of a matter may be a material consideration, it was hard to see, in the context of the case, how it could have been, as the Secretary of State contended:[129]

---

123 [2003] UKHL 5, per Lord Hoffmann at [49]–[50]. See also Lord Bingham of Cornhill at [7].

124 [2003] UKHL 5, per Lord Millett at [99]. See also *Bubb v Wandsworth LBC* [2011] EWCA Civ 1285, [2012] PTSR 1011, [2012] HLR 13.

125 *Associated Provincial Picture Houses v Wednesbury Corporation* [1948] 1 KB 223, CA; *CCSU v Minister of State for the Civil Service* [1985] AC 374, HL.

126 (1991) 24 HLR 520, CA, at 527.

127 A factor the local authority is entitled to take into account in deciding whether or not it was reasonable to expect a homeless person to have remained in accommodation for the purposes of deciding whether or not that person is homeless and/or intentionally homeless. In *Ashton*, the relevant statutory provision was Housing Act 1985 s60(4); now, see Housing Act 1996 s177(2).

128 [1981] 1 WLR 1092, QBD.

129 [1981] 1 WLR 1092 at 1099.

... a vitally material consideration ... While the weight to be given to a particular consideration is for the Secretary of State, such a conclusion indicates that either the ... Secretary of State misdirected himself, or he was acting perversely.

6.71   These cases could also be classified as cases involving misdirections of law: the decision-maker had fallen into legal error by misunderstanding the difference between a relevant factor to be taken into account and a factor that was conclusive to the issue under consideration.

6.72   In *R (Daly) v Secretary of State for the Home Department*,[130] Lord Steyn suggested that the doctrine of proportionality differed from the principles of *Wednesbury* review in this regard, so that where the court was exercising a proportionality jurisdiction, it may be appropriate and necessary for the attention of the court to be directed to the relative weight attached to the various relevant interests and considerations.[131] In subsequent cases, the courts have held that, when conducting a proportionality review of a decision, it may be necessary for a court to consider and even determine matters of fact relevant to the proportionality of the decision for itself.[132]

What considerations?

6.73   Some considerations must be taken into account, or left out of account, because the legislation under which the decision is taken so provides, whether expressly or impliedly. Failure to take a statutorily relevant consideration into account, or leave a statutorily irrelevant one out of account, will invalidate the decision.[133]

6.74   **Public Sector Equality Duty** One of the most important general considerations that authorities are statutorily directed to take into account is provided by Equality Act 2010 s149: the Public Sector Equality Duty (PSED).[134]

130 [2001] UKHL 26, [2001] 2 AC 532.

131 See para 6.21 above.

132 See *Manchester CC v Pinnock* [2010] UKSC 45, [2011] 2 AC 104, per Lord Neuberger at [73] and [104]. See also *Corby BC v Scott* [2012] EWCA Civ 276, [2012] HLR 23, per Lord Neuberger MR at [28].

133 *Re Findlay* [1985] AC 318, HL, per Lord Scarman at 333–4 approving *CREEDNZ Inc v Governor-General* [1981] 1 NZLR 172. See also *R v Secretary of State for Transport ex p Richmond-upon-Thames LBC (No 1)* [1994] 1 WLR 74, QBD.

134 The PSED is the successor to individual duties in relation to race, disability and gender (Race Relations Act 1976 s71, Disability Discrimination Act 1995 s49A, Sex Discrimination Act 1975 s76A), which were repealed on 5 April 2011 (although Disability Discrimination Act 1995 s49A remains in force in Northern Ireland)). The first of these duties, the race equality duty (inserted

6.75   Section 149(1) provides that certain specified authorities[135] must, in the exercise of their functions, have 'due regard' to the need to eliminate unlawful discrimination, harassment and victimisation and to advance equality of opportunity[136] and foster good relations between persons with 'protected characteristics' and others.

6.76   The 'protected characteristics' for the purposes of the equality duty are:[137]

- age,
- disability,
- gender reassignment,
- pregnancy and maternity,
- race,
- religion or belief,
- sex, and
- sexual orientation.[138]

6.77   The duty to have 'due regard' is unqualified.[139] It applies not only to formulation of policies, but also to the application of those policies

into the Race Relations Act 1976 by Race Relations (Amendment) Act 2000 s2, to extend the previous general duty on local authorities) arose from the Macpherson Report (Home Office *The Stephen Lawrence Inquiry: Report of an Inquiry by Sir William Macpherson of Cluny* (Cm 4262–I, February 1999)), which found 'institutional racism' in the Metropolitan Police, following failures of the investigation into the racially-motivated murder of Stephen Lawrence. Until the introduction of the race equality duty, the legislative emphasis had been on dealing with cases of discrimination after the event. The race equality duty and the subsequent disability and gender equality duties were designed to bring about a shift towards promoting equality.

135 Set out in Equality Act 2010 Sch 19. Additionally, authorities not specified in Sch 19, but who exercise public functions are subject to the PSED in the exercise of those functions. A 'public function' is defined by reference to the HRA 1998 s6 test: Equality Act 2010 s150(5). On functions of a public nature see further paras 2.80–2.103.

136 Having due regard to the need to advance equality of opportunity involves, *inter alia*, having due regard, in particular, to the need to remove or minimise disadvantages suffered by persons who share a relevant protected characteristic that are connected to that characteristic, and taking steps to meet the needs of persons who share a relevant protected characteristic that are different from the needs of persons who do not share it: Equality Act 2010 s149(3). The steps involved in meeting the needs of disabled persons that are different from the needs of persons who are not disabled include, in particular, steps to take account of disabled persons' disabilities (s149(4)). Compliance with the s149 duties may involve treating some persons more favourably than others (s149(6)).

137 Equality Act 2010 s149(7).

138 The characteristics are defined in Equality Act 2010 ss5–7 and 9–12.

139 *R (Meany) v Harlow DC* [2009] EWHC 559 (Admin), [61].

in individual cases.[140] Due regard is the regard that is appropriate in all the circumstances, which is primarily a matter for the authority, subject to review by the court.[141] The court must ensure, however, that it does not micro-manage the process.[142]

6.78   In *R (Baker) v Secretary of State for Communities and Local Government*,[143] Dyson LJ said[144] that:

> The question in every case is whether the decision-maker has in substance had due regard to the relevant statutory need. Just as the use of a mantra referring to the statutory provision does not of itself show that the duty has been performed, so too a failure to refer expressly to the statute does not of itself show that the duty has not been performed. ... To see whether the duty has been performed, it is necessary to turn to the substance of the decision and its reasoning.

6.79   Compliance is important 'not as a rearguard action following a concluded decision but as an essential preliminary to any such decision. Inattention to it is both unlawful and bad government.'[145]

6.80   While section 149 of the 2010 Act imposes no specific duty to undertake a formal equality impact assessment,[146] the authority must be able to demonstrate in some way that it has fulfilled the substantive requirements of the duty during the decision-making process in issue. In *R (Brown) v Secretary of State for Work and Pensions*,[147] the Divisional Court laid down six general principles as to how a public authority may demonstrate that it has done so:[148]

> ... First, those in the public authority who have to take decisions that do or might affect disabled people must be made aware of their duty to have 'due regard' to the identified goals ... Thus, an incomplete or

---

140 *Pieretti v Enfield LBC* [2010] EWCA Civ 1104, [2011] PTSR 565, [2011] HLR 3. See also, *Barnsley MBC v Norton* [2011] EWCA Civ 834, [2012] PTSR 56, [2011] HLR 46 at [15].

141 *R (Baker) v Secretary of State for Communities and Local Government* [2008] EWCA Civ 141, [2009] PTSR 809 at [31].

142 *R (Greenwich Community Law Centre) v Greenwich LBC* [2012] EWCA Civ 496, [2012] EqLR 572, per Elias LJ at [30], referred to in *R (Buckley) v Sheffield CC* [2013] EWHC 512 (Admin), per Supperstone J at [38].

143 [2008] EWCA Civ 141, [2009] PTSR 809.

144 At [37].

145 *R (BAPIO) v Secretary of State for the Home Department* [2007] EWCA Civ 1139 at [3] (on Race Relations Act 1976 s71).

146 *R (Brown) v Secretary of State for Work and Pensions* [2008] EWHC 3158 (Admin), [2009] PTSR 1506 at [89].

147 [2008] EWHC 3158 (Admin), [2009] PTSR 1506.

148 [2008] EWHC 3158 (Admin) at [90]–[96].

erroneous appreciation of the duties will mean that 'due regard' has not been given to them ...

Secondly, the 'due regard' duty must be fulfilled before and at the time that a particular policy that will or might affect disabled people is being considered by the public authority in question. It involves a conscious approach and state of mind. ... Attempts to justify a decision as being consistent with the exercise of the duty when it was not, in fact, considered before the decision, are not enough to discharge the duty ...

Thirdly, the duty must be exercised in substance, with rigour and with an open mind. The duty has to be integrated within the discharge of the public functions of the authority. It is not a question of 'ticking boxes'...

However, the fact that the public authority has not mentioned specifically section 49A(1)[149] in carrying out the particular function where it has to have 'due regard' to the needs set out in the section is not determinative of whether the duty under the statute has been performed ... But it is good practice for the policy or decision maker to make reference to the provision and any code or other non-statutory guidance in all cases where section 49A(1) is in play. ...

Fourthly, the duty imposed on public authorities that are subject to the section 49A(1) duty is a non-delegable duty. The duty will always remain on the public authority charged with it. ...

Fifthly, and obviously, the duty is a continuing one.

Sixthly, it is good practice for those exercising public functions in public authorities to keep an adequate record showing that they had actually considered their disability equality duties and pondered relevant questions. Proper record-keeping encourages transparency and will discipline those carrying out the relevant function to undertake their disability equality duties conscientiously. If records are not kept it may make it more difficult, evidentially, for a public authority to persuade a court that it has fulfilled the duty imposed by section 49A(1)....

6.81   In *R (Harris) v Haringey LBC*,[150] the Court of Appeal rejected an argument by the local authority that equality duty considerations were effectively built into the decision-making process because the development brief for the area and the relevant planning policies themselves reflected those considerations. The court emphasised the need for the authority to consider actively in the context of the duty the material that was before it.

---

149 Disability Discrimination Act 1995 s49A(1), a predecessor to the current PSED.

150 [2010] EWCA Civ 703, [2011] PTSR 931.

6.82   There is no formal duty for an authority to carry out a formal equality impact assessment,[151] nor need express reference to the PSED be made for the duty to be properly discharged, although it is good practice to do so: *R (Brown) v Secretary of State for Work and Pensions,*[152]. Indeed, where an authority is discharging its functions under other statutory provisions, which expressly direct their attention to the needs of disabled persons, it may be entirely superfluous to make express reference to the PSED.[153]

6.83   The due regard duty is not theoretical, or an exercise in speculation.

> ... it is only if a characteristic or combination of characteristics is likely to arise in the exercise of the public function that they need be taken into consideration. I would only add the qualification that there may be cases where that possibility exists in which case there may be a need for further investigation before that characteristic can be ignored: see the observations of Elias LJ in *Hurley and Moore* para 96.[154] (Perhaps more accurately it may be said that whilst the Council has to have due regard to all aspects of the duty, some of them may immediately be rejected as plainly irrelevant to the exercise of the function under consideration – no doubt often subliminally and without being consciously addressed. As Davis LJ observed in *Bailey,*[155] para 91, it is then a matter of semantics whether one says that the duty is not engaged or that it is engaged but the matter is ruled out as irrelevant or insignificant).[156]

6.84   Thus although the duty is imposed on the authority, and it is not for challengers to tell them how that should be done if a breach of

---

151 *R (Domb) v Hammersmith and Fulham LBC* [2009] EWCA Civ 941, per Rix LJ at [52].

152 [2008] EWHC 3158 (Admin), [2009] PTSR 1506 at [93]. See also *R (Luton BC) v Secretary of State for Education* [2011] EWHC 217 (Admin), [2011] BLGR 553

153 *R (McDonald) v Kensington and Chelsea RLBC* [2011] UKSC 33, [2011] PTSR 1266, per Lord Brown at [24]. This passage in *McDonald* concerned Disability Discrimination Act 1995 s49A, but the same principle should apply to any of the protected characteristics referred to in Equality Act 2010 s149 (although there are probably less statutory provisions expressly directed at other relevant characteristics than there are for disability). See also *R (Rajput) v Waltham Forest LBC* [2011] EWCA Civ 1577, [2012] BLGR 506 and *R (Greenwich Community Law Centre) v Greenwich LBC* [2012] EWCA Civ 496, [2012] Eq LR 572.

154 *R (Hurley and Moore) v Secretary of State for Business Innovation & Skills* [2012] EWHC 201 (Admin), [2012] HRLR 13.

155 *R (Bailey) v Brent LBC* [2011] EWCA Civ 1586, [2012] BLGR 530.

156 *R (Greenwich Community Law Centre) v Greenwich LBC* [2012] EWCA Civ 496, [2012] EqLR 572, per Elias LJ at [30].

duty is alleged, the claimant should at least identify some protected characteristic that might realistically be said to have been engaged and yet was not considered.[157] As Davis LJ said, in *Bailey*:

> Councils cannot be expected to speculate on or to investigate or to explore such matters *ad infinitum*; nor can they be expected to apply, indeed they are to be discouraged from applying, the degree of forensic analysis for the purpose of an EIA and of consideration of their duties under s.149 which a QC might deploy in court.[158]

6.85 **Other examples** Some examples of other statutorily relevant/irrelevant matters are as follows.

- Housing Act 1996 ss169(1) and 182(1) require that a local authority in performing its functions under Parts 6 (allocations) and 7 (assistance for homeless persons) of that Act must have regard to any guidance given by the Secretary of State.[159]
- Local planning authorities are obliged to have regard to the applicable development plan and any local finance considerations when considering planning applications.[160]
- Social services authorities must have regard to the views of specified categories of person when accommodating or looking after a child.[161]

6.86 In *R v Oadby and Wigston BC ex p Dickman*,[162] Buxton J, construing housing benefit regulations, held that factors described in a regulation as 'the relevant factors' in relation to whether a claimant could be expected to move, were the only factors that an authority were entitled to take into consideration:[163]

> Otherwise, the implication is that the authority is bound to take into account a factor which has been said to be not irrelevant, or at least not to be relevant. That is a conclusion I do not think is likely or even lawful.

157 *R (Greenwich Community Law Centre) v Greenwich LBC* [2012] EWCA Civ 496, [2012] Eq LR 572, per Elias LJ at [34].
158 *R (Bailey) v Brent LBC* [2011] EWCA Civ 1586, [2012] BLGR 530, per Davis LJ at [102].
159 And see on this point *R v Wandsworth LBC ex p Hawthorne* [1994] 1 WLR 1442, CA.
160 Town and Country Planning Act 1990 s70.
161 Children Act 1989 ss20(6) and 22(4).
162 (1996) 28 HLR 806, QBD.
163 (1996) 28 HLR 806 at 817.

Subsequently, however, this analysis was not followed; the statutory factors were intended to be no more than matters that were relevant.[164]

6.87   See also *R v Secretary of State for the Environment ex p Lancashire CC*,[165] in which it was held that mandatory statutory criteria could not be supplemented by guidance.[166]

6.88   Conversely, statute may provide for matters that a decision-maker is not to take into account when reaching a decision. For example, if public supply or works contracts are under consideration, a local authority is statutorily prohibited from taking account of 'non-commercial considerations'.[167]

Non-specified factors

6.89   Where statute has not intervened, it will be for the decision-maker to decide what matters are relevant for consideration or should be left out of account as irrelevant. The court will only intervene in that decision on the ground of *Wednesbury* unreasonableness,[168] although the position may be different where fundamental rights are at stake and the court approaches the issue under the rubric of proportionality.[169]

6.90   In this situation, it is extremely difficult and almost inevitably misleading to attempt to make general propositions regarding factors that may or may not be relevant. The courts have, on occasion, suggested factors that must generally be considered. In *R v Lincolnshire CC and Wealden DC ex p Atkinson*,[170] for example, Sedley J stated that

---

164 See *R v Housing Benefit Review Board for Allerdale District Council ex p Doughty* (CO/2362/98), (2000) 25 May, unreported, per Elias J at [54]–[64].

165 [1994] 4 All ER 165, QBD.

166 See also, eg, *R v Highbury Corner Metropolitan Stipendiary Magistrate ex p Di Matteo* [1991] 1 WLR 1374; *London Residuary Body v Lambeth LBC* [1990] 1 WLR 744; *R v Secretary of State for Trade and Industry ex p Lonrho plc* [1989] 1 WLR 525, HL.

167 Local Government Act 1988 s17(1), although non-commercial matters can be taken into account to the extent necessary to comply with the public sector equality duty (1988 Act s17(10)), and to the extent required by s1, Public Services (Social Value) Act 2012 s1 (1988 Act s17(11)).

168 See, eg, *R v Secretary of State for Transport ex p Richmond upon Thames LBC* [1994] 1 WLR 74, per Laws J at 95. See also *R v Southwark LBC ex p Cordwell* (1994) 26 HLR 107, QBD. See also *South Buckinghamshire DC v Porter* [2003] UKHL 26, [2003] 2 AC 558.

169 See the discussion of *R (Daly) v Secretary of State for the Home Department* [2001] UKHL 26, [2001] 2 AC 532, and of *Manchester CC v Pinnock* [2010] UKSC 45, [2011] 2 AC 104, and *Corby BC v Scott* [2012] EWCA Civ 276, [2012] HLR 23 at paras 6.20–6.28 above.

170 (1995) 8 Admin LR 529, QBD, at 535.

government guidance would be of relevance in any case, regardless of whether there was a statutory obligation to consider it, on the basis that such guidance will indicate matters which are themselves relevant. In *R (Ali) v Newham LBC*,[171] Kenneth Parker J said that:[172]

> ... the weight that should be given to particular guidance depends upon the specific context in which the guidance has been produced. In particular (without intending to create an exhaustive list) I believe that it is necessary to give due regard to the authorship of the guidance, the quality and intensity of the work done in the production of the guidance, the extent to which the (possibly competing) interests of those who are likely to be affected by the guidance have been recognised and weighed, the importance of any more general public policy that the guidance has sought to promote, and the express terms of the guidance itself. In my view, it would be unwise for the court to descend into the intrinsic merits of the guidance, unless it was seriously contended that it was unlawful or very obviously defective.

6.91 It has also been said that local authorities are, absent any statutory inhibition, entitled to act in the best interests of their inhabitants.[173] Where fundamental needs are in issue, considerations of 'common humanity' have also been held to be relevant.[174] A recommendation of the Local Government Ombudsman does not have to be implemented by the local authority concerned but in deciding whether to do so the authority must take into account relevant considerations, such as if it has been guilty of maladministration or if the individual concerned has suffered serious distress or anxiety.[175]

6.92 A person's Convention rights would now appear, inevitably, to be relevant.

6.93 Beyond this, however, the question of what is or is not relevant will depend on the specific decision that falls to be made and the statutory framework within which it arises. The relevance of certain considerations that decision-makers have taken into account has repeatedly come before the courts in different contexts. Even the general points made above are heavily dependent on context. Common humanity, for example, will not always be relevant. In *R v Somerset*

---

171 [2012] EWHC 2970 (Admin), [2013] Eq LR 40.
172 [2012] EWHC 2970 (Admin) at [39].
173 *South Hams DC v Slough* (1992) 25 HLR 189, (1992) 91 LGR 202, CA, adopted in *R v South Hams DC ex p Gibb* [1995] QB 158, CA. See now Local Government Act 2000 ss2–3 and Localism Act 2011 ss1–2.
174 *R v Lincolnshire CC and Wealden DC ex p Atkinson* (1995) 8 Admin LR 529, QBD. See also *South Buckinghamshire DC v Porter* [2003] UKHL 26, [2003] 2 AC 558; *R v Hillingdon LBC ex p McDonagh* (1998) 31 HLR 531.
175 *R (Gallagher) v Basildon DC* [2010] EWHC 2824 (Admin), [2011] PTSR 731.

CC ex p Fewings,[176] for example, it was held that questions of cruelty and morality were not capable of being relevant to a decision to ban fox-hunting on the authority's land in the context of an obligation to manage that land for the 'benefit, improvement or development of their area'. The same conclusion may not be reached today.

Financial resources

6.94   This consideration has been held to be relevant in some contexts but not in others. In *R v Gloucestershire CC ex p Barry*,[177] the House of Lords held that an authority could take account of its limited financial resources in deciding whether a person was in need of services under Chronically Sick and Disabled Persons Act 1970 s2, and as to the services necessary to meet any identified needs. Once it had been decided that specific services were necessary, however, a lack of resources could not excuse a failure to provide them. See also *R v Sefton MBC ex p Help the Aged*,[178] holding that resources were relevant to whether a person needed services under the National Assistance Act 1948; and *R v Norfolk CC ex p Thorpe*,[179] where resources were held to be relevant to a decision whether it was necessary or desirable to provide a pedestrian footway under the Highways Act 1980.

6.95   The Supreme Court has recently held that, generally, when deciding whether to exercise a statutory power, an authority must have regard to the cost to the public of so doing, at least to the extent of considering more economic ways of achieving the same objective: *Health and Safety Executive v Wolverhampton CC*.[180] Lord Carnwath said:[181]

> ... In simple terms, the question is whether a public authority, when deciding whether to exercise a discretionary power to achieve a public objective, is entitled to take into account the cost to the public of so doing.

---

176   [1995] 1 WLR 1037. Simon Brown LJ dissented from this proposition, holding that such factors were necessarily relevant and could even be treated as decisive so long as other relevant matters were not left out of account. On its facts, this case has now been overtaken by the Hunting Act 2004. See also *R (Countryside Alliance) v Attorney General* [2007] UKHL 52, [2008] 1 AC 719.

177   [1997] AC 584, HL.

178   [1997] 4 All ER 532, CA.

179   (1998) 96 LGR 597, CA.

180   [2012] UKSC 34, [2012] 1 WLR 2264.

181   [2012] UKSC 34 at [24]–[25]. See also *R (McDonald) v Kensington and Chelsea RLBC* [2011] UKSC 33, [2011] PTSR 1266; *R (KM) v Cambridgeshire CC* [2012] UKSC 23, [2012] PTSR 1189.

Posed in that way, the question answers itself. As custodian of public funds, the authority not only may, but generally must, have regard to the cost to the public of its actions, at least to the extent of considering in any case whether the cost is proportionate to the aim to be achieved, and taking account of any more economic ways of achieving the same objective. Of course, the weight attributable to cost considerations will vary with the context. Where, for example, the authority is faced with an imminent threat to public security within its sphere of responsibility, cost could rarely be a valid reason for doing nothing, but could well be relevant to the choice between effective alternatives. So much is not only sound administrative practice, but common sense.

6.96   Conversely, in *R v East Sussex CC ex p Tandy*,[182] the House of Lords held that the question of resources was irrelevant to the question of what constituted a suitable education for a child with special educational needs. The fact that there may have been other calls on the authority's resources did not establish that the authority enjoyed insufficient resources to comply with the statutory duty, but rather that the authority preferred to use its resources for other purposes. To permit this would be to downgrade a duty to provide a suitable education to a mere power.[183] See also *R v Birmingham CC ex p Mohammed*,[184] where resources were held to be irrelevant to the question of whether to award a disabled facilities grant; *R v Bristol CC ex p Penfold*,[185] where resources were not relevant to the issue of whether a person may be in need of community care services; *R (Khan) v Newham LBC*,[186] in which the authority's resources were not relevant to the issue of whether the court should require it to comply with its duty to secure suitable accommodation for a homeless person. Similarly, in *R (Conville) v Richmond upon Thames LBC*,[187] it was held that when an authority decides the period for which it should secure that accommodation is available so as to give a homeless applicant a reasonable opportunity of securing accommodation for himself, it may not have regard to considerations peculiar to itself, such as the extent of its resources.[188]

182 [1998] AC 714, HL.
183 [1998] AC 714, per Lord Browne Wilkinson at 891–2.
184 [1999] 1 WLR 33, QBD.
185 (1997–98) 1 CCLR 315, CA.
186 [2001] EWHC 589 (Admin).
187 [2006] EWCA Civ 718, [2006] 1 WLR 2808.
188 A duty owed under Housing Act 1996 s190(2)(a).

Forthcoming legislation

6.97 Future legislation that will affect the powers of a decision-maker is a factor that has been held relevant to the exercise of a current power.[189]

6.98 Current powers may also be used to prepare for the coming into force of new powers.[190] Thus, where a local authority's licensing officer had delegated functions to a sub-committee under powers contained in the Licensing Act 2003, but before those powers had come into force, the sub-committee's decision was upheld because the delegation was consistent with the authority's need to take preparatory steps before the 2003 Act came into force, and the authority did in fact enjoy current power to delegate, albeit under a different legislative scheme (the Local Government Act 1972).[191]

6.99 The intention of forthcoming legislation to abolish regional strategies was a material consideration for a local planning authority to take into account when determining a planning application.[192]

Frustrating the policy of an Act

6.100 The decision-maker must act to promote, rather than to defeat the policy and objects of an Act, or other source that created the power in question.

6.101 In *Padfield v Minister of Agriculture, Fisheries and Food*,[193] Lord Reid said:[194]

> ... [the Minister] contends that his only duty ... is to consider a complaint fairly and that he is given an unfettered discretion with regard to every complaint either to refer it or not to refer it to the committee as he may think fit ... It is implicit in the argument for the Minister ... that either he must refer every complaint or he has an unfettered discretion to refuse to refer any case. I do not think that is right. Parliament must have conferred the discretion with the intention that it should be used to promote the policy and objects of the Act ... [I]f the Minister, by reason of his having misconstrued the Act or for any

189 See *R v Secretary of State for the Environment ex p Birmingham CC* [1987] RVR 53, DC. Such legislation does not act as a prohibition on the use of current powers: *Re Westminster CC* [1986] AC 668, HL.

190 *R v Secretary of State for Health ex p Keen* (1990) 3 Admin LR 180, QBD.

191 *R (Raphael) v Highbury Corner Magistrates' Court* [2010] EWHC 1502 (Admin), [2011] PTSR 152.

192 *R (Cala Homes (South) Ltd) v Secretary of State for Communities and Local Government* [2011] EWCA Civ 639, [2011] 2 EGLR 75. See also para 13.5 below.

193 [1968] AC 997, HL.

194 [1968] AC 997 at 1031–2.

other reason, so uses his discretion as to thwart or run counter to the policy and objects of the Act, then our law would be very defective if persons aggrieved were not entitled to the protection of the court.

6.102 This principle has been confirmed in numerous cases including *R v Secretary of State for the Home Department ex p Brind*,[195] where Lord Ackner stated that the Secretary of State's power could only be used 'to advance the purposes for which it was conferred' and 'to promote the policy and objects of the Act'.[196]

6.103 In *M v Scottish Ministers*,[197] the ministers were given a power under the Mental Health (Care and Treatment) (Scotland) Act 2003 to make regulations concerning the ability of patients compulsorily detained in hospital to make applications to a mental health tribunal. The ministers did not make any such regulations, which were necessary to give practical effect to provisions in the 2003 Act. It was held that their failure to do so had thwarted the intention of the Scottish Parliament and was therefore unlawful.

Fettering of discretion

6.104 A decision-maker must reach its own decision on each individual case. It must not fetter its discretion by approaching a decision with a predetermined policy on how all cases falling within a particular class will be treated. This, of course, does not mean that policies are unlawful per se; very little public administration could be conducted without them.[198] It simply means that the decision-maker must approach each case on its own merits and must leave its mind 'ajar'[199] and be prepared to listen to someone with something new to say.

6.105 In *British Oxygen Co Ltd v Minister of Technology*,[200] the Board of Trade had power to make grants towards capital expenditure for new

---

195 [1991] 1 AC 696, HL.

196 [1991] 1 AC 696 at 756. See also *R v Warwickshire CC ex p Williams* [1995] ELR 326; *R v Secretary of State for the Home Department ex p Fire Brigades Union* [1995] 2 AC 513, HL; *R v Secretary of State for the Home Department ex p Yousaf* [2000] 3 All ER 649, CA.

197 [2012] UKSC 58, [2012] 1 WLR 3386.

198 A point emphasised by the House of Lords in *R v Eastleigh BC ex p Betts* [1983] 2 AC 613, HL. Indeed, see *R v Secretary of State for the Home Department ex p Hepworth* [1998] COD 146, QBD, for a policy (of incentives for prisoners) which was upheld even though it admitted of no exceptions and operated as a 'black-and-white' rule. See below, para 6.108 and note 207.

199 *R v Secretary of State for the Environment ex p Brent LBC* [1982] QB 593, DC.

200 [1971] AC 610, HL.

machinery or plant. The Board adopted a policy of refusing grants for any item costing less than £25 each. Lord Reid stated:[201]

> ... the general rule is that anyone who has to exercise a statutory discretion must not 'shut his ears to an application' ... What the authority must not do is to refuse to listen at all. But a Ministry or large authority may have had to deal already with a multitude of similar applications and then they will almost certainly have evolved a policy so precise that it could well be called a rule. There can be no objection to that, provided the authority is always willing to listen to anyone with something new to say. Of course I do not mean to say that there need be an oral hearing.

6.106   In *R v Eastleigh Borough Council ex p Betts*,[202] Lord Brightman expressed the same concept in the following terms:[203]

> '... provided that the authority do not close their mind to the particular facts of the individual case ... a body which is charged with exercising an administrative discretion is entitled to promulgate a policy or guidelines as an indication of a norm which is intended to be followed ...

6.107   In *R v Secretary of State for the Home Department ex p Venables*,[204] Lord Browne-Wilkinson summarised the position in similar terms, stating that a discretionary power conferred by Parliament:[205]

> ... must be exercised on each occasion in the light of the circumstances at that time. In consequence, the person on whom the power is conferred cannot fetter the future exercise of his discretion by committing himself now as to the way in which he will exercise his power in the future ... These considerations do not preclude the ... [decision-maker] from developing and applying a policy as to the approach which he will adopt in the generality of cases ... But the position is different if the policy which he has adopted is such as to preclude the ... [decision-maker] from departing from the policy or from taking into account circumstances which are relevant to the particular case ... If such an inflexible and invariable policy is adopted, both the policy and the decisions taken pursuant to it will be unlawful ...

---

201 [1971] AC 610 at 625.
202 [1983] 2 AC 613, HL.
203 [1983] 2 AC 613 at 627H–628A.
204 [1998] AC 407, HL.
205 [1998] AC 407 at 496–7. See also, more recently, *R (Gujra) v Crown Prosecution Service* [2012] UKSC 52, [2013] 1 AC 484, per Lord Kerr at [76].

6.108   On the other hand, the position may be different where the function in question involves making a scheme with rules.[206] Thus, a rule was lawful that automatically debarred persons convicted of certain criminal offences from being treated as fit and proper for the purpose of obtaining a door supervisor's licence for a period of years after they became free from the effects of the conviction: *R (Nicholds) v Security Industry Authority.*[207]

6.109   A different aspect of the possible fettering of a decision-maker's discretion was discussed, somewhat more controversially, in *Bromley LBC v Greater London Council.*[208] The Greater London Council (GLC) had introduced a scheme of subsidised fares for public transport in London, causing it to increase its precept on the London borough councils. The House of Lords held that the GLC owed a fiduciary duty to the ratepayers to have regard to their interests, and that it was in breach of that duty in failing to balance fairly the interests of the ratepayers and transport users, thus casting an inordinate burden on the ratepayers. Lord Diplock, in the course of his speech, made the following remarks:[209]

> I see no difference between members of ... the majority party and those who are members of a minority party. In neither case, when the time comes to play their part in performing the collective duty of the GLC to make choices of policy or action on particular matters, must members treat themselves as irrevocably bound to carry out pre-announced policies contained in election manifestos even though, by that time, changes of circumstances have occurred that were unforeseen when those policies were announced and would add significantly to the disadvantages that would result from carrying them out.

206   There is also some suggestion that the rule against fettering does not apply to decisions made under prerogative powers: *R (Elias) v Secretary of State for Defence* [2006] EWCA Civ 1293, [2006] 1 WLR 3213 at [191].

207   [2006] EWHC 1792 (Admin), [2007] 1 WLR 2067. See also, *R v Secretary of State for the Home Department ex p Hepworth* [1998] COD 146, where it was permissible to have fixed criteria for incentives within a prison; and *R (P) v Secretary of State for the Home Department* (2002) 17 May, unreported, where a policy without exceptions relating to the escape of dangerous prisoners was also upheld. It is interesting that in two recent challenges to local authority schemes for reducing the liability for certain council taxpayers, no complaint was made about the schemes in question having fixed rules: *R (Stirling) v Haringey LBC* [2013] EWCA Civ 116; *R (Buckley) v Sheffield CC* [2013] EWHC 512 (Admin).

208   [1983] 1 AC 768, HL.

209   [1983] 1 AC 768 at 829.

Unlawful delegation or dictation

6.110　The decision must be made by the decision-maker to whom it has been entrusted. Decision-makers cannot avoid their duties by allowing themselves to be dictated to by, or simply accepting the decision of, another body. Furthermore, decision-makers may not delegate their decisions to others unless they have specific power to do so and have done so properly. Where a body or official, without the power to do so, purports to reach a decision, that decision is void in law and the true decision-maker has, as a matter of law, reached no decision at all.

Delegation

6.111　In *Barnard v National Dock Labour Board*,[210] the National Dock Labour Board had delegated to the port manager its power to suspend men. Denning LJ held that:[211]

> ... [n]o judicial tribunal can delegate its functions unless it is enabled to do so expressly or by necessary implication ... [T]here is nothing in this scheme authorising the board to delegate this function, and it cannot be implied ... [I]f the board have no power to delegate their functions to the port manager, they can have no power to ratify what he has done.

6.112　Similarly, in *Allingham v Minister of Agriculture and Fisheries*,[212] the minister, by regulations, delegated his powers to give directions for the use of agricultural land to a county war agricultural committee. The committee left selection of fields to its executive officer. Lord Goddard CJ said:

> I can find no provision in any order having statutory effect or any regulation which gives the executive committee power to delegate that which the Minister has to decide and which he has power to delegate to the committee to decide for him. If he has delegated, as he has, his power of making decisions to the executive committee, it is the executive committee that must make the decision, and, on the ordinary principle of *delegatus non potest delegare*, they cannot delegate their power to some other person or body.[213]

6.113　The full rigour of this doctrine has not, however, always been applied especially in relation to central government decisions. In *Carltona*

---

210 [1953] 2 QB 18, CA.
211 [1953] 2 QB 18 at 40.
212 [1948] 1 All ER 780, DC.
213 [1948] 1 All ER 780 at 781.

Ltd v Works Comissioners,[214] the Court of Appeal accepted that it was a concomitant of the Secretary of State's acceptance of responsibility for the decisions taken within his or her department that devolution to officials of decision-making powers was a practical necessity in the administration of government which did not infringe the rule against delegation.

6.114 An example of this is the case of *R v Secretary of State for the Home Department ex p Oladehinde,*[215] in which the House of Lords regarded it as 'obvious' that the Secretary of State could not take all deportation decisions personally but was entitled to delegate them to suitably senior persons within his department. In *R v Southwark LBC ex p Bannerman,*[216] the court described it as commonplace in central and local government for a decision to be taken in the name of a person who had not personally taken it. It declined to investigate the internal organisation of a department but was prepared to assume, in the absence of evidence to the contrary, that the writer of a letter had authority to do so.[217]

6.115 In *R (Chief Constable of West Midlands Police) v Birmingham Justices,*[218] the court held that a chief constable was entitled, within the *Carltona* doctrine, to discharge functions through another officer for whom he was responsible and answerable. The *Carltona* principle did not depend on the peculiar status of civil servants and ministers, but was a general principle predicated on the principle that the head of a department was responsible for things done under his authority.

Dictation

6.116 *Lavender & Sons v Minister for Housing and Local Government*[219] illustrates the principle that a person entrusted with decision-making powers cannot allow him or herself to be dictated to. In that case, the minister had refused to grant planning permission for gravel extraction on a farm unless the Minister for Agriculture consented. Willis J held that this was unlawful, stating:[220]

---

214 [1943] 2 All ER 560, CA.
215 [1991] 1 AC 254, HL.
216 (1989) 22 HLR 459, (1990) 2 Admin LR 381, QBD.
217 See also *R v Hertsmere BC ex p Woolgar* (1995) 27 HLR 703, QBD, where the court held an authority to be entitled to delegate investigative powers notwithstanding its inability to delegate the actual decision-making function.
218 [2002] EWHC 1087 (Admin), [2003] ACD 18.
219 [1970] 1 WLR 1231, QBD.
220 [1970] 1 WLR 1231 at 1240–1.

It seems to me that he has said in language which admits of no doubt that his decision to refuse permission was solely in pursuance of a policy not to permit minerals ... to be worked unless the Minister of Agriculture was not opposed to their working ... It seems to me that by adopting and applying his stated policy he has in effect inhibited himself from exercising a proper discretion (which would of course be guided by policy considerations) in any case where the Minister of Agriculture has made and maintained an objection ... Everything else might point to the desirability of granting permission, but by applying and acting on his stated policy, I think the Minister has fettered himself in such a way that in this case it was not he who made the decision for which Parliament has made him responsible. It was the decision of the Minister of Agriculture not to waive his objection which was decisive in this case, and while that might properly prove to be the decisive factor for the Minister when taking into account all material considerations, it seems to me quite wrong for a policy to be applied which in reality eliminates all the material considerations save only the consideration, when that is the case, that the Minister of Agriculture objects. This means, as I think, that the Minister has, by his stated policy, delegated to the Minister of Agriculture the effective decision ... where the latter objects ...

6.117   Similarly, in *R v Metropolitan Police Disciplinary Board ex p Director Complaints Bureau Metropolitan Police*,[221] it was unlawful for the Board, in deciding to dismiss a disciplinary charge brought on the same facts as a potential criminal charge, to have regarded as conclusive the decision by the Director of Public Prosecutions that there was insufficient evidence to justify a prosecution.[222]

6.118   In the same way, a decision-maker will act unlawfully if he or she simply rubber-stamps the decision of some other body, or acts under the influence of or pressure from an outside agency.[223]

---

221 [1996] COD 324.

222 See also *R v Secretary of State for Trade and Industry ex p Lonrho plc* [1989] 1 WLR 525, HL, per Lord Keith of Kinkel at 538C.

223 See, eg, *R v Parole Board ex p Watson* [1996] 1 WLR 906, in which it was held that the Board must exercise its own discretion and decide the matter for itself, and not simply review the reasons for revoking parole given by the Secretary of State; *Re Findlay* [1985] AC 318, HL; *R v City of Sunderland ex p Baumber* [1996] COD 211, QBD, where it was unlawful for a local authority to instruct educational psychologists not to consult other agencies for advice but to apply to the deputy chief education officer to justify why, exceptionally, access to other advice was necessary. On the other hand, however, it was lawful for the Audit Commission to 'adopt', in advance and without exception, certain ratings derived from the performance assessment processes of a different inspectorate. This did not infringe against *Lavender* because the ratings adopted were not a decision by an outside body in an individual case:

Secret policies

6.119   It is unlawful for a decision-maker to refrain from making a policy known to the persons to whom it applies. In *Salih v Secretary of State for the Home Department*,[224] Stanley Burnton J held that there exists a constitutional imperative that statute law be made known and that the policies of a public authority could well have an importance for an individual akin to that of a statute. It was, accordingly, inconsistent with the constitutional imperative referred to above, for the Secretary of State to withhold information about his policy concerning 'hard cases support' in immigration cases, which related to the exercise of statutory power.

6.120   This statement was approved by the Supreme Court in *R (Lumba) v Secretary of State for the Home Department*.[225] The Secretary of State had a published policy on detention, but also a separate, unpublished, policy. The Secretary of State unlawfully applied the unpublished policy.[226] Lord Dyson said:[227]

> The rule of law calls for a transparent statement by the executive of the circumstances in which the broad statutory criteria will be exercised. Just as arrest and surveillance powers need to be transparently identified through codes of practice and immigration powers need to be transparently identified through the immigration rules, so too the immigration detention powers need to be transparently identified through formulated policy statements.

> The individual has a basic public law right to have his or her case considered under whatever policy the executive sees fit to adopt provided that the adopted policy is a lawful exercise of the discretion conferred by the statute ... There is a correlative right to know what that currently existing policy is, so that the individual can make relevant representations in relation to it. ...

> There was a real need to publish the detention policies in the present context. ... The failure to publish these policies meant that individuals who may have been wrongly assessed as having committed a crime that rendered them ineligible for release would remain detained, when in fact, had the policy been published, representations could have been made that they had a case for release.

R (Ealing LBC) v Audit Commission [2005] EWCA Civ 556. This case is almost certainly wrongly decided.

224 [2003] EWHC 2273 (QB).
225 [2011] UKSC 12, [2012] 1 AC 245.
226 The policy was also unlawful because it was a blanket policy, see the discussion on fettering of discretion at paras 6.104–6.109 above.
227 [2011] UKSC 12 at [34]–[35], [37]–[38].

The precise extent of how much detail of a policy is required to be disclosed was the subject of some debate before us. It is not practicable to attempt an exhaustive definition. It is common ground that there is no obligation to publish drafts when a policy is evolving and that there might be compelling reasons not to publish some policies, for example, where national security issues are in play. Nor is it necessary to publish details which are irrelevant to the substance of decisions made pursuant to the policy. What must, however, be published is that which a person who is affected by the operation of the policy needs to know in order to make informed and meaningful representations to the decision-maker before a decision is made.

Irrationality

Improper purposes or motives

6.121 It is a fundamental principle of public law[228] that a decision-maker must not use the powers entrusted to him for purposes which fall outside the ambit of his authority. In *R v Tower Hamlets LBC ex p Chetnik Developments Ltd,*[229] Lord Bridge of Harwich stated: 'Statutory power conferred for public purposes is conferred as it were upon trust, not absolutely – that is to say, it can be validly used only in the right and proper way which Parliament when conferring it is presumed to have intended ....'[230]

6.122 In *Congreve v Home Office,*[231] the Home Secretary announced an increase in the television licence, to take effect from 1 April. The claimant, along with around 24,500 other people, purchased a new licence at the old price, before 1 April. The Home Secretary threatened to revoke this licence if the claimant did not pay the difference between the old and new prices.

6.123 The Court of Appeal (Lord Denning MR) held that although the Secretary of State had an undoubted discretion under the Act to revoke a licence, that discretion was limited to the extent that the

---

228 *Credit Suisse v Allerdale BC* [1997] QB 306, CA, per Neill LJ at 333, cited with approval by Lord Bingham of Cornhill in *Porter v Magill* [2001] UKHL 67, [2002] 2 AC 357, HL.

229 [1988] AC 858, HL, at 872.

230 [1988] AC 858 at 872. See also *R v Inland Revenue Commissioners ex p Preston* [1985] AC 835, HL (it would have been improper for the respondent to have delayed in order to render the applicant's claim time-barred); *R v St George's Healthcare NHS Trust ex p S* [1999] Fam 26, CA (the Mental Health Act 1983 could not properly be used to prevent a mother refusing medical intervention for an unborn child).

231 [1976] QB 629, CA.

courts would intervene if it were exercised arbitrarily or improperly. In view of the fact that the licence issued to the claimant on 26 March was valid on that date and the licensee had done nothing wrong at all, the Home Secretary could not lawfully revoke the licence, at any rate not without offering the plaintiff his money back, and not even then except for good cause. It was an improper use of a minister's discretionary power to propose to revoke a licence validly obtained as a means of levying money that Parliament had given the executive no authority to demand. Accordingly, the court could and should intervene to declare that the proposed revocation of the plaintiff's licence was unlawful, invalid and of no effect.[232]

6.124   In *Westminster Corporation v London and North Western Railway Co*,[233] the Corporation had power to build public conveniences on or under any street. They built an underground convenience under the middle of Parliament Street with access from the pavement on either side of the street. The appellant alleged that the Corporation had, in reality, wished to build a subway which it had no power to do. The Earl of Halsbury LC said:[234]

> It seems to me that the ... statute itself contemplates that ... conveniences should be made beneath public roads, and if beneath public roads some access underneath the road level must be provided; and if some access must be provided, it must be a measure simply of greater or less convenience when the street is a wide one, whether an access should be provided at only one or at both sides of the street. That if the access is provided at both sides of the street, it is possible that people who have no desire or necessity to use the convenience will nevertheless pass through it to avoid the dangers of crossing the carriageway seems to me to form no objection to the provision itself ... I quite agree that if the power to make one kind of building was fraudulently used for the purpose of making another kind of building, the power given by the Legislature for one purpose could not be used for another.

6.125   In *Porter v Magill*,[235] the House of Lords held that it was an improper purpose, and unlawful, for Westminster City Council to have exercised its powers to dispose of housing stock in certain wards of the borough in an attempt to secure electoral advantage for the ruling party (the so-called 'homes-for-votes' policy). Lord Bingham of Cornhill accepted that, in one sense, all policies are pursued for reasons of political advantage that may properly form part of the motives

232 [1976] QB 629, especially at 649 and 651.
233 [1905] AC 426, HL.
234 [1905] AC 426 at 427–8.
235 [2001] UKHL 67, [2002] 2 AC 357.

for acting in a particular way, in the sense that it is not improper to hope that a properly-exercised power will be popular and earn the gratitude and support of the electorate: '... but a public power is not exercised lawfully if it is exercised not for a public purpose for which the power was conferred but in order to promote the advantage of a political party.'[236]

6.126   Westminster's policy was a deliberate, blatant and dishonest misuse of public power; representing political corruption.[237]

Bad faith

6.127   A decision-maker must not act in bad faith or dishonestly. In this context, bad faith has a broader meaning than dishonesty.

6.128   In *Roberts v Hopwood*,[238] at a time when the cost of living and trade union scale wage rates had been falling for some time, Poplar Borough Council resolved not to reduce employees' wages and to pay male and female employees at the same rate. The council had power to pay 'such wages as ... [it] may think fit'. On a challenge to the resolution brought by the district auditor, the House of Lords held that it was unlawful. Lord Sumner said:[239]

> The respondents conceded that for wages fixed *mala fide* no exemption from review could be claimed and that the mere magnitude of the wages paid, relatively to the wages for which the same service was procurable, might be enough in itself to establish bad faith. This admission ... leads to two conclusions. Firstly, the final words of the section are not absolute, but are subject to an implied qualification of good faith – 'as the Board may *bona fide* think fit.' ... *Bona fide* here cannot simply mean that they are not making a profit out of their

236 [2001] UKHL 67 at [21].

237 Per Lord Scott at [132]. In *R v Waltham Forest LBC ex p Baxter* [1988] QB 419, CA, an elected member of a local authority was entitled to take account of party loyalty in deciding to vote in favour of a rates resolution, so long as such considerations did not dominate to exclude other considerations. Conversely, however, in *R v Local Commissioner for Administration in North and North East England ex p Liverpool CC* [2001] 1 All ER 462, it was unlawful for party political considerations and influence to have been the decisive factor in the approval of a planning application for the development of part of the Anfield stadium. See also *R v Ealing LBC ex p Times Newspapers Ltd* (1986) 85 LGR 316, DC, where the authority's refusal to provide the applicant's newspapers in its public libraries was due to its political hostility to the applicant because it had dismissed workers who had taken strike action. This was not a consideration that was relevant to the authority's duty to provide a comprehensive and efficient library service.

238 [1925] AC 578, HL.

239 [1925] AC 578 at 603–4.

office or acting in it from private spite, nor is *bona fide* a short way of saying that the Council has acted within the ambit of its powers and therefore not contrary to law. It must mean that they are giving their minds to the comprehension and their wills to the discharge of their duty towards that public, whose money and local business they administer.

6.129　In the *Westminster Corporation* case (above para 6.124) Lord Mac-Naghten added:[240]

In order to make out a case of bad faith it must be shown that the Corporation constructed this subway as a means of crossing the street under colour and pretence of providing public conveniences which were not really wanted at that particular place.

6.130　In *Smith v East Elloe RDC*,[241] it was said that the meaning of bad faith had never been precisely defined as its effects had remained mainly in the region of hypothetical cases, but that it covered fraud or corruption.[242] In *Cannock Chase DC v Kelly*,[243] it was suggested that the term should now only be used to denote dishonest misuse or abuse of power.

Imposing decision-maker's duty on a third party

6.131　Where Parliament has imposed a duty on the decision-maker, it is unlawful for the decision-maker to seek to require a third party to perform that duty instead.

6.132　In *Hall & Co v Shoreham by Sea UDC*,[244] the local authority acted unlawfully in requiring a developer to construct a road over the entire frontage of its own site at its own expense as a condition of obtaining planning permission for a development. The Court of Appeal held that this was utterly unreasonable and could not possibly have been intended by Parliament.

6.133　In *R v Hillingdon LBC ex p Royco Homes Ltd*,[245] the authority granted outline planning permission for a housing development, subject to planning conditions that the houses should be occupied by people on the authority's housing waiting list, with security of

---

240　[1905] AC 426 at 432.

241　[1956] AC 736, HL.

242　[1956] AC 736, per Lord Somervell at 770 (in a dissenting speech). And see *Porter v Magill* [2001] UKHL 67, [2002] 2 AC 357.

243　[1978] 1 WLR 1, CA.

244　[1964] 1 WLR 240, CA.

245　[1974] QB 720, DC.

tenure for ten years. Lord Widgery CJ said that the conditions were undoubtedly:[246]

> ... the equivalent of requiring the applicants to take on at their own expense a significant part of the duty of the council as housing authority. However well-intentioned and however sensible such a desire on the part of the council may have been, it seems to me that it is unreasonable in the sense in which Willmer LJ was using that word in *Hall's* case.

6.134 Bridge J added:[247] 'This is in my judgment as clear a case as one would expect to find of conditions being imposed which are ultra vires, because the council are seeking to impose on the citizen the performance of a duty which statute puts on them.'

6.135 In *Leeds CC v Spencer*,[248] the Court of Appeal applied this principle, holding that a local authority could not lawfully avoid performing its statutory duty under Environmental Protection Act 1990 s45, to collect household refuse by exercising its power under Prevention of Damage by Pests Act 1949 s4, to serve a notice requiring the owner of a house to clear the rubbish himself. This was to seek to place on the citizen the performance of a duty which Parliament had placed on the authority itself.

Substantive or Wednesbury unreasonableness

6.136 The modern approach to substantive unreasonableness as used in the *Wednesbury* sense, together with its applicability and relationship to other related doctrines such as proportionality, has been discussed above.[249] It is not proposed to repeat that discussion here. The basic principle, however, is that a decision must not be so unreasonable that no reasonable decision-maker, properly directing him or herself, could have come to it: if it is, it cannot have been taken properly. This ground is also sometimes also referred to as 'perversity' or 'irrationality'.[250] Its effect is to afford the decision-maker a range of responses within which the court will not be entitled to intervene, an

---

246 [1974] QB 720 at 732A–B.
247 [1974] QB 720 at 732H.
248 [2000] BLGR 68, CA.
249 See paras 6.7–6.41 above.
250 See Lord Greene MR in the *Associated Provincial Picture Houses v Wednesbury Corporation* [1948] 1 KB 223, CA, at 229–30 and *Lord Diplock in Council of Civil Service Unions v Minister for the Civil Service* [1985] AC 374, HL. Use of the term 'irrational' may be misleading if it suggests that *Wednesbury* unreasonableness and irrationality in the *CCSU* sense (above, paras 6.10–6.12) are synonymous.

effect in some ways similar to that of the European doctrine of 'margin of appreciation'.[251]

6.137   In *Re W (an infant)*,[252] Lord Hailsham of St Marylebone observed that:[253]

> ... unreasonableness can include anything which can objectively be adjudged to be unreasonable. It is not confined to culpability or callous indifference. It can include, when carried to excess, sentimentality, romanticism, bigotry, wild prejudice, caprice, fatuousness or excessive lack of common sense.

6.138   It is noteworthy that the concept of objectivity in the court's adjudication has emerged forcefully in recent times in the context of the 'anxious scrutiny'/proportionality debate,[254] though it may also be observed that many of the characteristics described in the list above are primarily subjective.[255]

6.139   As has been seen above, the courts will sometimes apply a more interventionist approach to this ground, whether by means of the 'anxious scrutiny' test, or by applying the principles of proportionality instead.[256] There are other occasions, however, on which it has been held that the *Wednesbury* ground may not be available at all.

6.140   In *R v Secretary of State for the Environment ex p Nottinghamshire CC*,[257] for example, Lord Scarman, with whom the rest of the House of Lords agreed, stated that in matters of public financial administration, it was not constitutionally appropriate, save in very exceptional circumstances, for the courts to intervene on the ground of 'unreasonableness' to quash guidance which had been approved by resolution of the House of Commons. Provided that the minister did not exceed the scope of his powers, or abuse them, these were matters of political judgment for him and the House of Commons. Accordingly, an examination by the courts of the detail of the guidance or its consequences would only be justified:[258]

> ... if a *prima facie* case were to be shown for holding that the Secretary of State had acted in bad faith, or for an improper motive, or that the

---

251 See para 1.56 and this chapter at para 6.29 above.

252 [1971] AC 682, HL.

253 [1971] AC 682 at 688.

254 See paras 6.18–6.28 above.

255 See Arden QC et al *Local Government, Constitutional and Administrative Law* (1999), p156, note 92.

256 See paras 6.18–6.37 above.

257 [1986] AC 240, HL.

258 [1986] AC 240 at 247.

consequences of his guidance were so absurd that he must have taken leave of his senses.

6.141 This statement was approved by the House of Lords in *R v Secretary of State for the Environment ex p Hammersmith and Fulham LBC.*[259]

6.142 In much the same way, the courts will not interfere readily on *Wednesbury* grounds with central government decisions concerning areas of macro-economic policy. In *R (Luton BC) v Secretary of State for Education,*[260] Holman J held that the Secretary of State's decision to stop the previous government's school-building programme could not be challenged on a discrete *Wednesbury* ground. It was a decision with a patently political and heavy macro-economic content. Any irrationality in such a decision would be obvious and would not require sophisticated or detailed enquiry.

6.143 It is an approach that may be contrasted with that adopted in another House of Lords decision: *R v Greater London Council ex p Bromley LBC,*[261] in which it was held that the GLC had acted unlawfully and in breach of its fiduciary duty in implementing a policy to award a grant to the London Transport Executive so that concessionary fares may be offered on public transport in London, the grant to be paid for by the ratepayers of the London boroughs (by way of a precept issued by the GLC). While part of the decision turned on the construction of the relevant legislation, Lord Diplock described the policy as 'clearly' a 'thriftless use of moneys obtained by the GLC'.[262]

6.144 There are plainly both constitutional and legal differences between central and local government, in the sense that Parliament is sovereign whereas local authorities are not, and that local authorities may only act within the statutory powers that have been conferred upon them, whereas Parliament is not subject to such constraints – it may change the law. It can, nonetheless, legitimately be observed that to the extent that the courts are required to adjudicate on the legality of policy, a deference appears to extend to central government policies that is not accorded to those of local authorities, even when operating within the authority's legal powers.[263]

---

259 [1991] 1 AC 521, per Lord Bridge of Harwich at 595–7.
260 [2011] EWHC 217 (Admin), [2011] BLGR 553; see also *R (Hurley and Moore) v Secretary of State for Business, Innovation and Skills* [2012] EWHC 201 (Admin), [2012] HRLR 13.
261 [1983] 1 AC 768, HL.
262 [1983] 1 AC 768 at 830F.
263 See also, eg, *Roberts v Hopwood* [1925] AC 578, HL, in which Lord Atkinson (at 594) referred to the authority as having failed in their duty to administer funds that did not belong to it alone, by having allowed itself 'to be guided ... by

Proportionality

6.145 In essence, the principle of proportionality is that a measure must be proportionate to the legitimate aim it is intended to address. How the principle falls to be applied in individual cases, the tests involved in its application, and the courts' enthusiasm for it, have been considered above.[264] It is fair to say, however, that save for where it arises under the HRA 1998, it has not yet found general acceptance in English administrative law, although the courts have usually left open the possibility that it may do so in the future.

6.146 In particular, Lord Diplock in *CCSU*, said:[265]

'One can conveniently classify under three heads the grounds upon which administrative action is subject to control by judicial review. The first ground I would call 'illegality', the second 'irrationality' and the third 'procedural impropriety'. That is not to say that further development on a case-by-case basis may not in course of time add further grounds. I have in mind the possible adoption in the future of the principle of 'proportionality' which is recognised in the administrative law of several of our fellow members in the EEC.

6.147 The House of Lords in *R v Secretary of State for the Home Department ex p Brind*[266] considered the application of the principle. Lord Templeman said:[267]

It seems to me that the courts cannot escape from asking themselves whether a reasonable Secretary of State, on the material before him, could reasonably conclude that the interference with freedom of expression which he determined to impose was justifiable. In terms of the Convention, as construed by the European Court, the interference with freedom of expression must be necessary and proportionate to the damage which the restriction is designed to prevent.

6.148 Lord Roskill added some 'observations' on the subject:[268]

I am clearly of the view that the present is not a case in which the first step can be taken for the reason that to apply that principle in the present case would be for the court to substitute its own judgment of

some eccentric principles of socialistic philanthropy, or by a feminist ambition to secure equality of the sexes in the matter of wages in the world of labour'. The decision in *Roberts* would almost certainly be different today (see *Pickwell v Camden LBC* [1983] QB 962, CA).

264 See paras 6.18–6.37 above.

265 *Council of Civil Service Unions v Minister for the Civil Service* [1985] AC 374, HL at 410.

266 [1991] 1 AC 696, HL.

267 [1991] 1 AC 696 at 751.

268 [1991] 1 AC 696 at 750.

what was needed to achieve a particular object for the judgment of the Secretary of State on whom that duty has been laid by Parliament. But to so hold in the present case is not to exclude the possible future development of the law in this respect.

6.149   In spite of such comments, however, the courts appeared to take the view that the principle added little to the *Wednesbury* doctrine in any event,[269] a view that would no longer seem tenable, in the light of subsequent authority.[270]

Procedural impropriety

Natural justice; duty to act fairly

6.150   In all cases, a decision-maker must act fairly, or in accordance with the principles of natural justice. The nature, content and extent of this duty will depend on the circumstances and the nature of the decision-maker and the decision in question. They are not 'engraved on tablets of stone'.[271] Natural justice has also been described as 'fairness writ large and juridically ... "fair play in action"'.[272] The two fundamental concepts of natural justice are the rule against bias and the right to be heard.

Natural justice and article 6 of the European Convention on Human Rights

6.151   The content of the common law principles of natural justice has now been supplemented by HRA 1998 Sch 1, art 6.[273] In non-criminal matters, article 6 applies in the determination of a person's 'civil

---

269 *R v Brent LBC ex p Assegai* (1987) 11 June, unreported, DC, per Woolf LJ: 'Where the response is out of proportion with the cause to this extent, this provides a very clear indication of unreasonableness in a *Wednesbury* sense.' See also the judgment of Lord Donaldson MR in the Court of Appeal in *ex p Brind* [1991] 1 AC 696 at 721–2.

270 See, eg, *R (Daly) v Secretary of State for the Home Department* [2001] UKHL 26, [2001] 2 AC 532, and the discussion at paras 6.30–6.37 above, although note *R (McGrath) v Secretary of State for Work and Pensions* [2012] EWHC 1042 (Admin), [2012] ACD 87, where Cranston J said, at [33], that an 'exercise of discretion which is disproportionate is indicative of administrative action which is *Wednesbury* unreasonable'.

271 See *Lloyd v McMahon* [1987] AC 625, HL, per Lord Bridge of Harwich at 702H.

272 *Furnell v Whangarei High Schools Board* [1973] AC 660, PC, per Lord Morris of Borth y Gest at 679G.

273 That is, article 6 of the European Convention on Human Rights.

rights and obligations'.[274] Strasbourg has construed the word 'civil' to mean, in effect, 'private law'. Unfortunately, the meaning given to that term by Strasbourg, and the boundaries between private and public law are not the same as those that exist in the UK and have been described above.[275]

6.152 Different states have set different boundaries between their concepts of private law and public law, and the Strasbourg court has, over time, developed its own concepts of those rights that exist in private law and those that do not; this has been said to depend only on the 'character of the right'.[276]

6.153 In cases where it is held to apply, the scope of article 6 seems to be broader in some respects than the common law duty to act fairly, in terms of the rights conferred.[277] The court has emphasised that article 6 does not control or affect the content of, or rights granted under, national law, but provides purely procedural guarantees in relation to how such rights as are accorded to an individual, under his own national law, may be determined. Moreover, in order for article 6 to apply at all, there must be a 'contestation' (ie a dispute between the individual and a public authority as defined under the Act) as to civil rights and obligations that are (at least arguably) recognised in national law, and a decision that will be determinative of such civil rights and/or obligations.

Civil rights and obligations

6.154 Strasbourg case-law has determined that cases concerning rights existing in contract and tort, commercial and insurance law, family law and the law of succession, employment law (but not most public sector employment) and the law of real property are treated as private law rights and hence within the scope of article 6. The court has also held that social security and welfare assistance are both private law rights to which article 6 applies, at least to the extent that the benefit in question is a statutory right rather than a discretionary payment.[278]

---

274 Article 6(1).
275 See chapter 3.
276 *König v Federal Republic of Germany* (1978) 2 EHRR 170 para 90.
277 So far as civil litigation is concerned, Lord Judge CJ said in *R (Khaled) v Secretary of State for Foreign and Commonwealth Affairs* [2011] EWCA Civ 250, [2012] QB 477 at [32], that he 'would need a great deal of persuasion to accept that the standard of fairness set by the common law for the determination of issues arising in civil litigation is any less robust than the standards set by article 6'.
278 See *Schuler-Zgraggen v Switzerland* (1993) 16 EHRR 405 para 46.

Conversely, matters concerning immigration and nationality, tax, legal aid in civil proceedings, state education, prisoners' and tenants associations' rights, state medical treatment, elections, etc, are outside the scope of article 6.

6.155   The UK courts are not bound to follow the Strasbourg classification of rights. The Court of Appeal, for instance, has stated explicitly that, under the HRA 1998, it is for the national courts to develop their own human rights jurisprudence rather than simply to follow that developed in Europe.[279]

6.156   The HRA 1998 applies to all acts of courts and tribunals, however they be categorised, and there should therefore be little or no difficulty applying article 6 in relation to litigation before these bodies.

6.157   As to the acts of those public authorities falling within HRA 1998 s6(3)(b), it cannot be asserted that these will necessarily amount to determinations of civil rights. In *Ali v Birmingham CC*, for example, which concerned a local authority's homelessness functions, Lord Hope said:[280]

> I would be prepared now to hold that cases where the award of services or benefits in kind is not an individual right of which the applicant can consider himself the holder, but is dependent upon a series of evaluative judgments by the provider as to whether the statutory criteria are satisfied and how the need for it ought to be met, do not engage article 6(1). In my opinion they do not give rise to 'civil rights' within the autonomous meaning that is given to that expression for the purposes of that article. The applicants' right to accommodation under section 193 of the 1996 Act falls into that category. I would hold that article 6 was not engaged by the decisions that were taken in the applicants' cases by the reviewing officer.

6.158   In *R (Khaled) v Secretary of State for Foreign and Commonwealth Affairs*, Sedley LJ said:[281]

> 'What seems to me to emerge from the present Strasbourg jurisprudence is that, while civil rights within the autonomous meaning of article 6 can be brought into play either by direct challenge or by administrative action, it is the nature and purpose of the administrative action which determines whether its impact on private law rights is such that a legal challenge to it involves a determination of civil rights. Thus, for example, the nature and purpose of taxation are such that, despite its direct impact on property rights, taxation falls outside article 6; while the nature and purpose of professional regulation are

---

279 See *Begum v Tower Hamlets LBC* [2002] 1 WLR 2491, CA, and HRA 1998 s3.
280 [2010] UKSC 8, [2010] 2 AC 39 at [49].
281 [2011] EWCA Civ 350, [2012] QB 477.

such that its impact on the right to earn a living may bring it within article 6.

6.159 The Supreme Court has considered whether an employee's civil rights were engaged when he was refused legal representation during a disciplinary hearing at the school where he was employed.[282] The employee's civil right to practise his profession would be directly determined by a separate decision of the Independent Safeguarding Authority.[283] The test to be applied was whether the school's disciplinary proceedings would directly determine or exert a substantial influence over that decision. As their decisions and procedures were directed at different issues, the employee's civil rights were not engaged by the school's disciplinary hearing.

6.160 The courts have considered whether certain types of decision have involved a determination of a person's civil rights and obligations, to decide the applicability of article 6: a decision about admissions to primary school did not;[284] nor did a decision to exclude a student from school.[285] Determinations of civil rights and obligations do not take place in an immigration appeal,[286] (although, if an appellate structure is established it must comply with the essential guarantees provided by article 6);[287] or in decisions of the state regarding the entry, stay and deportation of nationals of other countries[288] (from which it follows that civil rights are also not determined in decisions concerning detention pending deportation or bail conditions imposed as an alternative to such detention).[289] A decision to extradite a UK citizen does, however, involve a determination of civil rights.[290]

6.161 Applications for judicial review of decisions of the Secretary of State about including individuals on a list of those suspected of a connection with terrorism, resulting in their assets being frozen, do

---

282 *R (G) v X School Governors* [2011] UKSC 30, [2012] 1 AC 167.

283 Which would involve a determination of a civil right. See also *R (Wright) v Secretary of State for Health* [2009] UKHL 3, [2009] 1 AC 739.

284 *R v Richmond upon Thames LBC ex p JC* [2001] BLGR 146, [2001] ELR 21, CA.

285 *R (B) v Head Teacher of Alperton Community School* [2001] EWHC 229 (Admin), [2002] BLGR 132; *R (V) v Independent Appeal Panel for Tom Hood School* [2010] EWCA Civ 142, [2010] PTSR 1462.

286 *MNM v Secretary of State for the Home Department* [2000] INLR 576.

287 *R v Secretary of State for the Home Department ex p Saleem* [2001] 1 WLR 443.

288 *Maaouia v France* (2000) 33 EHRR 42.

289 *R (BB (Algeria)) v Special Immigration Appeals Commission* [2012] EWCA Civ 1499.

290 *Pomiechowski v Poland* [2012] UKSC 20, [2012] 1 WLR 1604.

not involve the determination of article 6 civil rights;[291] nor does a decision to award a contract;[292] nor a decision to withdraw a prisoner's privileges of associating with other prisoners;[293] nor a refusal of compensation under an ex gratia scheme;[294] nor a decision by an employer to dismiss an employee under a contract of employment.[295]

6.162   While the decision to transfer a patient from a medium secure hospital to high security conditions was not a determination of his civil rights, the decision-making process engaged the common law duty of fairness because of the serious nature of the actual and potential adverse consequences flowing from it.[296]

Independent and impartial tribunal: 'full jurisdiction'

6.163   A person's article 6 right of access to an independent and impartial tribunal with full jurisdiction is closely related to the concept of 'civil rights'.[297] In *Begum*, Lord Bingham commented on this point, stating:

> The narrower the interpretation given to 'civil rights' the greater the need to insist on review by a judicial tribunal exercising full powers. Conversely, the more elastic the interpretation given to 'civil rights', the more flexible must be the approach to the requirement of independent and impartial review if the emasculation (by over-judicialisation) of administrative welfare schemes is to be avoided.[298]

6.164   'Full jurisdiction' does not means that the tribunal must have power to reconsider every issue in dispute for itself, but only that it must have 'jurisdiction to deal with the case as the nature of the decision requires'.[299]

---

291   *R (Khaled) v Secretary of State for Foreign and Commonwealth Affairs* [2011] EWCA Civ 350, [2012] QB 477.

292   *R v Secretary of State for the Home Department ex p Venture International Projects Ltd* (2000) 20 October, unreported, CA.

293   *R (King) v Secretary of State for Justice* [2012] EWCA Civ 376, [2012] 1 WLR 3602.

294   *R (Tawfick) v Secretary of State for the Home Department* [2001] ACD 28.

295   *Mattu v University Hospitals of Coventry and Warwickshire NHS Trust* [2012] EWCA Civ 641, [2012] 4 All ER 359, contrary to Smith LJ's obiter remarks in *Kulkarni v Milton Keynes Hospital NHS Trust* [2009] EWCA Civ 789, [2010] ICR 101. The right to carry on one's profession was accepted, in *Mattu* to be a civil right.

296   *R (L) v West London Mental Health NHS Trust* [2012] EWHC 3200 (Admin).

297   *Begum v Tower Hamlets LBC* [2003] UKHL 5, [2003] 2 AC 430.

298   [2003] UKHL 5 at [5].

299   *R (Alconbury) v Secretary of State for the Environment, Transport and the Regions* [2001] UKHL 23, [2003] 2 AC 295, per Lord Hoffmann at [87]; *Begum* [2003] UKHL 5 at [33].

6.165   This issue has, in the years since the introduction of the HRA 1998, focused principally on the issue of whether judicial review is an adequate remedy for the purposes of article 6, bearing in mind that – traditionally at any rate and on whatever approach may be appropriate in individual case – the judicial review court does not have power to re-examine the merits of the case before it, but only the legality of the decision and the process by which it was made.

6.166   In *Bryan v United Kingdom*,[300] the ECtHR held that the remedy of judicial review was satisfactory to meet the requirements of article 6(1) in circumstances where there was no dispute of primary fact and, therefore, the powers of the court on judicial review were sufficient to provide the safeguards guaranteed by article 6(1).

6.167   In *R (Alconbury) v Secretary of State for the Environment, Transport and the Regions*,[301] the House of Lords considered this issue for the first time after the coming into force of the HRA 1998. The judicial committee took the view that full jurisdiction did not necessarily require the availability of a full merits review of the decision under challenge. The requirement (as stated in such cases as *Albert and le Compte v Belgium*)[302] meant only that the court should have sufficient powers to deal with a case as the nature of that case demanded, as distinct from there being an entitlement to a full rehearing.[303] The statutory scheme under which the Secretary of State determines planning applications is not incompatible with the right to a fair hearing guaranteed by article 6. The powers of the court when reviewing those decisions were the same as those developed by the common law for

---

300 (1995) 21 EHRR 342, ECtHR.

301 [2001] UKHL 23, [2003] 2 AC 295.

302 (1983) 5 EHRR 533, ECtHR.

303 See also *R (Kathro) v Rhondda Cynon Taff CBC* [2001] EWHC 527 (Admin), [2002] Env LR 15, QBD, where the court held that the determination by the authority of their own planning decision was not a violation of article 6: *Alconbury* could not be distinguished on the basis that the planning authority's procedure contained fewer fact-finding powers. See also *R (Friends Provident Life Office) v Secretary of State for the Environment, Transport and the Regions* [2001] EWHC 820 (Admin), [2002] 1 WLR 1450: although *Alconbury* was not expressly directed to the human rights of a third party for planning permission, the administrative decision-making process affected a third party in a similar manner and there was therefore no reason in principle why the claimant's rights under article 6 should not be engaged. There was, however, no violation of article 6. The initial decision-making process, in which the authority were obliged to act fairly, was, when combined with the High Court's powers of review, sufficient to ensure that the procedure was compatible with article 6: applying *Bryan v United Kingdom* (1995) 21 EHRR 342, ECtHR.

the review of other administrative acts and were adequate for that purpose as they entitled the court to set aside a decision if it considered the decision to be perverse or wrong in law or procedure.

6.168   The Court of Appeal, in *R (McLellan) v Bracknell Forest DC*,[304] adopted a similar approach, holding that judicial review was an adequate remedy in relation to a statutory procedure whereby once the decision was properly taken to terminate an introductory (ie probationary) tenancy,[305] the court could not refuse to make a possession order. The tenant, however, had the right to seek an internal review of the decision taken by a senior officer (or a panel of elected members) not involved with the taking of the original decision, followed by judicial review. The court held that there was no reason to hold that the statutory review procedure could not be operated fairly, nor that judicial review would not provide an adequate safeguard to tenants, enabling them to challenge any unfairness and/or infringement of their Convention rights. Whether or not judicial review could satisfy the requirements of 'full jurisdiction' depended on a number of factors including whether any material facts were in dispute. In the context of introductory tenancies, this was not the case:

> ... under the introductory tenancy scheme it is not a requirement that the council should be satisfied that breaches of the tenancy agreement have in fact taken place. The right question under the scheme will be whether in the context of allegation and counter-allegation it was reasonable for the council to take a decision to proceed with termination of the introductory tenancy. That is again a matter which can be dealt with under judicial review either of the traditional kind or if it is necessary so to do intensified so as to ensure that the tenant's rights are protected.[306]

6.169   While the subject-matter of these cases now enables the county court to conduct a proportionality review of such decisions, the quotation from *McLellan* set out above has recently been approved by the Supreme Court.[307]

6.170   A similar two-stage review process relating to decisions concerning a local authority's duties to a homeless person (stage 1: internal;

---

304 [2001] EWCA Civ 1510, [2002] QB 1129.

305 Housing Act 1996 Pt 5.

306 [2001] EWCA Civ 1510 at [97]. See also *R (Bewry) v Norwich CC* [2001] EWHC 657 (Admin), [2002] HRLR 2; *R (Bono) v Harlow DC* [2002] EWHC 423 (Admin), [2002] 1 WLR 2475.

307 See *Hounslow LBC v Powell* [2011] UKSC 8, [2011] 2 AC 186, per Lord Phillips at [93].

stage 2: appeal on a point of law to the county court)[308] was challenged in *Begum v Tower Hamlets LBC*.[309] The House of Lords held that, assuming article 6 even applied, it was not breached by the operation of the statutory procedures. The officer of the authority conducting the internal review was not an independent tribunal because she was not a tribunal at all, not being part of the judicial branch of government, but an administrator.[310] In the context of the two-stage process, the second stage (in this case the county court entertaining an appeal on a point of law) did have full jurisdiction, which did not always require a complete rehearing. Accordingly, while the officer must of course act impartially and fairly, there was no need for independent findings of fact and a full appeal.

6.171   Whether an independent finder of facts would be necessary did not depend on the extent to which the particular administrative scheme was likely to involve resolution of disputes of fact. Rather, the relevant issue was whether, consistently with the rule of law and constitutional propriety, the decision-making powers in question could be entrusted to administrators. If they could, it was not relevant whether there would be many or few occasions on which findings of fact needed to be made.[311] Parliament was entitled to take the view that it was not in the public interest that an excessive proportion of the public funds available for a welfare scheme should be consumed in administration and legal disputes.[312] Strasbourg, moreover, would accord the contracting states a margin of appreciation in this regard.[313]

6.172   Moreover, the appropriate intensity of article 6 judicial review in the context of a statutory welfare scheme had to be consistent with that scheme. Article 6 did not provide the basis for more intensive judicial review. Where no Convention rights were engaged, other than under article 6, conventional judicial review was sufficient to comply with that article's requirements in a homelessness case.

6.173   *Begum* was considered by the ECtHR in *Tsfayo v United Kingdom*.[314] The Strasbourg court held that the process at that time of challenging

---

308 Housing Act 1996 Pt 7 and particularly ss202–204.

309 [2002] EWCA Civ 239, [2002] 1 WLR 2491, CA. The House of Lords decision is reported at [2003] UKHL 5, [2003] 2 AC 430. See also *Adan v Newham LBC* [2001] EWCA Civ 1916, [2002] 1 WLR 2120 (not followed in *Begum*).

310 [2003] UKHL 5, per Lord Hoffmann at [27].

311 [2003] UKHL 5 at [59].

312 [2003] UKHL 5 at [44]–[48].

313 [2003] UKHL 5 at [55].

314 (2006) 48 EHRR 18, [2007] HLR 19.

housing benefit decisions by appeal to a housing benefit review board comprised of elected members of the same local authority whose officers had made the original decision was incompatible with article 6.[315] The board was not an independent and impartial tribunal and a challenge to a review board decision by way of judicial review was not an appeal to a court of full jurisdiction as the High Court did not have power to review findings of fact.

6.174   The ECtHR drew a distinction between cases where 'the issues to be determined required a measure of professional knowledge or experience and the exercise of administrative discretion pursuant to wider policy aims' and cases where what was being decided was 'a simple question of fact' determination of which did not require specialist experience.[316] In the first type of case judicial review would be sufficient, but in the second type of case it was not.

6.175   The Supreme Court considered this theme in *Ali v Birmingham CC*.[317] As noted above, the court held that article 6 did not apply to homelessness decision-making, but went on to say that, even if it did, the absence of a full fact-finding jurisdiction in the county court[318] did not contravene the requirements of article 6 because the factual issues concerned in such cases were merely staging posts on the way to the much broader judgments that had to be made. Similarly, in *R (King) v Secretary of State for Justice*,[319] a decision to withdraw a prisoner's privileges of association with other prisoners did not engage article 6, but, even if it had, the decision-making processes within the prison, which included a review board and the availability of judicial review, were sufficient to comply with article 6.

Elements of procedural fairness

The rule against bias

6.176   The rule against bias is, in essence, that no one may be a judge in his own cause. Of course, where actual bias can be proved[320] that is

---

315   That system was repealed after the decision complained about in *Tsfayo*, by Child Support, Pensions and Social Security Act 2000 s68 and Sch 7.

316   (2006) 48 EHRR 18 at [45].

317   [2010] UKSC 8, [2010] 2 AC 39.

318   The jurisdiction in that case was that of the county court on a statutory appeal under Housing Act 1996 s204, which is the same as the High Court in judicial review. See further chapter 9 below.

319   [2012] EWCA Civ 376, [2012] 1 WLR 3602.

320   Which will probably require cross-examination, see *R (Berky) v Newport City Council* [2012] EWCA Civ 378, [2012] 2 CMLR 44 at [30]; and *EU Plants Ltd v Wokingham BC* [2012] EWHC 3305 (Admin) at [63].

a plain ground for the grant of relief. In the absence of actual bias, it seems that there are two different tests, applicable to different situations.

Apparent bias – direct pecuniary interest

6.177 Where the judge of a cause has a direct pecuniary interest in the outcome, the court will not enquire as to the likelihood of bias, but will proceed to quash the decision. In *Dimes v Proprietors of Grand Junction Canal*,[321] the court set aside a decree of the Lord Chancellor on the basis of his interest in the canal company, notwithstanding that 'no one can suppose that Lord Cottenham could be, in the remotest degree, influenced by' it. The court stated that this would have a 'most salutary influence' on inferior tribunals when it became known that the court was prepared to take such action.[322] See also the comments of Lord Goff of Chieveley in *R v Gough*.[323]

Other cases

6.178 In all other cases where apparent bias is alleged, the test is based on the approach set out in *R v Gough*,[324] but modified to comply with the requirements of article 6.[325] Under *Gough*, the test was expressed to be whether there was a 'real danger' of bias 'on the part of a relevant member of the tribunal in question, in the sense that he might unfairly regard (or have unfairly regarded) with favour or disfavour, the case of a party to the issue under consideration by him'.

6.179 In *Director General of Fair Trading v Proprietary Association for Great Britain*[326] Lord Phillips MR suggested a 'modest adjustment' to the test, expressed in the following terms:[327]

> When the Strasbourg jurisprudence is taken into account, we believe that a modest adjustment of the test in *R v Gough* is called for, which makes it plain that it is, in effect, no different from the test applied in most of the Commonwealth and in Scotland. The court must first ascertain all the circumstances which have a bearing on the suggestion that the judge was biased. It must then ask whether those

---

321 (1852) 3 HL Cas 759, HL.
322 (1852) 3 HL Cas 759, per Lord Campbell at 793–4.
323 [1993] AC 646, HL, at 661 (though the *Gough* test itself is no longer applicable, see below).
324 [1993] AC 646, per Lord Goff at 670.
325 The jurisprudence of the ECtHR, to which the court must now have regard (HRA 1998 s2) was to the effect that the test should be an objective one: see, eg, *Hauschildt v Denmark* (1989) 12 EHRR 266 at 279, para 48.
326 Also known as *Re Medicaments (No 2)* [2001] 1 WLR 700, CA.
327 [2001] 1 WLR 700 at [85].

circumstances would lead a fair-minded and informed observer to conclude that there was a real possibility, or a real danger, the two being the same, that the tribunal was biased.

6.180   In other words, the test was now to be expressed in objective terms, it was a question of whether the fair-minded and informed observer would conclude that there was a real danger of bias, not whether the court considered this to be so.

6.181   In *Porter v Magill*,[328] the House of Lords approved the 'modest adjustment' to the *Gough* test with a further minor amendment. Lord Hope of Craighead stated:

> I respectfully suggest that your Lordships should now approve the modest adjustment of the test in *R v Gough* set out in [*Director General of Fair Trading*]. It expresses in clear and simple language a test which is in harmony with the objective test which the Strasbourg court applies when it is considering whether the circumstances give rise to a reasonable apprehension of bias. It removes any possible conflict with the test which is now applied in most Commonwealth countries and in Scotland. I would however delete from it the reference to 'a real danger'. Those words no longer serve a useful purpose here, and they are not used in the jurisprudence of the Strasbourg court. The question is whether the fair-minded and informed observer, having considered the facts, would conclude that there was a real possibility that the tribunal was biased.[329]

6.182   The current test for apparent bias is, therefore, whether a fair-minded and informed observer, in possession of all the relevant facts, would consider there to be a 'real possibility' of bias.

6.183   The, hypothetical, fair-minded and informed observer is someone who adopts a 'balanced approach'[330] and who is 'neither complacent not unduly sensitive or suspicious'.[331]

Bias or predetermination?

6.184   There is considerable overlap between the concepts of apparent bias and predetermination, although the two do not cover entirely the same ground.[332] Some examples may help to illustrate the approach

---

328   [2001] UKHL 67, [2002] 2 AC 357.

329   [2001] UKHL 67 at [103].

330   *R (PD) v West Midlands and North West Mental Health Review Tribunal* [2004] EWCA Civ 311, [2004] MHLR 174, approving Silber J at first instance ([2003] EWHC 2469 (Admin), [2004] MHLR 25).

331   *Lawal v Northern Spirit Ltd* [2003] UKHL 35, [2003] ICR 856.

332   It is only in rare cases that the distinction will be significant, see Wade and Forsyth *Administrative Law* (10th edn, 2009), p390.

taken by the courts on an application for judicial review on the ground of apparent bias or predetermination.[333]

6.185 In *R (Georgiou) v Enfield LBC*,[334] the decision of a local authority to grant listed building and planning consents was quashed by Richards J because the voting patterns of councillors who were members of the conservation advisory group and the planning committee gave rise to a real possibility of predetermination.

6.186 The same judge quashed another planning decision in *Ghadami v Harlow DC*[335] where he held that remarks made by the chairman of the planning committee, which had been secretly recorded, suggested a strong predisposition in favour of the planning application.

6.187 The *Georgiou* and *Ghadami* decisions can be contrasted with *Condron v National Assembly for Wales*,[336] where the Court of Appeal held that an impromptu remark made by the chairman of the Welsh Assembly's planning decision committee that he was 'going to go with the Inspector's report' did not amount to predetermination of the issue.

6.188 *R (Port Regis School Ltd) v North Dorset DC*[337] also concerned a planning application. A local masonic lodge agreed to provide financial help to the developer in exchange for a room in the development being given over to its use. The claimant argued that the grant of planning permission was affected by apparent bias because two of the councillors who voted to approve planning permission were themselves freemasons. Newman J accepted that masonic practices were secretive and were difficult for independent, fair-minded observers to be informed about, but did not believe that this amounted to an appearance of bias. The applicant had placed great stress on the masonic oath, which required a mason to assist fellow masons. Newman J felt that, read in context, the oath was little more than an exhortation to charity and, in any event, required masons to observe the law of the land.

---

333 Also relevant are *Helow v Advocate General for Scotland* [2008] UKHL 62, [2008] 1 WLR 2416; *R (Lewis) v Redcar and Cleveland BC* [2008] EWCA Civ 746, [2009] 1 WLR 83; *R (Kaur) v Institute of Legal Executives Appeal Tribunal* [2011] EWCA Civ 1168, [2012] 1 All ER 1435, where Rix LJ explained, at [49], that 'the doctrines with which we are here concerned are to guard against the insidious effects of which those concerned are not even conscious'; and *EU Plants Ltd v Wokingham BC* [2012] EWHC 3305.

334 [2004] EWHC 779 (Admin), [2004] BLGR 497, [2004] 2 P&CR 21.

335 [2004] EWHC 1883 (Admin), [2005] BLGR 24, [2005] 1 P&CR 19.

336 [2006] EWCA Civ 1573, [2007] BLGR 87, [2007] 2 P&CR 4.

337 [2006] EWHC 742 (Admin), [2006] BLGR 696, [2007] 1 P&CR 29.

Limitation of challenges

6.189 Concerns over the number of bias challenges brought in respect of local government decisions, led to the enactment of section 25 of the Localism Act 2011 which provides:

(1) Subsection (2) applies if –
   (a) as a result of an allegation of bias or predetermination, or otherwise, there is an issue about the validity of a decision of a relevant authority, and
   (b) it is relevant to that issue whether the decision-maker, or any of the decision-makers, had or appeared to have had a closed mind (to any extent) when making the decision.

(2) A decision-maker is not to be taken to have had, or to have appeared to have had, a closed mind when making the decision just because –
   (a) the decision-maker had previously done anything that directly or indirectly indicated what view the decision-maker took, or would or might take, in relation to a matter, and
   (b) the matter was relevant to the decision.[338]

6.190 It is not at all clear what effect section 25 will have or what, if anything, it adds to the pre-existing position, which Collins J had explained in the following terms:[339]

... Councillors will inevitably be bound to have views on and may well have expressed them about issues of public interest locally. Such may, as here, have been raised as election issues. It would be quite impossible for decisions to be made by the elected members whom the law requires to make them if their observations could disqualify them because it might appear that they had formed a view in advance. ...

The reality is that Councillors must be trusted to abide by the rules which the law lays down, namely that, whatever their views, they must approach their decision-making with an open mind in the sense that they must have regard to all material considerations and be prepared to change their views if persuaded that they should. ... unless there is positive evidence to show that there was indeed a closed mind, I do not think that prior observations or apparent favouring of a particular decision will suffice to persuade a court to quash the decision. ...

338 Section 25(2) only applies if the decision-maker is a member of the authority (elected or not) or a co-opted member of the authority: s25(3).
339 *R (Island Farm Development) v Bridgend County BC* [2006] EWHC 2189 (Admin), [2007] BLGR 60 at [30]–[31].

The right to be heard

6.191　The main components of the right to be heard are, briefly, as follows. A person is entitled to have notice of the case against him or her, which he or she will have to meet, and to have the opportunity to meet the case including a reasonable time to prepare. If there is to be a hearing, the person is also entitled to know the details of the time and date of at which it will take place and to attend.

6.192　In *Ridge v Baldwin*,[340] a chief constable was suspended for conspiracy to obstruct the course of justice. He was acquitted and applied to be reinstated. The committee considering his application, however, decided that he had been negligent and dismissed him. No specific charge was formulated against him, but the committee considered his statements in evidence at his trial and the judge's comments. The House of Lords held that the decision to dismiss him was null and void. The respondent could only dismiss the chief constable on the grounds set out in the enabling Act and was bound to observe the principles of natural justice, to inform him of the charges made against him and give him an opportunity of being heard. It had failed to do so.

6.193　In another case, Lord Denning said: 'He must know what evidence has been given and what statements have been made affecting him; and he must be given a fair opportunity to correct or contradict them.'[341]

6.194　A recent example of a decision being quashed for a lack of fairness is *R (Shoesmith) v Ofsted*.[342] Directions given by the Secretary of State to a local authority removing the claimant from her statutory post of Director of Children's Services, and her summary dismissal, were unlawful as the claimant had not been given an opportunity to put her case.[343]

6.195　The precise content of the right to be heard will depend upon the circumstances of the case. Sometimes it is sufficient to inform the person of the substance of the case against him, without disclosing the precise evidence or sources of information. The requirement

---

340　[1964] AC 40, HL.

341　*Kanda v Government of the Federation of Malaya* [1962] AC 322, PC, at 337, where an application for citizenship had been refused without the grounds being disclosed. See also *R v Chief Constable of North Wales Police ex p Evans* [1982] 1 WLR 1155, HL, where a probationary constable who resigned to avoid dismissal was neither told the allegations against him nor given the chance to answer them.

342　[2011] EWCA Civ 642, [2011] PTSR 1459.

343　This case is discussed in more detail at paras 2.73–3.23.

for natural justice must be weighed against the detriment disclosure may cause to the function of the decision-maker.[344]

6.196 A person must be given sufficient time to prepare his case,[345] and must have an opportunity to put that case. Usually there must be an oral hearing, though this is not always necessary. Decision-makers are, in general, masters of their own procedure. In *Lloyd v McMahon*,[346] the House of Lords held that a district auditor had acted fairly in disclosing his case to councillors and offering them only the chance to make representations in writing, when deciding whether or not to surcharge them for wilful misconduct. As a general rule, however, the more important the rights at stake, the more likely it is that fairness will require an oral hearing.

6.197 Failure to allow cross-examination may be unfair, but is more likely to be held to be so in formal as opposed to informal hearings.[347] It now seems that where it is decided to hold an oral hearing, cross-examination ought usually to be permitted, as the testing of witnesses is usually the purpose of such a hearing.[348]

6.198 There is no right to legal representation in all cases. The Court of Appeal has held that while most hearings permit representation, it was not 'self-evident that that was an advantage'. That is particularly so in relation to specialist tribunals adopting a hands-on approach. Such tribunals 'might well be able to reach the right conclusion just as often and much more cheaply and quickly, without as with such formal representation'.[349]

6.199 In *R (Alliss) v Legal Services Commission*,[350] the court considered that the failure to provide a person with a lawyer may contravene the requirements of article 6 (see below) where a lawyer's assistance was indispensable to secure the right to effective access to a court or where, for reasons of fairness, the appearance of the fair administra-

---

344 See *R v Gaming Board for Great Britain ex p Benaim and Khaida* [1970] 2 QB 417; *R v Monopolies and Mergers Commission ex p Matthew Brown Plc* [1987] 1 WLR 1235.

345 See *R v Thames Magistrates Court ex p Polemis* [1974] 1 WLR 1371, QBD.

346 [1987] AC 625, HL.

347 See *R v Board of Visitors of Hull Prison ex p St Germain (No 2)* [1979] 1 WLR 1401, QBD (breach where cross-examination refused, but disputed evidence the applicant wished to contest was taken into account by the visitors); *Herring v Templeman* [1973] 3 All ER 569, CA (no necessity for witnesses).

348 *R v Army Board of the Defence Council ex p Anderson* [1992] 1 QB 169, DC, per Taylor LJ at 188.

349 *R v Secretary of State for the Home Department ex p Cheblak* [1991] 1 WLR 890, CA, per Lord Donaldson MR at 906.

350 [2003] ACD 16.

tion of justice must be sustained, and to ensure that a party to civil proceedings could participate effectively. A similar conclusion was reached in relation to article 2 of the Convention in *R (Khan) v Secretary of State for Health*.[351]

6.200 It has been held that fairness requires that a person be given all reasonable facilities to help exercise the right to be heard. Such facilities include the help of a friend to take notes and give advice, unless the court orders otherwise in the interests of justice, maintaining order and controlling its own procedure.[352] On the other hand, the failure by a person to attend a hearing, resulting in him being unable to put his case, due to the default of his professional adviser, did not entitle him to complain of any failure by the tribunal to act fairly.[353]

6.201 In a planning context, it has been held that there was a breach of natural justice where an interested party to an appeal against the refusal of planning permission was deprived of an opportunity to respond to expert evidence relied on by the developer because it had only been submitted on the last day on which representations could be made. The grant of planning permission was therefore quashed.[354]

6.202 A policy that provides for opportunities for individuals to put their case, but which could be applied in such a way as to remove those opportunities may be an unlawful policy if it gives rise to an unacceptable risk of unlawful decision-making (aside from the possibility of challenging individual unlawful decisions as they arise).[355]

Article 6 of the European Convention on Human Rights

6.203 Article 6 adopts a different formulation, entitling a person 'in the determination of his civil rights and obligations or of any criminal

351 [2003] EWCA Civ 1129, [2004] 1 WLR 971. In so far as it related to a death before the HRA 1998 came into force, *Khan* was disapproved in *Re McKerr's Application for Judicial Review* [2004] UKHL 12, [2004] 1 WLR 807, but that case in turn was doubted in *Re McCaughey's Application for Judicial Review* [2011] UKSC 20, [2012] 1 AC 275. The Supreme Court held in *McCaughey* that article 2 did not compel an investigation into deaths which had occurred before the 1998 Act came into force, but where it was decided that an inquest should take place, that inquest did have to comply with the procedural requirements of article 2.

352 *R v Leicester City Justices ex p Barrow* [1991] 2 QB 260, CA.

353 *Al-Mehdawi v Secretary of State for the Home Department* [1990] 1 AC 876, HL.

354 *R (Ashley) v Secretary of State for Communities and Local Government* [2012] EWCA Civ 559, [2012] JPL 1235.

355 *R (Refugee Legal Centre) v Secretary of State for the Home Department* [2004] EWCA Civ 1481, [2005] 1 WLR 2219; *R (Medical Justice) v Secretary of State for the Home Department* [2010] EWHC 1925 (Admin), *R (Suppiah) v Secretary of State for the Home Department* [2011] EWHC 2 (Admin).

charge against him' a right to a 'fair and public hearing within a reasonable time by an independent and impartial tribunal established by law'.

6.204 The question of what will amount to a determination of a person's civil rights and obligations and whether a tribunal is independent and impartial and has full jurisdiction has been discussed elsewhere.[356]

Reasons

6.205 At common law, there is no general duty on decision-makers to give reasons for their decisions. However, in many cases, statute has now provided such a duty.[357]

A general duty?

6.206 In *R v Secretary of State for the Home Department ex p Doody*,[358] the House of Lords approached the question of whether there was a duty to give reasons by asking what fairness required, and whether the scheme operated by the Secretary of State fell below the minimum standards of fairness. It was held that where, in deciding whether or not to release a life prisoner on licence, the Secretary of State departed from the judicial recommendation, he was required to give reasons for so doing.

6.207 In *R v Higher Education Funding Council ex p Institute of Dental Surgery*,[359] Sedley J declined to hold that there was a general legal duty to give reasons for all administrative decisions. Instead, he held that there was a spectrum of decision-making, at one end of which the importance of the rights at stake would be such that reasons would always be required, while at the other end, reasons would not generally be necessary.

Article 6

6.208 The right to a fair hearing guaranteed by article 6 does, so far as the ECtHR is concerned, require that the decision-maker must 'indicate with sufficient clarity the grounds on which they base their decision'

---

356 See paras 6.154–6.175 above.
357 See, for example, Tribunals and Inquiries Act 1992 s10; Housing Act 1996 s184; Tribunal Procedure (Upper Tribunal) Rules 2008 SI No 2698 rr22, 30 and 40; Town and Country Planning (Development Management Procedure) (England) Order 2010 SI No 2184) art 31, etc.
358 [1994] 1 AC 531, HL.
359 [1994] 1 WLR 242, DC.

in order that the individual may be in a position usefully to exercise any right of appeal.[360]

6.209 This general obligation has not, however, received unqualified acceptance by the UK courts. In *R (Asha Foundation) v Millenium Commission*,[361] Lightman J, applying the *Institute of Dental Surgery* case[362] and *R v Professional Conduct Committee of the GMC ex p Salvi*,[363] stated that it was well-established that there was a category of decisions for which no reasons need be given other than those implicit in the decision itself. The Commission's decision, like academic judgments, fell into this class of case.

6.210 The judge enunciated the following principles concerning the giving of reasons:

(a) the requirement to give reasons was inextricably linked with the decision-making process and must be considered in that context;

(b) where, in the course of that process, the decision-maker was obliged to give reasons for the decision, an obligation could be imposed requiring those reasons to be disclosed to the parties affected by it;

(c) if there was no obligation to articulate reasons other than those implicit in the decision itself, there would be no scope to impose any further obligation to give reasons where the decision-maker did no more that he was legally bound to do;

(d) the obligation to give reasons was to give the actual reasons for the decision at the time and not reasons that had later been reconstructed: accordingly if no, or no fully articulated, reasons were given at the time, they could not be given later;

(e) if an obligation to give reasons could be identified, or had been accepted, that obligation must relate back and require reasons to be given when making the decision.[364]

---

360 See *Hadjianastassiou v Greece* (1992) 16 EHRR 219 para 33. That does not require every point raised in argument to be dealt with, but submissions that would, if accepted, be decisive must be dealt with: see *Van der Hurk v Netherlands* (1994) 18 EHRR 481 and *Hiro Balani v Spain* (1994) 19 EHRR 566.

361 [2002] EWHC 916 (Admin), [2002] ACD 79 upheld on appeal to the Court of Appeal at [2003] EWCA Civ 88, [2003] ACD 50.

362 [1994] 1 WLR 242, DC.

363 (1999) 46 BMLR 167, QBD.

364 See also, *R (Tucker) v Director General of the National Crime Squad* [2002] EWHC 832 (Admin), [2002] ACD 80.

6.211   The Court of Appeal, upholding Lightman J's decision, did not express a view about these principles, save to confirm that the duty to give detailed reasons will depend on the circumstances.[365]

Content of the duty

6.212   Where a duty to give reasons has been established, the reasons given must be 'proper, adequate and intelligible' and must deal with the substantial points that have been raised.[366] Lord Brown explained the requirement, in a planning context, in *South Buckinghamshire DC v Porter (No 2)*:[367]

> The reasons for a decision must be intelligible and they must be adequate. They must enable the reader to understand why the matter was decided as it was and what conclusions were reached on the 'principal important controversial issues', disclosing how any issue of law or fact was resolved. Reasons can be briefly stated, the degree of particularity required depending entirely on the nature of the issues falling for decision. The reasoning must not give rise to a substantial doubt as to whether the decision-maker erred in law, for example by misunderstanding some relevant policy or some other important matter or by failing to reach a rational decision on relevant grounds. But such adverse inference will not readily be drawn. The reasons need refer only to the main issues in the dispute, not to every material consideration. They should enable disappointed developers to assess their prospects of obtaining some alternative development permission, or, as the case may be, their unsuccessful opponents to understand how the policy or approach underlying the grant of permission may impact upon future such applications. Decision letters must be read in a straightforward manner, recognising that they are addressed to parties well aware of the issues involved and the arguments advanced. A reasons challenge will only succeed if the party aggrieved can satisfy the court that he has genuinely been substantially prejudiced by the failure to provide an adequately reasoned decision.[368]

---

365 [2003] EWCA Civ 88, [2003] ACD 50. In *RWE Npower Renewables Ltd v Welsh Ministers* [2011] EWHC 1778 (Admin), Beatson J held a decision to be unlawful because the defendant had given no reasons for their rejection of expert evidence on the principal important issue.

366 *Westminster CC v Great Portland Estates plc* [1985] 1 AC 661, per Lord Scarman at 673, approving *In re Poyser and Mills' Arbitration* [1964] 2 QB 467, per Megaw J at 478.

367 [2004] UKHL 33, [2004] 1 WLR 1953.

368 [2004] UKHL 33 at [36]. On the approach to decision letters, see also *Holmes-Moorhouse v Richmond upon Thames LBC* [2009] UKHL 7, [2009] 1 WLR 413 at [45]–[52], in the context of homelessness review decisions under Housing Act 1996 s202.

6.213 A failure to give such reasons, where there is an obligation to do so, may, on its own, be a sufficient ground to quash the decision.[369] In some challenges to local authority planning decisions, however, the courts have exercised a certain amount of restraint and have refused to quash decisions if there is no prospect of the authority coming to a different decision if required to give proper reasons or if there has been no prejudice caused by the failure.[370]

6.214 The statutory obligation may itself frame the extent of the duty to give reasons, eg notice granting planning permission only has to include a summary of reasons for granting permission, unless the grant of permission is subject to conditions, in which case full reasons must be given for each condition imposed.[371] If, however, permission is refused, full reasons must be given for the refusal.[372]

Reasons in court

6.215 Where an applicant seeks judicial review of the decision, a duty to explain it arises, in order to facilitate the adjudication of the issue.[373] In *Padfield*,[374] Lord Upjohn was of the view that a minister:

> ... is a public officer charged by Parliament with the discharge of a public discretion ... If he does not give any reason for his decision it maybe, if circumstances warrant it, that a court may be at liberty to come to the conclusion that he had no good reason for reaching that conclusion ....

6.216 In *R v Lancashire CC ex p Huddleston*,[375] the court considered that, in general, authorities should give sufficient reasons as are adequate to enable the court to ascertain whether or not the authority had erred in law. For instance, where it is alleged that irrelevant considerations

---

369 *R v Westminster CC ex p Ermakov* [1996] 2 All ER 302, (1995) 28 HLR 819.

370 *R (Smith) v Cotswold DC* [2007] EWCA Civ 1341; *R (Siraj) v Kirklees MBC* [2010] EWCA Civ 1286, [2011] JPL 571; *R (Telford Trustee No 1 Ltd) v Telford and Wrekin Council* [2011] EWCA Civ 896, [2012] PTSR 935.

371 Town and Country Planning (Development Management Procedure) (England) Order 2010 SI No 2184 art 31(1)(a). See also *R (Telford Trustee No 1 Ltd) v Telford and Wrekin Council* [2011] EWCA Civ 896, [2012] PTSR 935.

372 Town and Country Planning (Development Management Procedure) (England) Order 2010 SI No 2184 art 31(1)(b).

373 See, eg, *Padfield v Minister for Agriculture and Fisheries* [1968] AC 997, HL, where the House of Lords commented that if the Secretary of State refused to give reasons for his decision, the court may conclude that there was no good reason for it.

374 [1968] AC 997, HL, at 1061–2.

375 [1986] 2 All ER 941, CA.

were considered, this will generally entail explaining what the authority did and did not take into account.[376]

6.217   The Crown Court, sitting in its appellate capacity, must give sufficient reasons to demonstrate that it has identified the issues in contention in the case before it and how it has resolved each of those issues.[377] Where a compelling point had been raised by the defence, it was incumbent on the Crown Court to deal with the point.[378]

6.218   Where there is a statutory obligation to give reasons, the court will not entertain explanations, additional to the statutory reasons given, otherwise than by way of elucidation or correction of those statutory reasons.[379] In particular, *ex post facto* explanations or rationalisations that seek to contradict the original reasons given will not be admitted. The decision of the Court of Appeal to this effect in *R v Westminster CC ex p Ermakov*,[380] was followed by Stanley Burnton J in *R (Nash) v Chelsea College of Art and Design*.[381] In that case, the judge indicated the court would only accept later reasons in exceptional circumstances, the relevant considerations being as follows:

- whether the new reasons were consistent with those originally given;
- whether it was clear that the new reasons were the original reasons of the decision-maker;
- whether there was a real risk that the new reasons had been composed subsequently or in order to justify the decision retrospectively;
- the delay before the new reasons were advanced; and
- the circumstances in which they were advanced.

---

376 [1986] 2 All ER 941, per Parker LJ at 947.

377 *R v Harrow Crown Court ex p Dave* [1994] 1 WLR 98, DC.

378 *R (Taylor) v Maidstone Crown Court* [2003] EWHC 2555 (Admin), [2004] ACD 19.

379 See, eg, *Hijazi v Kensington and Chelsea RLBC* [2003] EWCA Civ 692, [2003] HLR 72 (decision-maker allowed to rely on a subsequent statement explaining that certain matters had been taken into account even though they were not referred to in the decision letter); and *Keane v Law Society* [2009] EWHC 783 (Admin) (decision-maker allowed to rely on subsequent statement which was consistent with original reasons and dealt with an issue raised for the first time in judicial review proceedings). See also *Hall v Wandsworth LBC* [2004] EWCA Civ 1740, [2005] HLR 23 (decision-maker allowed to rely on a subsequent statement but that statement still failed to provide an adequate explanation for the rejection of medical evidence).

380 See *R v Westminster CC ex p Ermakov* [1996] 2 All ER 302, (1995) 28 HLR 819. See further at paras 20.29–20.34 below and the cases there cited.

381 [2001] EWHC 538 (Admin); (2001) *Times* 25 July.

6.219 In *R (Leung) v Imperial College of Science, Technology and Medicine*,[382] Silber J suggested two additional considerations:

- whether the decision-maker would have been expected to state in the decision document the reasons that he or she later sought to advance;
- the 'over-arching factor' of whether it would be just in all the circumstances to refuse to admit the subsequent reasons.[383]

6.219 In the context of homelessness appeals, where witness statements from both parties have sometimes tended to proliferate, the Court of Appeal[384] has reminded county court judges (hearing appeals on a point of law), of the need to:

> be astute to ensure that evidential material ... is limited to that which is necessary to illuminate the points of law that are to be relied on in the appeal, or the issue of what, if any, relief ought to be granted. An undisciplined approach to the admission of new evidence may lead to the danger that the reviewing officer is found guilty of an error of law for not taking into account evidence that was never before her, notwithstanding the applicant's opportunity to make representations about the original decision.

Appeals

6.220 Natural justice does not require that there should be a right of appeal.[385] An appeal may, however, sometimes cure defects in the procedure at an earlier stage.

6.221 In *Calvin v Carr*,[386] a horse owner had been disqualified by Australian Jockey Club stewards for one year. The club committee dismissed the appeals. Lord Wilberforce held that although there is no general rule regarding whether appellate proceedings could cure a defect due to a failure of natural justice, there was a broad spectrum of domestic proceedings between those at one end where the inquiry stage could be said to have merged into the appellate stage (such as social clubs) and those where a complainant has the right to nothing less than a fair hearing at both the original and appeal stages (such as

---

382 [2002] EWHC 1358 (Admin), [2002] ACD 100, [2002] ELR 653.

383 The purpose of these additional factors was said to be that the court may be less cautious about admitting later reasons where there was no obligation to give reasons at the time. *Ermakov* and *Nash* were both cases where there was such a duty.

384 *Cramp v Hastings BC* [2005] EWCA Civ 1005, [2005] HLR 48, per Brooke LJ at [71].

385 *Ward v Bradford Corporation* (1971) 70 LGR 27.

386 [1980] AC 574, PC.

trade union membership, planning, employment, etc). Intermediate cases exist where a person who had joined in an organisation or contract was to be taken to have agreed to accept what in the end is a fair decision, reached after a consideration of the case on its merits, notwithstanding some initial defect. In such cases, the test is whether after both original and appellate stages the complainant has had a fair deal of the kind he or she bargained for when he or she joined the organisation or entered into the contract.

6.222　In *R (DR) v Head Teacher of St George's Catholic School*,[387] the claimant was permanently excluded from school and appealed. His application for judicial review of the decision to exclude him, confirmed on appeal, was dismissed. The Court of Appeal considered the issue of the extent to which unfairness at an early stage of the three-stage appeal process could be cured by utilising the final stage of appeal.

6.223　The court held that it was necessary to construe the statutory scheme as a whole, in order to ascertain the intention of Parliament concerning the effect of unfairness in an early part of the process. In this case, although Parliament did not intend any stage of the process to be unfair, nor did it intend a party aggrieved at a decision at the first stage to seek judicial review rather than appeal. Although the appeal did not give redress in respect of the earlier unfairness, the aggrieved party obtained a new, fair decision on the merits from the 'custom-built' expert and independent statutory body, following a full rehearing. Unless the prior procedural unfairness complained of had somehow tainted the subsequent appeal, in which case the appeal decision itself would necessarily fall, the right to a fair determination of a person's case would be satisfied by the appeal hearing and decision. On a judicial review application brought instead of an appeal, the court would usually leave the claimant to his statutory remedy.

A fair hearing would have made no difference

6.224　In some circumstances, the courts have been prepared to hold that there has been no breach of natural justice where a fair hearing could have made no difference. In *Malloch v Aberdeen Corporation*,[388] Lord Wilberforce stated that the court does not act in vain. It need not determine whether a hearing was required where it could only be a useless formality because there was nothing the applicant could

---

387　[2002] EWCA Civ 1822, [2003] BLGR 371, [2003] ELR 104.
388　[1971] 1 WLR 1578, HL.

have said that would have affected the decision.[389] In fact, these decisions, and those concerning mixed motives and partial invalidity,[390] are closely related to those concerning the discretionary nature of the remedy in judicial review proceedings.[391]

Exclusion of natural justice

6.225　It is clear that the principles discussed above do not apply in all cases. First, there is no right to be heard before the passing of legislation, whether primary or delegated, unless statute so provides.[392] Secondly, it appears that the right to be heard can be excluded, for instance in cases involving national security.[393] In addition, some classes of applicant, such as prisoners and immigrants, are similarly not always accorded the same rights as are generally applicable.

Other procedural irregularities

Legitimate expectation

6.226　The principles concerning legitimate expectations are one aspect of the duty to act fairly and are rooted in the concept of fairness.[394] Where a decision-maker has indicated that he or she will proceed in a particular manner, whether by express promise, implication or past practice, it may be unlawful to fail to do so. Where a promise is made by a person who has no power to make it, another decision-maker will not be bound to take it into account, even if it could amount to a legitimate expectation.[395]

389　See also *Cinnamond v British Airports Authority* [1980] 1 WLR 582, CA.

390　See chapter 7.

391　See, eg, *R v Islington LBC ex p Hinds* (1995) 28 HLR 302, CA, where relief was refused because failure to give proper reasons had not substantially prejudiced the applicant. This case is no longer good law on the issues of reasons, however, see paras 6.205–6.219 above.

392　See Consultation at paras 6.225–6.265 below.

393　*Council of Civil Service Unions v Minister of State for the Civil Service* [1985] AC 374, HL.

394　See *R v North and East Devon Health Authority ex p Coughlan* [2001] QB 213, CA.

395　See *R (Bloggs 61) v Secretary of State for the Home Department* [2003] EWCA Civ 686, [2003] 1 WLR 2724, where the prison service was held not to be bound by a police promise that, in exchange for information, a prisoner would be kept in protective witness custody rather than mainstream prison. The police had no power to make the promise and the prison service did not have to take it into account in deciding to move the prisoner back to mainstream custody.

6.227   In order to invoke the doctrine, however, and to have an 'expectation' in the first place, the claimant must have known of the publicised procedure, promise or representation, and relied on it.

6.228   In *R (Zeqiri) v Secretary of State for the Home Department*,[396] the House of Lords confirmed that conduct by a public officer which was akin to breach of contract or representation could be an abuse of power for which judicial review was appropriate, the denial of a legitimate expectation being one form of the more general concept of abuse of power. A representation must be construed in the context in which it was made, and must be 'clear, unambiguous and devoid of relevant qualification'.[397] The question was not whether in private law the representation would give rise to an estoppel but whether, by acting contrary to it, the decision-maker would be acting with 'conspicuous unfairness'[398] and so abusing its power.

6.229   The requirement for reliance does not mean that detriment or a change of position are necessarily required. In *R (Bibi) v Newham LBC*,[399] Schiemann LJ, giving the judgment of the court, held that these matters had a factual rather than a legal significance: 'In a strong case, no doubt, there will be both reliance and detriment; but it does not follow that reliance (that is, credence) without measurable detriment cannot render it unfair to thwart a legitimate expectation.'[400]

6.230   In considering the weight to be given to the fact that the appellants, a homeless refugee family who had relied on a promise of priority for local authority housing by waiting for such housing to materialise, could not show what the court described as 'concrete detriment', or change of position, Scheimann LJ said that the fact that someone had not changed their position did not mean that they had not relied on the promise; indeed the absence of change of position could demonstrate reliance on the promise.[401] Moreover, while no concrete detriment had been shown, there was 'moral detriment' in the continued disappointment of the expectation and 'potential detriment' in the deflection of the possibility that the family could have found somewhere else to settle in the UK where housing was less hard to come by:[402]

396 [2002] UKHL 3, [2002] Imm AR 296, [2002] ACD 60.
397 See *R v Inland Revenue Commissioners ex p MFK Underwriting Agents Ltd* [1990] 1 WLR 1545, DC.
398 *R v Inland Revenue Commissioners ex p Unilever Plc* [1996] STC 681, CA.
399 [2001] EWCA Civ 607, [2002] 1 WLR 237.
400 At [31].
401 At [53].
402 At [55].

In our view these things matter in public law, even though they might not found an estoppel or actionable misrepresentation in private law, because they go to fairness and through fairness to possible abuse of power. To disregard the legitimate expectation because no concrete detriment can be shown would be to place the weakest in society at a particular disadvantage. It would mean that those who have a choice and the means to exercise it in reliance on some official practice or promise would gain a legal toehold inaccessible to those who, lacking any means of escape, are compelled simply to place their trust in what has been represented to them.

6.231   In *R v North and East Devon Health Authority ex p Coughlan*,[403] the Court of Appeal held that three categories of expectation are now recognised by law: (a) cases where the decision-maker is only obliged to bear in mind its promise, giving the promise whatever weight it considers, before deciding whether to depart from it; (b) cases where the promise induces a legitimate expectation that a certain procedure will be followed before taking a decision, such as a promise of consultation (procedural expectation); and (c) cases where the promise has induced a legitimate expectation of a substantive benefit (substantive expectation).[404]

6.232   In *Coughlan*,[405] Lord Woolf explained the courts' approach to these three types of expectation.

There are at least three possible outcomes. (a) The court may decide that the public authority is only required to bear in mind its previous policy or other representation, giving it the weight it thinks right, but no more, before deciding whether to change course. Here the court is confined to reviewing the decision on *Wednesbury* grounds. This has been held to be the effect of changes of policy in cases involving the early release of prisoners (see *Re Findlay* [1985] AC 318; *R v Home Secretary ex p Hargreaves* [1997] 1 WLR 906). (b) On the other hand the court may decide that the promise or practice induces a legitimate expectation of, for example, being consulted before a particular decision is taken. Here it is uncontentious that the court itself will require *the opportunity for consultation* to be given unless there is an overriding reason to resile from it (see *A-G for Hong Kong v Ng Yuen Shiu* [1983] 2 AC 629) in which case the court will itself judge the adequacy of the reason advanced for the change of policy, taking into account what fairness requires. (c) Where the court considers that a lawful promise or practice has induced a legitimate expectation of a *benefit which is substantive*, not simply procedural, authority now establishes

403 [2001] QB 213, CA.
404 [2001] QB 213, per Lord Woolf MR at [57].
405 [2001] QB 213, CA, at [57]

that here too the court will in a proper case decide whether to frustrate the expectation is so unfair that to take a new and different course will amount to an abuse of power. Here, once the legitimacy of the expectation is established, the court will have the task of weighing the requirements of fairness against any overriding interest relied upon for the change of policy. (Emphasis in original.)

6.233 The second and third categories differ from the first in that the court will consider the issue of fairness for itself and is not limited, as in the first class of case, to scrutiny on the basis of *Wednesbury* review. In cases falling within the third category, the court will have to decide, when necessary, whether there is a sufficient overriding interest to justify a departure from what has been previously promised.[406] Since *Coughlan*, the courts have emphasised that the categories of legitimate expectation are not closed.[407]

Substantive expectations

6.234 Traditionally, the expectation that a claimant could acquire was said to be purely procedural. A claimant could not acquire a legitimate expectation that a substantive decision would be in his favour, but only that the decision would be reached in a particular manner.

6.235 In *R v Devon CC ex p Baker*,[408] a pre-*Coughlan* decision, Simon Brown LJ identified two types of substantive expectation that would be recognised by the courts:[409]

(1) Sometimes the phrase is used to denote a substantive right: an entitlement that the claimant asserts cannot be denied him. It was used in this sense and the assertion upheld in cases such as *R v Secretary of State for the Home Department ex p Khan* [1984] 1 WLR 1337 and *R v Secretary of State for the Home Department ex p Ruddock* [1987] 1 WLR 1482 ... [T]he claimant's right will only be found established when there is a clear and unambiguous representation upon which it was reasonable for him to rely. Then the administrator or other public body will be held bound in fairness by the representation made unless only its promise or undertaking as to how its power would be exercised is inconsistent with the statutory duties imposed upon it. The doctrine employed in this sense is akin to an estoppel ...

(2) Perhaps more conventionally the concept of legitimate expectation is used to refer to the claimant's interest in some ultimate benefit which he hopes to retain (or, some would argue, attain). Here, therefore, it

---

406 [2001] QB 213 at [58].
407 See paras 6.245–6.251 below and see *Zeqiri* and *Bibi* above (notes 396 and 399).
408 [1995] 1 All ER 73, CA.
409 [1995] 1 All ER 73, CA at 89–90.

is the interest itself rather than the benefit that is the substance of the expectation. In other words the expectation arises not because the claimant asserts any specific right to a benefit but rather because his interest in it is one that the law holds protected by the requirements of procedural fairness; the law recognises that the interest cannot properly be withdrawn (or denied) without the claimant being given an opportunity to comment and without the authority communicating rational grounds for any adverse decision. Of the various authorities drawn to our attention, *Schmidt v Secretary of State for Home Affairs* [1969] 2 Ch 149, *O'Reilly v Mackman* [1983] 2 AC 237 and the recent decision of Roch J in *R v Rochdale Metropolitan BC ex p Schemet* [1993] 1 FCR 306 are clear examples of this head of legitimate expectation.

6.236   Thus where, for example, a decision-maker announces that a substantive benefit will be conferred on persons meeting certain specified criteria who apply for the benefit by a specified date, it would be an unlawful breach of the substantive expectations of those claimants who meet the published criteria and apply for the benefit for the decision-maker to change the criteria after the closing date for applications has passed, by which time it is too late to reapply.[410]

6.237   The Court of Appeal in *Coughlan*[411] confirmed the existence of substantive expectations, not necessarily limited in the way suggested by the court in *Baker*, but generally sustainable on the basis of the requirements of fairness. Lord Woolf MR said:[412]

> The fact that the court will only give effect to a legitimate expectation within the statutory context in which it has arisen should avoid jeopardising the important principle that the executive's policy-making powers should not be trammelled by the courts (see *Hughes v DHSS* [1985] AC 766, 788, per Lord Diplock). Policy being (within the law) for the public authority alone, both it and the reasons for adopting or changing it will be accepted by the courts as part of the factual data – in other words, as not ordinarily open to judicial review. The court's task – and this is not always understood – is then limited to asking whether the application of the policy to an individual who has been led to expect something different is a just exercise of power. In many cases the authority will already have considered this and made appropriate exceptions (as was envisaged in *British Oxygen v Board of Trade* [1971] AC 610 ...), or resolved to pay compensation where money alone will suffice. But where no such accommodation is made, it is for the court to say whether the consequent frustration of the individual's expectation is so unfair as to be a misuse of the authority's power.

410   See, eg, *R v Secretary of State for the Home Department ex p Khan* [1984] 1 WLR 1337, CA.

411   [2001] QB 213, CA.

412   [2001] QB 213 at [82].

6.238   In *R (Godfrey) v Southwark LBC*,[413] the Court of Appeal held that a rigorous standard was to be applied when a substantive legitimate expectation was claimed on the basis of a representation or promise by a public authority and that the duty of public authorities to exercise powers in the public interest had to be kept in mind.[414]

Procedural expectation

6.239   In *Attorney-General of Hong Kong v Ng Yuen Shiu*,[415] a senior immigration officer had announced that before deporting illegal immigrants, each would be interviewed and his case 'treated on its merits'. The applicant was arrested and a removal order made against him without him having any opportunity to make representations as to why he should not be removed. The Privy Council held that the ordinary principle applied that when a public authority charged with the duty of making a decision promised to follow a certain procedure before reaching that decision, good administration required that it should act by implementing the promise provided the implementation did not conflict with the authority's statutory duty. Accordingly, assuming an alien had no general right to be heard before being deported, the making of the promise to interview each illegal immigrant and decide each case on its merits required the applicant to be given an opportunity to state his case. The failure to ask him whether he wished to make representations why he should not be removed was a sufficient ground for setting aside the decision.[416]

6.240   In *R (Weaver) v London & Quadrant Housing Trust*,[417] the Divisional Court rejected an argument that a tenant had acquired a legitimate expectation arising from the landlord's standard terms and conditions of tenancy. The court held that it was too tenuous and general in character to be enforceable in public law. No evidence had been provided that the claimant had had the expectation alleged or even that she had known of the term of the contract. The expectation was an artificial construction derived from the landlord's standard terms and conditions and attributed to the claimant.

---

413 [2012] EWCA Civ 500, [2012] BLGR 683.
414 See also *R (Niazi) v Secretary of State for the Home Department* [2008] EWCA Civ 755, (2008) *Times* 21 July.
415 [1983] 2 AC 629, PC.
416 See also *Council of Civil Service Unions v Minister of State for the Civil Service* [1985] AC 374, HL.
417 [2008] EWHC 1377 (Admin), [2009] 1 All ER 17 (not in issue on appeal to the Court of Appeal: [2009] EWCA Civ 587, [2010] 1 WLR 363.

6.241 Nor did the British Medical Association enjoy any procedural legitimate expectation of consultation before the General Medical Council withdrew a benefit, where the Council had received advice that the benefit constituted unlawful discrimination.[418]

6.242 Conversely, in *R (Vieira) v Camden LBC*,[419] a local authority breached the legitimate expectations of objectors to a grant of planning permission by granting permission without consulting the objectors on a proposed amendment to the application and without placing an officer's briefing on the amended plan on its website for comment.

When departure may be permitted

6.243 In *R (Bibi) v Newham LBC*,[420] the Court of Appeal identified three questions that would arise in all legitimate expectation cases, whether procedural or substantive:

(a) To what has the public authority, whether by practice or by promise, committed itself?
(b) Has the authority acted or does it propose to act unlawfully in relation to its commitment?
(c) What should the court do?[421]

6.244 It is probably the last of these questions that has received the most judicial attention since *Bibi*.

6.245 In *R (Nadarajah) v Secretary of State for the Home Department*,[422] Laws LJ noted Lord Woolf's comments in *Coughlan* that the limits of legitimate expectation had yet to be finally determined. Laws LJ offered some obiter[423] suggestions to answer the third question in *Bibi* to move the law's development 'a little further down the road':[424]

---

418 *R (British Medical Association) v General Medical Council* [2008] EWHC 2602 (Admin), (2009) *Times* 19 January.
419 [2012] EWHC 287 (Admin).
420 [2001] EWCA Civ 607, [2002] 1 WLR 237. See also *R (National Association of Guardians ad Litem and Reporting Officers) v Children and Family Court Advisory and Support Service* [2001] EWHC 693 (Admin), [2002] 1 FLR 255, [2001] Fam Law 877; *R (Galligan) v University of Oxford* [2001] EWHC 965 (Admin), [2002] ACD 33, [2002] ELR 494.
421 *R (Bibi) v Newham LBC* [2001] EWCA Civ 607, [2002] 1 WLR 237, per Schiemann LJ at [19].
422 [2005] EWCA Civ 1363, (2005) *Times* 14 December.
423 In *R (Lumba) v Secretary of State for the Home Department* [2011] UKSC 12, [2012] 1 AC 245, Lord Phillips noted, at [312] of his dissenting judgment, that his approval of [68]–[69] in *Nadarajah* as a 'compelling analysis of the law' was also obiter.
424 [2005] EWCA Civ 1363 at [68]–[69].

The search for principle surely starts with the theme that is current through the legitimate expectation cases. It may be expressed thus. Where a public authority has issued a promise or adopted a practice which represents how it proposes to act in a given area, the law will require the promise or practice to be honoured unless there is good reason not to do so. What is the principle behind this proposition? It is not far to seek. It is said to be grounded in fairness, and no doubt in general terms that is so. I would prefer to express it rather more broadly as a requirement of good administration, by which public bodies ought to deal straightforwardly and consistently with the public. In my judgment this is a legal standard which, although not found in terms in the European Convention on Human Rights , takes its place alongside such rights as fair trial, and no punishment without law. That being so there is every reason to articulate the limits of this requirement – to describe what may count as good reason to depart from it – as we have come to articulate the limits of other constitutional principles overtly found in the European Convention. 'Accordingly a public body's promise or practice as to future conduct may only be denied, and thus the standard I have expressed may only be departed from, in circumstances where to do so is the public body's legal duty, or is otherwise, to use a now familiar vocabulary, a proportionate response (of which the court is the judge, or the last judge) having regard to a legitimate aim pursued by the public body in the public interest. The principle that good administration requires public authorities to be held to their promises would be undermined if the law did not insist that any failure or refusal to comply is objectively justified as a proportionate measure in the circumstances.

This approach makes no distinction between procedural and substantive expectations. Nor should it. The dichotomy between procedure and substance has nothing to say about the reach of the duty of good administration. Of course there will be cases where the public body in question justifiably concludes that its statutory duty (it will be statutory in nearly every case) requires it to override an expectation of substantive benefit which it has itself generated. So also there will be cases where a procedural benefit may justifiably be overridden. The difference between the two is not a difference of principle. Statutory duty may perhaps more often dictate the frustration of a substantive expectation. Otherwise the question in either case will be whether denial of the expectation is in the circumstances proportionate to a legitimate aim pursued. Proportionality will be judged, as it is generally to be judged, by the respective force of the competing interests arising in the case. Thus where the representation relied on amounts to an unambiguous promise; where there is detrimental reliance; where the promise is made to an individual or specific group; these are instances where denial of the expectation is likely to be harder to justify as a proportionate measure. ... On the other hand where the government decision-maker is concerned to raise wide-ranging or 'macro-political' issues of policy, the expectation's enforcement in the courts will encounter a steeper climb. All these considerations, whatever their direction, are pointers not rules. The balance between an individual's fair treatment in particular circumstances, and the vindication of other ends having a proper claim on the public interest (which is the essential dilemma posed by the law of legitimate expectation) is not precisely calculable, its measurement not exact. ... These cases have to be judged in the round.

6.246   In *R (Bancoult) v Secretary of State for Foreign and Commonwealth Affairs (No 2)*,[425] Lord Mance preferred to reserve for another case his 'opinion as to whether it is helpful or appropriate to rationalise the situations in which a departure from a prior decision is justified in terms of proportionality, with its overtones of another area of public law'.[426]

6.247   Lord Dyson considered how the court should approach legitimate expectation decisions in *Paponette v Attorney General of Trinidad and Tobago*.[427] He said:[428]

> The initial burden lies on an applicant to prove the legitimacy of his expectation. This means that in a claim based on a promise, the applicant must prove the promise and that it was clear and unambiguous and devoid of relevant qualification. If he wishes to reinforce his case by saying that he relied on the promise to his detriment, then obviously he must prove that too. Once these elements have been proved by the applicant, however, the onus shifts to the authority to justify the frustration of the legitimate expectation. It is for the authority to identify any overriding interest on which it relies to justify the frustration of the expectation. It will then be a matter for the court to weigh the requirements of fairness against that interest.
>
> If the authority does not place material before the court to justify its frustration of the expectation, it runs the risk that the court will conclude that there is no sufficient public interest and that in consequence its conduct is so unfair as to amount to an abuse of power.

6.248   Lord Dyson approved Laws LJ's suggestion in *Nadarajah*[429] that departure from a legitimate expectation should only be allowed where it

---

425   [2008] UKHL 61, [2009] 1 AC 453.
426   [2008] UKHL 61 at [182].
427   [2010] UKPC 32, [2012] 1 AC 1.
428   [2010] UKPC 32 at [36]–[38].
429   [2005] EWCA Civ 1363 at [68], quoted above, para 6.245.

can be objectively justified as a proportionate measure in the circumstances.[430] His Lordship said:[431]

> It is for the authority to prove that its failure or refusal to honour its promises was justified in the public interest. There is no burden on the applicant to prove that the failure or refusal was not justified.

> How an authority justifies the frustration of a promise is a separate question which is of particular significance in the present case ...

> ...[T]he Attorney General has provided the court with no ... reasons why the 1997 Regulations were made notwithstanding that their effect would be in conflict with [representations which had been made]. [Counsel] submits that it is possible to infer from the mere fact that the 1997 Regulations were made that there had been a change of policy and that this must have been in response to some public interest which overrode the expectations generated by the representations. The Board rejects the proposition that the court can (still less, should) infer from the bare fact that a public body has acted in breach of a legitimate expectation that it must have done so to further some overriding public interest. So expressed, this proposition would destroy the doctrine of substantive legitimate expectation altogether, since it would always be an answer to a claim that an act was in breach of a legitimate expectation that the act must have been in furtherance of an overriding public interest.

6.249   Accordingly, unless an authority provided evidence to explain why it had acted in breach of a representation or promise made to an applicant, it would be:[432]

> unlikely to be able to establish any overriding public interest to defeat the applicant's legitimate expectation. Without evidence, the court is unlikely to be willing to draw an inference in favour of the authority. This is no mere technical point. The breach of a representation or promise on which an applicant has relied often, though not necessarily, to his detriment is a serious matter. Fairness, as well as the principle of good administration, demands that it needs to be justified. Often, it is only the authority that knows why it has gone back on its promise. At the very least, the authority will always be better placed than the applicant to give the reasons for its change of position. If it wishes to justify its act by reference to some overriding public interest, it must provide the material on which it relies. In particular, it must give details of the public interest so that the court can decide how to strike the balance of fairness between the interest of the applicant and the overriding interest relied on by the authority. As Schiemann LJ

---

430 At [38].
431 At [39], [41].
432 At [42].

put it in *R (Bibi) v Newham London Borough Council* [2002] 1 WLR 237, para 59, where an authority decides not to give effect to a legitimate expectation, it must 'articulate its reasons so that their propriety may be tested by the court'.

6.250 Lord Dyson accepted that there may be circumstances, though it would be a rare case, in which it would be possible to identify the relevant overriding public interest from the terms of the decision that is inconsistent with an earlier promise and the context in which it is made. In such a case, the terms of, and background to, the decision itself may provide enough material to enable the court to decide how the balance should be struck.[433]

6.251 Where an authority is considering whether to act inconsistently with a representation or promise that it has made and that has given rise to a legitimate expectation, good administration as well as elementary fairness demands that it takes into account the fact that the proposed act will amount to a breach of the promise. Put in public law terms, the promise and the fact that the proposed act will amount to a breach of it are relevant factors that must be taken into account.[434]

Consistency

6.252 This is another aspect of the duty to act fairly that is akin to the principle of legitimate expectation. Decisions must not be indiscriminate and decision-makers must act consistently in their dealings with the public; reaching inconsistent or contradictory decisions on similar facts is a misuse of power.

6.253 In *HTV v Price Commission*,[435] the respondent changed its basis for calculating the percentage of HTV's profits that must be paid to the Exchequer. Denning LJ held that:[436]

It is ... the duty of the Price Commission to act with fairness and consistency in their dealing with manufacturers and traders ... if they regularly interpret the words of the code in a particular sense – or regularly apply the code in a particular way – they should continue to interpret it and apply it in the same way thereafter unless there is good cause for departing from it. At any rate, they should not depart from it in any case where they have, by their conduct, led the manufacturer or trader to believe that he can safely act on that interpretation of the code or on that method of applying it, and he does so act

---

433 *Paponette v Attorney General of Trinidad and Tobago* [2010] UKPC 32 at [43].
434 *Paponette*, per Lord Dyson at [46].
435 [1976] ICR 170, CA.
436 [1976] ICR 170 at 185.

on it. It is not permissible for them to depart from their previous interpretation and application where it would not be fair or just for them to do so ... It is a misuse of power for [the Commission] to act unfairly or unjustly to a private citizen when there is no overriding public interest to warrant it.

6.254 In *Inland Revenue Commissioners v Preston*,[437] however, the House of Lords held that a taxpayer could not complain of unfairness merely because the Inland Revenue Commissioners decided to perform their statutory duties, even though they had previously agreed, before receiving new information, that they would not do so. While conduct by the Commissioners equivalent to a breach of contract or representation could amount to an abuse or excess of power, it is only in exceptional circumstances that the courts could decide that something which the Commissioners had, by taking action against the taxpayer, determined to be fair, is unfair.

Consultation

6.255 In *Coughlan*,[438] the Court of Appeal restated the principles of consultation as follows. Where statute or previous practice establishes an obligation on a decision-maker to consult prior to making a decision, the following principles apply:

- The consultation must take place while the proposals are still at a formative stage (ie when the results of the consultation may still make a difference).
- The consultee must be given sufficient information about, and reasons for, the proposal to be able to respond in a meaningful and intelligent way and sufficient time to be able to respond.
- There must then be sufficient time for the responses to be considered properly, and the responses must be considered conscientiously, in the course of taking the ultimate decision.[439]

6.256 In the absence of a statutory duty or a legitimate expectation of consultation, there is no obligation to consult.[440] In *R (BAPIO Action*

---

437 [1985] AC 835, HL.

438 [2001] QB 213, CA.

439 See also eg, *R v Brent LBC ex p Gunning* (1985) 84 LGR 168, QBD. See also *Council of Civil Service Unions v Minister for the Civil Service* [1985] AC 374, HL; *R v Secretary of State for Social Services ex p AMA* [1986] 1 WLR 1, QBD; *R (Breckland DC) v Electoral Commission Boundary Committee for England* [2009] EWCA Civ 239, [2009] PTSR 1611, [2009] BLGR 589.

440 *R (Stamford Chamber of Commerce) v Secretary of State for Communities and Local Government* [2009] EWHC 719 (Admin), [2009] 2 P&CR 19.

Ltd) v Secretary of State for the Home Department,[441] however, while it was held that there was no express duty to consult, the Court of Appeal stated that it would be wrong not to consult a body that has previously been regularly consulted.

6.257 The courts will not strike down a consultation exercise merely because it could have been done better. Some clear unfairness must be shown to have been caused to some people affected by the consultation process. What fairness requires by way of consultation, however, will depend on the circumstances of the individual case.[442] In *R (Royal Brompton and Harefield NHS Foundation Trust) v Joint Committee of Primary Care Trusts*,[443] the Court of Appeal adopted the formulation, derived from an earlier case,[444] that for a consultation process to be held unlawful, it must be shown that any error made was such as to have the effect that there could have been no proper consultation and that something had 'gone clearly and radically wrong'.[445]

6.258 The requirement that sufficient information be given about a proposal includes the obligation to provide such information in a form that those consulted will be able to understand.[446] It is not permissible to leave it to other, more expert, consultees to 'mediate' the information for those with less expertise: the consulting body must do that exercise itself, especially where there are likely to be widely differing views among consultees.[447]

6.259 Where consultation is required about a proposal, the need to provide sufficient information does not always oblige a body to give details of alternative options or to explain why such alternatives have not been or are not being pursued. In *Vale of Glamorgan Council v Lord Chancellor and Secretary of State for Justice*,[448] the Divisional Court considered a challenge to the Lord Chancellor's decision to close Barry Magistrates Court, a decision that required prior consultation. One of the grounds of challenge was that the Lord Chancellor

---

441 [2007] EWCA Civ 1139, [2008] ACD 7 (not in issue on appeal to the House of Lords: [2008] UKHL 27, [2008] 1 AC 1003).

442 *R (Stirling) v Haringey LBC* [2013] EWCA Civ 116.

443 [2012] EWCA Civ 472, (2012) 126 BMLR 134

444 *R (Greenpeace) v Secretary of State for Industry* [2007] EWHC 311 (Admin), per Sullivan J.

445 *Brompton and Harefield* at [13].

446 *R (Breckland DC) v Boundary Committee* [2009] EWCA Civ 239, [2009] PTSR 1611 at [46].

447 *R (Breckland DC) v Boundary Committee* (above) at [69].

448 [2011] EWHC 1532 (Admin).

had failed to consult about any alternative scheme. The Court rejected that argument. Elias LJ, giving the judgment of the Court, said:

> ... there is no general principle that a Minister entering into consultation must consult on all the possible alternative ways in which a specific objective might arguably be capable of being achieved. It would make the process of consultation inordinately complex and time consuming if that were so.

6.260 Likewise, in *R (Stirling) v Haringey LBC*,[449] the Court of Appeal rejected an argument that a local authority, consulting on a draft scheme for reducing council tax liabilities for those in financial need ought to have informed consultees of alternative options, even if those had been rejected. Sullivan LJ said:

> It is one thing to say that when options for change are presented in a consultation paper ... they must be fairly presented, it is quite another to submit, as [counsel] submitted on behalf of the Appellant, that in order to be fair a consultation paper must present information about other options that have been rejected. What fairness requires depends on the circumstances of the particular case.

6.261 A failure to consult in accordance with the terms of a statutory obligation is likely to render the subsequent decision unlawful, even if some consultation was in fact carried out.[450]

6.262 Likewise, a statutory exemption from the general requirement of consultation in cases of urgency cannot be relied on by a body to justify its failure to consult in circumstances where it delayed before taking action for so long that the urgency relied on could properly be described as 'self-induced': *R v Secretary of State for Social Security ex p AMA*.[451]

6.263 Where there has been an earlier, full, consultation, a later consultation may not be unlawful even if it is less extensive. In *R (Milton Keynes Council) v Secretary of State for Communities and Local Government*,[452] the Secretary of State's failure to consult local authorities directly during a limited consultation process concerning a proposed statutory instrument did not mean that the consultation process was unlawful. This was because there had been a full and formal consultation a year earlier, during which local authorities had had the opportunity to make submissions.

449 [2013] EWCA Civ 116. See also *R (Buckley) v Sheffield CC* [2013] EWHC 512(Admin).

450 *R (Peat) v Hyndburn BC* [2011] EWHC 1739 (Admin).

451 (1992) 25 HLR 131, QBD.

452 [2011] EWCA Civ 1575, [2012] ACD 40.

6.264   Likewise, where, circumstances change during a consultation process (or immediately following it) the authority will not necessarily need to consult again. In *Stirling* (above), Sullivan LJ said that:[453]

> '..there would often be a 'moving target', and a decision maker was not obliged to draw each and every change of circumstance during what might be a lengthy consultation process to the attention of consultees. It is easy to postulate the test – that the new factor must be of such significance that, in all the circumstances, fairness demands that it must (not may) be drawn to the attention of consultees; it is much more difficult to decide what fairness demands in any particular set of circumstances. A holistic approach should be adopted, all relevant factors should be considered, and these may include, in addition to the nature and significance of the new material, such matters as the extent to which the new material is in the public domain, thereby affording consultees the opportunity to comment upon its relevance to the proposal the subject of the consultation, and the practical implications, including cost and delay, of further consultation.

6.265 Where, following consultation, the decision-maker decides that it wishes to adopt a different proposal than that which was consulted on, a slightly different test has been adopted by the courts. In *R (Smith) v East Kent NHS Hospital Trust*,[454] Silber J said that '... there should only be re-consultation if there is a fundamental difference between the proposals consulted on and those which the consulting party subsequently wishes to adopt'.[455]

Miscellaneous

Estoppel

6.266 It seems that estoppel will not lie against the Crown.[456] Moreover, a local authority cannot be estopped from performing its statutory powers or duties.[457]

6.267   An authority can, however, by its conduct or representations, waive a procedural requirement. Where power has been delegated to an officer, whom the authority has held out as having delegated

---

453 At [24]. See also *R (Buckley) v Sheffield CC* [2013] EWHC 512 (Admin).

454 [2002] EWHC 2640 (Admin), (2003) 6 CCLR 251.

455 At [45].

456 But see *Gowa v Attorney General* (1985) 82 LS Gaz 681, CA, which held that it could. The House of Lords in *Gowa* [1985] 1 WLR 1003 expressly left the point open.

457 *Western Fish Products Ltd v Penwith DC* (1978) 77 LGR 185, CA; *R v Lambeth LBC ex p Clayhope Properties Ltd* [1988] QB 563, CA.

authority, and that officer makes a representation in reliance upon which a person acts to his or her detriment, the effect may be to bind the authority.[458]

458 *Downderry Construction Ltd v Secretary of State for Transport, Local Government and the Regions* [2002] EWHC 2 (Admin), [2002] ACD 62. See also *Western Fish* (above); and *Wells v Minister for Housing and Local Government* [1967] 1 WLR 1000, CA.

Refusal of relief, invalidity and finality

Discretionary remedy and refusal of relief

Delay

7.1 Even where one or more grounds of challenge may be made out, relief may be refused at the discretion of the court. The time limits set out in SCA 1981, s31(6), and CPR r54.5 must be adhered to strictly, and undue delay may result in the refusal of permission or, even if not, the refusal of any relief. Factors that the court must statutorily take into account in deciding whether or not to grant relief, where there has been delay, include whether the delay is such that to grant relief would cause hardship or prejudice to the respondent or would be detrimental to good administration.[1]

7.2 In *O'Reilly v Mackman*,[2] Lord Diplock said:

> The public interest in good administration requires that public authorities and third parties should not be kept in suspense as to the legal validity of a decision the authority has reached in purported exercise of decision-making powers for any longer period than is absolutely necessary in fairness to the person affected by the decision.

7.3 It was emphasised in *R v Secretary of State for Health and Elmfield Drugs Ltd ex p Furneaux, Skinner and Knox*,[3] that the causal connection must be between the grant of relief and any prejudice suffered by the respondent and not between the actual delay and the prejudice.

7.4 The phrase 'detrimental to good administration' has not been defined by the courts. In *R v Dairy Produce Quota Tribunal ex p Caswell*[4] the Court of Appeal offered some guidance as to its meaning which was, briefly, as follows:

- administrative inconvenience is not sufficient reason to deny relief: the consequence of granting it must be positive harm;
- the court can take into account the effect on other potential applicants and the effects if their applications were successful;

---

1 SCA 1981 s31(6). Detriment to good administration may be relevant to the exercise of discretion if there has not been delay, see *Bahamas Hotel Maintenance and Allied Workers Union v Bahamas Hotel Catering and Allied Workers Union* [2011] UKPC4; *R (South West Care Homes Ltd) v Devon CC* [2012] EWHC 1867 (Admin).

2 [1983] 2 AC 237 at 280H–281A.

3 [1994] 2 All ER 652, CA. See also *R v Swale BC ex p Royal Society for the Protection of Birds* (1990) 2 Admin LR 790.

4 *R v Dairy Produce Quota Tribunal ex p Caswell* [1989] 1 WLR 1089, CA.

- there must be affirmative evidence of such detriment or at least evidence from which it can be inferred.[5]

7.5 The House of Lords upheld the decision of the Court of Appeal.[6] Lord Goff of Chievely said:[7]

> I do not consider that it would be wise to attempt to formulate any precise definition or description of what constitutes detriment to good administration. This is because applications for judicial review may occur in many different situations, and the need for finality may be greater in one context than in another. But it is of importance to observe that section 31(6) recognises that there is an interest in good administration independently of hardship, or prejudice to the rights of third parties, and that the harm suffered by the applicant by reason of the decision which has been impugned is a matter which can be taken into account by the court when deciding whether or not to exercise its discretion under section 31(6) to refuse the relief sought by the applicant. In asking the question whether the grant of such relief would be detrimental to good administration, the court is at that stage looking at the interest in good administration independently of matters such as these. In the present context, that interest lies essentially in a regular flow of consistent decisions, made and published with reasonable dispatch; in citizens knowing where they stand, and how they can order their affairs in the light of the relevant decision. Matters of particular importance, apart from the length of time itself, will be the extent of the effect of the relevant decision, and the impact which would be felt if it were to be re-opened. ...

7.6 In *R (Lichfield Securities Ltd) v Lichfield DC*,[8] the Court of Appeal also considered the scope of detriment to good administration, describing it as 'relatively unexplored ground'. Potter LJ continued that this was:[9]

> no doubt partly for the reasons indicated in Lord Goff's speech in *R v Dairy Produce Quota Tribunal, ex p Caswell* ... But a further reason for the relative infrequency of decisions based on good administration is in our view that it can come into play only (a) where undue delay has occurred, and (b) – in practice – where the consequent hardship or

5 For an example of a case where the evidence was insufficient, see *R (Peat) v Hyndburn BC* [2011] EWHC 1739 (Admin).
6 *R v Dairy Produce Quota Tribunal ex p Caswell* [1990] 2 AC 738, HL.
7 [1990] 2 AC 738 at 749F–750A. Cited with approval in *Bahamas Hotel Maintenance and Allied Workers Union v Bahamas Hotel Catering and Allied Workers Union* [2011] UKPC 4, per Lord Walker at [40].
8 [2001] EWCA Civ 304, (2001) 3 LGLR 35.
9 Embarrassment for the defendant is not the same thing as detriment to good administration: *R (Peat) v Hyndburn BC* [2011] EWHC 1739 (Admin), per McCombe J at [63].

prejudice to others is insufficient by itself to cause relief to be refused. In such a situation it can rarely, if ever, be in the interests of good administration to leave an abuse of public power uncorrected. Indeed ... May J in *R v Mid-Warwickshire Licensing Justices ex p Patel* [1994] COD 251 [held] that, despite undue delay, the interests of good administration were served not by withholding but by granting relief.

7.7   In *Lichfield*,[10] the Court of Appeal also considered more generally the way in which the courts should approach the issue of delay under the (then) new procedural regime. The court held that,[11] regardless of whether it involves repetition of the arguments about promptness canvassed at the permission stage, SCA 1981 s31(6)(b) places the issue of undue delay on the agenda at the substantive hearing. It does not follow from this, however, that the judge at the substantive hearing should consider the matter as if the issue had never previously arisen, at least where the matter was properly argued at the permission stage. It was undesirable that one Administrative Court judge should act, in effect, as a court of appeal from another or decide an issue without reference to a fellow judge's earlier decision. The matter was one of practical case management under the CPR. In addition, the second judge must have in mind the need to prevent circumvention of CPR r54.13, which prohibits applications to set aside the grant of permission.

7.8   Accordingly, although ultimately a matter for the judge hearing the substantive application, the appropriate course in such cases would generally be that the defendant should be permitted to recanvass by way of undue delay, an issue of promptness which has been decided at the permission stage in the claimant's favour only if:

- the permission judge has expressly so indicated;
- new and relevant material is introduced on the substantive hearing;
- exceptionally, the issues have developed at the full hearing in such a way as to put a different aspect on the question of promptness; or if the first judge has plainly overlooked some relevant matter or reached a decision per incuriam.

7.9   Applying these principles, it would seem that it will not generally be open to the defendant at the substantive hearing to argue for the refusal of relief, under SCA 1981 s31(6)(b), on the ground of hardship, prejudice or detriment to good administration, where these

10   [2001] EWCA Civ 304, (2001) 3 LGLR 35.
11   [2001] EWCA Civ 304 at [34].

issues have been explored fully at the permission stage, even though the question at that stage was whether or not to grant permission rather than whether or not to grant relief.[12]

7.10 There is of course a distinction between the issues of whether there has been undue delay and whether, if there has, relief should be refused.[13] Unless delay can be shown, however, the court will not be called upon to address whether the grant of relief will cause prejudice, hardship or detriment to good administration, and so the approach of the Court of Appeal in *Lichfield*, limiting reconsideration of delay at the relief stage, will clearly have an impact on the frequency with which it is called upon to consider refusing relief.

7.11 Having said this, although *Lichfield* considered the position under the CPR, it was a feature of that case that the permission application was adjourned into open court where it was fully argued. It must be doubted whether a permission decision taken on the papers, even with the benefit of the defendant's summary of grounds for resisting the application, would be considered to be a proper argument on the issue of delay so as to debar the judge at the substantive hearing with the benefit of detailed argument and evidence from the defendant, from considering the issue of refusal of relief. Such a situation would, in any event, seem to fall within the second of the exceptions to the general rule enunciated in *Lichfield* – new and relevant evidence introduced at the substantive hearing.[14] This is separate from the question of whether or not the judge may reopen the question of the grant of permission to proceed, which is generally prohibited.[15]

7.12 Sometimes, notwithstanding delay, relief will be granted. The courts have held that illegality of a policy is a good reason for doing so, where otherwise the unlawful policy would continue in operation, particularly where only prospective relief is sought. In *R v Westminster CC ex p Hilditch*,[16] Nicholls LJ said that:

> If the policy is unlawful, prima facie it should be discontinued. The mere fact that the policy has been in place for nearly three years is not a sufficient reason for the court countenancing its continuing

12 See, eg, *Lichfield* [2001] EWCA Civ 304, per Sedley LJ at [37]: 'We take the same view [ie, that the claimant had acted promptly in that case], whether the question is regarded as one of promptness in applying for leave or of undue delay in seeking relief.'

13 See *Lichfield* at [39]–[40].

14 *Lichfield* [2001] EWCA Civ 304 at [34].

15 *R v Criminal Injuries Compensation Board ex p A* [1999] 2 AC 330, HL. See also CPR r54.13.

16 [1990] COD 434, CA.

implementation for the indefinite future. There is here good reason for extending time for the making of an application for judicial review, at any rate so far as the relief sought is directed at retraining the further implementation of the allegedly unlawful policy.

7.13   In *R v Rochdale BC ex p Schemet*,[17] Roch J cited Nicholls LJ's comments, although the court refused mandatory relief that would have affected the budget of the respondent education authority for the previous two years, granting only declarations on the illegality of the impugned decisions.[18] In *R v East Sussex CC ex p Ward*,[19] permission was granted on the express basis that no relief would be granted in respect of any period prior to six months before the grant of permission itself (in fact only declaratory relief was granted for various reasons).[20]

7.14   In *R (Blakey) v Secretary of State for Work and Pensions*,[21] however, a delay of a five and half years was partly responsible for the court refusing relief.[22]

Alternative remedies

7.15   The court may refuse relief on the basis that the claimant has not used an alternative remedy (such as an internal or statutory appeal) that would be more convenient for the disposal of the issue in question.[23] Judicial review is often referred to as a remedy of last resort, and the court will usually be extremely reluctant to embark upon enquiries into disputes of fact, especially where an alternative forum, better equipped to do so, exists. In *R v Secretary of State for the Home Department ex p Swati*,[24] Sir John Donaldson MR said:[25]

> ... in giving or refusing leave to apply for judicial review, account must be taken of alternative remedies available to the applicant ...

---

17 [1994] ELR 89, QBD, at 100–1.
18 See also *R v Warwickshire CC ex p Collymore* [1995] ELR 217.
19 (2000) 3 CCLR 132, QBD.
20 (2000) 3 CCLR 132 at 140A–C.
21 [2009] EWHC 172 (Admin), [2009] PTSR 1645.
22 The claimant had also failed to make use of a statutory appeal process, as to which see further below.
23 See, eg, *R v Inland Revenue Commissioners ex p Preston* [1985] AC 835, HL.
24 [1986] 1 WLR 477, CA.
25 [1986] 1 WLR 477 at 485. See also *R v Chief Constable of Merseyside Police ex p Calveley* [1986] QB 424, CA, to the same effect; and *R (Lim) v Secretary of State for the Home Department* [2007] EWCA Civ 773, [2008] INLR 60.

[T]he jurisdiction [will] not be exercised where there [is] an alternative remedy by way of appeal, save in exceptional circumstances. By definition, exceptional circumstances defy definition, but where Parliament provides an appeal procedure, judicial review will have no place, unless the applicant can distinguish his case from the type of case for which the appeal procedure was provided.

7.16 Generally, a right of appeal must be exhausted before resort may be had to judicial review. In *R v Birmingham CC ex p Ferrero*,[26] Taylor LJ emphasised that it would be exceptional to permit judicial review in such cases and stated that it would therefore be necessary, where the exception was sought to be invoked, to look carefully at the suitability of the statutory appeal in the context of the particular case.[27]

7.17 Where, however, proceeding by way of judicial review is genuinely more appropriate, this will be permitted, even where an alternative remedy is available. Examples of valid reasons for using judicial review have been:

- where the applicant seeks not to challenge the individual decision so much as the underlying legality of some determination of which the instant decision is just one manifestation;[28]
- where the decision in question was, on its face, made without jurisdiction or contained an error of law;[29]
- where the alternative remedy was nowhere near as convenient, beneficial and effectual;[30]

26 [1993] 1 All ER 530, CA.
27 An example of the application of this approach can be found in *R (Al-Le Logistics Ltd) v Traffic Commissioner for the South Eastern and Metropolitan Traffic Area* [2010] EWHC 134 (Admin), where in the circumstances judicial review was an appropriate remedy.
28 See *R v Paddington Valuation Officer ex p Peachey Property Corporation Ltd* [1966] 1 QB 380, CA; *R (Singh) v Cardiff CC* [2012] EWHC 1852 (Admin).
29 *R v Hillingdon LBC ex p Royco Homes Ltd* [1974] QB 720, DC, and see also *R (Taylor) v Maidstone BC* [2004] EWHC 257 (Admin), where *Royco* was applied to hold that judicial review was not an appropriate remedy where there was a statutory right of appeal, even though there had been procedural irregularities in the decision making process.
30 *R (C) v Financial Services Authority* [2012] EWHC 1417 (Admin), [2012] ACD 97. The error alleged was a failure to give proper reasons. The appellate tribunal proceeded by way of full rehearing and so did not have power to order the SFA to give fuller reasons. The reasons were necessary to enable the claimant to know whether or not to appeal, given that the appellate tribunal could increase the penalties imposed by the SFA. But cf eg *R v Falmouth and Truro Port Health Authority ex p South West Water* [2001] QB 445, CA.

- where costs were available on judicial review but would not be on appeal;[31] and
- where there are 'exceptional circumstances'.[32]

7.18   These examples of potential exceptions to the general rule must, however, be treated with caution. The difficulty lies not in stating that there are exceptions to the general rule, nor even in establishing some general principles on the basis of which an exception may be made (such as where the alternative remedy is less effective or where the circumstances are exceptional) but in identifying a consistent approach to the application of these principles so as to be able to predict with any degree of certainty when judicial review will be permitted and when it will not. This can be explained, to some extent, by the fact-sensitive nature of decisions on this issue, but it could be argued that the jurisprudence in this area has developed in a way that is more fact-sensitive than it needed to be or, indeed, that the courts have been more defensive of the exclusionary general rule than they need to be. Thus examples can be given of cases which have fallen on one side of the line but which could quite easily have fallen on the other. The following paragraphs therefore attempt to set out the main parameters for the individual decisions that the courts have taken.

7.19   In *R (Sivasubramaniam) v Wandsworth County Court*,[33] the appellant sought to challenge by way of judicial review decisions of a circuit judge, refusing permission to appeal from a decision of a district judge and refusing to set aside a district judge's order. The Court of Appeal held that the only exception to the general rule that judicial review of a discretionary decision would not be permitted where there was an alternative remedy, was where the alternative remedy was less satisfactory than judicial review.[34] Litigants should not be permitted to circumvent the sensible and proportionate statutory

---

31   *R v Inspector of Taxes ex p Kissane* [1986] 2 All ER 37, QBD.

32   *Arslan v Secretary of State for the Home Department* [2006] EWHC 1877 (Admin), where leave to enter the UK as a self-employed businessman was refused and the decision was challenged by judicial review rather than by appeal which could only be brought from outside the UK. The combination of damage to the business caused by requiring the claimant to leave the UK to appeal and the lateness of the defendant taking an alternative remedy point crossed the exceptional circumstances threshold: at [34].

33   [2002] EWCA Civ 1738, [2003] 1 WLR 475. And see paras 2.5–2.12 above.

34   This is a less restrictive formulation of the test than in the other cases referred to above. The judgment as a whole does not, however, indicate that the court was seeking to relax the test; rather, the court's other comments suggest the contrary. Other decisions have also sought to reinforce the strictness of the test: see, eg, *R (Cowl) v Plymouth CC* [2001] EWCA Civ 1935, [2002] 1 WLR 803.

scheme of appeals under the Access to Justice Act 1999, and thereby defeat the objects of the Act, save in truly exceptional cases. Refusals of permission to appeal were not susceptible to judicial review save in exceptional cases where the challenge to the decision was founded on a claim of jurisdictional error or procedural irregularity.

7.20   In *R (Strickson) v Preston County Court*,[35] the Court of Appeal went further, holding that before the High Court should entertain a judicial review of a county court order, there must a defect even more fundamental than an error of law.[36] Laws LJ said:[37]

> How should such a defect be described in principle? I think a distinction may be drawn between a case where the judge simply gets it wrong, even extremely wrong (and wrong on the law, or the facts, or both), and a case where, as I would venture to put it, the judicial process itself has been frustrated or corrupted. This, I think, marks the truly exceptional case. It will or may include the case of pre-*Anisminic* jurisdictional error, where the court embarks upon an enquiry which it lacks all power to deal with, or fails altogether to enquire or adjudicate upon a matter which it was its unequivocal duty to address. It would include substantial denial of the right to a fair hearing, and it may include cases where the lower court has indeed acted 'in complete disregard of its duties' (*Gregory*)[38], and cases where the court has declined to go into a point of law in a particular area which, against a background of conflicting decisions of a lower tribunal, the public interest obviously requires to be decided (*Sinclair*)[39]. ... The courts will have to be vigilant to see that only truly exceptional cases – where there has indeed, as I have put it, been a frustration or corruption of the very judicial process – are allowed to proceed to judicial review in cases where further appeal rights are barred by section 54(4).[40]

7.21   Where the Upper Tribunal refuses permission to appeal, so that there is no further right of appeal, judicial review may be relied upon in limited circumstances, the ambit of which has been defined not by reference to the *Sivasubramanium* line of cases but, instead, relying

---

35 [2007] EWCA Civ 1132. And see para 2.13 above.

36 [2007] EWCA Civ 1132 at [31].

37 [2007] EWCA Civ 1132 at [32]. For an example of a rare case in which a judicial review application succeeded, on the basis that the circuit judge appeared to have decided to refuse permission to appeal before having even heard argument, see *R (Sharing) v Preston County Court* [2012] EWHC 515 (Admin), discussed at para 2.14 above. Perhaps coincidentally, both *Strickson* and *Sharing* concerned challenges to decisions of the same circuit judge.

38 *Gregory v Turner* [2003] EWCA Civ 183, [2003] 1 WLR 1149.

39 *R (Sinclair Gardens Investments (Kensington) Ltd) v Lands Tribunal* [2005] EWCA Civ 1305, [2006] 3 All ER 650.

40 Access to Justice Act 1999 s54(4).

on other principles. In *R (Cart) v Upper Tribunal*,[41] the Supreme Court held that the tribunal system established by the Tribunals, Courts and Enforcement Act 2007 deserved a restrained approach to judicial review, but that the test to be applied to the issue of whether judicial review should be permitted was the same as that applicable to whether a second appeal would be permitted to the Court of Appeal.[42] The test would therefore be whether the challenge raised an important point of principle or practice, or whether there was some other compelling reason to hear it.[43]

7.22   There are numerous examples of the courts refusing relief on the basis that an alternative remedy, especially a right of appeal, ought to have been used in preference to judicial review.

7.23   In *R v Falmouth and Truro Port Health Authority ex p South West Water*,[44] the Court of Appeal re-emphasised the court's distaste, in general terms, for permitting judicial review to be a means of circumventing the usual, and statutorily prescribed procedures. The court rejected an argument that judicial review was appropriate because the statutory procedures, by way of appeal to the magistrates' court, were so protracted and subject to delay that they were not a realistic alternative remedy, especially given that the abatement notice which was challenged would have remained in operation pending an appeal to the magistrates so that the works required by the notice would have had to be carried out before the appeal had been heard. The court stated that the aim must be to make the statutory remedy effective rather than 'to surmise that it is so ineffective that judicial review is permitted'. There was no reason why the procedure laid down by Parliament should not be made an effective procedure. It was the duty of the courts to ensure that it was. Cases where judicial review was appropriate would be rare.

7.24   Similarly, in *M v Bromley LBC*,[45] the Court of Appeal upheld the refusal of relief on judicial review, on the ground of a more suitable alternative remedy. *M* challenged a finding of an investigation by the authority that he had abused children in his care while employed by the authority as a care-worker, alleging procedural impropriety. The court held that an appeal to the Care Standards Tribunal[46] was

---

41   [2011] UKSC 28, [2012] 1 AC 663. See also paras 7.75–7.78 below.

42   See CPR r52.13. See also CPR r54.7A, inserted as a consequence of *Cart*.

43   See para 2.15 above.

44   [2001] QB 445, CA.

45   [2002] EWCA Civ 1113, [2002] 2 FLR 802, CA.

46   The jurisdiction is now exercised by the First-tier Tribunal (Health, Education and Social Care Chamber).

the more appropriate course because it would enable the merits of the finding – which was the most important aspect – and not just the legality, to be examined in the round.

7.25 In *R (DR) v Headteacher of St George's Catholic School*,[47] the claimant was permanently excluded from school, and appealed in accordance with a statutory right of appeal which had three stages. Before reaching the final stage, he sought judicial review of the decision to exclude him. The application was dismissed as was an appeal to the Court of Appeal.

7.26 The Court of Appeal considered the extent to which unfairness at an early stage of the three-stage appeal process could be cured by utilising the final stage of appeal, and held that it was necessary to construe the statutory scheme as a whole, in order to ascertain the intention of Parliament regarding the effect of unfairness in an early part of the process. In this case, although Parliament did not intend any stage of the process to be unfair, nor did it intend a party aggrieved at a decision at the first stage to seek judicial review rather than appeal. Although the appeal did not give redress in respect of the earlier unfairness, the aggrieved party obtained a new, fair decision on the merits from the 'custom-built' expert and independent statutory body, following a rehearing. Unless, therefore, the prior procedural unfairness complained of had somehow tainted the subsequent appeal, in which case the appeal decision itself would necessarily fall, the right to a fair determination of a person's case would be satisfied by the appeal hearing and decision. On a judicial review application brought instead of an appeal, the court would usually leave the claimant to his statutory remedy.[48]

7.27 In some circumstances, the Secretary of State has power under statute to make an order declaring a local authority to be in breach of its statutory duties and to give directions to ensure that the duties are properly carried out.[49] It appears that whether or not such powers amount to an alternative remedy sufficient to preclude judicial review until they have been exhausted, will, like so much else in this area of the law, depend on the circumstances. In *R v Durham CC ex p*

---

47 [2002] EWCA Civ 1822, [2003] 3 BLGR 371.

48 See also *R (B) v Brent LBC Independent Appeal Panel* [2009] EWHC 1189 (Admin); [2009] ELR 390. See also generally *R (Sivasubramaniam) v Wandsworth County Court* [2002] EWCA Civ 1738, [2003] 1 WLR 475.

49 See, eg, Children Act 1989 s84; Local Authority Social Services Act 1970 s7D (inserted by National Health Service and Community Care Act 1990); Adoption and Children Act 2002 s14.

Curtis,[50] the Court of Appeal held that the power under Local Authority Social Services Act 1970 s7D did constitute an alternative remedy that must be exhausted, save where what was required was an authoritative resolution of a legal issue, in which case judicial review would be appropriate.

7.28   That decision may, however, be contrasted with *R v Brent LBC ex p Sawyers*,[51] in which a differently constituted Court of Appeal dealt with Children Act 1989 s84, which was identical in all material respects to Local Authority Social Services Act 1970 s7D, holding that although the existence of the default power could properly be taken into account as an avenue of redress alternative to judicial review, it did not amount to a right of appeal. Therefore, in the circumstances of that case, it was wrong to treat it as a more suitable remedy than judicial review.[52]

7.29   Cases such as *Sawyers*[53] must now be treated with considerable caution. The modern approach is generally to require claimants to make use of any alternative remedy, even if it would not afford all the relief that the claimant seeks and could not even consider all the issues. The reasons for this are essentially resources-based: High Court litigation is expensive (and often publicly funded on both sides) and the courts' resources are themselves limited.[54] This is closely related to the requirement that the courts have imposed that prospective parties to a judicial review claim must attempt alternative dispute resolution before embarking on litigation, even where ADR can do no more than to narrow the issues. This issue is considered in more detail elsewhere.[55]

7.30   On a procedural note, in *R (Wilkinson) v Chief Constable of West Yorkshire*,[56] the question of whether an alternative remedy was more appropriate than judicial review had been fully argued at the permission stage. The judge, in granting permission, had indicated that the point was arguable and the trial judge would have regard to his observations. The court at the substantive hearing could not, therefore,

---

50 [1995] 1 All ER 73, CA, (heard with and reported under *R v Devon CC ex p Baker*), per Simon Brown LJ at 92.

51 [1994] 1 FLR 203, CA. But see *R v Kingston-upon-Thames RLBC ex p T* [1994] FLR 798, DC, in relation to the Children Act 1989 s26 complaints procedure as an alternative remedy. See also paras 15.40–15.44 below.

52 [1994] 1 FLR 203, per Peter Gibson LJ at 214.

53 [1994] 1 FLR 203.

54 See *R (Cowl) v Plymouth CC* [2001] EWCA Civ 1935, [2002] 1 WLR 803, and paras 17.9–17.21.

55 See *R (Cowl) v Plymouth CC* [2001] EWCA Civ 1935; [2002] 1 WLR 803, and paras 17.9–17.21.

56 [2002] EWHC 2353 (Admin), [2002] Po LR 328.

decline jurisdiction to entertain the claim and consider the issue. Conversely, however, the grant of permission in an alternative remedy case was not an inviolate ruling. Alternative remedy arguments could still be considered in relation to the grant of relief.[57]

Other factors relevant to relief

7.31   Other factors the court will consider include whether the grant of a remedy appears futile, academic or otherwise unnecessary, whether the claimant has waived any breach, and the nature of the matter challenged.

7.32   In *R v Secretary of State for Social Services ex p Association of Metropolitan Authorities*,[58] the court refused to quash Housing Benefit Regulations on various grounds, primarily related to the general administrative inconvenience and, in the particular circumstances of the case, the futility of so doing. This was also associated with the facts that the challenge was against delegated legislation, that the principal complaint was not over the substance of the instrument but the non-compliance with a mandatory duty of consultation, and that the Secretary of State had, by the time of the hearing, issued further regulations that were accepted by the claimant to be lawful and that superseded the challenged instrument. Accordingly, only a declaration that the Secretary of State had acted unlawfully in failing to consult was granted.

7.33   In another case involving the Secretary of State and the Association of Metropolitan Authorities, *R v Secretary of State for Social Security ex p Association of Metropolitan Authorities*,[59] the court granted only a declaration for similar reasons. In this case, however, the effect was that the regulations remained in force in spite of the unlawful manner of their implementation.

7.34   By contrast, in *R (C) v Secretary of State for Justice*,[60] a challenge was made to the Secure Training Centre (Amendment) Rules 2007, partly on the basis that no race equality impact assessment had been carried out before their adoption. The claimant succeeded before the

---

57 Compare the position concerning delay and refusal of relief considered in *R (Lichfield Securities Ltd) v Lichfield DC* [2001] EWCA Civ 304, (2001) 3 LGLR 637.

58 [1986] 1 WLR 1, QBD.

59 *R v Secretary of State for Social Security ex p Association of Metropolitan Authorities* (1992) 25 HLR 131, QBD.

60 [2008] EWCA Civ 882, [2009] QB 657.

Divisional Court, but that court declined to quash the Rules.[61] The claimant appealed to the Court of Appeal. Shortly before the hearing before the Court of Appeal the Secretary of State produced an equality impact assessment. Buxton LJ considered that the Divisional Court had been wrong not to quash the Rules. Even though an equality impact assessment had now been produced, it nonetheless continued 'to be of the first importance to mark that failure by an appropriate order'.[62] The Court of Appeal therefore quashed the Rules.[63]

7.35   In *R v Chief Constable for the North Wales Police ex p Evans*,[64] the House of Lords refused the applicant, a probationary constable who had been dismissed in breach of his right to a fair hearing, an order of mandamus even though the judicial committee accepted that that would have been the only satisfactory remedy to obtain his reinstatement to the constabulary. To grant such an order, however, was impractical and would border upon usurpation of the chief constable's role.

7.36   Objections to the grant of relief may be raised by the court or by the defendant, either at the permission stage or on the full application. If there is to be an argument at the full hearing over whether it is appropriate to grant relief and, if so, the form it should take, it is not uncommon for the court to adjourn such argument until after judgment has been given.

Invalidity

7.37   One of the most difficult issues in judicial review is that of the status of an unlawful decision. On the one hand, ultra vires decisions and acts are frequently said to be void and of no effect, or described as nullities. On the other hand, as Hobhouse LJ observed in *Crédit Suisse v Allerdale BC*,[65] even unlawful decisions plainly do have effects until

---

61 [2008] EWHC 171 (Admin), [2010] 1 Prison LR 146.

62 [2008] EWCA Civ 882 at [49]–[55]. See also Keene LJ at [85].

63 In *R (Peat) v Hyndburn BC* [2011] EWHC 1739 (Admin), McCombe J described quashing a selective licensing scheme designated by the authority as the 'natural consequence' of the authority's failure to consult in accordance with the requirements of the statute.

64 [1982] 1 WLR 1155, HL.

65 [1997] QB 306, CA at 352B–355H.

they are quashed and even afterwards.[66] The court may, in its discretion, refuse any mandatory relief, or any relief at all, for a variety of reasons, which will almost inevitably have little or nothing do with the legality of the decision itself, as the issue of relief only arises if a decision has been found to be unlawful.[67] In addition, the presumption of regularity is sometimes invoked to the effect that a decision will be presumed lawful until proved to be invalid.[68]

7.38   In *London & Clydeside Estates v Aberdeen DC*,[69] Lord Hailsham referred to a spectrum of unlawful decisions, some being so obviously unlawful that the citizen may take no action to challenge them until action is taken by the decision-maker to seek to enforce them; others defective in such trivial respects that the decision-maker can safely rely on them nonetheless, in the knowledge that the court would reject any challenge. In between, there will be cases where the citizen needs to take action to protect her or his rights and the decision-maker will need to attempt to remedy the fault.

7.39   Hobhouse LJ, in *Crédit Suisse*, resolved the problems he had identified (para.7.37 above) by reference to this passage from Lord Hailsham's speech in *London & Clydeside Estates*, concluding that terms such as 'ultra vires', 'void' and 'nullity' bore different meanings in public law from those they had in private law:[70] 'It is not correct to take terminology from administrative law and apply it without the necessary adjustment and refinement of meaning to private law.'

7.40   In *Boddington v British Transport Police*,[71] the House of Lords considered the issue in the context of a challenge by a defendant in criminal proceedings to the validity of the byelaw for breach of which the prosecution had been brought. Lord Irvine LC stated that it was

---

66   See, eg, the cases where relief has been granted only prospectively, explicitly on the basis that the court was not prepared to undo the prior effects of the impugned act or decision: *R v Rochdale BC v Schemet* [1994] ELR 89, QBD; *R v Westminster CC ex p Hilditch* [1990] COD 434, CA.

67   See, eg, *R v Secretary of State for Social Security ex p Association of Metropolitan Authorities* (1992) 25 HLR 131, QBD, where a declaration that the Secretary of State had unlawfully introduced housing benefit regulations by reason of a failure to comply with the mandatory duty of consultation deliberately left the regulations themselves in force. See also the cases on refusal of relief referred to at paras 7.31–7.35 above.

68   *Omnia praesumuntur rite essa acta*: recently applied in eg *Saint Aubin Limitee v Alain Jean Francois Doger de Speville* [2011] UKPC 42, per Lord Phillips at [10].

69   [1980] 1 WLR 182, HL, at 189–90: see para 7.54 below.

70   [1997] QB 306, CA, at 355H. See also *Charles Terence Estates Ltd v Cornwall Council* [2012] EWCA Civ 1439, [2013] 1 WLR 466.

71   [1999] 2 AC 143, HL.

permissible to challenge the validity of the byelaw in this manner and considered some of the issues discussed above. He said:[72]

> Subordinate legislation, or an administrative act, is sometimes said to be presumed lawful until it has been pronounced to be unlawful. This does not, however, entail that such legislation or act is valid until quashed prospectively. That would be a conclusion inconsistent with the authorities ... In my judgment, the true effect of the presumption is that the legislation or act which is impugned is presumed to be good until pronounced to be unlawful, but is then recognised as never having had any legal effect at all.

7.41 This was, said Lord Irvine, a consequence of the judiciary's place in the legal system, as Lord Diplock had recognised in *Hoffmann-la Roche & Co v Secretary of State for Trade and Industry*,[73] where he had said:

> Under our legal system, however, the courts as the judicial arm of government do not act on their own initiative. Their jurisdiction to determine that a statutory instrument is ultra vires does not arise until its validity is challenged in proceedings ... Unless there is such a challenge and, if there is, until it has been upheld by a judgment of the court, the validity of the statutory instrument and the legality of acts done pursuant to the law declared by it are presumed. It would, however, be inconsistent with the doctrine of ultra vires ... if the judgment of a court ... that a statutory instrument was ultra vires were to have any lesser consequence in law than to render the instrument incapable of ever having had any legal effect ...

7.42 Thus, said Lord Irvine in *Boddington*,[74] Lord Hailsham, in *London & Clydeside Estates*,[75] was simply observing how the parties may feel it safe and/or prudent to react to differing degrees of unlawful action. That was a matter for the putative parties to decide:[76]

> Subject, however, to any statutory qualification upon his right to do so, the citizen could ... choose to accept the risk of uncertainty, take no action at all, wait to be sued or prosecuted by the public body and then put forward his arguments on validity and have them determined by the court hearing the case against him. That is a matter of right in a case of ultra vires action by the public authority, and would not be subject to the discretion of the court ... [A]ny other interpretation of Lord Hailsham LC's speech could not be reconciled with the decision of this House in the *Anisminic* case ...

72 [1999] 2 AC 143 at 155B–D.
73 [1975] AC 295, HL, at 365.
74 [1999] 2 AC 143, HL.
75 [1980] 1 WLR 182, HL.
76 [1999] 2 AC 143 at 157H–158D.

7.43   In the context of a challenge in criminal proceedings to the validity of the measure in reliance on which the prosecution was brought, this reasoning is, with one *caveat*, wholly convincing and constitutes a welcome and long overdue clarification of the applicable principles. The *caveat* relates to the fact that, in *Boddington* itself, the House of Lords held that an individual will not always be entitled to raise a defence by way of challenge to the validity of the instrument form-ing the basis of the prosecution. Whether or not such a defence is permissible depends on an analysis of the particular statutory con-text; legislation may be construed as having the effect of precluding such challenges being brought by way of defence. This is particularly likely where the acts sought to be challenged by way of defence were administrative acts which were aimed specifically at the defendant who had enjoyed had ample opportunity under the scheme to chal-lenge those acts.[77]

7.44   The main difficulty with Lord Irvine's analysis, however, in other contexts, is that it does not address the issues to which Hobhouse LJ referred in *Crédit Suisse*.[78] In particular, the granting of declaratory relief may leave an unlawful decision in being with full effect, and the court's decision whether or not to quash a decision will frequent-ly be influenced by any action taken in reliance on it by third parties. Even the quashing of a decision does not in many cases result in the undoing of all the prior effects of that decision.[79]

7.45   Thus a tenancy granted pursuant to an illegal housing allocations policy does not become 'ungranted' or otherwise liable to be set aside when the policy itself is quashed.[80] In *Birmingham CC v Qasim*,[81] the Court of Appeal held that where tenancies had been granted to per-sons in contravention of the authority's housing allocation scheme, the tenancies granted were not void or ineffective. The public law illegality of the allocation did not affect the private law validity of the grant.

---

77 *Boddington* (above) at 161G-H.
78 [1997] QB 306, CA.
79 See the cases referred to at para 7.13 above.
80 *R v Port Talbot BC ex p Jones* [1988] 2 All ER 207, (1987) 20 HLR 265, QBD.
81 [2009] EWCA Civ 1080, [2010] PTSR 471. In a passage which was probably obiter Lord Neuberger doubted, without actually referring to *Jones*, the conclusion in that case: see [34].

Second actors

7.46 A different approach to that suggested by Lord Irvine (above) was enunciated by Lord Steyn in *Boddington*, based on an essay entitled 'The Metaphysic of Nullity' – Invalidity, Conceptual Reasoning and the Rule of Law':[82]

> ... it has been argued that unlawful administrative acts are void in law. But they clearly exist in fact and they often appear to be valid; and those unaware of their invalidity may take decisions and act on the assumption that these acts are valid. When this happens the validity of these later acts depends upon the legal powers of the second actor. *The crucial issue to be determined is whether that second actor has legal power to act validly notwithstanding the invalidity of the first act.* and it is determined by an analysis of the law against the background of the familiar proposition that an unlawful act is void. (Emphasis supplied.)

7.47 In *Boddington*,[83] Lord Steyn described this explanation as 'the best explanation that I have seen'.

Triumph of Pragmatism?

7.48 Neither Lord Irvine's nor Lord Steyn's approach commanded a majority of the House of Lords in that case, and Lord Browne-Wilkinson advanced his own suggestion:[84]

> I am far from satisfied that an ultra vires act is incapable of having any legal consequence during the period between the doing of that act and the recognition of its invalidity by the court. During that period people will have regulated their lives on the basis that the act is valid. The subsequent recognition of its invalidity cannot rewrite history as to all the other matters done in the meantime in reliance on its validity.

7.49 In *Mossell (Jamaica) Ltd v Office of Utilities Regulations*.[85] Lord Phillips of Worth Matravers PSC referred to *Boddington* but declined to reach a firm view as to the issue. He said:[86]

> What it all comes to is this. Subordinate legislation, executive orders and the like are presumed to be lawful. If and when, however, they are successfully challenged and found ultra vires, generally speaking it is as if they had never had any legal effect at all: their nullification is

---

82 By Dr Christopher Forsythe, in the collection by Forsythe and Hare *The Golden Metwand and the Crooked Cord* (1998) 159.

83 At 172B-D.

84 At 164B–C.

85 [2010] UKPC 1.

86 At [44].

ordinarily retrospective rather than merely prospective. There may be occasions when declarations of invalidity are made prospectively only or are made for the benefit of some but not others. Similarly, there may be occasions when executive orders or acts are found to have legal consequences for some at least (sometimes called 'third actors') during the period before their invalidity is recognised by the court: see, for example, *Percy v Hall* [1997] QB 924. All these issues were left open by the House in the *Boddington* case. It is, however, no more necessary that they be resolved here than there.

7.50   In *R (Shoesmith) v Ofsted*,[87] Maurice Kay LJ was concerned with an argument that a decision to dismiss the claimant by her local authority employer, based on an unlawful direction from the Secretary of State, was, by reason of the illegality of the direction itself, rendered void and of no effect. He said:[88]

> The case ... now [put] on behalf of Ms Shoesmith ... is that ... the Secretary of State's unlawful direction vitiates the decision ... to dismiss her; accordingly, her dismissal is 'null, void and without legal effect'... In these circumstances she is entitled to ... arrears of salary and pension contributions ... until her employment is lawfully terminated.
>
> 119 This is an attractive submission but I do not feel able to accept it. It seems to me that there is an area, admittedly ill-defined but left open by ... *Boddington* ... and *Mossell* ...., in which the act of a public authority which is done in good faith on the reasonably assumed legal validity of the act of another public authority, is not *ipso facto* vitiated by a later finding that the earlier act of the other public authority was unlawful. I consider the present case, which involves the termination of an employment relationship, is within that ill-defined area. ...

7.51   The result of all this therefore seems to be that we are no closer to a definitive answer from the courts to the questions of validity raised at the beginning of this section. The most recent decisions demonstrate that there is little consensus as to the answer, but the courts have adopted an approach based on pragmatism, telling us little more than we already knew, ie that some unlawful decisions will, when quashed, be recognised as never having had any legal effect; others will be understood to have had legal effects, some or all of which will not be undone; yet others will continue to have legal effects. The relationship between the ruling on unlawfulness (including the basis for the ruling) and the decision as to what if any relief to grant in all the circumstances of the case will determine into which category of case any given unlawful decision will fall.

87 [2011] EWCA Civ 642, [2011] PTSR 1459.
88 At [118]–[119].

Mandatory and directory requirements and substantial compliance

7.52   This is another aspect of the topic of validity and the effect of a decision that is taken in an unlawful manner.[89] Failure to comply with the procedures laid down by Parliament will not always have as its corollary that the resulting decision or act will be void and of no effect. Where Parliament does not specify the result of such a failure, it will be for the courts to determine what that result should be. The mechanism the courts have evolved for doing this is to decide whether or not compliance with the provision in question is mandatory, and the extent of compliance with that requirement.

7.53   At one time, the courts held that if the requirement in question was mandatory the failure would result in the decision being rendered void: if it was simply a directory requirement, then the decision would not be rendered void. That approach has now been refined somewhat into a doctrine of substantial compliance but the essential position that a failure to comply fully with Parliament's requirements will not necessarily invalidate the decision taken continues to apply. At one level, it might seem surprising that the courts are in a position to hold that compliance with some of Parliament's requirements is not mandatory. On the other hand, this doctrine may be seen as necessary to avoid the administrative chaos that could ensue if decisions were struck down for the most technical, minor or immaterial of failures of compliance.

7.54   There is a danger of over-simplification in this matter. The courts have warned against attempting to fit the facts of any case into fixed categories, whether labelled 'mandatory' and 'directory' or 'void' and 'voidable' (or anything else). In *London and Clydeside Estates v Aberdeen DC*,[90] Lord Hailsham LC said:[91]

> When Parliament lays down a statutory requirement for the exercise of legal authority it expects its authority to be obeyed down to the minutest detail. But what the courts have to decide in a particular case is the legal consequence of non-compliance on the rights of the subject viewed in the light of a concrete state of facts and a continuing chain of events. It may be that what the courts are faced with is not so much a stark choice of alternatives but a spectrum of possibilities in which one compartment or description fades gradually into another. At one end of this spectrum there may be cases in which a fundamen-

---

89   See also 'Severability', at paras 7.62–7.69 below.
90   [1980] 1 WLR 182, HL.
91   [1980] 1 WLR 182 at 189–90.

tal obligation has been so outrageously or flagrantly ignored or defied that the subject can safely ignore what has been done and treat it as having no legal consequences upon himself ... At the other end of the spectrum the defect in procedure may be so trivial and nugatory that the authority can safely proceed without remedial action, confident that if the subject is so misguided as to rely on the fault, the court will decline to listen to his complaint. But in a very great number of cases ... it may be necessary for a subject, in order to safeguard himself, to go to court for a declaration of his rights, the grant of which may well be discretionary, and ... it may be wise for the authority ... to do everything in its power to remedy the fault in its procedure so as not to deprive the subject of his due or themselves of their power to act.

7.55   In *R v Secretary of State for the Home Department ex p Jeyeanthan*,[92] the Court of Appeal reconsidered the conventional approach to mandatory and directory requirements. Lord Woolf said that the position was more complex than simply considering whether a statutory provision was mandatory or directory. That approach distracted attention from the important question of what the legislator should be judged to have intended to be the consequence of the non-compliance. That question has to be assessed on a consideration of the language of the legislation against the factual circumstances of the non-compliance. In the majority of cases it would provide limited, if any, assistance to inquire whether the requirement was mandatory or directory; the requirement is never intended to be optional if a word such as 'shall' or 'must' is used.[93] Yet frequently, the court's investigation involved doing no more than deciding the sense in which the word 'shall' was used as part of a particular procedural requirement. As the word 'shall' would normally be inserted to show that something was required to be done, the exercise tended to be 'an unrewarding one.'[94]

7.56   Lord Woolf continued:[95]

> Bearing in mind Lord Hailsham L.C.'s helpful guidance I suggest that the right approach is to regard the question of whether a requirement is directory or mandatory as only at most a first step. In the majority of cases there are other questions which have to be asked which are more likely to be of greater assistance than the application of the mandatory/directory test. The questions which are likely to arise are as follows.

92 [2000] 1 WLR 354, CA. See also *Haringey LBC v Awaritefe* (1999) 32 HLR 517, CA; *R v Thanet DC ex p Warren Court Hotels Ltd* (2000) 33 HLR 32.
93 At 358G–H.
94 At 360C–D
95 At 362C–G.

1. Is the statutory requirement fulfilled if there has been substantial compliance with the requirement and, if so, has there been substantial compliance in the case in issue even though there has not been strict compliance? (The substantial compliance question.)
2. Is the non-compliance capable of being waived, and if so, has it, or can it and should it be waived in this particular case? (The discretionary question.) I treat the grant of an extension of time for compliance as a waiver.
3. If it is not capable of being waived or is not waived then what is the consequence of the non-compliance? (The consequences question.)

Which questions arise will depend upon the facts of the case and the nature of the particular requirement. The advantage of focusing on these questions is that they should avoid the unjust and unintended consequences which can flow from an approach solely dependant on dividing requirements into mandatory ones, which oust jurisdiction, or directory, which do not. If the result of non-compliance goes to jurisdiction it will be said jurisdiction cannot be conferred where it does not otherwise exist by consent or waiver.

7.57 In *R v Soneji*,[96] Lord Steyn adopted the same approach as had Lord Woolf, though largely by reference to *London and Clydeside Estates* itself,[97] and mentioning *Jeyeanthan* only in passing. Lord Steyn said[98] that Lord Hailsham had laid down,

> an important and influential dictum. It led to the adoption of a more flexible approach of focusing intensely on the consequences of non-compliance, and posing the question, taking into account those consequences, whether Parliament intended the outcome to be total invalidity. In framing the question in this way it is necessary to have regard to the fact that Parliament *ex hypothesi* did not consider the point of the ultimate outcome. Inevitably one must be considering objectively what intention should be imputed to Parliament.

7.58 Lord Steyn continued that:[99]

> ... the rigid mandatory and directory distinction, and its many artificial refinements, have outlived their usefulness. Instead, ... the emphasis ought to be on the consequences of non-compliance, and posing the question whether Parliament can fairly be taken to have intended total invalidity. That is how I would approach what is ultimately a question of statutory construction.

---

96 [2005] UKHL 49, [2006] 1 AC 340.
97 And another House of Lords case: *Attorney-General's Reference (No.3 of 1999)* [2001] 2 AC 91, HL.
98 [2005] UKHL 49 at [15].
99 [2005] UKHL 49 at [23].

7.59   In *Greenweb Ltd v Wandsworth LBC*,[100] the dispute concerned the appropriate basis for calculating compensation under the Land Compensation Act 1961, and whether certain statutory assumptions referred to by the Act in mandatory language were in fact directory only.[101] Without referring to *London and Clydeside Estates, Jeyeanthan,* or *Soneji*, the Court of Appeal concluded that the statutory language was clear and unambiguous, and that the consequences of its application was not so absurd that Parliament must have made a drafting mistake so as to permit the court to read the mandatory language as directory. Moreover, given the original purpose of the 1961 Act, mandatory provisions were appropriate. The authority therefore had to pay compensation of £1.6 million, rather than of around £15,000.

7.60   More recently, in *R (E (Russia)) v Secretary of State for the Home Department*,[102] the claimant's indefinite leave to remain in the UK was cancelled while he was abroad. The decision notice incorrectly stated that he could only exercise a right of appeal out of the country, whereas it should have stated that he had ten days to return to the UK and make an in-country appeal.[103] Although the claimant could still exercise his right to an out of country appeal, the Court of Appeal considered, applying *Soneji*, that Parliament would have intended that a failure to comply with the requirement to advise the recipient of his right to an in-country appeal would render the decision notice invalid. It was relevant that a claimant who had to pursue an appeal while out of the country faced considerable and well-established disadvantages.[104]

7.61   Although the reasoning in cases adopting the conventional mandatory/directory dichotomy may no longer be safely relied on, it is still worth noting the outcomes in some of those cases. Where Parliament provided for consultation before legislation, the courts held such a requirement to be mandatory.[105] Duties to give notice were usually held to be mandatory, although in *Langridge*,[106] the particular

100 [2008] EWCA Civ 910, [2009] 1 WLR 612.
101 Land Compensation Act 1961 ss14–15.
102 [2012] EWCA Civ 357, [2012] 1 WLR 3198.
103 See Immigration (Notices) Regulations 2003 SI No 568, Special Immigration Appeals Commission (Procedure) Rules 2003 SI No 1034, and *R (MK (Tunisia)) v Secretary of State for the Home Department* [2011] EWCA Civ 333, [2012] 1 WLR 700.
104 [2012] EWCA Civ 357 at [43].
105 *R v Secretary of State for Social Services ex p Association of Metropolitan Authorities* [1986] 1 WLR 1; *R v Secretary of State for Social Security ex p Association of Metropolitan Authorities* (1992) 25 HLR 131, DC.
106 *Secretary of State for Trade and Industry v Langridge* [1991] Ch 402, CA.

duty was held to be directory only. A requirement to inform a person of a right of appeal has also generally been held to be mandatory on both old and new approaches.[107]

Severability

7.62   Where a decision-maker has acted partly lawfully and partly unlawfully, eg has made an order partly within jurisdiction and partly in excess of it, or partly for lawful purposes and partly for unlawful ones, or in breach of some procedural rules, the court may decide not to quash the decision if the lawful part or purpose, etc, is the dominant one and the unlawful one is cleanly severable.[108]

7.63   The following have been severed:

- planning conditions;[109]
- an order of a disciplinary board;[110]
- an order of a licensing authority.[111]

7.64   Where a training board was under a duty to consult trade unions before making an order, the order was declared to be valid against those that had been consulted but invalid against those that had not.[112]

7.65   Similarly, where a statutory body gives reasons for a decision which may be clearly disentangled, and where the court is satisfied that although one reason may be bad in law, the body would have reached precisely the same decision for the remaining, valid reasons, the court may well refuse to intervene.[113]

---

107 *London and Clydeside Estates v Aberdeen DC* [1980] 1 WLR 182, HL. See also *R (E (Russia)) v Secretary of State for the Home Department* [2012] EWCA Civ 357, [2012] 1 WLR 3198 above.

108 See *R v Secretary of State for Transport ex p Greater London Council* [1986] QBD 556, QBD (upheld on appeal: [1986] JPL 513), although in that case the result of the impugned decision was an indivisible lump sum, so the whole decision was quashed.

109 *Hartnell v Minister of Housing and Local Government* [1965] AC 1134, HL.

110 *Bowman v State and State Services Commission* [1972] NZLR 78.

111 *R v Bournemouth Justices ex p Maggs* [1963] 1 WLR 320, DC.

112 *Agricultural, Horticultural and Forestry Industry Training Board v Aylesbury Mushrooms Ltd* [1972] 1 WLR 190, QBD.

113 See *R v Broadcasting Complaints Commission ex p Owen* [1985] QB 1153, DC; *R v Rochdale MBC ex p Cromer Ring Mill Ltd* [1982] 3 All ER 761, QBD; *R (UNISON) v First Secretary of State* [2006] EWHC 2373 (Admin), [2007] BLGR 188.

7.66   In *R (Lumba) v Secretary of State for the Home Department*,[114] the claimants were only entitled to nominal damages despite being detained pursuant to an unlawful, unpublished, blanket policy, because they would still have been detained if the lawful, published policy had been applied to their circumstances.

7.67   Where, however, the good and the bad, or the motives, etc, overlap, then the courts will hold that the power has not been properly exercised and the decision must be quashed.[115] In *London and Clydeside Estates v Aberdeen DC*,[116] the House of Lords held that a planning certificate which did not include notice of a right of appeal was not severable, because of the mandatory nature of the duty to give the applicant the appeal information.

7.68   In relation to instruments and, in particular, delegated legislation, the test now appears to be one of substantial severability rather than the old 'blue pencil' test. Where the bad words can be severed from the good and still leave a valid text unaffected by the presence of the invalid, the court may sever the good from the bad, and leave the valid part of the text to take effect. (This is the 'blue pencil' test.) Where this is not possible, the court may apparently 'modify the text' and grant a declaration that the instrument shall not take effect to the extent that the maker of it exceeded his or her powers. This can only be done, however, if the court is satisfied that in so doing it is effecting no change to the substance and purpose of the impugned provision.[117]

---

114 [2011] UKSC 12, [2012] 1 AC 245.

115 See *Westminster Corporation v London and North Western Railway Company* [1905] AC 426, HL; *R v Brighton Corporation ex p Shoosmith* (1907) 5 LGR 584; (1907) 96 LT 762, CA; *Webb v Minister of Housing and Local Government* [1964] 1 WLR 1295, QBD.

116 [1980] 1 WLR 182, HL.

117 See *DPP v Hutchinson* [1990] 2 AC 783, HL, per Lord Bridge of Harwich at 811; *R v Inland Revenue Commissioners ex p Woolwich Equitable Building Society* [1990] 1 WLR 1400, HL, per Lord Goff of Chieveley at 1418; *Oakley Inc v Animal Ltd* [2005] EWHC 210 (Pat), [2005] 1 CMLR 51; *R (Public and Commercial Services Union) v Minister for the Civil Service* [2010] EWHC 1463 (Admin), [2011] 3 All ER 73. See also *Crédit Suisse v Allerdale BC* [1997] QB 306, CA (contract); *R v Southwark LBC ex p Dagou* (1995), QBD 28 HLR 72 (decision letter).

Ouster and finality clauses

7.69   This is an extremely complex topic, to which much space could be
        devoted. In brief, however, provisions may be included in statutes
        that purport to exclude the court's supervisory jurisdiction by means
        of a variety of phrases. Such examples include statements that a deci-
        sion shall be 'final', that a delegated decision 'shall take effect as if
        enacted' in the Act, that certiorari[118] 'shall not issue' in respect of
        particular decisions, or that they 'shall not be questioned in any pro-
        ceedings whatever'.[119]

7.70   In general, the courts have accepted that such clauses prevent any
        appeal, but do not exclude the operation of judicial review where a
        decision-maker has acted in excess of jurisdiction. It has been held,
        for instance, that the so-called 'no-certiorari' clause does not prevent
        the court from quashing the act or decision where it was made in
        excess of jurisdiction (though it may prevent quashing for mere error
        on the face of the record).[120] Similarly, the 'as if enacted' formula only
        protects decisions in conformity with the Act (ie lawful decisions),
        since these were the only ones contemplated by the Act, and does not
        impede judicial control of irregular decisions.[121]

7.71   In particular, the House of Lords, in *Anisminic Ltd v Foreign Com-
        pensation Commission*,[122] held that a statutory provision that stated
        that a 'determination ... shall not be questioned in any court of law',
        the most common form of the modern ouster clause, was subject to
        the same doctrine as 'no-certiorari' clauses: it did not exclude judicial
        control in cases of excess of jurisdiction. Lord Reid said:[123]

> It is a well established principle that a provision ousting the ordi-
> nary jurisdiction of the court must be construed strictly – meaning,
> I think, that, if such a provision is reasonably capable of having two
> meanings, that meaning shall be taken which preserves the ordinary
> jurisdiction of the court.

---

118 That is, a quashing order.
119 As to provisions which on their true construction are not ouster clauses, see,
     eg, *Farley v Secretary of State for Work and Pensions (No 2)* [2006] UKHL 31,
     [2006] 1 WLR 1817; *A v B (Investigatory Powers Tribunal: jurisdiction)* [2009]
     UKSC 12, [2010] 2 AC 1.
120 See *R v Medical Appeal Tribunal ex p Gilmore* [1957] 1 QB 574, CA, and the
     cases there referred to by Denning LJ.
121 *Minister of Health v Yaffé* [1931] AC 494, HL.
122 [1969] 2 AC 147, HL.
123 [1969] 2 AC 147 at 170.

7.72 The House of Lords held that no tribunal has jurisdiction to make an error of law:[124]

> Lack of jurisdiction may arise in various ways ... [W]hile engaged on a proper inquiry, the tribunal may depart from the rules of natural justice; or it may ask itself the wrong questions; or it may take into account matters which it was not directed to take into account. Thereby it would step outside its jurisdiction. It would turn its inquiry to something not directed by Parliament and fail to make the inquiry which Parliament did direct. Any of these things would cause its purported decisions to be a nullity ...

7.73 It was held that the term 'determination' did not include everything which purported to be a determination but which was in fact not one at all because of an error of law. This fundamental public law decision therefore renders all errors of law, jurisdictional errors.

7.74 In *R v Secretary of State for the Home Department ex p Fayed*,[125] the Court of Appeal held that a provision that a decision 'shall not be subject to appeal to, or review in, any court' did not preclude judicial review on traditional grounds. In *R v Bradford MBC ex p Sikander Ali*,[126] the court suggested that judicial review proceedings were not civil proceedings, in circumstances where challenge to a decision was prohibited in 'civil or criminal' proceedings. In *Sivasubramaniam*,[127] the Court of Appeal declined to hold that the Civil Procedure Rules and in particular Part 52 (appeals) had ousted the supervisory jurisdiction of the Administrative Court. The court held that such an ouster would require the clearest of words and could not be achieved by implication.

7.75 Most recently, the Supreme Court came to consider a possible ouster clause in *R (Cart) v Upper Tribunal*.[128] The Tribunals, Courts and Enforcement Act 2007 introduced a new system of First-tier and Upper Tribunals. Appeals against decisions of First-tier Tribunals lie to the relevant Upper Tribunal. An appeal from the Upper Tribunal is to the Court of Appeal,[129] on any point of law arising from a decision of the Upper Tribunal, other than an 'excluded decision.' Among the categories of excluded decision is any decision of the

---

124 [1969] 2 AC 147, per Lord Pearce at 195.

125 [1998] 1 WLR 763, CA.

126 [1994] ELR 299.

127 *R (Sivasubramaniam) v Wandsworth County Court* [2002] EWCA Civ 1738, [2003] 1 WLR 475.

128 [2011] UKSC 28, [2012] 1 AC 663.

129 Tribunals, Courts and Enforcement Act 2007 s13.

Upper Tribunal refusing permission to appeal from a decision of a First-tier Tribunal.[130]

7.76 The claimants in *Cart* all sought judicial review of refusals of permission to appeal to the Upper Tribunal. The Supreme Court considered that the 2007 Act did not contain the clear words necessary to oust or exclude the court's supervisory jurisdiction in relation to unappealable Upper Tribunal decisions.

7.77 Baroness Hale said: [131]

> ... the scope of judicial review is an artefact of the common law whose object is to maintain the rule of law – that is to ensure that, within the bounds of practical possibility, decisions are taken in accordance with the law, and in particular the law which Parliament has enacted, and not otherwise. Both tribunals and the courts are there to do Parliament's bidding. But we all make mistakes. No-one is infallible. The question is, what machinery is necessary and proportionate to keep such mistakes to a minimum? In particular, should there be any jurisdiction in which mistakes of law are, either in theory or in practice, immune from scrutiny in the higher courts?

7.78 In concluding that there should be no immunity from judicial review, the Supreme Court considered that it would be proportionate to adopt the second appeals criteria found in CPR r52.13,[132] as the basis for limiting the availability of judicial review without excluding it altogether.[133]

Partial ouster

7.79 Partial ouster clauses, such as those contained in the Town and Country Planning Act 1990 ss285 and 286 onwards, to the effect that a decision shall not be questioned in any proceedings whatsoever except by way of the appeal mechanism provided by the Act itself, are enforced by the courts without resistance, given that judicial review is a remedy of last resort, in any event.

7.80 Moreover, in *R v Acting Returning Officer for Devon and East Plymouth European Constituency ex p Sanders*,[134] the court declined jurisdiction to review a decision of the respondent that a candidate's election nomination paper was valid, on the basis that the Parliamentary Election Rules provided that such a decision was 'final and shall

---

130 Tribunals, Courts and Enforcement Act 2007 s11(4)(b).
131 [2011] UKSC 28 at [37].
132 And now in CPR r54.7A.
133 [2011] UKSC 28 at [56].
134 [1994] COD 497, QBD.

not be questioned in any proceeding whatsoever'. The court held that, unlike *Anisminic*, this was only a partial ouster clause since it did not apply to decisions that a nomination paper was invalid. Furthermore, once the result of the voting was known, there was a right of appeal by electoral petition, and so recourse to law was only postponed by the rules and not precluded by them. The intention was to protect the integrity of the electoral process so that it could only be undone by objection brought once voting was over.

CHAPTER 8

Judicial review and immigration and asylum law

Introduction

8.1　Non-British citizens are subject to immigration control. Generally, they will require leave to enter, and/or to remain in, the UK (unless they possess a right of abode).[1] Leave may be granted for a limited or an indefinite period. The relevant legislation creates separate procedures for asylum and non-asylum applications and provides for appeals from decisions made in respect of such applications. Together with the Immigration Rules, they are intended to form a comprehensive code for immigration control.[2]

8.2　The role of judicial review within immigration law has been extensively circumscribed by a comprehensive system of statutory appeals. Generally, a right of appeal against an asylum or immigration decision lies to the First-tier Tribunal,[3] while decisions of the First-tier Tribunal are themselves subject to a right of appeal on a point of law to the Upper Tribunal.[4] Not all decisions are, however, appealable. In particular, the Secretary of State retains a residual discretion to determine who may enter or remain in the UK, and it is primarily these decisions that provide the scope for judicial review within immigration.

Principal Acts and Immigration Rules

8.3　The structure of immigration control, including the duties and powers of immigration officers and system of appeals, is set out in a variety of different statutes, as supplemented by regulations and orders made under their authority. The principal Acts currently governing immigration and asylum law are:[5]

1　Citizens of the Republic of Ireland are not subject to British immigration controls as the Republic of Ireland is located with the Common Travel Area. Although immigration controls do apply to EU nationals, they are subject to the freedom of movement and the freedom to supply services provisions of the Treaty of Lisbon; in relation to immigration control, these freedoms have been transposed into domestic law by the Immigration Act 1988 s7 and the Immigration (European Economic Area) Regulations 2006 SI No 1003, the effect of which is to exempt EU nationals with a right to reside from the requirement of leave to enter the United Kingdom.

2　Although the secretary of state does retain a residual discretion outside the Immigration Rules. The Rules are published as a House of Commons Paper. See further at para 8.5 below.

3　NIAA 2002 ss82(1) and 83.

4　Tribunals, Courts and Enforcement Act 2007 s11.

5　Note that some of the provisions of these Acts have been repealed and/or amended by subsequent legislation.

- Immigration Act 1971;
- British Nationality Act 1981;
- HRA 1998;
- Immigration and Asylum Act 1999;
- Nationality, Immigration and Asylum Act (NIAA) 2002;
- Asylum & Immigration (Treatment of Claimants) Act 2004;
- Immigration, Asylum and Nationality Act 2006;
- UK Borders Act 2007;
- Borders, Citizenship and Immigration Act 2009.

8.4   Reference should also be made to the National Assistance Act 1948, as this may still – in certain circumstances – impose duties to provide assistance to asylum-seekers.[6]

8.5   The Immigration Rules are statements published by the Secretary of State for the Home Department, which set out how she proposes to exercise the executive powers of the Crown to control immigration.[7] The power derives from the royal prerogative[8] rather than the Immigration Act 1971 (although the Act does provide what the Immigration Rules must contain and how Parliamentary approval of the Immigration Rules is to be obtained).[9]

8.6   Accordingly, other than in circumstances where the Immigration Rules are not compliant with requirements of the Immigration Act 1971, they cannot be vitiated on the ground that they are ultra vires. Particular rules may, however, be quashed or varied on other administrative law grounds or on the basis that they are incompatible with the HRA 1998.

8.7   The Immigration Rules are a source of legal rights[10] and a decision of the Secretary of State must be overturned by the First-tier Tribunal if it is not in accordance with the Rules.[11] The Secretary of State does, however, retain a residual discretion to make decisions – in favour of applicants – that depart from the Rules in exceptional or compassionate circumstances.[12] This exceptional discretion aside, the Secretary of State must ensure that the Immigration Rules are

---

6 This is considered in more detail in the context of housing (paras 9.43–9.55 below).

7 *Odelola v Secretary of State for the Home Department* [2009] UKHL 25, [2009] 1 WLR 1230, per Lord Hoffmann at [6].

8 See paras 2.55–2.65 above.

9 Immigration Act 1971 s1(4).

10 *Secretary of State for the Home Department v Pankina* [2010] EWCA Civ 719, [2011] QB 376.

11 NIAA 2002 s86(3)(a).

12 *Pearson v Immigration Tribunal* [1978] Imm AR 212, CA.

followed so as to ensure fairness between applicants.[13] In deciding whether to depart from the Rules, the Secretary of State must exercise her discretion intelligently, with common sense and humanity.[14]

8.8 It is not uncommon for the Secretary of State to adopt general, and sometimes unpublished, policies and practices that depart from the Immigration Rules. The existence of any such policy normally gives rise to a legitimate expectation that it will be followed, irrespective of whether or not it has been published.[15] The Secretary of State may not, however, operate guidance or codes of practice, not contained within the Immigration Rules, that require an applicant to satisfy certain requirements before he may be granted leave to enter or remain, as any requirement that must be satisfied is an 'immigration rule' within the meaning of the Immigration Act 1971 and must therefore be laid before Parliament.[16]

General scheme of the legislation

8.9 Immigration law confers decision-making functions on a variety of individuals and bodies. Historically, immigration officers were responsible for granting a person leave to enter the UK, while the Secretary of State was responsible for granting or varying a person's leave to remain and for making any decision to remove or deport the person.[17] The Secretary of State may now, however, grant a person leave to enter the UK[18] and immigration officers have the powers of

---

13 *R v Secretary of State for the Home Department ex p Ahmed (Irfan)* [1995] Imm AR 210, CS(OH).

14 *R (Kobir) v Secretary of State for the Home Department* [2011] EWHC 2515 (Admin).

15 *R (Rashid) v Secretary of State for the Home Department* [2004] EWHC 2465 (Admin).

16 Immigration Act 1971 and *R (Alvi) v Secretary of State for the Home Department* [2012] UKSC 33, [2012] 1 WLR 2208. This does not, however, apply to any guidance that governs the circumstances in which leave to enter will be granted outside the Immigration Rules: *R (Munir) v Secretary of State for the Home Department* [2012] UKSC 32, [2012] 1 WLR 2192.

17 The actual administration of support for persons entering the UK – as distinct from the control of immigration and asylum – is similarly apportioned between distinct bodies, although with less clarity than the control over entry. The issue is particularly acute with regard to asylum-seekers, the support of which is principally the duty of the Secretary of State but duties also fall on local authorities in certain circumstances (see *R (Westminster CC) v Secretary of State for the Home Department* [2002] UKHL 38, [2002] HLR 58 and *R (VC) v Newcastle CC* [2011] EWHC 2673 (Admin), [2012] PTSR 546).

18 NIAA 2002 s62.

the Secretary of State if they are delegated to them in accordance with the *Carltona* principle.[19]

8.10   The precise details of the law relating to permission to enter and remain in the UK and control over those who are granted such permission is beyond the scope of this work.[20] If, however, a person requires leave to enter the UK (and, where necessary, entry clearance),[21] such leave may be granted for limited or an indefinite period.[22] Limited leave to enter and/or remain may – and often is – subject to conditions and restrictions such as that the recipient may not have recourse to public funds and/or may not take up employment.[23]

8.11   An application for leave to enter is determined in accordance with the Immigration Rules, which prescribe circumstances in which it is to be refused and those in which it may be granted. There is a general right of appeal against a refusal of leave to enter or entry clearance,[24] but, save for in circumstances where an applicant's leave to enter has been refused in the UK when s/he had been granted entry clearance, the appeal must be brought by the applicant out of the UK.[25] An appeal may only be brought on specified grounds, eg the decision is not in accordance with the Immigration Rules or is a breach of the HRA 1998.[26]

8.12   Once leave to enter has been granted, it may be extended, either indefinitely or for a specified period, revoked or amended.[27] It is for the Secretary of State to decide whether to vary a person's leave and on what conditions, provided it is in accordance with the Immigration Act 1971.[28] Her decision must be informed by the Immigration Rules.

---

19 See *R v Secretary of State for the Home Department ex p Oladehinde* [1991] AC 254, HL, per Lord Griffiths at 300. The *Carltona* principle is explained at paras 6.113–6.115 above.

20 Reference should be had to the major works on this area, such as Macdonald and Toal, *Macdonald's Immigration Law and Practice* (Butterworths, 8th edn, 2010).

21 Leave to enter is – in most instances – granted or refused in the country of departure: Immigration (Leave to Enter and Remain) Order 2000 SI No 1161). Note that entry clearance is also required for a wider class of persons.

22 Immigration Act 1971 s3(1)(b).

23 Immigration Act 1971 s3(1).

24 NIAA 2002 s82(1)(a)(b).

25 NIAA 2002 s92. See para 8.27 below.

26 NIAA 2002 s84(1). See para 8.30 below.

27 Immigration Act 1971 s3(1)(b).

28 Immigration Act 1971 s3(3). A person's leave to remain may be extended by statute if an applicant to vary is made prior to the original leave expiry, but, owing to the decision not being made by the Secretary of State, that person's leave to remain expires: Immigration Act 1971 s3C.

An application is therefore likely to be refused where the variation or extension of leave is sought for a purpose not covered by the Immigration Rules.[29]

8.13   In prescribed circumstances, an extension of leave must be refused.[30] A refusal of an extension or variation of leave to remain will mean that the applicant is an 'overstayer' and liable to be removed or deported from the UK by the Secretary of State. Persons whose leave to remain has expired, or persons who entered the UK without leave to enter, may nonetheless, in limited circumstances, be able to regularise their immigration status in the UK by obtaining leave to remain outside the Immigration Rules.[31] In such circumstances applicants will be granted discretionary leave to remain.[32]

8.14   Applicants who have been granted indefinite leave to remain may remain in the UK indefinitely with no restrictions unless their leave to remain is revoked by the Secretary of State[33] or has lapsed.[34]

Asylum-seekers

8.15   An asylum-seeker is defined by the Immigration Rules as being any person who makes a request to be recognised as a refugee on the basis that it would be contrary to the UK's obligations under the Geneva Convention for him to be removed from the UK.[35] A refugee is defined by the Geneva Convention as anyone who, owing to a well-founded fear of being persecuted for reasons of race, religion, nationality, or membership of a particular social group or political opinion, is unable to return to their country of origin.[36]

8.16   An application for asylum may be made at any time either at the port of entry or anywhere in the UK. After making an application for

29 Subject to the Secretary of State's residual discretion to reach a decision favourable to the applicant which is not in accordance with the Immigration Rules. See para 8.7 above.
30 Immigration Rules para 322.
31 Most commonly by arguing that their removal would amount to a disproportionate interference with their (or members of their family's) article 8 rights.
32 Asylum Practice Instruction: 'Discretionary Leave'.
33 NIAA 2002 s76. A person's leave to remain is, however, extended by Immigration Act 1971 s3D, until his/her in country appeal rights have expired.
34 A person's indefinite leave to remain lapses if s/he remains out of the UK for a period of two years or more: Immigration (Leave to Enter and Remain) Order 2000 SI No 1161 art 13(4)(a).
35 Immigration Rules para 327.
36 Geneva Convention art 1A(2).

asylum, an asylum-seeker may either be granted temporary admission[37] or be detained.[38] Applicants with straightforward claims,[39] or who come from countries that are deemed to be safe,[40] will be 'fast tracked', ie sent to specific detention centres where their claims will be determined quickly.

8.17 Once an application has been made, the Immigration Rules require it to be determined by the Secretary of State[41] as soon as possible.[42] In the event that an application for asylum is refused, the Immigration Rules require the Secretary of State to give reasons (of fact and law) for rejecting the claim.[43]

Support for asylum-seekers

8.18 The Secretary of State may provide accommodation and financial support to asylum-seekers, over the age of 18,[44] and their dependants,[45] who are present in the UK, who have made a claim for asylum,[46] which has yet to be decided, if it appears to her that the asylum-seeker is likely to be destitute if such support is not provided.[47]

8.19 In principle, the Secretary of State must decline to provide support if she is of the view that the applicant's claim for asylum was not made as soon as reasonably practicable after the asylum-seeker entered the UK.[48] In practice, however, the Secretary of State must provide support where a failure to do so would result in the applicant becoming destitute.[49] Accordingly, as asylum-seekers are precluded

---

37 Immigration Act 1971 Sch 2 para 21.
38 Immigration Act 1971 Sch 2 para 16.
39 Currently defined by Asylum Process Instruction: Suitability for Detained Fast Track (DFT).
40 NIAA 2002 s94.
41 Immigration Rules para 328.
42 Immigration Rules para 333A.
43 Immigration Rules para 336.
44 Local social services authorities are required by Children Act 1989 to provide support to unaccompanied asylum seekers under the age of 18. See chapter 15.
45 Immigration and Asylum Act 1999 s94(1).
46 This definition includes applicants seeking leave to remain in the UK on the basis that a return to their country of origin would amount to a breach of art 3, ECHR: Immigration and Asylum Act 1999 s94(1)
47 Immigration and Asylum Act 1999 s95.
48 NIAA 2002 s55(1).
49 NIAA 2002 s55(5) requires the Secretary of State to provide support in circumstances where a failure to provide support would amount to a breach of an applicant's rights under the ECHR.

from entering employment[50] and are otherwise ineligible for benefits,[51] the Secretary of State is to all intents and purposes under a duty to provide support.[52]

8.20 The Secretary of State may also provide support to asylum-seekers whose claims have been refused.[53] A failed asylum-seeker will be entitled to support provided that he appears to be destitute and is either taking all reasonable steps to leave the UK or is unable to leave the UK either because there is no viable route of return to his country of origin or because he is unable to travel for medical reasons.[54]

The appeals structure

8.21 The statutory provisions relating to appeals are governed by the NIAA 2002 and Tribunals, Courts and Enforcement Act 2007. The rules of procedure for the First-tier Tribunal are set out in the Asylum and Immigration Tribunal (Procedure Rules) 2005[55] and the Asylum and Immigration Tribunal (Fast Track Procedure) Rules 2005.[56]

8.22 Appeals against decisions made on the basis that the exclusion, departure, deportation, etc, of the appellant is conducive to the public good or in the interests of national security are made to the Special Immigration Appeals Commission.[57] Appeals made under this Act are subject to their own procedure rules: the Special Immigration Appeals Commission (Procedure) Rules 2003.[58]

---

50 Immigration, Asylum and Nationality Act 2006 s15(1).

51 Immigration and Asylum Act 1999 s115.

52 In *R (Limbuela) v Secretary of State for the Home Department* [2006] UKHL 10, [2006] 1 AC 396, the House of Lords held that the failure to provide accommodation and support to someone who was unable to return to their country of origin, had no alternative means of support and was incapable of supporting himself amounted to a breach of article 3.

53 Immigration and Asylum Act 1999 s4(2).

54 Immigration and Asylum (Provision of Accommodation to Failed Asylum Seekers) Regulations 2005 SI No 930 reg 3.

55 SI No 230.

56 SI No 560.

57 Special Immigration Appeals Commission Act 1997 s2 and Sch 1. The Commission is made up of at least one judge or former judge who has held 'high judicial office' within the meaning of the Appellate Jurisdiction Act 1876 (ie High Court or above); and at least one former or current member of the Upper Tribunal. Customarily, there is a third member of any panel who is usually a high-ranking (or former) civil servant. The Lord Chancellor is now the Secretary of State for Constitutional Affairs.

58 SI No 1034.

Appeals to the First-tier and Upper Tribunal[59]

8.23　A right of appeal from the refusal of an asylum claim,[60] an immigration decision,[61] a refusal to provide support to an asylum-seeker,[62] or the refusal of bail to anyone detained under Immigration Act 1971[63] lies to the First-tier Tribunal. An applicant may appeal against a decision of the First-tier Tribunal, with the permission of the First-tier or Upper Tribunal, on a point of law, provided that the decision is not an excluded decision.[64] The following are excluded decisions:

- a decision of the First-tier Tribunal to review its own decision;[65]
- a decision made under s103 Immigration and Asylum Act 1999, to uphold the Secretary of State's refusal to provide support to under Immigration and Asylum Act 1999 s4 or s95;[66] and
- the refusal of bail under Immigration Act 1971 Sch 2.[67]

8.24　An applicant may appeal to the Court of Appeal against a decision of the Upper Tribunal, provided it is not a refusal of permission to appeal to the Upper Tribunal itself.[68] Judicial review is available against the refusal of permission by the Upper Tribunal, but should be refused unless the case raises an important point of principle or practice or there is some other compelling reason for a judicial review to be entertained.[69]

8.25　The Tribunal, Courts and Enforcement Act 2007 has also conferred upon the Upper Tribunal the power to grant public law remedies (ie declarations, injunctions, mandatory, quashing and prohibiting orders).[70] The Upper Tribunal may only exercise such powers in very limited contexts, in the field of immigration, pursuant to orders made by the Lord Chief Justice.[71]

59　This structure is not applicable in national security or public good cases, see note 57 above.

60　NIAA 2002 s83.

61　NIAA 2002 s82.

62　Immigration and Asylum Act 1999 s103.

63　Immigration Act 1971 Sch 2.

64　Tribunals, Courts and Enforcement Act 2007 s11(1), (4).

65　Tribunals, Courts and Enforcement Act 2007 s11(5).

66　Appeals (Excluded Decisions) Order 2009 SI No 275 art 2(a).

67　Appeals (Excluded Decisions) Order 2009 SI No 275 art 2(b).

68　Tribunals, Courts and Enforcement Act 2007 s13(3), (4), (8).

69　*R (Cart) v Upper Tribunal* [2011] UKSC 28, [2012] 1 AC 663.

70　Tribunals, Courts and Enforcement Act 2007 s15.

71　Tribunals, Courts and Enforcement Act 2007 s18. The powers of the Upper Tribunal are considered further in chapter 19, below. See also Practice Directions [2009] 1 WLR 527 and [2012] 1 WLR 16 (reproduced in appendix C).

Appeals process

8.26   An 'immigration decision' is one of the following decisions:[72]

- refusal of leave to enter the UK;
- refusal of entry clearance;
- refusal of a certificate of entitlement under NIAA 2002 s10 (ie right of abode);
- refusal to vary a person's leave to enter or remain in the UK if the result of the refusal is that the person has no leave to enter or remain;
- variation of a person's leave to enter or remain in the UK if, when the variation takes effect, the person has no leave to enter or remain;
- revocation, under NIAA 2002 s76, of indefinite leave to enter or remain in the UK;
- a decision that a person is to be removed from the UK by way of directions under Immigration and Asylum Act 1999 s10(1)(a), (b) or (c) (removal of a person unlawfully in the UK);
- a decision that an illegal entrant is to be removed from the UK by way of directions under Immigration Act 1971 Sch 2 paras 8–10;
- a decision that a person is to be removed from the UK by way of directions under Immigration, Asylum and Nationality Act 2006 s47 (removal: persons with statutorily extended leave);
- a decision that a person is to be removed from the UK by way of directions given by virtue of Immigration Act 1971 Sch 2 para 10A (family);
- a decision that a person is to be removed from the UK by way of directions under Immigration Act 1971 Sch 2 para 12(2) (seamen and aircrews);
- a decision to make an order under Immigration Act 1971 s2A (deprivation of right of abode);
- a decision to make a deportation order under Immigration Act 1971 s5(1); and
- a refusal to revoke a deportation order under Immigration Act 1971 s5(2).

8.27   As a general rule a person may not appeal against an immigration decision while present in the UK. A person may, however, appeal within the UK against:

- a refusal to vary his leave to remain in the UK;
- the revocation of his indefinite leave to remain;

---

72 NIAA 2002 s82(2).

- a decision to make a deportation order;
- a refusal to grant leave to enter where the applicant is in the UK and had been granted entry clearance;
- a refusal of an asylum or human rights claim; and
- a decision that breaches his EU rights.[73]

8.28 The Secretary of State may, however, preclude a person from bringing an appeal within the UK if she certifies that it is clearly unfounded.[74]

8.29 Where a person has made an asylum claim that has been rejected by the Secretary of State but he has been granted leave to enter or remain in the UK for a period of more than one year, he may appeal to the First-tier Tribunal against the rejection of his asylum claim.[75]

8.30 An appeal to the First-tier Tribunal must be brought on one or more of the statutory grounds and on a 'point of law',[76] although where the applicant appeals from outside the UK against his removal from the UK, his grounds for doing so are restricted.[77] The general (ie the non-restricted) grounds for appeal are as follows:[78]

- that the decision is not in accordance with immigration rules;
- that the decision is unlawful under HRA 1998 s6 as being incompatible with the appellant's Convention rights;
- that the appellant is an EEA national or a member of the family of an EEA national and the decision breaches the appellant's rights under the Community Treaties in respect of entry to or residence in the UK;
- that the decision is otherwise not in accordance with the law;
- that the person taking the decision should have exercised differently a discretion conferred by immigration rules;
- that removal of the appellant from the UK in consequence of the immigration decision would breach the UK's obligations under the Refugee Convention or would be unlawful under HRA 1998 s6 as being incompatible with the appellant's Convention rights.

---

73 NIAA 2002 s92(1), (2), (3).
74 NIAA 2002 s94(1), (2). In the context of an asylum or human rights claim there is a presumption that the claim is clearly unfounded if the removal is to a 'safe country' (ie a country listed in s94(4)): s94(3).
75 NIAA 2002 s83.
76 Tribunals, Courts and Enforcement Act 2007 s11(1), (4).
77 NIAA 2002 s95, which removes the right to appeal under s82(1) on the ground that the removal of the applicant would amount to a breach of the UK's obligations under the Geneva Convention or ECHR, except in cases where a person has been removed to a 'safe country' of which s/he is not a national.
78 NIAA 2002 s84(1)(a)–(g).

8.31   On an appeal, the First-tier Tribunal must treat the appeal against a decision 'as including an appeal against any decision in respect of which an appellant has a right of appeal'.[79] The First-tier Tribunal may, therefore, have to consider the legality of a different decision (or a number of different decisions) from that against which the appeal on its face is brought.[80] Moreover, an immigration judge may consider evidence about any matter that he thinks relevant to the substance of the decision, including evidence that concerns a matter arising after the date of the decision.[81]

8.32   The Secretary of State or an immigration officer can certify that an appeal against a new immigration decision may not be brought if it could have been raised on an earlier appeal against a prior immigration decision and there is no satisfactory explanation for why the appeal against the new decision was not raised at the previous appeal.[82]

Judicial review and immigration and asylum law

8.33   Decisions of the Secretary of State, immigration officers and the First-tier and Upper Tribunal may be subject to judicial review in the High Court on the usual principles of administrative law. In general, however, judicial review will not be an appropriate remedy where a statutory right of appeal exists,[83] and therefore – save in exceptional circumstances – the courts will require the statutory appeal to be pursued and will not entertain a judicial review claim. This means that judicial review may not be used even if it is very inconvenient for a person to exercise a right of appeal from outside the UK.[84]

8.34   There are unlikely to be exceptional circumstances, unless an applicant can point to any danger or practical obstacle to pursuing his appeal,[85] such as political pressure preventing an appeal in the appellant's country of origin.[86]

---

79 NIAA 2002 s85(1).
80 Though it must still, of course, be an immigration decision within NIAA 2002 s82(2).
81 NIAA 2002 s85(4).
82 NIAA 2002 s96(1).
83 *R v Secretary of State for the Home Department ex p Swati* [1986] 1 WLR 477, CA.
84 *R v Secretary of State for the Home Department ex p Pulgarin* [1992] Imm AR 96, QBD
85 *Grazales v Secretary of State for the Home Department* [1990] Imm AR 505, CA.
86 *R v Chief Immigration Officer, Gatwick Airport ex p Kharrazi* [1980] 1 WLR 1396, CA.

8.35   Despite the tribunal structure, judicial review remains relevant within the context of immigration decisions.[87] Generally, judicial review will be available where:

- the challenge is to the Immigration Rules or a statutory instrument;
- the challenge is to a practice or policy;
- the Secretary of State has failed to follow a policy or procedure;
- there is no statutory right of appeal;
- the Secretary of State and/or a local social services authority has determined that a child is an adult.

Challenge to Immigration Rules/statutory instrument/ practice or policy

8.36   The Tribunal may only decide whether the Secretary of State has applied the Immigration Rules correctly; it may not decide whether the rules themselves are lawful.[88] Challenges may therefore be brought on grounds that a rule is not in accordance with Immigration Act 1971, eg it has not been laid before Parliament,[89] it is incompatible with the HRA 1998 or is discriminatory under the Equality Act 2010.

8.37   Challenges may also be brought against statutory instruments, eg the rationality of a designation of a particular country as 'safe'[90] for the purposes of NIAA 2002 s94[91], or policies or procedures, eg the use of the fast-track detention centres[92], on administrative law grounds.

Failure of Secretary of State to follow a policy or procedure

8.38   The failure of the Secretary of State to follow a published policy, not contained within the Immigration Rules, will be judicially reviewable

---

87 It remains to be seen whether judicial review in the Administrative Court for immigration cases will be circumscribed further by requiring such claims to be heard in the Upper Tribunal. See para 8.25 above.

88 NIAA 2002 s84(1). See para 8.30 above.

89 *R (Alvi) v Secretary of State for the Home Department* [2012] UKSC 33, [2012] 1 WLR 2208. See para 8.8 above.

90 See note 74 above.

91 *R (Javed) v Secretary of State for the Home Department* [2001] EWCA Civ 789, [2002] QB 129.

92 *R (Refugee Legal Centre) v Secretary of State for the Home Department* [2004] EWCA Civ 1481, [2005] 1 WLR 2219.

on the grounds that an applicant has a legitimate expectation that any published policy will be applied.[93] This principle has also been held to extend to unpublished policies.[94] Claimants may also rely on unpublished policies that have since been revoked if, at the date the adverse decision was taken (eg a refusal leave to enter), the policy was in existence and the Secretary of State's failure to apply it amounted to an abuse of power.[95] An abuse of power will exist where there has been 'flagrant and prolonged incompetence'[96] on the part of the Secretary of State or she has acted unlawfully within established public law principles.[97]

No right of appeal

8.39 Judicial review remains available against decisions of immigration officers, the Secretary of State and the Tribunal itself where there is no right of appeal. Judicial review may therefore be potentially available in respect of the following:

- the decision is not an 'immigration decision',[98] eg the decision is to issue removal directions, or the refusal of a fresh claim for asylum or a request that the Secretary of State exercise her discretion to grant leave outside the Immigration Rules;
- the Secretary of State has certified an appeal as clearly unfounded;[99]
- the Secretary of State has certified that the appeal could have been brought earlier;[100]
- the decision of a First-tier Tribunal is an excluded decision, eg a refusal of support to an asylum-seeker or a decision to refuse a detained person bail;[101]
- permission to appeal from the First-tier Tribunal has been refused;[102]

---

93 See paras 6.226–6.251 above.
94 *R (Rashid) v Secretary of State for the Home Department* [2005] EWCA Civ 744, [2005] Imm AR 608.
95 *Rashid*, above.
96 *Rashid*, above.
97 *R (S) v Secretary of State for the Home Department* [2007] EWCA Civ 546, [2007] Imm AR 781.
98 See para 8.26 above.
99 See para 8.28 above.
100 See para 8.32 above.
101 See para 8.23 above.
102 See para 8.24 above.

- the Secretary of State has chosen to detain an applicant;
- a preliminary ruling of the First-tier Tribunal which resulted in the denial of justice that could not be remedied by an appeal.[103]

8.40　The Administrative Court has refused to entertain challenges to preliminary rulings in circumstances where a right of appeal exists against the final decision.[104] Judicial review will be available, however, where a preliminary ruling results in a denial of justice which is incapable of remedy on appeal to the Upper Tribunal,[105] eg decisions that prevent an appeal from being brought[106] or that bring the appeal to an end before a decision is made that could have been appealed to the Upper Tribunal.[107]

Unaccompanied asylum-seeking children

8.41　In recent years it has become increasingly common for asylum-seekers to challenge the age attributed to them by immigration officers or local authorities. This is of particular importance because local authorities, rather than the Secretary of State, are responsible for accommodating and providing support to children, and not only is such accommodation likely to be of better quality than that provided to adults, but the additional benefits of being accommodated under Children Act 1989 s20 will also be available.[108]

8.42　Before the decision of the Supreme Court in *R (A) v Croydon LBC*,[109] the courts had proceeded on the basis that the question of whether a person was a child was a matter for the local authority and that such a decision could only be challenged in the courts on traditional grounds for judicial review.[110] In *A*, however, the Supreme Court held that this was incorrect: the question of whether a person was a child was a question of jurisdictional, or precedent, fact and was therefore

---

103　See para 8.40 below.
104　*R (AM (Cameroon)) v Secretary of State for the Home Department* [2008] EWCA Civ 100, [2008] 1 WLR 2062.
105　*AM (Cameroon)*, above.
106　Eg a refusal to extend time for appealing or a refusal to accept a notice of appeal on the ground that there is no appealable decision.
107　Eg a decision to treat an appeal as withdrawn or abandoned.
108　See paras 15.7–15.9 below.
109　[2009] UKSC 8, [2009] 1 WLR 2557.
110　See for example *R (B) v Merton LBC* [2003] EWHC 1689 (Admin), [2003] 4 All ER 280.

a matter for the court to decide on the balance of probabilities after considering all of the evidence.[111]

8.43   Thus a hearing on such an issue, while still formally a judicial review hearing, will be akin to a civil trial on the merits, with both the claimant and social worker required to attend to give evidence under cross examination.[112] Neither party is subject to any burden of proof as the hearing is inquisitorial; the court is simply required to determine, on all of the evidence before it, the age of the child.[113]

8.44   Permission for judicial review in these cases will be refused only if the court concludes that the material before it raises a factual case which, taken at its highest, could not properly succeed at a contested factual hearing.[114]

8.45   Unsurprisingly, owing to the length and therefore cost of the hearings in the Administrative Court, art 11(c)(ii) of the First-tier Tribunal and Upper Tribunal (Chambers) Order 2010[115] has since required that all age assessment disputes must now be heard in the Upper Tribunal, with the Upper Tribunal exercising its judicial review jurisdiction. Where an application is made in the Administrative Court, however, the court must decide the question of permission before referring the case to the Upper Tribunal.[116]

---

111 See paras 6.49–6.56.
112 *R (F) v Lewisham LBC* [2009] EWHC 3542 (Admin), [2010] 1 FLR 1463.
113 *R (CJ) v Cardiff CC* [2011] EWCA Civ 1590, [2012] PTSR 1235.
114 *R (FZ) v Croydon LBC* [2011] EWCA Civ 59, [2011] PTSR 748.
115 2010 SI No 2655.
116 2010 SI No 2655.

CHAPTER 9

Judicial review and housing law

Introduction

9.1   The duty to provide public housing has historically fallen principally on local authorities. Although there is now a range of social landlords providing such accommodation, local authorities still have a central role to play in this area, whether by exercising specific housing functions (eg those contained in the Housing Acts 1985 and 1996) or housing-related social services functions (eg under the Children Act 1989 and the National Assistance Act 1948).[1]

9.2   The scope for judicial review of decisions made in exercise of these functions has been significantly reduced over the last 15 or so years by the introduction of a more extensive system of reviews and appeals (although the introduction of the HRA 1998 led to a considerable number of claims on the basis of alleged breaches of the article 8 right to respect for the home, and/or the article 6 right to a fair hearing).[2]

9.3   This chapter will focus principally on judicial review of local authorities, although following *R (Weaver) v London & Quadrant Housing Trust,*[3] judicial review challenges may now also be brought against some decisions of some private registered providers of social housing (formerly registered social landlords, or housing associations). The circumstances in which such claims may be brought are discussed in detail elsewhere.[4] So far, such challenges have been relatively few and far between. In *R (McIntyre) v Gentoo Group Ltd,*[5] the High Court held that the defendant housing association was, in theory, amenable to judicial review but that the decision under challenge (a refusal to consent to a mutual exchange of properties between two tenants) involved a contractual relationship, albeit one that possessed a public law dimension. Judicial review was refused because the available private law remedies had not been used.

1 For a general overview of housing law, reference should be made to Arden and Dymond, *Manual of Housing Law* (Sweet & Maxwell, 9th edn, 2012) and Astin, *Housing law: an adviser's handbook* (LAG, 2nd edn, 2011).
2 Notable in this regard was the line of cases seeking to challenge eviction decisions where there was no security of tenure (eg *R v Bracknell Forest BC ex p McLellan* [2001] EWCA Civ 1510, [2002] QB 1129; *R (Gangera) v Hounslow LBC* [2003] EWHC 794 (Admin), [2003] HLR 68; *R (Gilboy) v Liverpool CC* [2008] EWCA Civ 751, [2009] QB 699, [2009] HLR 11, which have to be viewed differently in the light of *Manchester CC v Pinnock* [2010] UKSC 45, [2011] 2 AC 104).
3 [2009] EWCA Civ 587, [2010] 1 WLR 363.
4 See paras 2.79–2.103 and 3.59–3.67 above.
5 [2010] EWHC 5 (Admin).

Homelessness

9.4   One of the principal housing duties imposed upon local authorities is the duty to provide assistance to homeless people.[6] In essence, where a person applies to an authority as homeless, the authority is under a duty to undertake enquiries into whether he or she is eligible for assistance, homeless or threatened with homelessness, in priority need and not homeless intentionally. If, following enquiries, the authority is satisfied that the applicant fulfils those requirements, it comes under a duty to secure that accommodation becomes available for the applicant and anyone who might reasonably be expected to live with her or him.[7]

9.5   The role of judicial review in the context of homelessness decision-making has been reduced significantly by the introduction of a procedure for the review of and appeal against such decisions.[8] A housing applicant may seek an internal review of most decisions, including those regarding what, if any, duty is owed and/or the suitability of accommodation offered[9] and, thereafter, may appeal to the county court on a point of law.[10] The existence of this alternative remedy in relation to most homelessness decisions renders judicial review as a means of challenging an authority's actions, available only in very limited situations.

Provision for accepting applications

9.6   Authorities must make reasonable provision for receiving applications from the homeless (although they may not require an application

---

6   Housing Act 1996 Pt 7 (as amended). It is not possible in this work to give a detailed explanation of the law governing homeless applications or homelessness in general – a detailed and complex area of law. Reference should be made in particular to Arden, Orme and Vanhegan *Homelessness and Allocations* (Legal Action Group, 9th edn, 2012).

7   The authority may also inquire into whether the person has a local connection with its area and/or with the area of another local authority and may, in certain circumstances, refer an applicant with a local connection elsewhere back to the other authority to be accommodated: see 1996 Act ss184, 198–200.

8   Housing Act 1996 ss202–204A.

9   Housing Act 1996 s202.

10 Housing Act 1996 s204 – the county court's jurisdiction in this regard is akin to the High Court's jurisdiction on judicial review and therefore a 'point of law' includes not only matters of legal interpretation but also the full range of issues akin to those which would otherwise be the subject of judicial review: *Nipa Begum v Tower Hamlets LBC* [2000] 1 WLR 306, (2000) 32 HLR 445, CA.

to take any particular form)[11] and failure to do so may give rise to a claim for judicial review on the ground that the arrangements are not reasonable.[12] Moreover, an authority cannot refuse to consider an application simply on the basis that the claimant does not live in its area or have a local connection with that area – such considerations can only be taken into account in the course of determining the application.[13] A refusal to consider an application, or an abnormal delay in considering an application, is an issue that may be resolved on judicial review.

9.7   A common reason for judicial review claims in relation to homelessness functions concerns the material submitted in support of the application; although there is no duty on the local authority to reconsider in the light of additional information in support of an application, where such information amounts to a material change in circumstances such a duty does arise.[14] Similarly, if the authority determines the application, there is no duty to reconsider the decision on the basis of fresh information, save where that information amounts to a material change in circumstances since the original application.[15] A fresh application must be accepted, however, unless the second application is based on facts that are identical to those of the first application.[16]

Enquiries

9.8   There are certain procedural rules and principles that must be followed when making enquiries; these broadly reflect the principles of procedural fairness that must be adopted by any person or body exercising statutory decision-making powers.[17] Accordingly, an authority is obliged to make the necessary enquiries and to pursue them rigorously and fairly;[18] an applicant is entitled to an opportunity to explain

---

11 *R v Chiltern DC ex p Roberts* (1991) 23 HLR 387, QBD; see also *R v Northavon DC ex p Palmer* (1994) 26 HLR 572, QBD.

12 *R v Camden LBC ex p Gillan* (1988) 21 HLR 114, QBD.

13 Although it is best practice for a claimant to apply to the local authority in which he or she lives – see *Hackney LBC v Sareen* [2003] HLR 54, CA.

14 *R v Tower Hamlets LBC ex p Nadia Saber* (1992) 24 HLR 611, QBD.

15 *R v Southwark LBC ex p Campisi* (1998) 31 HLR 560, CA. There may, of course, be a requirement to review the decision (Housing Act 1996 s202).

16 *Rikha Begum v Tower Hamlets LBC* [2005] EWCA Civ 340, [2005] 1 WLR 2103.

17 See *Ridge v Baldwin* [1964] AC 40, HL.

18 Although, there is no duty to conduct 'CID type' enquiries: *Lally v Kensington and Chelsea RLBC* (1980) *Times* 27 March, ChD; *R v Gravesham BC ex p Winchester* (1986) 18 HLR 207, QBD.

those matters that the authority considers to be adverse to his or her case;[19] where there is uncertainty the issue must be resolved in the applicant's favour;[20] and, enquiries must be current – and relate to the facts – as at the date of the decision.[21] Although failure to comply with these principles has previously given rise to grounds for judicial review,[22] such matters are more likely now to lead to a request for a review, and thereafter an appeal to the county court. This is not to exclude the possibility of judicial review where the authority fundamentally fails to conduct sufficient enquiries, to the point where they can be said to have failed to complete a lawful assessment.[23]

Interim accommodation

9.9   Pending determination of the enquiries necessary to determine what, if any, duty is owed, an authority must – if it believes or has reason to believe that the applicant may be homeless, eligible for assistance and in priority need – secure that accommodation is made available for his occupation.[24] Such accommodation must be suitable.[25] In securing accommodation for the applicant, the authority must therefore have regard to what is suitable and not simply what is available.[26] The suitability of accommodation is a matter that used frequently to be considered in judicial review proceedings but is now a matter for review and appeal to the county court. Whatever the forum, a wide discretion as to suitability is afforded to authorities.[27]

---

19 *R v Hackney LBC ex p Decordova* (1994) 27 HLR 108, QBD; *R (Begum) v Tower Hamlets LBC* [2002] EWHC 633 (Admin), [2003] HLR 8, QBD.

20 *R v Thurrock BC ex p Williams* (1981) 1 HLR 129, QBD.

21 *Mohammed v Hammersmith and Fulham LBC* [2001] UKHL 57, [2002] 1 AC 547.

22 See, for example, *R v Tynedale DC ex p McCabe* (1991) 24 HLR 385, QBD (decision quashed because the authority failed to direct their attention to the correct enquiries); *R v Brent LBC ex p Babalola* (1995) 28 HLR 196, QBD (decision quashed because the authority required the applicant to substantiate her allegations of neighbour nuisance, rather than investigating the matter themselves).

23 *R (Begum) v Tower Hamlets LBC* [2002] EWHC 633 (Admin), [2002] HLR 8, QBD.

24 Housing Act 1996 s188(1).

25 Housing Act 1996 ss205 and 206(1). See also *R v Ealing LBC ex p Surdonja* (1998) 31 HLR 686, QBD.

26 *R v Newham LBC ex p Ojuri (No 3)* (1998) 31 HLR 452, QBD.

27 But see, eg, *R v Brent LBC ex p Omar* (1991) 23 HLR 446, QBD for a suitability challenge that succeeded.

Decision on application

9.10   Similarly, the decision made by the authority is properly challenged by way of a request for a review under Housing Act 1996 s202, whether the challenge concerns the substance of the decision (ie whether the applicant was eligible, homeless, in priority need and not intentionally homeless) or the procedure followed in making it (including claims that the authority gave insufficient reasons for their decision or that the decision-making process was flawed and/or unfair).[28] Where an authority receives a request for a review but fails to make a decision on review within the statutory time-frame[29] the appeal may be brought against the original decision: judicial review therefore is still inappropriate.[30] A decision by an authority not to extend the time for requesting a review is, however, one that can be challenged by way of judicial review.[31]

The 'full' housing duty: suitability

9.11   Where an authority is under a duty to secure that accommodation becomes available for the applicant, that accommodation must be 'suitable'. The authority is therefore required to have regard to the applicant's circumstances and those of his family,[32] including their needs with regard to work, education and health.[33] Although accommodation outside an authority's area may be suitable[34] the decision to offer such accommodation must be made rationally and having regard to all the circumstances. In *R (Yumsak) v Enfield LBC*,[35] the claimant successfully argued that the decision to place her in bed and breakfast accommodation outside the authority's area was irrational because the authority knew the social, medical and educational needs

---

28 *R v Merton LBC ex p Sembi* (1999) 32 HLR 439, QBD.

29 The decision must be made within eight weeks of receipt of the request – see Housing Act 1996 s203(1) and (7) and the Allocation of Housing and Homelessness (Review Procedures) Regulations 1999 SI No 71.

30 Similarly, an authority's refusal to exercise its discretion to undertake a further, non-statutory review, is a matter for challenge by way of appeal to the county court and not on judicial review: *R v Westminster CC ex p Ellioua* (1998) 31 HLR 440, CA.

31 *R (C) v Lewisham LBC* [2003] EWCA Civ 927, [2003] 3 All ER 1277.

32 *R v Haringey LBC ex p Karaman* (1996) 29 HLR 366, QBD.

33 *R v Newham LBC ex p Sacupima* (1999) 33 HLR 1, QBD; *R v Newham LBC ex p Ojuri (No 3)* (1998) 31 HLR 452, QBD.

34 *R v Newham LBC ex p Sacupima* [2001] 1 WLR 563, (2000) 33 HLR 2, CA.

35 [2002] EWHC 280, [2003] HLR 1.

of her and her family would best be met in their area and because the authority had failed to demonstrate that there was no suitable accommodation available in its area.

9.12   Compliance with a full housing duty may not be deferred.[36] Accordingly, where a duty has been accepted but no progress made towards its fulfilment (ie no accommodation identified or offered) it may be possible to bring judicial review proceedings to compel the performance of the duty, although the court will take account of the realities of the situation, including the length of time that has elapsed since the acceptance of the duty, and will not order a local authority to do the impossible.[37]

9.13   Local authorities with limited housing stock may continue to accommodate successful applicants in interim bed and breakfast accommodation, pending the availability of temporary or permanent accommodation, although bed and breakfast accommodation can only be used for a maximum of six weeks for any applicants with family commitments.[38] As noted above, there are various considerations to which an authority must have regard when determining suitability and it is for the authority to determine – on the date on which the offer is made[39] – what is suitable for the applicant, having regard to all of the applicant's circumstances.[40] An applicant who is dissatisfied with the suitability of accommodation may appeal against the suitability of an offer, whether or not he accepts the offer.[41]

---

36   *R v Newham LBC ex p Begum* (1999) 32 HLR 808, QBD.

37   (1999) 32 HLR 808, per Collins J at 815–6.

38   Homelessness (Suitability of Accommodation) (England) Order 2003 SI No 3326. Slightly different provisions apply in Wales: Homelessness (Suitability of Accommodation) (Wales) Order 2006 SI No 650.

39   *R v Lambeth LBC ex p Ekpo-Wedderman* (1998) 31 HLR 498, QBD.

40   *R v Wycombe DC ex p Hazeltine* (1993) 25 HLR 313, CA. There is guidance on what amounts to suitable accommodation – Homelessness (Suitability of Accommodation) Order 1996 SI No 3204 and Homelessness (Suitability of Accommodation) (England) Order 2003 SI No 3326 – but the final decision is a composite assessment of all relevant factors: *R v Lewisham LBC ex p Dolan* (1992) 25 HLR 68, QBD.

41   See Housing Act 1996 s202 as amended by Homelessness Act 2002 s8(2). For examples of such challenges (brought under the old procedure by way of judicial review) see *R v Tower Hamlets LBC ex p Subhan* (1992) 24 HLR 541, QBD – authority failing to consider racial harassment problems on the estate in which the applicant was to be housed; *R v Haringey LBC ex p Karaman* (1996) 29 HLR 366, QBD – failure to consider the proximity of the accommodation to the applicant's estranged husband, who had previously been violent towards her; *R v Tower Hamlets LBC ex p Kaur, Ali et al* (1994) 26 HLR 597, QBD – affordability of accommodation.

Review and appeal

9.14 Following the introduction of the HRA 1998, questions arose as to whether the review and appeals procedures contained in the Housing Act 1996 were adequate to afford an applicant access to an independent and impartial tribunal so as to comply with the requirements of article 6 of the Convention. In *Adan v Newham LBC*,[42] the Court of Appeal commented (obiter) that the procedure may not be article 6 compliant, on the basis that the appeal to the county court under Housing Act 1996 s204 is, in effect, equivalent to a claim for judicial review in that the county court may only interfere with the local authority's decision on judicial review principles and may not conduct a full merits appeal.[43] This view was, however, subsequently rejected in *Runa Begum v Tower Hamlets LBC*.[44] The House of Lords held that, although the review process was not a review by an independent and impartial person, the right of appeal to the county court was an appeal to a court of full jurisdiction.[45] In *Ali v Birmingham CC*,[46] the Supreme Court concluded that article 6 did not apply, but that, even if it did, the statutory appeal process was still compatible with it, notwithstanding the absence of a full fact-finding jurisdiction.

Accommodation pending review or appeal

9.15 An issue that has frequently given rise to judicial review proceedings is the provision of accommodation pending review and/or appeal.[47] The local authority has a discretion to provide such accommodation and so must consider whether to exercise that discretion. When considering this issue, the authority must take account of three matters that will always be relevant: the merits of the applicant's case that the

---

42 [2001] EWCA Civ 1916, [2002] 1 WLR 2120.
43 *Nipa Begum v Tower Hamlets LBC* [2000] 1 WLR 306, CA. This reflects the issue in *Runa Begum v Tower Hamlets LBC* [2003] UKHL 5, [2003] 2 AC 430, ie whether a court exercising a supervisory jurisdiction could constitute a court of full jurisdiction to provide the necessary safeguards to comply with article 6 of the Convention – compare *R (Alconbury Developments Ltd) v Secretary of State for the Environment, Transport and the Regions* [2001] UKHL 23, [2003] 2 AC 295, which raised similar issues in the planning context and was applied in *Runa Begum*.
44 [2003] UKHL 5, [2003] 2 AC 430.
45 The requirements of article 6 are discussed further at paras 6.151–6.175 above.
46 [2010] UKSC 8, [2010] 2 AC 39.
47 The statutory duty to provide accommodation pending enquiries ends when the applicant is notified of the outcome of her or his decision: Housing Act 1996 s188(3).

decision under review/on appeal was flawed; whether there exists any new material that might well have affected the decision; and the applicant's personal circumstances.[48]

9.16 A distinction falls to be drawn between the appropriate methods of challenging decisions not to provide interim accommodation pending a review under Housing Act 1996 s202, and decisions not to do so pending appeal under Housing Act 1996 s204. Where the decision has been taken pending an appeal, there is a statutory right of appeal to the county court under Housing Act 1996 s204A.[49] The existence of this right will preclude the availability of judicial review to require accommodation pending an appeal.[50]

9.17 There is no right of appeal, however, in relation to a refusal of accommodation pending a section 202 review, and any challenge can only be brought by way of judicial review.[51]

Cases where applicant has no recourse to public funds

9.18 Normally, a person who has entered the UK with a condition that he may not have recourse to public funds will be ineligible for homelessness assistance (and for an allocation under Part 6)[52] There is now a limited category of cases in which such people, if they are carers for their dependent children who are EU nationals, may be entitled to homelessness assistance.

9.19 In *Pryce v Southwark LBC,*[53] the Court of Appeal, applying *Zambrano v Office national de l'emploi,*[54] held that a person who could rely on directly effective EU treaty rights to move and reside freely within the EU,[55] was not 'subject to immigration control' for the purposes

---

48 *R v Camden LBC ex p Mohammed* (1997) 30 HLR 315, QBD; *R v Newham LBC ex p Lumley* (2000) 33 HLR 11, QBD. In *R v Brighton and Hove Council ex p Nacion* (1999) 31 HLR 1095, CA, the Court of Appeal expressly approved the application of this test in relation to accommodation pending appeal. See also *Francis v Kensington and Chelsea RLBC* [2003] EWCA Civ 443, [2003] 1 WLR 2248.

49 Introduced by Homelessness Act 2002.

50 The same approach as was identified in *Mohammed* (1997) 30 HLR 315; *Lumley* (2000) 33 HLR 11; and *Nacion* (1999) 31 HLR 1095, will be applied on a statutory appeal: *Francis v Kensington and Chelsea RLBC* [2003] EWCA Civ 443, [2003] 1 WLR 2248.

51 See the cases referred to at notes 48 and 50 above.

52 See paras 9.22–9.23 below.

53 [2012] EWCA Civ 1572, [2013] 1 WLR 996.

54 Case C-34/09, [2012] QB 265, ECtHR Grand Chamber.

55 Ie the right to move and reside freely within the EU: Treaty on the Functioning of the European Union art 20(2).

of Pt 7, Housing Act 1996. *Zambrano* established that such people could include a parent who was a carer of a child where the child was a citizen of an EU member state and was within the state of which he was a citizen. In such cases, the child's citizenship of the EU could have consequential effects even for a parent who was not a national of any EU member state and who had no leave to remain and no right to work in that state. A '*Zambrano* carer' ie a third-party national carer of a UK national child, derived a right of residence from EU law and was eligible for homelessness assistance.

9.20 It should be noted that, in *Pryce*, the court heard no opposing submissions as to the effect of *Zambrano* as both parties and the Secretary of State as intervener agreed with the analysis set out above. The authority had conceded that the parent in that case satisfied the *Zambrano* criteria and, indeed, ultimately conceded the appeal itself. The Court of Appeal observed that the application of *Zambrano* was fact-sensitive, and its principles were likely to be subject to further analysis.

9.21 The Secretary of State has acted to acknowledge the right of residence of *Zambrano* carers,[56] but has amended the social security legislation to exclude them from welfare benefits including housing assistance unless they had already claimed such assistance prior to 8 November 2012.[57]

Allocations

9.22 The allocation of housing accommodation is governed by Housing Act 1996, Pt 6.[58] An authority must have a scheme for determining priorities in the allocation of its housing stock and may not allocate introductory or secure tenancies[59] other than in accordance with that scheme.[60] An allocation that is unlawful because it is made outside the scheme does not, however, render the grant of the tenancy void or ineffective in private law.[61]

---

56 Immigration (European Economic Area) (Amendment) Regulations 2012 SI No 1547.
57 Child Benefit and Child Tax Credit (Miscellaneous Amendments) Regulations 2012 SI No 2612.
58 As amended by the Homelessness Act 2002.
59 Or nominate a housing applicant to a private registered provider of social housing with whom the authority has nomination rights.
60 Housing Act 1996 s166A(1) in England, s167(1) in Wales.
61 *Birmingham CC v Qasim* [2009] EWCA Civ 1080, [2010] PTSR 471.

9.23   Although the scheme must be framed to secure that a reasonable preference is given to persons with housing needs specified in statute (eg homeless people and those with a medical or a welfare need for accommodation),[62] authorities have a wide discretion regarding the rules and priorities that may be included within their schemes.[63] In particular, so long as an authority's allocation scheme complies with the statutory requirements, the court will be very slow to interfere with it on the grounds of irrationality.[64]

9.24   Accommodation may only be allocated to 'eligible and qualifying persons' as defined in Housing Act 1996, Pt 6.[65] Eligibility is primarily a matter of immigration status; qualification is a matter for the local authority to decide.[66] In Wales, qualification does not arise, but, aside from immigration status, an authority may decide to treat someone as ineligible if he, or a member of his household, has been guilty of unacceptable behaviour rendering him unsuitable to be a tenant.[67] In England and in Wales, the authority may determine priorities between applicants within its scheme by reference to any behaviour of a person (or of a member of his or her household) which affects suitability to be a tenant, or their financial resources or local connection with the authority's area.[68]

9.25   The scope for judicial review in relation to the allocation of accommodation relates, primarily, to the legality of the allocation scheme adopted by the authority, the application of the scheme to the claimant's particular circumstances and the assessment of the claimant's housing needs carried out by the authority. It has been considerably constrained by the decision in *R (Ahmad) v Newham LBC*.[69]

---

62 Housing Act 1996 s166A(3) in England, s167(2) in Wales. Though the authority is entitled to depress the preference that would otherwise have been given by reference to factors such as previous rent arrears: *R v Wolverhampton MBC ex p Watters* (1997) 29 HLR 931, CA.

63 Housing Act 1996 ss 160ZA, 160A, 166A(5) and (6), and 167(5) and (6).

64 *R (Ahmad) v Newham LBC* [2009] UKHL 14, [2009] PTSR 632.

65 Housing Act 1996 s160ZA. In Wales the requirement is only to be an eligible person: s160A.

66 Housing Act 1996 s160ZA(7).

67 That is behaviour that would entitle an authority to possession under Housing Act 1985 grounds 1 to 7: Housing Act 1996 s160A.

68 Housing Act 1996 s166A(5) (England); s167(2A) (Wales).

69 [2009] UKHL 14, [2009] PTSR 632.

9.26   Prior to *Ahmad*, the courts had considered a number of judicial review challenges allocation schemes and decisions.[70] Those cases were doubted by Lord Neuberger in *Ahmad* itself and, as a result of the Supreme Court's conclusion in that case, that the courts should generally leave the design of an allocation scheme to the local authority, there have been many fewer challenges to allocation schemes. In *R (van Boolen) v Barking and Dagenham LBC*,[71] an authority's scheme was not unlawful for not including the detailed terms of an administrative practice, operated under the scheme, for deciding whether an applicant had a local connection. In *R (Tout a Tout) v Haringey LBC*,[72] an authority's procedure was held to be lawful whereby bids for available properties were placed automatically on behalf of applicants occupying temporary accommodation.

9.27   Some of the decisions prior to *Ahmad* may withstand that decision. In *R (Lin) v Barnet LBC*,[73] an authority's scheme was held to be unlawful to the extent that it failed to explain how points were awarded to applicants living in leased homelessness accommodation provided by housing associations when such accommodation fell to be returned to its owners. Likewise, it would still seem to be unlawful for an authority to adopt policies or rules so rigid that they have the effect of excluding an applicant's individual circumstances from consideration.[74]

9.28   It may also be observed that the interaction between anti-social behaviour and allocations, whether in terms of qualification for allocation under the scheme (in England) or eligibility (in Wales), or the priority to be accorded to those admitted to the scheme (England and Wales) may lead to challenges to decisions concerning anti-social behaviour. The procedure to be followed in making findings that affect qualification/eligibility or priority within a scheme must conform with the general public law concepts of rationality, reasonableness and fairness.

---

70   See eg *R (A) v Lambeth LBC; R (Lindsay) v Lambeth LBC* [2002] EWCA Civ 1084, [2002] HLR 57; *R (Giles) v Fareham BC* [2002] EWHC 2951 (Admin), [2003] HLR 36; *R (Begum) v Tower Hamlets LBC* [2002] EWHC 633 (Admin), [2003] HLR 8; *R (Lin) v Barnet LBC* [2007] EWCA Civ 132, [2007] HLR 30.

71   [2009] EWHC 2196 (Admin).

72   [2012] EWHC 873 (Admin).

73   [2007] EWCA Civ 132, [2007] HLR 30.

74   See *R v Canterbury CC ex p Gillespie* (1986) 19 HLR 7, QBD.

Other duties to provide housing

Children Act 1989[75]

9.29   Local authorities' social services departments are under a duty to provide services, which can include accommodation, to children in need in their area.[76]

9.30   The principal duties are contained in Children Act (CA) 1989, ss17 and 20. The former imposes a general duty to safeguard and promote the welfare of children in an authority's area; the latter imposes a specific duty to accommodate a child who appears to require accommodation for certain specified reasons, including that his carer has been prevented from providing him with suitable accommodation. A failure to comply with these provisions – or to exercise the powers and duties contained within them – may give rise to a claim for a judicial review.[77]

Section 17

9.31   A number of judicial review claims have focused on the scope of the duties imposed by these powers. In *R (G) v Barnet LBC*,[78] the claimant sought judicial review of the authority's decision to discharge their duty under CA 1989 s17, by funding the cost of returning the claimant and her son to their country of origin. The House of Lords held that section 17 duties were not owed individually to every child in need so that section 17(1) did not oblige the authority's social services department to meet every child's assessed needs regardless of resources. The provision of housing was a function of the local housing authority and was governed by the detailed provisions of the Housing Acts. Accordingly, section 17 could not be set up as a duty requiring the provision by social services authorities of accommodation for children so as to enable those children to live with their parents (the claimants). Lord Hope said:

> 91 I think that the correct analysis of section 17(1) is that it sets out duties of a general character which are intended to be for the benefit of children in need in the local social services authority's area in general. The other duties and the specific duties which then follow

75   See also chapter 15 below.
76   Children Act 1989 s20.
77   This appears to be so notwithstanding the right under CA 1989 s84 to apply to the secretary of state to exercise his or her default powers under the Act: *R v Brent LBC ex p Sawyers* [1994] 1 FLR 203, CA.
78   [2003] UKHL 57, [2004] 2 AC 208.

must be performed in each individual case by reference to the general duties which section 17(1) sets out. What the subsection does is to set out the duties owed to a section of the public in general by which the authority must be guided in the performance of those other duties ... As ... the defendants accepted, members of that section of the public have a sufficient interest to enforce those general duties by judicial review. But they are not particular duties owed to each member of that section of the public of the kind described by Lord Clyde in *R v Gloucestershire County Council, Ex p Barry* [1997] AC 584, 610a which give a correlative right to the individual which he can enforce in the event of a failure in its performance.

9.32   The Children Act 1989 s17 has now been amended to confirm that the powers it confers are wide enough to encompass the provision of accommodation.[79]

9.33   A related area of some importance to local authorities, which has given rise to a number of challenges ,is the duty that arises under section 17 when a child is in need but his family is ineligible for housing assistance due to their immigration status. This is particularly likely to arise where the family's immigration status is such that they are not entitled to have recourse to public funds.

9.34   Section 17 may play a significant role in such circumstances as, without the right to have recourse to public funds, the family will not have access to benefits, including housing benefit, or accommodation under Parts 6 and 7 of the Housing Act 1996.[80] Unlike the section 20 duty, which is to accommodate the child only, section 17 may be used to provide accommodation for families, where it is necessary to provide such assistance to an ineligible person in order to avoid a breach of that person's Convention rights.[81]

9.35   In *R (Kimani) v Lambeth LBC*,[82] the claimant was a Kenyan national with a four-year-old son, who applied for leave to reside in the UK. This application was refused, and the local authority declined to provide further support for the claimant and her child, on the basis that she was not eligible for such support. The claimant's challenge to that decision was refused. The Court of Appeal held that the objective of NIAA 2002 Sch 3 was to discourage from coming to, remaining in and consuming the resources of the UK certain classes of person

---

79 See Adoption and Children Act 2002 s16(1), which has amended Children Act 1989 s17(6).
80 See paras 9.18–9.21 above.
81 NIAA 2002 Sch 3 paras 1 and 7.
82 [2003] EWCA Civ 1150, [2004] 1 WLR 272.

who could reasonably be expected to look to other countries for their livelihood. Lord Phillips MR said:[83]

> There is no obvious reason why [a foreign national seeking to establish a right of residence] should expect to receive support from this country, rather than her home state, pending the determination of her claim to a right of residence.

9.36　As to the claimant's article 8 rights, the Court of Appeal said that respect for her family life did not require that she should remain in this country while her appeal was considered:[84]

> We do not consider that either article 3 or article 8 imposes a duty on the state to provide the claimant with support. She has not been granted leave to enter or remain in this country. She has been permitted to remain here to pursue an appeal in which she advances, *inter alia*, an article 8 claim ... [N]o infringement of article 8 would result from requiring her to return to her own country pending the determination of her appeal. ... A state owes no duty under the Convention to provide support to foreign nationals who are permitted to enter their territory but who are in a position freely to return home ...

9.37　In *R (M) v Islington LBC*,[85] the Court of Appeal held that an authority could not lawfully refuse assistance to a person whose child was a British citizen and who was destitute while her appeal against a refusal of indefinite leave to remain was pending. The authority had assessed the child's needs under CA 1989 s17 and considered paras 1(1)(g) and 7 of Sch 3 to the NIAA 2002.[86] The authority decided to

---

83　[2003] EWCA Civ 1150, per Lord Phillips MR at [24], [26].

84　[2003] EWCA Civ 1150, per Lord Phillips MR at [40], [49]. See also, eg, *R (Grant) v Lambeth LBC* [2004] EWCA Civ 1711, [2005] 1 WLR 1781 concerning a Jamaican national who had one child who was a British citizen. The local authority considered that it was in the best interests of the claimant and her family to return to Jamaica and offered to pay travel costs and to accommodate pending departure. Although the claimant was successful in her judicial review, the Court of Appeal allowed the authority's appeal: '... the claimant and her two elder children are illegally here, and have no right to be accommodated. The claimant cannot create such a right by making an application for leave to remain, or by appealing against a decision which has gone against her. On the other hand Lambeth, which has provided her with accommodation thus far, cannot act in such a way as to interfere with her Convention rights. The offer it has made seems ... to safeguard those rights' (at [31]).

85　[2004] EWCA Civ 235, [2005] 1 WLR 884.

86　That particular part of the schedule provides that a person who is in the UK in breach of the immigration laws and who is not an asylum-seeker is not eligible for support or assistance under CA 1989 s17.

exercise its power under Regulations[87] to offer the claimant and her child travel tickets to her home country and to accommodate them pending removal. The Court of Appeal held that under NIAA 2002 Sch 3, and the Regulations, the authority's power was limited to the provision of accommodation to a person who was unlawfully in the UK with a dependent child; but as there were ongoing immigration proceedings and the dependent child was British, the power had to be exercised in the light of their rights and the rights of the father to respect for family life under article 8.

9.38   In *R (Clue) v Birmingham City Council*,[88] the Court of Appeal discussed the considerations to which an authority must have regard when assessing a family including a person who:

- was unlawfully present in the UK within the meaning of NIAA 2002 Sch 3,
- was destitute and would (Schedule 3 aside) be eligible for services of the kind listed in paragraph 1 of Schedule 3; and
- had made an application for leave to remain which expressly or implicitly raised grounds under the European Convention on Human Rights:

9.39   The Court held that:[89]

> ... when applying Schedule 3, a local authority should not consider the merits of an outstanding application for leave to remain. It is required to be satisfied that the application is not 'obviously hopeless or abusive' ... Such an application would, for example, be one which is not an application for leave to remain at all, or which is merely a repetition of an application which has already been rejected. But obviously hopeless or abusive cases apart, in my judgment a local authority which is faced with an application for assistance pending the determination of an arguable application for leave to remain on Convention grounds, should not refuse assistance if that would have the effect of requiring the person to leave the UK thereby forfeiting his claim.

9.40   In cases where the three conditions referred to above[90] are present, financial considerations should not enter into an authority's decision-

---

87 Withholding and Withdrawal of Support (Travel Assistance and Temporary Accommodation) Regulations 2002 SI No 3078 reg 3.

88 [2010] EWCA Civ 460, [2011] 1 WLR 99.

89 [2010] EWCA Civ 460, per Dyson LJ at [66]. The Court of Appeal relied upon the approach applied in *R (W) v Croydon LBC* [2005] EWHC 2950 (Admin), [2006] BLGR 159 (see [74]–[76]); *R (B) v Haringey LBC* [2006] EWHC 2255 (Admin), [2007] HLR 13 (see [60]); and *Binomugisha v Southwark LBC* [2006] EWHC 2254 (Admin), [2007] 1 FLR 91 (see [53]).

90 At para 9.38.

making as this would be arbitrary and unfair.[91] The Court of Appeal in *Clue* noted, however, that different considerations applied where a person does not have an outstanding application for leave to remain. In such a situation, a local authority would be entitled to have regard to its resources in deciding whether an interference with a person's rights under article 8 would be justified and proportionate.[92]

Section 20

9.41   As noted above, authorities have a discrete duty to provide accommodation for a child in need who appears to require it because there is no person who has parental responsibility for the child, the child has been lost or abandoned, or the person who has been caring for the child is prevented from providing them with suitable accommodation or care.[93]

9.42   The duties under both CA 1989 ss17 and 20 are owed by authorities to children within the area of the authority. An issue that frequently arises between authorities is as to whose area the child concerned is in. This approach has been severely criticised at the highest judicial level:[94]

> ... Local authorities have to look after the children in their area irrespective of where they are habitually resident. ... [T]here should be no more passing the child from pillar to post while the authorities argue about where he comes from.

National Assistance Act 1948

9.43   National Assistance Act 1948 s21, provides a last resort for those in need of accommodation.[95] It imposes a duty on local authorities, to the extent directed by the Secretary of State, to provide assistance to

---

91 [2010] EWCA Civ 460 at [72].
92 [2010] EWCA Civ 460 at [73]. See also, eg, *R (KA) v Essex CC* [2013] EWHC 43 (Admin) which applied *Clue* (the local authority had acted unlawfully by withdrawing financial support and assistance from a family provided under the CA 1989 where the family was intending to appeal against an immigration decision raising human rights issues), but cf *MN and KN v Hackney LBC* [2013] EWHC 1205 (Admin).
93 CA 1989 s20(1). See also *R (G) v Southwark LBC* [2009] UKHL 26, [2009] 1 WLR 1299.
94 *R (G) v Southwark LBC* [2009] UKHL 26, [2009] 1 WLR 1291, per Baroness Hale at [28].
95 *R v Wandsworth LBC ex p O, R v Leicester CC ex p Bhikha* [2000] 1 WLR 2539; (2000) 33 HLR 39, CA.

those 'in need of care and attention' that is not otherwise available to them.[96]

9.44 The duty extends to those in need of care and attention by reason of:

- age,
- illness,
- disability,
- any other circumstances.[97]

9.45 The Secretary of State has directed that 'any other circumstances' criterion will entitle to assistance people who are or have been suffering from mental disorder and those who are dependent on alcohol or drugs.[98]

9.46 The section 21 duty also extends to expectant and nursing mothers who are in need of care and attention.[99]

9.47 Section 21 may therefore be used, in particular, to provide accommodation for older people, either in local authority owned or private care homes.[100] Judicial review in respect of the exercise of this power may challenge either the results of an assessment as to what, if any, needs the person has[101] or the continued discharge of the duty. In *R v Servite Houses and Wandsworth LBC ex p Goldsmith and Chatting*,[102] the claimants had been placed by an authority in a care home. The owners of the care home wished to close the home and relocate the residents. The claimants sought judicial review on the ground that the decision to close the home breached their legitimate expectation of a home for life. The judgment focused on whether the care-home owner – as a private landlord – was a public body and therefore

96 The Secretary of State's direction is, in England, contained within Department of Health Circular, LAC (93)10, App 1 (reproduced as appendix B in Clements & Thompson *Community Care and the Law* (LAG, 5th edn, 2011)). In Wales the relevant direction is contained in Welsh Officer Circular, WOC 35/93.

97 National Assistance Act 1948 s21(1)(a).

98 Department of Health Circular, LAC (93)10, App 1, para 2.

99 National Assistance Act 1948 s21(1)(aa).

100 In *R v Wandsworth LBC ex p Beckwith (No 1)* [1996] 1 WLR 60, HL, it was held that the duty imposed by National Assistance Act 1948 s21 could be discharged by entering into arrangements with other bodies.

101 Such assessments are conducted under the National Health Service and Community Care Act 1990 s47(1).

102 (2000) 33 HLR 35, (2000) 3 CCLR 325, QBD. See also *R (Chatting) v Viridian Housing* [2012] EWHC 3595 (Admin).

susceptible to judicial review: the court held that it was not.[103] This conclusion was reinforced by the Court of Appeal decision in *R (Heather) v Leonard Cheshire Foundation*,[104] although the court confirmed in the latter case that it was not inappropriate to have pursued the action by means of a judicial review claim.[105] The House of Lords held in *YL v Birmingham CC*[106] that private care-home owners were not public authorities for the purposes of the HRA 1998 s6. The effect of this decision was overturned by Health and Social Care Act 2008 s145.

9.48　　　Persons not entitled to receive certain state benefits[107] are expressly excluded from the ambit of the duty under National Assistance Act 1948 s21. The purpose of this exclusion is to prevent persons subject to immigration control, those who overstay in the UK after the expiration of their leave to remain here, and asylum-seekers[108] from obtaining assistance under the 1948 Act. Where an applicant is caught by this exclusion, he will only qualify for assistance under section 21 if his need for care and attention arises for some reason other than solely destitution: National Assistance Act 1948 s21(1A).[109]

9.49　　　Whether a local authority is obliged to discharge its duty under section 21 in such circumstances is largely a matter of fact and degree, regard being had to the situation of the applicant and whether his need for care and attention arises solely from destitution.[110] Where a local authority receives an application for assistance under section 21, it is a matter for it to conduct the necessary assessments and to determine – in the circumstances – whether the applicant's

103　See also *R v North and East Devon Health Authority ex p Coughlan* [2001] QB 213, (1999) 2 CCLR 285, CA, and contrast *R (Heather) v Leonard Cheshire Foundation* [2002] EWCA Civ 366, [2002] 2 All ER 936, [2002] HLR 49, (2002) 5 CCLR 317.

104　[2002] EWCA Civ 366, [2002] 2 All ER 936, [2002] HLR 49, (2002) 5 CCLR 317.

105　See paras 3.36–3.39 and 3.59–3.67 above for further consideration of this issue.

106　[2007] UKHL 27, [2008] 1 AC 95.

107　The prohibition applies to 'a person to whom section 115 of the Immigration and Asylum Act 1999 apples' – in essence this excludes asylum-seekers and those subject to immigration control.

108　Support for asylum-seekers is provided by the UK Border Agency: Immigration and Asylum Act 1999, see further paras 8.9–8.20.

109　See *R v Wandsworth LBC ex p O, R v Leicester CC ex p Bhikha* [2000] 1 WLR 2539, (2000) 33 HLR 39, CA.

110　'Destitution' is defined in Immigration and Asylum Act 1999 s95(3). The circumstances that will engage the duty under National Assistance Act 1948 s21 occur where destitution is made more acute by reason of age, illness or disability: *Bhikha* (above).

destitution is made more acute by some other factor. Such a decision will be susceptible to judicial review.

9.50 Accordingly, judicial review is often used as a remedy for those who are prima facie excluded from assistance under National Assistance Act 1948 s21 but seek to claim that their need for care and attention, although primarily arising from destitution, is made more acute by some other factor such as age, illness or disability. In *R v Wandsworth LBC ex p O, R v Leicester CC ex p Bhikha*,[111] both claimants had overstayed their leave to remain in the UK and sought to challenge the respective authorities' refusals to provide them with assistance under s21, arguing that they suffered from health problems. Allowing the appeal, Simon Brown LJ said:[112]

> Assistance under the 1948 Act is, it need hardly be emphasised, the last refuge for the destitute. If there are to be immigrant beggars on our streets, then let them at least not be old, ill or disabled.

9.51 Given that section 21 does not, therefore, completely exclude the provision of accommodation to those who are prima facie excluded, claims are often brought by asylum-seekers – or by local authorities – for a declaration as to whether the local authority or the UK Border Agency falls under a duty to provide accommodation and/or assistance.[113]

9.52 A need for care and attention is a pre-condition to the existence of the duty under section 21(1) of the 1948 Act. In *R (Wahid) v Tower Hamlets LBC*,[114] Hale LJ said that the words 'care and attention' in section 21 should be given their natural and ordinary meaning and meant 'looking after'.

9.53 Baroness Hale (as she had by then become) returned to this theme in *R (M) v Slough BC*,[115] where she said:[116]

> But 'care and attention' must mean something more than 'accommodation'. Section 21(1)(a) is not a general power to provide housing. That is dealt with by other legislation entirely, with its own criteria for eligibility. If a simple need for housing, with or without the means of subsistence, were within s.21(1)(a), there would have been no need for the original s.21(1)(b) . Furthermore, every homeless person who did not qualify for housing under the Housing Act 1996 would be

111 [2000] 1 WLR 2539, (2000) 33 HLR 39, CA.
112 [2000] 1 WLR 2539 at [36].
113 *R (Westminster CC) v National Asylum Support Service* [2002] UKHL 38, [2002] HLR 58; *R (Mani) v Lambeth LBC* [2003] EWCA Civ 836, (2003) 6 CCLR 376.
114 [2002] EWCA Civ 287, [2003] HLR 2 at [32].
115 [2008] UKHL 52, [2008] 1 WLR 1808.
116 [2008] UKHL 52 at [33].

able to turn to the local social services authority instead. That was definitely not what Parliament intended ... I remain of the view which I expressed in *Wahid*, at [32], that the natural and ordinary meaning of the words 'care and attention' in this context is 'looking after'. Looking after means doing something for the person being cared for which he cannot or should not be expected to do for himself: it might be household tasks which an old person can no longer perform or can only perform with great difficulty; it might be protection from risks which a mentally disabled person cannot perceive; it might be personal care, such as feeding, washing or toileting. This is not an exhaustive list. ...

9.54   In *R (SL) v Westminster CC*,[117] the Supreme Court held that the words 'care and attention' must take some colour from the association with the duty to provide residential accommodation. Something more than the service provided in that particular case (ie monitoring an individual) was required. The words 'not otherwise available' governed 'care and attention' not 'accommodation'; services that were entirely independent of accommodation arrangements would not, therefore, fall within s21. Whether the criterion of 'not otherwise available' was satisfied in any particular case was best left to the judgment and common sense of the local authority.[118]

9.55   It is for the authority to assess the risk to an applicant for assistance under section 21, based on the risk at the date of assessment.[119]

Housing grants

General

9.56   Local housing authorities have powers and duties to provide grants for home improvements. The award of these grants is now discretionary, save for disabled facilities grants which are mandatory where certain, prescribed conditions are met.[120] Authorities are required to prepare a grants policy – which must be prepared in accordance with

---

117 [2013] UKSC 27.

118 [2013] UKSC 27, per Lord Carnwath at [41]–[49].

119 *R (Nassery) v Brent LBC* [2011] EWCA Civ 539, [2011] PTSR 1639. For an example of a case where the authority's assessment was irrational, see *R (de Almeida) v Kensington and Chelsea RLBC* [2012] EWHC 1082 (Admin), (2012) 15 CCLR 318.

120 The grants regime is now contained in the Housing Grants, Construction and Regeneration Act 1996 and the Regulatory Reform (Housing Assistance) (England and Wales) Order 2002 SI No 1860.

guidance issued by the Secretary of State – and are only able to award grants in accordance with that policy.[121] This is conceptually similar to the housing allocation scheme, which must be adopted and complied with under Housing Act 1996 Part 6.[122] Accordingly, judicial review is likely to arise in similar situations, ie to challenge the vires of the grants policy itself or the application of that policy in specific cases. The award of a grant may be made subject to conditions,[123] which may, themselves, give rise to grounds for challenge.

9.57   Local authority grants are funded by central government, which enjoys considerable discretion in respect of awarding funding to, and recovering it from, local authorities.[124] As with any public discretion, these ministerial powers must be exercised in accordance with the general principles of administrative law.

Disabled facilities grants

9.58   Disabled facilities grants present a different form of potential challenge. The local authority has no discretion over the award of a grant – the award of grant is mandatory if the prescribed conditions are met – and so judicial review may be used to ensure the proper discharge of the duty. In *R v Greenwich LBC ex p Glen International*,[125] the application for a (then) mandatory renovation grant was not accompanied by the two estimates required by the legislation in force at the time.[126] Accordingly, the authority refused to award a grant. The claimants successfully sought judicial review of that decision on the basis that the grant sought was a mandatory grant and the authority were therefore obliged to exercise their discretion to dispense with the need for two estimates.

121   Regulatory Reform (Housing Assistance) (England and Wales) Order 2002 SI No 1860 arts 3(1) and 4.

122   See paras 9.22–9.29 above.

123   Regulatory Reform (Housing Assistance) (England and Wales) Order 2002 SI No 1860 art 3(4).

124   Regulatory Reform (Housing Assistance) (England and Wales) Order 2002 SI No 1860 arts 7 and 8.

125   (2001) 33 HLR 87, CA. The legislation under which this decision was reached was repealed by the Housing Grants, Construction and Regeneration Act 1996, which in turn was amended by the Regulatory Reform (Housing Assistance) (England and Wales) Order 2002 SI No 1860 and the Housing Act 2004, but the principles remain relevant – in particular with regard to disabled facilities grants.

126   Local Government and Housing Act 1989 s102(2)(b).

Defective housing grants

9.59   Defective housing grants may also be available from local authorities.[127] Such grants are only payable where the Secretary of State has designated a dwelling – or a class (or classes) of dwelling – as defective. Moreover, only those people who have purchased such a dwelling from a local authority may claim the grant.[128] There is some scope for judicial review as a remedy in relation to the operation of this grant regime,[129] although provision is made for appeals that militate against the availability of judicial review.[130]

Housing conditions

Statutory nuisance

9.60   Although not primarily related to housing law, the provisions of Environmental Protection Act 1990 Pt 3 are a useful means of enforcing housing conditions, where the problem does not constitute disrepair for the purposes of Landlord and Tenant Act 1985 s11. Because a statutory nuisance claim under section 82 of the 1990 Act is, in law, a criminal prosecution before the magistrates, the remedy of judicial review to challenge a decision of the magistrates will apply as it does to any other case heard by the magistrates' court. The courts have, however, indicated that an appeal by way of case-stated is likely to be more appropriate, unless the claimant's grounds include a breach of natural justice.[131]

9.61   Similarly, if a local authority serves an abatement notice under Environmental Protection Act 1990 s80, the court will generally expect the recipient to challenge the notice by way of the statutory appeal route under the Act, and there will only be very limited room for judicial review claims. The fact that the appeal route is not generally considered effective (due primarily to the delay in obtaining a hearing) will not be a reason for permitting claimants to seek judicial review instead.[132]

---

127 Housing Act 1985 Pt 16.
128 That is, people who have exercised the right to buy or who have otherwise purchased from an authority's housing stock.
129 See, for example, *R v Thurrock BC ex p Welham* (1991) 23 HLR 434, QBD.
130 See *R v Sandwell MBC ex p Cashmore* (1993) 25 HLR 544, QBD.
131 See *R (Clark-Darby) v Highbury Magistrates' Court* [2001] EWHC 959 (Admin).
132 See *R v Falmouth and Truro Port Health Authority ex p South West Water* [2001] QB 445, CA.

9.62   A refusal to serve an abatement notice does not confer a right of appeal on a person who sought the service of such a notice. In *R (Vella) v Lambeth LBC*,[133] a tenant unsuccessfully sought judicial review of the local authority's refusal to serve an abatement notice on his landlord to require the landlord to install sound insulation between his and a neighbouring flat.

Licensing

9.63   The Housing Act 2004 confers powers on local authorities to introduce landlord licensing schemes for privately let accommodation, including houses in multiple occupation, and to make other orders and give notices in relation to housing conditions in their area.[134]

9.64   In principle, the exercise (or non-exercise) of any of these functions is challengeable by way of judicial review, although some statutory rights of appeal have been created.[135]

9.65   In *R (Peat) v Hyndburn BC*,[136] 2004 Act landlords successfully challenged a local authority's designation of part of its area as an area of selective landlord licensing, on the grounds that there had been a failure to conduct any proper consultation exercise and that the information given to the Secretary of State to obtain his confirmation of the designation had been incorrect.

9.66   Where the validity of a notice served by a local authority on a person in control of a house in multiple occupation is challenged on the basis that the house is not in multiple occupation, it is not necessary to use judicial review proceedings. The county court has jurisdiction to determine that question.[137] This is not to say that judicial review may not be used in appropriate circumstances.[138]

Housing benefit

9.67   This topic is dealt with elsewhere.[139]

---

133 [2005] EWHC 2473 (Admin), [2006] Env LR 33.
134 Housing Act 2004 Pts 1–4.
135 Eg *ss*45 and 48.
136 [2011] EWHC 1739.
137 *Nolan v Leeds CC* (1991) 23 HLR 135.
138 See, eg, *R v Lambeth LBC ex p Clayhope Properties Ltd* [1988] QB 563, CA (judicial review granted of refusal to pay mandatory repair grant).
139 See paras 11.22–11.29 below.

Other housing functions

9.68   The significance of housing law, in its widest sense, as a series of local authority functions should not be underestimated. A detailed analysis of all of the applicable powers and duties is, however, beyond the scope of this work.

9.69   It should not be forgotten, however, in the context of judicial review, that local authorities have complex financial obligations in respect of their housing stock. Authorities are, for example, obliged to maintain a ring-fenced housing revenue account[140] relating to all sums falling to be credited or debited in respect of, among other things, properties provided in discharge of their functions under the Housing Acts 1985 and 1996. The account must be kept, broadly, in balance and may not be subsidised from other funds.[141]

9.70   This financial obligation provides scope for judicial review in respect of those items that may be credited or debited to the account. Thus, in *R v Ealing LBC ex p Lewis*,[142] the applicant successfully challenged the authority's attempt to debit from the account various items relating to the salaries of staff employed by them. Although such claims are rare, they do demonstrate the potential breadth of housing law as a source of judicial review claims.

Impermissible challenges

Secure, introductory and demoted tenancies

9.71   Questions arising under Housing Act 1985 Pt 4, relating to secure tenancies, or Housing Act 1996 Pt 5 Chs 1 and 1A, concerning introductory and demoted tenancies, may all be determined by the county court.[143] The use of judicial review is firmly discouraged by provisions that have the effect that any person commencing proceedings in the High Court which could have been commenced in the county court is not entitled to any costs at all.[144]

---

140   See Local Government and Housing Act 1989 s75 and Sch 4, as substantially amended by the Local Government Act 2003.

141   Local Government and Housing Act 1989 ss79–88 provided for a system of central government subsidy. Localism Act 2011 s167 and Sch 15 will abolish the subsidy in England, while it will remain in Wales.

142   (1992) 24 HLR 484, CA.

143   See Housing Act 1985 s110 and Housing Act 1996 ss138 and 143N.

144   See Housing Act 1985 s110(3); Housing Act 1996 ss138(3) and 143N(4).

9.72   Introductory and demoted tenancies were, however, treated differently until the decisions of the Supreme Court in *Manchester CC v Pinnock*[145] and *Hounslow LBC v Powell*.[146] Until those cases the position had been that because the county court has no jurisdiction to refuse to grant a possession order where the notice given to the tenant that proceedings are to be commenced is valid, any challenge to the merits of the decision to evict or to the conduct of the statutory review to which the tenant is entitled could only be brought by way of judicial review, and could not be relied on as a defence to the possession proceedings themselves.[147]

9.73   That approach was swept away in *Pinnock* and *Powell*. Introductory and demoted tenants, and, indeed, any other occupier of land,[148] can now rely on a public law defences or raise breaches of their rights under article 8 of the European Convention as a potential defence to possession proceedings, although it can be expected that such a defence will rarely succeed.[149] Such defences can be raised, in principle, at any stage of the proceedings, although an occupier will be expected to do so at the possession hearing and not at some later stage (eg, warrant), absent a material change of circumstances or some other exceptional circumstance.[150]

---

145 [2010] UKSC 45, [2011] 2 AC 104.

146 [2011] UKSC 8, [2011] 2 AC 1186.

147 See, eg, *Manchester CC v Cochrane* [1999] 1 WLR 89, (1999) 31 HLR 810, CA; *R (McLellan) v Bracknell Forest BC* [2001] EWCA Civ 1510, [2002] QB 1129; *R (Gilboy) v Liverpool CC* [2008] EWCA Civ 751, [2009] QB 699.

148 Eg a trespasser: *Birmingham CC v Lloyd* [2012] EWCA Civ 969, [2012] HLR 44.

149 See eg *Corby BC v Scott* [2012] EWCA Civ 276, [2012] HLR 23.

150 See *R (JL) v Secretary of State for Defence* [2013] EWCA Civ 449, per Briggs LJ at [38]–[42].

CHAPTER 10

Judicial review and education law

continued

10.1 Judicial review has become an increasingly important method of challenging decisions relating to education, and there is now a considerable body of case-law in this area. Moreover, due to changes made by the Education Act 2011, in force since 1 September 2012, judicial review principles will play an important role in relation to challenges, before the Independent Review Panel, to the permanent exclusion of pupils from maintained schools.[1]

Legislation and developments

10.2 The law on education is complex, with a sizeable number of statutes and regulations governing the area. Prior to the Education Act 2002, the statutory framework of education was set out in the Education Act 1996 which, although substantially repealed, still provides for important matters such as compulsory education, certain local authority functions, school attendance, school transport and special education needs. Other legislation which is still relevant includes the School Standards and Framework Act (SSFA) 1998, the Education Act 2005, the Education and Inspections Act 2006, and the Academies Act 2010.

10.3 The Education Reform Act 1988, Further and Higher Education Act 1992, Higher Education Act 2004, Education and Skills Act 2008 and Apprentices, Skills, Children and Learning Act 2009 govern the provisions of higher education, training and adult skills. The Apprentices, Skills, Children and Learning Act 2009 provides for apprenticeships for 16–18-year-olds with suitable qualifications.

10.4 The Equality Act 2010 replaced all previous equalities legislation. In its application to schools, the Equality Act 2010 does not substantially depart from the previous legislative regime. Schools may not unlawfully discriminate against pupils on the grounds of their sex, race, disability, religion or belief, sexual orientation, pregnancy or gender reassignment. Exceptions to the discrimination provisions for schools relate, for example, to the content of the curriculum and to collective worship.

10.5 On 3 November 2008, the Special Educational Needs and Disability Tribunal (SENDIST) became part of the unified tribunal system under the Tribunals, Courts and Enforcement Act 2007. SENDIST forms part of the First-tier Tribunal (Health, Education and Social Care Chamber (HESC)) together with the Care Standards Tribunal

---

1 Replacing the Independent Appeal Panel. See further below.

and the Mental Health Tribunal. The First-tier Tribunal hears all special educational needs appeals against local education authority (LEA) decisions.[2] Appeals from the tribunal are to the Upper Tribunal (Administrative Appeals Chamber).[3]

General duties of local education authorities

10.6 The general functions of LEAs are contained in the Education Act 1996.[4] Section 14 of that Act requires authorities to secure that sufficient primary and secondary schools are available for their area, which means sufficient in number, character and equipment to provide all pupils with the opportunity of an appropriate education.[5] In carrying out their functions local authorities must have a view to increasing the opportunity for parental choice and the need for diversity in the provision of schools.[6] Moreover, the authority must have regard to the need to have primary and secondary education in separate schools, securing boarding accommodation for those for whom it is deemed desirable and securing special educational needs provision within schools.[7] They must also contribute towards the spiritual, moral, mental and physical development of the community, by securing that efficient primary, secondary and further education is available to meet the needs of the population of their area.[8]

Human rights

10.7 By article 2 of the first protocol to the European Convention on Human Rights (the Convention):

> No person shall be denied the right to education. In the exercise of any functions which it assumes in relation to education and to teaching, the state shall respect the right of parents to ensure such education

---

2 In relation to procedure see generally Tribunal Procedure (First-tier Tribunal) (Health, Education and Social Care Chamber) Rules 2008 SI No 2699 as supplemented by the *Practice Direction: Health, Education and Social Care Chamber Special Educational Needs or Disability Discrimination in Schools Cases 2008.*

3 For a discussion on judicial review in the Upper Tribunal see chapter 19.

4 Education Act 1996 ss13–19 and Sch 1.

5 This term is defined by Education Act 1996 s14(3).

6 Education Act 1996 s14(3A).

7 Education Act 1996 s14(6).

8 Education Act 1996 s13(1).

and teaching in conformity with their own religious[9] and philosophical convictions.

10.8 The UK entered a reservation in respect of this provision to the effect that the second sentence of article 2 was only accepted so far as it was compatible with the provision of efficient instruction and training, and the avoidance of unreasonable public expenditure.[10]

10.9 In *A v Head Teacher and Governors of Lord Grey School*,[11] article 2 of the first protocol was said by Lord Bingham to be a weak guarantee when compared with others provided by the Convention; this was, he said, 'deliberately so':[12]

> There is no right to education of a particular kind or quality, other than that prevailing in the state. There is no Convention guarantee of compliance with domestic law. There is no Convention guarantee of education at or by a particular institution. There is no Convention objection to the expulsion of a pupil from an educational institution on disciplinary grounds, unless (in the ordinary way) there is no alternative source of state education open to the pupil[13] ... The test, as always under the Convention, is a highly pragmatic one, to be applied to the specific facts of the case: have the authorities of the state acted so as to deny to a pupil effective access to such educational facilities as the state provides for such pupils?

10.10 In *Lord Grey School*, it was held that an excluded pupil was not denied access to education in circumstances where the school sent work home for him, or where he was referred to the LEA that had arranged for him to attend a pupil referral unit.[14]

---

9 In *R (K) v Newham LBC* [2002] ELR 390, a decision of the independent appeals panel (as it was then known) not to allow a daughter of a devout Muslim admission into a single-sex school was quashed, the court stating that parental convictions must be (and had not been) given due weight, although plainly there would be cases where there were other considerations and article 2 of protocol 1 did not guarantee a right to admission. See also, eg, *R (T) v Leeds City Council* [2002] ELR 91 and *R (R) v Leeds City Council* [2006] ELR 25.

10 Human Rights Act 1998 s15(1) and Pt II Sch3. The treaty reservation reads 'At the time of signing the present (First) Protocol, I declare that, in view of certain provisions of the Education Acts in the United Kingdom, the principle affirmed in the second sentence of Article 2 is accepted by the United Kingdom only so far as it is compatible with the provision of efficient instruction training, and the avoidance of unreasonable public expenditure.'

11 [2006] 1 AC 363.

12 [2006] 1 AC 363 at [24].

13 Lord Bingham cited *Eren v Turkey* (App No 60856/00) 7 February 2006 as an example of this proposition.

14 [2006] 2 AC 363 at [25].

10.11   The Supreme Court considered article 2 of the first protocol in
A v Essex County Council,[15] and approved Lord Bingham's dictum in
Lord Grey School.[16] The case concerned an autistic boy with profound
needs and requirements. The Court held that the article 2 right was
a right to effective access to educational facilities without discrimination. Accordingly, a child with special educational needs would not
have been denied his article 2 right unless he was denied access to the
educational facilities the state provided for such pupils. A required
very specialist resources which had led to an 18-month delay before
he was placed in an educational institution that met his needs. The
court held that such a time to find such resources was hardly surprising, and, given that A was eventually provided with high quality
education, no breach of his article 2 rights had occurred.[17]

10.12   Article 2 does not provide a right to be education at a particular
school.[18] It does apply to higher education.[19]

10.13   There are, in addition, a number of rights arising from other articles of the Convention that are important in the education context.
These include:

- article 8 – respect for private and family life (it has been held that
  article 8 cannot be relied upon in cases concerning corporal punishment, sex education, choice of school, exclusion from a particular school or the language of instruction in the classroom);[20]
- article 9 – the right to freedom of thought, conscience and religion (in the exercise of its functions, the state must respect the
  rights of parents to ensure that education conforms with their
  own religious and philosophical convictions);[21]
- article 10 – the right to freedom of expression;
- article 14 – the right to freedom from discrimination.

---

15 [2010] UKSC 33, [2010] 3 WLR 509.

16 [2010] 3 WLR 509 at [12] and [20].

17 [2010] 3 WLR 509 at [21], [47], [51], [81], [85]–[89] and [128]. Note too the
dissenting judgments of Lord Philips and Baroness Hale who held, *inter alia*, A
had an arguable claim under article 2.

18 *S, T and P v London Borough of Brent* [2002] EWCA Civ 693, [2002] ELR 556.

19 *R (Douglas) v North Tyneside MBC* [2004] 1 WLR 2363. See also, *R (Hurley and
Moore) v Secretary of State for Business Innovation and Skills* [2012] EWHC 201
(Admin) which concerned an argument that article 2 of protocol 1 and Article
14 of the Convention were violated by the introduction of increased fees for
universities. The Divisional Court held it was not disproportionate to impose
such fees and as such there was no violation.

20 See further paras 10.18–10.40 and 10.51–10.55.

21 See further paras 10.37–10.40 below.

10.14 Article 9 has been the focus of a number of challenges involving school uniform requirements.[22] In *R (SB) v Governors of Denbigh High School*,[23] a maintained school, with a very diverse intake, had a school uniform policy that allowed pupils to choose from three options, one of which was the *shalwar kameeze*: a sleeveless smock-like dress with a square neckline, revealing the wearer's collar and tie, with the *shalwar*, loose trousers, tapering at the ankles which had been worn by some Muslim, Hindu and Sikh female pupils. The governors also approved the wearing of head scarves of a specified colour and quality. This uniform policy was explained to all parents and pupils at various stages of the educational process. SB was Muslim. She attended school one day wearing a *jilbab* which she insisted was the only clothing that met her religious requirements. The assistant head teacher told SB to return home and change into the school uniform. SB subsequently said she would not attend school if she could not wear Islamic clothing and contended she had been excluded/suspended from the school. Eventually, SB brought judicial review proceedings.

10.15 The House of Lords, by a majority, held that although article 9 was engaged it did not require that people should be allowed to manifest their religion at any time and place of their choosing. When considering what amounted to an interference with art 9(1) rights, the court has to consider all the circumstances of the case, including the extent to which an individual could reasonably be expected to be at liberty to manifest his beliefs in practice:

> The Strasbourg institutions have not been at all ready to find an interference with the right to manifest religious belief in practice or observance where a person has voluntarily accepted an employment or role

22 See also, eg, *R (X) v Head Teacher and Governors of Y School* [2007] EWHC 298 (Admin), [2008] 1 All ER 249 (a school refusing to allow a pupil to wear a *niqab* veil did not amount to a breach of article 9); and *R (Playfoot) v Millais School Governing Body* [2007] EWHC 1698 (Admin), [2007] HRLR 34 (a school's general prohibition on wearing jewellery was legitimate; article 9 was not even engaged where a pupil was not allowed to wear a purity ring). Although not concerned with article 9, in relation to school uniform challenges, see also *R (Watkins-Singh) v Aberdare Girls' High School Governors* [2008] EWHC 1865 (Admin), [2008] ELR 561 (a school's refusal to allow a Sikh pupil to wear a religious steel bangle constituted indirect discrimination under the Race Relations Act 1976 and Equality Act 2006); and *G v St Gregory's Catholic Science College Governors* [2011] EWHC 1452 (Admin), [2011] ELR 446 (a school's refusal to allow a pupil to wear his hair in cornrows which was contrary to the uniform policy amounted to indirect racial discrimination and could not be justified).

23 [2006] UKHL 15, [2007] 1 AC 100.

which does not accommodate that practice or observance and there are other means open to the person to practise or observe his or her religion without undue hardship or inconvenience ... [Strasbourg has developed] a coherent and remarkably consistent body of authority which our domestic courts must take into account and which shows that interference is not easily established.[24]

10.16 In SB's case there had been no interference: her family chose the school, which went to unusual lengths to inform parents of its uniform policy. The *shalwar kameeze*, and not the *jilbab*, was worn by SB's elder sister throughout her time at the school, and by SB for her first two years, without objection. SB could, of course, modify her beliefs but there were schools accessible to her that would have allowed the *jilbab*.[25] In the alternative, if there had been an interference with SB's article 9(1) rights then, since Parliament had given the governors the power to make decisions about school uniforms, the insistence on adherence to their policy was a limitation prescribed by law that was proportionate to its purpose and objectively justified under article 9(2).[26]

Judicial review

10.17 Where an education body, such as an LEA or board of governors, or a head teacher, is alleged to have acted beyond its powers or contrary to the principles of natural justice, it is susceptible to judicial review. In addition to such bodies, funding authorities and the Office of the Independent Adjudicator for Higher Education[27] are also susceptible to judicial review.

10.18 The decisions of independent schools are only susceptible to judicial review in extremely limited circumstances, because their authority derives from either contract or the consent of parents. As such, any remedy must be sought in contract.[28] Where, however, an

---

24 [2006] UKHL 15, [2007] 1 AC 100, per Lord Bingham at [23].
25 [2006] UKHL 15, [2007] 1 AC 100, per Lord Bingham at [25].
26 [2006] UKHL 15, [2007] 1 AC 100, per Lord Bingham at [32]–[34].
27 See, *R (Siborurema) v Office of the Independent Adjudicator for Higher Education* [2007] EWCA Civ 1365, [2008] ELR 209. The Office of the Independent Adjudicator for Higher Education was established under the Higher Education Act 2004 for the purpose of reviewing complaints made against higher education institutions. Although amenable to judicial review, it appears the court has limited powers on review: *R (Maxwell) v Office of the Independent Adjudicator for Higher Education* [2011] EWCA Civ 1236, [2012] ELR 538.
28 See *R v Panel on Takeovers and Mergers, ex p Datafin Ltd* [1987] QB 815, CA.

independent school was participating in an assisted places scheme, judicial review was held to be available. In *R v Cobham Hall School ex p G*,[29] Dyson J held that head teacher's decision to withdraw an assisted place from a pupil on the basis of unacceptable behaviour was amenable to judicial review. The school was exercising a public function within a statutory framework that set admission criteria and gave the Secretary of State a power to control the school's funding.[30]

10.19   Universities may be amenable to review but, again, in limited circumstances. Chartered universities are private bodies, but may be susceptible to judicial review in relation to their statutory functions. Where a university has a 'visitor', however, claimants will be expected to make use of that procedure before coming to court.[31] Students wishing to make a complaint that falls within the jurisdiction of the Office of the Independent Adjudicator for Higher Education will also be expected to use that route prior to commencing judicial review proceedings.[32]

10.20   The following areas of decision-making can give rise to applications for judicial review:

- admission and readmission of pupils;
- exclusion of pupils;
- admission, readmission and exclusion appeals;
- special education needs;
- reorganisation of schools, including school closures, the establishment of new schools, amalgamations and changes in the 'character' of schools;
- the school curriculum;
- school transport;
- financial and other support for pupils;
- grants and awards for pupils.

---

29 [1998] ELR 389, QBD.
30 See also *ex p T* [1995] ELR 356, QBD.
31 *R v Lord President of the Privy Council ex p Page* [1993] AC 682, HL. See also *Clark v University of Lincolnshire and Humberside* [2000] 1 WLR 1988, CA.
32 See below at paras 10.141–10.149.

Categories of maintained schools

Maintained schools

10.21　Under the SSFA 1998, schools maintained by LEAs on or after 1 September 1999 fall into five categories:[33]

- community schools;[34]
- foundation schools;[35]
- voluntary schools (voluntary-aided and voluntary-controlled);[36]
- community special schools;[37] and
- foundation special schools.[38]

10.22　Where a maintained school had selective admission arrangements at the beginning of the 1997–98 school year, the Secretary of State may designate the school as a grammar school.[39] Where a school is so designated, it must comply with specific procedures if it wishes to alter its admission arrangements so that they will no longer be selective.[40]

10.23　　Nursery schools and pupil referral units may also be maintained.

Academies

10.24　Academies are all-ability state-funded schools, originally established by the Learning and Skills Act 2000 (amending the Education Act 1996). Since their establishment, the legislative provisions governing

---

33　SSFA 1998 s20(1) and Sch 2 (as amended).
34　These are schools controlled by the local council and are free from business or religious group influence. County schools became community schools: SSFA 1998 Sch 2 para 1.
35　Grant-maintained schools which were formerly county schools or were established by the Funding Agency for Schools became foundation schools: SSFA 1998 Sch 2 para 3.
36　Controlled schools became voluntary-controlled schools. Aided and special agreement schools became voluntary-aided schools. Grant-maintained schools which were formerly aided or special agreement schools or were established by promoters also became voluntary-aided schools: SSFA 1998 Sch 2 paras 1 and 3.
37　Maintained special schools became community special schools: SSFA 1998 Sch 2 para 1.
38　Grant-maintained special schools became foundation special schools: SSFA 1998 Sch 2 para 3.
39　SSFA 1998 s104.
40　SSFA 1998 ss105–109.

academies have been substantially altered by the Academies Act 2010 and the Education Act 2011.

10.25   Academies have sponsors from a wide range of backgrounds, including universities and colleges, the business sector, charities and faith communities. They have largely replaced city technology colleges and city colleges for the technology of the arts, which were set up by the Education Reform Act 1988.[41] They enjoy greater freedom than maintained schools as they are not controlled by the local authority. They do, however, have to adhere to the same legislative provisions and guidance as maintained schools in relation to admissions,[42] exclusions and special educational needs.

10.26   The Academies Act 2010[43] contains provisions for all maintained schools, including primary and special schools, to apply to the Secretary of State to become academies.[44] The Secretary of State may, subject to certain conditions, make an academy order in relation to the school.[45] Prior to making an application, the governing body of a foundation school (or voluntary school that has a foundation) must consult the foundation.[46] Before a maintained school in England is converted to an academy, consultation must take place as to whether conversion should take place. The consultation exercise may take place before or after an order is made by the Secretary of State.[47] Generally, the consultation must be carried out by the school's governing body and must seek the views of such persons as it deems appropriate.[48]

---

41 See Academies Act 2010 explanatory notes para 3.
42 Although academies are not maintained schools for the purposes of Part III of the SSFA 1998, and so are not statutorily required to adhere to the Admissions Code or the Admissions Appeal Code, they are required to apply those Codes as part of the funding arrangements entered into with the Secretary of State: see para 4 of the Admission Code 2012.
43 As amended by the Education Act 2011.
44 Academies Act 2010 s3(1).
45 Academies Act 2010 s4.
46 Academies Act 2010 s3(3).
47 Academies Act 2010 s5.
48 Academies Act 2010 s5(4) and (5). In the case of a school that is eligible for intervention (within the meaning of Part 4 of the Education and Inspections Act 2006), the consultation may be carried out by the school's governing body, or by a person with whom the Secretary of State proposes to enter into Academy arrangements in respect of the school or an educational institution that replaces it. See Academies Act 2010 s10, in relation to consultation provisions in relation to entering into arrangements for a new and expanded educational institution.

10.27 The requirement for consultation plainly leaves governing bodies open to challenge by way of judicial review, should the consultation exercise fail to comply with the requirements of public law.[49] In *R (Moyse) v Secretary of State for Education*,[50] the Administrative Court rejected an application for permission to apply for judicial review of the decision of the Secretary of State to enter into a funding agreement so that a primary school would become an academy. The claimant contended that the Secretary of State's decision to approve the arrangement was unlawful as the consultation exercise that had taken place had failed to make mention of the governing body's decision – which decision it was said to be obliged to make – about whether the school should be converted to an academy. Refusing permission, Parker J described this argument as fundamentally flawed.

> There is simply nothing in section 5 of the 2010 Act that permits, let alone obliges, the governing body to take a decision on the question of whether conversion should take place. On the contrary, the only relevant decision maker is the Secretary of State, who, by section 1(1), may enter into academy arrangements with any person. Indeed, if a governing body were to purport to make a decision on the relevant question of conversion into an academy such a decision would lack the typical quality of a public law decision, namely an act having binding effect on the person to whom the decision is directed. ...'[51]

Admissions

Parental preference: Education Act 1996 s9

10.28 In carrying out their powers and duties, LEAs should take account, so far as may be compatible with the provision of efficient education, of the wishes of parents of the pupils. Education Act 1996 s9, as amended, provides:

> In exercising or performing all their respective powers and duties under the Education Acts, the Secretary of State and local authorities shall have regard to the general principle that pupils are to be educated in accordance with the wishes of their parents, so far as that is compatible with the provision of efficient instruction and training and the avoidance of unreasonable public expenditure.

49 In relation to consultation challenges, generally, see chapter 6.
50 [2012] EWHC 2758 (Admin), [2012] ELR 551.
51 [2012] EWHC 2758 (Admin) at [54]–[55].

10.29   On 1 February 2012, the following regulations came into force:[52]

- School Admissions (Admission Arrangements and Co-ordination of Admission Arrangements) (England) Regulations 2012;[53]
- School Admissions (Appeal Arrangements) (England) Regulations 2012;[54] and
- School Admissions (Infant Class Sizes) (England) Regulations 2012.[55]

10.30   On the same day, a new School Admission Code and School Admission Appeals Code were issued.[56] For applications in the normal admissions round, under the School Admissions Code, local authorities must provide a common application form that enables parents to express their preference for a place at any state-funded school, with a minimum of three preferences in rank order, allowing them to give reasons for their preferences. The Code notes, however, that while parents may express a preference admission authorities must not give any guarantees that a preference will be met.[57] Indeed, despite the general duty under EA 1996, s9, to educate in accordance with parents' wishes, such wishes have been held to be merely one factor that the authority should take into account. It is free to take into account and give greater priority to other factors.[58]

10.31   In *Watt v Kesteven CC*,[59] a Roman Catholic father declined, on religious grounds, to send his children to an independent secondary grammar school that was in the LEA's area and at which the authority had agreed to pay their tuition fees. Instead, he sent his children to a Roman Catholic boarding school that was located elsewhere and applied to the authority to pay the tuition fees (which were, in fact, less than at the school proposed by the authority). The authority refused

---

52 Consolidating with amendments the School Admissions (Admissions Arrangements) (England) Regulations 2008 SI No 3089, the School Admissions (Local Authority Reports and Admissions Forums) (England) Regulations 2008 SI No 3091 and the School Admissions (Co-ordination of Admission Arrangements) (England) Regulations 2008 SI No 3090 and revoking the Education (Admission Appeals Arrangements) (England) Regulations 2002 SI No 2899.

53 SI No 8.

54 SI No 9.

55 SI No 10.

56 Both issued under SSFA 1998 s84.

57 School Admissions Code 2012 para 2.1.

58 *Watt v Kesteven CC* [1955] 1 QB 408. See also, eg, *CM v Bexley LBC* [2011] UKUT 215 (AAC), [2011] ELR 413 which considered *Watt* in the context of the current statutory provision in Education Act 1996 s9.

59 [1955] 1 QB 408.

and the father sought a declaration that this refusal constituted a breach of statutory duty to provide secondary school education for his children at a school to which he had chosen to send them.

10.32   The Court of Appeal held that the duty of the LEA to secure that there are sufficient schools available for their area[60] only required that schools be made available in the authority's area. If a parent wished to send his child to a school of his own choice, with which the education authority had no arrangement, he could not claim as of right that the authority should pay the fees. Denning LJ said:[61]

> [The section] does not say that pupils must in all cases be educated in accordance with the wishes of their parents. It only lays down a general principle to which the county council must have regard. This leaves it open to the county council to have regard to other things as well, and also to make exceptions to the general principle if it thinks fit to do so. It cannot therefore be said that a county council is at fault simply because it does not see fit to comply with the parent's wishes.

10.33   In *Cummings v Birkenhead Corporation*,[62] Lord Denning MR said:

> There are many other things to which the education authority may have regard and which may outweigh the wishes of the parents. They must have regard, for instance, not only to the wishes of the parents of one particular child, but also to the wishes of the parents of other children and of other groups of children.

10.34   In *Cummings*, a parent unsuccessfully challenged an LEA's admission policy that, save in exceptional circumstances, children from Roman Catholic primary schools would only be considered for Roman Catholic secondary schools, because there were only enough spaces in non-Roman Catholic schools for pupils from county and Church of England schools.

10.35   The difficulty in challenging a decision that does not accord with a parent's wishes was explained by Lord Keith of Kinkel in *Harvey v Strathclyde Regional Council*:[63]

> In order to succeed in securing judicial review, the applicant must show either that the respondents paid no regard at all to the general principle …, or that they paid to it a degree of regard lesser than any reasonable education authority would have paid.

---

60 Education Act 1944 s8; now Education Act 1996 s14.
61 [1955] 1 QB 408 at 424.
62 [1972] Ch 12 at 36.
63 [1989] SLT 612 at 615. This case concerned the Education (Scotland) Act 1980 s28(1) – a provision almost identical to Education Act 1996 s9.

10.36 In *R v Birmingham CC ex p Youngson*,[64] where the parents of an aspiring ballet dancer wanted their LEA to pay for him to attend a private ballet school outside the authority's area, the court upheld the principle that parental preference under section 9 of the 1996 Act and article 2, protocol 1, Schedule 1 to the HRA 1998 are both qualified by the avoidance of unreasonable expenditure.[65]

10.37 The court referred to a comment by Slade LJ in *R v Surrey County Council Education Committee ex p H*,[66] to the effect that Parliament has not placed local authorities under an obligation to provide a child with the best possible education. There is no duty on an authority to provide such a utopian system or to educate him to his maximum potential.

10.38 In *R (K) v Newham LBC*,[67] Collins J said: '... the religious conviction of a parent is something to which due weight must be given in considering admission to a particular school'. On the fact of that case, therefore, the LEA had been obliged to give due weight to the parents' religious convictions, namely that their child should be educated in a single-sex school.

10.39 More recently, in *CM v Bexley LBC*,[68] the Upper Tribunal, acknowledging the view that this interpretation of s9 of the 1996 Act, may mean that the section adds little in most cases, observed that section 9 was not a strong provision and that even a situation where there would be no adverse implication for public expenditure would not mean that parental preference would necessarily prevail.[69]

Parental preference: SSFA 1998 s86

10.40 Under section 86, an LEA is obliged to make arrangements for enabling the parent of a child in its area to express a preference as to the school at which he wishes education to be provided. The authority must comply with a preference duly expressed, save where compliance with the preference would prejudice the provision of efficient education or the efficient use of resources.[70]

---

64 [2001] BLGR 218 (affirmed by the Court of Appeal: [2001] EWCA Civ 287).
65 See Human Rights Act 1998 Sch 3, Pt II for the UK's qualified acceptance.
66 (1984) 83 LGR 219 at 235.
67 [2002] EWHC 405 (Admin), [2002] ELR 390, QBD, at [29].
68 [2011] UKUT 215 (AAC), [2011] ELR 413.
69 [2011] UKUT 215 (AAC) at [47], [51] and [62].
70 SSFA 1998 s86(1), (2). See further paras 10.51–10.57 below.

Admission to maintained schools

10.41   The law in this area is governed by SSFA 1998 Pt III, although the Education Act 2002 and the Education Act 2011 have brought about a number of changes concerning admissions. In particular, admission appeals are governed by regulations rather than primary legislation.[71] The Secretary of State is under a duty to issue a Code of Practice on admissions, to be laid before Parliament; local authorities, admission authorities, schools adjudicators, admission appeal panels and governing bodies are under a duty to have regard to the provisions of that Code. On 1 February 2012, the Department for Education issued a new School Admission Code and a new School Admission Appeals Code.

10.42   Academies are required by their funding agreements to comply with these Codes and the law relating to admissions generally, although the Secretary of State may, by regulations, make different provision.

10.43   Since 1 April 2012, where admission arrangements have been determined by an admission authority for a maintained school in England, or have been determined by the proprietor of an academy school, and a body or person wishes to make an objection about those admission arrangements, the objection may be referred to the Schools Adjudicator. The Adjudicator must then decide whether, and, if so, to what extent, the objection should be upheld.[72] The Secretary of State may also refer admission arrangements to the Adjudicator where he is of the view that they do not, or may not, conform with the requirements relating to admission arrangements.[73]

10.44   The Schools Adjudicator is unable to entertain an objection:

- seeking an alteration to admission arrangements for a grammar school so that it no longer has selective admission arrangements;
- seeking an alteration to admission arrangements for a selective academy so as to remove selection;
- that the admission number has not been changed or has been increased for any school whose admission authority are not the local authority; or for an Academy;
- in respect of an increase, or decision not to change, the admission number for a community or voluntary controlled school other than an objection by the governing body of that school; or

---

71 Education Act 2002 ss50–51.
72 SSFA 1998 s88H.
73 SSFA 1998 s88I.

- to an agreement that the admission arrangements for an academy may vary from the School Admissions Code.[74]

10.45 It is likely that the availability of the Adjudicator as an alternative remedy in those areas over which he has jurisdiction will restrict the possibilities for seeking judicial review, although it may be possible to challenge a decision made by the Adjudicator.

10.46 Parents have increasingly sought to challenge, by way of judicial review, decisions taken by schools or LEAs refusing to admit a pupil to a particular school.[75] Prior to the introduction of the Schools Adjudicator, parents also sought to challenge admission decisions by way of attacking the school's admissions policy. Given the more limited remit of the Schools Adjudicator in this regard, judicial review may continue to be widely sought in relation to this aspect of the admissions procedure.

10.47 In the event of over-subscription, a school is entitled to have a policy on admissions, in order to determine which applications will be successful. A policy cannot discriminate between those children within the local authority area and those outside the area,[76] but can discriminate between religious persuasions in order to preserve the character of a church school.[77] A policy that considers applications from Roman Catholic children for places at non-denominational schools only after all other applicants have been placed has also been held to be lawful where the school is oversubscribed: *R v Lancashire CC ex p Foster.*[78]

10.48 In *R v Brighouse School Appeal Committee ex p G and B,*[79] the court rejected a school appeals committee's argument that a child could not be admitted to the school because it had already admitted the maximum number of pupils under its admissions policy and to allow more children to enter the school would prejudice the provision of efficient education and/or the use of resources. The court held that the committee had improperly restricted its consideration to the policy and numbers and had thereby fettered its discretion when reaching its decision.

---

74 School Admissions (Admission Arrangements and Co-ordination of Admission Arrangements) (England) Regulations 2012 SI No 8 reg 21(a)–(e).
75 See Parental preference, paras 10.28–10.40 above.
76 See para 10.53 below.
77 See paras 10.54–10.55 below.
78 [1995] 1 FCR 212, [1995] COD 45, DC.
79 [1997] ELR 39, QBD.

10.49   In *Hounslow LBC v School Admission Appeals Panel for Hounslow LBC*,[80] the issue of admissions to maintained schools was considered. The Court of Appeal held[81] that each case must be considered on its individual facts and that there was,

> nothing intrinsically unlawful about admission arrangements that favour on the one hand children who have a brother or sister at the school, or on the other hand those who live close to it. But inflexible application of either criterion – or, in another case, of other criteria – may produce a perverse decision in an individual case.

10.50   Significantly, the Court of Appeal commented that the circumstances would need to be 'quite exceptional' for the courts to interfere with a decision on an admissions appeal.[82]

10.51   In *R (Hampshire CC) v Independent Appeal Panel for Hampshire*,[83] a local authority's past failure to plan ahead, in respect of educational provision arising from a recent housing development, was held not to be a relevant factor when considering whether parental preferences under s86, SSFA 1998, must be complied with. The complaint, in that case, was that the school had failed to comply with the preference expressed by the children of seven families on the grounds that there were no places available at the preferred school. The appeal panel allowed the parents' appeal but the local authority's application for judicial review was granted.

10.52   The panel had failed to address the relevant primary issue, which was whether the local authority's decision was perverse, having regard to the preference of the parents, the admission arrangements and the evidence of prejudice to the school and to the efficient use of the authority's resources. The court said that, while it would be going too far to say that the past actions of a local authority could never be relevant to judging perversity, it was difficult to see how a failure of past planning could be relevant to the decision that had to be made under section 86. The relevant issues related to parental preference and prejudice to the child, or difficulties that the child would face now and in the future if the parental preference was not acceded to.

---

80 [2002] EWCA Civ 900, [2002] 1 WLR 3147, CA.
81 [2002] EWCA Civ 900, per May L at [60].
82 Hounslow has since been a applied in relation to the principles that should be considered by appeal panels. See, eg, *R (Hampshire CC) v Independent Appeal Panel for Hampshire* [2006] EWHC 2460 (Admin), [2007] ELR 266; *R (Haringey LBC) v School Admission Appeals Panel for Haringey LBC* [2005] EWHC 2338 (Admin), [2006] ELR 10; *R (Khundakji) v Cardiff CC Admissions Appeal Panel* [2003] EWHC 436 (Admin), [2003] ELR 495.
83 [2006] EWHC 2460 (Admin), [2007] ELR 266.

This fell to be set against the statutory requirement for considering prejudice to the provision of efficient education or the efficient use of resources. The reasons why parents were given a preference; the impact on the child if the preference was not acceded to; the disadvantageous position they might find themselves in compared to the general run of pupils within the county, etc, were all relevant matters. On the other hand, the reason why the problem had arisen and whether the education authority was at fault would not normally fall within the scope of relevant factors.[84]

10.53   In *R v Greenwich LBC ex p Governors of John Ball Primary School*,[85] the governing body of a primary school in Lewisham sought judicial review of a policy, adopted by the neighbouring authority of Greenwich, to give first preference to children resident in Greenwich together with residents in other areas with a sibling connection to the school applied for. The Court of Appeal held that LEAs were under a duty, subject to the statutory exceptions, to comply with the expressed preference of parents as to the school at which they wished their children to be educated, without distinction between children resident within and outside an authority's area. The borough's decision to adopt a school admissions policy giving priority to children within their own area was, therefore, ultra vires. Lloyd LJ said:[86]

> I do not regard efficient education or the efficient use of resources as being the sole source of lawful policy ... In my judgment an LEA can have any reasonable policy they think fit, provided it does not conflict with their duties ... Sibling priority and the proximity rule are sound and lawful policies whether or not they promote efficient education ... It may well be understandable for Greenwich to give their own residents priority over all other areas in Greenwich schools. But it conflicts with the clear provisions of [the Act].

10.54   In *Choudhury v Governors of Bishop Challoner Roman Catholic Comprehensive School*,[87] the applicants (parents of a Hindu child and parents of a Muslim child) sought judicial review of the Governors' and Appeal Committee's decisions to refuse to admit their daughters to an oversubscribed (voluntary-aided) Roman Catholic girls' school. Admission was refused on the basis that it would prejudice the provision of efficient education and that the girls did not meet the admission criteria, which gave priority to Roman Catholics and

---

84 *R (Hampshire CC) v Independent Appeal Panel for Hampshire* [2006] EWHC 2460 (Admin), [2007] ELR 266 at [29]–[33].

85 (1990) 88 LGR 589, CA.

86 (1990) 88 LGR 589 at 599.

87 [1992] 2 AC 182, HL.

other Christians. The issue to be decided was whether the governors of an oversubscribed voluntary-aided school were entitled to operate an admissions policy that gave preference to children of a particular religious persuasion, notwithstanding the preference expressed by the parent.

10.55 The House of Lords held that where a school was oversubscribed, compliance with the preference of all the applicants would necessarily prejudice efficient education and, in such circumstances, the school had to have an admissions policy, which would – whatever the criteria adopted – inevitably result in defeating the preference of some applicants. Since the school was oversubscribed there was, therefore, no duty on the governors to give effect to the applicants' preferences. Lord Browne-Wilkinson, delivering the only opinion,[88] adopted the following passage from the judgment of Taylor LJ in the Court of Appeal:

> ... if compliance with all parental preferences would result in overcrowding then the governors may apply any reasonable criteria to make the necessary reduction in numbers. Those criteria include sibling priority and geographical proximity. Likewise, in a church school, priorities such as those stated in the admissions policy here can properly be applied.

10.56 Other admissions policies that are prima facie lawful include catchment areas and feeder primary or nursery schools. It has, however, been held to be unlawful for an LEA to fail to ascertain parental preferences at the beginning of the process of placing a child, before addressing the question of the catchment area into which the child might fall.[89]

10.57 In *R v Cleveland CC ex p Commission for Racial Equality*,[90] the Commission sought judicial review of the council's decision under the Education Act 1980 to allow, in accordance with parental preference, the transfer of a pupil from a predominantly Asian school to a predominantly white school. The Court of Appeal held, upholding the decision of Macpherson J,[91] that the decision did not contravene the power granted by the Act and so was not based on any error of law. Nor did the transfer of the child amount to an act of segregation on racial grounds, so the council had not committed an act of discrimination contrary to the Race Relations Act 1976.

88 [1992] 2 AC 182 at 191–2.
89 *R v Rotherham MBC ex p Clark* [1998] 1 FCR 509, [1998] ELR 152, QBD.
90 (1993) 91 LGR 139, CA.
91 In the same case (1992) 4 Admin LR 417, QBD.

Admissions appeals

10.58 Under the SSFA 1998 s94(1), a local authority must make arrangements for parents (and/or for a child of sixth form age) to appeal against:

- any decision made by or on behalf of the authority – where the local authority is the admissions authority – refusing a child admission to a school;
- any other decision made by or on behalf of an authority as to the school at which education is to be provided for a child; and
- any decision made by or on behalf of the governors of a county or controlled school maintained by an authority, refusing a child admission to such a school.

10.59 SSFA 1998 s94(1A) provides a right of appeal to a child who has been admitted to a community or voluntary controlled school maintained by the authority against any decision made by or on behalf of the governing body refusing permission for the child to enter the school's sixth form.

10.60 SSFA 1998 s94(2)–(2A) provides a right of appeal for parents against any decision made by or on behalf of the governors of any foundation or voluntary-aided school refusing to admit the child to the school or to enter its school's sixth form.

10.61 SSFA 1998 s95, removes the right of appeal by a parent or child of sixth form age against a refusal to admit a child to a school, if that child has been permanently excluded from two or more schools, the last exclusion being within the previous two years. Instead, the governing body of a school now has a right of appeal against a decision by the LEA to admit such a child.[92] The governing body cannot appeal against a decision to admit to a school a child who is looked after by an authority, but may instead refer the matter to the Adjudicator.[93]

10.62 Appeals are heard by an independent appeal panel.[94] For appeals issued on or after 1 February 2012, the School Admissions (Appeal Arrangements) (England) Regulations 2012[95] and the new Admissions Appeal Code apply.[96] Decisions of an appeal panel are susceptible to

---

92 SSFA 1998 s95(2).
93 SSFA 1998 ss95(2A) and 95A.
94 School Admissions (Appeals Arrangements) (England) Regulations 2012 SI No 9 Sch 1.
95 SI No 9.
96 SSFA 1998 s84(3).

judicial review on normal public law principles, although there are,
to a limited extent, alternative remedies available:[97]

- the Secretary of State may consider whether the appeal panel was
  correctly constituted and the admission authority has acted reasonably in exercising its functions in respect of the appeals process or failed to discharge a duty in relation to that process;[98]
- a complaint may be made in relation to any alleged maladministration on the part of an appeal panel to the Local Government
  Ombudsman in respect of maintained schools, or to the Secretary
  of State in respect of appeal panels for Academies.

Exclusions

10.63   The law relating to school exclusions is now[99] governed by section
51A of the Education Act 2002.[100] In England, the head teacher of a
maintained school, the principal of an Academy,[101] or, the teacher in
charge of a pupil referral unit, may exclude a pupil from the school,
for disciplinary reasons,[102] whether for a fixed period or permanently.[103] The power must not be exercised so as to exclude a pupil for one
or more fixed periods if the pupil would be excluded for more than 45
school days in any school year.[104]

10.64   The section also makes provision for regulations to govern
appeals procedures.[105] The School Discipline (Pupil Exclusions and

---

97 See Education Act 1996 ss496, 497 and 497A and the School Admissions
Code.

98 See Education Act 1996 ss496, 497 and 497A. The Secretary of State has the
same power under an Academy's funding agreement.

99 Ie from 1 September 2012.

100 As inserted by the Education Act 2011 s4 and the School Discipline (Pupil
Exclusions and Reviews) (England) Regulations 2012 SI No 1033.

101 See the modifications made under Education Act 2002 s51A(12) in School
Discipline (Pupil Exclusions and Reviews) (England) Regulations 2012 SI
No 1033 regs 21–29 so that s51A and regulations made under it also apply to
academies.

102 *Exclusions from maintained schools, Academies and pupil referral units in England:
A guide for those with legal responsibilities in relation to exclusion* (Department for
Education, April 2012) at para 12.

103 Education Act 2002 s51A(1)–(2).

104 School Discipline (Pupil Exclusions and Reviews) (England) Regulations 2012
SI No 1033 regs 4, 13 and 22.

105 Education Act 2002 s51A(3).

Reviews) (England) Regulations 2012[106] make provision for, among other things, the provision of information relating to consideration of a person's reinstatement, the making of arrangements by the local authority to enable certain people to apply to a review panel for a review of a decision not to reinstate a pupil, and the procedure to be followed by a panel on such a review.[107] Any fact that needs to be established before a head teacher, principal or teacher in charge; or a governing body,[108] proprietor[109] or management committee;[110] or the review panel, must be established to the civil standard.[111]

10.65   The Secretary of State has published new guidance in relation to exclusions: *Exclusions from maintained schools, Academies and pupil referral units in England: A guide for those with legal responsibilities in relation to exclusion.*[112] This replaced the previous guidance on 1 September 2012.[113]

10.66   Judicial review is not available to challenge the decision of an independent school to expel a pupil.[114] Such schools are not public bodies and, while they operate within a statutory framework of control, the relationship between private schools and their pupils is founded on the contract made between the schools and those paying for the education of the pupils (ie the matter is based in a private law contract and has no statutory underpinning).[115]

---

106 SI No 1033, in force from 1 September 2012.

107 In relation to maintained schools see the School Discipline (Pupil Exclusions and Reviews) (England) Regulations 2012 SI No 1033 regs 4–11; for pupil referral units the relevant regulations are regs 12–20. The regulations also make provisions for academies: regs 21–29.

108 Maintained schools: see School Discipline (Pupil Exclusions and Reviews) (England) Regulations 2012 SI No 1033 regs 6–7.

109 Academies: see School Discipline (Pupil Exclusions and Reviews) (England) Regulations 2012 SI No 1033 regs 24–25.

110 Pupil referral units: see School Discipline (Pupil Exclusions and Reviews) (England) Regulations 2012 SI No 1033 regs 15–16.

111 School Discipline (Pupil Exclusions and Reviews) (England) Regulations 2012 SI No 1033 regs 10, 19 and 28.

112 Department for Education, April 2012. The guidance does not apply to independent schools, sixth form colleges, 16–19 academies, City Technology Colleges or City Colleges for the Technology of the Arts.

113 *Improving behaviour and attendance: guidance on exclusions for schools and pupil referral units,* September 2008.

114 *R v Fernhill Manor School ex p A* [1993] 1 FLR 620, [1994] 1 FCR 146.

115 *R v Incorporated Froebel Educational Institute ex p L* [1999] ELR 488. See also, eg, *R v Stanbridge Fairs School* [2003] ELR 400.

Appeals against permanent exclusions

10.67   An Independent Review Panel (IRP) will hear challenges brought against a decision not to reinstate a pupil. The IRP has replaced the Independent Appeals Panel, which formerly heard (and, in Wales, still hears) such challenges by virtue of the Education Act 2002 s52[116] and previous regulations.[117] The IRP consists of a lay member, a current or former head teacher and a current or former governor.[118] The IRP's powers on review are to:[119]

  (i)   uphold the decision of the responsible body,
  (ii) recommend that the responsible body reconsiders the matter, or
  (iii) if it considers that the decision of the responsible body was flawed when considered in the light of the principles applicable on an application for judicial review, quash the decision of the responsible body and direct the responsible body to reconsider the matter.

10.68   The last of these powers is the most interesting, especially given the additional power that where a direction is given under that section, the IRP may, in certain circumstances, order an adjustment of the school's budget share for a funded period.[120]

10.69   The new exclusions guidance refers to the IRP's powers. It states:[121]

   The panel may only quash the decision where it considers that it was flawed when considered in the light of the principles applicable on an application for judicial review ...

10.70   It then sets out the 'principles applicable on an application for judicial review'[122] by reference, solely, to the three headings set out by

116 Education Act 2002 s52 (as amended) still applies to Wales alongside the Education (Pupil Exclusions and Appeals) (Maintained Schools) (Wales) Regulations 2003 SI No 3227 and the Education (Pupil Exclusions and Appeals) (Pupil Referral Units) (Wales) Regulations 2003 SI No 3246.

117 The previous regulations were the Education (Pupil Exclusions and Appeals) (Maintained Schools) (England) Regulations 2002 SI No 3178 and the Education (Pupil Exclusions and Appeals) (Pupil Referral Units) (England) Regulations 2002 SI No 3179.

118 School Discipline (Pupil Exclusions and Reviews) (England) Regulations 2012 SI No 1033 Sch 1 para 3. An authority may appoint a clerk to advise the members of a review panel and the parties to a review on the procedure of a review and the law and statutory guidance relating to exclusions: Sch1 para 4.

119 Education Act 2002 s51A(4).

120 Education Act 2002 s51A(6).

121 Exclusions from maintained schools, Academies and pupil referral units in England: A guide for those with legal responsibilities in relation to exclusion, April 2012 at para 132.

122 Guidance paras 148–9.

Lord Diplock in *CCSU v Minister for the Civil Service*,[123] namely: illegality, irrationality and procedural impropriety.[124] It is, perhaps, a little disappointing that the Guidance goes no further than this, not least given the importance of the decisions that will fall to be made by panel members who may have little experience in matters of public law. Doubtless, IRP decisions will be challenged on judicial review, on the basis that decisions ought to have been, or ought not to have been, quashed.

10.71   New evidence may be presented to the IRP. The school, however, cannot introduce new reasons for the exclusion and it is expressly provided that panels must disregard any new reasons that are introduced.[125] The Guidance, however, states that the panel must only take account of the evidence that was reasonably available to the governing body at the time of making the decision. This includes any evidence that the panel considers would, or should, have been available to the governing body if they had been acting reasonably.[126]

10.72   Where a decision is not to be quashed, the IRP should consider whether to recommend that the governing body reconsiders the decision not to reinstate the pupil.[127] The Guidance states this should not be the default option, but should be used where evidence or procedural flaws have been identified that do not meet the criteria for quashing the decision but which the panel believes justify reconsideration.[128] In all other cases, the exclusion must be upheld.[129]

10.73   The question arises, given the ability to challenge exclusion decisions before the IRP, whether the Administrative Court will entertain judicial review proceedings before a review by the IRP has been requested. The courts have become less sympathetic to judicial review applications made without first having exhausted the appeal

123 [1984] 3 All ER 935.
124 See chapter 6 at para 6.10.
125 *Exclusions from maintained schools, Academies and pupil referral units in England: A guide for those with legal responsibilities in relation to exclusion* (April 2012) at para 133.
126 *Exclusions from maintained schools, Academies and pupil referral units in England: A guide for those with legal responsibilities in relation to exclusion* (April 2012) at para 134.
127 Education Act 2002 s51A(4)(b).
128 *Exclusions from maintained schools, Academies and pupil referral units in England: A guide for those with legal responsibilities in relation to exclusion* (April 2012) at para 150.
129 Education Act 2002 s51A(4)(a) and *Exclusions from maintained schools, Academies and pupil referral units in England: A guide for those with legal responsibilities in relation to exclusion* (April 2012) at para 151.

procedure. In *R v Governing Body of the Rectory School and Richmond LBC ex p WK (a minor)*,[130] where significant procedural unfairness was alleged, the court held that the appeal procedure was not appropriate for dealing adequately with such issues.

10.74　　On the other hand, in *R (DR) v Head Teacher of St George's Catholic School*,[131] where the claimant sought judicial review of an exclusion decision, alleging procedural unfairness in the early stages of the appeal process and without completing the final stage of that process, the application judicial review application was dismissed. The Court of Appeal held that the statutory appeals procedure needed to be considered as a whole in order to ascertain the intention of Parliament regarding the effect of unfairness in an early part of the process. Unfairness at an early stage could normally be cured by utilising the final stage of the procedure because, although Parliament did not intend any stage to be unfair, overall the intention was that the appellant should have a fair decision on the merits by the end of the process. Parliament did not intend a party aggrieved at a decision at the first stage to seek judicial review rather than appeal. Instead, it intended appellants to use the 'custom-built' expert and independent statutory appeals body. Unless, therefore, the prior procedural unfairness complained of either had tainted or would somehow taint any subsequent appeal, in which case the appeal decision itself would necessarily fall, the right to a fair determination of a person's case would be satisfied by the appeal hearing and decision. On a judicial review application brought instead of an appeal, the court would usually leave the claimant to his or her statutory remedy.[132]

10.75　　The High Court has, however, been prepared to entertain challenges to policies operated in relation to exclusions,[133] and against some alleged procedural impropriety during the appeal process (which did or would taint the fairness of the final stage of the process).[134]

10.76　　Under the new regime, it is plain from the powers of the IRP and the Guidance issued that allegations of procedural impropriety, or

---

130　[1997] ELR 484.

131　[2002] EWCA Civ 1822, [2003] ELR 104.

132　See also *R (Sivasubramaniam) v Wandsworth County Court* [2002] EWCA Civ 1738, [2003] 2 All ER 160.

133　See, eg, *C v London Borough of Brent* [2006] EWCA Civ 728, [2006] ELR 435.

134　See, eg, *R (A) v North Westminster Community School Head Teacher* [2002] EWHC 2351 (Admin), [2003] ELR 378 (use of anonymous witness statements); and *R (S) v Birmingham City Council Independent Appeal Panel* [2006] EWHC 2369 (Admin), [2007] ELR 57 (consideration of appeals arising out of the same incident should be heard together).

unfairness, will fall squarely within the IRP's review remit, and it is therefore to be expected that the court will expect litigants to use to statutory review route before commencing any legal challenge.

10.77 This does not rule judicial review out of exclusion decisions altogether. A decision of a governing body, for example refusing to comply with a recommendation to reconsider a decision not to reinstate may well be amenable to review.[135] The availability of an alternative remedy does not, after all, oust the jurisdiction of the High Court;[136] it is simply a matter to be taken into account when the court considers whether to allow a challenge to proceed (or succeed).[137]

10.78 Decisions of the IRP are, themselves, amenable to review on normal principles.[138] It has been held that other panels in the education law sphere are subject to public law control (and must give adequate reasons and take into account all relevant considerations),[139] and it would be surprising if these principles were not to apply to IRP decisions.

Special educational needs and discrimination

10.79 LEAs have various duties to identify, assess and provide for the special educational needs of children with learning difficulties, for whom they are responsible.[140] By Education Act 1996 s321, authorities are also obliged to identify those children with special educational needs

---

135 The IRP, unlike its predecessor, the Independent Appeals Panel, does not have power to order reinstatement of excluded pupils. In respect of reinstatement under the old regime, various challenges were brought in the context of threats of industrial action after reinstatement was ordered. In *R v Governors of B School ex p C* [2001] ELR 285, the court held that reinstatement does not necessarily entail full integration into the classroom, even when that was the previous state of affairs. Threatened strike action by members of staff if full reinstatement were to occur was a relevant matter a governing body could consider. See also *R (O) v the Governing Body of Parkview Academy and Another* [2007] ELR 388, an unsuccessful judicial review by a pupil, where the head teacher formulated a package for reinstatement which did not include being educated at the school due to threatened strike action by staff.

136 See *Leech v Deputy Governor of Parkhurst Prison* [1988] AC 533.

137 See paras 7.15–7.30 above.

138 See chapter 6 above.

139 See, eg, *R v Governors of Bacon's City Technology College ex p W* [1998] ELR 488, QBD; *R (I) v Independent Appeal Panel for G* [2005] EWHC 558, [2005] ELR 490; and *W v Independent Appeal Panel of Bexley LBC* [2008] EWHC 758 (Admin), [2008] ELR 301.

140 'Learning difficulties' is defined in Education Act 1996 s312(2).

where it is necessary for the authority to determine the special educational provision required by any learning difficulty the child may have. Once the authority has identified a child with special educational needs, it must assess that child's needs,[141] which may lead to a statement of special educational needs.[142] The authority also has a duty to assess a child's needs at the request of the parents.[143]

10.80   In its 2011 Green Paper *Support and aspiration: A new approach to special educational needs and disability*,[144] the Government put forward and explained its aims and proposals for change:[145]

> We want to give children the best chance to succeed by spotting any problems early, extending early education and childcare, and bringing together the services they need into a single assessment and a single plan covering education, health and care.

> We want to make the system less stressful for families and less costly to run by promoting mediation before appeals, giving parents more information about the services and expertise available locally and more support in navigating their way through the assessment system. Our proposals will also mean that children themselves can appeal if they feel they aren't getting the support they need.

> We want to give parents more control by offering every family with a single plan the right to a personal budget by 2014, making a wider range of short breaks available in all areas, and ensuring more choice by allowing parents to name in their child's plan, a preference for any state-funded school.

10.82   The proposals include a new approach to identifying special educational needs in early years settings and schools, and to transfer power to professionals on the front line and to local communities in order to facilitate giving parents a real choice when it comes to schooling.[146]

10.83   In May 2012, the Government published its response to the Green Paper consultation, entitled *Support and aspiration: A new approach to special educational needs and disability – Progress and next steps*.[147]

---

141 Education Act 1996 s323.

142 Education Act 1996 s324 and Sch 27.

143 Education Act 1996 s329.

144 11 March, 2011, Department for Education. Available at: https://www.education.gov.uk/publications/eOrderingDownload/Green-Paper-SEN.pdf accessed 20 January 2013.

145 Foreword by Michael Gove (Secretary of State for Education) and Sarah Teather (Minister of State for Children and Families).

146 See para 5 of the executive summary for the full scope of the proposals consulted upon.

147 Department of Education. Available at: https://www.education.gov.uk/publications/standard/publicationDetail/Page1/DFE-00046–2012

These papers culminated in the Children and Families Bill, which was presented to Parliament on 4 February 2013. One of the most significant proposed changes in relation to special educational needs is the replacement of statements with an education, health and care plan running from birth to 25 years of age.[148]

Special educational needs and disability discrimination appeals

10.84 The availability of judicial review in this field was first limited by the introduction of the Special Educational Needs Tribunals (SENTs) in 1993.[149] Subsequently, a new appellate body, SENDIST was introduced. From November 2008, however, SENDIST, in England, became part of a new unified tribunal system under the Tribunals, Courts and Enforcement Act 2007 and forms part of the First-tier Tribunal (Health, Education and Social Care Chamber) together with the Care Standards Tribunal and the Mental Health Review Tribunal.

10.85 There are two tiers of tribunal: the First-tier (the 'tribunal') hears all special educational needs appeals against local authority decisions. Appeals from the tribunal are to the Upper Tribunal (Administrative Appeals Chamber). Permission to appeal must be sought from the tribunal in the first instance.[150] An appeal from the Upper Tribunal on a point of law lies to the Court of Appeal,[151] other than in relation to excluded decisions.[152] The Upper Tribunal is also amenable to judicial review in limited circumstances.[153]

10.86 The old SENDIST rules have been replaced for all cases commenced after 3 November 2008, by the Tribunal Procedure (First-tier Tribunal) (Health, Education and Social Care Chamber) Rules

---

148 Children and Families Bill Part 3.
149 Education Act 1993 s177, then Education Act 1996 Pt IV s333 (now only applicable to Wales), and now Education Act 1996 Pt IV, specifically, ss325, 326 and 328A and the Tribunal, Courts and Enforcement Act 2007.
150 Prior to 3 November, 2008, appeals were made to the High Court. Practitioners should bear in mind that High Court case law may still be of significance. In relation to procedure see generally the Tribunal Procedure (Upper Tribunal) Rules 2008 SI No 2698 and chapter 19.
151 Tribunal, Courts and Enforcement Act 2007 s13.
152 An excluded decision includes any decision of the Upper Tribunal on an application for permission to appeal from a First-Tier tribunal: Tribunal, Courts and Enforcement Act 2007 s11(4)(b). See paras 2.48–2.51 and 7.75 above.
153 See *R (Cart) v Upper Tribunal* [2011] UKSC 28, [2011] 3 WLR 107 discussed at paras 2.50, 7.21 and 7.75–7.78.

2008.[154] The 2008 Rules are supplemented by the Practice Direction: Health Education and Social Care Chamber Special Educational Needs or Disability Discrimination in Schools Cases.

10.87   The local authority must notify the child's parent of:

- the parent's right of appeal to the tribunal;
- the time limit within which the appeal must be made;
- the availability of dispute resolution arrangements;
- the fact that use of such arrangements does not prejudice the right to appeal.[155]

10.88   In relation to special educational needs, the following matters may be appealed to the tribunal:

- following a statutory assessment, a refusal to issue a statement of special educational needs;[156]
- the contents of a statement when it is first made or when it has been amended;[157]
- a refusal to amend a statement after reassessment;[158]
- the description in the statement of the assessment of the child's special educational needs;[159]
- the description of special educational provision in the statement;[160]
- the school named in the statement or the fact that a school is not named;[161]
- a determination not to amend a statement following a review;[162]
- a refusal to change the name of the school to another maintained school;
- a refusal to undertake a statutory assessment or reassessment (in the latter event, provided there has been no new assessment within the preceding six months);[163] and
- the decision to cease to maintain a statement.[164]

---

154 SI No 2699.
155 Education (Special Educational Needs) (England) (Consolidation) Regulations 2001 SI No 3455 regs 12(2)(b), (4)(b), 17(1)(b), (2)(b), (2)(c) and (9).
156 Education Act 1996 s325.
157 Education Act 1996 s326(1)(a)–(b).
158 Education Act 1996 s326(1)(c).
159 Education Act 1996 s326(1A)(a).
160 Education Act 1996 s326(1A)(b).
161 Education Act 1996 s326(1A)(b)–(c).
162 Education Act 1996 s328A.
163 Education Act 1996 ss328 and 329.
164 See, eg, *Essex County Council v Williams* [2011] EWCA Civ 1315, [2012] ELR 1, and *LB v Kent County Council* [2011] UKUT 405, [2012] ELR 3.

10.89 The time limit for appealing is two months from the date on which the decision complained of was sent to the applicant.[165]

10.90 Disability is one of the 'protected characteristics' within the Equality Act (EA) 2010 and discrimination on that ground is prohibited.

10.91 The EA 2010 also prohibits discrimination arising from the other 'protected characteristics': age,[166] race, religion or belief, sex, sexual orientation and gender reassignment, but the tribunal cannot consider claims relating to these characteristics.

10.92 The Act defines a disability as: 'A physical or mental impairment which has a substantial and long-term adverse effect on a person's ability to carry out normal day-to-day activities.'[167]

10.93 A school must not discriminate against a pupil, because of disability, in relation to admissions, the provision of education, access to any benefit, facility or service, or, exclusions. It is also unlawful for a school to harass or victimise an applicant or pupil because of disability.[168] As with claims under the Disability Discrimination Act 1995, a complaint can be made to the tribunal, save in respect of an admissions decision in respect of a non-statemented pupil to a maintained school. The former exclusion from the tribunal's jurisdiction in respect of permanent exclusions of pupils from maintained schools no longer applies, except in Wales, if the exclusion occurred on or after 1 September 2012.[169]

10.94 The time limit for making a claim to the tribunal is six months from the date of the alleged discrimination.[170] The tribunal has power to extend the time limits in relation to any application if it considers it just to do so.[171]

10.95 In *R v Special Educational Needs Tribunal ex p South Glamorgan CC*,[172] the Court of Appeal held that judicial review is not the correct forum in which to challenge a SENT decision because of the availability of an alternative route of appeal. This would still appear

165 See the Schedule (Time limits for providing application notices and responses) to the Tribunal Procedure (First-tier Tribunal) (Health, Education and Social Care Chamber) Rules 2008 SI No 2699.

166 Age and marriage and civil partnership are excluded from the discrimination in schools provisions: EA 2010 s84. Age is reincluded in relation to further and higher education, but marriage and civil partnership remain excluded: s.90.

167 EA 2010 s6.

168 See generally, EA 2010 Pt 6 and specifically s85.

169 See generally, EA 2010 Sch 17, especially paras 13 and 14.

170 EA 2010 Sch 17 para 4.

171 Tribunal Procedure (First-tier Tribunal) (Health, Education and Social Care Chamber) Rules 2008 SI No 2699 r7.

172 [1996] ELR 326.

to apply under the new tribunal regime.[173] Reference was made to *R v Inland Revenue Commissioners ex p Preston*,[174] and *R v Secretary of State for the Home Department ex p Swati*,[175] as authority for the proposition that statutory rights of appeal must be exhausted before judicial review is sought.[176]

10.96   Judicial review may still be available,[177] however, for challenging decisions that fall outside the jurisdiction of the tribunal. Such matters in relation to special educational needs include challenging policies adopted by the local authority in relation to the statementing procedure, failure to comply with statutory time limits, failure to have regard to the relevant codes of practice and failure of a maintained school named in a statement to admit the child.

Other discrimination claims

10.97   As noted above,[178] the EA 2010 has replaced all previous equality legislation and now provides the code as to how educational institutions must operate to promote equality and prevent discrimination. Part 6 of the Act, alongside the more general provisions of Part 1, provide the framework for schools,[179] further and higher education establishments, qualifications bodies and educational charities.

10.98   The EA 2010 lists a number of protected characteristics, in relation to which discriminatory (and certain other) conduct is prohibited.[180] With regard to education the relevant protected characteristics are:[181]

---

173 See *R (Cart) v Upper Tribunal* [2011] UKSC 28, [2012] 1 AC 663, for the principles on which judicial review will be available to challenge a refusal of permission to appeal to the Upper Tribunal.

174 [1985] AC 835, HL.

175 [1986] 1 WLR 477, CA.

176 See also *Re M (a minor)* [1996] ELR 135, CA, which reaffirmed this principle.

177 There are other alternative remedies such as a complaint to the Local Government Ombudsman which could also be considered.

178 Paragraphs 10.90–10.92.

179 Generally, this includes a maintained school, an independent educational institution, an alternative provision academy and a non-maintained special school.

180 EA 2010 s4.

181 Part 6 does not apply to the protected characteristic of marriage and civil partnership or, in relation to schools, age: EA 2010 s84.

- age,[182]
- disability;[183]
- gender reassignment;[184]
- pregnancy and maternity;
- race, which includes colour, nationality and ethnic or national origins;[185]
- religion or belief, which includes the lack of religion;[186]
- sex and sexual orientation.[187]

10.99 The EA 2010 provides for various types of prohibited conduct.[188] Those most relevant to education are direct[189] and indirect discrimination (including disability discrimination) and the duty to make adjustments. Victimisation and harassment are also prohibited.[190]

10.100 Indirect discrimination relates to provisions, criteria or practices that are discriminatory. This, of course, will be of relevance to areas such as admissions or exclusion decisions. A provision, criterion or practice will be discriminatory if:

- it applies, or would apply, to persons who do not share the protected characteristic,
- it puts, or would put, persons who share the protected characteristic at a disadvantage when compared with persons who do not share it,
- it puts, or would put, the person with the protected characteristic at that disadvantage, and
- it cannot be shown to be a provision, criterion or practice that is a proportionate means of achieving a legitimate aim.[191]

10.101 The duty to make adjustments is a duty to take such steps as it is reasonable to have to take to avoid a substantial disadvantage to someone with a protected characteristic. This includes a disadvantage relating

---

182 Age is not a protected characteristic in relation to schools: EA 2010 s84, but is in relation to further and higher education: s90.
183 See above at para 10.92.
184 As defined by EA 2010 s7.
185 As defined by EA 2010 s9.
186 As defined by EA 2010 s10.
187 As defined by ss11 and 12.
188 See generally, EA 2010 Pt 1, chapter 2.
189 As defined by EA 2010 s13: a person discriminates against another if he treats him less favourably because of a protected characteristic.
190 EA 2010 ss26–27 and s85(3)–(5).
191 EA 2010 s19(2).

to access to a benefit, facility or service or deciding who is offered admission as a pupil.[192]

10.102   More specifically, in relation to schools and higher education establishments, discrimination is unlawful:

- in the arrangements made for deciding who is offered admission as a pupil;
- in the terms of an offer of admission;
- by not admitting the person as a pupil;
- in the way an establishment provides education or by not providing education;
- in the way in which access is afforded to any benefits, facilities or services or by not affording the benefit;
- by exclusion from an establishment; or
- by subjecting a person to any other detriment.[193]

10.103   It is also unlawful for a local authority to do anything which constitutes discrimination, harassment or victimisation in carrying out its public functions.[194] It is unlawful for a responsible body to discriminate in the performance of any of its other functions under the Education Acts, although some important exceptions are made,[195] including the ability of:

- single-sex schools to discriminate on the grounds of sex,[196]
- foundation or voluntary schools with a religious character and independent schools with a religious ethos to discriminate on the grounds of religion or belief,[197] and
- maintained schools,[198] grammar schools and independent schools, who select pupils on the basis of ability and aptitude, to discriminate on the grounds of disability.[199]

---

192 EA 2010 s20(3) and Sch 13 para 2.

193 EA 2010 ss84 and 91.

194 EA 2010 s29(6). Note also the public sector equality duty contained within EA 2010 s149: a public authority must, in the exercise of its functions, have due regard to the need to: eliminate discrimination, harassment, victimisation and any other conduct that is prohibited by or under this Act; advance equality of opportunity between persons who share a relevant protected characteristic and persons who do not share it; and foster good relations between persons who share a relevant protected characteristic and persons who do not share it (s149(1)).

195 EA 2010 Sch 11.

196 EA 2010 Sch 11 Pt 1.

197 EA 2010 Sch 11 Pt 2.

198 See School Standards and Framework Act 1998 s99(2) and (4).

199 EA 2010 Sch 11, Pt 3.

10.104 EA 2010 Pt 6, does not apply to the content of the curriculum. Nor will discrimination occur on the grounds of sex in relation to participation in a 'gender-affected activity'[200] ie a sport, game or other activity of a competitive nature in circumstances where the physical strength, stamina or physique of average persons of one sex would put them at a disadvantage when compared with the other sex as competitors in such activities.[201] A school would also be allowed to take positive action where, by reason of a protected characteristic, a person is suffering from some sort of disadvantage.[202]

10.105 Any contravention of the discrimination provisions referred to above can be remedied by the Secretary of State under his default powers.[203] Claims relating to discrimination – other than disability which, as discussed above, are brought before the First-tier tribunal – can also be made to the county court. The remedies available in the county court include a declaration in relation to any discrimination, victimisation or harassment, and compensation.[204] This will limit the availability of any challenge by way of judicial review although, as seen above, arguments in relation to religious discrimination have been raised in challenges concerned with school uniform policies and school transport.

Discriminatory selection procedures

10.106 Given the similarity between the provisions of EA 2010 and previous anti-discrimination legislation, earlier case-law examining the nature of discrimination within selection procedures will still be relevant. In *R v Birmingham CC ex p Equal Opportunities Commission*,[205] the Equal Opportunities Commission challenged a local authority's selection procedure for the provision of secondary education in its area. The Commission alleged that in carrying out its duties under the legislation, the authority was discriminating against girls (female pupils required higher marks in the entrance examination to enter grammar schools as fewer places were available for them) and was therefore in breach of the relevant statutory provisions. The House of Lords confirmed that this procedure was discriminatory and unlawful.

---

200 EA 2010 s195.
201 EA 2010 s195(3).
202 See generally, EA 2010 s158 (positive discrimination).
203 EA 2010 s87. This does not apply to independent educational institutions that are not special schools or alternative provision academies: s87(2).
204 EA 2010 ss113–119.
205 [1989] AC 1155, HL.

10.107   Further proceedings were brought against the authority as a result of its failure adequately to comply with the House of Lords ruling: see *R v Birmingham CC ex p Equal Opportunities Commission (No 2)*.[206] The authority had attempted to remedy the illegality found by the House of Lords by changing the status of one of the boys' schools from grammar school to grant-maintained school, which meant that the school was no longer maintained by the authority and had the effect, by leaving it out of account, that the number of grammar school places available to boys and girls became broadly similar.

10.108   The Court of Appeal held that in complying with its duty to secure sufficient places in its area for secondary education, the authority could not ignore a school that had obtained grant-maintained status and offered places only to boys, but must have regard to all schools in the area, whether or not maintained by the authority itself. The fact that the number of places available to boys and girls was broadly the same, leaving that school out of account, was therefore irrelevant.

10.109   Neill LJ said:[207]

> It seems to us ... in considering whether sufficient schools are available, the LEA has to take account, and only take account, of places which are available free. The relevant 'pool', as we would term it, is the pool of free places in single-sex schools providing a grammar school education. The pool may include assisted places at independent schools, but in our judgment it certainly includes grant-maintained schools.

> The duty of securing that sufficient schools are available for providing secondary education of a suitable kind is a different duty from the duty to provide such schools.

10.110 In *R (E) v JFS Governing Body*,[208] the Supreme Court considered a challenge to a Jewish school's oversubscription admissions policy where preference was given to children recognised as Jewish by the Office of the Chief Rabbi by virtue of matrilineal descent from a woman who was born Jewish or converted to Judaism. The prospective pupil's mother had converted to Judaism but in a manner that was not recognised by the Office of the Chief Rabbi, and the school refused to admit him. A nine-judge Supreme Court held, by a majority of five to four, that whether there was direct discrimination for the purposes of the Race Relations Act 1976 s1(1)(a), on grounds of race, in this case ethnic origins, required a determination of the factual criteria that led to the decision taken by the person alleged to have

206 [1994] ELR 282, CA.
207 [1994] ELR 282 at 297.
208 [2009] UKSC 15, [2010] 2 WLR 153.

discriminated. The factual criterion for admission in this case, had been based on the pupil's ethnic origins and, therefore, the school's admissions policy constituted direct discrimination.

Reorganisation of schools

10.111 The Education and Inspections Act 2006 replaced the provisions for the establishment, alteration and discontinuance of schools contained in the SSFA 1998 for England.[209] It has recently been amended by the Education Act 2011 with amendments coming into force on 1 February and 1 April 2012.

10.112 Since 1 February 2012, if a local authority is of the view that a new school needs to be established in its area, it must seek proposals for the establishment of an academy and specify a date for such proposals.[210] After the date for proposals, the local authority must inform the Secretary of State of the steps taken to seek proposals for the establishment of an academy, and of any proposals submitted to it (or, if it is the case, that there have been no proposals).[211]

10.113 In relation to the establishment of a new foundation, voluntary or foundation special school, or an academy school, a local authority may, providing it has the consent of the Secretary of State, publish a notice inviting proposals from persons for the establishment of any such new school.[212] Before the closing date for proposals, a notice can be withdrawn with the consent of the Secretary of State. The Secretary of States also has power to direct that a notice be withdrawn.[213] The procedure for the establishment of new schools also involves the publication of the proposals and consultation.[214]

10.114 Where a local authority wishes to discontinue a community, foundation or voluntary school, a community or foundation special school, or a maintained nursery school (or, indeed, the governing body of a foundation or voluntary school, or a foundation special school wishes to discontinue a school) the procedure also involves a

---

209 The provisions within the SSFA 1998 (as amended) ss28–35 are still applicable to Wales.

210 Education and Inspections Act 2006 s6A(1)–(2).

211 Education and Inspections Act 2006 s6A(3).

212 Education and Inspections Act 2006 s7. A local authority in England cannot propose to establish a school in Wales which is proposed to be maintained by a local authority in England: Education and Inspections Act 2006 s14.

213 Education and Inspections Act 2006 s7A.

214 Education and Inspections Act 2006 ss9–11.

process of publication and consultation.[215] The *Gunning* criteria for lawful consultation have been applied in this context, so that consultation will need to be conducted while proposals are still at a formative stage, giving consultees adequate time and adequate information to enable them to prepare a meaningful response. The authority must give conscientious consideration to responses before making a decision.[216]

School transport

10.115   Until April 2007, local authorities were under a mandatory duty to consider whether transport arrangements were necessary to secure a child's attendance at school and to provide that transport free of charge or fund the child's travel arrangements.[217]

10.116   The current provisions in relation to school transport can now be found in the Education Act 1996 as amended by the Education and Inspections Act 2006.[218] Under these provisions, a local authority must:

- assess the school travel needs in its area and assess the facilities and services for sustainable modes of travel to, from and within their area in order to prepare and publish a strategy for each academic year to promote the use of sustainable modes of travel to meet the school travel needs of its area, those being the needs of children and persons of sixth form age as regards travel to

---

215   Education and Inspections Act 2006 ss15–16. In relation to alterations, the Education and Inspections Act 2006 contains provisions as to publications and how such alterations can be implemented: Education and Inspections Act 2006 ss18–24.

216   See, eg, *R v Brent LBC ex p Gunning* (1985) 84 LGR 168, where judicial review was granted on the ground of inadequate consultation. *Gunning* was applied *R v Secretary of State for Education and Employment ex p McCarthy* (1996) *Times* 24 July; QBD, a case concerning a decision by the Secretary of State to withdraw the school's approved status under the Education Act 1993 and *R v Lambeth LBC ex p N* [1996] ELR 299, a case concerning a proposal to close a maintained boarding school for children with special educational need. See too, the recent permission decision in *R (Moyse) v Secretary of State for Education* [2012] EWHC 2758 (Admin), [2012] ELR 551 and generally paras 6.255–6.265 above.

217   See Education Act 1944 s55 and subsequently the Education Act 1996 s509.

218   There have also been relatively minor amendments made by the Education Act 2011. It should be noted that different provisions apply to Wales: see Learner Travel (Wales) Measure 2008 SI No 2.

and from schools, institutions or other places where they receive education;[219]

- make any suitable home to school travel arrangements that the authority considers necessary to facilitate an eligible child's attendance at his educational establishment and provide such travel arrangements free of charge for that child;[220]
- have regard to the Secretary of State's guidance;[221]
- make arrangements for transport (free of charge) as is considered necessary to facilitate adults receiving education at further and/or higher education establishments maintained or assisted by the authority or within the further education sector;[222]
- consult, prepare a transport policy statement and make arrangements for transport (free of charge) as is considered necessary to facilitate attendance by relevant young adults[223] at institutions outside the further and higher education sectors in cases where the authority has secured the relevant provision for the adult;[224]
- prepare and publish a transport policy statement for the provision of transport for persons of sixth form age for each academic year and ensure that the arrangements under the policy are given effect;[225] and
- have regard, when exercising its travel functions, to any wish of a parent or a person of sixth form age to be educated at a particular school or institution based on religion or belief.[226]

10.117 The Education Act 1996 also provides authorities with a discretion to make school travel arrangements, which they deem necessary, for a child who is not an eligible child,[227] to make arrangements to help

---

219 Education Act 1996 s508A(1)–(2), (5)–(6). 'Sustainable modes of travel' is defined in s508A(3) and 'school travel needs' is defined in subs(4) of the same section.
220 Education Act 1996 s508B. 'Eligible child' is defined in Sch 35B of the 1996 Act and 'home to school travel arrangements' and 'travel arrangements' are defined within s508B.
221 Education Act 1996 ss508A(9), 508D, 508H and 509AB. The current guidance is *Home to School Travel and Transport Guidance* (May 2007 and 2010) *Post-16 Transport Guidance* (June 2010).
222 Education Act 1996 s508F(1)–(2) and (4).
223 An adult who is aged under 25 and is subject to learning difficulty assessment: Education Act 1996 s508F(9).
224 Education Act 1996 ss508F(1) and (3)–(4) and 508G.
225 Education Act 1996 ss509AA–509AC.
226 Education Act 1996 s509AD.
227 Education Act 1996 s508C.

with travel for early years education[228] and to create a school travel scheme for its area.[229]

10.118   The possibility of judicial review is limited by the availability of an alternative remedy under the Education Act 1996. Sections 496–497B provide the Secretary of State with powers to prevent the unreasonable exercise of functions by a local authority, the governing body of any community, foundation or voluntary school, or of any community or foundation special school, or of any maintained nursery school. These powers, together with those under sections 508I and 509AE (transport provision for adults subject to learning difficulty assessment and persons of sixth for age, respectively), give the Secretary of State a wide discretion to direct a local authority to provide school transport. These alternative remedies must be exhausted before making an application for judicial review: *R v Essex CC ex p EB*.[230] This does not mean that judicial review will never be available but, generally, the Secretary of State should be the first port of call.

10.119   One issue in relation to which there has been a number of judicial review challenges is that of 'suitability' in relation to transport arrangements,[231] as even under the current legislative provisions, the arrangements made by authorities must be 'suitable' arrangements.[232] Related to this requirement is the fact that the Education Act 1996 makes a child's parents liable for a criminal offence if they fail to secure the regular attendance of registered pupil at school; a defence to such a charge being that the authority has failed to make suitable transport arrangements or, in relation to independent schools, that no suitable arrangements have been made and the child's school is not within walking distance of his home.[233]

10.120   In *Essex County Council v Rogers*,[234] the child's parent had been convicted of an offence under the Education Act 1944 for refusing to

---

228   Education Act 1996 s509A.

229   Education Act 1996 s508E and Sch 35C.

230   [1997] ELR 327. See also para 10.129 below.

231   See, eg, *R v Carmarthenshire ex p White* [2001] ELR 172; *R v Vale of Glamorgan ex p J* [2001] EWCA Civ 593, [2001] ELR 758; and *R (Jones) v Ceredigion County Council* [2004] EWHC 1376 (Admin) (considered by the Court of Appeal [2005] EWCA Civ 986, [2005] ELR 565 but not on the point of suitable arrangements. The House of Lords gave permission for a leapfrog appeal on that point but it was not pursued: [2007] UKHL 24, [2007] 1 WLR 1400). It should be noted that the challenges in these cases strayed into the realms of suitability of the school as part of considering whether the transport arrangements were suitable.

232   See generally, Education Act 1996 s508B and Sch 35B.

233   Education Act 1996 s444.

234   [1987] AC 66, [1986] 3 WLR 689.

send her daughter to school on the basis the shortest walking route available was unsuitable for the child to use unaccompanied and the alternative route was over three miles. The defendant successfully appealed against her conviction to the Divisional Court, but the House of Lords allowed the authority's appeal, concluding that an available walking route was a route along which a child accompanied as necessary could walk with reasonable safety to school; a route did not fail to qualify as available because of dangers that would arise if the child used it unaccompanied.[235]

10.121 In *R v Dyfed CC ex p S (Minors)*,[236] the children and their family lived in Dyfed, Wales having moved there from England. The area in which the family lived, was a rural area where the schools educated children predominantly in Welsh. The authority had been providing free transport for the children to attend a school some 10 miles from their home which, in accordance with the parents' wishes, was not a predominantly Welsh-speaking school. The authority proposed to change the educational provision and provide suitable transport arrangements for the children to attend a Welsh-speaking school closer to their home. The Secretary of State refused to intervene. An application for judicial review was dismissed and the children appealed. The children's case involved the contention that the school had to be suitable for transport arrangements to be suitable. The court held that the transport arrangements were what had to be suitable, not the school. To suggest otherwise would run contrary to what Parliament had intended in relation to a defence concerning the lack of suitable arrangements for ensuring a pupil attended school.[237]

10.122 In *R (R) and others v Leeds City Council*,[238] nine claimants, all of whom resided within Leeds, brought challenges to a decision by Leeds City Council to decline to provide free school transport for the purpose of facilitating their attendance at schools they currently attended in Manchester. The claimants' parents wished their children to attend an orthodox Jewish school, which was unavailable in the Leeds area. There were, however, schools in Leeds offering Hebrew studies adapted for the Jewish community along with the

---

235 [1987] AC 66 at 77–8. See too, *R v Devon CC ex p George* [1989] AC 573, [1988] 3 WLR 1386 (it was for a local authority's judgment, based on all the circumstances, whether free transport was necessary for the purpose of facilitating attendance at school).

236 [1995] ELR 98.

237 By way of contrast see, eg, *R v Rochdale MBC ex p Schemet* [1993] 1 FCR 306.

238 [2005] EWHC 2495 (Admin), [2006] BLGR 579.

national curriculum.[239] Wilkie J held that the authority's decision was neither unlawful nor *Wednesbury* unreasonable. The authority was entitled to decide that the Leeds schools offering the national curriculum were suitable alternative schools so that it was not necessary to provide free school transport to facilitate the attendance of persons receiving education at schools in Manchester.[240]

10.123   The position may, however, be different where a school is named in Part 4 of a special educational needs statement.[241]

Judicial review, appeals and default powers

10.124   As stated above,[242] the Secretary of State has default powers under Education Act 1996 ss496 and 497B and a general reserve power to secure proper performance.[243]

10.125   When considering whether the powers of the Secretary of State preclude resort to the courts, the older cases demonstrate a distinction between unlawful acts and omissions to exercise functions. In *Cummings v Birkenhead Corporation*,[244] for example, it was held that what is now the section 496 power excludes the jurisdiction of the courts except where an ultra vires act, such as a breach of the principles of natural justice, is alleged. Similarly, in *Herring v Templeman*,[245] the court held that although what is now the section 496 power precluded resort to the courts where a mere wrong exercise of discretion was alleged (in that case a failure to hold an oral hearing), but not where an ultra vires act was alleged.

10.126   More recently, however, the courts appear not to have regarded the existence of default powers as automatically precluding an

---

239 [2005] EWHC 2495 (Admin) at [19].

240 [2005] EWHC 2495 (Admin) at [29].

241 See, *R v Havering ex p K* [1998] ELR 402; (1997) *Times* 18 November; and *R v Islington ex p GA* [2000] EWHC 390. In the latter case it was suggested that the situation may well be avoided by the authority including more than one school in the statement. This has since been considered by the Upper Tribunal in *MH v Nottinghamshire County Council* [2009] UKUT 178 (AAC) and the Court of Appeal in *S v Dudley Metropolitan Borough Council* [2012] EWCA Civ 346, [2012] PTSR 1393. Note too the position in relation to a child with special education needs at sixth form age: *R (A) v North Somerset Council* [2009] EWHC 3060 (Admin), [2010] ELR 139.

242 At para 10.118.

243 Education Act 1996 ss197A–197B.

244 [1972] Ch 12, CA.

245 [1973] 2 All ER 581.

application for judicial review. In *R v Inner London Education Authority ex p Ali,*[246] the applicant alleged that the authority had breached its duty under what was then Education Act 1944 s8, to secure provision of sufficient schools in the area. The applicant complained to the Secretary of State, who declined to exercise his default power. As a preliminary point, the court considered the nature of the duty imposed by section 8 and the relevance of the existence of the Secretary of State's default power. The Court of Appeal held that the existence of the default power did not preclude an application for judicial review. Where the Secretary of State had decided not to exercise his default power in a particular case, moreover, and then an application was made for judicial review, the court would not be bound by the Secretary of State's decision, although it would be a factor to be taken into account when considering whether or not to grant relief.

10.127   Woolf LJ said that he:[247]

> ... would not accept that the language of the default powers contained in sections 68 and 99 of [the Education Act 1944, now sections 496–497 of the Education Act 1996] indicates that Parliament intended the jurisdiction of the courts to be ousted from considering the issues which can be considered by the Secretary of State under those sections.

10.128 In *R v Newham LBC ex p R,*[248] however, the court reached a different conclusion. The applicants were parents of a child with special educational needs. They appealed against a statement of special educational needs, which was then remitted back to the LEA for reconsideration. The parents then sought judicial review of the second statement. One question for the court was whether the applicants had an alternative remedy by way of appeal to the Secretary of State. The Divisional Court held that it was not its function to redraft the statement and that the Secretary of State was better placed than the court to form a view as to what should be in the statement and thus dispose of the outstanding issues.

10.129   Schiemann J stated:[249]

> The law as to the circumstances in which the court will refuse relief by way of judicial review on the ground that an alternative remedy is available is now well settled. However, I think the following may be regarded as uncontroversial. Judicial review is a discretionary remedy

---

246 (1990) 2 Admin LR 822.
247 (1990) 2 Admin LR 822 at 831B–C.
248 [1995] ELR 156.
249 (1990) 2 Admin LR 822 at 165.

and relevant factors in deciding whether to exercise the discretion to grant leave to move for judicial review or to grant particular relief include a consideration of:

(1) whether a refusal to quash will be to leave the applicant without remedy; and, in particular,

(2) whether there is available an alternative forum in front of which the applicant can argue his substantive and legal points and which can dispose of them;

(3) whether the court's judgment will dispose of the outstanding issues;

(4) the chance of a point of law sought to be raised in the judicial review proceedings surfacing again in any alternative forum;

(5) the time implications of allowing the judicial review procedure to start or continue.

Where the matter justifies the making of a general declaration, then the appropriate way of proceeding, if the declaration would be of value to the applicant, would be to go by way of judicial review. That is because this court is the only one having power to make such a declaration. Insofar as the complaint is that a particular child has been the subject of a mistaken value judgment by the LEA then the appropriate way of proceeding is by way of appeal to the Secretary of State. Even if the complaint is that the mistaken value judgment by the LEA was arrived at in part by reason of mistakes of law, it is in general appropriate to proceed by way of appeal rather than by judicial review unless the alleged mistakes of law are likely to be repeated by the Secretary of State.

10.130 In *R v Essex CC ex p EB*,[250] the Divisional Court refused permission to apply for judicial review of an LEA's decision regarding whether school transport was 'necessary', as the Secretary of State was best placed to determine the question under Education Act 1996 ss496–497. McCullough J said:[251]

It is not for the court to judge safety. The court could not go to the route and look at it itself. The Secretary of State, on the other hand, through his officials, could do exactly that and, if need be, on different occasions. He is in a far better position to assess safety by watching the traffic, considering visibility, taking into account width, and perhaps the absence of verges and so on – all matters more suitable for decision by the Secretary of State.

10.131 In *R v Brent LBC ex p F*,[252] the Divisional Court held that where the issues were really educational ones, the best person to resolve them

250 [1997] ELR 327, DC.
251 [1997] ELR 327 at 329.
252 [1999] ELR 32.

was the Secretary of State, using his far-reaching powers under EA 1996 s497.

Who should be the claimant?

10.132 A final point to consider in judicial review applications in the field of education is who should bring the claim. Either the parents or the child could be the claimant. There are important ramifications, however, regarding funding where the claimant is a child.

10.133   In the context of school admissions cases, it has been held that while the child may well have a sufficient interest to mount a challenge, nevertheless the parent(s) should usually be named as the claimant(s), as the only reason for bringing a challenge in the name of the child is usually to be able to obtain public funding for the challenge and to protect the parents in costs should the challenge fail. This was an abuse and a device and a reason for refusing permission to apply for judicial review.[253]

10.134   In relation to school closure, however, the position appears to be somewhat different. In *R (WB and KA) v Leeds School Organisation Committee*,[254] Scott Baker J held that that issue was relevant not to standing but to abuse and therefore the court's discretion. Both parents and children had a sufficient interest to bring judicial review proceedings in school closure or reorganisation cases, and while in many cases it may be the parents who had the real interest and while it may be an abuse of process to name the child as the claimant for the purposes of obtaining funding and protection against a possible costs order, clear evidence would be needed to establish such an abuse. The school admissions cases, referred to above, were distinguished on the basis that the appellate regime there under consideration made it clear that the right of appeal was that of the parent and not the child. There was no indication that the court's decisions in those cases were intended for any wider application.[255]

253 *R v Richmond LBC ex p JC* [2001] ELR 21; and *B v Head Teacher of Alperton Community School* [2001] ELR 359.
254 [2002] EWHC 1927 (Admin), [2003] ELR 67.
255 [2002] EWHC 1927 (Admin), [2003] ELR 67 at [32]–[37].

Higher education

10.135   For the purposes of judicial review, distinctions are drawn between the different origins in law of the various universities and colleges. Many universities are chartered bodies created by Royal Charter issued pursuant to the royal prerogative. Traditionally, a chartered body was not subject to the ultra vires rule, as the charter simply grants corporate capacity to the body, not statutory power, and so they have been treated as domestic institutions. The internal affairs of these universities are regulated by a 'visitor', who is appointed in accordance with the statutes and other instruments which govern the university's constitution. As the visitor has sole and exclusive jurisdiction over internal matters, the courts will usually lack the jurisdiction to intervene: *Thomas v University of Bradford*.[256]

10.136   Visitors no longer have jurisdiction to hear complaints made in respect of an application for admission as a student or a complaint made by a student or former of a qualifying institution.[257] In addition, visitors cannot hear complaints by a student or former student of a different institution but who is undertaking a course of study which will lead to an award from the qualifying institution. These complaints are now heard by the Office of the Independent Adjudicator.[258] Where the remedy of appeal to the visitor exists, however, it will constitute an alternative remedy, precluding judicial review.

10.137   In *R v Lord President of the Privy Council ex p Page*,[259] a majority of the House of Lords held, on the facts, that the visitor of Hull University was not susceptible to judicial review, as he had been acting within his jurisdiction. Judicial review would lie, however, if he had acted outside his jurisdiction in the sense that he had no power under the regulating documents to adjudicate on the dispute or, more importantly, if he had abused his power or acted in breach of the rules of natural justice.

10.138   It has also been said by the House of Lords, albeit by way of obiter dicta and in a different context, that relief by way of judicial review

256 [1987] 1 AC 795, HL.
257 Higher Education Act 2004 s20. Qualifying institutions are as defined in s11: a university whose entitlement to grant awards is conferred or confirmed by an Act of Parliament, a Royal Charter, or by order of the Privy Council; a constituent college, school or hall or other institution of a university whose entitlement is by an Act of Parliament; an institution conducted by a higher education corporation; and an institution designated by the Secretary of State.
258 See below, paras 10.141–10.149.
259 [1993] AC 682, HL.

is available to restrain a chartered corporation – in that case a local authority – from carrying out unauthorised acts,[260] that is acts inconsistent with the charter. However, universities will not automatically be considered public bodies as the powers derived from their charter are not derived from the prerogative, even though the charter itself is. Moreover, there has never been any doubt that a local authority is susceptible to review. In practice, the courts will rarely intervene in the exercise of the visitor's discretion or judgment unless it is satisfied that it is wrong in law: *R v University of London ex p Vijayatanga*.[261]

10.139 The second way in which a university may have been created is by an Act of Parliament, such as the Universities of Oxford and Cambridge Act 1571. Universities created by statute can be the subject of judicial review.

10.140 Finally, modern institutions of higher education are usually higher education corporations, which are conducted in accordance with the instruments and articles of government. Some are companies, usually limited by guarantee.[262] Judicial review may lie where a university fails to act in accordance with its own regulations.[263]

Office of the Independent Adjudicator for Higher Education

10.141 The Office of the Independent Adjudicator for Higher Education (OIA) was established under the Higher Education 2004 and is an independent body operating a scheme to hear students' complaints. Although the OIA was set up only to hear complaints in relation to qualifying institutions[264] it was given a power to extend the scheme to non-qualifying institutions and has a protocol that sets out the terms upon which such institutions may apply to join and may be admitted to membership of the scheme.[265]

10.142 Under the Higher Education Act 2004, a qualifying institution must comply with any obligation imposed upon it by the OIA under

---

260 *Hazell v Hammersmith and Fulham LBC* [1992] 2 AC 1, HL.

261 [1988] QB 322.

262 Education Reform Act 1988 ss121, 124 and 129.

263 See, eg, *R v Board of Governors of Sheffield Hallam University ex p R* [1995] ELR 267; *R v Manchester Metropolitan University ex p Nolan* [1994] ELR 380.

264 See above at para 10.136.

265 The current protocol can be found at: www.oiahe.org.uk/media/35819/protocol_for_nqis.pdf.

the scheme for the review of qualifying complaints.[266] A qualifying complaint is defined in section 12 of the Act as a complaint about an act or omission of a qualifying institution which is made by a person as a student or former student at that institution, or as a student or former student at any another institution undertaking a course of study, or programme of research, leading to the grant of an award from the qualifying institution. A complaint will not fall within the OIA's remit if it relates to matters of academic judgment.[267]

10.143 The jurisdiction of the OIA will constitute an alternative remedy and will therefore restrict the availability of judicial review against further and higher education institutions. Importantly, however, it has been held that the OIA's decisions are amenable to judicial review.

10.144 _R (Siborurema) v Office of the Independent Adjudicator_[268] was the first case to consider the powers of the OIA and whether it was amenable to judicial review. The Court of Appeal had no difficulty in concluding that the OIA would be susceptible to judicial review:[269]

(a) Though it is not necessarily determinative, the entire procedure for dealing with student complaints about the decisions of [Higher Education Institutions (HEIs)] is set up by statute. That is an important aspect.

(b) The Secretary of State (and the Assembly in Wales), may designate a body corporate as the designated operator for review of student complaints ...

(c) OIA has been so designated.

(d) The body must not be designated unless the designating body is satisfied that it is providing a scheme for the review of qualifying complaints that meets conditions set out in Schedule 2 to the Act ...

(e) The designated operator must comply with duties set out in Schedule 3 (Section 14).

(f) The governing body of every qualifying institution must comply with any obligation imposed on it by the scheme ... There is a strong public element and public interest in the proper determination of complaints by students to HEIs.

(g) The range of potential complaints is broad and the function contemplated for OIA cannot be categorised merely as regulating contractual arrangements between student and HEI.

---

266 Higher Education Act 2004 s15. The rules of the scheme can be found at: www.oiahe.org.uk/media/1258/oia-rules.pdf (accessed on 3 February 2013). For further information about the scheme see www.oiahe.org.uk/.

267 Higher Education Act 2004 s12(2).

268 [2007] EWCA Civ 1365, [2008] ELR 209.

269 [2007] EWCA Civ 1365, [2008] ELR 209 at [49].

10.145 The court also held that the designated operator should be subject to the supervision of the High Court and that it would not be impeded in its role by the existence of a limited remedy in the courts if it had exceeded its powers or acted in a manner inconsistent with the legislation. It would, however, be contrary to the statutory regime if the OIA was to become a law unto itself without the court being able to intervene where necessary.[270]

10.146   It appears, nonetheless, that any challenge to a decision of the OIA will be difficult:[271]

> Parliament has conferred on the designated operator a broad discretion. It is not prescriptive as to how complaints should be considered when making a decision whether they are justified. OIA is able, both in defining its scheme and in deciding whether particular complaints are justified, to exercise a discretion in determining how to approach the particular complaint. OIA is entitled to operate on the basis that different complaints may require different approaches. In assessing whether a complaint has been approached in a lawful manner, the court will have regard to the expertise of OIA, which in turn should have regard to the expertise of the [Higher Education Institution (HEI)]. OIA is entitled in most cases, if it sees fit, to take the HEI's regulations and procedures as a starting point and to consider, when assessing a complaint, whether they have been complied with ...

10.147 Accordingly:[272]

> Decisions may, however, be challenged where, for example, there have been breaches of the rules of natural justice, by way of bias or relevant procedural injustice, or where there has been such scant or inappropriate consideration of a complaint that what had occurred could not fairly be described as a review.

> In its decision on complaints, OIA is expected to follow rational and fair procedures and to give adequate reasons for its decisions and recommendations. Thus the procedures followed and the decision letters which emerged can properly be scrutinised with that object in mind.

10.148 The scope of the OIA's scheme was further considered in *R (Maxwell) v Office of the Independent Adjudicator*.[273] The Court of Appeal said that:[274]

> ... the practice and procedures for the review and resolution of a wide range of student complaints under the independent scheme operated

---

270 [2007] EWCA Civ 1365, [2008] ELR 209 at [50].
271 [2007] EWCA Civ 1365, [2008] ELR 209 at [53].
272 [2007] EWCA Civ 1365, [2008] ELR 209 at [55]–[56].
273 [2011] EWCA Civ 1236, [2012] PTSR 884.
274 [2011] EWCA Civ 1236, [2012] PTSR 884 at [32]–[33].

free of charge and largely as an inquisitorial process on a confidential basis by the OIA under the 2004 Act, is quite different from civil proceedings. Its informal inquisitorial methods, which are normally conducted on paper without cross examination and possibly leading to the making of recommendations in its Final Decision, mean that the outcome is not the product of a rigorous adversarial judicial process dealing with the proof of contested facts, with the application of the legislation to proven facts, with establishing legal rights and obligations and with awarding legal remedies, such as damages and declarations ...

... the courts are not entitled to impose on the informal complaints review procedure of the OIA a requirement that it should have to adjudicate on issues, such as whether or not there has been disability discrimination. Adjudication of that issue usually involves making decisions on contested questions of fact and law, which require the more stringent and structured procedures of civil litigation for their proper determination.

10.149 As long as the OIA's decision is within the range of judgments available to it in the particular circumstances it will be difficult to succeed in establishing that the OIA has erred in law.[275] Conversely, however, where the OIA's decision is inadequately reasoned in relation to compensation, the decision may be quashed to be determined again by the OIA.[276]

---

275 See, eg, *R (Arratoon) v Office of the Independent Adjudicator for Higher Education* [2008] EWHC 3125 (Admin), [2009] ELR 186.

276 *R (Cardao-Pito) v Office of the Independent Adjudicator for Higher Education* [2012] EWHC 203 (Admin), [2012] ELR 231.

CHAPTER 11

Judicial review and social security law

Introduction

11.1   The law surrounding social security is, at the time of writing, in a state of flux. A complex system of numerous different social security benefits is about to be replaced by a single benefit with a large number of different elements, known as 'universal credit'.

11.2   As such, much of the old law in this chapter will shortly become of, primarily, historical interest. The new law is, however, to be phased in over a period of years, and the detail of the new law is, moreover, neither in force at the time of writing nor, in relation to some aspects, even published.

11.3   This chapter will therefore outline, first, the current system and then, so far as they are known, the new arrangements.[1] Under both regimes, the role for judicial review is considerably constrained by the comprehensive appeals system that exists in relation to decisions concerning most benefits.

The legislation

The old primary legislation

11.4   The principal Acts concerning the social security system are the Social Security Contributions and Benefits Act 1992 and the Social Security Administration Act 1992. Together, these Acts consolidated the bulk of the pre-existing legislation.[2]

11.5   Subsequent statutory provisions that amend and/or supplement the principal Acts include the:

- Social Security (Mortgage Interest Payments) Act 1992 s2;
- Social Security (Contributions) Act 1994 ss1 and 3;
- Statutory Sick Pay Act 1994;
- Social Security (Incapacity for Work) Act 1994;

---

1   For more detail on the 'old' law, see chapter 11 in the 2nd edition of this work. On social security law generally, see the 'Recent developments in social security law' series in *Legal Action* (LAG) and CPAG's annual *Welfare benefits and tax credits handbook* and *Housing Benefit and Council Tax Legislation*. For more detail on the 'new' law, see Kennedy *Universal Credit: an introduction* (House of Commons Library Standard Note SN06469, 2012) and CPAG, *Universal Credit: what you need to know* (CPAG, 3rd edn, forthcoming 2013).

2   Many of these provisions, which are superseded by the introduction of universal credit, will be repealed from 1 April 2013, albeit with extensive saving and transitional provisions; others will be subject to amendment: Welfare Reform Act 2012 and its associated commencement orders.

- Jobseekers Act 1995;
- Pensions Act 1995 ss126–129, 131–134, 148, 177, Sch 4 and Sch 7 Pt 11;
- Social Security Act 1998;
- Welfare Reform and Pensions Act 1999;
- Immigration and Asylum Act 1999 ss115 and 123;
- Child Support, Pensions and Social Security Act 2000;
- Tax Credits Act 2002;
- Welfare Reform Act 2007.

Delegated legislation

11.6   The Social Security and Child Support (Decisions and Appeals) Regulations 1999[3] provided the procedural rules and other requirements for the unified appeals system introduced by the Social Security Act 1998 concerning social security, contracted-out pensions, child support and vaccine damage decisions. Following the transfer of appeal functions to the Social Security and Child Support Tribunal within the Social Entitlement Chamber of the First-tier Tribunal,[4] the relevant procedural rules are now to be found in the Tribunal Procedure (First-tier Tribunal) (Social Entitlement Chamber) Rules 2008.[5]

Benefits

11.7   The principal social security benefits with which this chapter is concerned are:

- income support;
- jobseeker's allowance;
- employment and support allowance;
- housing benefit;
- child tax credit;
- working tax credit; and
- council tax reduction.

11.8   Each of these benefits is addressed briefly in turn below.

---

3   SI No 991, as amended.
4   Under the Tribunals, Courts and Enforcement Act 2007 and the Transfer of Tribunal Functions Order 2008 SI No 2833.
5   SI No 2685.

Income support

11.9   Income support is administered by the Secretary of State for Work and Pensions. It is provided for by the Social Security Contributions and Benefits Act 1992.[6] Income Support is an income-related benefit.[7]

11.10   Detailed provision for the assessment and payment of income support is made by the Income Support (General) Regulations 1987.[8]

11.11   It is a means-tested benefit payable to people who are either unemployed or in part-time employment, who are not eligible for certain other state benefits.[9] Claimants whose capital exceeds £16,000 cannot receive Income Support.[10]

11.12   The Secretary of State is responsible for decisions in relation to Income Support.[11] There is a right of appeal to the First-tier Tribunal (Social Entitlement Chamber) against most such decisions.[12] There is a further right of appeal to the Upper Tribunal (Administrative Appeals Chamber) from decisions of the First-tier Tribunal on a point of law. An appeal from the Upper Tribunal is to the Court of Appeal.[13]

Jobseeker's allowance

11.13   The Jobseekers Act 1995 governs the scheme of jobseeker's allowance (JSA). Generally speaking JSA is payable to those who are either unemployed or who work for less than 16 hours a week and who are seeking full-time employment.[14] JSA payments are calculated by reference to either contribution-based JSA or income-based JSA.[15]

11.14   The assessment and payment of JSA is governed by the Jobseeker's Allowance Regulations 1996.[16]

---

6 Social Security Contributions and Benefits Act 1992 s124.
7 Social Security Contributions and Benefits Act 1992 s123.
8 SI No 1967.
9 Such as jobseeker's allowance, considered at paras 11.15–11.19 below.
10 Social Security Contributions and Benefits Act 1992 s134 and Income Support (General) Regulations 1987 SI No 1967 reg 45.
11 Social Security Act 1998 s8.
12 Social Security Act 1998 s12.
13 Social Security Act 1998 s14 and Tribunals, Courts and Enforcement Act 2007 ss11 and 13.
14 Jobseekers Act 1995 ss1–3.
15 Jobseekers Act 1995 ss2–3.
16 SI No 207.

11.15   JSA is a means-tested benefit. The amount to which a claimant is entitled depends, in part, on their income and capital. A claimant with capital in excess of £16,000 is ineligible for JSA.[17]

11.16   The Secretary of State is responsible for decisions in relation to JSA.[18] There is a right of appeal to the First-tier Tribunal (Social Entitlement Chamber) against most such decisions.[19] There is a further right of appeal to the Upper Tribunal (Administrative Appeals Chamber) from decisions of the First-tier Tribunal on a point of law. An appeal from the Upper Tribunal is to the Court of Appeal.[20]

Employment and support allowance

11.17   Employment and support allowance (ESA) was introduced for most new claimants on 27 October 2008,[21] replacing incapacity benefit.

11.18   Incapacity benefit was a contributory benefit payable in respect of any day of incapacity to work, provided that certain conditions were met.[22] Incapacity benefit was either short-term, for periods of up to 364 days, or long-term, for periods of longer than 364 days.

11.19   The basic conditions for eligibility for ESA are that the claimant:[23]

- has limited capability for work,
- is at least 16 years old,
- has not reached pensionable age,
- is in Great Britain,
- is not entitled to income support,[24] and
- is not entitled to JSA.[25]

11.20   Provision for the assessment and calculation of ESA are made by the Employment and Support Allowance Regulations 2008.[26]

---

17 Jobseekers Act 1995 s13 and Jobseeker's Allowance Regulations 1996 reg 107.
18 Social Security Act 1998 s8.
19 Social Security Act 1998 s12.
20 Social Security Act 1998 s14 and Tribunals, Courts and Enforcement Act 2007 ss11 and 13.
21 Welfare Reform Act 2007 s1 and Welfare Reform Act 2007 (Commencement No 6 and Consequential Provisions) Order 2008 SI No 787.
22 Social Security Contributions and Benefits Act 1992 s30A.
23 Welfare Reform Act 2007 s1(3).
24 See paras 11.9–11.12 above.
25 See paras 11.13–11.16 above.
26 SI No 794. See also Employment and Support Allowance (Work-Related Activity) Regulations 2011 SI No 1349.

11.21   The Secretary of State is responsible for decisions in relation to ESA.[27] There is a right of appeal to the First-tier Tribunal (Social Entitlement Chamber) against most such decisions.[28] There is a further right of appeal to the Upper Tribunal (Administrative Appeals Chamber) from decisions of the First-tier Tribunal on a point of law. An appeal from the Upper Tribunal is to the Court of Appeal.[29]

Housing benefit

11.22   Provision for the scheme of housing benefit is made by the Social Security Contributions and Benefits Act 1992.[30] Housing benefit is administered by local housing authorities. Where rent is payable to a local housing authority, it is provided by way of rent rebate; in all other cases it is provided by way of a rent allowance.[31]

11.23   Detailed provision for the assessment and payment of housing benefit is made by the Housing Benefit Regulations 2006.[32]

11.24   There is a right of appeal against decisions by authorities in respect of housing benefit to the First-tier Tribunal.[33] That right of appeal may be exercised by any person affected by such a decision.[34] In limited circumstances only will a landlord or an agent acting on behalf of that landlord be treated as a person affected by a decision of a relevant authority.[35] Otherwise, a landlord has no right of appeal.[36]

11.25   The Secretary of State, the authority and any person affected by the decision appealed against have a right to appeal on a point of law from a decision of the First-tier Tribunal to the Upper Tribunal, and thereafter to the Court of Appeal.[37]

---

27 Social Security Act 1998 s8.
28 Social Security Act 1998 s12.
29 Social Security Act 1998 s14 and Tribunals, Courts and Enforcement Act 2007 ss11 and 13.
30 Social Security Administration Act 1992 s130.
31 Social Security Administration Act 1992 s134.
32 SI No 213. See also Housing Benefit and Council Tax (Decisions and Appeals) Regulations 2001 SI No 1002.
33 Child Support, Pensions and Social Security Act 2000 s68 and Sch 7.
34 Child Support, Pensions and Social Security Act 2000 Sch 7 para 6(3).
35 Housing Benefit and Council Tax (Decisions and Appeals) Regulations 2001 SI No 1002 reg 3(1)(e).
36 *Wirral MBC v Salisbury Independent Living Ltd* [2012] EWCA Civ 84, [2012] PTSR 1221, [2012] HLR 25.
37 Child Support, Pensions and Social Security Act 2000 Sch 7 para 8 and Tribunals, Courts and Enforcement Act 2007 s13.

11.26   In addition to housing benefit, a local housing authority may make discretionary housing payments to a person if that person is entitled to housing benefit and/or council tax benefit and if they appear to the authority to require some additional financial assistance to meet their housing costs.[38]

11.27   The total amount of discretionary housing payments that an authority can make in any year is subject to a cap.[39]

11.28   The payments are – rather unusually in the field of social security – wholly discretionary. There is no right of appeal against a refusal to award a discretionary payment, but authorities are required to operate a review procedure and to give written notice with reasons for any decision on review.[40]

11.29   The absence of a defined appeal structure leaves open the possibility of judicial review in respect of any failure to award a discretionary payment, on the usual administrative law principles, although the wide discretion conferred on authorities will make it more difficult to succeed on a challenge to a decision under this scheme, unless the authority has made a clear legal error in its decision-making process.[41]

Child tax credit and working tax credit

• 11.30   Tax credits were introduced by the Tax Credits Act 1999, as part of an attempt to modernise the social security system and a movement away from the traditional use of the Department for Work and Pensions (formerly the Department of Social Security) to administer all state benefits. The Tax Credits Act 2002 repealed and replaced the 1999 Act.

11.31   Under the 2002 Act, there are two types of tax credit – child tax credit and working tax credit. Both credits are aimed at encouraging benefit claimants into work (and thus away from reliance on JSA) and rewarding those who continue in full-time work. Child tax credit replaced several previous forms of benefit in respect of children such

---

38 Child Support, Pensions and Social Security Act 2000 s69, and Discretionary Financial Assistance Regulations 2001 SI No 1167.

39 Discretionary Housing Payments (Grants) Order 2001 SI No 2340 art 7.

40 Discretionary Financial Assistance Regulations 2001 SI No 1167 regs 6(3) and 8.

41 The suitability, or otherwise, of discretionary housing payments to meet a shortfall in housing costs not covered by housing benefit was considered by the Court of Appeal in *Burnip v Birmingham CC* [2012] EWCA Civ 629, [2013] PTSR 117.

as the child element in income support and income-based JSA. Working tax credit replaced working families tax credit, disabled persons tax credit and the New Deal 50 plus.

Initial decisions

11.32 Tax credits are administered by the Commissioners for Her Majesty's Revenue and Customs and, accordingly, the initial decision as to the entitlement to and amount of any award are made by the Board.[42] Once an initial decision has been made, a notice is served on the applicant requiring a declaration to be made that there has been no relevant change in circumstances and that the applicant is accordingly entitled to the tax credit at the rate assessed.[43]

Revised decisions

11.33 Once that declaration has been received, the Board must make a decision as to whether the applicant was entitled to tax credit at the rate assessed[44] and may – within the specified time limit – institute an enquiry to satisfy themselves that the applicant was so entitled.[45] Where that time limit has expired, but the applicant's tax liability is revised or the Board has reasonable grounds for believing that a decision regarding entitlement was wrong, due to fraud or neglect, it may make a 'decision on discovery' – a decision to revise that decision.[46]

11.34 If notified of a change in the applicant's circumstances, the Board are under a duty to make a revised decision as to the rate of the award.[47] Likewise, where, during the period for which an award is made, the Board has reasonable grounds for believing that an applicant is receiving a tax credit to which he is not entitled or at a rate to which he is not entitled, it may, of its own motion, amend or

---

42 Tax Credits Act 2002 s14. The Board is defined by s67 as being the Commissioners of the Inland Revenue. Detailed provision in relation to entitlement to the two benefits is to be found in the Child Tax Credit Regulations 2002 SI No 2007 and the Working Tax Credit (Entitlement and Maximum Rate) Regulations 2002 SI No 2005.

43 Tax Credits Act 2002 s17(2).

44 Tax Credits Act 2002 s18.

45 Tax Credits Act 2002 s19. Inherent in this power of enquiry are the general powers of the Inland Revenue, among other things, to demand a personal tax return under Taxes and Management Act 1970.

46 Tax Credits Act 2002 s20. This power is subject to a long-stop time-limit of five years after the end of the tax year to which the decision relates.

47 Tax Credits Act 2002 s15.

terminate the award.[48] Where there are not reasonable grounds for that belief, but the Board holds the belief nonetheless, it may serve the applicant with notice requiring such information or evidence as it considers necessary.[49]

Appeals

11.35 The applicant must be notified of any revised decision and of his right to appeal.[50] The right of appeal relates to initial decisions, revised decisions, a decision following enquiry or on discovery, a decision imposing a penalty and a decision to charge interest on an overpayment of tax credit.[51] Appeals are now dealt with by the First-tier Tribunal (Social Security and Child Support).[52]

11.36 Accordingly, as with a majority of social security benefits, there is little scope for judicial review in relation to tax credits given the comprehensive statutory appeals system. There may, however, be scope for a challenge on general public law grounds in relation to the extensive powers of the Board to conduct enquiries, further enquiries and discovery into the validity of entitlement. It is also to be noted that there is no right of appeal against a decision to recover overpayments of tax credits.

Council tax reduction

11.37 From 1 April 2013, council tax benefit has been abolished.[53] In its place, each local billing authority is obliged to consult on and adopt its own council tax reduction scheme, making provision to reduce the liability of council tax payers in its area whom it considers to be in financial need or who are members of a class whom it considers to be in financial need.[54] If an authority had not adopted a scheme by 31

---

48 Tax Credits Act 2002 s16.
49 Tax Credits Act 2002 s16(2).
50 Tax Credits Act 2002 s23. See also the Tax Credits (Claims and Notifications) Regulations 2002 SI No 2014.
51 Tax Credits Act 2002 s38. Note that there is no right of appeal against a decision to recover an overpayment. Detailed provision in relation to appeals is contained in the Tax Credits (Appeals) Regulations 2002 SI No 2926, the Tax Credits (Appeals) (No 2) Regulations 2002 SI No 3196 and the Tax Credits (Claims and Notifications) Regulations 2002 SI No 2014.
52 Tax Credits Act 2002 ss39 and 63.
53 Welfare Reform Act 2012 s33(1)(e).
54 Local Government Finance Act 1992 (inserted by Local Government Finance Act 2012) s13A(2).

January 2012, the Secretary of State's default scheme (mirroring the previous council tax benefit scheme) was imposed on it.[55]

11.38 The most controversial aspect of this change is that central government, which had fully funded council tax benefit, has reduced by 10 per cent[56] the amount of funding it will provide to support the new arrangements, on the basis that:

- local authorities should be able to identify savings through efficiency and fraud reduction; and
- claimants should be encouraged by the benefit system to find work (an overarching premise of the welfare reform policy).[57]

11.39 Appeals from decisions relating to reductions in council tax liability are to the Valuation Tribunal.[58] Where a local authority has introduced a hardship scheme in addition to its council tax reduction scheme, and that hardship scheme operates not by way of reducing a person's liability but by way of assisting a person to meet that liability, no appeal to the Valuation Tribunal will be possible. In those circumstances, judicial review will be the only available remedy.[59]

Relationship between the appeal structure and judicial review

11.40 While, as stated above, the role of judicial review is plainly limited in the field of social security, it is not ousted altogether. In most cases, however, where the statutory rights of appeal provide an effective remedy, a claimant would need to persuade the High Court that there was a good reason why he should be permitted to bring a judicial review claim instead of an appeal. It is likely to be difficult to do so in the majority of cases, given the principle that all available alternative remedies must be exercised before bringing judicial review proceedings.

---

55 Local Government Finance Act 1992 Sch 1A(4); Council Tax Reduction Scheme (Default Scheme) (England) Regulations 2012 SI No 2886.

56 Ie 10% of the amount it provided for each authority in the final year of council tax benefit.

57 See Public Spending Review 2010, *Localising Support for Council Tax, A Statement of Intent* (DCLG, May 2012), especially at paras 1.3–1.4.

58 Local Government Finance Act 1992 ss13A(1) and 16(1)(b).

59 See paras 11.26–11.29 above in relation to housing benefit discretionary hardship payments.

11.41   In some cases, however, a judicial review claim may be properly brought. It may be appropriate, for instance, to challenge the validity of regulations.[60] It is not only the validity of legislation that may be challenged by judicial review but also the legality of guidance. In *R (National Association of Colliery Overman Deputies and Shot-firers) v Secretary of State for Work and Pensions*,[61] the claimant sought and was granted judicial review of the Secretary of State's refusal to modify his guidance for medical assessors, or to issue new guidance, concerning the diagnostic utility of tests for vibration-induced white finger, when determining whether a person suffered from that disease and was therefore eligible for industrial injuries benefit.

11.42   Judicial review may also be available where, for example, an authority promises to carry out a review but fails to do so. In *R v Lambeth LBC ex p Ogunmuyiwa*,[62] no formal application for a review had been made, but the authority had raised an expectation that one would be carried out. Poppelwell J stated that:[63]

> although it does not strictly come within the statutory framework of the regulations, it seems to me that that is a particular reason why the ordinary rule of exploring every other avenue should in the instant case be rejected.

11.43   Judicial review may also be available to challenge a practice of the Secretary of State. In *R (Child Poverty Action Group) v Secretary of State for Work and Pensions*,[64] the Supreme Court upheld a declaration that overpayments of certain benefits could only be recovered pursuant to statutory powers, so that the Secretary of State's practice of requesting in writing the repayment of overpayments from benefit recipients even where he had no right to recover such overpayments was unlawful.

---

60 See eg *R (Child Poverty Action Group) v Secretary of State for Work and Pensions* [2011] EWHC 2616 (Admin), [2011] Eq LR 1233. See also eg *R v Secretary of State for Social Security ex p Association of Metropolitan Authorities* [1986] 1 WLR 1; *R v Secretary of State for Social Services ex p Association of Metropolitan Authorities* (1993) 25 HLR 131, QBD.

61 [2003] EWHC 607 (Admin), [2004] ACD 14.

62 (1997) 29 HLR 950, DC.

63 (1997) 29 HLR 950 at 955.

64 *R (Child Poverty Action Group) v Secretary of State for Work and Pensions* [2010] UKSC 54, [2011] 2 AC 15.

11.44   As noted elsewhere, judicial review may be permissible to challenge a decision of the Upper Tribunal to refuse permission to appeal a decision of the First-tier Tribunal.[65]

Universal credit

11.45   Universal credit is a new benefit, to be administered by the Department for Work and Pensions, which will be phased in over the period from April 2013 to 2017. It is being introduced following a Green Paper, *21st Century Welfare*[66] and a White Paper, *Universal Credit: welfare that works.*[67]

11.46   It is the Government's intention that, by 2017, universal credit will have completely replaced the following benefits:

- income support;
- income-based JSA;
- income-related employment and support allowance;
- housing benefit;
- child tax credit; and
- working tax credit.

11.47   Universal credit will apply to new claimants from October 2013.[68] Where an existing claimant experiences a change of circumstances, he will be moved on to universal credit. Other existing claimants will be moved to universal credit as part of a managed process phased in between 2013 and 2017.

11.48   The principal piece of primary legislation governing universal credit is the Welfare Reform Act 2012, although it needs to be considered as part of a package of reforms, such as the introduction of council tax reduction schemes.[69]

11.49   The Welfare Reform Act 2012 is supplemented by a large number of pieces of delegated legislation, which set out the detail of how the

---

65   See *R (Cart) v Upper Tribunal* [2011] UKSC 28, [2012] 1 AC 663, paras 2.50, 7.21 and 7.75–7.78 above.

66   Department for Work and Pensions, Cm 7913, 2010.

67   Department for Work and Pensions, Cm 7957, 2010.

68   Universal credit will apply to a limited 'Pathfinder Group' of claimants from 29 April 2013: Universal Credit (Transitional Provisions) Regulations 2013 SI No 386.

69   Under Local Government Finance Act 2012. See paras 11.37–11.39 above.

new system will operate in practice. At the time of writing, the delegated legislation made includes the: [70]

- Universal Credit Regulations 2013; [71]
- Universal Credit, Personal Independence Payment, Jobseeker's Allowance and Employment and Support Allowance (Claims and Payments) Regulations 2013 ('Claims and Payments Regulations'); [72]
- Universal Credit, Personal Independence Payment, Jobseeker's Allowance and Employment and Support Allowance (Decisions and Appeals) Regulations 2013 ('Decisions and Appeals Regulations'). [73]

11.50 So far as the scope for judicial review is concerned, the most important regulations are probably the Decisions and Appeals Regulations. These Regulations provide for a decision-making process that is broadly similar to that contained in the Social Security and Child Support (Decisions and Appeals) Regulations 1999. [74] Accordingly, it is likely that the role of judicial review will be very limited.

11.51 In particular, the Decisions and Appeals Regulations, make provision for the Secretary of State to issue revised decisions on any grounds at certain times; [75] or, on specified grounds, at any time, [76] including in cases of:

- an official error or mistake; [77]
- a decision against which no appeal lies; [78]
- a decision that has been appealed against, but where the appeal has not been determined; [79]
- certain decisions relating to sanctions. [80]

---

70 The Department of Work and Pensions has compiled a list of regulations at www.dwp.gov.uk/policy/welfare-reform/legislation-and-key-documents/welfare-reform-act-2012/welfare-reform-regulations/.
71 SI No 376.
72 SI No 380.
73 SI No 381.
74 SI No 991.
75 SI No 381 reg 5.
76 SI No 381 reg 8.
77 SI No 381 reg 9.
78 SI No 381 reg 10.
79 SI No 381 reg 11(1). Regulation 11(2) makes provision for the slightly more complicated scenario where a claimant has more than one appeal ongoing.
80 SI No 381 reg 14.

11.52   In specified circumstances, the Secretary of State may make decisions superseding other decisions.[81] The Secretary of State has power to correct an accidental error in a decision, or in any record of a decision, at any time.[82]

11.53   Some decisions of the Secretary of State made under the Claims and Payments Regulations may be appealed under the Decisions and Appeals Regulations.[83] Appeals will lie to the First-tier Tribunal and from there to the Upper Tribunal.

11.54   There are, however, a sizeable number of decisions against which there is no right of appeal.[84]

11.55   Where an appeal is available under the Decisions and Appeals Regulations, this can be expected to preclude an application for judicial review in most circumstances. Where the right of appeal is expressly excluded, however, claimants may be able to rely on judicial review instead.

11.56   Some benefit claimants will be required to request a revision of the Secretary of State's decision before they can exercise a right of appeal to the First-tier Tribunal.[85] Where the Secretary of State gives a claimant a written notice of a decision and the notice contains a statement that a right of appeal against the decision only exists if the Secretary of State has considered an application for revision of the decision, a claimant cannot appeal against that decision until the Secretary of State has considered whether to revise it. In a case where an appeal is brought without a revision having first been sought, the Secretary of State may treat the purported appeal as a request for a revision of the decision.[86]

11.57   Given that the right of appeal in such cases is dependent not only on the Secretary of State having been asked to revise the decision, but on his having actually given consideration to so doing,[87] it may be permissible to use judicial review proceedings as a means of compelling the Secretary of State to consider revising a decision in a case in which he has failed to do so for an unreasonably long period or for no good reasons.

---

81 SI No 381 reg 22.
82 SI No 381 reg 38.
83 SI No 381 reg 50 and Sch 2.
84 SI No 381 reg 50 and Sch 3.
85 Social Security Act 1998 s12 as amended by Welfare Reform Act 2012 s102.
86 SI No 381 reg 7.
87 SI No 381 reg 7(2).

CHAPTER 12

Judicial review and police powers

General

12.1   Judicial review is available to supervise the statutory and non-statutory duties and discretionary powers of the police. In *D'Souza v DPP*,[1] for example, a case that concerned police powers of entry under the Police and Criminal Evidence Act 1984 (PACE), the appeal was allowed since the purpose for which the police had in fact been exercising their powers of entry was not a purpose within the Act, so that they had not been exercising any valid power at all. In *R v Commissioner of the Police of the Metropolis ex p Blackburn (No 1)*,[2] judicial review was granted of a decision by the Commissioner not to enforce certain gaming laws, contrary to the general duty on chief constables to enforce the law; in *R v Chief Constable of Kent County Constabulary ex p L*,[3] a decision to prosecute rather than caution was held to be reviewable.

12.2   It has also been held that the statutory powers of arrest that confer executive discretion are subject to judicial review.[4] If this is so, it may be that, likewise, the common law power of arrest should be subject to the supervisory jurisdiction; it is difficult to determine any reason in principle why the availability of judicial review should be limited to the statutory power. What is clear, however, is that operational decisions will not usually be susceptible to judicial review.

Circumstances where judicial review may arise

12.3   Judicial review most frequently arises in relation to two areas of decision-making (which may also include human rights and EA 2010 challenges):

- internal disciplinary proceedings; and
- the exercise of police powers, such as the power to caution; arrest; execute a search warrant; and other statutory powers, eg the Crime and Security Act 2010, the Serious Organised Crime and Police Act 2005, the Terrorism Act 2000, the Public Order Act 1986 and the Police and Criminal Evidence Act 1984.

---

1   [1992] 1 WLR 1073. *D'Souza* was in fact an appeal by way of case stated, but judicial review principles are applied in such cases.
2   [1968] 2 QB 118.
3   [1993] 1 All ER 756.
4   See *Holgate-Mohammed v Duke* [1984] AC 437, HL.

12.4 A challenge by way of judicial review may be brought where the police have taken a decision not to act,[5] where there is a clear duty to act, or where they have acted but have done so unreasonably.[6] Judicial review may also be sought in respect of a general policy decision, where there has been improper exercise of discretion, or in relation to a specific police decision made by an individual officer.[7] In practice, however, the courts are generally reluctant to interfere with the exercise of police discretions.

12.5 A police authority may bring a claim for judicial review against an executive order of central government.[8]

Internal disciplinary proceedings

12.6 In *R v Chief Constable of Merseyside Police ex p Calveley*,[9] complaints were made against five police officers. The officers concerned did not receive formal notice of the complaints, under the Police (Discipline) Regulations 1977,[10] until some two years later. The chief constable proceeded with disciplinary hearings and the officers were found guilty and dismissed or required to retire. The officers enjoyed a right of appeal against the chief constable's decision under Police Act 1964 s37, which they proceeded to exercise. Before the appeal was heard, however, the officers sought judicial review of the decision.

---

5 For example, in *R v Chief Constable of Devon and Cornwall ex p Central Electricity Generating Board* [1981] 3 All ER 826, CA, the applicant applied for judicial review seeking an order to compel the chief constable to remove or assist in the removal of protesters who were obstructing a survey being conducted by the applicant. The court refused to make the order, on the ground that although the police had powers to intervene in the removal of persons who resisted removal by CEGB and were under a duty to uphold the law, they could not be compelled to remove all persons interfering with CEGB's work.

6 In this respect, judicial review may also lie against a court's decision to compel an individual to comply with police powers: see *R v Bristol Crown Court ex p Bristol Press and Picture Agency Ltd* (1986) *Times* 11 November, CA, where the claimant sought judicial review of an order made under PACE 1984 s9, compelling them to produce photographs taken during a public order offence (see also *R v Central Criminal Court ex p Adegbesan* [1986] 1 WLR 1292, DC).

7 *R v Cambridge Chief Constable ex p Michel* (1991) 91 Cr App R 325, for example, concerned the decision of a custody officer to detain a juvenile under PACE 1984 s38. Leave to apply for judicial review was refused.

8 See *R v Secretary of State for the Home Department ex p Northumbria Police Authority* [1988] 1 All ER 556, CA, concerning the Home Secretary's decision to issue certain riot equipment against the wishes of the police authority.

9 [1986] QB 424, CA.

10 SI No 508.

12.7   The Court of Appeal held that judicial review should not be attempted where there was an alternative remedy, save in exceptional circumstances. In considering exceptional circumstances, the court would have regard to the speed of the alternative procedure, whether it was convenient and whether the matter depended on particular technical knowledge available to the appellate body. The delay of two years in the instant case was a serious departure from the disciplinary procedure that amounted to an abuse of process. The five officers had been prejudiced and, consequently, judicial review in these circumstances was justified.

12.8   In *R v Chief Constable of Merseyside Police ex p Merrill*,[11] the court quashed disciplinary proceedings against a detective constable where the chief constable had erroneously concluded that the service of a complaint notice on him under the disciplinary rules could be deferred until after his criminal trial (at which he was acquitted). The court held that prima facie delay caused prejudice and the greater the delay (in this case 18 months), the greater the prejudice.

12.9   A right of appeal against dismissal is contained in Police Act 1996 s85, as amended. Appeals are heard by the Police Appeals Tribunal (PAT).[12] A PAT can hear an appeal where the grounds formulated contend that the finding or disciplinary action imposed was unreasonable, or there is evidence that could not reasonably have been considered at the original hearing and that could have materially affected the decision, or there was a breach of procedure or other unfairness that could have materially affected the decision.[13] There is no right of appeal from a PAT decision and, therefore, the only route of challenge will normally be by way of judicial review.

12.10   A number of decisions has considered what amounts to an unreasonable finding or unreasonable disciplinary action within r4(4)(a), Police Appeals Tribunal Rules 2008.[14] Although the 2008 Rules have

---

11 [1989] 1 WLR 1077.

12 In relation to the PAT see the Police Act 1996 s85 and Sch 6 and also, generally, the Police Appeals Tribunal Rules 2012 SI No 2630.

13 Police Appeals Tribunal Rules 2012 SI No 2630 r4. In relation to a breach of procedure, see the Police (Complaints and Misconduct) Regulations 2012 SI No 1204, and the Police Reform Act 2002 Sch 3.

14 SI No 2863. Replaced by Police Appeals Tribunal Rules 2012 SI No 2630. The recent cases include *R (Montgomery) v PAT* [2012] EWHC 936 (Admin), *R (Chief Constable of Hampshire) v PAT* [2012] EWHC 746 (Admin), *R (Chief Constable of the Derbyshire Constabulary) v PAT* [2012] EWHC 2280 (Admin), [2012] ACD 126 and *R (Chief Constable of Durham) v PAT* [2012] EWHC 2733 (Admin), [2013] ACD 20.

now been revoked and replaced by the Police Appeals Tribunal Rules 2012,[15] the new r4(4)(a) is analogous and retains the reasonableness element. In *R (Chief Constable of Derbyshire Constabulary) v PAT*,[16] Beatson J, expressed the view that whether or not a finding or disciplinary action was reasonable should be assessed by asking whether the finding or sanction was one within the range of reasonable findings or sanctions on the material considered.

12.11   In *R (Chief Constable of Durham) v PAT and Cooper*,[17] the Divisional Court considered the appropriate standard of review to be adopted by the PAT in relation to appeals alleging 'unreasonable' findings or sanctions. The court held that, as a specialist tribunal, the PAT was not limited to a *Wednesbury* approach when considering the unreasonableness of the finding appealed against. The PAT could not, on the other hand, substitute its own view for that of the original misconduct panel, or substitute its own approach, unless and until it had reached that view or made findings that the previous decision was unreasonable.[18]

Complaints

12.12   The Police Reform Act 2002 introduced the Independent Police Complaints Commission (IPCC), which replaced the Police Complaints Authority in April 2004. The IPCC consists of a chairman and not less than five other members. The IPCC must investigate complaints, 'conduct matters' and death and serious injury matters.[19] The IPCC

---

15 SI No 2630.
16 [2012] EWHC 2280 (Admin), [2012] ACD 126.
17 [2012] EWHC 2733 (Admin), [2013] ACD 20, applied in *R (Chief Constable of Wiltshire Police) v PAT* [2012] EWHC 3288 (Admin).
18 [2012] EWHC 2733 (Admin) at [6]–[7]. Also note, *R (Chief Constable of Avon and Somerset) v PAT* [2004] EWHC 220 (Admin), [2004] Po LR 116 at paras [28]–[29] where it was held that it was inherent in the powers of the PAT to consider all matters before it and reach its own conclusions rather than being restricted to a power of review. In *R (Chief Constable of Hampshire Constabulary) v PAT* [2012] EWHC 746 (Admin), however, it was common ground that r4(4)(a), Police Appeals Tribunal Rules 2008 contained a right to review only with the test being 'a *Wednesbury* test shorn of technicality' but, in relation to r4(4)(b) and (c) (new evidence or procedural error), the role of the PAT went further than review (at para [25]).
19 Police Reform Act 2002 ss9, 12(2A) and 13, and Sch 3. In relation to the IPCC's statutory power to investigate deaths that may well implicate the police, it has been said that it is 'inescapable that the function of the IPCC forms part of the art.2, European Convention on Human Rights (right to life), process when

do not have jurisdiction to investigate a complaint about the exercise of police functions under Part VIII of the Immigration and Asylum Act 1999.[20]

12.13   The decisions of the IPCC are susceptible to challenge by way of judicial review. It is clear, however, that any such challenge should only be brought after a claimant has exhausted the statutory appeals process.[21] A lack of confidence in the IPCC would not justify the bringing of a premature challenge in the Administrative Court and short-circuiting the appellate regime.[22]

12.14   In *R (Muldoon) v IPCC*,[23] the Administrative Court considered the approach that should be taken when a claimant seeks to challenge an appeal decision of the IPCC. Parker J stated that, as the IPCC is an independent statutory appeal body whose decision are likely to involve matters of judgment, the Administrative Court,[24]

> will allow the IPCC a discretionary area of judgment and will not intervene unless satisfied that the IPCC has gone beyond that permissible area to reach a conclusion not fairly and reasonably open to it. This function of the court is important because an appellant is ... entitled to have a proper review because it is important that the functions of the IPCC are carried out properly to maintain public confidence in the system and the police force and to ensure that if there are lessons to be learnt, that that happens ...

conducting an independent investigation': *R (IPCC) v HM Coroner for Inner North London* [2009] EWHC 2681 (Admin), [2009] Inquest LR 232 at [30].

20   *R (Salimi) v Secretary of State for the Home Department* [2012] EWCA Civ 422, where the Court of Appeal also held that immigration officials had used excess force when escorting a man from the UK.

21   The time period for appealing a decision of the IPCC is 28 days commencing on the day after the date of the letter giving notification of the decision: reg 11, Police (Complaints and Misconduct) Regulations 2012 SI No 1204. These Regulations, which came into force from 22 November 2012, appear to take into account the decision in *R (Burke) v IPCC* [2011] EWCA Civ 1665 in which it was held that the time to bring an appeal started to run from the date when the notification was sent rather than from when it was received. Although *Burke* was decided under the old Regulations (reg 10, Police (Complaints and Misconduct) Regulations 2004 SI No 643), the power to extend the time limit is retained in the new Regulations and, therefore, it is important to note that delay in receipt would be a weighty factor in deciding whether or not to exercise the power to extend the period; it is not, however, conclusive (*Burke* at [31]).

22   *R (Pewter) v Commissioner of Police of the Metropolis* [2010] EWHC 3927 (Admin); (2011) *Legal Action* (May) 23.

23   [2009] EWHC 3633 (Admin). The approach was endorsed by the Court of Appeal in *R (Cubells) v IPCC* [2012] EWCA Civ 1292.

24   At [19]–[20].

... what is important and necessary is that the conclusion should be clear and the reasons for those conclusions can be readily understood by the complainant, the police officers concerned and the relevant police authority, who may need to review their procedures in the light of the decision.

Investigations

12.15   In *R (Reynolds) v Chief Constable of Sussex Police*,[25] a man suffered serious injury while in police custody. It became clear, however, that the injury may not have been caused by the police but by events prior to any police action. The IPCC investigated the circumstances following the police involvement while the police investigated the potentially criminal matters that may have occurred before they were called. The Court of Appeal held that the IPCC had a power and a duty under s10 and Sch 3 of the Police Reform Act 2002 to investigate, and determine the form of that investigation, where there had been serious injury to a person detained in police custody. This duty extended to the examination of anything that had occurred prior to any police involvement that may have caused the injury as it would not otherwise be possible to evaluate whether it was the conduct of police that resulted in the injury. While this did not include investigating criminal conduct, which was a matter for the police, and while there may well be overlap between the enquiries of the police and those of the IPCC, the IPCC had to carry out its own inquiry into the causation of the injury in order to comply with Convention requirement that an enquiry into matters concerning articles 2 and 3 be an independent inquiry.[26]

12.16   As to the possibility of challenging the way that the IPCC conducted an investigation, in its discretion, the court said:[27]

No doubt that discretion can, in theory, be challenged on well-known public law principles but any litigant who wishes to challenge its discretion will have an uphill task.

---

25 [2008] EWCA Civ 1160, [2009] 3 All ER 237 (CA).

26 At [16]–[17], [21]–[33]. See also, eg, *Ramsahai v Netherlands* App No 52391/99, 15 May 2007, (2007) 26 EHRR 43.Note also, *R (IPCC) v HM Coroner for Inner North London* [2009] EWHC 2681 (Admin), [2009] Inquest LR 232, where it was declared that the art 2, ECHR jurisprudence showed that the investigative obligation may be achieved by a number of procedures and, therefore, a coroner should look favourably on a request by the IPCC to attend a post-mortem (at [30]–[31]).

27 [2008] EWCA Civ 1160, [2009] 3 All ER 237 at [30].

12.17   The case of *R (Saunders and Tucker) v IPCC*[28] also highlighted the uphill task faced by litigants challenging the manner in which IPCC investigations are carried out. In *Saunders*, judicial review was sought following investigations into two separate police incidents where two men were fatally shot. The IPCC accepted it had a power to direct that officers must not confer when making a statement about the incident but had not used it as they were negotiating with the Association of Chief Police Officers regarding its guidance on exactly this area ie conferring following police shootings. The challenge was brought on the basis that the IPCC had failed to prevent the police officers involved from liaising with one another before making notes of the incident and, as such, there had been a breach of article 2 of the Convention.

12.18   The Administrative Court dismissed the claims. The fact there had been collaboration was not enough for the investigations to fall foul of article 2, and each case required individual consideration to adjudge whether or not the investigation had been adequate. The IPCC's power to direct that officers should not confer before making their first statements about an incident was a power exercisable in individual cases, not a general power to direct chief officers to put procedures in place to prevent officers conferring.[29]

12.19   The Court also considered the policy of the Police Reform Act 2002 in relation to the importance of the IPCC keeping interested parties appropriately informed:[30]

> ... it is part of the policy of the 2002 Act that the Commission should be as open as is reasonably possible in the communication of information to interested persons. ... Having said that, what degree of information is necessary to satisfy the obligation under the 2002 Act inevitably requires an exercise of judgment as to what is necessary to keep interested persons 'properly informed' and as to what truly affects 'the progress of the investigation'. It is plainly not the case that interested persons are entitled to be informed of every minor development or twist and turn of the investigation: that would place quite unreasonable burdens on the authority conducting the investigation (which might be the police or the Commission) and be of little value to complainants or (in the case of a fatality) their families.

28 [2008] EWHC 2372 (Admin), [2009] HRLR 1 (decided two weeks before *Reynolds*).

29 At [38]–[40], [48], [53].

30 [2008] EWHC 2372 (Admin), [2009] HRLR 1 at [81]–[82]. See also, eg, *McKerr v UK* App No 28883/95, 4 May 2001, (2002) 34 EHRR 20, where the European Court of Human Rights noted that complainants should be involved in the investigations.

The judgment of what information requires to be disclosed can in the nature of things only be made by the body conducting the investigation ... though of course subject to the intervention of the court where that judgment is exercised irrationally or otherwise unlawfully ...

Further representations and review of decisions

12.20 In *R (Coker) v IPCC*[31] the IPCC investigated the behaviour of a police officer following an arrest where the arrested man was seriously ill and subsequently died in custody. The investigator produced a report that recommended formal misconduct action. The report was sent to the Commissioner of the Metropolitan Police who disagreed with the recommendation and instead thought the case was appropriate for 'words of advice' to be given to the officer. The IPCC reviewed the case and decided that a written warning should be provided. A written warning can only be given, however, if the officer is willing to accept it; the officer in this case refused. The IPCC, again, reconsidered the situation and decided that words of advice would suffice. The claimant, whose brother was the man who had died, challenged the IPCC's decision not to direct misconduct proceedings. The court held that the IPCC was entitled to accept further representations and to keep any disciplinary proceedings under review. The decision was not unlawful or irrational.

12.21 Where the IPCC has reached and promulgated an appeal decision, there appears to be no power to vary it following further representations.[32]

---

31 [2010] EWHC 3625 (Admin). See also, *R (Wilkinson) v Police Complaints Authority* [2004] EWHC 678 (Admin), [2004] Po LR 189, a case concerning the old Police Complaints Authority where it was held that the authority had the power to review a decision to dispense with an investigation and, having looked at it again, to revoke the decision.

32 *R (Dennis) v Independent Police Complaints Commission* [2008] EWHC 1158 (Admin), where the claimant challenged an appeal decision of the IPCC that was based on a misunderstanding of the facts. The judicial review was successful and the appeal decision quashed: an appeal decision should not be looked at as if it were a judgment but should be clear and the reasons readily understood by those affected by the decision. In this case, the decision was flawed and irrational as it had been based upon factual errors.

Police powers[33]

Cautions and decisions to prosecute

12.22   In *R v Chief Constable of Kent ex p L,*[34] the applicant, a juvenile, sought judicial review of a decision to prosecute rather than caution him, contrary to the police's general policy of cautioning instead of prosecuting juveniles in circumstances such as those pertaining in his case. It was held that the discretion whether to prosecute was reviewable, but would only be interfered with if the decision to prosecute was clearly contrary to the settled policy of the Director of Public Prosecutions.

12.23   Watkins LJ said:[35]

> I have come to the conclusion that if judicial review lies in relation to current criminal proceedings, in contrast to a failure to take any action against a person suspected of a criminal offence, it lies against the body which has the last and decisive word, the CPS.
>
> A refusal to prosecute or even possibly to caution by the police is another matter. In that event the police may be vulnerable to judicial review, but only upon a basis which, the cases show, is rather severely circumscribed.

12.24   In *R v Commissioner of Police of the Metropolis ex p P,*[36] a 12-year-old boy of good character sought judicial review of a decision to caution him, contrary to Home Office guidance. The Divisional Court held that where a formal caution was administered in clear breach of Home Office guidelines, the court could properly exercise its jurisdiction to review the legality of the caution. In that case, the caution was quashed as there was a clear breach of the condition that an offender had to admit the offence before a caution could be appropriately administered. The police had failed to apply the further condition that where the suspect was under 14 years of age, it was necessary to establish whether he knew that what he was doing was seriously wrong.[37]

---

33   The powers of police officers and of police authorities are contained principally in the PACE (especially section 24 – arrest without warrant) as amended by the Serious Organised Crime and Police Act 2005, the Police Acts 1996 and 1997, the Police Reform Act 2002, and the Criminal Justice Act 2003.

34   [1993] 1 All ER 756.

35   [1993] 1 All ER 756 at 767.

36   (1996) 8 Admin LR 6, (1995) *Times* 24 May, QBD.

37   See also *R v DPP ex p C* [1995] 1 Cr App R 136, (1994) *Times* 7 March. That case also involved a decision not to prosecute, contrary to guidelines. The Divisional Court held that it had power to review a decision not to prosecute, but the power to review should be used sparingly. See also *R v DPP ex p Manning* [2001] QB 330.

12.25　Where the discretion to prosecute is concerned, it can therefore be seen that the court will be reluctant to intervene unless there has been a clear breach of settled policy.[38] It has also been held, given the number of challenges to the decision to prosecute, that the appropriate forum in relation to pending prosecutions is, save for in exceptional circumstances, the criminal courts by way of defence.[39]

Arrest and subsequent detention

12.26　An arresting officer, under s24 of PACE (as amended), may arrest without a warrant anyone who is about to commit or is committing an offence and anyone whom he has reasonable grounds for suspecting to be about to commit or to be committing an offence. The officer must also have reasonable grounds to believe it is necessary to arrest the person for one of the reasons set out in section 24(5):

* to enable the name or address of the person to be ascertained in circumstances where the officer does not know, and cannot readily ascertain, the person's name or address, or has reasonable grounds for doubting whether the information given by the person is correct;
* to prevent the person causing physical injury to himself or others, suffering physical injury, causing loss of or damage to property, committing an offence against public decency, or causing an unlawful obstruction of the highway;
* to protect a child or other vulnerable person;
* to allow the prompt and effective investigation of the offence or of the conduct of the person; or
* to prevent any prosecution for the offence from being hindered by the disappearance of the person.

38　See, eg, *R (Mondelly) v Commissioner of Police of the Metropolis* [2006] EWHC 2370 (Admin), [2007] Crim LR 298 (no clear and settled policy not to arrest or prosecute for possession of cannabis); *R (A) v South Yorkshire Police* [2007] EWHC 1261 (Admin), (2007) 171 JP 465 (the decision to prosecute, rather than to warn youths in a criminal damage case was not a departure from the statutory guidance); *R (Guest) v Director of Public Prosecutions* [2009] EWHC 594 (Admin), [2009] 2 Cr App R 26 (successful challenge to the decision to issue a conditional caution rather than prosecute); *R (E) v DPP* [2011] EWHC 1465 (Admin), [2012] 1 Cr App R 6 (the policy relevant to the case was not unlawful but the CPS had failed to give a proper decision as the prosecutor had failed to follow and apply the guidance).

39　*R (Pepushi) v Crown Prosecution Service* [2004] EWHC 798 (Admin), [2004] INLR 638 at [49] mentioning *R v Director of Public Prosecutions ex p Kebilene* [2000] 1 Cr App R 275, [2002] 2 AC 326.

12.27   Section 37 of PACE confers powers on the custody officer to decide whether or not to detain a person following his arrest.

12.28   Under these sections, officers are exercising discretions that can be challenged by way of judicial review,[40] although any such challenge presents a high hurdle for the claimant to surmount given the low statutory threshold for the exercise of the discretions in question. Moreover, if a challenge would require the calling of evidence due to factual disputes, the Administrative Court may not be the appropriate forum.[41]

12.29   In *Holgate-Mohammed v Duke*,[42] the Court of Appeal[43] considered the reasonableness of an arrest that was contended to be unlawful. Sir John Arnold P said:[44]

> As to the proposition that there were other things which [the officer] might have done, no doubt there were other things which he might have done first ... But the fact that there were other things which he might have done does not ... make that which he did do into an unreasonable exercise of the power of arrest if what he did do, namely to arrest, was within the range of reasonable choices available to him.'

12.30   In *Castorina v The Chief Constable of Surrey*,[45] Woolf LJ – citing Lord Diplock's speech in *Holgate-Mohammed v Duke*,[46] – posed three questions to be answered in cases in which it is alleged there has been an unlawful arrest:

> 1. Did the arresting officer suspect that the person who was arrested was guilty of the offence? The answer to this question depends entirely on the findings of fact as to the officer's state of mind.
> 2. Assuming the officer had the necessary suspicion, was there reasonable cause for that suspicion? This is a purely objective requirement to be determined by the judge if necessary on facts found by a jury.

40 See, eg, *R (Redknapp) v Commissioner of City of London Police Practice Note* [2008] EWHC 1177 (Admin), [2009] 1 WLR 2091; and *R (Rawlinson and Hunter trustees) v Central Criminal Court* [2012] EWHC 2254 (Admin), [2013] Lloyd's Rep FC 132.

41 See, eg, *Sher v Chief Constable of the Greater Manchester Police* [2010] EWHC 1859 where a challenge to arrest and subsequent detention under the Terrorism Act 2000 failed. Permission was refused on the basis that the Administrative Court was an inappropriate forum given the fact-sensitive nature of the application which related to matters over a year old, and given also that a private law claim for unlawful imprisonment was available.

42 [1984] QB 209.

43 Subsequently approved by the House of Lords at [1984] AC 437, HL.

44 [1984] QB 209, per Sir John Arnold P at 216C.

45 (1996) 160 LG Rev 241.

46 [1984] AC 437, HL at 442–3.

3. If the answer to the two previous questions is in the affirmative, then the officer has a discretion which entitles him to make an arrest and in relation to that discretion has been exercised in accordance with the principles laid down by Lord Greene MR in *Associated Provincial Picture Houses Ltd v Wednesbury Corporation.*[47]

12.31   More recently, in *Hayes v Chief Constable of Merseyside Police,*[48] the Court of Appeal held that the following two-stage test applied when a court was considering whether or not an arrest was lawful: the police have to show first, that the officer had reasonable grounds for suspecting that an offence had been committed and that the claimant was guilty of it and, secondly, that the officer had reasonable grounds for believing that it was necessary to arrest the person to allow the prompt and effective investigation of the offence or of the conduct of the claimant. The case also illustrated the difficulty claimants may have in challenging such decisions. Hughes LJ said:[49]

> But the challenge, if it comes, is not one which requires the officer's decision to be subjected to a full-blown public law reasons challenge. It is one which requires it to be shown that on the information known to the officer he had reasonable grounds for believing arrest to be necessary, for an identified s24(5) reason. To require of a policeman that he pass through particular thought processes each time he considers an arrest, and in all circumstances no matter what urgency or danger may attend the decision, and to subject that decision to the test of whether he has considered every material matter and excluded every immaterial matter, is to impose an unrealistic and unattainable burden. Nor is it necessary.

12.32   In *R (Hicks) v Commissioner of Police of the Metropolis,*[50] the Divisional Court considered a judicial review concerning policing at the time of and immediately prior to the Royal Wedding on 29 April 2011. The claim included a challenge asserting that the practice of pre-

---

47 [1948] 2 KB 223, CA. See also *Richardson v Chief Constable of West Midlands Police* [2011] 2 Cr App R 1, where Slade J at [60] commented that the *Castorina* principles could be adopted and applied to questions concerning reasonable belief and necessity in s24 of PACE; and *Al Fayed v Commissioner of Police* [2004] 1 Pol LR 370 (also relied upon in the judgment in *Richardson*), where Auld LJ at [83] stated that a subjective approach should be taken as to whether the arresting officer was of the belief that the arrest was necessary but an objective approach should be applied to whether the officer had reasonable grounds for that belief and whether his discretion was exercised in a *Wednesbury* unreasonable manner.

48 [2011] EWCA Civ 911, [2012] 1 WLR 517, considering the provisions of s24 of PACE in their current form.

49 [2012] 1 WLR 517 at [39]–[40].

50 [2012] EWHC 1947 (Admin), [2012] ACD. 102.

emptive arrests on the basis of imminent breach of the peace was unlawful as it operated an impermissibly low threshold of tolerance for public protest. The court disagreed and held, *inter alia*, that not only was the police policy lawful but the arrests were also lawful even where the arresting officer had been told to make the arrests by his superiors.[51]

Search warrants

12.33   In *R v Chief Constable of Lancashire ex p Parker*,[52] the Divisional Court reviewed the execution of a search warrant, granting permission to apply for judicial review, on the basis that the police had failed to produce or supply a copy of the warrant to the person whose premises were being searched. The search was therefore declared unlawful, as consequently was the seizure and retention of materials taken during the search.

12.34   In *R v Chief Constable of Warwickshire ex p Fitzpatrick*,[53] the Divisional Court held that judicial review was not an appropriate remedy where an individual complained of excessive seizure of material pursuant to a search warrant. Jowett J emphasised that judicial review was not a fact-finding exercise and was an extremely unsatisfactory tool by which to determine, in any but the clearest cases, whether there had been a seizure of material not permitted by a search warrant. He said:[54]

> In my judgment a person who complains of excessive seizure ... should not, save in such cases, seek his remedy by way of judicial

---

51 It should be noted that an appeal is pending in this case. See also in relation to pre-emptive actions, *R (Laporte) v Chief Constable of Gloucestershire* [2006] UKHL 55, [2007] 2 AC 105. The claimant, in *Laporte*, was travelling by coach from London to join an anti-war demonstration in Gloucestershire. The police stopped the coach and escorted it back to London. The claimant contended this action was unlawful especially given the chief superintendent had concluded that a breach of the peace was not imminent but decided to send the coaches back to prevent a breach of the peace. At first instance the claimant was successful but the police were successful on appeal to the Court of Appeal. The House of Lords allowed the claimant's appeal and held, *inter alia*, that there was nothing in domestic authority to support action short of arrest being taken when a breach of the peace was not imminent. The decision of the chief superintendent was therefore unlawful. Had there been a reasonable apprehension that a breach of the peace was imminent the question would then have been whether the action taken was reasonable and proportionate.

52 [1993] QB 577, DC.

53 [1999] 1 WLR 564, DC.

54 [1999] 1 WLR 564 at 579.

review but should rely on his private law remedy when he will have a tribunal which will be able to hear evidence and make findings of fact unfettered by *Wednesbury* principles. In an appropriate case the court in a private law action is able to grant interlocutory relief on a speedy basis on well recognised principles so that in all but the clearest cases ... judicial review has only disadvantages and no advantages when compared with the private law remedy.

12.35 In *R (Rottman) v Commissioner of Police for the Metropolis*,[55] the police arrested the claimant, on the driveway outside his house, under a magistrates' warrant issued under the Extradition Act 1989. The police went with the claimant into his house and, on doing so, searched the house and seized certain computer equipment. The claimant sought judicial review on the ground that the search had been illegal as there had been no warrant permitting the police to search the property or seize goods.

12.36 The Divisional Court held that an officer only had power to enter and search a property for the purposes of executing a warrant of arrest and that there was no common law power entitling him or her to conduct the search. The House of Lords allowed an appeal by the police,[56] on the ground that the power to search an arrested person logically and as a matter of common sense also permitted the police officer to search the premises in which he was arrested. Moreover, there was a common law power to search and seize property after the execution of a warrant of arrest. The contention that the seizure of goods amounted to a violation of the claimant's rights under article 8 (right to respect for the home and family life) of the Convention was also rejected on the basis that the seizure had been in accordance with the law and was justified, proportionate and necessary to promote the legitimate aim of preventing crime.

12.37 *R (Cronin) v Sheffield Justices*[57] was another case concerning article 8 of the Convention. The claimant sought a declaration that, under article 8, justices were required to record their reasons for issuing a search warrant (to search the claimant's home for drugs) and to keep a record of the proceedings. The only record of the proceedings

---

55 [2002] UKHL 20, [2002] 2 AC 692.
56 Lord Hope of Craighead dissented on the basis that the common law powers of search and seizure following execution of a warrant did not extend to warrants issued under the Extradition Act 1989.
57 [2002] EWHC 2568 (Admin), [2003] 1 WLR 752. See also in relation to court records and reasons, eg, *Burgin v Commission of Police of the Metropolis* [2011] EWHC 1835 (Admin); and *R (Glenn and Co (Essex) Ltd) v Revenue and Customs Commissioners* [2011] EWHC 2998 (Admin), [2012] 1 Cr App R 22 at [33]–[34].

in question was the information and warrant, which were signed, despite the application for the warrant having been supported by oral evidence. The claimant accepted that the application itself was lawful. Lord Woolf CJ dismissed the application, as the position was amplified by affidavits from the defendant. He said:[58]

> A citizen's home should not be entered unless there is lawful justification for this being done or the citizen has given permission. In the absence of permission or lawful justification, it would clearly be an unlawful trespass in relation to which the citizen is entitled to damages.

A person would usually, therefore, have a private law remedy which may well mean that judicial review is not the appropriate claim to make. Advisors should turn their minds to the appropriate venue for a claim (judicial review is likely also to be inappropriate where the case turns on conflicts of evidence and the court has to carry out a fact finding exercise). Where there has been procedural error, however, the Administrative Court have seen fit to intervene and have made it plain that obtaining a search warrant should never be treated as a formality.[59]

Persons in custody

12.38   In *R v Chief Constable of Avon and Somerset ex p Robinson*,[60] the Divisional Court rejected a challenge by way of judicial review to the refusal of the police to afford access to police stations to unqualified legal clerks so that they might interview clients.

---

58 [2003] 1 WLR 752 at [2].

59 See *R (Redknapp) v Commissioner of City of London Police Practice Note* [2008] EWHC 1177 (Admin), [2009] 1 WLR 2091 approved in *R (Wood) v North Avon Magistrates' Court* [2009] EWHC 3614 (Admin). See also, eg, *R v Preston Crown Court ex p Faisaltex Ltd* [2008] EWHC 2832; and *R v HMRC ex p Mercury Tax Group Ltd* [2008] EWHC 2721 (Admin) (material non-disclosure). Further, in relation to disclosure, note the decision in *R (Rawlinson & Hunter Trustees SA) v Central Criminal Court* [2012] EWHC 3218 (Admin) where the Divisional Court ordered that indemnity costs be paid where the Serious Fraud Office materially misstated the position on an *ex parte* application for search warrants which were quashed following a finding that they were unlawful.

60 [1989] 1 WLR 793, (1991) 90 Cr App R 27, DC.

12.39   In *R v Chief Constable of South Wales ex p Merrick*,[61] the Divisional Court granted judicial review of the police's refusal to permit an applicant to consult a solicitor after 10 am while on remand in custody at a magistrates' court. It was held that, although the right to consult a solicitor under PACE 1984 s58(1) did not extend to a person on remand in custody, there was a common law right to consult a solicitor that was in no way abrogated by PACE 1984. The right was on request, to see a solicitor as soon as reasonably practicable. The police policy to refuse such a request on the sole ground that the request was made after 10 am was unlawful.

12.40   In *R (Bloggs) v Secretary of State for the Home Department*,[62] a prisoner sought judicial review of the Home Secretary's decision to move him from a protected witness unit and place him in mainstream prison, on the ground that – following his arrest – the police had promised that he could remain in protected witness custody for the duration of his sentence if he provided them with information, which promise amounted to a legitimate expectation. The court dismissed the application on the ground that the police had no power to make such a promise and that the prison service were not, therefore, obliged to take that promise into account, even if it did amount to a legitimate expectation.

Duty to enforce the law

12.41   In *R v Commissioner of Police for the Metropolis ex p Blackburn*,[63] the Commissioner made a policy decision, circulated to senior officers in a confidential instruction, not to take proceedings against gaming clubs unless there were complaints of cheating or they had become the haunts of criminals. On a challenge to the policy, the Court of Appeal held that the police owed the public a duty to enforce the law and that the court could, if necessary, compel performance of that duty. While the Commissioner had a discretion not to prosecute, his discretion to make policy was not absolute.

---

61 [1994] 1 WLR 663, DC. See also, eg, *R (Malik) v Chief Constable of Greater Manchester* [2006] EWHC 2396 (Admin) which concerned the police excluding a solicitor from acting for the claimant. Permission for judicial review was granted but the application ultimately failed on the basis of the information available and, specifically, the reasons given by the police on the custody record.

62 [2003] EWCA Civ 686, [2003] 1 WLR 2724.

63 [1968] 2 QB 118, CA.

12.42   Lord Denning MR stated:[64]

I hold it to be the duty of ... every Chief Constable, to enforce the law of the land. He must take steps so to post his men that crime may be detected; and that honest citizens may go about their affairs in peace. He must decide whether or no suspected persons are to be prosecuted; and, if need be, bring the prosecution or see that it is brought ...

12.43   He continued:[65]

Although ... chief officers of police are answerable to the law, there are many fields in which they have a discretion with which the law will not interfere. For instance, it is for the Commissioner ... to decide in any particular case whether inquiries should be pursued, or whether an arrest should be made, or a prosecution brought. It must be for him to decide on the disposition of his force and the concentration of his resources on any particular crime or area. No court can or should give him direction on such a matter. He can also make policy decisions and give effect to them, as, for instance, was often done when prosecutions were not brought for attempted suicide. But there are some policy decisions with which I think, the courts can, if necessary, interfere. Suppose a chief constable were to issue a directive to his men that no persons should be prosecuted for stealing any goods less than £100 in value. I should have thought that the court could countermand it. He would be failing in his duty to enforce the law ...

12.44   In *R v Oxford ex p Levey*,[66] however, the Court of Appeal dismissed an appeal against the judge at first instance's refusal to quash a decision of the chief constable of Merseyside not to pursue a suspect into the Toxteth area of Liverpool. The claimant had been robbed in Liverpool, and a police car gave chase but withdrew when the suspect entered Toxteth. The court held that there was no evidence of any breach or failure of duty by the chief constable in policing the Toxteth area and the application failed on its merits. Sir John Donaldson MR stated that it was not for the courts to review the chief constable's choice of methods provided that he did not exceed the limits of his discretion.

12.45   *Blackburn*[67] was also distinguished by the Court of Appeal in *R v Chief Constable of Sussex ex p International Trader's Ferry Ltd*.[68] Live animal exporters were afforded police protection against demonstrators at a port. The ferry company sought judicial review of the chief

---

64   [1968] 2 QB 118 at 136A–B.
65   [1968] 2 QB 118 at 136D–G.
66   (1987) 151 LG Rev 371, CA affirming (1985) *Times* 18 December, QBD.
67   [1968] 2 QB 118, CA.
68   [1998] QB 477, CA.

constable's decision to reduce the level of protection afforded. The court held that the chief constable was entitled to conclude that he could not provide effective policing throughout his police area and maintain the level of policing at the port without significant extra resources, which he had no realistic prospect of obtaining. Accordingly, he had to decide how best to deploy his limited resources in order to keep the peace and enforce the law and, in the circumstances, his decision to reduce policing at the port was not unreasonable.

12.46   Kennedy LJ, delivering the judgment of the court, said:[69]

> The situation cannot be compared with that which was considered by this Court in ... *ex p Blackburn* ... where as a result of a policy decision, the police did not attempt to enforce one section of the Betting, Gaming and Lotteries Act 1963.

12.47   In the House of Lords, Lord Slynn described the applicable principles in the following way:[70]

> The courts have long made it clear that, though they will readily review the way in which decisions are reached, they will respect the margin of appreciation or discretion which a chief constable has. He knows through his officers the local situation, the availability of officers and his financial resources, the other demands on the police in the area at different times: *Chief Constable of the North Wales Police v Evans* [1982] 1 WLR 1155, 1174. Where the use of limited resources has to be decided the undesirability of the court stepping in too quickly was made very clear by Sir Thomas Bingham MR in *R v Cambridge Health Authority ex parte B* [1995] 1 WLR 898, 906 and underlined by Kennedy LJ in the present case. In the former the Master of the Rolls said in relation to the decisions which have to be taken by health authorities 'difficult and agonising judgments have to be made as to how a limited budget is best allocated to the maximum advantage of the maximum number of patients. That is not a judgment which the court can make.' The facts here are different and the statutory obligations are different but *mutatis mutandis* the principle is relevant to the present case. It seems to me that it is the right principle and that, whilst the courts must be astute to condemn illegal acts by the police yet, as was said by Balcombe LJ in *Harris v Sheffield United Football Club Ltd* [1988] QB 77, 95:
>
> > 'The true rule, in my judgment, is as follows. In deciding how to exercise his public duty of enforcing the law, and of keeping the peace, a chief constable has a discretion, which he must exercise even-handedly. Provided he acts within his discretion, the courts

---

69 [1998] QB 477 at 492.
70 [1999] 2 AC 418 at 430D–G.

> will not interfere ... In exercising that discretion a chief constable
> must clearly have regard to the resources available to him.'

12.48   In *R v Greater Manchester Police Authority and Chief Constable of Police
for Greater Manchester ex p Central Motors (Farnworth) Ltd,*[71] the police
authority had, historically, discharged its duty to remove vehicles from
the road by an informal agreement with local contractors including
the claimant. In 1994, that agreement was varied and the police
entered into a contract with the third defendant for the removal of
vehicles. The claimant brought judicial review proceedings on the
ground that this contract was unlawful as the police authority and/or
the chief constable were acting ultra vires when they entered it.

12.49   The Court of Appeal dismissed the claim on the basis that statute
permitted a police authority to delegate certain functions,[72] and that
they were therefore entitled to enter into a contract with a private
company in order to discharge their statutory duty to remove vehicles
from the road.

Operational decisions: disclosure of information

12.50   The courts are reluctant to interfere with an operational decision. In
R v Chief Constable of North Wales ex p AB,[73] the police had adopted
a policy of disclosing information about paedophiles to people in the
locality where it was in the public interest to do so and necessary for
the protection of persons who might otherwise become the victims
of crime. In pursuance of this policy, the police informed a caravan
site owner that two convicted paedophiles were staying at the caravan
site. The owner required the paedophiles to leave. They sought judicial review of the police policy.

12.51   The Court of Appeal held that the decision to disclose the names
was not irrational, nor was the original policy or its implementation
unlawful. Lord Woolf MR stated:[74]

> ... the court would be slow to characterise as irrational an operational
> decision such as the NWP [North Wales Police] made here to disclose

---

71 (1998) 3 March, unreported, CA.
72 Local Government Act 1972 ss101 and 111. See also *R v South Yorkshire Police
ex p Chief Constable of South Yorkshire* [2000] 1 WLR 55, CA, where s111 was
said to provide the power for the police authority to fund individual officers'
criminal defences to private prosecutions brought against them in respect of
the Hillsborough disaster.
73 [1999] QB 396, CA.
74 [1999] QB 396, CA, at 430A.

information about sex offenders where their motive was to protect children.

12.52 Similarly, in *Woolgar v Chief Constable of Sussex Police*,[75] the Court of Appeal held that the police were entitled to release details of an interview with a registered nurse who had been arrested but against whom no charges had been brought. The claimant sought an injunction to prevent the details being disclosed to the UK Central Council for Nursing who were conducting their own investigation. Where a regulatory body operating in the field of public health and safety sought access to confidential material in the possession of the police, the police were entitled to release the information if they were reasonably persuaded that it was of some relevance to the subject matter of the enquiry being conducted by the regulatory body.

12.53 By contrast, however, in *R v A Local Authority in the Midlands and A Police Authority in the Midlands ex p LM*,[76] the claimant had entered into a contract with an education authority, subject to submitting to a police check, to provide school bus services. He sought judicial review and an injunction to prohibit the police, on the check, from disclosing information that allegations of child abuse had been made against him ten years previously in respect of which no further action had been taken. Dyson J allowed the claim, holding that even though the claimant had agreed to submit to a police check, it could not be said that he had no grounds of complaint. Disclosure of such allegations should only be made where there was a pressing need for it; it should be the exception and not the rule because the consequences of disclosure could be very damaging for the subject of the allegations. Article 8 of the Convention was relevant because one of the consequences of disclosure would be to interfere with the claimant's private life. The decision in this case to disclose was irrational, as nothing in the information suggested that the claimant posed any risk to children on school buses.

12.54 Authorities must examine the facts and balance the public interest in the need to protect children against the need to safeguard the individual's right to a private life. In particular, they must consider their belief in the truth of the allegations (the greater the conviction that an allegation was true, the more pressing would be the need to disclose it); the interest of the third party in obtaining the information (the greater the legitimacy of that interest, the more pressing

75 [2000] 1 WLR 25, CA.
76 (1999) 2 LGLR 1043, QBD.

would be the need for disclosure); and the degree of risk posed by the person if disclosure was not made.

12.55   In *R (X) v Chief Constable of the West Midlands Police*,[77] Lord Woolf CJ stated that, having regard to the language of s115(7), Police Act 1997,[78] a chief constable was under a duty to disclose information for the purposes of inclusion on an enhanced criminal record certificate (ECRC) if the information might be relevant, unless there was some good reason for not making such disclosure.[79] Section 115:[80]

> ... was obviously required by Parliament because it was important (for the protection of children and vulnerable adults) that the information should be disclosed even if it only might be true. If it might be true, the person who was proposing to employ the claimant should be entitled to take it into account before the decision was made as to whether or not to employ the claimant. This was the policy of the legislation in order to serve a pressing social need.

12.56   In *R (L) v Commissioner of Police of the Metropolis*,[81] the Supreme Court considered what information is to be provided by the chief officer of a police force to the Secretary of State for inclusion in an ECRC, focusing on whether the legislative provisions were compatible with the right to respect for a person's private life under article 8 of the Convention. Finding article 8 was clearly engaged, the Court commented that the effect of the approach taken in *R (X) v Chief Constable of the West Midlands Police*

> has been to tilt the balance against the applicant too far. It has encouraged the idea that priority must be given to the social need to protect the vulnerable as against the right to respect for private life of the applicant.

12.57   The Court held that the relevant statutory provision could be read, without the need for words to be added or for it to be read down, so that decisions taken are compatible with article 8 rights.[82]

12.58   Lord Neuberger listed factors which would normally be relevant and should be taken into account when coming to a decision, although they were only examples: in some cases, other matters

---

77 [2004] EWCA Civ 1068, [2005] 1 WLR 65.
78 Section 115 has since been replaced by s113B of the Police Act 1997 which was inserted by s163(2) of the Serious Organised Crime and Police Act 2005.The new section does not differ in any material respect from the former section 115 and, therefore, the decisions relating to the previous provision are still relevant.
79 [2005] 1 WLR 65 at [36].
80 [2005] 1 WLR 65 at [37].
81 [2009] UKSC 3, [2010] 1 AC 410.
82 [2010] 1 AC 410 at [44] and [47].

would also need to be taken into account; in other cases, some of the listed examples may not require consideration. The factors were:

- the gravity of the material involved,
- the reliability of the information,
- whether the applicant has had a chance to rebut the information,
- the relevance of the information to the job role,
- the period that has elapsed since the relevant events occurred, and
- the impact on the applicant of including the material in the ECRC, both in terms of the prospects of obtaining the employment and more generally.[83]

12.59   In a recent decision, however, the Court of Appeal has held that the disclosure provisions of the Police Act 1997 and the Rehabilitation of Offenders Act 1974 (Exceptions) Order 1975 are incompatible with article 8 of the Convention. In *R (T) v Chief Constable of Greater Manchester*,[84] the appellant, T, received two warnings from Manchester Police when he was 11 years old, regarding stolen bicycles. At the age of 18, and having never reoffended, T enrolled on a sports course at college. An ECRC was obtained because he would have contact on the course with minors. In the light of the applicable case law,[85] the police considered that they had no discretion not to disclose the warnings, and included them on the ECRC.

12.60   T's appeal was heard with *JB v Secretary of State for the Home Department*. In *JB*, the appellant had failed to pay for an item while shopping despite paying for another item. She was apprehended by a member of staff after leaving the premises and said that she had made an honest mistake. The police decided that a caution would be appropriate and JB accepted it. Sometime later, JB saw that there were job vacancies in the care sector and completed a training course. After completing the course she was subject to a criminal records

---

83 Ibid, at [81]. The factors to be weighed into the balancing exercise and the general guidance given in *L* was endorsed in *R (J) v Chief Constable of Devon and Cornwall* [2012] EWHC 2996 (Admin) which was a challenge brought in relation to the new s113B of the Police Act 1997. The case also highlighted that it would be good practice under s113B in borderline cases to provide the opportunity to the person who may be subject to a ECRC to make representations and, if this is not done, to record the reasoning for not doing so. See also, eg, *R (W) v Chief Constable of Warwickshire* [2012] EWHC 406 (Admin).

84 [2013] EWCA Civ 25, [2013] 1 Cr App R 27, [2013] HRLR 14.

85 *Chief Constable of Humberside v Information Commissioner* [2010] 1 WLR 1136.

check, which revealed the caution, preventing her from obtaining employment.[86]

12.61   The Court of Appeal[87] accepted that the interference with T's article 8 rights pursued both the general aim of protecting employers and, in particular, children and vulnerable adults who are in their care and the particular aim of enabling employers to make an assessment as to whether an individual is suitable for a particular kind of work. It concluded, however, that the statutory regime requiring the disclosure of all convictions and cautions relating to recordable offences was disproportionate to that legitimate aim.

> It is true that disclosable offences do not include offences which are so insignificant that they are not even recorded on the PNC: the offences recorded on the PNC are those for which sentences of imprisonment may be imposed, but also a substantial number of other specified offences. We do not, however, consider this to be a proportionate filtering scheme in the context of article 8 considerations ...

> The fundamental objection to the scheme is that it does not seek to control the disclosure of information by reference to whether it is relevant to the purpose of enabling employers to assess the suitability of an individual for a particular kind of work. Relevance must depend on a number of factors including the seriousness of the offence; the age of the offender at the time of the offence; the sentence imposed or other manner of disposal; the time that has elapsed since the offence was committed; whether the individual has subsequently re-offended; and the nature of the work that the individual wishes to do. These same factors also come into the picture when the balance is to be struck (as it must be) between the relevance of the information and the severity of any impact on the individual's article 8(1) right.

> The force of this fundamental objection is well demonstrated by the facts of T's case. ... It is difficult to see what relevance the fact that, as a young child, he had received these warnings could have to the question whether he was suitable to be enrolled on a sports course and have contact with children when he was 18 years of age. The disclosure regime was introduced in order to protect children and

---

86 The appeal also involved a third appellant, AW, but she was refused permission to appeal. At 16, AW agreed with her boyfriend to carry out a 'car-jacking' which led to the driver being stabbed by her boyfriend. AW knew that he was carrying what she thought to be a knife. AW was charged and pleaded guilty to manslaughter and robbery. AW wanted to serve in the army and challenged the scheme (that her conviction will never be considered as spent) as incompatible with article 8. The Court of Appeal held that the decision of Parliament fell within its area of discretionary judgment. It was entitled to take the view that some offences are so serious that they should never be regarded as 'spent'. This was not a blanket policy (at [73])

87 At [37]–[39].

vulnerable adults. That objective is not furthered by the indiscriminate disclosure of all convictions and cautions to a potential employer, regardless of the circumstances. A blanket requirement of disclosure is inimical to the [Rehabilitation of Offenders Act] and the important rehabilitative aims of that legislation. Disclosure that is irrelevant (or at best of marginal relevance) is 'counter to the interests of re-integrating ex-offenders into society so that they can lead positive and law-abiding lives'...

12.62 Although JB was an adult at the time of her caution, the court held that she too was entitled to a declaration of incompatibility based upon the same reasons as applied in T's case; her offence was of a trivial nature and around eight years had passed by the time she applied for employment working with vulnerable people.[88]

Operational decisions: other decisions

12.63 In *R v Chief Constable of Devon and Cornwall ex p Central Electricity Generating Board*,[89] the Court of Appeal refused to interfere with a chief constable's decision not to assist the claimant electricity generating company by removing protesters from land on which they were obstructing the claimant's officers. The applicant was considering possible sites for a nuclear power station – one such site being in Cornwall. Protesters on the land prevented the claimant's officers from carrying out its statutory duties to investigate and survey the land. Accordingly, the claimant wrote to the chief constable asking for assistance. The chief constable declined to assist on the basis that there had been no actual or apprehended breach of the peace or unlawful assembly and that he therefore enjoyed no power to arrest the protestors. The claimant sought an order of mandamus.

12.64 Lord Denning MR, in the Court of Appeal, declined to interfere with the chief constable's decision. He said:[90]

I would not give any orders to the Chief Constable or his men. It is of the first importance that the police should decide on their own responsibility what action should be taken in any particular situation ... the decision of the Chief Constable not to intervene in this case was a policy decision with which I think the courts should not intervene.

---

88 Current reports suggest that the Government will seek permission to appeal against this decision.
89 [1982] 1 QB 458, CA.
90 [1982] 1 QB 458 at 472. Compare his judgment in *R v Commissioner of Police for the Metropolis ex p Blackburn* [1968] 2 QB 118, CA, discussed at paras 12.41–12.43 above.

12.65   On 1 April 1 2009, two demonstrations were held in London outside the Royal Exchange and in Bishopsgate (the 'Climate Camp') to protest against a G20 summit that was to be held on 2 April. The protest outside the Royal Exchange was disorderly to the point of serious violence and police decided to cordon off the area blocking all exits followed by dispersal. The Climate Camp demonstrators were disorderly and violent to a much lesser extent but the police decided to contain the demonstrators not because they believed there would be an imminent breach of the peace in the Climate Camp itself but because they believed a breach was imminent because of the likelihood that violent protestors from the Royal Exchange would move to the Climate Camp within a few minutes. A claim for judicial review, *R (McClure and Moos) v Commissioner of Police for the Metropolis,*[91] was brought by two people at the Climate Camp on the basis that the police action was unnecessary and unlawful.

12.66   The protestors succeeded at first instance, but the Court of Appeal allowed the Commissioner's appeal. The High Court had applied the incorrect test when assessing the issue of whether the police were entitled to apprehend an imminent breach of the peace; the court should have considered the reasonableness of the police officer's apprehension of an imminent breach of the peace, but had instead wrongly formed its own assessment of the imminence of a breach. There was nothing to suggest the apprehension of the police was unreasonable or the decision unlawful especially given that no less intrusive measure would have prevented the apprehended breach.[92]

Operational decisions: duties to members of the public

12.67   In *R (Bryant) v Commissioner of Police of the Metropolis,*[93] the Administrative Court considered a challenge relating to the well-documented allegations of telephone 'hacking' by journalists. The applicants sought permission to bring judicial review proceedings contending that their article 8 Convention rights had been infringed by the police during its investigations into hacking by persons linked to the *News of the World* newspaper, as they had not been informed that they may have been targeted by private investigators.

---

91   [2012] EWCA Civ 12.
92   [2012] EWCA Civ 12 at [68]–[76] and [93]–[96].
93   [2011] EWHC 1314 (Admin), [2011] HRLR 27.

12.68   In granting permission, and ruling that the article 8 challenge was arguable, Foskett J acknowledged that there were circumstances[94] in which the police are under a positive obligation to take steps to safeguard a person's physical integrity, an obligation that appears to be regarded as capable of being embraced within article 8.[95] The court warned, however, that the merits of the case were to be kept under review referring the parties to the statement on the standard form when a judge grants permission.[96]

12.69   In *Van Colle v Chief Constable of Hertfordshire*,[97] a witness in a criminal trial was murdered by the defendant, following threats and intimidation that had been reported to the police. The claimant sought to establish that the failure of the police to protect the witness breached their positive obligation under article 2 of the Convention, particularly given that the state had put him in danger by deciding to use him as a witness. The House of Lords held, following *Osman v UK*,[98] that a violation of the positive obligation under article 2 of the Convention would only be established if it could be shown that a public authority had, or ought to have, known of a real and immediate risk to the life of an identified person from the criminal acts of a third party, and had failed to take reasonable measures within its powers which might have been expected to avoid that risk. There was no other test and, in particular, no lower test for people who were witnesses for the state in criminal proceedings.

12.70   The ECtHR rejected an appeal.[99] The police had not known, nor ought they to have known, of a real and immediate risk to the life of the witness who was murdered.

---

94 *Osman v United Kingdom* (2000) 29 EHRR 245.
95 [2011] HRLR 27 at [51]–[61]. See also *Van Colle v Chief Constable of Hertfordshire* [2008] UKHL 50, [2009] 1 AC 225.
96 [2011] HRLR 27 at [75]–[76].
97 [2008] UKHL 50, [2009] 1 AC 225.
98 See para 12.68 above.
99 *Van Colle v UK* App No 7678/09 (Judgment 13 November 2012) (2013) *Times* 22 January.

CHAPTER 13

Judicial review and planning law

Introduction

13.1 Planning law covers a range of matters, from development control to compulsory purchase to decisions concerning the environment. Accordingly, it is an area of law that affects society as a whole, in one form or another, and decisions must, naturally, be subject to a system of review. Most planning decisions, in common with an increasing number of areas of public law decision-making, are subject to a statutory system of appeals, which has thereby relegated judicial review proceedings to a subordinate role.

13.2 A right of appeal, however, is not conferred on every party who may be affected by a planning decision. Despite the potential impact on, and rights afforded to, members of the public who may be affected by a planning decision, the planning process remains essentially a matter between an applicant (the developer) and the decision-maker (the local authority, or the Secretary of State).[1] In particular, where a proposed development is granted permission, there are likely to be many people, and/or groups of people, who objected to the grant of permission and who may wish seek to challenge the decision. Such people do not, however, enjoy statutory rights of appeal because they do not apply to challenge the grant of planning permission, only its refusal. Accordingly, judicial review remains of relevance in this situation, the supervisory jurisdiction exerting some control over the exercise of planning functions.

13.3 Equally importantly, judicial review can provide a second stage of review, where an appeal lies to a body that is not, in all the circumstances, independent or impartial for the purposes of article 6 of the European Convention on Human Rights.[2]

Legislation

Town and Country Planning Act 1990

13.4 The principal legislation governing the planning process is contained in the TCPA (TCPA) 1990, as amended, and in secondary legislation

---

1 Or, in some cases, the Mayor of London: see Greater London Authority Acts 1999 and 2007.

2 As found in HRA 1998 Sch 1.

made under its authority.[3] The TCPA 1990 confers the initial decision-making powers in relation to planning control on local planning authorities, which, in most instances, will be the local district (or unitary) authority in whose area the development is proposed.[4] Part 3 makes provision for the control of development, including applications for planning permission,[5] the determination of applications by planning authorities,[6] the Secretary of State's powers to call in applications,[7] and the right to appeal to the Secretary of State against a refusal of planning permission.[8]

13.5   Part 2 of the TCPA 1990 created the duty to compile development plans. This is now found in Planning and Compulsory Purchase Act 2004, Pt 3.[9]

13.6   The enforcement of planning control is governed by Part 7. Part 12 of the TCPA 1990 makes provision, among other things, for a statutory right of appeal, on a point of law to the High Court,[10] against a decision by the Secretary of State. The TCPA 1990 is supplemented by secondary legislation and by the National Planning Policy Framework, issued by the government department with responsibility for planning.[11]

---

3 See also the Planning (Listed Buildings and Conservation Areas) Act 1990, which makes special provision for buildings listed by the Secretary of State and for conservation areas; the Planning and Compulsory Purchase Act 2004; and the Planning Act 2008.

4 The definition of 'local planning authority' is contained in TCPA 1990 s1. The Mayor of London may direct that he is to be the local planning authority in respect of applications relating to land in Greater London which are of 'potential strategic importance': TCPA 1990 s2A.

5 TCPA 1990 s6.

6 TCPA 1990 ss70–75.

7 TCPA 1990 ss76A–77.

8 TCPA 1990 s78.

9 The Secretary of State announced that the geographically broader regional strategies were revoked on 6 July 2010. Existing regional strategies actually need to be revoked by Order. See also *R (Cala Homes (South) Ltd) v Secretary of State for Communities and Local Government* [2010] EWHC 2866 (Admin), [2011] BLGR 204; and *R (Cala Homes (South) Ltd) v Secretary of State for Communities and Local Government* [2011] EWCA Civ 639, [2011] 2 EGLR 75; and the repeals in Localism Act 2011.

10 Such statutory appeals are dealt with by the Administrative Court.

11 Department for Communities and Local Government *National Planning Policy Framework* (NPPF). The NPPF was issued in March 2012. One of its aims was to replace over 1,000 pages of national policy (Planning Policy and Statement and Planning Policy Guidance Notes) with one document of around 50 pages.

Decision-making and the role of judicial review

13.7　In most cases, applications for planning permission are determined by the local planning authority. The Secretary of State has a discretion, however, to call in applications and determine them himself, following a public inquiry, if so requested by the applicant or the planning authority.[12] Where planning permission is granted, it may be as outline permission, with the details of the development still to be approved, or as full planning permission, and it may be unconditional or with conditions attached.[13]

13.8　Where the local planning authority refuses permission, grants conditional permission or does not determine an application within the applicable time limits, the applicant may appeal to the Secretary of State. Such an appeal is, in the majority of cases, determined by a planning inspector, appointed by the Secretary of State, following an inquiry, although the Secretary of State may decide to take the decision himself, following the inquiry.[14] Where the appeal is dismissed by the Secretary of State – or where the Secretary of State determines a called-in application adversely to the applicant – there is a statutory right of appeal on a point of law to the High Court.[15]

13.9　Judicial review has no role in this process, save in the sense that an appeal on a point of law is conducted on judicial review principles.[16] There is, however, no right of appeal against the grant of permission and therefore an objector has no remedy other than to seek judicial review of the decision to grant permission.

13.10　Such claims frequently concentrate on an alleged failure by the decision-maker to have regard to relevant considerations, or to give a

---

12　TCPA 1990 s77.

13　Some applications do not require formal planning consent, such as a change of use of land that is governed by the Town and Country Planning (Use Classes) Order 1987 SI No 764 (as amended) or where an applicant applies simply for a certificate of lawful use (TCPA 1990 s192).

14　The procedure of inquiries conducted by an inspector is governed by the Town and Country Planning Appeals (Determination by Inspectors) (Inquiries Procedure) (England) Rules 2000 SI No 1625. See, eg, *R (Alconbury) v Secretary of State for the Environment, Transport and the Regions* [2001] UKHL 23, [2003] 2 AC 295 for an example of an appeal decided by the secretary of state rather than an inspector.

15　TCPA 1990 s289.

16　Judicial review is also relevant in that it is the only route for challenging costs orders made by a planning inspector on an appeal under TCPA 1990 s78: see *Golding v Secretary of State for Communities and Local Government* [2012] EWHC 1656 (Admin).

consideration sufficient weight,[17] or to comply with the requirements of procedural fairness. It is for the court to decide whether a consideration is material but usually a matter for the decision-maker to determine what weight is to be afforded to relevant considerations.[18]

13.11   In *R (Jones) v Mansfield DC*,[19] the claimant sought to challenge the grant of planning permission on the ground that the authority had failed properly to consider the environmental impact of their decision to grant permission.[20] The court held that it was a matter for the planning authority, in the circumstances of each case, to decide whether a development was likely to have significant environmental effects. While the authority must have regard to any uncertainties and the impact they may have on its ability to reach a reasonable conclusion, the local authority had been entitled in that case to consider that the large body of information available to it, even though incomplete, was nevertheless sufficient for it to make a decision about the likelihood of significant environmental effects.[21]

13.12   A claim for judicial review may also be brought to challenge an authority's decision to grant a certificate of lawful use or proposed use under TCPA 1990 ss191 and 192.[22]

---

17 TCPA 1990 s70(2) provides that, in determining a planning application, the authority must have regard to (a) the provisions of the development plan, (b) any local finance considerations and (c) any other material consideration. Decision-makers must have regard to any relevant EU provisions that impact on the decision to grant or refuse permission, including the impact the development would have on the environment – Town and Country Planning (Environmental Impact Assessment) Regulations 2011 SI No 1824 and Town and Country Planning (Environmental Impact Assessment) (England and Wales) Regulations 1999 SI No 293; the protection of natural habitats – Conservation of Habitats and Species Regulations 2010 SI No 490; and, waste management – Waste (England and Wales) Regulations 2011 SI No 988.

18 *Bolton MBC v Secretary of State for the Environment* (1991) 61 P&CR 343, CA. But see *South Oxfordshire DC v Secretary of State for the Environment* [1981] 1 WLR 1092, QBD, where a decision was quashed for giving conclusive weight to a relevant consideration (described by the decision-maker as a 'vitally material consideration').

19 [2003] EWHC 7 (Admin), [2003] 1 P&CR 31.

20 See also *R (Barker) v Bromley LBC* [2006] UKHL 52, [2007] 1 AC 470; *R (Lebus) v South Cambridgeshire DC* [2002] EWHC 2009 (Admin), [2003] 2 P & CR 5; *R (Catt) v Brighton and Hove CC* [2007] EWCA Civ 298, [2007] BLGR 331; *R (Brown) v Carlisle CC* [2010] EWCA Civ 525, [2011] Env LR 5.

21 See *British Telecommunications plc v Gloucester City Council* [2001] EWHC 1001 (Admin), [2002] 2 P&CR 33.

22 See, eg, *R v Thanet DC ex p Tapp* [2001] EWCA Civ 559, [2002] 1 P&CR 7; and *R (North Wiltshire DC) v Cotswold DC* [2009] EWHC 3702 (Admin).

13.13   Similarly, where a developer successfully applies to have the grant of permission varied[23] – eg by the removal of a condition originally attached to the permission – it is open to an interested party to seek to challenge that decision by way of judicial review.[24] In *R (Barker) v Waverley BC*,[25] the claimant sought judicial review of the authority's decision to remove a condition as to future use attached to planning consent on the grounds, among other things, that he had a legitimate expectation that the land would be restored to its original use and that the authority's decision was therefore *Wednesbury* unreasonable. The Administrative Court allowed the claim, but the authority's appeal to the Court of Appeal was allowed: the applicant's legitimate expectation did not have legal primacy over the authority's need to have regard to all material considerations and their decision to remove the condition was not, therefore, unreasonable.

13.14   Judicial review is also the appropriate forum for challenging the validity of planning legislation. It is open to a local planning authority to challenge secondary legislation made by the Secretary of State[26] as well as to an individual affected by a decision flowing from the legislation. In *R (Alconbury) v Secretary of State for the Environment, Transport and the Regions*,[27] the claimants applied for judicial review of the Secretary of State's decision to call in a planning application, on the grounds that the power to do so was contrary to article 6 of the European Convention on Human Rights as the Secretary of State was not an independent and impartial tribunal.[28]

---

23 The power to make such an application is conferred by TCPA 1990 s73.

24 The legality and rationality of conditions is a matter that may be challenged by way of judicial review. See *Newbury DC v Secretary of State for the Environment* [1981] AC 578, HL, for guidance as to the legal validity of planning conditions. Conditions must fulfil a planning purpose (*R v Hillingdon LBC ex p Royco Homes Ltd* [1974] QB 720); should fairly and reasonably relate to the permitted development; and, should not be manifestly unreasonable. See also, generally, *R (Ayres) v Secretary of State for the Environment, Transport and the Regions* [2002] EWHC 295 (Admin) and Department of the Environment *Circular 11/95: Use of conditions in planning permission* (now reissued by Department of Communities and Local Government).

25 [2001] EWCA Civ 566, [2002] 1 P&CR 6. See also *R (Godfrey) v Southwark LBC* [2012] EWCA Civ 500, [2012] BLGR 683.

26 See *R (Spelthorne BC) v Secretary of State for the Environment Transport and the Regions* (2000) 82 P&CR 10, QBD.

27 [2001] UKHL 23, [2003] 2 AC 295.

28 Conjoined applications related to the secretary of state's power to recover appeals for consideration by himself (under TCPA 1990 Sch 6 para 3) and to the secretary of state's powers of compulsory purchase, on the basis that appeals against both types of decision would be contrary to article 6 of

13.15   The Divisional Court found that the legislation was incompatible with article 6 and made a declaration of incompatibility under HRA 1998 s4. The House of Lords allowed an appeal, stating that, although the Secretary of State was not an independent and impartial tribunal, any decisions made by him were reviewable on a statutory appeal to the High Court, which was a court of full jurisdiction.

Time limits

13.16   For some time, a judicial doctrine was applied that an application for judicial review of a grant of planning permission must be brought within six weeks of the substantive decision (probably the resolution to grant permission rather than the formal grant itself) on the basis that the time limit for a developer to bring a statutory appeal to the High Court was six weeks and objectors should not be afforded any more generous time limit.[29]

13.17   In *R (Burkett) v Hammersmith and Fulham LBC*, however, the House of Lords decided that the courts had been wrong to adopt the principles described above. In particular, it was a misconception that the statutory three-month long-stop period for bringing a claim could in fact be judicially shortened to six weeks; a statutory time limit could not be 'counteracted by a judicial policy decision'.[30]

13.18   The Government has, however, recently brought forward proposals to introduce an equivalent statutory time limit, ie six weeks for all planning challenges.[31]

13.19   While the requirement to act promptly normally provides a time limit for the bringing of a judicial review claim,[32] this may not be the case, and different considerations may come into play, when issues of EU law are raised.[33] In *Uniplex (UK) Ltd v NHS Business Service Authority*,[34] the ECJ disapproved of the requirement of promptness. Consequently, it appears that, where a breach of EU law is relied

the Convention as they would lie to the secretary of state, who was not an independent or impartial tribunal.

29 See *R v Secretary of State for Trade and Industry ex p Greenpeace* [1998] EuLR 48, CA; *R v North Somerset DC ex p Garnett* [1997] JPL 1015, QBD; *R v Ceredigion CC ex p McKeown* [1998] 2 PLR 1 at 2.

30 [2002] UKHL 23, [2002] 1 WLR 1593, per Lord Steyn at [53]. See, generally, as to time limits, paras 18.18–18.23 below.

31 Ministry of Justice *Reform of Judicial Review: the Government Response* April 2013 (Cm 8611), para 14 and annex.

32 Senior Courts Act 1981 s31, CPR r54.4.

33 See generally 18.25–18.29 below.

34 C-406/08 [2010] PTSR 1377, [2010] 2 CMLR 47.

upon, the only requirement is that the claim be brought within three months.[35] Time limits for challenges based on domestic law are unchanged.[36]

13.20   Note that, in the specific context of a challenge to a local planning authority's adoption of a development plan document,[37] it has been held that the statutory six-week time limit starts to run on the day that the plan is adopted, rather than the following day.[38]

Planning enforcement decisions

13.21   Judicial review may also be available against a local authority's decision to – or not to – enforce planning control on a developer.[39] In *R (Prokopp) v London Underground Ltd* and others,[40] the claimant sought to prevent the first defendant from undertaking demolition works in connection with a proposed extension of one of its railway lines. He sought judicial review against them, and against the two relevant local authorities, whose decisions not to take enforcement action against the railway company he challenged on the basis that the railway company did not have planning permission for the demolition. (The permission that had been granted had expired because, due to a mistake in its implementation rendering that implementation unlawful, it had not been lawfully implemented within the requisite five-year period). The claimant obtained an interim injunction against the railway company prohibiting them from commencing work, notwithstanding concerns about his standing as a private individual to seek to enforce breaches of planning control in circumstances where the authorities charged with doing so had decided not to take action.

13.22   The court held that it could be appropriate to grant interim relief to a private individual against a developer, to prevent the taking of irrevocable steps which the claimant contended to be unlawful but which were not being enforced by the local planning authority. In

---

35 *R (Buglife: The Invertebrate Conservation Trust) v Medway Council* [2011] EWHC 746 (Admin), [2011] 3 CMLR 39, [2011] Env LR 27. See also *R (Berky) v Newport CC* [2012] EWCA Civ 378, [2012] 2 CMLR 44.

36 *Finn-Kelcey v Milton Keynes BC* [2008] EWCA Civ 1067, [2009] Env LR 17; *R (Berky) v Newport CC* [2012] EWCA Civ 378, [2012] 2 CMLR 44.

37 Planning and Compulsory Purchase Act 2004 s113.

38 *Hinde v Rugby BC* [2011] EWHC 3684 (Admin), [2012] JPL 861; and *Barker v Hambleton DC* [2012] EWCA Civ 610, [2012] CP Rep 36, [2013] 1 P&CR 1.

39 See, eg, *R (McCarthy) v Basildon DC* [2009] EWCA Civ 13, [2009] BGLR 1013.

40 [2003] EWHC 960 (Admin), [2003] 19 EGCS 119. Hackney LBC and Tower Hamlets LBC were the second and third defendants.

such a case, while the claim would initially be brought against the developer, the local authority must be added as a defendant and the claim would proceed against the authority with the developer taking part as an interested party. A private individual could not, however, obtain a permanent injunction in a public law claim, which would, in effect, amount to an enforcement action, which was the responsibility of the local authority and which carried with it procedural safeguards for the developer such as a right of appeal.

13.23　　The Court of Appeal reversed the judge's decision on other grounds but did not comment on these issues.[41]

41　[2003] EWCA Civ 961, [2004] Env LR 8.

CHAPTER 14

Judicial review and information

Introduction

14.1   On 1 January 2005, the Freedom of Information Act (FOIA) 2000 came into force in England, Wales and Northern Ireland.[1] The aim of the Act, as described in the White Paper, *Your Right to Know*,[2] was to strike a balance between extending people's access to information held by public authorities and preserving confidentiality in circumstances where disclosure of the information would be contrary to the public interest. The balance was to weigh in favour of openness which was described as 'fundamental to the political health of a modern state'.[3]

14.2   The FOIA provides individuals and companies with a right to request that a public authority inform them whether or not certain information is held. If the authority does hold the information, the Act confers a right on the person who made the request to be provided with it. The Act does not, however, provide a right of access to personal data.

14.3   The right to access personal files and medical records is governed by the Data Protection Act (DPA) 1998. In addition, certain information held by public authorities falls outside the scope of both the FOIA 2000 and the DPA 1998 and is regulated by other enactments, such as the Environmental Information Regulations 2004,[4] which makes provision for access to environmental information.

Data Protection Act 1998[5]

14.4   The DPA[6] (as amended) makes provision for regulating the processing of information relating to individuals. This includes the obtaining,

1   The position in Scotland is governed by the similar provisions of the Freedom of Information (Scotland) Act 2000.

2   Cm 3818, December 1997.

3   See the Foreword to *Your Right to Know* by the then Chancellor of the Duchy of Lancaster. The Act, however, was criticised as a substantial retreat from the White Paper. Critics highlighted the broad categories of exemptions covering policy advice and decision-making, and the heavy reliance on discretionary disclosure. Further criticism concerned the failure to adopt an overriding 'public interest' test for the disclosure of information.

4   SI No 3391.

5   Minor provisions came into force on Royal Assent; commencement of the remainder of the Act was on 1 March 2000: DPA 1998 (Commencement) Order 2000 SI No 183.

6   The Act gives effect to the requirements of EU Council Directive 95/46 EC on the protection of individuals with regard to the processing of personal data, and on the free movement of such data. The directive required implementation within

holding, use or disclosure of such information. The Act also contains provisions as to rights of access to processed personal information.

14.5 In essence, the rights created by the DPA 1998 entitle an individual, on request, to be informed[7] by a data controller if any personal data relating to him is being processed and, if it is, to be provided with a description of the data, the purpose for which it is being processed and the person(s) to whom it may be disclosed.[8] The individual is also entitled to be provided with the information held by the data controller and to be informed of the source of that data.[9]

Terminology

14.6 'Data' means[10] information that:

- is being processed[11] by means of equipment operating automatically in response to instructions for that purpose (ie data held on computers);
- is recorded with the intention that it should be processed by means of such equipment;
- is recorded as part of a relevant filing system or with the intention that it should form part of a relevant filing system (ie data that is manually filed in a filing system and is easily accessible);
- does not fall within any of the above but forms part of an 'accessible record';
- does not fall within any of the above but is recorded information held by a public authority.[12]

---

three years of its adoption (ie by 24 October 1998); processing 'already underway' must be brought into compliance within a further three years (ie by 2001); and (although at the discretion of member states) information already held in manual files must be brought into compliance within 12 years of the directive's adoption (ie by 2007), except for subject access which applied from 2001.

7 The data controller may charge a reasonable fee for supplying any information in response to a request (see Data Protection (Subject Access) (Fees and Miscellaneous Provisions) Regulations 2000 SI No 191, as amended by 2001 SI No 3223) and is under no obligation to disclose any information until the fee is paid or until he has verified the identity of the individual by requesting such information as he considers necessary: DPA 1998 s7(2)(b), (3).

8 DPA 1998 s7(1)(a) and (b).

9 DPA 1998 s7(1)(c).

10 DPA 1988 s1(1).

11 DPA 1998 s1(1), for the definition of 'processed'.

12 'Public authority' means a public authority as defined by the FOIA 2000 or a Scottish public authority as defined by the Freedom of Information (Scotland) Act 2002 (DPA 1998 s1(1)) (see below).

14.7   'Relevant filing system' means any set of information relating to individuals to the extent that, even if the information is not processed by means of computer equipment, the set is structured, either by reference to individuals or by reference to criteria relating to individuals, in such a way that specific information relating to a particular individual is readily accessible.[13]

14.8   The inclusion of information that is not processed by means of computer gives the DPA 1998 wide scope. Indeed, it has been said that on the basis of this definition of 'relevant filing system' that:[14]

> ... manual files held by a Local Authority Housing Department which relate to individual tenants, manual files held by the Home Office which relate to immigration applications, and personnel files held by employers would be covered. All the above will comprise of sets of information relating to, and structured by reference to, individuals. Certainly an efficient manual filing system, conventionally arranged alphabetically, should ensure that information relating to a particular individual would be accessible.

14.9   'Accessible record' means:[15]

- a health record;[16]
- an educational record;[17]
- an accessible public record.[18] This term refers to information held by a local housing authority for the purposes of any of the authority's functions, as well as to information held by a local social services authority for any purpose relating to that authority's functions.

14.10   'Personal data' means data that relate to individuals who can be identified from that data or that data with other information held by the data controller. The data includes an expression of an opinion about the person and any indication of the intention of the data controller or other person in respect of the individual. That individual is referred to as the 'data subject'.[19]

---

13   DPA 1998 s1(1).
14   See House of Commons Library Research Paper 98/48 (available online at www.parliament.uk).
15   DPA 1998 s68.
16   As defined by DPA 1998 s68(2).
17   As defined by DPA 1998 Sch 11.
18   As defined by DPA 1998 Sch 12. See also DPA 1998 Sch 12 para 3 which provides that accessible records are governed by separate rules.
19   DPA 1998 s1(1).

Rights of access

14.11 The Act confers on data subjects the following rights:[20]

- the right to be informed by any data controller (ie the person who holds the data) whether personal data of which he or she is the data subject are being processed by or on behalf of the data controller;
- if so, the right to be given a description, by the data controller, of the personal data concerned, the purposes for which they are being processed and the recipients or classes of recipients to whom they are disclosed or may be disclosed;
- the right to be told in an intelligible form the information constituting the personal data, and any information available to the data controller as to the source of the data; and
- where data relating to the data subject is processed by automatic means for the purpose of evaluating matters relating to the data subject, such as her or his performance at work, creditworthiness, reliability or conduct, and that processing was or is likely to be the sole basis for the taking of a decision significantly affecting the data subject, the right to be informed by the data controller of the 'logic involved in that decision-taking'.[21]

Exclusions from the right of access

14.12 There are a number of exclusions from the right of access.[22] These include:

- national security;[23]
- crime and taxation;[24]
- health, education and social work;[25]

---

20 DPA 1998 s7(1).
21 DPA 1998 s12.
22 DPA 1998 Pt IV.
23 DPA 1998 s28. A ministerial certificate will be conclusive of the fact it asserts that the information is excluded by reason of national security (although there is a right of appeal against a certificate: see DPA 1998 Sch 6).
24 DPA 1998 s29.
25 DPA 1998 s30, which does not itself provide this exemption but instead permits the secretary of state to make such exemptions by order. See Data Protection (Subject Access Modification) (Health) Order 2000 SI No 413; Data Protection (Subject Access Modification) (Education) Order 2000 SI No 414; Data Protection (Subject Access Modification) (Social Work) Order 2000 SI No 415.

- regulatory activity;[26]
- journalism, literature and art;[27]
- research, history and statistics;[28]
- manual data held by public authorities;[29]
- information made available to the public by or under another enactment;[30]
- disclosures required by law;[31]
- Parliamentary privilege;[32]
- confidential references given by the data controller;[33]
- armed forces;[34]
- judicial appointments and honours;[35]
- Crown employment and Crown or ministerial appointments;[36]
- management forecasts;[37]
- corporate finance;[38]
- negotiations with the data subject;[39]
- examination marks and/or scripts;[40]
- legal professional privilege;[41]
- self-incrimination.[42]

14.13   A request for information need only be complied with where the individual makes the request in writing; pays any applicable fee (which must not exceed the prescribed maximum);[43] and gives the data controller such information as he or she reasonably requires in order

---

26 DPA 1998 s31.
27 DPA 1998 s32.
28 DPA 1998 s33.
29 DPA 1998 s33A.
30 DPA 1998 s34.
31 DPA 1998 s35.
32 DPA 1998 s35A.
33 DPA 1998 Sch 7 para 1.
34 DPA 1998 Sch 7 para 2.
35 DPA 1998 Sch 7 para 3.
36 DPA 1998 Sch 7 para 4.
37 DPA 1998 Sch 7 para 5.
38 DPA 1998 Sch 7 para 6.
39 DPA 1998 Sch 7 para 7.
40 DPA 1998 Sch 7 paras 8 and 9.
41 DPA 1998 Sch 7 para 10.
42 DPA 1998 Sch 7 para 11.
43 Currently £10: Data Protection (Subject Access) (Fees and Miscellaneous Provisions) Regulations 2000 SI No 191 reg 3 (these regulations have been amended by 2001 SI No 3223).

to identify the person making the request and locate the information requested.[44] The Act prescribes time limits for complying with requests – generally 40 days, provided that all of the information referred to above has been supplied to the data controller.[45]

14.14   There is no obligation to disclose information requested if to do so would also necessitate disclosure of information relating to another individual, unless that individual consents or it is reasonable in all the circumstances to comply with the request without her or his consent.[46] In determining the reasonableness of disclosing information without consent, the data controller must have regard to any duty of confidentiality, any steps taken to obtain consent, any express refusal of consent and the question whether the individual is capable of giving consent.[47]

Unstructured data

14.15   There is no general right of access to unstructured data, ie any recorded information held by a data controller that is not structured by reference to individuals or criteria relating to individuals. There is, however, a limited right if the request contains a description of such data.[48] Public authorities will not be obliged to disclose unstructured data, in any event, if they estimate that the cost of doing so would exceed a prescribed limit.[49]

Right to prevent processing

14.16   A data subject may require a data controller not to process information, or to stop processing it, on the ground that its being processed would – or would be likely to – cause substantial and unwarranted distress to him or to another person.[50] The data controller may decline to comply with such a request if the data subject has previously given

---

44   DPA 1998 s7.
45   DPA 1998 s7.
46   DPA 1998 s7(4). Information relating to another individual includes a reference to information that would identify the individual as the source of the information: DPA 1998 s7(5).
47   DPA 1998 s7(6).
48   DPA 1998 s9A.
49   DPA 1998 s9A(5). The prescribed limit is currently £600 for public authorities listed in the FOIA Pt 1 Sch 1 (see below) and £450 for any other public authority: Freedom of Information and Data Protection (Appropriate Limit and Fees) Regulations 2004 SI No 3244.
50   DPA 1998 s10.

consent, or if the processing is necessary for the performance of a contract, compliance with a legal obligation or the protection of the vital interests of the data subject.[51] The data subject also has the right to restrict processing of personal data for the purposes of direct marketing[52] and to require the data controller not to make any decision affecting the data subject based solely on automatic processing of personal data.[53]

Remedies and enforcement

14.17　Where a data controller refuses to comply with a data subject's request for information, or has refused, on request, to stop processing data for marketing purposes or otherwise, or has, in spite of a request not to do so, taken a decision against the data subject solely on the basis of automatically processed data, the data subject may apply to the county court or High Court for an order that the data controller must comply with the request.[54]

14.18　Other enforcement provisions, contained in the DPA 1998, include the power of the Information Commissioner to issue an enforcement notice where he considers that a data controller is acting in breach of one of the data protection principles.[55] A data subject may request the Information Commissioner to assess whether or not personal data is being processed in accordance with provisions of the Act.[56] If the Information Commissioner decides that data is being processed otherwise than in accordance with those provisions, he may serve a variety of notices requiring compliance or further information.[57]

51　DPA 1998 s10(2) and Sch 2 paras 1–4.
52　DPA 1998 s11.
53　DPA 1998 s12.
54　DPA 1998 ss7(9), 10(4), 11(2), 12(8) and 15(1).
55　DPA 1998 s40. The data protection principles are contained in DPA 1998 Sch 1. They are, in summary, that: 1) personal data must be processed fairly and lawfully; 2) personal data must only be obtained for specified and lawful purposes; 3) personal data must be adequate, relevant and not excessive in relation to the purpose for which it is processed; 4) personal data must be accurate and kept up to date; 5) personal data must not be kept for longer than is necessary; 6) personal data must be processed in accordance with the DPA 1998; 7) adequate technical and organisational measures must be taken to protect against unlawful or unauthorised processing, and accidental loss or destruction, of personal data; and 8) personal data must not be transferred to a non-EEA country, unless that country ensures an adequate level of protection for the rights and freedoms of data subjects.
56　DPA 1998 s42.
57　DPA 1998 ss40, 43 and 44.

The Commissioner may also serve an assessment notice as a way of investigating whether or not a data controller has complied or is complying with the data protection principles.[58] The recipient of such a notice has a right to appeal to the Information Rights Tribunal and, thereafter, to the Upper Tribunal.[59]

14.19   There is no right of appeal, however, from a decision of the Information Commissioner not to serve a notice or take any other enforcement action. Accordingly, the only means of challenging such a decision is likely to be by way of judicial review.

Freedom of Information Act 2000

14.20   The FOIA 2000 makes provision for a general right of access to information held by public authorities in the course of carrying out their public functions, subject to certain conditions and exemptions.

14.21   The term 'public authority'[60] includes:

- government departments (other than the Office for Standards in Education, Children's Services and Skills);[61]
- the House of Commons, House of Lords and National Assembly for Wales but not in relation information relating to: any residential address of a member of either House of Parliament; travel arrangements not yet undertaken or regular in nature by a member of either House of Parliament;[62] the identity of any person who delivers or has delivered goods, or provides or has provided services, to a member of either House of Parliament; or expenditure on security arrangements by a member of either House of Parliament;[63]

---

58 DPA 1998 ss41A and 41B.
59 DPA ss48–49 and Sch 6 (see also discussion of the Information Rights Tribunal below). Further rights of appeal lie where data is not disclosed on the ground of national security.
60 Defined in FOIA 2000 s3, s6 (publicly owned companies) and Sch 1.
61 FOIA 2000 Sch1 para 1. The Office for Standards in Education, Children's Services and Skills is a public authority, in respect of information held for purposes other than those of the functions exercisable by Her Majesty's Chief Inspector of Education, Children's Services and Skills under s5(1)(a)(iii) of the Care Standards Act 2000: FOIA 2000 Sch 1 para 1A.
62 This does not include information relating to the total amount of expenditure incurred on regular travel during any month.
63 FOIA 2000 Sch1 paras 2, 3 and 5.

- the Northern Ireland Assembly and the Welsh Assembly Government;[64]
- the armed forces;[65]
- local authorities,[66] the Greater London Authority, the Common Council of the City of London and the Council of Sicily; [67]
- the National Health Service;[68]
- police;[69]
- maintained schools and other educational institutions;[70]
- Inner Temple's sub-treasurer or the under-treasurer of the Middle Temple, in respect of information held in his capacity as a local authority;[71]
- bodies and authorities constituted or established by way of order under various statutory provisions;[72]
- the Broads Authority;[73]
- Transport for London, the London Transport Users Committee and a Passenger Transport Executive for an integrated transport area;[74]
- a National Park authority;[75]
- other prescribed bodies.[76]

14.22 A request for information under FOIA 2000 must be made in writing, state the name of the applicant and an address for correspondence,

64 FOIA 2000 Sch1 paras 4 and 5A.
65 This does not include the special forces or any unit who is assisting the Government Communications Headquarters in the carrying out of its functions: FOIA Sch1 para 6.
66 As defined in the Local Government Act 1972. A joint committee under s102(1)(b) of the Local Government Act 1972 is also a public authority for the purposes of the FOIA 2000: FOIA 2000 Sch 1 para 25.
67 FOIA 2000 Sch1 paras 7–9 and 11. In relation to the Common Council they are only a public authority with regards to information held when acting as a local authority, a police authority or a port health authority.
68 As provided for in FOIA 2000 Pt III Sch1 paras 36A–45A (England and Wales). For Northern Ireland see paras 48–51D.
69 As provided for in FOIA 2000 Pt V Sch1 paras 57–59 (England and Wales) and 62–64. For Northern Ireland also see paras 60–61.
70 As provided for in FOIA 2000 Pt IV Sch1 paras 52–53 (England and Wales). For Northern Ireland see paras 54–56.
71 FOIA 2000 Sch1 para 10.
72 FOIA 2000 Sch1 see paras 12–13, 15, 15A, 16, 18, 19A-19B, 21–23, 26–27, 31, 33 and 35B-35E.
73 FOIA 2000 Sch1 para 24.
74 FOIA 2000 Sch1 paras 28–30.
75 Established under s63 of the Environment Act 1995: FOIA 2000 Sch1 para 32.
76 See FOIA Pt VI Sch1 (England and Wales) and Pt VII Sch1 (Northern Ireland).

and describe the information requested. A public authority must treat a request as being made in writing where it is sent by electronic means (eg a request sent by e-mail), is received in a form that is legible and is capable of being used for reference.[77] A public authority may charge a fee for information in accordance with prescribed regulations.[78] If a public authority does charge a fee, it must give the applicant a notice in writing stating the amount of the fee. Where a notice is given, the public authority is not obliged to comply with the request for information unless the fee is paid within the period of three months beginning with the day on which the notice is given to the applicant.[79]

14.23   Generally, a public authority must provide an applicant with the information requested promptly and, in any event, within 20 working days following the date of receipt of the request (or, where applicable, the fee).[80]

14.24   A public authority must adopt a scheme, approved by the Information Commissioner, relating to its publication of information. An authority must publish information in accordance with its scheme, and must review its scheme having regard to the public interest in allowing access to information, and the publication of reasons for decisions taken by the authority. A scheme must specify:

- classes of information the authority publishes or intends to publish;
- the manner in which information is, or is intended to be, published; and
- whether the material is, or is intended to be, available to the public free or on payment of a fee.[81]

77 FOIA 2000 s8.
78 In deciding upon a fee to comply with a request under s1(1), FOIA 2000, a public authority must have regard to reg6 of the Freedom of Information and Data Protection (Appropriate Limit and Fees) Regulations 2004 SI No 3244: the maximum fee must not be in excess of the total costs the authority reasonably expects to incur informing the person making the request whether it holds the information, and communicating the information to the person. The authority may take into account the costs of the means or form of communicating the information, reproducing any document containing the information, and postage and other forms of transmitting the information (this list is not exhaustive). A public authority may not, however, take into account costs that are attributable to the time it will take or the time it will take to redact the information. In respect of the latter see, eg, *Chief Constable of South Yorkshire v Information Commissioner* [2011] EWHC 44 (Admin), [2011] 1 WLR 1387.
79 FOIA 2000 s9.
80 FOIA 2000 s10(1).
81 FOIA 2000 s19.

Limitations and exclusions

14.25   The Act applies similar limitations to the right to information to those applicable under the DPA 1998. A public authority is, accordingly, not obliged to provide information unless it has been given sufficient details to identify the information requested[82] and is not obliged to provide information where it estimates that the cost of doing so will exceed the prescribed limit.[83] Nor is an authority required to comply with a vexatious or repetitious request.[84]

14.26   The Information Commissioner's Office (ICO) has published guidance in relation to vexatious requests,[85] which suggests that the following five questions will aid public authorities in deciding whether or not a request is vexatious:

- Can the request fairly be seen as obsessive?
- Is the request harassing the authority or causing distress to staff?
- Would complying with the request impose a significant burden?
- Is the request designed to cause disruption or annoyance?
- Does the request lack any serious purpose or value?

14.27   Although a useful guide, the criteria suggested by the ICO should not be used by public authorities as a 'tick-box' exercise. Rather, the authority must look at all the surrounding circumstances and apply them to the question of whether the request is vexatious.[86]

14.28   In *Independent Police Complaints Commission v Information Commissioner,* [87] the First-tier Tribunal gave some useful examples of when a request may be vexatious, which, interestingly, included a request that 'may be so grossly oppressive in terms of the resources and time demanded by compliance ... regardless of the intentions or *bona fides* of the requester' even where FOIA 2000 s12 would not

---

82   FOIA 2000 s1(3).

83   FOIA 2000 s12. The prescribed limit is currently £600 for public authorities listed in the FOIA Pt 1 Sch 1 and £450 for any other public authority: Freedom of Information and Data Protection (Appropriate Limit and Fees) Regulations 2004 SI No 3244.

84   FOIA 2000 s14.

85   *FOIA Vexatious or repeated requests*, ICO, 3 December 2008 (version 4) available at www.ico.gov.uk/upload/documents/library/freedom_of_information/ detailed_specialist_guides/awareness_guidance_22_vexatious_and_repeated_ requests_final.pdf.

86   *Independent Police Complaints Commission v Information Commissioner* (EA/2011/0222).

87   EA/2011/0222 at [15].

operate to exempt the authority from compliance with the request. The case concerned a request to the IPCC that involved 438 cases, followed by a second request for further information. In the period of around two years preceding the requests, the same person had made 25 requests for information to the IPCC regarding their investigations. The requests were unfocussed and extremely wide ranging. The First-tier Tribunal held:[88]

> The present requests were ... not just burdensome and harassing but ... wholly unreasonable and of very uncertain purpose and dubious value, given the undiscriminating nature of the first request [and the tribunal were in no way convinced the requests were made in good faith] ... we should have regarded any one of those findings as sufficient to describe these requests as vexatious ....

14.29   There are also numerous exclusions to the right to information some of which are absolute, and others of which are qualified and subject to a public interest test.[89] The information subject to the public interest test will not have to be provided to the applicant if the public authority is of the view that, in all the circumstances, the public interest in maintaining the exemption outweighs the public interest in disclosing the information.[90] Aside from the familiar exemptions relating to such matters as national security, defence, international relations, etc, an authority is not required to provide information that is accessible by other means[91] or that relates to any investigation into the possibility of prosecution for an offence[92] or to any documents that are in the authority's possession as a consequence of court proceedings.[93]

---

88 EA/2011/0222 at [20].

89 The exemptions are set out at FOIA 2000 Pt II. The provisions within Pt II where there is an absolute restriction on disclosure are listed at FOIA 2000 s2(3).

90 FOIA 2000 s2(2). Section 2(1) contains a similar provision as to whether or not the information has to be confirmed or denied as being held by the public authority. On the public interest test see, eg, *Hogan v Information Commissioner* (EA/2005/0026) at paras 54–61; *Guardian Newspapers v Information Commissioner* [2007] UKIT EA/ 2006/0011 at paras 81–92; and *Secretary of State for Work and Pensions v Information Commissioner* [2007] UKIT EA/2006/013.

91 FOIA 2000 s21. A public authority will, however, have to provide advice and assistance to the applicant so they can obtain the information from the relevant source.

92 FOIA 2000 s30.

93 FOIA 2000 s32.

14.30   There is no right to information that contains personal data of which the person requesting disclosure is not the subject.[94] It has been held, however, that information containing personal data can be disclosed under the FOIA where it is capable of undergoing the statistical process of 'Barnardisation' or redaction, or where it was already anonymised.[95]

Codes of practice

14.31   The FOIA 2000 requires the Secretary of State[96] to produce a code of practice providing guidance on the practices that public authorities should adopt in connection with the discharge of their functions under the Act. In particular, the code of practice must include guidance about:

- procedures for giving advice and assistance to people who have made or propose to make requests for information;
- transferring a request to another authority which holds the information requested;
- consulting with people to whom the information requested relates or who are likely to be affected by its disclosure;
- inserting terms into contracts concerning the disclosure of information; and
- the introduction by public authorities of complaints procedures relating to their compliance with their obligations under the Act.[97]

---

94 FOIA 2000 s40. A public authority does not even have to confirm or deny whether it is the holder of such information if to do so would mean personal information was disclosed.

95 See, eg, *Department of Health v Information Commissioner* [2011] EWHC 1430 (Admin), [2011] Med LR 363, where it was held that anonymised statistical information held by the Department of Health as to patients who had had late terminations on medical grounds was not personal data; and, *Common Services Agency v Scottish Information Commissioner* [2008] UKHL 47, [2008] 1 WLR 1550, where a researcher sought information on incidents of childhood leukaemia in certain postal areas.

96 Secretary of State for Constitutional Affairs.

97 FOIA 2000 s45. The current code of practice is: *Secretary of State for Constitutional Affairs' Code of Practice on the discharge of public authorities' functions under Part I of the FOIA 2000*, November 2004 available on the Ministry of Justice website at www.justice.gov.uk/information-access-rights/foi-guidance-for-practitioners/code-of-practice.

14.32　The Lord Chancellor must also produce a code of practice, offering guidance to relevant authorities[98] on the practice that would be desirable for them to follow in respect of the keeping, management and destruction of their records.[99]

14.33　　A further obligation is placed on the Information Commissioner to promote good practice and, in particular, the observance by public authorities of the requirements of the Act and the codes of practice laid down under it.[100]

Enforcement and appeals

14.34　Where a person (the 'complainant') has requested information from a public authority, he may apply to the Information Commissioner for a decision on whether, in any specified respect, the request has been dealt with in accordance with the Act.[101] The Commissioner must make a decision on the application unless it appears to him that the complainant has not exhausted any complaints procedure operated by the authority under the Secretary of State's code of practice, or has delayed unduly, or that the application is frivolous or vexatious (or has been abandoned or withdrawn).[102]

14.35　　If the Information Commissioner considers that the complaint is made out, he must serve on the complainant and the public authority a 'decision notice', specifying steps that should be taken and the time limit within which they must be taken.[103] Where the Commissioner does not make a decision on the application, he or she must notify the complainant of this and of his or her grounds for not doing so.[104]

14.36　　If, independently of any application from a complainant, the Commissioner is satisfied that a public authority has failed to comply

---

98　A 'relevant authority' means a public authority or any other office or body, not a public authority, whose administrative and departmental records are public records for the purposes of the Public Records Act 1958 or the Public Records (Northern Ireland) Act 1923: FOIA 2000 s46(7).

99　FOIA 2000 s46. The current code of practice is: *Lord Chancellor's Code of Practice on the management of records issued under section 46 of the FOIA 2000*, July 16, 2009 available on the Ministry of Justice website at www.justice.gov. uk/information-access-rights/foi-guidance-for-practitioners/code-of-practice.

100　FOIA 2000 s47.

101　FOIA 2000 s50.

102　FOIA 2000 s50(2). The Information Commissioner also has power to request information from a public authority, by means of serving an 'information notice', before reaching a decision on the application: FOIA 2000 s51.

103　FOIA 2000 s50(3)(b).

104　FOIA 2000 s50(3)(a).

with any of the requirements of the Act, he may issue an 'enforcement notice', which specifies the provision(s) of the Act that have not been complied with, and the steps that must be taken to remedy that non-compliance.[105] If the authority fails to comply with the Commissioner's requirements, the Commissioner may certify that non-compliance, which may then be dealt with by the High Court as if it were a contempt of court,[106] although the court enquires into the matter for itself, including hearing evidence and reading statements, and does not merely accept the Commissioner's decision in that regard.[107] The Act creates no right of action in civil proceedings, however, for a failure to comply with any duty it imposes.[108]

14.37   In certain circumstances, particular public authorities[109] are not required to comply with either a decision notice or an enforcement notice. Where a notice is served on such an authority, in relation to a failure to confirm or deny the existence of information (falling within the exclusions contained in Pt II, FOIA 2000), or failing to disclose information (that is exempt), the 'accountable person'[110] within that authority may give the Commissioner a certificate signed by him or her stating that on reasonable grounds he or she has formed the opinion that there was no failure to comply with the Act.[111] Such certificate, if given, causes the notice to cease to have effect.[112]

14.38   The complainant or the public authority has a right of appeal against a decision notice to the Information Rights Tribunal (First-

---

105 FOIA 2000 s52.

106 FOIA 2000 s54.

107 FOIA 2000 s54.

108 FOIA 2000 s56.

109 Namely, any central government department, the National Assembly for Wales or any other public body so designated by an order of the secretary of state: FOIA 2000 s53(1)(a).

110 The 'accountable person' is the First Minister for Wales (in relation to the Assembly), the First Minister and Deputy First Minister in Northern Ireland acting jointly (in relation to a Northern Ireland public authority), or (in relation to any other public authority) a Minister of the Crown who is also a member of the Cabinet, or the Attorney-General or Advocate-General in Scotland or Attorney-General for Northern Ireland: FOIA 2000 s53(8).

111 FOIA 2000 s53. Such a certificate should not be confused with a certificate under FOIA 2000 s23 or s24 stating that information cannot be disclosed on the ground of national security. An appeal against the latter type of certificate lies to the Information Rights Tribunal: FOIA 2000 s60.

112 FOIA 2000 s53(2).

tier Tribunal (Information Rights)).[113] The question of whether the tribunal has jurisdiction where the Commissioner, by letter, declines to entertain a complaint was considered in *British Broadcasting Corporation v Sugar*.[114] The High Court's view was that the tribunal did not have jurisdiction, because if the Commissioner decided not to serve a decision notice, there was nothing that could be appealed to the tribunal. The remedy in such situations, it was said, would be to bring judicial review proceedings.[115] The House of Lords, however, disagreed:[116] section 50 of the Act does not prescribe the form of a decision notice and the term 'decision notice' simply describes a letter setting out the commissioner's decision. The tribunal, therefore, did have jurisdiction in such cases.[117]

14.39   A public authority may also appeal to the tribunal against an information or enforcement notice.[118] The tribunal has power to allow or dismiss an appeal and to substitute an alternative notice where appropriate. In reaching its decision on appeal, the tribunal can review any finding of fact made by the Commissioner on which the notice appealed against was based.[119]

14.40   An appeal lies from the tribunal to the Upper Tribunal on a point of law.[120] The procedure is governed by the Tribunal Procedure (First-tier Tribunal) (General Regulatory Chamber) Rules 2009.[121]

14.41   There is no right of appeal against a certificate issued by the 'accountable person', and it therefore seems that the only method of challenging such a certificate will be judicial review. Given the narrow scope of the discretion and the fact that it relates to exempt information, challenges are likely to be rare and difficult to establish. Moreover, the comprehensiveness of the appeals structure set up by

---

113 The Information Rights Tribunal is part of the First-tier Tribunal in the General Regulatory Chamber and is known as the First-tier Tribunal (Information Rights).

114 [2009] UKHL 9, [2009] 1 WLR 430.

115 See *R (Sugar) v Information Commissioner* [2007] EWHC 905 (Admin), [2007] 1 WLR 2583 and affirmed by the Court of Appeal [2008] EWCA Civ 191, [2008] 1 WLR 2289.

116 Lord Hoffmann and Baroness Hale dissenting.

117 *British Broadcasting Corporation v Sugar* [2009] UKHL 9, [2009] 1 WLR 430 (at [37]).

118 FOIA 2000 s57. Appeals are governed by the procedure set down in DPA 1998 Sch 6: FOIA 2000 s61.

119 FOIA 2000 s58.

120 See chapter 19. Decisions made by the tribunal can be found at www. informationtribunal.gov.uk/Public/search.aspx.

121 SI No 1976.

the Act will probably rule out judicial review save in the exceptional case.

Access to information from local authorities

14.42   The Local Government Act 1972 provides for access to meetings and certain information of a local authority.[122] The general principle is that meetings must be open to the general public, but authorities are entitled to exclude the public from all or part of a meeting, in specific circumstances. If a meeting is being held in public, members of the public may not be excluded, except to prevent disorderly conduct or other misbehaviour. Accredited newspaper representatives must also be afforded reasonable facilities for reporting and for making telephone calls at their own expense.

14.43   The Local Government Act 1972 does not, however, require or authorise the disclosure of confidential information in breach of confidence. The public must be excluded from meetings during items of business where it is likely that their presence would result in such disclosure to them. They may also be excluded during items of business where it is likely that their presence would result in the disclosure to them of 'exempt' information.

Agendas and reports

14.44   Copies of the agenda for a meeting must be open to public inspection, generally at least three clear days before the meeting, at the authority's offices. This also applies to copies of any report for the meeting except parts of a report relating to items to be discussed in private, which may be excluded. Where a meeting must be held in public, a reasonable number of copies of agendas and reports must be made available for members of the public present at the meeting. After a meeting, a copy of the minutes of – and reports relating to – the public parts of the meeting and of the agenda, must be open to inspection by the public for six years.[123]

14.45   Documents must be open to inspection at all reasonable hours and free of charge, although a fee may be charged for copying them. It is a criminal offence to refuse to provide copies to a person entitled

122 See Local Government Act 1972 Pt VA, inserted by the Local Government (Access to Information) Act 1985.
123 Local Government Act 1972 ss100B and 100C.

to them or intentionally to obstruct a person exercising his rights to inspect or copy documents.[124]

Health

14.46   Access to medical and health records is governed by the Access to Medical Reports Act 1988 (which permits an individual to see medical reports prepared about him for employment or insurance purposes, subject to certain exclusions) and the Access to Health Records Act 1990 (which gives a general right of access to health records, again, subject to exclusions). There is also a non-statutory code of practice: Code of Practice on Openness in the NHS.

Access to information concerning the environment

14.47   Access to environmental information may be obtained under the Environmental Information Regulations 2004.[125] These regulations make provision for access to any information relating to the environment (as defined) that is held by a relevant person in an accessible form, and otherwise than for the purposes of any judicial or legal functions. The regulations apply to any information not already required to be disclosed under any other enactment. In addition, the INSPIRE Regulations 2009 make provision for public access to spatial data sets and services.[126]

---

124   Local Government Act 1972 s100H.

125   SI No 3391. This implements EC Council Directive 2003/4/EC on public access to environmental information and repeals Council Directive 90/313/EEC. Note to the Convention on Access to Information, Public Participation in Decision-making and Access to Justice in Environmental Matters, Aarhus, Denmark, 25 June 1998.

126   SI No 3157. This implements Directive 2007/2/EC, which concerns the creation and operation of national and European Union infrastructures relating to spatial information for the purposes of EU environmental policies and other policies or activities which may have an impact on the environment.

CHAPTER 15

Judicial review and children

The legislation

15.1   The law relating to the care and upbringing of children is contained within the Children Act (CA) 1989 (as amended).

15.2   Part 3 of CA 1989 obliges local authorities to assist people who have parental responsibility for children with their care. This includes the responsibility to provide services for families within the authority's area and can include power to provide accommodation for children and for their families.

Duties to children

Duties to children in need

15.3   Section 17(1) of the CA 1989 creates a duty to 'safeguard and promote the welfare' of children who are in need and to promote the upbringing of such children by their parents by providing a range and level of services 'appropriate to those children's needs'.

15.4   This is a general duty imposed on local authorities, the performance of which is facilitated by the more specific duties and powers conferred by CA 1989 Pt 3.[1] This includes, for example, the duty to identify children in need in their area;[2] to assess those children's needs;[3] to maintain a register of disabled children;[4] and to provide accommodation where necessary to protect the child.[5] Local authorities must provide services for children living with their families 'as they consider appropriate', including advice, counselling and guidance, home help and assistance to enable such children to have a holiday.[6]

15.5   A child is defined as 'in need' if:

- he is unlikely to achieve or maintain, or have the opportunity of achieving or maintaining, a reasonable standard of health or development without provision for him of services by a local authority under the Act; or

---

1   CA 1989 s17(2) and Sch 2 Pt I. For more information see Wise, Broach, Gallagher, Pickup, Silverstone and Suterwalla, *Children in Need: local authority support for children and families* (LAG, 2011).
2   CA 1989 Sch 2 para 1.
3   CA 1989 Sch 2 para 3.
4   CA 1989 Sch 2 para 2.
5   CA 1989 Sch 2 para 5.
6   CA 1989 Sch 2 para 8.

- if his health or development is likely to be significantly impaired, or further impaired without the provision of such services; or
- he is disabled.[7]

15.6   The duty under Children Act 1989 s17 has been described as a 'target' duty.[8] In *R (G) v Barnet LBC*,[9] the House of Lords held that section 17 imposes a general duty on a local authority, in addition to other more specific duties, to safeguard and promote the welfare of children in their area. Accordingly, while this does not take the decision-maker outside the scope of judicial review altogether, a challenge would need to show that a decision had been taken in contravention of the established principles of public law, such as the obligation to take account of all relevant matters, ignore the irrelevant, not to fetter a discretion, not to act perversely, etc. It would not be sufficient for a claimant simply to allege that he, or his child, had not been safeguarded or that his welfare had not been promoted. There is no specific duty enforceable at the suit of the individual. The House of Lords agreed with the analysis of Scott Baker J, in *R (A) v Lambeth LBC*,[10] at first instance, where he said:[11]

> ... the duty owed under section 17 of the Children Act 1989 is a target duty owed to children in general and is not justiciable by judicial review.[12] It is to be distinguished from a specific duty such as that in section 20 to provide accommodation for the whole family.

7   CA 1989 s17(10). By section 17(11), a child is disabled if he is blind, deaf or dumb or suffers from mental disorder of any kind or is substantially and permanently handicapped by illness, injury or congenital deformity or such other disability as may be prescribed. For these purposes, 'development' means physical, intellectual, emotional, social or behavioural development; and 'health' means physical or mental health.

8   *R (G) v Barnet LBC* [2003] UKHL 57, [2004] 2 AC 208; *R v Bexley LBC, ex p B* (2000) 3 CCLR 15; *X (Minors) v Bedfordshire CC* [1995] 2 AC 633. As to target duties generally, see *R v Inner London Education Authority ex p Ali* (1990) 2 Admin LR 822, QBD where Woolf LJ described the duty imposed on local education authorities by Education Act 1944 s8 (to secure the provision of sufficient schools in their area) as a target duty. See also generally, paras 3.69–3.71 above.

9   [2003] UKHL 57, [2004] 2 AC 208.

10 [2001] EWHC 376 (Admin), (2001) 33 HLR 60.

11 The specific principles involved in *A* and *G* relating to the provision of accommodation are considered elsewhere (see paras 9.29–9.42 above in the context of housing and judicial review.

12 It is submitted that this is not intended to go further than the propositions set out at para 15.6 above. It is not suggesting that the duty is non-justiciable in the sense that the court cannot entertain a challenge to a decision under section 17(1), however tainted by conventional public law illegality, improper purposes, bad faith, bias etc that decision may be.

Duty to provide accommodation

15.7   A local authority must comply with specific duties in relation to the provision of accommodation and placements. In particular, CA 1989 s20 provides that authorities 'shall' provide accommodation for any child in need in their area who 'appears to them to require accommodation' as a result of specified circumstances,[13] and for any child aged 16 or above whose welfare the authority 'considers is likely to be seriously prejudiced' if accommodation is not provided.[14] The Children Act 1989 does not provide the courts with a power to review the decision of a local authority in relation to the placement of a child. Judicial review, or a complaint to the Secretary of State, would therefore be the only remedy.[15]

15.8   The position is different in relation to the use of the authority's powers under CA 1989 s17. *R (G) v Barnet* LBC[16] confirmed that local authorities may use their powers under section 17 to provide accommodation. While judicial review is not available to enforce a section 17 duty,[17] a challenge may be brought against a decision of an authority as to what powers to use (or, more usually in this situation, what powers not to use) on conventional public law principles.[18]

15.9   The differences between the statutory provisions have led to a number of challenges as to which duty the local authority is actually discharging when it provides accommodation: section 17, section 20

---

13 CA 1989 s20(1)(a)–(c). The accommodation duty arises in respect of: any child in need within the authority's area who appears to them to require accommodation as a result of – (a) there being no person who has parental responsibility for him; (b) his being lost or having been abandoned; or (c) the person who has been caring for him being prevented (whether or not permanently, and for whatever reason) from providing him with suitable accommodation or care. The condition in sub-para (c) is interpreted by the courts in a broad, purposive way: see, eg, *R (S) v Sutton LBC* [2007] EWHC 1196 (an appeal to the Court of Appeal was on a different point: [2007] EWCA Civ 790, (2007) 10 CCLR 615), referred to with approval in *R (M) v Hammersmith and Fulham LBC* [2008] UKHL 14, [2008] 1 WLR 535); and *R (RO) v East Riding of Yorkshire Council and Secretary of State for Education* [2011] EWCA Civ 196.

14 CA 1989 s20(3).

15 See *R (G) v Barnet LBC* (above), per Lord Scott at [137].

16 [2003] UKHL 57, [2004] 2 AC 208.

17 See the discussion of *R (G) v Barnet LBC*, at paras 9.31–9.32 above.

18 See *R (G) v Barnet LBC* (above), per Lord Hope of Craighead at [91].

or some other duty.[19] In *R (M) v Hammersmith and Fulham LBC*,[20] the question was whether the claimant (who had never been in care) was accommodated under the local authority's section 20 powers (so as to trigger other duties) rather than s188, Housing Act 1996 (interim homelessness accommodation).[21] Giving the judgment of the court, Baroness Hale said:[22]

> I am entirely sympathetic to the proposition that where a local children's services authority provide or arrange accommodation for a child, and the circumstances are such that they should have taken action under section 20 of the 1989 Act, they cannot side-step the further obligations which result from that duty by recording or arguing that they were in fact acting under section 17 or some other legislation. The label which they choose to put upon what they have done cannot be the end of the matter. But in most of [the previous][23] cases that proposition was not controversial. The controversy was about whether the section 20 duty had arisen at all.

She went on:[24]

> It is one thing to hold that the actions of a local children's services authority should be categorised according to what they should have done rather than what they may have thought, whether at the time or in retrospect, that they were doing. It is another thing entirely to hold that the actions of a local housing authority should be categorised according to what the children's services authority should have done had the case been drawn to their attention at the time ...

Duties to children 'looked after' by an authority

15.10 Local authorities are under certain, specific, duties to children who are looked after by them. 'Looked after' means in their care or

---

19 See, eg, *Southwark LBC v D* [2007] 1 FLR 2181; *R (H) v Wandsworth LBC* [2007] 2 FLR 822; *R (S) v Sutton LBC* (2007) 10 CCLR 615; *R (L) v Nottinghamshire County Council* [2007] ACD 372; and *R (RO) v East Riding of Yorkshire Council and Secretary of State for Education* [2011] EWCA Civ 196 (a case concerning a conflict between section 20 and provisions within the Education Act 1996).

20 [2008] UKHL 14, [2008] 1 WLR 535.

21 As to the relevant provisions of the Housing Act 1996, see chapter 9 above.

22 [2008] UKHL 14, [2008] 1 WLR 535 at [42].

23 Baroness Hale referred in her judgment to *Southwark LBC v D* [2007] 1 FLR 2181; *R (H) v Wandsworth LBC* [2007] 2 FLR 822; *R (S) v Sutton LBC* (2007) 10 CCLR 615; and *R (L) v Nottinghamshire County Council* [2007] ACD 372.

24 [2008] UKHL 14, [2008] 1 WLR 535 at [44].

accommodated by them (for a period longer than 24 hours) in the exercise of any social services functions.[25]

15.11   Authorities must safeguard and promote the welfare of such children and provide such services for children cared for by their parents as appear reasonable.[26] Other duties imposed include those to accommodate and maintain children by, among other things, placing them with foster parents.[27]

15.12   There also are continuing duties owed to by local authorities to looked-after children.[28] Section 24 of CA 1989 includes children looked after by local authorities within the definition of 'persons qualifying for advice and assistance'. Accordingly:

- a person between the age of 16 and 21 who was being looked after when he became 16, where there is a special guardianship order in place (or where such an order was in force prior to his reaching 18) and who needs help; or
- a person who is under 21 who was, after turning 16 but while still a child, but is no longer, looked after, accommodated or fostered and who needs help,

must be advised and befriended by the authority as if he were being looked after by them.[29]

15.13   There is also a discretionary duty to provide financial assistance to persons qualifying for advice and assistance in seeking employment and in attending education or training.[30] In relation to full-time further education or higher education, the local authority must provide suitable accommodation during vacations periods or provide financial assistance to allow the person to secure such accommodation.[31]

---

25 CA 1989 s22(1) and (2). See also, *R (D) v Southwark LBC* [2007] EWCA Civ 182, [2007] 1 FCR 788 at [53], where it was held that a child is 'looked after' from the time that the duty under section 20(1) arose (see below). Parliament cannot have intended that a child would have to be looked after for 24 hours before either a placement or an arrangement could be made under section 23.

26 CA 1989 s22(3).

27 CA 1989 ss22A-22F.

28 A looked-after child may become an 'eligible child': see CA 1989 Sch 2 para 19B. Local authorities must assess the needs of an eligible child and prepare a pathway plan for him, which must be kept under review: CA 1989 Sch 2 para 19B(4) and (5). See also section 23E (pathway plans). Such plans should clearly state 'who does what, where and when': see *R (J) (by his litigation friend MW) v Caerphilly County Borough Council* [2005] EWHC 580 (Admin), [2005] 2 FLR 860, per Munby J at [45].

29 CA 1989 s24A(3).

30 CA 1989 s24B(1) and (2).

31 CA 1989 s24B(5).

15.14 Given the various duties that are owed to children, depending, among other things, on whether they are children in need, looked after children,[32] eligible children,[33] or relevant children,[34] disputes can arise as to what, if any, category a child falls within and so what, if any, duties may be owed. In *R (Berhe) v Hillingdon LBC*,[35] the authority provided social services assistance under CA 1989 s17 (including accommodation) to a child who was an unaccompanied asylum-seeker. On turning 18, the child requested assistance from the authority asserting that, as a person formerly 'looked after' by the authority, she now fell within the scope of assistance owed to a 'former relevant child', ie a formerly looked after 18- to 21-year-old.[36]

15.15 The authority refused such assistance on the ground that the claimant was not a former relevant child, having been provided not with accommodation under CA 1989 s20, but merely with services (including accommodation) under section 17. The claimant had therefore not been looked after and so was not now a former relevant child. The Administrative Court held that there no legitimate distinction could be drawn between providing housing by way of a service and accommodating a child, and that therefore the claimant had been looked after by the authority.

Duties to all children

15.16 Local authorities have a duty to provide some services where appropriate – and a power to provide others – to all children and their

---

32 CA 1989 ss22A–22F.

33 CA 1989 Sch 2 para 19B. An eligible child is a child who a child who (a) is aged 16 or 17; and (b) has been looked after by a local authority for a prescribed period, or shorter periods which amount in aggregate to a prescribed period, which began after he reached a prescribed age and ended after he reached the age of 16, or a child within a category prescribed as eligible by the Secretary of State (England) or the Welsh Ministers (Wales): Sch 2 para 19B(2)–(3).

34 CA 1989 s23A. A relevant child is a child who a child who (a) is not being looked after by any local authority; (b) was, before last ceasing to be looked after, an eligible child (see above, last footnote); and, (c) is aged 16 or 17: s23A(2).

35 [2003] EWHC 2075 Admin, [2004] 1 FLR 439. See also, *R (W) v Essex CC* [2003] EWHC 3175 (Admin).

36 CA 1989 s23C. This section defines a former relevant child as either (a) a person who has been a relevant child for the purposes of s23A (and would be one if he were under 18), and in relation to whom the authority from which the duties are being claimed was the last responsible authority; or (b) a person who was being looked after by the authority when he attained the age of 18, and immediately before ceasing to be looked after was an eligible child.

families, whether or not they are in need. They must, for example, provide family centres,[37] and may provide day care and/or supervised activities,[38] financial help,[39] and recreational facilities.[40] Certain services must be provided for children under the age of five, whether or not they are in need. An example is such day care as is appropriate for children who are not yet attending school.[41] This provision may also be extended to other children. Local authorities must also take reasonable steps to prevent neglect and abuse,[42] and to reduce the need for legal proceedings in respect of children in their area.[43]

Other duties

15.17   Local authorities also have functions and responsibilities, both within and outside the CA 1989, which may give rise to judicial review claims. Such functions include: making the enquiries they consider necessary to decide whether to take action to safeguard or promote a child's welfare,[44] convening child protection conferences,[45] maintaining local safeguarding children boards,[46] proactively preventing sexual exploitation[47] and arranging sufficient provision of children's centres to meet local need.[48]

---

37 CA 1989 Sch 2 para 9.
38 CA 1989 s18.
39 CA 1989 s17(6).
40 Local Government (Miscellaneous Provisions) Act 1976 s19(1).
41 CA 1989 s18.
42 CA 1989 Sch 2 para 4.
43 CA 1989 Sch 2 para 7.
44 CA 1989 s47.
45 See *Working Together to Safeguard Children: A guide to inter-agency working to safeguard and promote the welfare of children*, 21 March 2013 (HM Government), especially chapter 1. This is binding guidance issued by the Secretary of State under Local Authority Social Services Act 1970 s7. This guidance replaced that issued under the same title in March 2010, and came into force on 15 April 2013 (para 5). See also CA 1989 s47.
46 See *Working Together to Safeguard Children* (fn 45 above), at chapter 3. Local safeguarding children boards had to be established by 1 April 2006 under the CA 2004. The functions of the local safeguarding children board are set out in ss14 and 14A, CA 2004 and the Local Safeguarding Children Boards Regulations 2006 SI No 90.
47 See *Safeguarding Children and Young People from Sexual Exploitation* (HM Government, June 2009). This is binding guidance issued by the Secretary of State under Local Authority Social Services Act 1970 s7.
48 Childcare Act 2006 s5A (as amended by the Apprenticeships, Skills, Children and Learning Act 2009).

15.18   In *R (ET) v Islington LBC*,[49] a challenge to an assessment of the risk posed to three children by a sex offender, Cranston J applied an enhanced scrutiny approach to a CA 1989 case, on the basis that:[50]

> the consequences of the council falling into error is the possible sexual abuse of children and young people. The profundity of the impact, to use that phrase, is equivalent, indeed potentially greater, than in community care ... In my view, a notion of heightened review does not undermine the *Wednesbury* test. The court is simply saying that the public authority must exercise its discretion with a due appreciation of its responsibilities. In effect, given the context, the public authority must tread more carefully than usual. Heightened review calibrates *Wednesbury* unreasonableness to the matter at issue.

The Court of Appeal reversed the High Court's decision.[51] In respect of the passage cited above, Black LJ (with whom the rest of the Court agreed) said, at [48]:

> Cranston J held that 'the intensity of *Wednesbury* review is ... heightened under the Children Act 1989 in circumstances like the present, where the consequence of the council falling into error is the possible sexual abuse of children and young people' ... He approached his review ... from this perspective. A Respondent's Notice was filed by the local authority arguing that the judge should have taken a conventional *Wednesbury* approach. The time estimate for the appeal hearing was insufficient to permit argument on this point and we indicated that we would have to reconvene to deal with it if a determination of the issue was necessary for our decision. As it turns out, it is not. My own consideration of the case has been shaped by ordinary *Wednesbury* principles ... Our decision in this case does not therefore develop the law on this point, or indeed on any other point, turning as it does on its own facts.

Child protection conferences

15.19   The conduct of child protection conferences (formerly known as case conferences) has given rise to challenge by way of judicial review. In *R v Cornwall County Council ex p H*,[52] the local authority had a policy not to allow solicitors to attend child protection conferences except to read out a prepared statement. Parents who had attended the conference were not entitled to minutes of the meeting. H challenged the policy, both aspects of which were held to be unlawful. It was

49 [2012] EWHC 3228 (Admin).
50 At [26].
51 [2013] EWCA Civ 323
52 [2000] 1 FLR 236.

unlawful to have a blanket ban on the attendance of solicitors, and the guidance made it clear that parents and their legal representatives should be provided with minutes of the part of the conference that they had attended.

15.20   An 18-year-old autistic male failed, however, in his challenge to the procedure of a local authority panel under which he was not allowed to have legal representation or an independent note-taker. The court did not accept that this was unfair: the panel had a discretion and had acted reasonably by (a) giving the parents the option of an adjournment so all parties could seek legal advice; and (b) deciding there was no prejudice in relation to refusing an independent note-taker as an experienced note-taker was already present at the meeting.[53]

15.21   In *R v Norfolk County Council ex p M*,[54] the applicant sought to challenge the local authority's decision to follow the recommendation of a case conference and place his name on the child abuse register.[55] The applicant was a married man of good character against whom no charges had been brought following a police investigation into the allegation of abuse. He complained that he had enjoyed no opportunity to refute the allegations and that his employers had wrongly been informed. The Divisional Court held that the consequences of registration were sufficiently serious to impose a duty on the council to act fairly. Waite J said:[56]

> It has to be remembered ... that Parliament has entrusted virtual autonomy to local authorities in the discharge of their statutory duties of child care, and the powers of judicial intervention have to be made to fit into that framework. I have held that it is the duty of a case conference (or other agency of local government) exercising a discretion whether or not to enter the name of an alleged child abuser on the child abuse register to act fairly ... It is not the function of the courts – vigilant though they will always be to restrain an oppressive use of these registers – to substitute their own view as to how such a balance is to be resolved for that of the informed and specialist authorities who have been charged by statute with the duty of resolving it. If, therefore, it can be demonstrated in future cases that the particular procedure or range of inquiry followed by a local authority in the course of registering the name of an alleged abuser had represented a genuine attempt, reasonable in all the circumstances, to reconcile

---

53   *R (LP) v Barnet LBC* CO/670/00 (2000) 17 November, unreported.
54   [1989] QB 619, DC.
55   Child abuse registers no longer exist, but the case is still informative as to the approach of the courts where a child protection conference has made a recommendation.
56   [1989] QB 619 at 629–30.

the duty of child protection on the one hand and the duty of fairness to the alleged abuser on the other, it is unlikely that the courts will intervene through judicial review to strike the registration down.

15.22 In *R v Harrow LBC ex p D*,[57] a local authority decided to place the names of a mother and her children on the 'at risk' register, following the recommendation of a case conference. The mother had not been permitted to attend the case conference but had been able to submit written representations. She sought to challenge the decision by way of judicial review. The authority contended that judicial review would not lie in relation to a decision to place a name on the register.

15.23 The Court of Appeal rejected the submission of the local authority and held that if it could be shown that the decision was utterly unreasonable (which had not been shown in the instant case), judicial review would lie. The court emphasised, however, that recourse to judicial review should be rare and, furthermore, that in proceedings involving children, the welfare of that child was a paramount consideration over and above the interests of any individual who might have been prejudiced or any decision-maker which might be criticised. Butler-Sloss LJ said:[58]

> Unless there are exceptional features leading to a conclusion, such as in the Norfolk case, I for myself would hesitate long before encouraging a review of the way in which a particular case conference arrived at the recommendation required before the register entry is made ... It would also seem that recourse to judicial review is likely to be, and undoubtedly ought to be, rare. Local authorities have laid on them by Parliament the specific duty of protection of children in their area. ... Unlike other areas of judicial review, the considerations are not limited to the individual who may have been prejudiced and the tribunal or organisation being criticised. In this field, unusually, there is a third component of enormous importance: the welfare of the child who is the purpose of the entry on the register. In proceedings in which the child is subject, his or her welfare is paramount.

15.24 In *R v Hampshire CC ex p H*,[59] the court adopted a very similar line to that in *D*.[60] In *H*, however, the application for judicial review – which concerned the decision to place a child's name on the child protection register and the decision, following a recommendation of a case conference, to continue that registration – was granted on the basis that there was insufficient material to justify the registration.

---

57 [1990] Fam 133.
58 [1990] 1 FLR 79 at 85.
59 [1999] 2 FLR 359, CA.
60 [1990] Fam 133.

The court, however, reiterated the principle that recourse to judicial review should be rare in the field of child protection.

15 25   Moreover, Butler-Sloss LJ, giving the judgment of the Court, said:[61]

> There were adequate alternative remedies to judicial review available to the applicants. Those remedies were quicker, cheaper and more satisfactory. The appeal and complaints procedures in Hampshire were well able to correct procedural irregularities and to give consistent and informed advice on good practice in sharing and running case conferences and were far more suitable to do so than the court hearing a judicial application. The criticisms of the case conference, other than the lack of material upon which to reach a decision, taken at the highest and cumulatively, did not amount to matters in respect of which judicial review should be available. They were the subject of an appeal and that was the appropriate procedure to adopt.

15.26   These conclusions from *D* and *H* were applied in *R (A) v Enfield LBC*,[62] in which the court reiterated that judicial review challenges to child protection decisions should be rare, and that the claimants ought to have made use of the available complaints procedure rather than commence court proceedings.[63]

Compliance with guidance

15.27   Another potential area of challenge relates to breaches of statutory guidance (much of which in this area is binding). In *R (B) v Barnet LBC*,[64] the claimant applied for judicial review alleging, *inter alia*, that the local authority had failed to have regard to, and provide appropriate support under, *Safeguarding Children and Young People from Sexual Exploitation*.[65] The court held that the guidance required a proactive approach, whereas the approach of the authority had been entirely reactive, offering support only in response to specific incidents. Accordingly, the authority was in breach of its duties.[66]

---

61 [1999] 2 FLR 359 at 366C–E.
62 [2008] EWHC 1886 (Admin), [2008] 2 FLR 1945.
63 Per Blair J at [23]–[26], [29]–[32].
64 [2009] EWHC 2842 (Admin), (2009) 12 CCLR 679.
65 *Safeguarding Children and Young People from Sexual Exploitation* (HM Government, June 2009). This is binding guidance issued by the Secretary of State under Local Authority Social Services Act 1970 s7.
66 [2009] EWHC 2842 (Admin) at [41].

Reviews, complaints and appeals

Reviews of cases

15.28 The Secretary of State (in England) or the Welsh ministers (in Wales) may make regulations requiring the case of each child who is being looked after by a local authority to be reviewed in accordance with the provisions of regulations.[67]

15.29 The regulations[68] may make provision for a number of matters, including:[69]

- the manner in which each case is to be reviewed;
- the considerations to which the local authority are to have regard in reviewing each case;
- the time when each case is to be first reviewed and the frequency of subsequent reviews;
- the people whose views the authority must seek, before conducting any review (including the child, persons with parental responsibility and other persons whose views the authority consider relevant).

Complaints procedures

15.30 Various persons[70] may complain to the local authority, under CA 1989 s26, in relation to the authority's powers and duties to provide support for families and children under Part III[71] of that Act.

15.31 By CA 1989 s26(3) local authorities are obliged to establish a procedure for considering any representations, including complaints, made by the following persons:

- a child in need or a child being looked after by the local authority;
- a parent or other person with parental responsibility;
- any foster parent; or
- any other person as the authority consider has a sufficient interest in the child's welfare to warrant representations being considered by them concerning the discharge by them of any of their functions under CA 1989 Pt III.[72]

---

67 CA 1989 s26(1).
68 Arrangements for Placement of Children by Voluntary Organisations and Others (England) Regulations 2011 SI No 582 (Pt 5); Review of Children's Cases (Wales) Regulations 2007 SI No 307.
69 CA 1989 s26(2).
70 See paras 15.31–15.33 below.
71 And such of its functions under Parts IV and V as the Secretary of State may specify in regulations made under CA 1989 s26(3A).
72 Inserted by Adoption and Children Act 2002 s117.

15.32 Children Act 1989 s26(3B) specifies two additional categories of potential complainant:

- a person for whose needs provision is made by the Adoption Service[73] and any other person to whom arrangements for the provision for adoption support services extends; and
- any other person as the authority consider has sufficient interest in a child who has been or may be adopted to warrant his representations being considered.

15.33 This complaints procedure is clearly intended to deal with a wide range of issues that may be raised by a wide range of persons. Children other than those in need or those being looked after (or those for whom needs or support provision is being made by the Adoption Service), are not, however, specified as potential complainants.

15.34 The complaints procedure must have an independent element,[74] and the local authority must have due regard to the findings of those who have considered the representations and must notify the child, the person making the representations and other affected persons of their decision, of their reasons and of any action taken or to be taken.[75] The procedure to be followed is set out in the Children Act 1989 Representations Procedure (England) Regulations 2006[76] and the Children Act 1989 Representations Procedure (Wales) Regulations 2005.[77]

15.35 In addition to the section 26 complaints procedure, there are two further avenues of complaint:

- a complaint in relation to children's homes or voluntary organisations may be made within their own procedures;[78] and
- a complaint in relation to all matters not within the scope of the CA 1989 s26(3) may be made to the local authority under Local Authority Social Services Act 1970 s7B.

Default powers of the Secretary of State

15.36 Under Children Act 1989 s84, the Secretary of State may declare a local authority to be in default, where he or she is satisfied that they

---

73 Adoption and Children Act 2002 s3(1).
74 CA 1989 s26(4). The requirement for an independent element will be circumscribed in cases prescribed the appropriate national authority in regulations made under CA 1989 s26(4A).
75 CA 1989 s26(7).
76 SI No 1738.
77 SI No 3365.
78 Arrangements for Placement of Children by Voluntary Organisations and Others (England) Regulations 2011 SI No 582.

have, without reasonable cause, failed to comply with a duty under the CA 1989. The Secretary of State then has power to issue directions to compel the local authority to comply with the duty and may enforce these directions by a mandatory order.[79]

Appeals

15.37   A right of appeal lies to the county court against the making by a magistrates' court of any order under the CA 1989, or the Adoption and Children Act 2002, or the refusal to make such an order. This includes care and supervision orders (including an interim order).[80]

Judicial review and the appeal structure

Judicial review of Children Act 1989 duties

15.38   The CA 1989 has conferred wide discretionary powers on local authorities and social workers, and has thereby increased the possibilities for using judicial review in child cases, particularly in relation to authorities' duties under Part III of the Act (local authority support for children and their families). The other parts of the CA 1989 are less significant in the field of administrative law and are, consequently, not dealt with in this chapter.

15.39   The use of judicial review is, however, limited by the availability of the case review and complaints procedure under CA 1989 s26, and by the Secretary of State's default powers under section 84.[81] Each of these procedures will usually provide an alternative remedy. The wide discretion conferred on local authorities in performance of many of their duties under the Act often makes it difficult to bring a successful challenge by way of judicial review. There remains, obviously, the ability to challenge the vires of any subordinate legislation, and/or the failure of an authority to acknowledge that any duty is owed to a child.[82]

79   This power is similar to that conferred by Education Act 1996 s497 (as amended).
80   CA 1989 s94(1) as amended.
81   And by the reluctance of the courts to permit judicial review to become a common means of challenging decisions about children (see paras 15.24–15.26 above). See generally, paras 7.15–7.30.
82   An interesting example of the latter was *R (B) v Merton LBC* [2003] EWHC 1689 (Admin), in which the local authority refused to accept a duty to the claimant on the basis that they were not satisfied that he was a child at all, as he could not prove his age. The approach to age assessments, however, has

Children Act 1989 s26 as an alternative remedy

15.40 It has been held that the complaints procedure under s26, CA 1989 is an appropriate alternative remedy which ought to be exhausted before any application for judicial review is made. In *R v Kingston upon Thames RLBC ex p T,*[83] the Divisional Court refused permission to apply for judicial review of a local authority's decision regarding the placement of the applicant's daughter as a child in need, stating that the complaints procedure under section 26 offered an appropriate alternative remedy.

15.41 Ward J held that the section 26 procedure was quicker and cheaper than judicial review, no specialist knowledge was required and the members of the panel would consider the matter anew, exercising their own independent judgment of the facts on the merits, including any new facts placed before them. The panel was not confined to finding *Wednesbury* unreasonableness or that the decision was plainly wrong. There was little difference between the effectiveness of judicial review to bring about change, and the due regard to the recommendations of the panel that the Act and the regulations required the local authority to have. If the local authority failed to heed the panel's recommendations, judicial review could then be invoked. He continued:[84]

> By far the most compelling argument for first requiring these panel procedures to be enforced before intervening by way of judicial review is that such an order of priority would seem to me to fall within the broad legislative purpose of the Act. Parliament has quite clearly assigned certain functions in controlling the lives of our children to the local authorities. Parliament has most definitely denied the court power to intervene. That is quite clear from the whittling down of the inherent jurisdiction of wardship. It is quite clear from the provisions of section 37 of the Act, which gives the court no other power than to invite the local authority to intervene in a case where the court wishes there to be consideration of care or supervision. Part III is intended to operate in a new climate of partnership between the local authorities and the family. It is part of the philosophy of sitting down and trying to work things out together. It is better than adversarial contest in the courts. The door of the court is the last door that should be opened.

since been altered by the Supreme Court in *R (A) v Croydon LBC* [2009] UKSC 8, [2009] 1 WLR 2557 and now, where a dispute arises about a person's age, it must be determined as a matter of fact by the court rather than on pure review principles. For further discussion on the approach to age assessments, see chapter 19.

83 [1994] 1 FLR 798, DC. See also the cases referred to above, at paras 15.24–15.26.
84 [1994] 1 FLR 798 at 815.

15.42 This approach was reiterated in *R (S) v Hampshire CC*,[85] where permission was to apply for judicial review was refused as the Regulations under section 26 provided an alternative remedy by way of the complaints procedure, which was there to provide a speedy, informal and cheap way of resolving disputes.

15.43 In *R v Birmingham CC ex p A*,[86] Sir Stephen Brown held that judicial review was not the appropriate remedy for a complaint of unreasonable delay in placing a child in appropriate accommodation. This was not a case that sought to clarify the law, but rather a case that sought to find the local authority in breach of CA 1989 s20 in failing to act with reasonable diligence and expedition. The more appropriate remedy was the complaints procedure under section 26, which provided for a wide-ranging procedure to investigate cases where there was an allegation of culpable neglect on the part of the local authority.

15.44 The cases that have been decided concerning the compliance of complaints and review procedures with article 6 of the Convention have indicated, however, that judicial review provides an important procedural safeguard, given that internal procedures cannot, in their nature, comprise independent and impartial tribunals. Exceptional cases may exist where a person will not be obliged to use them before resorting to the Administrative Court.[87] Judicial review may, therefore, continue to have a relevance in Children Act 1989 proceedings, notwithstanding the availability of a complaints process.

Children Act 1989 s84 as an alternative remedy

15.45 In *R v Brent LBC ex p Sawyers*,[88] the Court of Appeal held that an alleged breach of an authority's duty under CA 1989 s23(8) – the duty, where an authority provides accommodation for a child it is looking after, to secure, so far as is reasonably practicable, that the accommodation is not unsuitable for the child's needs – was properly litigated by way of judicial review, notwithstanding the Secretary of State's default powers under CA 1989 s84. The court, overruling Owen J at first instance, held that these default powers did not provide an alternative remedy to deprive the applicant of the right to apply to the High Court.

85 [2009] EWHC 2537 (Admin).
86 [1997] 2 FLR 841, DC.
87 See *R (Alconbury Developments Ltd) v Secretary of State for the Environment, Transport and the Regions* [2001] UKHL 23, [2003] 2 AC 295.
88 [1994] 1 FLR 203, CA.

15.46   While the Court of Appeal in *Sawyers* did consider that the procedure under CA 1989 s26, where available, would provide an alternative
remedy, section 84, by contrast, did not confer either an express or
implied right of 'appeal' from a decision by a local authority by which
a person was aggrieved.

15.47   Peter Gibson LJ said:[89]

> In my judgment it is manifest from those provisions [sections 26(3)
> and 84] that Parliament intended that a person aggrieved by the way
> a local authority exercised its functions (including powers as well
> as duties) would have a remedy by making a representation to the
> authority and so setting in train the representations procedure. That
> remedy is available to a person ... as of right, and it is to be contrasted
> with the absence of a corresponding right under section 84.

15.48   Although relating to local authorities' social services functions and
the Secretary of State's default power under Local Authority Social
Services Act 1970 s7D, *R v Devon CC ex p Baker*[90] is another example
of a case in which the Court of Appeal held that a statutory default
power was not an adequate alternative remedy so as to preclude the
use of judicial review.

15.49   The Court of Appeal held that it was not clear whether or not the
default power was available because it was not clear whether the subject-matter of the claim – an alleged failure to consult properly prior
to the decision to close a residential home – was a social services
function. Given this, and that the essence of the complaint was a
matter of law in a developing field, it was particularly appropriate for
decision by the court.

15.50   This does not mean, however, that the existence of a default power
will always be disregarded by the court on the question of alternative
remedies, particularly in the current judicial climate of insistence that
alternative methods of dispute resolution be attempted, even where
those methods will be unlikely to resolve all the issues between the
parties.[91]

89 [1994] 1 FLR 203 at 212.
90 [1995] 1 All ER 73, CA.
91 See, eg *R (Cowl) v Plymouth CC* [2001] EWCA Civ 1935, [2002] 1 WLR 803;
    (2002) 5 CCLR 42; and *R (C) v Nottingham City Council* [2010] EWCA Civ 790,
    [2011] 1 FCR 127. In the *Nottingham City Council* case, the court reminded
    parties to litigation that judicial review was a remedy of last resort and should
    only be used where there is no question of the dispute being resolved outside
    litigation. In that case, although the local authority had offered to provide the
    assistance sought under the CA 1989 on a without prejudice basis as opposed
    to formally accepting any duties; judicial review, therefore, was academic and
    should not have been pursued.

CHAPTER 16

Judicial review and public funding

Structure

16.1   The Access to Justice Act 1999, Pt 1, created the Legal Services Commission (LSC), which – in relation to the administration of public funds for litigation – replaced the Legal Aid Board. On 1 April 2013, new provisions for of civil and criminal legal aid came into force under the Legal Aid, Sentencing and Punishment of Offenders Act (LASPOA) 2012. In particular, the LSC was renamed the Legal Aid Agency (LAA) and became an executive agency of the Ministry of Justice. In place of the old Funding Code, Regulations now govern whether a matter will qualify for legal aid and the applicable procedures.[1]

16.2   The administration of legal aid remains separated into two branches, both controlled by the LAA:

- civil legal aid, formerly known as the Community Legal Service, which is concerned with funding for civil actions; and
- criminal legal aid, formerly known as the Criminal Defence Service, which deals with criminal cases.

Civil legal aid

16.3   The essential features of the civil legal aid system are as follows:[2]

- public funding will only be available to approved contractors who meet certain, specified quality control standards;[3]

---

1   See Civil Legal Aid (Merits Criteria) Regulations 2013 SI No 104, Civil Legal Aid (Procedure) Regulations 2012 SI No 3098 and Criminal Legal Aid (General) Regulations 2013 SI No 9. The sets of (civil) regulations referred to above, replace the old Funding Code Pts 1 and 2 made under s8, Access to Justice Act 1999 and apply to all applications (save for cases that attract criminal legal aid) made on or after 1 April 2013. It should be noted that existing cases, ie cases where legal aid was granted before 1 April 2013 under the Access to Justice Act 1999 or any earlier Act, will continue to be governed by the provisions of the earlier provisions. Transitional provisions are contained within the Legal Aid, Sentencing and Punishment of Offenders Act 2012 (Consequential, Transitional and Saving Provisions) Regulations 2013 SI No 534 regs 6–13. This means that the Funding Code including the *Guidance* will continue to be relevant to currently funded cases for some time. See, generally, *LSC Manual* (Sweet & Maxwell), which contained all the relevant legislation, guidance and directions relating to LSC funding. See also Ling and Pugh, *LAG Legal aid handbook 2013/14* (LAG, 2013).

2   The details of legal aid funding is complex and beyond the scope of this chapter, which is intended only to provide an overview of the aspects that may affect judicial review. For a more detailed analysis, see the *Lord Chancellor's Guidance under section 4 of Legal Aid, Sentencing and Punishment of Offenders Act 2012* and the Ministry of Justice website (www.justice.gov.uk/).

3   LASPOA 2012 s3.

- the LAA – established by the Lord Chancellor under a power within LASPOA 2012 – is to commission and administer legal aid services in line with the relevant provisions of LASPOA 2012 and the policy and strategy set by ministers and the Ministry of Justice;[4]
- the LAA must fund any services referred to Pt 1 of Sch 1 to LASPOA 2012,[5] if the individual person qualifies for legal aid, or in cases in which the director of legal aid casework:[6]
  - has made an exceptional case determination,[7] and the individual qualifies for legal aid; or
  - has, in relation to an inquest concerning the death of a member of the person's family, the director has made a wider public interest determination,[8] and the individual qualifies for legal aid;[9]
- the Lord Chancellor has power to make an exceptional case determination that an individual qualifies for the services in relation to cases that would otherwise be excluded under Pt 1 of Sch 1 to LASPOA 2012; he may authorise the funding of services in specified circumstances in individual cases;[10]
- the allocation of civil legal aid automatically places a first statutory charge, equal to (or in some cases greater than) the amount spent on funding services, over any property recovered or preserved in the course of the proceedings,[11] although there are exceptions to this general rule and some property is excluded.[12] One such

---

4 See LASPOA 2012 s2, Hansard, HC Deb, 28 February 2013, c34WS, the Legal Aid Agency Framework Document (para 2.1) and the Legal Aid Agency Business Plan.

5 LASPOA 2012 s9.

6 See LASPOA 2012 s4.

7 LASPOA 2012 s10. An exceptional case determination is a determination that a failure to provide legal aid would breach the person's Convention rights or enforceable EU rights, or that it is appropriate to provide legal aid because of the risk of such a breach: LASPOA 2012 s10(3).

8 Ie a determination that the provision of advocacy services at the inquest would produce significant benefits for a class of person other than the individual or a member of his family: LASPOA 2012 s10(4)–(5).

9 See para 16.10 below. See also LASPOA 2012 s11.

10 LASPOA 2012 s10. See also the *Lord Chancellor's Guidance under section 4 of Legal Aid, Sentencing and Punishment of Offenders Act 2012*.

11 LASPOA 2012 s25 – this may include circumstances where a person recovers possession of a property as a result of the proceedings: *Parkes v Legal Aid Board* [1994] 2 FLR 850 confirmed on appeal [1997] 1 WLR 1547.

12 See LASPOA 2012 s25(3) and Civil Legal Aid (Statutory Charge) Regulations 2013 SI 2013 No 503, Pt 2, regs 5–6, 8–9.

exception arises where the director is satisfied that the proceedings had a wider public interest (eg test cases).[13]

Criminal legal aid

16.4   Similar provisions apply in relation to criminal legal aid (formerly the Criminal Defence Service). Services may only be provided by accredited bodies; initial advice and assistance must be available to any individual who has been arrested or who is held in custody if the director has determined that the individual qualifies for such advice and assistance,[14] and funding for representation in court is also available where the director determines an individual qualifies.[15] In principle, the individual may choose which representative he wishes to represent him, so long as that representative is able to provide criminal legal aid services.[16]

16.5   In relation to both civil and criminal legal aid, detailed provision relating to the administration of funding is contained in regulations,[17] and in the *Lord Chancellor's Guidance under section 4 of Legal Aid, Sentencing and Punishment of Offenders Act 2012*.[18]

Funding assessments and appeals

16.6   Where costs are subject to assessment by the court, the provisions of CPR Pt 47 apply. A person dissatisfied with the assessment may apply for permission to appeal.[19]

---

13 Civil Legal Aid (Statutory Charge) Regulations 2013 SI No 503 Pt 2 reg 9.
14 LASPOA 2012 s13 and Criminal Legal Aid (General) Regulations 2013 SI No 9 Pt 2.
15 Access to Justice Act 1999, LASPOA 2012 ss14, 16 and Sch 3 and Criminal Legal Aid (General) Regulations 2013 SI No 9 Pt 5.
16 LASPOA 2012 s27(4), and Criminal Legal Aid (Determinations by a Court and Choice of Representative) Regulations 2013 SI No 614 Pt 3.
17 Civil Legal Aid (Procedure) Regulations 2012 SI No 3098; Civil Legal Aid (Merits Criteria) Regulations 2013 SI No 104; Criminal Legal Aid (General) Regulations 2013 SI No 9.
18 The *Guidance* is reproduced on the Ministry of Justice website: www.justice. gov.uk/.
19 Civil Legal Aid (Costs) Regulations 2013 SI No 611 reg 18.

16.7   Where either civil or criminal legal aid is provided, the Lord Chancellor is obliged to pay any remuneration properly due.[20] Public funding is, however, subject to assessment by the area director,[21] the procedure for which varies depending on the nature of the action. A client who has a financial interest in his solicitor's costs has a right of review or appeal against remuneration decisions, at which he can make representations to a costs committee.[22]

16.8   Similarly, solicitors or counsel may appeal against the assessment of their costs.[23] In the first instance, such an appeal is by way of a request for a review to a funding review committee, which may vary or confirm the original assessment. Thereafter, if there is a point of principle or of general importance that needs to be considered, there is a right of appeal to a freshly constituted costs committee. A final right of appeal lies to the costs appeal committee. Thereafter challenge is by way of judicial review.[24]

16.9   It is also open to the LSC to challenge an award of costs made against them: *R (Gunn) v Secretary of State for the Home Department (recovery of costs).*[25] *Gunn* was applied in *LSC v F,*[26] where the court dismissed the LSC's appeal against a costs order on the basis that it would normally be just and equitable to award a successful non-funded party his costs to be recovered from public funds where a funded party could not meet such costs unless there were facts which rendered such a result unjust or inequitable.[27]

---

20 See the Civil Legal Aid (Remuneration) Regulations 2013 SI No 422 regs 6 and 7. See also Criminal Legal Aid (Remuneration) Regulations 2013 SI No 435.

21 Civil Legal Aid (General) Regulations 1989 SI No 339 reg.105.

22 Civil Legal Aid (General) Regulations 1989 SI No 339 reg 105A. See also *R (Wulfsohn) v LSC* [2002] EWCA Civ 250, [2002] CP Rep 34 where a litigant-in-person successfully appealed against the High Court's refusal to order the defendant to pay him his costs for research involved in a claim for judicial review against a decision of the LSC to refuse him funding.

23 Civil Legal Aid (General) Regulations 1989 SI No 339 reg 105.

24 As to which see paras 16.16–16.21 below.

25 [2001] EWCA Civ 891, [2001] 1 WLR 1634.

26 [2011] EWHC 899 (QB), [2011] 5 Costs LR 740.

27 A costs order cannot be made against the Lord Chancellor in relation to a first instance claim unless the non-funded party is the defendant, is an individual and would suffer hardship if a costs order were not made. The last two these requirements do not apply on appeal: CPR r47 and see the Costs Practice Direction para.21.

Applications, reviews and appeals

16.10 The Lord Chancellor must appoint a director of legal aid casework[28] to consider applications for funding and make the initial determination on whether funding should be granted, having regard to the Regulations and Guidance. As part of this process, the director must decide whether the individual 'qualifies for legal aid', taking into account both the financial resources of the individual and any criteria contained within regulations made by the Lord Chancellor.[29] In some circumstances, an authorised solicitor may grant funding under devolved powers. Where this is the case, the same appeal process arises against a decision to refuse funding. Provision is also made for emergency representation and emergency certificates, which may be granted subject to certain conditions.[30]

16.11 Where the director is satisfied that all relevant criteria and procedures have been complied with,[31] and that the applicant is financially eligible, he or she must issue a certificate to that effect,[32] unless the actual or likely costs of the case exceed a defined threshold, in which case he must refer the matter to the Special Cases Unit.[33] Where the

---

28 LASPOA 2012 s4. By s5(3), the functions conferred on the director may be exercised by a person authorised by the director or by such a person's employees.

29 See Civil Legal Aid (Merits Criteria) Regulations 2013 SI No 104. When setting the criteria, the Lord Chancellor must reflect the following factors (which for the most part reflect the provisions that were within the Funding Code) within the regulations: (a) the likely cost and benefit of providing the services; (b) the availability of resources to provide the services; (c) the appropriateness of applying those resources to provide the services, having regard to present and likely future demands for the provision of civil legal services; (d) the importance for the individual of the matter; (e) the nature and seriousness of the act, omission, circumstances or matter in relation to which the services are sought; (f)the availability to the individual of non-legal aid services and the likelihood of his being able to make use of such services; (g) if the matter relates to a dispute, the prospects of success; (h) the conduct of the individual in connection with services or an application for them; (i) the conduct of the individual in connection with any legal or other proceedings for resolving disputes about legal rights or duties; and (j) the public interest: LASPOA 2012 s11(3).

30 Civil Legal Aid (Procedure) Regulations 2012 SI No 3098 Pt 5.

31 The criteria and procedures are set out, respectively, in the Civil Legal Aid (Merits Criteria) Regulations 2013 SI No 104 and Civil Legal Aid (Procedure) Regulations 2012 SI No 3098 which should be read together with the Lord Chancellor's Guidance, especially at para 8.15.

32 Civil Legal Aid (Procedure) Regulations 2012 SI No 3098 reg 37.

33 Civil Legal Aid (Procedure) Regulations 2012 SI No 3098 Pt 6 and the Lord Chancellor's Guidance.

director considers that the applicant is not eligible, he or she must notify the applicant (and his solicitor) and provide a brief statement of his reasons.[34]

16.12   The director also has power to amend or withdraw a certificate;[35] the latter power may be exercised if the applicant no longer satisfies the criteria under which funding was granted, if his or her conduct justifies withdrawal, or if he or she is no longer eligible financially.[36]

16.13   Where an application is refused, or a certificate withdrawn or amended, the applicant may ask the director to review the decision.[37] The director must consider any representations made on the review and may decide to affirm or amend his earlier determination or substitute a new determination.

16.14   An applicant who is dissatisfied with the determination on review or with the determination of a special cases unit may ask for the determination to be referred to the adjudicator.[38] The adjudicator may:

- determine certain issues of fact, such as the prospects of success and the cost/benefit analysis;
- consider whether the determination under review was unlawful or unreasonable;
- confirm the determination on review; or
- refer the matter back to the decision-maker for a further review, the decision on which is final.[39]

Legal aid for public law claims[40]

16.15   Under the Civil Legal Aid (Merits Criteria) Regulations 2013, judicial review proceedings are defined as falling within public law claims along with habeas corpus proceedings and homelessness cases.[41]

---

34 Civil Legal Aid (Procedure) Regulations 2012 SI No 3098 reg 43.
35 Civil Legal Aid (Procedure) Regulations 2012 SI No 3098 regs 37 and 42.
36 Civil Legal Aid (Procedure) Regulations 2012 SI No 3098 reg 42(1). It would appear that it is not open to a director to place an embargo on funding, pending the outcome of enquiries into the applicant's continued eligibility – *R (Machi) v LSC* [2001] EWCA Civ 2010, [2002] 1 WLR 983.
37 Civil Legal Aid (Procedure) Regulations 2012 SI No 3098 reg 44.
38 Civil Legal Aid (Procedure) Regulations 2012 SI No 3098 reg 45.
39 Civil Legal Aid (Procedure) Regulations 2012 SI No 3098 regs 46–48.
40 The funding of judicial review claims, including standard limitations, is considered in more detail in paras 17.60–17.70.
41 Civil Legal Aid (Merits Criteria) Regulations 2013 SI No 104 reg 2.

There are two types of funding available: funding in relation to investigative help; and funding for full representation.

16.16   An application for civil legal aid in relation to investigative help (as distinct from assistance by way of representation) may be refused

- if the act under challenge does not appear to be amenable to judicial review;[42] or
- where there are administrative appeals or other procedures available, and such remedies should have been pursued prior to commencing judicial review proceedings.[43]

16.17   No distinction between the funding considerations is drawn on the basis of whether permission for judicial review has been granted.

16.18   An application for full representation funding may be refused if:

- judicial review is unavailable as a remedy for the act or decision subject to complaint; or
- there are administrative appeals or other procedures which should have been attempted prior to the consideration of proceedings.[44]

16.19   Legal aid will also be refused unless the proposed defendant has had a reasonable opportunity to respond to the challenge (in accordance with the pre-action protocol), save in circumstances where it would be impracticable to afford the proposed defendant such an opportunity, for example, in extremely urgent applications.[45]

16.20   Prospects of success and cost–benefit criteria are also applied to applications for funding of judicial review proceedings.[46] When considering prospects of success, the LAA are concerned with the prospects of obtaining the substantive remedy sought rather than the prospects of obtaining permission (although the latter is plainly relevant to the prospects of obtaining substantive relief, as the higher the risk of failure at an earlier stage, the higher the risk of overall failure).[47]

16.21   Funding for full representation will be refused if the prospects of success are poor or unclear. If prospects are borderline, funding may be refused unless there is:

---

42 Civil Legal Aid (Merits Criteria) Regulations 2013 SI No 104 reg 53.
43 Civil Legal Aid (Merits Criteria) Regulations 2013 SI No 104 reg 54.
44 Civil Legal Aid (Merits Criteria) Regulations 2013 SI No 104 reg 56.
45 Civil Legal Aid (Merits Criteria) Regulations 2013 SI No 104 regs 54 and 56
46 Civil Legal Aid (Merits Criteria) Regulations 2013 SI No 104 chapter 2.
47 Civil Legal Aid (Merits Criteria) Regulations 2013 SI No 104 reg 56.

- a significant wider public interest; or
- a significant human rights issues; or
- an overwhelming importance to the client.[48]

16.22 So far as cost–benefit is concerned, funding may be refused if the likely costs of proceedings are disproportionate to any likely benefit to be gained from bringing the proceedings.[49]

16.23 On 27 February 2013, the LSC announced that, from 1 April 2013, solicitors will no longer have delegated powers to grant themselves emergency funding in judicial review cases, save where the challenge falls within one of a very few categories of case, the most important of which relates to challenges under Pt 7 of the Housing Act 1996 – homelessness.[50] In all other cases, save where a specific delegation of the function has been granted to a provider by way of an authorisation[51] (which can only be exercised in relation to the cases and the circumstances specified in the authorisation),[52] providers must seek prior approval from the LAA before judicial review work is undertaken. The LAA has put into place operational provisions to deal with emergency funding applications.[53] Where a provider requires an emergency funding certificate in order to undertake work in less than 48 hours the LAA have set up two email addresses to which the application[54] should be sent:

- For immigration cases: emergency-immigrationapps@legalaid.gsi.gov.uk.
- For non-immigration cases: emergency-apps@legalaid.gsi.gov.uk.

48 Civil Legal Aid (Merits Criteria) Regulations 2013 SI No 104 reg 56.
49 Civil Legal Aid (Merits Criteria) Regulations 2013 SI No 104 reg 56.
50 LSC announcement, 27 February 2013; see also the Standard Civil Contract Specification 2013, section 5.3, in force from 1 April 2013. By section 5.3(a), the other categories in which devolved powers may still be used are: s21 National Assistance Act 1948 (as amended), s20 Children Act 1989 (as amended) or s47(5) National Health Service and Community Care Act 1990 (as amended). For new emergency applications that do not require a grant of legal aid immediately, form CLS APP 1 needs to be submitted by DX or post: see generally, Legal Aid Agency, *Application for emergency funding in Judicial review cases, Processes and procedures from 1 April 2013* (available at www.justice.gov.uk/downloads/legal-aid/funding-code/judicial-review-emergency-funding-process.pdf).
51 LASPOA 2012 ss5(5)–(7) and 6.
52 Standard Civil Contract Specification 2013 s5.3(a).
53 Legal Aid Agency, *Application for emergency funding in Judicial review cases, Processes and procedures from 1 April 2013* (available at www.justice.gov.uk/downloads/legal-aid/funding-code/judicial-review-emergency-funding-process.pdf).
54 Form CLS APP 6.

The email addresses are not, however, to be used in respect of emergency applications to the out of hours duty judge. In relation to immigration out of hours cases, the LAA will accept applications between 5pm and 8pm, Monday to Friday and 10am to 2pm on the weekend and Bank Holidays. The application should be sent to: asylum-out-of-hours@legalaid.gsi.gov.uk.[55]

Challenging funding decisions

16.24   Clearly, given the relatively comprehensive nature of the appeals and review system, the scope for judicial review of a decision by the LAA is restricted and, in any event, such a claim will normally only be permissible after rights of appeal and review have been exhausted. There remains, however, the possibility of challenging a refusal to award funding on public law grounds.[56]

16.25   Challenges to the legality or rationality of a decision of the LAA (or the decisions of Funding Review Committees on appeal) are not limited to decisions to refuse funding; judicial review may equally be sought of a decision to discharge a certificate before the proceedings have reached a conclusion, or on a matter of statutory interpretation.

16.26   In *R (Machi) v LSC*,[57] the LSC informed the claimant on the day before the hearing that his entitlement to funding was being reviewed and that, until a decision had been made, no further work could be undertaken under the certificate unless expressly approved by the LSC itself. The result was that the claimant was unrepresented at

---

55 Legal Aid Agency, *Application for emergency funding in Judicial review cases, Processes and procedures from 1 April 2013* (available at www.justice.gov.uk/downloads/legal-aid/funding-code/judicial-review-emergency-funding-process.pdf).

56 In *R (Bateman) v LSC* [2001] EWHC 797 (Admin), [2002] ACD 29, the court held that the LSC's decision to withdraw the claimants' funding certificates on the ground that the claimants had failed to disclose material facts was irrational because the facts that had not been disclosed would not have affected the claimants' eligibility for funding. The claimants' costs awards, however, were significantly reduced as they had pursued some 'hopeless', 'futile' and 'untenable' arguments. Errors of law, in this context, may include the giving of inadequate reasons, or an alleged failure to consider the effect of other statutory provisions (*R v Legal Aid Board ex p W (Children)* [2000] 1 WLR 2502, CA; and *Martin v LSC* [2007] EWHC 1786 (Admin)). See also the older case of *R v Legal Aid Board ex p Hughes* (1992) 24 HLR 698.

57 [2001] EWCA Civ 2010, [2002] 1 WLR 983.

the hearing. He applied for judicial review of the LSC's decision on the ground that they had acted unfairly or irrationally by effectively discontinuing his funding on the day before the hearing and, in any event, that they did not have power to withdraw funding pending a review of entitlement.[58] The court held that a funding certificate was valid until it was discharged and that there was no statutory power to embargo the use of the certificate pending review of eligibility. Accordingly, the claim was allowed.[59]

16.27   In *R (Toth) v LSC*,[60] Hooper J dismissed an argument that the cost–benefit analysis used when determining whether the claimant's funding certificate should be discharged was ultra vires.

16.28   Claims relating to the construction and/or legality of legislation may also involve arguments relating to human rights. In *R (Alliss) v LSC*,[61] the claimant successfully sought judicial review of the withdrawal of his funding on the ground, among other things, that this deprived him of effective access to a court and thus the right to a fair hearing for the purposes of HRA 1998 Sch 1, art 6(1).

---

58 The relevant legal power derived from the Civil Legal Aid (General) Regulations 1989 SI No 339, and the Legal Aid Act 1988.

59 As to statutory interpretation, see also *R v LSC ex p Burrows (t/a David Burrows (a firm))* [2001] EWCA Civ 205, [2001] 2 FLR 998, where the claimant sought to challenge the LSC's decision to limit the amount of costs payable to him (as a legal representative) on the basis that the word 'limitations' in Legal Aid Act 1988 s15(4) did not include financial limitations but extended only to limitations on the scope of assistance. See also *R (Pearson) v LSC* [2001] EWHC 1048 (Admin), which concerned the interpretation of Civil Legal Aid (General) Regulations 1989 SI No 339 reg 46(3) and was brought after a review by a funding review committee; *R (Patel) v Lord Chancellor* [2010] EWHC 2220 (Admin), [2011] ACD 5, which considered the threshold for illustrating a 'wider public interest' and held it was a high threshold because it required the benefits of other individuals other than the claimant to be substantial (see now LASPOA 2012 s10(4)–(6)); and *LSC v Loomba* [2012] EWHC 29 (QB), [2012] 1 WLR 2461, where the court considered three test cases considering the interpretation of, and interplay between, the Legal Aid Act 1988 s4(1)(b) and the Civil Legal Aid (General) Regulations 1989 SI No 339. In *Loomba*, the court held that the LSC was entitled to assess a final costs bill 'nil' and could recoup payments made on account.

60 [2002] EWHC 5 (Admin).

61 [2002] EWHC 2079 (Admin).

16.29   It should be noted, however, that litigants in civil proceedings that will determine their civil rights have no automatic Convention right to public funding.[62] In *X v United Kingdom*,[63] it was held that,[64]

> only in exceptional circumstances, namely where withholding of legal aid would make the assertion of a civil claim practically impossible, or where it would lead to an obvious unfairness of the proceedings, can ... article 6(1) of the Convention [be invoked].

16.30   In *Martin v LSC*,[65] the court made it clear that no obligation was to be derived from article 6 requiring the state to provide legal aid for every dispute concerning a civil right or for every case that could not be adequately presented without the provision of public funds.[66]

16.31   More recently, in *LSC v Loomba*,[67] the court considered whether art 1 of Prot 1 to the Convention – the right to peaceful enjoyment of possessions – was engaged in relation to payments made by the LSC on account to solicitors. The court held that it was not: payments on account were subject to the limitation that they were only paid on account of a final assessment of entitlement. The LSC was entitled to assess at 'nil' a final costs and to recoup the payments made on account.

---

62   *P, C and S v United Kingdom*, ECHR, 16 July 2002. See also *Airey v Ireland* (1979) 2 EHRR 305, ECHR.

63   (1984) 6 EHRR 136.

64   It should also be noted that, in applying the test laid down in *X v United Kingdom*, the LAA must act reasonably – *R (Jarrett) v LSC and others* [2001] EWHC 389 (Admin). See now the power of the director of legal aid casework to make an exceptional case determination (or a wider public benefit determination): LASPOA 2012 s10.

65   [2007] EWHC 1786 (Admin).

66   The challenge in *Martin* succeeded, however, on the basis that the LSC had provided inadequate reasons for its decision to withdraw funding.

67   [2012] EWHC 29 (QB), [2012] 1 WLR 2461.

Pre-application procedure

Introduction

17.1   Since the introduction of the CPR (and due as much to the philosophy that led to their introduction as to the provisions of the rules themselves), the courts have placed much greater emphasis on requiring litigants to follow procedures and take all possible alternative measures to resolve their dispute prior to having resort to legal proceedings.[1] Despite the very strict time limits involved,[2] this is no less true of judicial review claims than of any other type of civil action. Nor is it simply a matter of following the judicial review pre-action protocol. Although compliance with the protocol is plainly important, the court's requirements go much further, including that, at the very least, active consideration is given to attempting alternative dispute resolution,[3] including the use of any available alternative remedies,[4] before a claim is brought.[5]

17.2   Where proceedings are necessary, the court may decide to take a proactive stance in relation to the issues that it will permit to be raised (active case-management).[6] Alternatively, it may adjudicate on the issues and then penalise one or more of the parties in costs for raising those it considers to have been unreasonably litigated.[7]

17.3   Much, including the grant or refusal of permission, the availability of legal aid and the costs orders made at the end of proceedings, may ultimately depend on the attention that the parties, particularly the claimant, have paid to these matters before the commencement of proceedings. These issues do not, however, concern only the claimants' advisers. There is now a clear, and openly expressed,[8] judicial agenda that all parties must recognise and take account of the cost

1   See eg CPR r1.4(2)(e) and (f).
2   See paras 18.18–18.23 below.
3   CPR r1.4(2)(e) provides that the court's duty to manage cases includes 'encouraging the parties to use an alternative dispute resolution procedure if the court considers that appropriate and facilitating the use of such procedure'.
4   See paras 7.15–7.30.
5   The approach of the Upper Tribunal, in its public law jurisdiction, is discussed in chapter 19.
6   See eg CPR r1.4(2)(c) and r54.12(b). See also *R (Opoku) v Southwark College Principal* [2002] EWHC 2092 (Admin), [2003] 1 WLR 234 as to an attempt to raise grounds at the full hearing for which permission to apply had been refused.
7   See eg *R (Bateman) v Legal Services Commission* [2001] EWHC 797 (Admin), [2002] ACD 29.
8   See eg *Bateman* (above, note 7); *R (Cowl) v Plymouth CC* [2001] EWCA Civ 1935, [2002] 1 WLR 803; *Dunnett v Railtrack PLC* [2002] EWCA Civ 303, [2002] 1 WLR 2434.

of and time taken by judicial proceedings (especially in terms of the public money that is involved in every case – even if the claimant is not publicly funded, the defendant as a public body is likely to be; even if neither party is publicly funded, the court itself is funded by public taxation) and consider these matters in relation to what is likely to be achieved by litigation as compared with other, cheaper means of resolving disputes.

17.4 This, together with other requirements (such as, for the defendant, the requirement of a pleaded summary of the grounds of defence in the acknowledgement of service[9]) is likely to make it imperative that both parties have properly considered the strengths and weaknesses of their own case, and indeed what they hope to achieve by litigation (and what possible opportunities there may be for avoiding proceedings) at a far earlier stage than was formerly (or traditionally) the case.[10]

17.5 One, perhaps ironic, effect of this is likely to be that both claimants and defendants will be involved in the expenditure of not inconsiderable sums of money at a much earlier stage in a dispute, which costs are likely to be wholly irrecoverable if proceedings do not result. This may affect defendants disproportionately, given that it will be a dangerous, not to say reckless, response to first notification of a potential claim simply to deny the legitimacy of the claim and wait and see if proceedings develop. Defendants as well as claimants run the risk of adverse costs orders, even if they ultimately succeed in the proceedings where, for instance, the court does not consider that they have engaged sufficiently with the possibility of alternative dispute resolution at a sufficiently early stage.[11]

17.6 Moreover, in many cases, it will be essential for the claimant's adviser to obtain as much information as possible about the circumstances of the decision, and the facts about the claimant known to the

9 CPR r54.8(4)(a)(i).

10 And see the comments of the Court of Appeal concerning the costs consequences for defendants of late concessions and settlements in judicial review proceedings, eg: *R (Bahta) v Secretary of State for the Home Department* [2011] EWCA Civ 895; *M v Croydon LBC* [2012] EWCA Civ 595, [2012] 1 WLR 2607.

11 See eg *Dunnett v Railtrack PLC* [2002] EWCA Civ 303, [2002] 1 WLR 2434 and *Halsey v Milton Keynes General NSH Trust* [2004] EWCA Civ 576. This has, in fact, been a risk for defendants for many years. In *R v Kensington and Chelsea RLBC ex p Ghebregiogis* (1995) 27 HLR 602, QBD, where costs were awarded against a local authority defendant which had conceded the claim prior to the permission hearing, as their failure to consider the merits of the claim properly on receipt of the letter before action caused the necessity for proceedings to be issued.

decision-maker when the decision was taken. This will often involve requesting to see the information held about the claimant in the decision-maker's files.[12]

17.7　Equally, it can be difficult to gauge the correct balance to strike between seeking to resolve the dispute in ways that do not involve resort to the judicial review court and seeking to follow the requirements of the pre-action protocol on the one hand, and acting promptly so as not to fall foul of the time limits on the other.

17.8　This chapter explores these issues.

Alternative dispute resolution

17.9　In spite of the necessity to act promptly to challenge a public law decision, and the greater need to do so where third party rights may be affected by any challenge,[13] nevertheless judicial review may be refused if the court considers that some form of alternative dispute resolution ought to have been attempted before proceedings were commenced, and would have been a satisfactory alternative remedy.

17.10　In R (Cowl) v Plymouth CC,[14] the Court of Appeal (Lord Woolf CJ) upheld the dismissal of a judicial review application concerning the closure of two residential homes, where the defendant authority had offered to treat the application as a complaint under the applicable statutory complaints procedure, to convene a panel with an independent chair to consider the complaint as soon as reasonably practicable and, while the conclusions of the panel would not be binding, to give them adequate weight. The offer had been contained in an open letter sent by the defendant to the claimants prior to the permission application having been dealt with.[15]

17.11　The claimants rejected the offer, on the basis that the complaints procedure was not a true alternative remedy in that it would not resolve all the issues that could be dealt with on judicial review, in particular the issues of law. Although permission was granted, the substantive claim was dismissed and the claimants appealed.

17.12　The Court of Appeal considered that the offer of the complaints procedure was 'very sensible' and could and should have formed the basis for negotiations, rather than being rejected.[16] The court stated

---

12　See 'Disclosure' below; paras 17.22–17.26.
13　See para 18.30 below.
14　[2001] EWCA Civ 1935, [2002] 1 WLR 803.
15　Cowl, per Lord Woolf CJ at [7]–[10].
16　Cowl, per Lord Woolf CJ at [11].

that both parties had been wrong to believe that the claimants were entitled to proceed with their judicial review claim unless either the parties agreed otherwise or the offer of a complaints procedure constituted an alternative remedy which would fulfil all the functions of judicial review. This was too narrow an approach. Under the CPR, parties do not have a right to the resolution of their respective contentions by way of judicial review absent an entirely equivalent alternative remedy. If the alternative procedure can resolve a significant part of the issues, the court should not permit judicial review proceedings to proceed, except for good reason. If a legal issue subsequently calls for resolution by the court, it can be examined at that stage and the court may be considerably assisted by the findings made in the course of the alternative procedure.[17]

17.13   The court went further. Lord Woolf CJ said:[18]

> ... What followed was due to the unfortunate culture in litigation of this nature of over-judicialising the processes which are involved. ... Without the need for the vast costs which must have been incurred in this case already being incurred, the parties should have been able to come to a sensible conclusion as to how to dispose of the issues which divided them. If they could not do this without help, then an independent mediator should have been recruited to assist. That would have been a far cheaper course to adopt. Today, sufficient should be known about ADR to make the failure to adopt it, in particular when public money is involved, indefensible.

17.14   Accordingly:[19]

> ... the courts should scrutinise extremely carefully applications for judicial review in the case of applications of the class with which this appeal is concerned. The courts should then make appropriate use of their ample powers under the CPR to ensure that the parties try to resolve the dispute with the minimum involvement of the courts. The legal aid authorities should co-operate in support of this approach.

> To achieve this objective the court may have to hold, on its own initiative, an *inter partes* hearing at which the parties can explain what steps they have taken to resolve the dispute without the involvement of the courts. In particular the parties should be asked why a complaints procedure or some other form of ADR has not been used or adapted to resolve or reduce the issues which are in dispute. If litigation is necessary the courts should deter the parties from adopting an unnecessarily confrontational approach to the litigation.

---

17 *Cowl*, per Lord Woolf CJ at [14].
18 *Cowl*, per Lord Woolf CJ at [25].
19 *Cowl*, per Lord Woolf CJ at [2]–[3].

17.15 It is a little difficult to know how far-reaching these last comments are intended to be, as *Cowl* contains no indication of what Lord Woolf meant by 'applications of the class' with which *Cowl* was concerned. It seems unlikely that he was referring solely to cases involving the closure of residential homes (ie the specific subject-matter of *Cowl* itself). If, on the other hand, he was talking about any applications that could reasonably and sensibly be dealt with by means other than litigation, then there can be little quarrel with the – on the face of it – somewhat extreme suggestion that the courts should ensure that their involvement is minimal.

17.16 The funding authorities (at least in a number of areas) do now apply a requirement that alternative means of resolving a dispute must generally be attempted before recourse is had to the courts, refusing funding for judicial review cases for this reason, even potentially in cases where there is no available alternative course of action which would necessarily amount to an alternative remedy.[20]

17.17 In *Dunnett v Railtrack PLC*,[21] the Court of Appeal adopted the same approach by reference, in part, to CPR r1.4(2)(e), obliging the court to manage cases actively, including 'encouraging the parties to use an alternative dispute resolution procedure if the court considers that appropriate and facilitating the use of such procedure'.

17.18 In that case, the court refused to make any order for costs in favour of the respondent, even though it had successfully resisted the appeal, because the respondent had rebuffed an advance from the appellant to consider ADR before expending costs on the appeal. Brooke LJ stated that it was to be hoped that any publicity given to this part of the court's judgment would draw the attention of lawyers to their duties to further the overriding objective in the way that is set out in CPR Pt 1 and to the possibility that, if they turn down out of hand the chance of alternative dispute resolution when suggested by the court, as had happened on this occasion, they may have to face uncomfortable costs consequences.[22]

17.19 The only safe conclusion to draw from these cases is that ADR is firmly on the agenda in judicial review cases, and cannot be ignored. The courts' role, however, is not to require parties to engage in ADR,

---

20 See paras 17.61–17.67 below and see *Funding Code* (April 2010) paras 7.2.3 and 7.3.3, and especially *Part C Funding Code: Guidance*, Release 08 (April 2010) para 16.5.4, where specific reference to *Cowl* is made and confirmation given of the funding authorities' support for that approach. The code, however, has since been replaced: see para 17.60 below.

21 [2002] EWCA Civ 303, [2002] 1 WLR 2434.

22 See also, eg, *Halsey v Milton Keynes General NHS Trust* [2004] EWCA Civ 576.

for example by way of court order, but rather to encourage parties to do so.[23] It will not always be appropriate or possible to engage in an ADR process (not least where there is a fundamental dispute on a point of law on which the defendant cannot compromise) but the parties must be in a position to demonstrate both to funding authorities and to the courts the consideration that has been given to the possibility of resolving the dispute without court proceedings and the reasons why this has not been successful or not even attempted. In cases where ADR was not attempted and there is an assertion by one party that it should have been when it comes to the position on costs, the court is unlikely to take the failure into account where the chance of ADR succeeding was no more than fanciful.[24]

Alternative remedies

17.20   That alternative remedies must generally be used in preference to judicial review has long been the position – judicial review is often referred to as a remedy of last resort.[25] It is therefore unsurprising that the Court of Appeal considered this issue as an integral part of its reasoning in *Cowl* (above). A full discussion of alternative remedies, their use and the potential consequences of failure to use them, appears elsewhere in this book.[26] Nevertheless, the availability of any such remedy, even if not wholly satisfactory from the claimant's point of view, must form part of the consideration of the possible alternative means of resolving the dispute.

17.21   This is, conceptually, different from the question of whether judicial review or private law proceedings are appropriate. Different principles apply, and the court's reaction has tended to be different.[27] That issue is considered elsewhere in this book.[28]

---

23 *Halsey v Milton Keynes General NHS Trust* [2004] EWCA Civ 576.

24 *R (A) v East Sussex County Council* [2005] EWHC 85 (Admin), (2005) 8 CCLR 228. See also *R (Rodriguez-Bannister) v Somerset Partnership NHS and Social Care Trust* [2003] EWHC 2184 (Admin), (2004) 7 CCLR 385.

25 See the statements to this effect in numerous cases, including *R v Secretary of State for the Home Department ex p Swati* [1986] 1 WLR 477; *R v Chief Constable of Merseyside Police ex p Calveley* [1989] AC 1228, HL, and the cases referred to at paras 7.15–7.30.

26 See paras 7.15–7.30 above.

27 See eg *R (Heather) v Leonard Cheshire Foundation* [2002] EWCA Civ 366, [2002] 2 All ER 936; *R (Clark-Darby) v Highbury Magistrates' Court* [2001] EWHC 959 (Admin), [2002] RVR 35; *Trustees of the Dennis Rye Pension Fund v Sheffield City Council* [1998] 1 WLR 840

28 See paras 3.29–3.39 above.

Pre-action disclosure

17.22   Claimants can now generally obtain information about themselves, held by public bodies (as data controllers) under the DPA 1998 s7. A specific right relating to information held by public bodies can also be found in the FOIA 2000 s1.[29]

17.23   By DPA 1998 s7 a person is entitled to be informed whether any personal data about him is held by a data controller and to have that information communicated to him in an intelligible form (ie he can have copies). Information can be withheld if its disclosure would involve disclosing personal data about a third party who has not consented to the release of that information about him.[30] The data controller can refuse to provide copies if to do so would involve disproportionate effort[31] and is not obliged to comply with any request where information has been reasonably requested from the person seeking the information and such information has not been forthcoming.[32] The data controller is entitled to charge a fee not exceeding a prescribed maximum, for the communication of the information.[33]

17.24   By FOIA 2000 s1(1) any person making a request for information to a public authority is entitled to be informed in writing as to whether the authority holds the information requested and, if it is held, to have that information communicated to him. If the information is communicated, the obligation to inform the person in writing whether it is held is treated as complied with.[34] A public authority is not obliged to provide the information where it reasonably requires further information from the person making the request, has asked for the information and has not been provided with it.[35] Information can be withheld if the cost of complying with a request would exceed a prescribed appropriate limit[36] or the request is vexatious or a repeat of a previous request and a reasonable period of time has not passed since the request.[37] The public authority is entitled to charge a fee,

29   See generally, on this topic, chapter 14.
30   DPA 1998 s7(4).
31   DPA 1998 s8(2).
32   DPA 1998 s7(3).
33   DPA 1998 s7(2).
34   FOIA 2000 s1(5).
35   FOIA 2000 s1(3).
36   FOIA 2000 s12.
37   FOIA 2000 s14.

which it must notify to an applicant in writing, not exceeding a prescribed amount.[38]

17.25 These rights can and often should be exercised by claimants prior to the commencement of proceedings. It is noteworthy that the standard form letter before claim annexed to the pre-action protocol provides for a request for information, while providing that the protocol itself confers no obligation on public bodies to provide information additional to their pre-existing obligations.[39] In many cases, it may be necessary to have sight of this information in order properly to formulate the grounds of challenge to be included in the pre-claim letter.

17.26 The practical difficulty is likely to be the length of time it can take actually to receive the information requested, especially given the strictness of the judicial review time limits, the obligation to consider alternatives to litigation, and the duty of full and frank disclosure.[40] It will normally be sensible for advisers to request all relevant information as early as possible and, where possible, prior to sending the letter before claim. Where time is pressing, however, the letter before claim can include the request for information.

Pre-action protocol

17.27 The judicial review pre-action protocol has been in force since 4 March 2002 and is to be read with CPR Pts 8 and 54. In substance, it imposes a requirement in most cases that the claimant should send a detailed letter before claim to the defendant and give the defendant time to respond before proceedings are issued. Fourteen days is usually sufficient time to respond. If the defendant does not consider that time to be sufficient, it should send an interim reply and propose a reasonable extension.

Contents of the letter before claim

17.28 The purpose of the letter before claim is expressed to be to identify the issues in dispute and establish whether litigation can be avoided. A *pro forma* letter is annexed to the protocol itself.[41] In essence,

---

38 FOIA 2000 s9.
39 See para 17.31 below.
40 See paras 18.115–18.127 below.
41 Protocol, Annex A (see appendix A, p616 below).

the matters with which the letter must deal are no more extensive than those that would normally be covered in a letter before action, namely:

- a clear summary of the facts on which the claim is based;
- the date and details of the decision or act or omission under challenge;
- the reason that decision is said to be wrong;
- the action that the defendant is expected to take, including the remedy sought (and the timescale for the taking of such action);
- the details of any information sought (including a more detailed explanation of the decision under challenge);
- the claimant's details and those of his or her legal advisers;
- the address for reply and service of court documents;
- the details of any interested parties known to the claimant;
- the defendant's reference details and/or the identity of those dealing with the matter in dispute;[42]
- the proposed reply date.[43]

The defendant's response

17.29   A standard format letter of response is also appended to the protocol.[44] Defendants should normally respond within 14 days and a failure to do so will be taken into account by the court in the absence of good reasons.[45] Where it is not possible to respond within this time limit, an interim reply and request for a reasonable extension

---

42 Section 3 of Annex A to the Protocol states that where the claim concerns an immigration, asylum or nationality case (dependent upon the nature of the case) public bodies have requested that certain references are used to ensure a prompt response, namely, Home Office reference number, the Port reference, the Asylum and Immigration Tribunal reference, the National Asylum Support Service reference or, if unavailable, the full name, nationality and date of birth of the proposed claimant. Further, if a claimant is challenging a decision by the Legal Services Commission, the certificate number should be recorded on the letter before claim as a reference.

43 It should be noted that s2 of Annex A to the Protocol records certain addresses and methods that must be used for service of the letter before claim to ensure a prompt response. The public bodies listed are the UK Border Agency, the Legal Services Commission and any department or body for which the Treasury Solicitor acts. It also notes that where the claim concerns a local authority, the letter must be sent to the address on the decision letter/notification and the legal department.

44 Protocol, Annex B (see appendix A, p622 below).

45 Protocol para 13 and note 5, referring to CPR Pre-Action Protocol Practice Direction paras 2–3.

of time should be sent, giving reasons for the need for an extension and, where necessary, additional information requested. The claimant will not be bound to grant the extension, particularly given the time limits for applying for judicial review, but if the court considers that the claimant has brought proceedings prematurely (ie in this instance because the extension ought to have been granted) it may impose sanctions.[46]

17.30 If the claim is being conceded in full, the response should say so 'in clear and unambiguous terms'.[47] If the claim is not being conceded at all, or only in part, the response should set this out clearly and:

- where appropriate, contain a new decision clearly identifying which aspects of the claim are, and which are not, conceded, or give a clear timescale within which a new decision will be issued;
- give a more detailed explanation of the original decision, if appropriate;
- address any points of dispute or explain why they cannot be addressed;
- enclose any relevant documents requested by the claimant or explain why they are not enclosed;
- where relevant, state whether or not any application for interim relief will be opposed.[48]

17.31 As to the provision of information or documentation requested by the claimant, the protocol states that it does not impose any greater obligation upon public bodies to disclose documents or give reasons for decisions than that already provided for in statute or at common law. Where, however, the court considers that the body ought to have provided a relevant document and/or information, it may impose sanctions, especially where the failure amounts to a breach of such statutory or common law obligations.[49]

17.32 The response should be sent to all interested parties identified by the claimant, and give details of any other parties the defendant considers to have an interest.[50]

---

46 Protocol para 14.
47 Protocol para 15. See also, eg *R (M) v Croydon LBC* [2012] EWCA Civ 595, where a claim is going to be conceded, that fact should be communicated before proceedings are issued.
48 Protocol para 16.
49 Protocol para 6.
50 Protocol para 17.

Applying the protocol

17.33   The protocol describes itself as a 'code of good practice' which 'contains the steps which parties should generally follow before making a claim for judicial review'.[51] In reality, as noted above, it is far more than that – many of its provisions, while stating that they do not impose obligations as such, warn of sanctions if the court considers that the parties should have behaved differently in applying those provisions.[52] Worthy of note is the warning that the judge may refuse to hear the case where alternative procedures have not been used, though all the circumstances, including the nature of the alternative remedy, will be taken into account.[53] Claimants are strongly advised to seek appropriate legal advice.[54]

17.34   The protocol is expressed not to be appropriate in two classes of case.[55] First is where the defendant does not have the legal power to alter the decision under challenge, such as a tribunal that, having exercised its powers, no longer enjoys any jurisdiction in relation to the case which was before it (the protocol cites the immigration appeal authorities as an example of this, but most tribunals will fall into the same category).

17.35   Secondly, the protocol will not be appropriate in urgent cases and/or where emergency interim relief is sought, such as where a person is to be removed from the UK, or where a homeless applicant has been refused – or is about to lose – temporary accommodation. Even in urgent cases, however, it is good practice for the claimant to fax a copy of the claim form to the defendant prior to issue of the proceedings.[56]

17.36   In other cases, however, it is left to claimants to 'satisfy themselves' whether or not they should follow the protocol, 'depending on the circumstances of the case'.[57] Where the court considers that the protocol ought to have been used, it will take account of compliance

---

51   Protocol para 5.
52   See Protocol, eg paras 3.1, 6, 7, 13, 14.
53   Protocol para 3. See also *R (Wilkinson) v Chief Constable of West Yorkshire* [2002] EWHC 2353 (Admin), where it was held that the court at the substantive hearing could not decline jurisdiction on the ground of an unused alternative remedy (where the permission judge had considered the point arguable), but that the issue would be relevant to relief.
54   Protocol para 4.
55   Protocol para 6.
56   See Protocol para 7 and Form N463, the 'urgency' form. See also paras 18.95–18.102 below.
57   Pre-action Protocol para 7.

or non-compliance in making case management directions and/or when making costs orders. This will apply both to claimants who do not send a letter before claim and defendants who do not respond.[58] It should be noted, in addition, that the Legal Aid Agency expects applicants for legal aid for judicial review claims to comply with the protocol.[59]

17.37 Accordingly, wherever it is even conceivable that use of the protocol would be considered appropriate by the court, it would seem sensible to follow the procedure it sets out, particularly given that that procedure involves nothing more than the sending of a letter before claim or, for defendants, a response to that letter. If strict compliance is not possible, moreover, it is still preferable for claimants to comply as closely as possible (for example by giving the defendant a shorter time to respond to the letter before claim, where 14 days is not available), rather than to send no letter at all.

The protocol and time limits

17.38 The protocol makes it clear that compliance with its terms will not of itself affect the application of the time limits for judicial review[60] (ie that claims must be made promptly and in any event within three months of the grounds for challenge first arising and that undue delay may lead to a refusal of permission or of any remedy). The introductory paragraph specifically states that the protocol 'does not affect the time limit specified by' the rules. It is also stated that while the court has a discretion under CPR r3.1(2)(a) to extend time to permit a late claim to be brought, this will only be used in 'exceptional circumstances' and that 'compliance with the protocol alone is unlikely to be sufficient to persuade the court to allow a late claim', though it is doubtful that 'exceptional circumstances' is in fact the correct test.[61]

---

58 Pre-action Protocol. See also the comments of Pill LJ concerning costs orders in *R (Bahta) v Secretary of State for the Home Department* [2011] EWCA Civ 895, at para 21.62 below.

59 See the Legal Aid (Merits Criteria) Regulations 2013 SI No 104 regs 54(b) and 56(2): a letter before claim giving a reasonable time for a response must be send in all cases save where the individual shows that it would be impracticable.

60 Senior Courts Act 1981 s31(6) and CPR r54.5. See also paras 18.18–18.69 below.

61 Protocol note 1. The reference to 'exceptional circumstances' is not found in CPR r3.1(2)(a) itself, nor in r3.9 or r3.10, which also confer power on the court to relieve a party from a sanction for failure to comply with a rule. Under RSC Ord 53 r4(1), the test was whether the court considered there to be 'good reason' to extend time.

17.39   Likewise, as noted above, the fact that the time limits are unaffected by the protocol is reflected in the statement that a defendant's request for an extension of time to serve a response may not be agreed by the claimant.[62]

17.40   It is difficult to know where this leaves claimants' advisers. In particular, this is likely to arise where a client only seeks legal advice for the first time well after the decision was made, so that there may be only a few days remaining before the claim would go outside the three-month long-stop period for commencing proceedings. Accordingly, using the protocol procedure and allowing 14 days for a response to the letter before claim would take the commencement of proceedings beyond the relevant time limits.

17.41   Lateness of this sort would not seem to bring the case within the urgency exception to the use of the protocol in that it would appear to be properly classified as delay rather than urgency: the need for permission or relief is not urgent, there is simply very little time left before the expiry of the time for bringing the claim. Indeed, the protocol makes it clear that it cannot be used as a means of extending time and thereby avoiding the application of the normal time limits, and warns that if those time limits are not observed, time will only be extended in exceptional cases.

17.42   On the other hand, the rules, the courts and the protocol itself insist that the parties must not commence proceedings prematurely or without exploring alternative methods of resolving the dispute, on pain of sanctions in costs or in the refusal of permission or relief or even funding.

17.43   In most cases, the following course would seem to be appropriate, and difficult for the courts to criticise. If there is any time left before the expiry of three months since the decision under challenge was made, a letter before claim in the form appended to the pre-action protocol should be sent to the defendant giving a time for a response shortened to meet the urgency of the case (and to reflect the need to act promptly, so far as it is possible to do so)[63] and that will in any event expire prior to the expiry of the three-month time limit. Proceedings should be issued within the three-month period in order to protect the claimant's position (though this will not protect the claimant from the possible consequences of having delayed, it will at least not be necessary to seek a formal extension of time beyond the three-month back-stop).

---

62 Protocol para 14.
63 Even if this means allowing only a few days or even hours for a response.

17.44   The defendant should be informed that proceedings are being issued for this reason but that the claimant will seek a stay of those proceedings from the court,[64] in order that the protocol procedure can be worked through and it can be established whether the proceedings need to be fully (or at all) contested.

17.45   In fact, there is no reason why a request for an extension of time by a defendant cannot be dealt with on a similar basis in appropriate cases: rather than simply refuse an extension, it may be more sensible to agree to it on the basis that proceedings will be issued but a stay sought for the period of the extension. The question of which party should bear the costs of issuing, in the event that the claim is ultimately conceded, can be agreed or resolved by the court.

17.46   In many ways, the pre-action protocol simply reflects pre-existing best practice in the manner in which judicial review claims are prepared. The court has, for many years, made plain its disapproval of claimants who seek permission to apply for judicial review without first serving a proper letter before action on the defendant. More than 20 years ago, in *R v Horsham District Council ex p Wenman*,[65] Brooke J, describing the following propositions as 'elementary', held that judicial review proceedings should not be embarked upon before the decision-maker has received a complaint and been given an opportunity to say whether or not that complaint is accepted and, if not, to give its reasons. Moreover, judicial review proceedings are wholly inappropriate as the forum for the resolution of issues of disputed fact, and all material matters, including the existence of an alternative, statutory remedy, must be placed before the judge invited to grant permission. Wasted costs orders may be made against legal representatives who fail to comply with these elementary propositions.

17.47   The same difficulties as those suggested above, particularly in relation to time limits, have therefore arisen for a considerable time and the pre-action protocol only exacerbates them in the sense that

---

64 By CPR r1.4(1), the court is under a duty to further the overriding objective by actively managing cases. CPR r1.4(2)(e) and (f) provide that active case management includes: encouraging the parties to use alternative dispute resolution if the court considers it appropriate and facilitating the use of such procedure; and helping the parties to settle the whole or part of the case. Thus while CPR r26.4 does not apply (application for a stay for the purpose of ADR on the filing of allocation questionnaires), the court has ample power under its case management functions to grant a stay for the purposes of ADR. Applications for a stay should generally comply with PD 24 para 3.1(a).

65 (1992) 24 HLR 669, QBD, and [1994] 4 All ER 681, QBD (not an alternative report of the same decision but a report of a subsequent decision in the same case).

the sanctions imposed retrospectively for what the court considers to have been an inappropriate exercise of judgment are potentially more far-reaching. While it is perhaps disappointing that the protocol has not provided any solutions to these difficulties, it is unlikely that the court will penalise parties who have acted sensibly and reasonably in all the circumstances.

Time limits and other letters

17.48   Sometimes before a decision is reached, a decision-maker will indicate his or her current view of the applicant's case, and give the applicant a chance to make comments on that view, in time to influence the decision. This is usual, for example, in immigration, and some homelessness, cases, where the decision-maker will usually send a 'minded to refuse' or a 'minded to find' letter, briefly setting out the reasons why the application as it stands is not accepted.

17.49   This is another occasion on which carefully worded representations are important, not only because such representations may change the decision-maker's view. It may be that the decision-maker's approach, as set out in its own letter, can be shown to be legally defective, so that even if that approach is persisted in, the groundwork for a challenge has been laid.

Where delay has occurred

17.50   Where it is thought that the applicant may have been guilty of some delay or, after the decision has been taken, more material is obtained that an applicant wishes to put before the decision-maker, it should be remembered that a person is always entitled to ask the decision-maker to reconsider his decision in the light of the new evidence or even just further representations. Any refusal to reconsider may become challengeable in the same way as a reconsideration that results in another refusal. Where a later decision is under challenge, it may be possible to include in that challenge the original decision, even though the applicant's delay might otherwise have led to the refusal of leave or relief. Accordingly, advisers should generally challenge all the decisions complained of in relation to the application, and not merely the latest in time.

17.51   The courts do look critically at the decisions that are challenged and the extent to which they reflect the reality of the situation, so that the course suggested in the previous paragraph will not save a claimant from a finding of delay if the court concludes that the real decision under challenge remained the original rather than the reviewed decision. Nonetheless it is always likely to be helpful if a reconsideration can be obtained; indeed, seeking a reconsideration, possibly on the basis of new material or new representations, is the most basic form of attempted ADR available in judicial review proceedings.

Drafting the letter before claim

17.52   The letter before claim is an important document, not only in that it is likely to be the first explicit statement of the errors that the decision-maker is alleged to have made, but also because the response it elicits from the defendant may amplify and further explain the reasons already given for the decision. This may help the claimant and his advisers to understand better the approach and procedure that the decision-maker adopted.

17.53   Moreover, any failure by the claimant, without good reason, to include an issue that is later included in the claim itself may lead to unnecessary costs arguments, particularly if the issue proves to be important or decisive, and the defendant can establish that the inclusion of that issue in the letter before claim would have led it to adopt a different approach to the litigation. Accordingly, letters before claim should generally be fully argued, setting out all the claimant's main contentions. This will include any representations that the claimant may have wished to have made to a decision-maker but was not afforded the opportunity to do so (which will provide the defendant with an opportunity to consider any such representations). The latter was discussed in *R (C) v Chief Constable of Greater Manchester*,[66] where Toulson LJ said:

> When considering how such disputes are handled, it is also right to bear in mind the pre-action protocol for judicial review applications. There may be cases [where a defendant], in good faith, does not think it necessary to afford an opportunity to make representations, but the [claimant] is aggrieved by the lack of opportunity given to him of doing so. In such circumstances one would expect the pre-action letter to set out the representations which the person would have wished to make, and, unless the [defendant] considers that they do not merit any consideration at all, one would expect ... at that stage [a defendant] to give consideration to them. All this is part of the modern process for dealing with public law complaints in a way which is just and does not involve unnecessary expense. In other words, I would hope that courts are not going to be burdened with judicial review applications

66 [2011] EWCA Civ 175, [2011] 2 FLR 383.

based on a failure of an opportunity to make representations, without the complainant first setting out the concerns and relevant considerations in correspondence ...

Responding to the letter before claim

17.54 As stated above, the defendant receiving a letter before claim ignores it, or pays it only cursory attention, at his own risk, and possibly at his peril.[67] The formal letter before claim may not be the first intimation of a possible claim, as correspondence often precedes such a letter, and so the defendant may have had some prior opportunity to investigate matters and reach a view on both the merits of the claim and the appropriate way of dealing with it.

17.55 The defendant's response should be as full as possible and should, even if not raised by the claimant, draw attention to any issues that the defendant may wish to raise in the summary grounds of defence, should proceedings be issued, including such matters as delay, the availabilities of alternative remedies etc. The response should also propose any possible methods aside from litigation of resolving or narrowing the issues between the parties (again, whether or not mentioned by the claimant) that would be acceptable to the defendant.

17.56 The defendant may quite properly also suggest that, even if any of the defendant's proposals are not acceptable to the claimant, the claimant should make her or his own proposals and the issue of proceedings should be held back for a period of time, while discussions about alternative means of resolving the dispute are explored.

Protective costs orders

17.57 This issue is dealt with at chapter 18 below.[68] Consideration of whether an application for a protective costs order (PCO) may properly be made, however, will generally be necessary prior to the issue of proceedings. Indeed, if an application is contemplated, the defendant should be alerted to this as early as possible. A reference to such an application is not out of place in the letter before claim.[69]

---

67 As to possible cost consequences see, eg, *R (Bahta) v Secretary of State for the Home Department* [2011] EWCA Civ 895, [2011] CP Rep 43.

68 Paras 18.171–18.184 below.

69 *R (Campaign for Nuclear Disarmament) v The Prime Minister (Costs)* [2002] EWHC 2777 (Admin); (2002) *Times* 27 December, per Maurice Kay J at [7].

Costs-only proceedings

17.58 CPR r44.12A provides for an unusual procedure whereby a party to a dispute that has been settled on all issues apart from that of costs (which settlement has been confirmed in writing), and where no proceedings have yet been commenced, may start proceedings in accordance with CPR Pt 8.[70]

17.59 The court must dismiss the claim, however, if it is opposed by the other party to the dispute.[71] Accordingly, it would seem that the procedure may only be invoked where all parties desire the court to resolve the costs position. It must be unlikely that the Legal Aid Agency would grant legal aid for such a claim.

Funding

Applications for legal aid

17.60 The funding criteria for judicial review proceedings are contained in chapter 2 of the Civil Legal Aid (Merits Criteria) Regulations 2013[72] and paragraphs 7.34–7.44 of the Guidance.[73] The criteria for both investigative representation and full representation are different from those applicable to other types of civil claim; the standard criteria for determinations for legal representation must be met[74] but public law claims also attract further criteria.

70 CPR r44.12A(1)–(2).
71 CPR r44.12A(4)(b).
72 SI No 104. See also the criteria for claims against public authorities ie claims involving the abuse of position or powers or breach of Convention rights at regs 57–59. For cases issued prior to 1 April 2013, the criteria are contained in s7 of the *Funding Code* (April 2010), and s16, *Part C Funding Code: Guidance* (Release 08, April 2010).
73 *Lord Chancellor's Guidance under section 4 of Legal Aid, Sentencing and Punishment of Offenders Act 2012.*
74 The standard criteria are: (a) the individual does not have access to other potential sources of funding (other than a conditional fee agreement) from which it would be reasonable to fund the case; (b) the case is unsuitable for a conditional fee agreement; (c) there is no other person, including a person who might benefit from the proceedings, who can reasonably be expected to bring the proceedings; (d) the individual has exhausted all reasonable alternatives to bringing proceedings including any complaints system, ombudsman scheme or other form of alternative dispute resolution; (e) there is a need for representation in all the circumstances of the case including (i) the nature and complexity of the issues; (ii) the existence of other proceedings; and (iii) the interests of other parties to the proceedings; and (f) the proceedings are not likely to be allocated to the small claims track: Civil Legal Aid (Merits Criteria) Regulations 2013 SI No 104 reg 39.

Investigative representation

17.61   As to investigative representation, in addition to the standard criteria, further specific criteria apply (but the minimum damages rule[75] is disapplied).[76] The further criteria are

- the prospects of success of the case are unclear and substantial investigative work is required before those prospects can be determined;[77]
- the director has reasonable grounds for believing that, once the investigative work to be carried out under investigative representation is completed, the case will satisfy the criteria for full representation and, in particular, will meet the cost benefit criteria in regulation 42 and the prospects of success criterion in regulation 43;[78]
- the act, omission or other matter complained of in the proposed proceedings appears to be susceptible to public law challenge;[79]
- the individual has exhausted all administrative appeals and other alternative procedures that are available to challenge the act, omission or other matter before bringing a public law claim;[80]
- the individual has:
  - notified the proposed defendant of the individual's potential challenge and given a reasonable time for the proposed defendant to respond; or
  - shown that doing so would be impracticable.[81]

17.62   Failure to satisfy any of these further criteria will provide a basis for the refusal of investigative representation, although it will not be refused on the basis that the decision is not judicially reviewable if there is an arguable case that the decision is susceptible to challenge.[82]

---

75   For the minimum damages rule, see Civil Legal Aid (Merits Criteria) Regulations 2013 SI No 104 reg 40(1)(c) and (2).

76   Civil Legal Aid (Merits Criteria) Regulations 2013 SI No 104 reg 55.

77   Civil Legal Aid (Merits Criteria) Regulations 2013 SI No 104 reg 40(1)(a).

78   Civil Legal Aid (Merits Criteria) Regulations 2013 SI No 104 reg 40(1)(b).

79   Civil Legal Aid (Merits Criteria) Regulations 2013 SI No 104 reg 53(a) applied by reg 54 (a).

80   Civil Legal Aid (Merits Criteria) Regulations 2013 SI No 104 reg 53(b) applied by reg 54 (a).

81   Civil Legal Aid (Merits Criteria) Regulations 2013 SI No 104 reg 54(b).

82   *Lord Chancellor's Guidance under section 4 of Legal Aid, Sentencing and Punishment of Offenders Act 2012* para 7.36.

17.63   If an alternative remedy or other procedure is, in principle, available, it is for the legal representative completing the application form to explain why it has not been followed in the particular case. Generally, where the matter can be challenged in an alternative tribunal or court, judicial review will not be deemed the most appropriate remedy. It is recognised, however, that there may be exceptional reasons as to why judicial review should be pursued in the circumstances of an individual case.[83] It will not be enough that judicial review is considered the more convenient remedy but it will be relevant to funding if the speed of alternative remedy will prevent an individual from obtaining the remedy he needs.[84]

17.64   As for the requirement to notify a proposed defendant of the potential challenge, the *Guidance* sets out two situations in which it may prove impracticable to comply with this criterion. These are: (a) where there is urgency so that the pre-action protocol does not have to be followed, and (b) where any delay would 'create a significant risk of prejudice to the applicant's prospects of a successful claim'.[85]

Full representation

17.65   The criteria for full representation are as follows:[86]

- the act, omission or other matter complained of in the proposed proceedings appears to be susceptible to public law challenge;[87]
- the individual has exhausted all administrative appeals and other alternative procedures that are available to challenge the act, omission or other matter before bringing a public law claim;[88]
- the director is satisfied that:
  - the individual has sent a letter before claim to the proposed defendant (except where this is impracticable), and where such a letter has been sent, the proposed defendant has been given a reasonable time to respond;

---

83 *Lord Chancellor's Guidance under section 4 of Legal Aid, Sentencing and Punishment of Offenders Act 2012* para 7.36(b).

84 *Lord Chancellor's Guidance under section 4 of Legal Aid, Sentencing and Punishment of Offenders Act 2012* para 7.37(i). See generally the entirety of para 7.37.

85 *Lord Chancellor's Guidance under section 4 of Legal Aid, Sentencing and Punishment of Offenders Act 2012* para 7.41(i) and (ii).

86 Civil Legal Aid (Merits Criteria) Regulations 2013 SI No 104 reg 56.

87 Civil Legal Aid (Merits Criteria) Regulations 2013 SI No 104 reg 53(a) applied by reg 56(1)(b).

88 Civil Legal Aid (Merits Criteria) Regulations 2013 SI No 104 reg 53(b) applied by reg 56(1)(b).

- the proportionality test is met;[89] and
- the director is satisfied that the prospects of successfully obtaining the substantive order sought in the proceedings are:
  - very good, good or moderate; or
  - borderline, and:
    (i) the case is of significant wider public interest;
    (ii) the case is one with overwhelming importance to the individual; or
    (iii) the substance of the case relates to a breach of Convention rights.[90]

17.66 Funding for full representation may be refused if the individual has not sent a letter before claim and given the proposed defendant a reasonable opportunity to respond. It may also be refused if the proportionality test is not met.[91] The proportionality test will be met if the director is satisfied that the likely benefits of the claim justify the likely costs.[92] In relation to the likely costs, generally regard will be had to CPR r44.3(5), ie whether the likely costs are reasonable when considering the sums in issue, the value of any non-monetary remedy and other factors, for example the public importance of the issues in the case.[93] In judicial review claims, where it is unlikely that the remedy sought will involve damages, the test will be satisfied if the reasonable private individual test is met.[94] The reasonable private individual test will be met where a reasonable privately paying client would bring or continue the proceedings in the same circumstances and with the same prospects of success.[95]

17.67 Regard is also had to the prospects of success although the cost–benefit considerations are disapplied.[96] The prospects of success are defined as the prospects of obtaining a successful outcome,[97] which is an objective test as to how likely the case would be to succeed at final hearing.[98] Funding will be refused where prospects are unclear[99] or

---

89 Civil Legal Aid (Merits Criteria) Regulations 2013 SI No 104 reg 56(2).
90 Civil Legal Aid (Merits Criteria) Regulations 2013 SI No 104 reg 56(3).
91 Civil Legal Aid (Merits Criteria) Regulations 2013 SI No 104 reg 56.
92 Civil Legal Aid (Merits Criteria) Regulations 2013 SI No 104 reg.8.
93 *Lord Chancellor's Guidance under section 4 of Legal Aid, Sentencing and Punishment of Offenders Act 2012* para 4.2.7.
94 *Lord Chancellor's Guidance* para 4.2.8.
95 Civil Legal Aid (Merits Criteria) Regulations 2013 SI No 104 reg 7.
96 Civil Legal Aid (Merits Criteria) Regulations 2013 SI No 104 reg 56(1)(a) and (3).
97 Civil Legal Aid (Merits Criteria) Regulations 2013 SI No 104 reg 5.
98 *Lord Chancellor's Guidance* para 4.1.1.
99 Investigative representation may be available where prospects are unclear.

poor, or where they are borderline and there is no significant wider public interest or overwhelming importance to the client or significant human rights issues raised. [100]

Certificate limitations

17.68 Where the director makes a determination that funding is available he must issue a certificate recording the determination.[101] Such a determination may be subject to limitations on the work to be carried out.[102] The *Guidance* provides for three types of limitation that are expected to be the typical limitations placed upon certificates. The three limitations are: (a) investigative limitations, (b) limitations for negotiations, and (c) proceedings limitations.[103]

17.69 In relation to judicial review proceedings it may be that a certificate is limited to compliance with the pre-action protocol (in cases that are not urgent). This limitation would seemingly fall under a negotiation limitation.[104]

Emergency funding

17.70 On 27 February 2013, the Legal Services Commission announced that, from 1 April 2013, solicitors will no longer have delegated powers to grant themselves emergency funding in judicial review cases, save where the challenge falls within one of a very few categories of case, the most important of which relates to challenges under Pt 7 of the Housing Act 1996 – homelessness.[105] In all other cases, save where a specific delegation of the function has been granted to a provider by way of an authorisation[106] (which can only be exercised in relation to the cases and the circumstances specified in the

---

100 Civil Legal Aid (Merits Criteria) Regulations 2013 SI No 104 reg 56(3).
101 Civil Legal Aid (Procedure) Regulations 2012 SI No 3098 reg 37.
102 Civil Legal Aid (Procedure) Regulations 2012 SI No 3098 reg 37(2)(g).
103 *Lord Chancellor's Guidance under section 4 of Legal Aid, Sentencing and Punishment of Offenders Act 2012* para 6.17.
104 *Lord Chancellor's Guidance* para 6.17(b).
105 Legal Services Commission announcement, 27 February 2013; see also the Standard Civil Contract Specification 2013 s5.3, in force from 1 April 2013. By se5.3(a), the other categories in which devolved powers may still be used are: National Assistance Act 1948 s21 (as amended), Children Act 1989 s20 (as amended) or National Health Service and Community Care Act 1990 s47(5) (as amended).
106 LASPOA 2012 ss5(5)–(7) and 6.

authorisation),[107] providers must seek prior approval from the LAA before judicial review work is undertaken. The LAA has put into place operational provisions to deal with emergency funding applications.[108] Where a provider requires an emergency funding certificate in order to undertake work in less than 48 hours the LAA have set up two email addresses to which the application[109] should be sent:

- For immigration cases: emergency-immigrationapps@legalaid. gsi.gov.uk.
- For non-immigration cases: emergency-apps@legalaid.gsi.gov.uk.

The email addresses are not, however, to be used in respect of emergency applications to the out of hours duty judge. In relation to immigration out of hours cases, the LAA will accept applications between 5pm and 8pm, Monday to Friday and 10am to 2pm on the weekend and Bank Holidays. The application should be sent to: asylum-out-of-hours@legalaid.gsi.gov.uk.[110]

---

107 Standard Civil Contract Specification 2013 s5.3(a).
108 Legal Aid Agency, *Application for emergency funding in Judicial review cases, Processes and procedures from 1 April 2013* (available at www.justice.gov. uk/downloads/legal-aid/funding-code/judicial-review-emergency-funding-process.pdf).
109 Form CLS APP 6.
110 Legal Aid Agency, *Application for emergency funding in Judicial review cases, Processes and procedures from 1 April 2013* (available at www.justice.gov. uk/downloads/legal-aid/funding-code/judicial-review-emergency-funding-process.pdf).

CHAPTER 18

The permission application

continued

The procedural regime

18.1 An application for judicial review cannot be made unless permission of the High Court has been obtained in accordance with the rules of the court.[1] Permission to apply for judicial review is made to a High Court judge, usually one of the Queen's Bench Division who has been assigned to hear matters listed in the Administrative Court List (formerly the 'Crown Office list').

18.2 Applications for judicial review are governed by the CPR Pts 8 and 54 together with the Pt 54 Practice Directions, and the Senior Courts Act (SCA) 1981 s31. Part 54 deals with, among other things, the claim form to be used for applications, the requirement to notify other parties that an application is to be made and provisions relating to the permission hearing itself, including early case management.

Requirement for permission

18.3 By CPR r54.4, the court's permission to proceed is required in a claim for judicial review, whether or not the claim has been commenced under the Part 54 procedure.

When to use the CPR Part 54 procedure

18.4 The question of whether the subject matter of a case is suitable to be litigated in judicial review proceedings (eg whether the claim involves private or public law rights; whether the decision-maker is susceptible to judicial review) is considered elsewhere.[2] There is also, however, a procedural aspect to the issue of whether a claim may, or indeed must, be brought by way of judicial review, which is considered here.

18.5 In procedural terms, the CPR Pt 54 procedure must be used where the claimant is seeking a quashing order, a mandatory order, a prohibiting order or an injunction under SCA 1981 s30 (ie to restrain a person from acting in an office in which he is not entitled to act).[3]

18.6 A claimant seeking a declaration or injunction in combination with a quashing, mandatory and/or prohibiting order must also use the judicial review procedure; where the only relief claimed is a declaration and/or injunction, the procedure may be used but is

1 SCA 1981 s31(3).
2 See above, chapters 2 and 3.
3 CPR r54.2, and see generally chapter 5.

not mandatory.[4] The court has power to grant a declaration and/or injunction where it considers that it would be just and convenient to do so having regard to the nature of the matters in respect of which relief could be granted (by a quashing, mandatory or prohibiting order), the nature of the persons/bodies against whom relief is sought and all the circumstances of the case.[5]

18.7　　A judicial review claim may include a claim for damages, but the procedure may not be used if damages are all that is claimed.[6] Moreover, a claim for damages will only be possible if the claimant already enjoys a right to damages in private law or, now, under the Human Rights Act (HRA) 1998:[7] the judicial review procedure itself creates no free-standing right to damages.[8]

Transfer to and from the Administrative Court

18.8　　CPR r54.20 confers power on the court to transfer proceedings out of the Administrative Court. The rule itself is in unlimited terms – that the court may order a claim brought under Part 54 to continue as if it had not been commenced under that Part, ie as an ordinary claim under CPR Pt 7 or Pt 8, and, where it does so, may give directions about the future management of the claim.

18.9　　This is much broader than the equivalent power contained in the old rules,[9] under which the court could only order that a judicial review application continue as an ordinary action where the relief claimed was a declaration, injunction or damages. Accordingly, the restrictive construction that the courts gave to this former power may no longer be wholly applicable, although the principle that at least some viable private law claim must already be discernible in the proceedings as drafted would seem to remain relevant.[10]

18.10　　In addition to the power referred to above, the provisions of the CPR,[11] concerning transferring cases, among other things, into and out of specialist lists, are also expressly applied to the Administrative

---

4　CPR r54.3(1), and see generally chapter 5.
5　SCA 1981 s31(2).
6　CPR r54.3(2), and see generally chapter 5.
7　HRA 1998 s8.
8　SCA 1981 s31(4)(b), and see generally chapter 5 above.
9　RSC Ord 53 r9(5).
10　See *R v East Berkshire Health Authority ex p Walsh* [1985] QB 152, CA, per Sir John Donaldson at p166. For a fuller discussion of this issue, see chapter 3 above at paras 3.13–3.23 and chapter 5 at paras 5.46–5.49.
11　CPR r30.5.

Court.[12] The effect of this is not entirely clear. CPR r30.5(2) provides simply that the High Court may 'order proceedings to be transferred to or from a specialist list'. On a broad construction, this could permit the court to transfer a claim commenced as an ordinary civil action into the Administrative Court. A narrow construction, however, would only entitle the court to transfer in what was in effect already a judicial review application that for some reason was not commenced in the Administrative Court.

18.11   In non-judicial review cases, the courts – when considering whether a case should be transferred – have looked at factors such as the complexity of the issues in the case, the value of any financial claim and where the balance of convenience and fairness lies.[13]

18.12   In judicial review cases, an indication of the probable answer may be found in the combination of CPR rr30.5(3), 54.4 and Practice Direction (PD) 54A para 14.2.

- The first of these provides that an application to transfer proceedings to or from a specialist list must be made to a judge dealing with claims in that list.
- CPR r54.4 states that permission to proceed is required in a claim for judicial review whether started under Part 54 or transferred to the Administrative Court.
- Paragraph 14.2 of PD 54A states that in deciding whether a claim is suitable for transfer to the Administrative Court, the court will consider whether it raises issues of public law to which Part 54 should apply.

18.13   It would seem, then, that the broader construction referred to above is that intended by the CPR. This construction also accords with the statements about the flexibility of the CPR, in the context of transfer, made in the cases referred to at paras 3.7–3.68 above.

18.14   In addition to consideration of the issue referred to in PD 54A, the court will take account of whether a transfer would circumvent the procedural safeguards for defendants which are implicit in the Part 54 procedure, to the prejudice of the defendant (especially delay), particularly bearing in mind that the use of the Part 54 procedure is mandatory where a quashing, mandatory and/or prohibition order are sought.[14] As stated above, it is also made explicit by CPR r54.4

12 CPR r54.20, which applies the provisions of CPR Part 30.
13 See: *Brynley Collins v Raymond J Drumgold* [2008] EWHC 584 (TCC), [2008] TCLR 5; and *Neath Port Talbot CBC v Currie* [2008] EWHC 1508 (TCC), [2008] CP Rep 39.
14 CPR r54.2.

that a transfer of proceedings to the Administrative Court cannot be effected in such a way as would enable the claimant to avoid the permission stage.

18.15   For these reasons, if a significant amount of redrafting would be necessary, the court may be cautious about transferring a case into the Administrative Court. This was certainly the general approach adopted by the court in relation to the power under RSC Ord 53 r9(5) (power to permit certain judicial review applications to continue as if commenced by writ).[15]

18.16   The court is likely to be sympathetic, however, to an application to transfer into the Administrative Court where, for example, the question of whether judicial review proceedings were appropriate is unclear,[16] the ordinary proceedings have been commenced promptly (in public law terms),[17] and the issues are already clearly defined in the claim form. In *R (Heather) v Leonard Cheshire Foundation*,[18] Lord Woolf CJ emphasised that the courts do not have an appetite, under the new rules, to embark on the kinds of dispute about forum, which took up so much judicial time under the old procedural regime:[19]

> ... there was ... reflected in the decision of the court below ... an idea that if LCF [Leonard Cheshire Foundation] was not performing a public function, proceedings by way of judicial review were wrong. This is an echo of the old demarcation disputes as to when judicial review was or was not appropriate under Order 53. Part 54 CPR is intended to avoid any such disputes which are wholly unproductive ...

> We wish to make clear that the CPR provides a framework which is sufficiently flexible to enable all the issues between the parties to be determined ... In view of a possibility of a misunderstanding as to the scope of judicial review we draw attention to this and the powers of transfer under Part 54.[20]

18.17   It therefore appears likely that claimants should no longer be vulnerable to the kind of procedural dispute regarding the appropriateness of the procedure adopted, which occupied so much of the courts' time in the 1980s and 1990s, so long as they have behaved reasonably. In such cases, where there is genuine difficulty as to the correct procedure, strike-out applications based on the use of the wrong procedure will not be viewed sympathetically by the courts,

---

15 See paras 3.31–3.39 above.
16 See the discussion of public and private law at paras 3.7–3.68.
17 See SCA 1981 s31(6) and CPR r54.5.
18 [2002] EWCA Civ 366, [2002] 2 All ER 936, (2002) 5 CCLR 317.
19 At [38]–[39].
20 See also the discussion at chapter 3 above.

but instead the power to transfer in and out of the Administrative Court will be used to ensure that valid claims are able to proceed in the most appropriate way.

Time limits[21]

18.18 Strict time limits are imposed on the making of applications, and they must be adhered to. By CPR r54.5(1), the claim form must be filed promptly and, in any event, not later than three months after the grounds for making the claim first arose (generally the date of the decision). This rule does not apply where any other enactment specifies a shorter time limit for bringing the claim.[22]

18.19 CPR r54.5(2) states that the time limit in rule 54.5(1) may not be extended by agreement between the parties. The question of extending time is one for the court and not for the parties. It is also important to note that compliance with the pre-action protocol does not absolve the claimant from the requirement to bring the application within the time limits set out in rule 54.5(1).[23]

---

21 On 13 December 2012, the Ministry of Justice launched a brief consultation exercise, closing on 24 January 2013, which made various proposals for the reform of certain aspects of judicial review procedure: *Judicial Review: proposals for reform*, Ministry of Justice, December 2012. The Government's response to the consultation – *Reform of Judicial Review: the Government response*, Cm 8611, Ministry of Justice, April 2013 (*Response*), proposes to reduce the time for applying for permission in certain classes of case: (a) procurement cases, where the long-stop period will be reduced to 30 days (presumably from the decision rather than the claimant's knowledge of it) so as to reflect the general time limit for appeals under the Public Contract Regulations 2006 (*Response* para 13 and annex); (b) planning cases, where the back-stop period is to be reduced to six weeks so as to reflect the six-week period available for a statutory appeal on a refusal of a planning application, ie reverting to the judicially-created 'rule' existing prior to *R (Burkett) v Hammersmith and Fulham LBC* [2002] UKHL 23, [2002] 1 WLR 1593 described below at paras 18.47–18.53 (*Response* para 14 and annex). In cases of continuing breach, the consultation had proposed amending CPR r54.5 to make time start to run from the first occurrence of the breach (while taking account of when the claimant became aware of the breach or ought to have become aware of it (consultation paper paras 61–65). *Response*, however, states that it has been decided not to alter the position where the grounds giving rise to the claim are the result of an ongoing breach, relate to a delay in making a decision or taking action, or relate to a case where there have been multiple points at which decisions have been made (*Response* para 15).

22 CPR r54.5(3).

23 See paras 17.38–17.51 above.

18.20　As mentioned below,[24] if there has been delay, even within the three-month period, then the reasons for that delay should be set out on the claim form.

18.21　Rule 54.5 must be read in conjunction with SCA 1981 s31(6) and (7). Section 31(6) provides:

> Where the High Court considers that there has been undue delay in making an application for judicial review, the court may refuse to grant–
> (a) leave for the making of the application; or
> (b) any relief sought on the application, if it considers that the granting of the relief sought would be likely to cause substantial hardship to, or substantially prejudice the rights of, any person or would be detrimental to good administration.

18.22　Section 31(6) is 'without prejudice to any enactment or rule of court which has the effect of limiting the time within which an application of judicial review may be made'.[25]

18.23　It is clear, then, that the question of delay arises in two contexts. The first relates to whether or not permission should be granted; the second to whether or not relief should be granted even if the decision under challenge is found to have been unlawful.

The permission decision

18.24　The effect of the provisions described above is not that an applicant has three months within which to make an application, as is the case, for instance, in an employment tribunal. The requirement is that an application be made promptly. The three-month period referred to is simply a long-stop. In *R v Lichfield DC ex p Lichfield Securities Ltd*,[26] the Court of Appeal stated that 'promptness' is 'simply a function of the factors, ranging from the systemic to the idiosyncratic, which affect the fairness of letting a particular application proceed in a particular situation after a particular lapse of time; and these will ordinarily be the same factors as determine whether there has been undue delay.'[27]

18.25　The question has been raised whether the requirement for promptness coupled with the three-month long stop is sufficiently

---

24　This is part of the duty to give full and frank disclosurre, see paras 18.115–18.127 below.

25　SCA 1981 s31(7).

26　[2001] EWCA Civ 304, (2001) 3 LGLR 637.

27　[2001] EWCA Civ 304, per Sedley LJ at [33].

certain to comply with EU law and the European Convention on Human Rights.[28]

18.26   The ECJ considered an analogous provision in *Uniplex (UK) Ltd v NHS Business Services Authority*.[29] The case concerned a requirement to bring proceedings 'promptly and in any event within three months' in relation to actions alleging breaches of public procurement rules. The ECJ held, considering the relevant Directives and national law applicable, that a national provision in such terms gave rise to uncertainty as a limitation period, the duration of which was at the discretion of the court, and which was not predictable in its effects.[30]

18.27   Domestically, it has been held that *Uniplex* applies to challenges to environmental impact assessments (generally challenges involving European Directives); the approach seemingly being to ignore the element of promptness, exercise the court's discretion to extend time and require that the proceedings are brought within three months from the date the claimant knew, or ought to have know, of the alleged breach.[31]

18.28   In relation to judicial review proceedings on purely domestic grounds, however, the courts have been reluctant to take the same approach as *Uniplex*. In *Finn-Kelcey v Milton Keynes BC*,[32] the claimant issued judicial review proceedings just within the three-month long-stop. The judge at first instance refused permission due both to delay and to poor merits. The Court of Appeal upheld the judge's decision that the application had not been made promptly. The claimant had been aware of the decision as soon as it was made and had failed to comply with the requirements of CPR r54.5. Compliance with the pre-action protocol did not affect the fact that proceedings had to be brought promptly.

---

28 See *R (Burkett) v Hammersmith and Fulham LBC* [2002] UKHL 23, [2002] 1 WLR 1593 at [6], [53] and [59]–[66].

29 [2010] 2 CMLR 47.

30 At [41]–[43].

31 See, eg *Sita UK Ltd v Greater Manchester Waste Disposal Authority* [2010] EWHC 680 (Ch), [2010] 2 CMLR 48; *R (Buglife: the Invertebrate Conservation Trust) v Medway Council* [2011] EWHC 746 (Admin) (the requirement of promptness was not enforceable in the domestic courts); and, *R (U & Partners (East Anglia) Ltd) v Broads Authority* [2011] EWHC 1824 (Admin), QBD: (a time limit that was subject to judicial discretion, such as that laid down by CPR r54.5, was not certain and would not represent a proper transposition of the relevant EU Directive).

32 [2008] EWCA Civ 1067, [2009] Env LR 17.

18.29   In *R (Berky) v Newport City Council*,[33] the Court of Appeal held that the importance of the promptness requirement in relation to challenges on domestic law grounds had been confirmed by the court in *Finn-Kelcey* (above) and, although that case preceded *Uniplex*, its authority in the domestic context was undiminished and the judge was right to refuse permission on the delay ground alone.[34]

18.30   Accordingly, permission (or relief) can be refused even where the application has been made within the three-month limit.[35] In *R v Independent Television Commission ex p TV NI Ltd*,[36] the Court of Appeal refused permission on the ground of delay to two television companies that had not been awarded licences, even though the applications were made only two months after the decision complained of. Permission was refused on the ground that, by the time the applications were made, those companies who had been awarded licences had acquired firm rights with which they could deal and on the strength of which they could spend money.

18.31   The subject matter and factual matrix of the application will also factor into whether or not delay will result in the refusal of permission. In *R (Crown Prosecution Service) v Newcastle Upon Tyne Youth Court*,[37] an application for judicial review was refused (even though the district judge had adopted the wrong approach in the case) where the claim was brought five weeks after the youth court's decision. The defendant had turned 18 years old with the consequence of being subject to additional penalties as an adult and, therefore, justice would not be served by requiring him to enter a plea again as an 18-year-old, but would instead be served by refusing the application.[38]

18.32   Where an application involves the public interest but could cause serious prejudice to the Secretary of State, it has been held to be

---

33   [2012] EWCA Civ 378, [2012] 2 CMLR 44.

34   At [35] and [53]. The court acknowledged that in relation to the ground of challenge relating to the Environmental Impact Assessment, delay, by itself, may not have been a sufficient basis to refuse permission.

35   See, eg, *R v Dairy Produce Quota Tribunal ex p Caswell* [1990] 2 AC 738, HL.

36   (1991) *Times* 30 December; see also *R v Secretary of State for Health ex p Alcohol Recovery Project* [1993] COD 344, DC.

37   [2010] EWHC 2773 (Admin).

38   At [27]–[31].

incumbent on the claimant to make the application promptly regardless of any funding difficulties.[39]

18.33 Conversely, in *R v Birmingham CC ex p Dredger and Paget*,[40] the applicants' delay in applying for permission until six weeks after the date of the decision relating to the rent to be charged to market traders, and two weeks after the decision was implemented, did not count against them.

18.34 CPR Pt 54 makes no specific reference to any power of the court to extend time beyond the three-month long-stop. The reference in the old rules to the long-stop being subject to the power of the court to extend time where it considered that 'there is good reason for extending the period',[41] is not reproduced in Part 54. This does not, however, mean that the court no longer enjoys any power to extend the period. CPR r3.1(2)(a), for example, confers express power to extend the time for compliance with any rule.[42] Indeed, in *Lichfield*,[43] the Court of Appeal indicated that the formal enlargement of time can, in practice, be restricted to applications made outside the three-month time limit.[44]

18.35 While it does not necessarily follow that the discretion under the rules will be exercised identically with that under the old rules, as the express requirement for 'good reason' no longer exists, it appears that the court will continue to apply substantially the same criteria, and follow its previous decisions recognising that claims for judicial review are different from general civil litigation and time limits should be adhered to. Indeed, the Administrative Court Guidance states that the court will only extend time for where it is satisfied there are 'very good reasons' for so doing.[45] Although the pre-action protocol suggests that time will only be extended 'in exceptional circumstances', it is submitted that this is not the appropriate test and

---

39 See, *R (Harrow Community Support Ltd) v Secretary of State for Defence* [2012] EWHC 1921 (Admin) at [52] and [54]–[56], where the claimant sought judicial review of the decision of the Secretary of State to locate a ground-based air defence system, including missiles, on the roof of a tower block as part of the 2012 London Olympics security. The claimant had known about the decision two months prior to making the application.

40 [1993] 91 LGR 532, [1993] COD 340, QBD.

41 RSC Ord 53 r4(1).

42 And see CPR rr3.9 and 3.10 regarding relief from sanctions for failure to comply with a rule.

43 [2001] EWCA Civ 304, (2001) 3 LGLR 637.

44 [2001] EWCA Civ 304, per Sedley LJ at para [33].

45 *Administrative Court Guidance, Notes for applying for judicial review* (1 April 2011) para 5.2.

is not a test suggested by SCA 1981 s31(6), or the rules themselves.[46] The onus for demonstrating good reason falls on the claimant.[47]

18.36 Delay caused by the necessity for obtaining legal aid can amount to good reason for extending time,[48] or at least go 'a very long way down that road',[49] but will not automatically do so, especially where the court is not satisfied as to the efforts made in that regard.[50] Where there has been delay caused by funding issues, the claimant or his legal representatives must act with 'particular promptitude thereafter'.[51]

18.37 Where an applicant has tried to obtain a remedy by other means, such as by pursuing an alternative remedy, it is suggested that this may also constitute good reason for delay.[52] Communications with the proposed defendant may be a good reason.[53] It appears that the 'general importance of the issues' and the public interest in the application can afford good reason, notwithstanding that the delay has

---

46 See Pre-action Protocol, note 1. There is no reference to a requirement of exceptional circumstances for an extension of time to be granted in provisions of CPR r3.1(2)(a) – the rule referred to in the note itself – or rr3.9 and 3.10 (relief from sanctions), nor was that the test under RSC Ord 53 r4(1) ('good reason'). See also the comments of Lord Steyn in *R (Burkett) v Hammersmith and Fulham LBC* [2002] UKHL 23, [2002] 1 WLR 1593 at [53], concerning the counteracting of statutory time limits by judicial policy decision.

47 See, eg, *R v Warwickshire CC ex p Collymore* [1995] ELR 217 at 228F.

48 See *Re Wilson* [1985] AC 750, HL, at 755B; *R v Stratford on Avon DC ex p Jackson* [1985] 1 WLR 1319; *R v Surrey Coroner ex p Wright* [1997] QB 786.

49 *R v Governors of La Sainte Union Convent School ex p T* [1996] ELR 98.

50 See *R v University of Portsmouth ex p Lakareber* [1999] ELR 135. In *R v Sandwell MBC ex p Cashmore* (1993) 25 HLR 544 Owen J was of the view that delay in obtaining legal aid cannot usually be a good reason for extending time, although if the applicant would be left with no other remedy, the two features, taken together, might constitute good reason.

51 *R (Rayner) v Secretary of State for the Home Department* [2007] EWHC 1028 (Admin), [2007] 1 WLR 2239 at [90].

52 See, eg, *R v Chief Constable of North Wales Police ex p Evans* [1982] 1 WLR 1155, where the applicant had first taken his case to the industrial tribunal; *R v Secretary of State for the Home Department ex p Oladehinde* [1991] 1 AC 254, where the applicant had utilised his statutory right of appeal; *R (Javed) v Secretary of State for the Home Department* [2001] EWCA Civ 789, [2002] QB 129. Note, however, *R (International Masters Publishers Ltd) v Commissioners of Her Majesty's Customs & Excise* [2006] EWHC 127, Admin, where Collins J held at [16]–[17] that the claimant was guilty of inexcusable delay where they had, *inter alia*, pursued an appeal based on a commercial decision that they need not spend money on judicial review proceedings.

53 *R v Harrow LBC ex p Carter* (1994) 26 HLR 32, QBD; *R v Greenwich LBC ex p Patterson* (1994) 26 HLR 159.

not been satisfactorily explained.[54] Lack of knowledge of a reviewable decision can amount to a good reason,[55] as can the strength of the challenge,[56] the absence of prejudice, including where there has been reasonable behaviour on the part of a claimant which has not caused prejudice,[57] and the importance of the rights at stake.[58] The default of a professional, non-legal adviser has been held not to constitute good reason.[59] Nor was good reason shown where a local authority had agreed to a deferment of proceedings, but the other defendant, a government department who funded the function in question and whose regulations were challenged, had not been approached to agree.[60]

18.38　　It cannot be asserted that a particular factor will always (or will never) amount to a good reason for extending time. For almost any case in which the court has extended time on the basis of a specific matter, another can be found in which the same matter has been held not to amount to good reason for doing so. The most important consideration, in any given case, is likely to be the court's view of the overall reasonableness of the claimant's conduct causing the delay, judged in the context of the length of the delay, the explanation for

---

54　*R v Secretary of State for the Home Department ex p Ruddock* [1987] 1 WLR 1482, DC. *R v Secretary of State for Trade and Industry ex p Greenpeace* [2000] Env LR 221, QBD. See also, eg, *R v Essex CC ex p Jackson Projects Ltd* [1995] COD 155, where one of the factors for refusing an extension of time was the absence of any point of general importance; and *R (Law Society) v Legal Services Commission* [2010] EWHC 2550 (Admin) at [126], where the court held the case to be exceptional so that the general importance of the issues amounted to a good reason to extend time.

55　See, eg, *R v Secretary of State for the Home Department ex p Ruddock* [1987] 1 WLR 1482; *R v Licensing Authority ex p Novartis Pharmaceuticals Ltd* [2000] COD 232; and *R (N) v A London Borough Council* [2010] EWHC 3602 (Admin) at [24], it was correct not to issue proceedings in circumstances where the claimant was unsure of the decision taken at a public meeting, but efforts were made to issue as soon as the minutes of the meeting were disclosed.

56　See, eg, *R v Warwickshire CC ex p Collymore* [1995] ELR 217 and *PJG v Child Support Agency* [2006] EWHC 423 (Fam), [2006] 2 FLR 857.

57　See, eg, *R (Burkett) v Hammersmith and Fulham LBC* [2002] UKHL 23, [2002] 1 WLR 1593; *R (Health & Safety Executive) v Wolverhampton City Council* [2010] EWCA Civ 892, [2011] PTSR 645, a case where the claimant had acted reasonably in the exploration of a solution which would avoid the matter coming to court; and, *R (Castle) v Metropolitan Police Commissioner* [2011] EWHC 2317 (Admin), [2012] 1 All ER 953. Contrast, *R (Ford) v Press Complaints Commission* [2001] EWHC 683, [2002] EMLR 95, the absence of prejudice alone was not enough for an extension of time.

58　*Ahmad v Secretary of State for the Home Department* [1999] Imm AR 356, CA.

59　*R v Tavistock General Commissioners ex p Worth* [1985] STC 564.

60　*R (Camacho) v Haringey LBC* [2003] EWHC 1497 (Admin).

it, and any hardship/prejudice or detriment to good administration relied on by the defendant or third parties.[61]

Delay at the substantive hearing: SCA 1981 and CPR

18.39   The courts have explored, in a number of decisions,[62] the relationship between the role of the court in relation to delay at the permission stage and that at the substantive hearing and, indeed, the somewhat obscure relationship between SCA 1981 s31(6) and the relevant rules of court. In *R v Dairy Produce Quota Tribunal ex p Caswell*,[63] Lord Goff of Chievely said:

> Even if the Court thinks there was a good reason for the delay, it may still refuse leave or, if leave has been granted, refuse substantive relief, where in the Court's opinion the granting of such relief is likely to cause hardship or prejudice or would be detrimental to good administration independently of hardship or prejudice.

18.40   The House of Lords and the Court of Appeal have both considered the issue again subsequently. What emerges from these decisions, in summary, is that if the question of delay is fully considered at the permission stage, and permission is granted, the court may only reconsider the issue at the substantive hearing in limited circumstances.

18.41   The House of Lords set out the following principles in *R v Criminal Injuries Compensation Board ex p A*:[64]

- on a permission application, permission to apply for judicial review out of time may be granted, refused or deferred to the substantive hearing;

- permission may be given if the court considers that good reason for extending the period has been shown. The good reason is generally to be seen from the standpoint of the claimant;

---

61   See, eg, *R v Commissioner for Local Administration ex p Croydon LBC* [1989] 1 All ER 1033, CA; *R v Durham CC ex p Huddleston* [2000] 1 WLR 1484, [2000] 2 CMLR 229, [2000] Env LR D20; *R (Gavin) v Haringey LBC* [2003] EWHC 2591 (Admin), [2004] 1 PLR 61; and, *R (UNISON) v NHS Wiltshire Primary Care Trust* [2012] EWHC 624 (Admin), [2012] ACD 84.

62   In *R (Burkett) v Hammersmith and Fulham LBC* [2002] UKHL 23 at [23], the dovetailing of s31(6) with the rules was described as 'inept'; in *R v Criminal Injuries Compensation Board ex p A* [1999] 2 AC 330, HL, Lord Slynn of Hadley described it, at 340, as 'perhaps curious'.

63   [1990] 2 AC 738, HL.

64   [1999] 2 AC 330, HL.

- it is possible, though unusual on a without notice application, that if the court considers that hardship, prejudice or detriment to good administration has been shown, permission may be refused even if good reason for extending time has been made out;
- if permission is given, an application to set it aside may be made, though this is not to be encouraged. Under the CPR, an application to set aside permission may not be made,[65] though the court retains an inherent jurisdiction in limited circumstances to set aside a grant of permission;[66]
- if permission is given then, unless set aside, it does not fall to be reopened at the substantive hearing on the basis that there is no ground for extending time. At the substantive hearing there is no application for permission to apply for judicial review, permission having already been given;
- the court is probably unable to refuse to 'grant ... leave' – ie to apply SCA 1981 s31(6)(a) – at the substantive hearing on the grounds of hardship, prejudice or detriment to good administration; by that stage it is too late to refuse permission unless it sets aside the original grant without a separate application having been made for that to be done;
- if the application is adjourned to the full hearing, the questions of good reason for extending time and of hardship, prejudice or detriment to good administration justifying a refusal of permission may both fall for determination.[67]

18.42   The Court of Appeal, in *Lichfield*,[68] considered this issue specifically in the context of the procedural regime under the CPR. The court held that,[69] regardless of whether it involves repetition of the arguments about promptness canvassed at the permission stage, s31(6)(b), SCA 1981 places the issue of undue delay on the agenda at the substantive hearing. It does not follow from this, however, that the judge at the substantive hearing should consider the matter as if the issue had never previously arisen, at least where the matter was properly argued at the permission stage. It was undesirable that one

---

65   CPR r54.13.

66   *R (Webb) v Bristol CC* [2001] EWHC 696 (Admin); *R (Enfield LBC) v Secretary of State for Health* [2009] EWHC 743 (Admin).

67   *R v Criminal Injuries Compensation Board ex p A* [1999] 2 AC 330, HL, per Lord Slynn at 341B–F.

68   *R v Lichfield DC ex p Lichfield Securities Ltd* [2001] EWCA Civ 304, (2001) 3 LGLR 637.

69   [2001] EWCA Civ 304 at [34].

Administrative Court judge should act, in effect, as a court of appeal from another, or decide an issue without reference to a fellow judge's earlier decision. The matter was one of practical case management under the CPR. In addition, the second judge must have in mind the need to prevent circumvention of CPR r54.13, which prohibits applications to set aside the grant of permission.

18.43   Accordingly, although ultimately a matter for the judge hearing the substantive application, the appropriate course in such cases would generally be that the defendant should be permitted to recanvass by way of undue delay, an issue of promptness which has been decided at the permission stage in the claimant's favour only if:

- the permission judge has expressly so indicated;
- new and relevant material is introduced on the substantive hearing;
- exceptionally, the issues have developed at the full hearing in such a way as to put a different aspect on the question of promptness; or
- if the first judge has plainly overlooked some relevant matter or reached a decision per incuriam.[70]

18.44   Applying these principles, it would seem that it will not generally be open to the defendant at the substantive hearing to argue for the refusal of relief, under SCA 1981 s31(6)(b), on the ground of hardship, prejudice or detriment to good administration, where these issues have been explored fully at the permission stage, even though the question at that stage was whether or not to grant permission rather than whether or not to grant relief.[71]

18.45   Having said this, although *Lichfield* considered the position under the CPR, Pt 54 was not yet in force, and it was a feature of that case that the permission application was adjourned into open court where it was properly argued. It must be doubted whether a permission decision taken on the papers, even with the benefit of the defendant's summary of grounds for resisting the application, should be considered to be a proper argument on the issue of delay to debar the judge at the substantive hearing, with the benefit of detailed argument and evidence from the defendant, from considering the issue of refusal of

---

70 At [34].
71 See, eg, *Lichfield* [2001] EWCA Civ 304, per Sedley LJ at [37]: 'We take the same view [ie, that the claimant had acted promptly in that case], whether the question is regarded as one of promptness in applying for leave or of undue delay in seeking relief'.

relief.[72] Such a situation would, in any event, seem to fall within the second of the exceptions to the general rule enunciated in *Lichfield* – new and relevant evidence introduced at the substantive hearing.[73] This is separate from the question of whether or not the judge may reopen the question of the grant of permission to proceed, which is generally prohibited.[74]

Refusal of relief

18.46   The considerations relating to refusal of relief on the grounds of hardship, prejudice or detriment to good administration are considered at chapter 7.[75]

When time starts to run

18.47   The House of Lords considered this issue, which had vexed the lower courts for a number of years, in *R (Burkett) v Hammersmith and Fulham LBC*.[76] In that case, the judicial committee decided that the claimants had not been guilty of delay by reason of their not having challenged the local authority planning committee's resolution to grant planning permission but instead having waited until the formal grant of planning permission.

The former position

18.48   The claimants, in *Burkett*, had been refused permission to apply for judicial review of the grant of planning permission on the ground that they had delayed too long before commencing proceedings. There had grown up a body of case-law to the effect that time would generally start to run from the date of the substantive decision of

---

72   Potential problems with the new approach have been identified by the courts: see, eg, *R v Local Commissioner ex p Field* [2000] COD 58; *R v Essex CC ex p Tarmac Roadstone Holdings Ltd* [1998] PLCR 56.

73   *Lichfield* [2001] EWCA Civ 304 at [34].

74   *R v Criminal Injuries Compensation Board ex p A* [1999] 2 AC 330, HL. See also, *R v Chief Constable of West Yorkshire ex p Wilkinson* [2002] EWHC 2353 (Admin), where it was held that the judge can, at the substantive stage, have regard to the question of delay when deciding what remedy, if any, to grant, but that that issue is different from contending at the substantive stage that permission should not have been granted due to delay which had already been the subject of argument at the permission stage.

75   At paras 7.1–7.14 above.

76   [2002] UKHL 23, [2002] 1 WLR 1593.

which complaint was made, and that it would not necessarily be safe to wait until the formal manifestation of that decision.

18.49 In *R v Secretary of State for Trade and Industry ex p Greenpeace*,[77] for example, Laws J stated:

> A judicial review applicant must move against the substantive act or decision which is the real basis of his complaint. If, after that act has been done, he takes no steps but merely waits until something consequential and dependent upon it takes place and then challenges that, he runs the risk of being put out of court for being too late ...

18.50 Thus, in planning cases, permission had been refused where the claimant challenged the formal grant of planning consent, rather than challenging the resolution to grant it.[78]

18.51 In addition, in certain types of case, the court had begun to impose particularly strict time limits for commencing judicial review challenges.[79] Where, for example, a related statutory scheme prescribes time limits shorter than three months for bringing a statutory appeal, such as Town and Country Planning Act 1990 s289 (six-week time limit for a statutory appeal to the High Court against a refusal of planning permission), the Administrative Court repeatedly refused permission where the claimant challenging the grant of planning permission (who enjoyed no statutory appeal rights) had waited more than six weeks before commencing the challenge.

18.52 In *R v Ceredigion CC ex p McKeown*,[80] Laws J stated that he found it 'nearly impossible to conceive of a case' in which permission to apply for judicial review would be granted where the application was lodged more than six weeks after the grant of the planning permission. This was because:

> I can see no rhyme or reason in permitting the common law remedy of judicial review to be enjoyed upon a timescale in principle more generous to an applicant than Parliament has seen fit to fix in relation to those who desire to challenge a refusal of [planning] permission or its grant subject to conditions. I do not say that there cannot be such a case, but in my judgment it would be a wholly exceptional one.

18.53 The Court of Appeal, in *Burkett*,[81] while disapproving the 'somewhat mathematical emphasis' that had sometimes been placed on Laws

---

77 [1998] ELR 415.
78 See *R (Burkett) v Hammersmith and Fulham LBC* [2001] Env LR 684, CA, at [12]; see also, eg, *R v North Somerset DC ex p Garnett* [1997] JPL 1015, QBD.
79 See also CPR r54.5(3).
80 [1998] 2 PLR 1 at 2.
81 [2001] Env LR 684 at [20].

J's dictum, stated that the time set by Town and Country Planning Act 1990 s288 'should be kept in mind as a touchstone of varying usefulness.

The law after Burkett

18.54 The House of Lords decided that the courts had been wrong to adopt the principles described above. In particular, it was a misconception that the three-month period was in fact shortened to six weeks by the planning cases referred to above, as a statutory time limit could not be 'counteracted by a judicial policy decision'.[82] As Lord Steyn pointed out, the importance of this issue is not limited to an obscure area of planning law but potentially applies across the board, whenever a decision-maker informs the citizen that he or she is minded to reach a decision adverse to that citizen. For time to run from the expression of that provisional view would 'plainly not be sensible and would involve waste of time and money'. It would also be contrary to principle to require the citizen to take such premature legal action.[83]

18.55 Lord Steyn said,[84] referring to the requirement of the rules that a claim must be brought not later than three months 'from the date when the grounds for the application first arose',[85] that the natural and obvious meaning was that the grounds for an application first arose when the decision was made. The fact that the illegality in a decision was foreseeable at some point before the decision was actually made did not detract from this meaning.

18.56 The contrary argument, that it was disruptive of good administration to permit a citizen to delay his challenge until the actual formal decision was made, could not prevail. While the court would have jurisdiction to entertain a challenge to a resolution to grant planning consent both before and after that decision was made formal by the actual grant, it was a 'jump in legal logic' to say that a person must challenge the resolution on pain of losing the right to bring a challenge to the actual grant which gives effect to the resolution and so is the decision which actually affects that person's rights.[86]

---

82 *Burkett* [2002] UKHL 23, per Lord Steyn at [53].
83 [2002] UKHL 23 at [43].
84 [2002] UKHL 23 at [39].
85 This was the language of RSC Ord 53 r4(1), but CPR r54.5(1)(b), the equivalent current procedural rule, is almost identical referring to the requirement that a claim be made not later than three months ('after the grounds to make the claim first arose').
86 *Burkett* [2002] UKHL 23, per Lord Steyn at [42].

18.57   There were a number of policy considerations which militated in favour of time starting to run only when a formal decision had been made:

- the context of the issue about when time began to run was a rule of court which, by imposing a time limit, may deprive the citizen of the right to challenge abuses of power not necessarily involving only individual rights but also potentially community interests. That context weighed heavily in favour of a clear and straightforward interpretation of the rule that would lead to a readily ascertainable start date. Allowing the courts to ascertain the start date retrospectively was antithetical to the context of a time limit barring proceedings;

- legal policy favours simplicity and certainty rather than complexity and uncertainty. In the absence of indications to the contrary, the legislature must be presumed to have intended to create a certain and predictable regime. The citizen and the decision-maker – and indeed an interested third party such as the developer – must know where they stand, particularly where the effect of the rule to be interpreted may result in the loss of the right to challenge an unlawful exercise of power. For the court retrospectively to assess the appropriate date by which proceedings ought reasonably to have been commenced, with the attendant lack of certainty, would be 'a recipe for sterile procedural disputes and unjust results';

- the preparation of judicial review cases was a burdensome task. Lord Steyn referred, in particular, to the duty of full and frank disclosure, and the obligation to present to the court a detailed statement of grounds, evidence, supporting documents in a paginated and indexed bundle, a list of essential reading with the relevant passages sidelined and legislative sources in a paginated indexed bundle. This was a heavy burden on individuals and (for funded claimants) the Legal Services Commission (now the Legal Aid Agency). A claimant is also at risk of having to pay substantial costs. All of these factors reinforced the view that it is unreasonable to require the citizen to challenge a decision that may never take effect and unfair to subject him to a retrospective decision by the court as to the date when the time limit for commencing proceedings was triggered.

18.58   *Burkett* has since been applied in other cases.[87] In the context of public procurement and European Law, however, dealing with questions of acting promptly, it has been held that time started to run from the date on which the claimant knew, or ought to have known, of the alleged breach of the procurement rules.[88] Further, in *R (Anufrijeva) v Secretary of State for the Home Department,*[89] a slightly adapted approach was taken when the House of Lords held that a notice of a decision was required before it would have the character of a determination with legal effect; time would therefore run from the date of such notice.[90] There also appears to be some leeway where the decision that has been made is unclear; a claimant being entitled to seek clarification of the decision before time starts to run.[91]

87 See, eg, *R (Garden Leisure Group Ltd) v North Somerset Council* [2003] EWHC 1605 (Admin); *Younger Homes (Northern) Ltd v First Secretary of State* [2003] EWHC 3058 (Admin) and *R (Catt) v Brighton and Hove County Council* [2007] EWCA Civ 298, [2007] Env LR 691.

88 See, eg, *Uniplex (UK) Ltd v NHS Business Authority* [2010] 2 CMLR 47. See also, *R (Parker Rhodes Hicknotts Solicitors) v Legal Services Commission* [2011] EWHC 1323 (Admin), *Allan Rutherford LLP v Legal Services Commission* [2010] EWHC 3068 (Admin) and *Hereward & Foster Ltd v Legal Services Commission* [2010] EWHC 3370 (Admin) where it was held that the relevant date to challenge a tender decision was at the time the selection criteria were published, and that the claimant was not entitled to ignore the defects in the criteria and enter the bidding process to see whether or not they would be successful despite the defects before bringing a challenge. The domestic decision are all based on *Jobsin Co UK Plc (t/a Internet Recruitment Solutions) v Department of Health* [2001] EWCA Civ 1241, [2002] 1 CMLR 44, however, which was decided before *Burkett.*

89 [2003] UKHL 36, [2004] 1 AC 604.

90 Ibid, at [26].

91 *R (Macrae) v Herefordshire DC* [2012] EWCA Civ 457, [2012] JPL 1356.

Continuing illegality[92]

18.59   An issue not dealt with in *Burkett* is when time begins to run, and indeed how the rules relating to delay apply generally, where what is challenged is a continuing failure to act lawfully. Examples of this may be a continuing failure to make a lawful decision in relation to an application for accommodation; a continuing failure to conduct an assessment of need under the community care legislation, or to make a statement of special educational need; or a continuing an act or policy which is unlawful.

18.60   Frequently, the allegation of a continuing failure to make a lawful decision is not based on a failure to make any decision at all. Instead, the illegality may arise from the making of a decision that is unlawful (hence the continuing failure to make a lawful one). It may be insufficient for the decision-maker simply to make a new decision, for example, where the illegality of the decision stems from its having been taken in accordance with, or having regard to, an unlawful policy that is still in place and that would therefore continue to inform and so invalidate any new decision.

18.61   The unlawful decision may have been taken, and indeed the policy is likely to have been adopted, some time – possibly years – prior to the challenge being brought. In the case of a policy, there would be no reason for the claimant ever to consider its legality until it was actually applied to his or her case.

18.62   The questions therefore arise when time starts to run in such cases. Are decisions and policies rendered immune from challenge, on the basis that they were implemented more than three months prior to the commencement of proceedings?

92 On 13 December 2012, the Ministry of Justice launched a brief consultation exercise, closing on 24 January 2013, which made various proposals for the reform of certain aspects of judicial review procedure: *Judicial Review: proposals for reform*, Ministry of Justice, December 2012. The Government's response to the consultation – *Reform of Judicial Review: the Government response*, Cm 8611, Ministry of Justice, April 2013 (*Response*), contains the government's final proposals. These do not include the proposal consulted on to amend CPR r54.5 to make clear that in cases of continuing breach, time starts to run from the first occurrence of the breach, while taking account of when the claimant became aware of the breach or ought to have become aware of it (consultation paper paras 61–65). The government has now decided not to proceed with this proposal, or to alter the current position where the grounds giving rise to the claim are the result of an ongoing breach, relate to a delay in making a decision or taking action, or relate to a case where there have been multiple points at which decisions have been made (*Response* para 15).

18.63   The courts have, in general, declined to accept this as the position, by adopting a variety of different responses. In principle, the continued failure to make a lawful decision over time can be analysed as a new failure arising each day, starting the running of time again.[93] Even so, this does not render it irrelevant to have regard, in considering delay, to the date when the breach began.[94] In other cases, the courts have simply stated that delay does not absolve a public authority from performing its duty.[95]

18.64   Where a continuing beach of obligation or unlawful state of affairs is not put right by a defendant, time will frequently not run against a claimant at least until that state of affairs has come to an end.[96]

18.65   In relation to a continuous, unlawful, positive act, in *R (Hammerton) v London Underground Ltd*,[97] the court considered when the grounds subject to review first arose as part of the requirement under CPR r54.5(1). Applying *Burkett*, however, the court considered that looking solely at the start date would be too narrow an approach. Where there was a continuing, positive breach of duty – in this case a continuous breach of planning controls – the grounds for review continued to arise each day, as the defendant committed a further unlawful act daily.[98]

18.66   Similarly, the courts have held that the illegality of a policy is a good reason for extending time, where otherwise the unlawful policy would continue in operation, particularly where only prospective relief is sought. In *R v Rochdale BC ex p Schemet*,[99] Roch J cited the comments of Nicholls LJ in *R v Westminster CC ex p Hilditch*,[100] that:

93 See, eg, *R v Islington LBC ex p Camp* [2004] LGR 58; *R (Hammerton) v London Underground Ltd* [2002] EWHC 2307 (Admin), [2003] JPL 984; and *Somerville v Scottish Ministers* [2007] UKHL 44, [2007] 1 WLR 2734, which concerned a continuing act of alleged incompatibility with a Convention right; the time limits being those contained in s7(5) HRA 1998.

94 See, eg. *R v Essex CC ex p C* [1994] ELR 54, QBD; and *R (Hammerton) v London Underground Ltd* [2002] EWHC 2307 (Admin), [2003] JPL 984 at [197].

95 See, eg, *London and Clydeside Estates v Aberdeen DC* [1980] 1 WLR 182. See also the cases on the importance of the issues at stake constituting good reason for extending time, eg, *R v Secretary of State for the Home Department ex p Ruddock* [1987] 1 WLR 1482; *R v Secretary of State for Foreign and Commonwealth Affairs ex p World Development Movement* [1995] 1 WLR 386.

96 See, eg, *R (Hammerton) v London Underground Ltd* [2002] EWHC 2307 (Admin), [2003] JPL 984; and *R (G) v Secretary of State for Justice* [2010] EWHC 3407 (Admin).

97 [2002] EWHC 2307 (Admin), [2003] JPL 984.

98 Ibid, at [194]–[197].

99 [1994] ELR 89, QBD, at 100–1.

100 (1990) 14 June, unreported, transcript p17.

... if a policy is unlawful, *prima facie* it should be discontinued. The mere fact that the policy has been in place for nearly three years is not a sufficient reason for the court countenancing its continuing implementation for the indefinite future. There is here good reason for extending time for the making of an application for judicial review, at any rate so far as the relief sought is directed at restraining the further implementation of the allegedly unlawful policy.

18.67   In *Schemet* itself, the court refused mandatory relief that would have affected the budget of the respondent education authority for the previous two years, granting only declarations as to the illegality of the impugned decisions.[101] In *R v East Sussex CC ex p Ward*,[102] permission was granted on the express basis that no relief would be granted in respect of any period prior to six months before the grant of permission itself (in fact only declaratory relief was granted for various reasons).[103]

Dealing with time limits

18.68   *R (Burkett) v Hammersmith and Fulham LBC*[104] clearly eases the burden on claimants by clarifying the position in relation to the start of the running of time. It has no easing effect, however, on the obligation to act promptly once the final decision to be challenged has been made. Having said this, advisers should remember that decision-makers may frequently communicate more than one reviewable decision, in any particular case, and where a reconsideration has been undertaken but has confirmed the original decision, the later decision can – and generally should – be challenged especially where it replaces or supersedes the original decision. This may well assist the claimant, even if he or she has been guilty of delay in relation to the initial decision.

18.69   If a request for a reconsideration has been refused, that decision may in itself be reviewable, although, absent any change of circumstances, the court is more likely in such a case to take the view that the substance of the claimant's complaint is the original adverse decision rather than the refusal on the part of the decision-maker to reconsider. In such cases, all decisions of the decision-maker should be included on the claim form. Apart from other considerations, it

---

101 See also *R v Warwickshire CC ex p Collymore* [1995] ELR 217.
102 (2000) 3 CCLR 132, QBD.
103 (2000) 3 CCLR 132 at 140A–C.
104 [2002] UKHL 23, [2002] 1 WLR 1593.

may be more difficult for a decision-maker to claim hardship, prejudice or detriment to good administration in relation to a challenge to his or her initial decision, if a reconsideration has recently been undertaken.

Commencement of proceedings

18.70 The claim form in proceedings in the Administrative Court may be issued at the Queen's Bench Division[105] of the High Court at:

- the Royal Courts of Justice in London; or
- the District Registry of the High Court at Birmingham, Cardiff,[106] Leeds, or Manchester.[107]

18.71 Any claim started in Birmingham will normally be determined at a court in the Midland region (geographically covering the area of the Midland Circuit); in Cardiff in Wales or Bristol; in Leeds in the North-Eastern Region (geographically covering the area of the North Eastern Circuit); in London at the Royal Courts of Justice; and in Manchester, in the North-Western Region (geographically covering the Northern Circuit).[108]

18.72 There are certain types of proceedings that can only be issued and heard at the Royal Courts of Justice in London. These are outlined at CPR PD 54D para 3.1 and include proceedings relating to control orders, proceedings relating to terrorism, proceedings under the Proceeds of Crime Act 2002, proceedings that must be heard by a Divisional Court and proceedings relating to the discipline of solicitors. If such proceedings are started at an Administrative Court office outside London they will be transferred to London.[109]

---

105 On 14 January, 2013, the Queen's Bench Division and Administrative Court Office merged despite CPR PD 54D Administrative Court (Venue) still referring to the Administrative Court Office.
106 Administrative Court hearings are now also held in Bristol, but the Cardiff Administrative Court Office serves the Bristol Court and so it seems that cases to be heard in Bristol need to be issued in Cardiff: see Judicial Office Press release dated 31 October 2012, referring to the opening of the Bristol Administrative Court on 5 November 2012, and estimating that around 200 claims per annum would be issued in Cardiff for hearing in Bristol: www.judiciary.gov.uk/media/media-releases/2012/admin-court-to-sit-in-bristol-31102012 (accessed on 28 March 2013).
107 CPR PD 54D para.2.1.
108 CPR PD 54D para.2.2.
109 CPR PD 54D para 3.2.

Court fees

18.73   The fee, payable on the commencement of the judicial review procedure, ie on filing the documents mentioned above, is currently £60.[110] If permission is granted, an additional fee of £215[111] becomes payable within seven days of the service on the claimant of the order granting permission.[112]

Formal requirements of the claim form

18.74   The formal requirements of the claim form are set out in CPR rr8.2; 54.6 and PD 54A. The matters that must be specified by virtue of rule 8.2 or Part 54 are as follows:

- that Part 8 applies to the claim,[113] although there appears to be no reference to this point in the claim form N461 (or in the notes to the form);
- the question which the court is asked to decide:[114] this appears to be dealt with at section 3 (details of the decision to be judicially reviewed) and section 6 (detailed statement of grounds) of the claim form;

---

110   Civil Proceedings Fees Order 2008 SI No 1053 (as amended by SI 2008/2853, SI 2009/1498 and SI 2011/586) Sch 1 para 1.9(a) and *Administrative Court Guidance, Notes for applying for Judicial Review* (1 April 2011) para 6.1.

111   It is currently proposed to increase this fee to £235. In addition, on 13 December 2012, the Ministry of Justice launched a brief consultation exercise, closing on 24 January 2013, which made various proposals for the reform of certain aspects of judicial review procedure: *Judicial Review: proposals for reform*, Ministry of Justice, December 2012. One of the proposals was to introduce a fee of £215 (rising to £235) for renewals of permission applications (see paras 18.143–18.147, below). The Government's response to the consultation – *Reform of Judicial Review: the Government response*, Cm 8611, Ministry of Justice, April 2013 (*Response*), includes this proposal (*Response*, para 18). Should permission be granted on the renewed application, no further fee will be payable (ie the fee referred to at para 18.73, above, will not be required).

112   Civil Proceedings Fees Order 2008 SI No 1053 (as amended by SI 2008/2853, SI 2009/1498 and SI 2011/586) Sch 1 para 1.9(b). By para 1.9(c), if the claim was commenced otherwise than by using the judicial review procedure, the additional fee payable within seven days of service of the order granting permission is £60. At first sight, it is not entirely clear when this provision may apply, although it could refer to the power of the court, pursuant to CPR r54.20, applying CPR r30.5, to transfer cases begun by ordinary civil process to the Administrative Court. As to this power, see further above at paras 18.8–18.17.

113   CPR r8.2(a).

114   CPR r8.2(b).

- the remedy sought (including any interim remedy) and the legal basis, or grounds, for the claim to that remedy:[115] again, see section 6 of the claim form as regards the grounds (note that PD 54A – reflected at section 6 – permits the grounds to be drafted as a document accompanying the claim form),[116] and section 7 on the remedy sought;
- the enactment, if any, under which the claim is made;[117]
- if the claimant is claiming in a representative capacity, what that capacity is;[118]
- if the defendant is being sued in a representative capacity, what that capacity is: these last three requirements, to the extent that they are applicable to a judicial review claim, would also, in practice, be dealt with by including the relevant information in the grounds;[119]
- that the claimant is requesting permission to apply for judicial review: see section 4 of the claim form;[120]
- the name and address of any person considered to be an interested party:[121] this is dealt with at section 2 of the claim form. Where the claim relates to proceedings before a court or tribunal, any other parties to those proceedings must be named as interested parties;[122]
- a statement of truth:[123] the statement of truth contained in the claim form, under its section 9, confirms the truth of the facts stated in section 8 (statement of facts relied on) of the form. Accordingly, where the statement of facts relied on (see below) is drafted as separate documents accompanying the claim form, it is probably unnecessary that it should include an additional statement of truth, as the facts stated in the separate document would still fall within section 8 of the form. The position concerning the grounds for review is not so clear. If it is drafted as a separate document and contains facts, as is likely, then these ought to

---

115 CPR r8.2(b). The requirement that any remedy claimed (including any interim remedy) and the grounds for the claim be included is repeated by CPR r54.6(1)(c) and CPR PD 54A para 5.6(1).
116 CPR PD 54A para 5.6(1), and see further below.
117 CPR r8.2(c).
118 CPR r8.2(d).
119 CPR r8.2(e).
120 CPR r54.6(1)(b).
121 CPR r54.6(1)(a).
122 CPR PD 54A paras 5.1–5.2.
123 CPR rr8.2 and 22.1.

be verified by a statement of truth,[124] though the form makes no provision for this. For this reason, the safest course would be to add a statement of truth where the grounds are drafted as a separate document attached to the claim form. Verification by a statement of truth is essential where the claimant wishes to rely on the contents of the claim form as evidence in the claim, whether in relation to a claim for interim relief or generally.[125]

18.75　The claim form must also include or be accompanied by the following information:

- a detailed statement of the grounds for seeking review:[126] given their probable length, it is likely to be more practical to draft the statement of grounds as a separate document accompanying the claim form, as is permitted by PD 54A, rather than to include the grounds at section 6 of the claim form itself. As stated above, where this practice is adopted, the grounds should probably contain their own statement of truth;
- a statement of the facts relied on:[127] section 8 of the claim form. Where the statement is contained in a separate document accompanying the claim form, it is probably not necessary to include an additional statement of truth, though no criticism would attach to including one;
- any application to extend the time limit for filing the claim form:[128] this would, in practice, generally be included at section 9 of the claim form. Likewise, if the contents of any application pleaded under section 9 of the claim form are to be used as evidence in the application, a statement of truth must be included in section 9;[129]
- any application for directions:[130] also included at section 9;
- a time estimate for the substantive (ie not a permission) hearing:[131] see section 5 of the claim form.

124　CPR rr8.2 and 22.1.
125　CPR r8.5(7) states that the matters set out in the claim form may be relied on as evidence if the claim form is verified by a statement of truth. In relation to claims for interim relief, an analogous provision is contained in CPR r32.6(2) and PD 32 paras 1.3 and 26.1. As to interim injunctions, see CPR PD 25A para 3.2.
126　CPR PD 54A para 5.6(1).
127　CPR PD 54A para 5.6(2).
128　CPR PD 54A para 5.6(3).
129　See note 122 above.
130　CPR PD 54A para 5.6(4).
131　CPR PD 54A para 5.6(5).

Additional requirements in human rights cases

18.76 In any case where the claimant seeks to raise any issue under the HRA 1998, or seeks a remedy available under that Act, the claim form must also:[132]

- state that fact;[133]
- give precise details of the right under the European Convention on Human Rights (the Convention) that is alleged to have been infringed and details of the alleged infringement;[134]
- specify the relief sought;[135]
- state if the relief sought includes a declaration of incompatibility under HRA 1998 s4 or damages in respect of a judicial act to which section 9(3) of that Act applies (ie damages for an arrest or for detention in breach of article 5 of the Convention);[136]
- where the relief sought does include a declaration of incompatibility, give precise details of the legislative provision alleged to be incompatible and details of the alleged incompatibility;[137]
- where the claim is founded on a finding of unlawfulness made by another court or tribunal, give details of that finding;[138]
- where the claim is founded on a judicial act alleged to have infringed a Convention right as provided by HRA 1998 s9, state the judicial act complained of and the court or tribunal alleged to have so acted.[139]

18.77 The discussion, above,[140] concerning statements of truth would appear also to apply to these requirements.

18.78 In cases where the claimant seeks damages for a judicial act and/or a declaration of incompatibility, the relevant Secretary of State (or, in the case of a judicial act, the Lord Chancellor)[141] should be listed in the claim form as an interested party.[142] In either case, CPR Pt 19 requires notice of such a claim to be given to the Crown and entitles

---

132 CPR PD 54A para 5.3.
133 CPR PD 16 para 15.1(1).
134 CPR PD 16 para 15.1(2)(a).
135 CPR PD 16 para 15.1(2)(b).
136 CPR PD 16 para 15.1(2)(c).
137 CPR PD 16 para 15.1(2)(d).
138 CPR PD 16 para 15.1(2)(e).
139 CPR PD 16 para 15.1(2)(f).
140 At para 18.74.
141 Or, in the case of courts martial, the Secretary of State for Defence: CPR PD 19A para 6.6(2).
142 See the list of authorised government departments annexed to CPR PD 66.

a minister, or person nominated by him, to be joined as a party to the proceedings. Indeed, no award of damages for a judicial act may be made unless the minister responsible for the court concerned or a person or government department nominated by him has been joined.[143]

18.79   In *Poplar Housing and Regeneration Community Association Ltd v Donoghue*,[144] the Court of Appeal set out the procedure to be adopted for notifying the Crown in cases where the possibility of a declaration of incompatibility arises.[145]

- The formal notice that the HRA and the CPR require should always be given by the court. This is because the court will be in the best position to assess whether there is a likelihood of a declaration of incompatibility being made.
- So as to give the Crown as much notice as possible, whenever a party is seeking a declaration of incompatibility or acknowledges that a declaration of incompatibility may be made, it should give as much informal notice to the Crown as practical of the proceedings and the issues that are involved.
- The formal and informal notice to the Crown should be given to a person named in the list published under s17, Crown Proceedings Act 1947.
- At the same time as the party gives notice informally to the Crown, it should send a copy of such notice to the court so that the court is alerted to the fact that it will have to consider whether a formal notice should be given. It should also send a copy of the notice to the other parties.
- In these circumstances, 'the court' means the court that will hear the proceedings. That is a trial court at the level of the High Court or, in the case of appeals, the Court of Appeal or the High Court

143 HRA 1998 s9(4). CPR r19.4A (3) provides that where a claim is made for damages in respect of a judicial act and no application to be joined is made by the minister or person nominated by him within 21 days, or such other period as the court directs, of notice having been served, the court may join the minister or other person as a party. CPR r19.4A(1)–(2) provides that a court may not make a declaration of incompatibility unless 21 days' notice, or such other period as the court directs has been given to the Crown, and that where notice has been given, a minister or other person nominated by him must be joined as a party to the proceedings on giving notice to the court. For the detailed provisions concerning these matters and, in particular, how notification to the Crown should be made in such cases, see: HRA 1998 ss4 and 9; CPR r19.4A; and CPR PD 19A paras 6.1–6.6.

144 [2001] EWCA Civ 595, [2001] 3 WLR 183.

145 [2001] 3 WLR 183, per Lord Woolf CJ at 191A–E.

(in the case of appeals to the High Court). The county court cannot make a declaration of incompatibility (HRA 1998 s4(5)).

Additional requirements in cases raising devolution issues

18.80 A devolution issue, in essence, is an issue concerning whether an act of the Scottish Parliament; the Welsh Government; or the Northern Ireland Assembly; or the exercise of a function by the Scottish Executive or any minister is within the devolved powers conferred by the relevant Acts of Parliament or breaches a Convention right or EU law.[146]

18.81 Where a devolution issue is raised, the claim form must:[147]

- specify that such an issue is being raised and identify the relevant provisions of the relevant Act;[148]
- contain a summary of the facts, circumstances and points of law on the basis of which a devolution issue is alleged to arise.

18.82 The discussion above,[149] concerning the need for statements of truth would appear also to apply to these requirements.

Documents to be filed with the claim form

18.83 The claim form must be accompanied by the following additional documents:

- any written evidence in support of the claim or application to extend time;[150]
- a copy of any order that the claimant seeks to have quashed;[151]
- where the judicial review claim relates to a decision of a court or tribunal, an approved copy of the court or tribunal's reasons for reaching the decision challenged;[152]
- copies of any documents on which the claimant proposes to rely;[153]

---

146 See Scotland Act 1998 s98 and Sch 6; Government of Wales Act 2006 s149 and Sch 9; Northern Ireland Act 1998 s79 and Sch 10.
147 CPR PD 54A para 5.4.
148 That is, the Scotland Act 1998, the Government of Wales Act 2006 or the Northern Ireland Act 1998.
149 At para 18.74.
150 CPR PD 54A para 5.7(1) and CPR r8.5(1).
151 CPR PD 54A para 5.7(2).
152 CPR PD 54A para 5.7(3).
153 CPR PD 54A para 5.7(4).

- copies of any relevant statutory material;[154]
- a list of essential documents for advance reading by the court with page references to the passages relied on.[155]

18.84   If it is not possible to file all of these documents with the claim form, the claimant must indicate the documents which have not been filed, and the reasons why they are not currently available.[156] Section 10 of the claim form contains a checklist with boxes that may be ticked to indicate whether a document is included in the body of the form, attached to it or will be filed later. Section 10 of the form requires not only a statement of the reasons why a document not available at the time of filing the claim form has not been supplied, but also the date when it is expected to be available.

Drafting the grounds or statement of facts

18.85   The grounds should be fully pleaded and include the reasons for any delay, even if an extension of time is not required because the three-month back-stop period for making the claim has not expired.[157] In practice, in most cases, claimants tend to incorporate the grounds and statement of facts[158] relied on into one document containing appropriate subheadings.[159] As regards the statement of facts, it is worth bearing in mind that as there is no longer any formal requirement for an affidavit or witness statement in support of the claim form,[160] the statement of facts must include a full statement of all those facts relied on.

18.86   The grounds should include any authorities to which the claimant intends to refer at the hearing. In citing authorities, however, it is necessary to comply with the Practice Directions (Citation of Authorities) 2001 and 2012[161] which prohibit the citing of certain types of authority (subject to exceptions)[162] and imposes requirements

---

154 CPR PD 54A para 5.7(5).

155 CPR PD 54A para 5.7(6).

156 139a CPR PD 54A para 5.8.

157 See under 'Delay' above at paras 18.39–18.45.

158 CPR PD 54A para 5.6(2).

159 For a precedent, see appendix A.

160 See under 'Evidence in support' below at paras 18.105–18.108.

161 [2001] 1 WLR 1001 (Sup Ct), [2012] 1 WLR 780. The 2012 Practice Direction was issued on 23 March and came into force on 24 March 2012.

162 Under the 2001 Practice Direction, which has not been repealed by the 2012 Practice Direction, the following categories of judgment may not be cited before any court unless it clearly indicates that it purports to establish a

concerning the appropriate methods of citing authorities,[163] and the use of authorities from other jurisdictions.[164]

18.87 The 2012 Practice Direction makes provision of the citation of authorities either by way of a photocopy of the published report or by way of a copy of a reproduction of the judgment in electronic form that has been authorised by the publisher of the relevant series. The report must be presented to the court in an easily legible form (a 12-point font is preferred but a 10- or 11-point font is acceptable), and the advocate presenting the report must be satisfied that the report has not been reproduced in a garbled form from the data source. In any case of doubt the court will rely on the printed text of the report (unless the editor of the report has certified that an electronic version is more accurate because it corrects an error contained in an earlier printed text of the report).[165]

18.88 The Practice Direction (Supreme Court: Judgments: Neutral Citations) must also be complied with.[166]

18.89 It has been held that authorities which are unfavourable to the claimant's case should be mentioned and where possible distinguished in the grounds,[167] and this is emphasised in the 2001 Practice

---

new principle of law or to extend the law (2001 Practice Direction para 6.1). Those categories are: applications attended by one party only; applications for permission to appeal; decisions on applications that only decide that the application is arguable; county court cases unless (a) cited to illustrate the measure of damages in personal injury cases (and presumably, by analogy, housing disrepair cases) or (b) cited in a county court on an issue in respect of which no authority of a higher court is available (2001 Practice Direction para 6.2). In addition, advocates will be required to justify a decision to cite a judgment in which it is indicated that it only applied decided law to the facts of the particular case; or that it does not extend or add to the existing law (2001 Practice Direction paras 7.1–7.2).

163 It is necessary to state, in respect of each authority cited, the proposition of law demonstrated by the authority, the parts of the judgment that support the proposition and, if more than one authority is cited for the same proposition, the reason for doing so (2001 Practice Direction para 8.1). Any list of authorities must bear a certification by the advocate responsible that these requirements have been complied with (2001 Practice Direction para 8.3).

164 See 2001 Practice Direction paras 9.1–9.2 (though they do not apply to decisions of the European Court of Justice or organs of the European Convention on Human Rights which are governed by the previous paragraphs: 2001 Practice Direction para 9.3).

165 2012 Practice Direction para 13.

166 [2002] 1 WLR 346.

167 See, eg, *R v Crown Prosecution Service ex p Hogg* [1994] COD 237, QBD and *Re V (A Child) (Care Proceedings: Human Rights Claims)* [2004] EWCA Civ 854, [2004] 1 All ER 997.

Direction (Citation of Authorities).[168] Statutory provisions ousting the jurisdiction of the court should also be mentioned in the grounds that should explain why it is claimed such clauses do not apply to the application in question.[169]

18.90   If damages are claimed, the usual rules of pleading apply and full particulars should be given.[170]

18.91   The claim form, as a statement of case, must, if drafted by a legal representative, be signed by him or her. If drafted by a legal representative as a member or employee of a firm, it must be signed in the name of the firm.[171]

18.92   In drafting the grounds, it should be borne in mind that they will form the basis not only of the argument on the permission application, but also of the full application if permission is granted. It is essential to set out precisely what is complained of in an intelligible manner. Although such matters always entail questions of individual style, it is probably better to draft the grounds more in the style, and with the detail, of a skeleton argument rather than that of a civil pleading. Although they may be amended, with permission,[172] at a later stage, and although the claimant's legal advisers are under an obligation to reconsider the merit of the claim (and where necessary amend it) on receipt of the defendant's evidence and detailed grounds of resistance)[173] it is imperative to spend time formulating the grounds properly, not least so as to increase the chances of permission being granted.

Interim relief

18.93   Any claim for interim relief must be included in the claim form together with the substantive relief sought.[174] Details of all remedies being sought, including interim remedies, are in practice, set out at section 7 of the claim form. By CPR r25.3(2), an application for interim relief must be supported by evidence unless the court orders otherwise. In general, evidence at hearings other than the trial is

---

168 [2001] 1 WLR 1001.

169 *R v Cornwall CC ex p Huntingdon* [1992] 3 All ER 566, DC, at 576.

170 Formerly RSC Ord 53 r7(2) applying RSC Ord 18 r12. No specific reference to this appears in CPR Pt 54, but it remains good practice.

171 CPR PD 5 para 2.1. See also para 2.2 for the general requirements as to the form of all court documents.

172 CPR r54.15.

173 See paras 20.20–20.34 below.

174 CPR r54.6(1)(c).

given by witness statement unless the court, a practice direction or an enactment requires otherwise,[175] although a party may if he or she wishes rely solely on the contents of his or her statement of case or application provided that they have been verified by a statement of truth.[176] The evidence must set out the facts on which the claimant relies for the claim for interim relief, including all facts (including adverse facts) of which the court should be aware.[177] If an application for interim relief is made without notice to the defendant, the evidence in support must state the reasons why notice was not given.[178]

18.94   In practice, the application will be made using sections 7 and 9 of the claim form, supported by evidence. This may be the evidence contained in the statement of facts (section 8) and/or that contained in a witness statement.[179] As stated above,[180] if the statement of facts is drafted to contain the evidence required to support the claim for interim relief, it is probably unnecessary for it to contain a separate statement of truth (though there is nothing to be lost by including one).

Urgent cases and interim injunctions

18.95   Even in urgent cases, and those in which interim injunctions are sought, the court will generally initially consider the matter on the papers. The Administrative Court has issued guidance on the procedure to be followed in all cases where the application for permission is urgent and/or where an interim injunction is sought.[181] Although stated to be guidance, it is the duty of the advocate for the claimant to comply with the procedure it sets out, and where a 'manifestly inappropriate' application is made, consideration will be given to the making of a wasted costs order.[182]

18.96   The procedure is as follows. Where an application is made for the permission application to be heard as a matter of urgency, and/or

---

175 CPR r32.6(1).
176 CPR r32.6(2), and see CPR 22.1(1) and (3), and see the discussion at para 18.74 above.
177 CPR PD 25A para 3.3.
178 CPR r25.3(3) and PD 25A para 3.4 (see also PD 25A paras 4.1–4.5).
179 See 'Evidence in support' at paras 18.105–18.108.
180 See paras 18.109–18.114.
181 Practice Statement (Administrative Court: Listing and Urgent Cases) [2002] 1 WLR 810 Scott Baker J, 1 February 2002.
182 [2002] 1 WLR 810 para 2.

where an interim injunction is sought, the prescribed form (N463) attached to the guidance,[183] must be completed, which sets out:

- the need for urgency;
- the timescale within which consideration of the permission application is sought (eg 72 hours or sooner if necessary); and
- the date by which the substantive hearing should take place.[184]

18.97 Where an interim injunction is sought, the claimant must also provide:

- a draft order; and
- the grounds for seeking the injunction.[185]

18.98 The claimant must serve, by email or fax, and post, the claim form and the application for urgency on the defendant and interested parties, advising them of the application and of their right to make representations.[186] Where an interim injunction is sought, the claimant must also serve, by e-mail or fax, and post, the draft order and grounds for the application, likewise advising the defendant and interested parties of the application and of their right to make representations.[187]

18.99 The Administrative Court currently allocates paper applications for permission on a daily basis, and one judge acts as the 'urgent judge'. The application will be considered within the timescale requested, and the judge may make such order as he or she considers appropriate. If an oral hearing within a specified time is directed, the Administrative Court will liaise with the representatives of the parties to fix a permission hearing within the time period directed.[188]

18.100 Where the matter is so urgent that the urgency procedure cannot be complied with because there is no time to issue proceedings, the claimant can still apply orally for permission and/or interim relief to the duty judge in court 37 at the Royal Courts of Justice. Alternatively, CPR PD 25A para 4.5 indicates that, where interim relief is urgently sought, the claimant's representative can telephone the Royal Courts of Justice on 020 7947 6000, between 10 am and 5 pm and ask to be put through to a judge available to deal with an emergency application in a judicial review matter (though in practice, this can be a difficult procedure to invoke).

---

183 See appendix A, p645 below.
184 [2002] 1 WLR 810 para 4 and form N463.
185 [2002] 1 WLR 810 para 5.
186 [2002] 1 WLR 810 para 6.
187 [2002] 1 WLR 810 para 7.
188 [2002] 1 WLR 810 paras 2, 8 and 9.

18.101   Urgent telephone applications out of hours may be made by telephoning the Royal Courts of Justice and asking security to be put through to the duty judge's clerk, who will contact the duty judge if the matter is sufficiently urgent. In any of these circumstances, the claimant will need to undertake to issue the claim and the injunction application with evidence in support in accordance with the judge's direction; the claim form should normally be served on the defendant with the sealed copy of the injunction order.

18.102   When conducting an urgent hearing before the judge, in the absence of the other party, especially when the hearing is by telephone out of hours, when there will be no official recording of the hearing, it is imperative that the claimant's advocate not only ensures that the judge has been specifically directed to all matters adverse to the claimant's case, but has keeps a record of the hearing, and of the documents to which the judge's attention was directed. This is not only a professional obligation (not to mislead the court) but is also an aspect of the duty to give full and frank disclosure.[189] The advocate will also need a draft order which can be transmitted to the judge, should the interim relief be granted.

Other matters

18.103   As stated above, the practice of the Administrative Court is that all applications will initially be considered by a judge on the papers, unless the court directs otherwise, so as to deal with permission applications more speedily and avoid unnecessary cost.[190] An application for interim relief may well be a reason why the court would direct an oral hearing. The previous practice that claimants should request an oral hearing if they are seeking interim relief,[191] is no longer applicable, particularly in the light of the guidance on urgent cases.[192] There is no provision in the rules, however, to prevent the claimant requesting an oral hearing in appropriate circumstances: if such an application is to be made, it should be set out in sections 7 and 9 of the claim form.

18.104   Where judicial review is sought in a matrimonial or family context, it is desirable for the claimant to request on the claim form

189 See eg, *R (Lawer) v Restormel BC* [2007] EWHC 2299 (Admin) [2008] HLR 20, esp at [63]–[65]. See paras 18.115–18.127 below.

190 See Practice Statement para 6(7) and form N461A para 9(ii).

191 See eg, *R v Kensington and Chelsea RLBC ex p Hammell* [1989] QB 518, per Parker LJ at 539.

192 See paras 18.95–18.102 above.

that the matter be heard by a judge of the Family Division.[193] Such a request may be included at sections 7 and 9 of the claim form. Even if no such request is included, it has been suggested that in sensitive family matters, the Administrative Court Office should always seek to put the claim before a judge with both Administrative Court and Family Division experience, or before the President of the Family Division.[194] It should also be noted that where care proceedings are already on foot, it would normally be wholly inappropriate to seek judicial review (and this is also applicable to family cases that involve human rights issues).[195]

Evidence in support

18.105 A statement of facts relied on must be included in or attached to the claim form, which must be verified by a statement of truth in any event.[196] The claimant may rely on the contents of the statement of case as evidence, provided the contents of the form have been verified by a statement of truth.[197] If written evidence is to be used on behalf of the claimant, however, it must be filed with the claim form.[198]

18.106 Despite of the absence of any formal requirement for evidence, in practice it will frequently be advisable to file evidence in support, not least in order to exhibit documents that may support the claimant's claim.[199]

18.107 The importance of a witness statement in support of the claim, made by the claimant, should not be underestimated. Even though the claim form will contain a statement of the relevant facts, a witness

---

193 R v Dover Magistrates Court ex p Kidner [1983] 1 All ER 475, QBD.

194 See, eg R (S) v Secretary of State for the Home Department [2002] EWHC 18 (Fam/Admin), [2002] Fam 213; and Re M (Care Proceedings: Judicial Review) [2003] EWHC 850 (Admin), [2003] FLR 171, per Munby J at [42]. In S, it was said that plainly there would be cases concerning the welfare of children or incompetent adults which involve public law and, therefore, the Administrative Court would be an appropriate venue but there are many cases that involve public and private law considerations and these cases should be litigated in the Family Division before judges of that division.

195 See, R (S) v Haringey LBC [2003] EWHC 2734 (Admin). In relation to relief sought under HRA 1998 s7(1)(a), see C v Bury MBC [2002] EWHC 1438 (Fam), [2002] 2 FLR 868 at [53]–[55], where it was said that such cases should be heard in the Family Division of the High Court before, if possible, judges with Administrative Court experience.

196 See para 18.74 above.

197 CPR r8.5(7).

198 CPR PD 54A para 5.7(1). See also CPR r8.5(1) and (2).

199 Especially documents referred to at CPR PD 54A paras 5.7(2)–5.7(4).

statement will still enable the claimant to raise matters which are more appropriately dealt with in evidence (such as statements of belief, feelings, etc) and indeed to emphasise matters that although dealt with in the statement of facts, will probably carry more weight if the claimant is willing to attest to them personally (such as denying allegations made against him or making allegations against the decision-maker).

18.108   The general position is that no written evidence may be relied on unless it has been served in accordance with any rule under CPR Pt 54 or a direction of the court[200] (the provisions of CPR r8.6(1) are disapplied)[201] or unless the court gives permission.[202] Accordingly, the court has power to allow statements to be used by the claimant, even if none has been filed with the claim form and such permission may be given where a claimant seeks to reply to evidence from the defendant or to inform the court of subsequent events. It may be, however, that this power would not be exercised in the case of a party who for no good reason has failed to file evidence at the proper time, unless there were strong reasons for doing so.

Formal requirements of written evidence

18.109 The majority of the formal requirements regarding the content of written evidence are contained in CPR Pt 32[203] and PD 32. In brief, the statement must include the heading of the case and,[204] in the top right-hand corner, must appear: the party on whose behalf the statement is made; the initials and surname of the witness; the number of the statement in relation to that witness; the identifying initials and number of each exhibit; and the date on which the statement was made.[205]

18.110   The statement must, if practicable, be in the witness's own words and should be expressed in the first person.[206] It must also state:

- the full name of the witness;
- the address at which he lives or, if the statement is made in his professional or business capacity, the address at which he works, the position he holds and the name of his firm or employer;

---

200 CPR r54.16(2)(a).
201 By CPR r54.16(1).
202 CPR r54.16(2)(b): see further below.
203 See, in particular, CPR r32.8.
204 PD 32 para 17.1.
205 PD 32 para 17.2.
206 PD 32 para 18.1.

- his or her occupation or, if none, description;
- if it is the case, the fact that he or she is a party or the employee of a party to the proceedings;[207]
- which of the statements are made from the witness' own knowledge and which are matters of information and belief;
- the source of any matters of information or belief.[208]

18.111 Exhibits should be verified and identified by the witness, and remain separate from the statement itself.[209] References in the statement to an exhibit should use the words 'I refer to the [description of exhibit] marked "...".[210] Where more than one statement to which there are exhibits is made by a witness in the proceedings, the exhibits should be numbered consecutively throughout the statements and not start again with each statement.[211]

18.112 Provision is also made for the format of the statement, the exhibits, and the statement of truth,[212] and other ancillary matters.[213]

18.113 Hearsay evidence is now generally admissible in civil proceedings, the quality of the evidence going to its weight rather than its admissibility.[214] This is subject to two qualifications: first, the power of the court to exclude evidence that would otherwise be admissible,[215] and secondly, the fact that hearsay evidence may remain inadmissible on other grounds, such as its relevance. In judicial review proceedings, hearsay evidence is commonly used in the form of information derived from the files and records of the decision-maker. The use of such evidence is usually uncontroversial.

18.114 Judicial review claims, particularly at the permission stage, are won and lost on the quality of the claimant's paperwork: these cases are very different from other civil cases, where deficiencies in the papers can frequently be overcome by oral evidence and submissions.

---

207 PD 32 para 18.1(1)–(4).
208 PD 32 para 18.2(1)–(2).
209 PD 32 para 18.3.
210 PD 32 para 18.4.
211 PD 32 para 18.6.
212 PD 32 paras 11.3–15.4; 19.1–20.3.
213 See generally Practice Directions 22 and 32.
214 Civil Evidence Act 1995, especially s2, and see the notice requirements contained in CPR Pt 33. It had previously been held that statements of information and belief were only admissible at the permission stage but not, without permission, at the substantive hearing: *R v Sandhutton Parish Council ex p Todd and Fox* [1992] COD 409, QBD. This has not, however, survived the Civil Evidence Act 1995.
215 CPR r32.1(2).

The foregoing applies, of course, with particular force where, as is now the general practice,[216] permission is considered on the papers alone.

Full and frank disclosure

18.115 Under the first modern codification of procedural rules for judicial review claims,[217] the permission application was formally made without notice to the defendant. At least in the later years of those rules, however, the application had in reality become, in most cases, a hybrid type of application in relation to which the court generally disapproved of claimants coming to court without – at the very least – notifying defendants of their intention to do so by a full letter before action, and at which defendants frequently submitted short written evidence and were represented.

18.116 Nevertheless, formerly, even applications at which both parties were present were made '*ex parte* on notice' rather than *inter partes*. This had implications for the contents of the documents, especially the witness statement, in that the claimant was under a duty to give full and frank disclosure of all relevant matters, even if unfavourable to his or her case. Failure to give such disclosure could constitute grounds for setting permission aside, or for refusing the relief sought at the full hearing. This duty extended not simply to matters of fact,[218] but also to the existence of alternative remedies, ouster clauses and other points of law, including case-law, which were adverse to the claim.[219]

18.117 The position under CPR Pt 54 appears to remain the same, notwithstanding the new requirement of service of the documents filed at court on the defendant, and the opportunity for the defendant to file an acknowledgement of service setting out the grounds for contesting the claim.[220] The essential nature and purpose of the

---

216 *Administrative Court Guidance, Notes for applying for Judicial Review* (1 April 2011) para 10.1.

217 RSC Ord 53.

218 As to which, see, eg, *R v Secretary of State for the Home Department ex p Comfort Henry* [1995] Imm AR 42; *R v Secretary of State for the Home Office ex p Shahina Begum* [1995] COD 176.

219 See, eg, *R v Crown Prosecution Service ex p Hogg* [1994] COD 237, QBD; *R v Cornwall CC ex p Huntingdon and another* [1992] 3 All ER 566, DC, at 576; *R v Secretary of State for the Home Department ex p Li Bin Shi* [1995] COD 135.

220 CPR rr54.7 and 54.8, and see further at paras 18.129–18.133 below.

permission hearing, as a mechanism for filtering out unarguable or otherwise improper claims, remains the same and defendants are not intended, in the acknowledgement of service, to file lengthy, fully argued, defences nor to file detailed evidence in reply. Accordingly, the court will still view with disapproval a judicial review claim that does not set out all the material facts known to the claimant whether or not they support the claimant's case.[221] It should also be noted, however, that a claimant may well seek pre-permission disclosure from a defendant. There is nothing wrong with such an approach although the courts will not entertain fishing expeditions.[222]

18.118 In any event, in urgent cases where permission is sought without any acknowledgement of service having been filed, the requirements of full and frank disclosure are plainly still applicable.[223] Having said this, it is extremely rare for permission to be granted without acknowledgements of service having been filed. It is far more common for interim relief to be granted pending consideration of the permission application and, where necessary, the time for filing and serving acknowlegdements of service will be abridged, sometimes to just a few days.[224]

Content of the duty to give full and frank disclosure

18.119 There is a general obligation on parties to judicial review claims to conduct the proceedings openly.[225] In *R (Lawer) v Restormel Borough*

---

221 A failure to give full and frank disclosure can lead to permission being set aside or interim relief being discharged: see, eg, *R (Webb) v Bristol CC* [2001] EWHC 696 (Admin); *R (Lawer) v Restormel BC* [2007] EWHC 2299 (Admin) [2008] HLR 20; *R (Khan) v Secretary of State for the Home Department* [2008] EWHC 1367 (Admin); *R (MS) v Secretary of State for the Home Department* [2010] EWHC 2400 (Admin); and *R (Konoyba) v Kensington and Chelsea RLBC* [2011] EWHC 2653 (Admin).

222 See, eg, *R (Hoppr Entertainment Ltd) v Office of Communications* [2011] EWHC 3693 (Admin), where it was held that a pre-permission application for disclosure was a mere fishing expedition and not allowed.

223 See, eg, CPR PD 25A para 3.3 in relation to the duty to disclose all material facts on applications for interim injunctions, and see *Memory Corp Plc v Sidhu (No 1)* [2000] 1 WLR 1143, CA; and *R (Lawer) v Restormel Borough Council* [2007] EWHC 2299 (Admin), [2008] HLR 20. See further paras 18.119–18.122 below. As to the procedure for making urgent applications, see paras 18.95–18.102 above.

224 See eg *R (Buckley) v Sheffield CC* [2013] EWHC 512 (Admin) where the time for filing the acknowledgement of service was abridged to just six days.

225 See *R (Gillan) v Commissioner of the Police for the Metropolis* [2004] EWCA Civ 1067, [2005] QB 388, CA at [54].

Council,[226] Munby J set out what was meant by a duty to make proper disclosure:[227]

> ... the duty to make proper disclosure requires more than merely including relevant documents in the court bundle. Proper disclosure for this purpose[228] means specifically identifying all relevant documents for the judge, taking the judge to the particular passages in the document which are material and taking particular steps to ensure that the judge correctly appreciates the significance of what he is being asked to read.

18.120 Munby J also made it clear that the burden on counsel was more onerous where an urgent telephone application was made and the judge had no papers before him.[229]

18.121 The courts have also indicated that, particularly where the case is to be considered on the papers, claimants should draw the attention of the judge to a body of authority that is contrary to the claimant's case and state why it is distinguishable.[230] This obligation is generally applicable to anything that may affect the outcome of the application, or affect any remedy granted, such as the existence of ouster clauses,[231] alternative remedies,[232] and delay. In *R v Bromley LBC ex p Barker*,[233] the judge set aside permission on the basis that the claimant's application notice had not dealt adequately with the question of delay, and had failed to request an extension of time or give reasons why such an extension should be granted.

18.122 It has also been held that the duty extends to disclosure of any defence the claimant has reason to anticipate may be advanced.[234] In practice, this last aspect of the duty is likely to be satisfied by explaining the defendant's position as it has been explained to the claimant, eg in the response to the letter before claim.

18.123 This is one aspect of the duty that arises particularly on the application for permission, although the provision for acknowledgement of service setting out summary grounds of resistance probably mitigates it to some extent. In *R v Jockey Club Licensing Committee ex p*

---

226 [2007] EWHC 2299 (Admin), [2008] HLR 20.

227 *Lawer* at [69].

228 *Lawer* concerned an application for interim relief on a without notice basis.

229 See generally *Lawer* at [63]–[65] and [69]–[70].

230 *R v Crown Prosecution Service ex p Hogg* [1994] COD 237, QBD; *R v Secretary of State for the Home Department ex p Li Bin Shi* [1995] COD 135

231 *R v Cornwall CC ex p Huntington* [1992] 3 All ER 566, DC.

232 For example, *R v Horsham DC ex p Wenman* [1995] 1 WLR 680.

233 [2001] Env LR 1, QBD.

234 *Lloyds Bowmaker Ltd v Britannia Arrow Holdings* [1988] 1 WLR 1337.

Wright (Barrie John),[235] Potts J considered the full extent of that duty on a paper application. He held that the applicant must show utmost good faith and make full and frank disclosure of the material facts; the material facts are those it is material for the judge to know, and materiality is to be decided by the court and not by the applicant's advisers. The applicant must make proper enquiries before applying for permission, and the duty of disclosure includes a duty to disclose such facts as would have been known to the applicant had he or she made such enquiries. The extent of the enquiries which would constitute 'proper' enquiries would depend on all the circumstances of the case, including the nature of the case and the relief sought, the degree of urgency and the amount of time available for such enquiries to be made.[236]

18.124   If it transpires that there has been a material non-disclosure, the court should be astute to ensure that the applicant is deprived of any advantage derived by obtaining permission, in breach of the duty of disclosure. Whether or not the fact that had not been disclosed warranted immediate and automatic discharge of the permission, without consideration of the merits, may depend on the importance of the fact to the issues involved in the application. The court has discretion in the matter and will not automatically discharge permission for every omission.[237] Nevertheless, it has been held that if a person does not comply with the obligation to make full and frank disclosure, he or she will be deprived of the fruits of his order whether or not, had the disclosure been made, he would still have obtained the order and whether the omission was deliberate or innocent, some limited latitude being allowed for a slip, though even then only where the party concerned had corrected it quickly.[238]

---

235 [1991] COD 306, QBD, and see *Brink's-MAT Ltd v Elcombe* [1988] 1 WLR 1350, CA.

236 See also, *R (Lawer) v Restormel BC* [2007] EWHC 2299 (Admin), [2008] HLR 20.

237 See *R v Secretary of State for the Home Department ex p Beecham (Grazyna)* [1996] Imm AR 87, QBD, and *R v Jockey Club Licensing Committee ex p Wright* [1991] COD 306, QBD.

238 *R (Tshikangu) v Newham LBC* [2001] EWHC 118 (Admin), [2001] NPC 33. In this case, permission was set aside on the basis that, among other things, the claimant's solicitors had failed to inform the court that judicial review was no longer required by the claimant, and had not sent a letter before action to the defendant. See also, eg, *Fitzgerald v Williams* [1996] QB 657, CA; *Network Telecom (Europe) Ltd v Telephone Systems International Inc* [2003] EWHC 2890 (QB); and *R (Khan) v Secretary of State for the Home Department* [2008] EWHC 1367 (Admin).

18.125   The courts have, quite apart from setting aside permission where appropriate, been prepared to discharge interim relief and to order wasted costs against legal representatives where there has been a failure by the claimant to comply with the spirit of full and frank disclosure. In *R (MS) v Secretary of State for the Home Department*,[239] an interim injunction preventing the claimant's removal from the United Kingdom was discharged because not only was there no arguable case but there had been material non-disclosure in a without notice application that had been made.[240] In *R (F) v Head Teacher of Addington High School*,[241] the court ordered that the claimant's solicitors pay wasted costs where a letter from the defendant had not been drawn to the attention of the judge at the permission stage.

18.126   The duty to keep the court informed does not cease once the application has been filed or even when permission has been granted. It continues for at least as long as the proceedings continue without notice to the other side.[242] In this respect, the rules on notification of the defendant and other interested parties[243] will render it unlikely that many claims will reach the permission stage on a 'without notice' basis.

18.127   The duty, at pre-permission stage, does not always fall solely on the claimant, particularly where a defendant has had notice and has completed an acknowledgment of service. *R (Evans) v Lord Chancellor*,[244] illustrates how a defendant can be at fault prior to permission being granted. In *Evans*, the defendant resisted the original application for permission for judicial review and succeeded in having permission limited to grounds which did not include the primary ground. After the permission hearing, the defendant 'very properly' disclosed documents which provided renewed weight to the ground

239 [2010] EWHC 2400 (Admin).
240 See also, eg, *R v Wealden District Council ex p Pinnegar* [1996] COD 64; *R (Konoyba) v Kensington and Chelsea RLBC* [2011] EWHC 2653 (Admin); and *R (F) v Westminster CC* [2012] EWHC 1357 (Admin) (even though permission was refused and, therefore, the interim relief would have been discharged in any event, the court held that had permission been granted, the interim relief would have been discharged due to a failure to disclosure relevant material on an urgent application).
241 [2003] EWHC 228 (Admin).
242 *Tshikangu* [2001] EWHC 118 (Admin).
243 See para 18.128 below.
244 [2011] EWHC 1146 (Admin), [2011] 1 WLR 838.

which had not been given permission. Permission was subsequently granted and the claim allowed.[245]

Service on the defendant and interested parties

18.128 By CPR r54.7, the claim form must be served on the defendant and, unless the court directs otherwise, any person the claimant considers to be an interested party (ie any person other than the claimant and the defendant who is directly affected by the claim)[246] within seven days after the date of issue. The court will not serve these documents.[247] Although the rule not does explicitly require service of the documents to be filed with the claim form (including any evidence in support), these documents should also be served, and failure to do so would be very likely to have costs consequences.

Acknowledgement of service

18.129 A person who has been served with the claim form and who wishes to take part in the judicial review proceedings must file and serve an acknowledgement of service.[248] Practice form N462 should be used for this purpose.[249] The acknowledgement must be filed not more than 21 days after the service of the claim form,[250] and served on the claimant and, unless the court directs otherwise, any other person named in the claim form not later than seven days after it is filed.[251] These time limits may not be extended by agreement between the parties[252] but, presumably, may be extended by the court pursuant to its general powers.[253]

---

245 For the duty of disclosure generally in relation to defendants, see also paras 20.26–20.28.
246 CPR r54.1(2)(f).
247 See PD 54A para 6.1.
248 CPR r54.8(1).
249 See appendix A, p648 below.
250 CPR r54.8(2)(a).
251 CPR r54.8(2)(b) and see CPR r54.7(b).
252 CPR r54.8(3).
253 See, eg, CPR r3.1(2)(a). See also CPR rr3.8–3.10 for the general power to relieve a party in default from the sanctions for failure to comply with the rules, and to rectify errors of procedure. See also CPR r6.9 for the power to dispense with service of a document.

18.130 The acknowledgement must state whether the person filing it contests the claim[254] and, if this is the case, must contain a summary of the grounds for doing so.[255] It must also state whether the person filing it (who may be an interested party wishing to support the claim) seeks a different remedy from that set out in the claim form and, if so, what remedy is sought.[256]

18.131 In all cases, the name of the filing party should be set out in full. Where that party's name has been set out incorrectly in the claim form, it should be correctly set out in the acknowledgement, followed by the words 'described as' and the incorrect name.[257] It must be signed by the party or its legal representative and include an address for service.[258] The acknowledgement must also state the name and address of any person the party filing it considers to be an interested party,[259] and may include or be accompanied by an application for directions.[260]

18.132 Other general provisions concerning acknowledgements of service are as follows:

- If two or more parties acknowledge service through the same legal representative at the same time, only one acknowledgement of service is necessary.[261]
- An acknowledgement may be withdrawn or amended only with the permission of the court: an application for this purpose must be made in accordance with the CPR Pt 23 procedure and supported by evidence.[262]

18.133 Although the wording of CPR r54.8(1) would suggest that failure to file and serve an acknowledgement of service within the specified time limits precludes a person from taking any part in the judicial review claim, this is not the effect of the sanctions provided by CPR

254 CPR r8.3(2)(a).
255 CPR r54.8(4)(a)(i).
256 CPR r8.3(2)(b).
257 CPR PD 10 paras 5.1–5.2.
258 CPR r10.5.
259 CPR r54.8(4)(a)(ii), and see CPR r54.1(2)(f) for the definition of 'interested party'.
260 CPR r54.8(4)(b). CPR r54.8(5) disapplies r10.3(2), which subjects the general provisions of CPR r10.3(1) concerning the time for filing acknowledgement of service to two other rules: CPR r6.22 (period for acknowledgement where claim form served out of the jurisdiction) and CPR r6.16(4) (period for responding to claim for served on agent of overseas principal).
261 CPR PD 10 para 5.3.
262 CPR PD 10 paras 5.4–5.5.

r54.9, which are far less draconian. A failure to file and serve an acknowledgement of service in time will, however, preclude a person served with the claim form from taking part in a permission hearing, unless the court allows him to do so.[263] Such a person will be able to take part at the substantive hearing, so long as he or she complies with the rules,[264] or any direction of the court, for filing and serving detailed grounds for resisting (or supporting) the claim and written evidence.[265] The failure to acknowledge service of the claim form may, however, be taken into account by the court in relation to costs.[266] The general rule, contained in CPR r8.4, concerning failure to file and serve an acknowledgement in time is disapplied.[267]

Evidence in reply

18.134 There is nothing in the rules preventing the defendant from filing evidence in reply at the permission stage. Indeed, there is something to be said for doing so where it would assist the court to make a decision on permission and perhaps prevent the pointless incurring of additional costs. Such evidence should be submitted sufficiently long before the permission decision for the claimant to be able to file further evidence, should this be necessary. The court is unlikely to be sympathetic to defendants bombarding it with material prior to the permission decision, or to the late filing of evidence causing delay in the making of the decision or necessitating a hearing that would otherwise have been unnecessary.

The test for permission

18.135 At the permission stage, the court must, in principle, be satisfied that there is an arguable case for review, and that the claimant has sufficient interest in the subject matter of the claim, or standing. The court may also consider questions of delay.[268] A favourable finding on standing is no guarantee that the court at the full hearing will not

---

263 CPR r54.9(1)(a).
264 CPR r54.14.
265 CPR r54.9(1)(b).
266 CPR r54.9(2).
267 CPR r54.9(3). The disapplied rule (CPR r8.4(2)) is that the defendant may attend the hearing of the claim but may not take part in it unless the court gives permission.
268 See paras 18.18–18.69 above.

take a different view of that issue. The court should generally not reconsider the issue of delay if it has been resolved in the claimant's favour at the permission stage.[269]

18.136 Consideration of the application for permission should be relatively brief, as its stated purpose is only to sift out the hopeless or frivolous cases. Permission hearings are listed for no more than 30 minutes. If a party considers that more time will be required, then a time estimate must be provided so that a special fixture can be arranged.[270] In practice, even where a special fixture is requested, applications will often be listed in the general permission list. Administrative Court judges frequently call all the cases in the list into court at the start of the morning's business and decide the running order by reference to the probable length of time each case is likely to take to be heard.

18.137 In practice, it not unusual for the court to go into the matter in some depth at the permission stage. Hearings can last considerably longer than the allotted time, particularly where the defendant attends. On occasion, oral applications for permission can last several hours, especially where (for instance, in deportation cases when a time for removal has been set) the issues involved are extremely important, and the permission hearing will effectively dispose of the matter.

The permission decision

18.138 The court will consider the permission application on the papers.[271] Where permission is granted, the court may also give directions, including ordering a stay of the proceedings to which the claim relates (ie the decision-making process challenged, not the judicial review proceedings).[272] The orders that may be made on the grant of permission are discussed elsewhere.[273]

18.139 On granting or refusing permission, whether on the papers alone or following an oral hearing, the court will serve its order to that effect, including any directions given, on the claimant, the defendant

---

269 See paras 18.39–18.45 above.

270 *Administrative Court Guidance, Notes for applying for Judicial Review* (1 April 2011) para 11.4.

271 CPR PD 54A para 8.4.

272 CPR r54.10(1)–(2).

273 Paras 5.53–5.71 above and paras 18.158–18.161 below.

and any other person who filed an acknowledgement of service.[274] Where the court decides on the papers to refuse permission, or to grant it subject to conditions or on certain grounds only, it will also serve its reasons for that decision at the same time as serving the order.[275]

Adjourning into open court

18.140   If the court is not sure whether permission should be granted on the papers, it has power to adjourn the permission application into open court for a hearing at which the defendant and other interested parties may – or must – attend.[276] This power is most likely to be used where the defendant is in possession of important information that will have a material influence on whether permission should or should not be granted, where the judge requires clarification of the defendant's position, or where issues of delay arise for consideration.[277]

18.141   An application for interim relief may, additionally, render an oral hearing appropriate, though this will no longer inevitably be the case, given the defendant's opportunity to state its case in the acknowledgement of service. (Under the old rules, the practice was for an oral hearing to be held whenever a claimant sought interim relief, as the means by which the defendant could make representations.[278])

Sensitive applications concerning children

18.142   In *Re M (Care Proceedings: Judicial Review)*,[279] the following guidance was suggested for dealing with cases (which were much to be deprecated) where judicial review claims were brought seeking to restrain the institution of care or other proceedings for the protection of a child, or otherwise to raise matters that were properly raised in such proceedings as were already on foot. To avoid delay, in such a situ-

---

274 CPR r54.11.

275 CPR r54.12(1)-(2).

276 There is nothing in CPR Pt 54 requiring the court to consider the application on the papers. This practice is referred to in PD 54A (paras 8.4–8.6) as a general rule but it is no more than that.

277 See paras 18.18–18.69 above.

278 *R v Kensington and Chelsea RLBC ex p Hammell* [1989] QB 518, per Parker LJ at 539.

279 [2003] EWHC 850 (Admin), [2003] FLR 171, per Munby J at [42].See also para 18.104 above.

ation, which could be extremely damaging to a child who may be urgently in need of the court's protection:

- the Administrative Court Office should upon receipt of the papers immediately issue the proceedings and then immediately place the file before an Administrative Court judge who is also a judge of the Family Division. If no such judge is immediately available, the file should be put before the President of the Family Division;

- the judge before whom the file is placed should give immediate directions, with a view, where appropriate, to the case being 'fast-tracked' and disposed of as quickly as possible. It may be appropriate to dispense both with the acknowledgement of service and with any preliminary decision by the judge on the papers, and to proceed immediately to an oral hearing before a judge (who should always be an Administrative Court and Family Division judge).

Renewal of applications[280]

18.143 There is no right of appeal against a paper refusal or conditional grant of permission, or a grant on restricted grounds only, but the claimant may request that it be reconsidered at an oral hearing. Such a request must be filed within seven days of the service of the reasons.[281] No

---

280 On 13 December 2012, the Ministry of Justice launched a brief consultation exercise, closing on 24 January 2013, which made various proposals for the reform of certain aspects of judicial review procedure: *Judicial Review: proposals for reform*, Ministry of Justice, December 2012. The Government's response to the consultation – *Reform of Judicial Review: the Government response*, Cm 8611, Ministry of Justice, April 2013 (*Response*), contains the government's final proposals. The consultation paper had proposed removing the right to an oral renewal of the permission application in two circumstances: (a) where there has already been a prior judicial process involving a hearing considering substantially the same issue as raised in the judicial review claim; and (b) where the judge, on written submissions, has determined the claim to be 'totally without merit'. The Government have decided to proceed in part with this proposal, removing the right to an oral reconsideration where a judge has determined the claim to be 'totally without merit' but not on the basis that substantially the same matter has been considered at a prior judicial hearing (*Response* paras.16 and 17). The Government has also decided to introduce a fee of £215 for an oral renewal hearing. The fee will rise to £235 if the consultation on fees results in the increase of fees generally to that level but at the time of writing the response to that consultation was not published. Should permission be granted on the renewed application, nor further fee will be payable (ie the fee referred to at para 18.73, above, will not be required).

281 CPR r54.12(3)–(4).

indication is given in the CPR or Part 54, or PD 54A, as to how the request is made. The Notes for Guidance, however, provide that a request for an oral hearing must be made on the notice of renewal, Form 86b, and a copy of the form should be sent to the claimant with the judge's decision to refuse permission.[282] A Practice Statement[283] has been issued which requires claimants, when completing the form used for renewing permission applications, to set out the grounds for renewal in the light of the reasons given by the single judge when refusing permission on the papers.

18.144 In practice, the Administrative Court Office will serve Form 86b, with the order and reasons for refusal/conditional/limited permission.

18.145 At least two days' notice of any hearing date will be given to the claimant, defendant and any other person who filed an acknowledgement of service.[284] This provision formalises what had historically been the position, namely that oral permission hearings (particularly those following the refusal of permission on the papers) are on notice to the defendant and all interested parties. The Practice Direction makes clear, however, that notification of a hearing does not oblige the defendant or other interested party to attend, unless the court directs otherwise, and that attendance will not generally lead to a costs order being made against the claimant.[285]

18.146 The oral hearing is treated as a new application. There is no additional burden on the claimant to demonstrate that the judge refusing, or granting conditional permission, was wrong to have done so. The test is the same as that which applied on the paper application: whether the claimant can demonstrate an arguable case. Where an application is renewed, however, it is usually sensible to prepare a skeleton argument for the hearing, although this is not required by the rules or practice directions. The advantage of doing so is to deal with the reasons given for the first decision and to put before the second judge points and arguments that have not already been rejected by the judge who considered the matter on the papers. It also offers the chance to set out the claimant's contentions more clearly or more persuasively.

---

282 *Administrative Court Guidance, Notes for applying for judicial review* (1 April 2011) paras 11.1–11.5.

283 *Practice Statement,* Scott Baker J, 1 February 2002, [2002] 1 All ER 633 at 636.

284 CPR r54.12(5).

285 CPR PD 54A paras 8.5–8.6. The defendant, if permission is refused following the hearing, will still be entitled to seek the costs of the acknowledgement of service: see paras 18.165–18.170 below.

18.147   In addition, where permission has been refused on a specific factual basis, such as that of undue delay, it will generally be necessary for further evidence to be submitted, in addition to any skeleton argument, dealing with the points of fact arising, eg explaining the reasons for the delay.

Appeals against the refusal of permission

Non-criminal applications

18.148 Where permission is refused following an oral hearing, in a non-criminal judicial review application, the claimant may apply to the Court of Appeal for permission to appeal against the refusal.[286] It is to be noted that the right of appeal to the Court of Appeal may be narrower than the right to request an oral hearing in the Administrative Court,[287] in that it appears to apply only to a refusal of permission (which will include refusal on some grounds and permission on others), but not to a conditional grant.

18.149   The application for permission to appeal must be made within seven – not the usual 21 – days of the judge's refusal of permission to apply for judicial review.[288] Permission to appeal is sought by completing an appellant's notice[289] in the usual way, but different provisions are made regarding the documents that must be filed with the appellant's notice.[290] The documents to be filed are:

- one additional copy of the appellant's notice for the Court of Appeal;[291]
- one copy of the appellant's notice for each respondent, to be sealed and returned;[292]
- the order refusing permission to apply for judicial review;[293]

---

286 CPR r52.15(1).
287 See paras 18.143–18.147 above, and CPR r54.12(3). CPR r52.15 states that it applies where permission has been refused at an oral hearing in the High Court. See further paras 20.17–20.19.
288 CPR r52.15(2). The general power to extend time applies to appeals, and an application to extend time should be made in the usual way.
289 Form N161 – see generally CPR Pt 52.
290 CPR PD 52 para 5.1.
291 CPR PD 52 para 5.6(2)(a) and 5.6A(1)(b).
292 CPR PD 52 para 5.6(2)(b).
293 CPR PD 52 para 5.6(2)(d).

- the Form N461 and statement of facts;[294]
- a copy of the original decision that is the subject of the judicial review application;[295]
- any witness statements or affidavits in support of any application included in the appellant's notice;[296]
- a copy of any order giving or refusing permission to appeal together with the judge's reasons; [297]one copy of the skeleton argument for each notice filed;[298] a transcript of the judgment;[299]
- any other documents the appellant reasonably deems necessary for the appeal court to reach a decision.[300]

18.150   Where it is not possible to file all the above documents, the appellant must indicate which documents have not yet been filed and the reasons why they are not currently available.[301]

18.151   Unless the Court of Appeal orders otherwise, a sealed copy of the appellant's notice, including any skeleton argument, must be served on all respondents to the application for permission to appeal as soon as practicable and, in any event, not later than seven days after it is filed.[302] Where it is impracticable for the appellant's skeleton argument to accompany the appellant's notice, it must be lodged and served on all respondents within 14 days of filing the notice.[303] An unrepresented appellant is not obliged to lodge a skeleton argument, but is encouraged to do so to assist the court.[304]

18.152   On an application for permission to appeal against the refusal of permission, the Court of Appeal may, instead of giving permission to appeal, grant permission to apply for judicial review. Where it does so, the case will proceed in the High Court unless the Court of Appeal orders otherwise.[305] In making the decision, the Court of Appeal should look to achieve the most convenient and costs effective

---

294 CPR PD 52 para 5.6A(1)(g). This paragraph requires the filing of statements of case where relevant to the subject of the appeal.

295 CPR PD 52 para 5.6A(1)(j).

296 CPR PD 52 para 5.6(2)(f) and 5.6A(1)(d).

297 CPR PD 52 para 5.6(2)(e).

298 CPR PD 52 para 5.6(2)(c).

299 CPR PD 52 para 5.6A(1)(f).

300 CPR PD 52 para 5.6A(1)(l).

301 CPR PD 52 para 5.7.

302 CPR r52.4(3) and PD 52 para 5.21.

303 CPR PD 52 paras 5.9(2).

304 CPR PD 52 para 5.9(3).

305 CPR r52.15(3)–(4).

course.[306] The Court of Appeal may deem it appropriate to retain cases where, for example, the Administrative Court would be bound by authority, an appeal to the Court of Appeal would be inevitable for some other reason, or it is the cost convenient course given the issue(s) raised by the claim.[307]The Court of Appeal should also consider whether or not the claim needs to be transferred to the Upper Tribunal in accordance with s31A of the SCA 1981.

18.153   The power to grant permission to apply for judicial review rather than permission to appeal against the refusal of permission is akin to the procedure under the old rules. It will generally be more appropriate for the Court of Appeal to adopt this course than to grant permission to appeal which would then require a further full appeal hearing on the issue of whether permission to apply for judicial review ought to have been refused. Such a course would incur additional costs and may be thought inappropriate bearing in mind that if the test for permission to appeal is satisfied – that the judge below was arguably wrong to refuse permission to apply – it is likely to follow that the judicial review claim was itself arguable and that no purpose would be served by a full appeal on this issue.[308] It is also considered undesirable to have a claim heard by two or three Court of Appeal judges before it has been adjudicated on by a first instance judge.[309]

18.154   The Court of Appeal will not always adopt such a course, particularly where the issue is not simply whether the judge at the permission stage wrongly decided that the claim was not arguable, but relates instead to a specific point of law or specific issue, such as delay. In *Burkett*,[310] for example, the Court of Appeal granted permission to appeal but dismissed the full appeal on the issue of delay.[311]

---

306 See *R (Shiner) v Commissioners of HM Revenue and Customs* [2010] EWCA Civ 558.

307 See, eg, *R (Shiner) v Commissioners of HM Revenue and Customs* [2010] EWCA Civ 558, where the Court of Appeal heard the substantive case due to issues of European law and Convention Rights which could be dealt with alongside linked cases.

308 See the notes to the *White Book* (Sweet & Maxwell, 2013) Vol 1 p1764–65 paras 52.15.2 and 52.15.3.

309 *White Book* (Sweet & Maxwell, 2013) Vol 1 p1764–65 para 52.15.3.

310 [2002] UKHL 23, [2002] 1 WLR 1593.

311 See also, eg, *R (M) v Homerton University Hospital* [2008] EWCA Civ 197, where permission to appeal was granted and followed by argument on appeal regarding the refusal to grant permission for judicial review; and *R (Omar) v Secretary of State for Foreign & Commonwealth Affairs* [2011] EWCA Civ 1589, where the Court of Appeal granted permission to apply for judicial review after hearing a substantive appeal against the refusal of permission.

Criminal applications

18.155   In criminal applications, there is no right to appeal to the Court of Appeal against the refusal of permission.[312]

Further appeal

18.156   It used to be thought that there was no right of appeal to the Supreme Court against a refusal of permission to appeal or to apply for judicial review. In *R (Burkett) v Hammersmith and Fulham LBC*,[313] however, the House of Lords held that it did indeed have jurisdiction to entertain an appeal from the Court of Appeal, where the Court of Appeal had granted permission to appeal against the refusal of permission to apply for judicial review, but had then dismissed the appeal on the merits after a full hearing, and so had refused permission to apply for judicial review.

18.157   In other cases, it appears that the formerly understood position still holds good: there is no right of appeal to the Supreme Court against a refusal of permission to appeal to the Court of Appeal,[314] nor any right to appeal against the refusal of permission to apply for judicial review itself on an application for permission to the Court of Appeal.[315] The rationale for this is that the only application before the Court of Appeal is for permission to appeal, which cannot be the subject of further appeal.

Directions and orders on the grant of leave

18.158   The court hearing the permission application has power to allow the applicant to amend his or her claim form.[316] Where permission is granted, the court has power to give directions, including imposing

---

312   SCA 1981 s18(1)(a), and see *R v Tottenham Justices ex p Ewing* (1986) 30 July, unreported.

313   [2002] UKHL 23, [2002] 1 WLR 1593.

314   See *R v Secretary of State for Trade and Industry ex p Eastaway* [2000] 1 WLR 2222, HL.

315   *Re Poh* [1983] 1 WLR 2, HL. Though this decision was doubted in *Kemper Reinsurance Co v Minister of Finance* [2000] 1 AC 1, PC, it was confirmed in *Eastaway* [2000] 1 WLR 2222. It was distinguished in *Burkett*, but not departed from, and is consistent with *Eastaway*.

316   CPR r17.1(2).

a stay on the decision-making process which is the subject matter of the application.[317]

18.159　The court may order that the hearing of the substantive application be expedited and abridge the defendant's time for filing detailed grounds of resistance and evidence in reply to the claim.[318] These powers may be of particular importance, for example, in homelessness cases if an injunction is refused.[319] In deciding whether to seek expedition, it should be remembered that in 2011 it took on average 11 weeks for a decision on permission to be taken on the papers, and a further 21 weeks if the matter went to an oral renewal. Overall, the average waiting time for non-expedited cases, from lodging to final decision was around 10 months.[320]

18.160　The court may otherwise grant permission on terms.[321] In *R v Westminster CC ex p Residents' Association of Mayfair*,[322] an order for security for costs was made. The court also has inherent jurisdiction to grant bail where permission is granted (or even pending the permission application), but not if permission is refused.[323]

18.161　More detailed consideration of the powers of the court to grant interim relief may be found in chapter 5.[324]

Costs

18.162　CPR Pt 54 makes no specific provision regarding costs. Ordinarily, if permission is granted, costs will be reserved to the full application, or will be ordered to be in the cause. The court may well consider the issue of costs, even on granting permission, if it is considered that the matter is likely to be resolved without the need for a full hearing. In particular, in these circumstances, it may be worthwhile seeking to obtain an order for a detailed assessment of a claimant's publicly

---

317　CPR r54.10(1)-(2).

318　CPR r3.1(2)(a) and (b).

319　Although see *R v Cardiff CC ex p Barry* (1990) 22 HLR 261, where it was held that, where necessary, an injunction ought ordinarily to follow from the grant of permission in homelessness cases.

320　*Management information, Administrative Court Office,* as cited in the consultation paper 'Judicial Review, Proposals for Reform' December 2012 para 33 and footnote 14. See www.official-documents.gov.uk/document/cm85/8515/8515.pdf.

321　CPR r54.12(b)(i).

322　[1991] COD 182, QBD.

323　See *R v Secretary of State for the Home Department ex p Turkoglu* [1988] QB 398.

324　See paras 5.53–5.71 above.

funded costs, although if this is not possible, any consent order filed
to seek to dispose of the application is likely to make provision for
costs (or else the court will be required to rule on the issue).

18.163　If the defendant concedes, or the application is not pursued for
other reasons, before the permission hearing, the starting position
is that it is unusual for the claimant to be awarded the costs even of
issuing the application.[325] For a full discussion of the issue of costs,
see chapter 21 below.[326]

18.164　Even if the defendant appears at an oral hearing and permission
is refused, CPR PD 54 para 8.6 provides that that the court will generally not make a costs order against the claimant in respect of the
hearing; neither the defendant nor any interested party is required to
attend such a hearing unless the court directs otherwise.[327] In making a decision about costs:

- the court will take account of the claimant's compliance or otherwise with the pre-action protocol, and the conduct of the parties
  generally;[328] and
- the defendant will generally be entitled to a limited amount of
  costs in respect of drafting the acknowledgement of service.[329]

325　See *R (Boxall) v Waltham Forest LBC* [2000] All ER (D) 2445, though see *R v
　　Kensington and Chelsea RLBC ex p Ghebregiogis* (1994) 27 HLR 602, [1994] COD
　　502, QBD; where costs were awarded against a respondent who conceded
　　before the permission hearing because of the failure to engage properly with
　　the claim at letter before action stage. It should also be noted that where a
　　claim is ultimately unsuccessful a judge should turn his mind to whether the
　　costs awarded in favour of a defendant should include pre-permission costs. If
　　these are sought, it is for the defendant to justify their inclusion: *R (Davey) v
　　Aylesbury Vale District Council* [2007] EWCA Civ 1166, [2008] 1 WLR 878). See
　　also paras 21.59–21.64 below.
326　See paras 21.34–21.66 below.
327　CPR PD 54A paras 8.5 and 8.6. Exceptionally, costs may be awarded (*R
　　(Davey) v Aylesbury Vale District Council* [2007] EWCA Civ 1166, [2008] 1
　　WLR 878). This may occur, for example, if the defendant has been required
　　by the court to attend, rather than merely notified of the hearing: see, eg, *R
　　v Committee of Advertising Practice ex p Bradford Exchange Ltd* [1991] COD
　　43, QBD, (although the applicant made no submissions to the contrary and
　　had sought interim relief). See also *R v Commissioners of Inland Revenue ex p
　　Mead and Cook* [1993] COD 324 (where costs were not awarded). Both of these
　　authorities relate to the old rules.
328　See paras 18.165–18.170 below. See paras 17.27–17.51 above; and see also
　　CPR r44.3(4)(a).
329　See paras 8.165–18.170 below.

Defendants' costs at the permission stage

18.165 In *R (Mount Cook Land Ltd) v Westminster City Council*,[330] the Court of Appeal held for the first time that, in principle, there was no reason why a defendant who incurred costs complying with the rules by filing an acknowledgement of service with summary grounds of resistance, should not be entitled to recover the costs of so doing should permission be refused, albeit that the general position that a defendant who attended a permission hearing would not ordinarily be entitled to the costs of that hearing remained good law.

18.166 Auld LJ said:[331]

> ... I would hold the following to be the proper approach to the award of costs against an unsuccessful claimant, and to the relationship of the obligation in CPR 54.8 on a defendant 'who wishes to take part in the judicial review' to file an acknowledgment of service with the general rule in paragraph 8.6 of the Practice Direction that a successful defendant at an oral permission hearing should not generally be awarded costs against the claimant:
>
> 1) ... certainly in a case to which the Pre-Action Protocol applies and where a defendant or other interested party has complied with it, ... a successful defendant or other party at the permission stage who has filed an acknowledgment of service pursuant to CPR 54.8 should generally recover the costs of doing so from the claimant, whether or not he attends any permission hearing.
>
> 2) The effect of paragraph 8.6, when read with paragraph 8.5, of the Practice Direction,[332] in conformity with the long-established practice of the courts in judicial review and the thinking of the Bowman Report giving rise to the CPR 54 procedure, is that a defendant who attends and successfully resists the grant of permission at a renewal hearing should not generally recover from the claimant his costs of and occasioned by doing so.
>
> 3) A court, in considering an award against an unsuccessful claimant of the defendant's and/or any other interested party's costs at a permission hearing, should only depart from the general guidance in the Practice Direction if he considers there are exceptional circumstances for doing so.
>
> 4) A court considering costs at the permission stage should be allowed a broad discretion as to whether, on the facts of the case, there are exceptional circumstances justifying the award of costs against an unsuccessful claimant.

---

330 [2003] EWCA Civ 1346, [2004] CP Rep 12.
331 *Mount Cook Land* at [76].
332 See above para 18.164.

5) Exceptional circumstances may consist in the presence of one or more of the features in the following non-exhaustive list:
   a) the hopelessness of the claim:
   b) the persistence in it by the claimant after having been alerted to facts and/or of the law demonstrating its hopelessness;
   c) the extent to which the court considers that the claimant, in the pursuit of his application, has sought to abuse the process of judicial review for collateral ends – a relevant consideration as to costs at the permission stage, as well as when considering discretionary refusal of relief at the stage of substantive hearing, if there is one; and
   d) whether, as a result of the deployment of full argument and documentary evidence by both sides at the hearing of a contested application, the unsuccessful claimant has had, in effect, the advantage of an early substantive hearing of the claim.
6) A relevant factor for a court, when considering the exercise of its discretion on the grounds of exceptional circumstances, may be the extent to which the unsuccessful claimant has substantial resources which it has used to pursue the unfounded claim and which are available to meet an order for costs.
7) The Court of Appeal should be slow to interfere with the broad discretion of the court below in its identification of factors constituting exceptional circumstances and in the exercise of its discretion whether to award costs against an unsuccessful claimant.

18.167   In *R (Ewing) v Deputy Prime Minister*, the Court of Appeal amplified the principles on which defendants may be awarded costs, and the practice for seeking such costs.[333]

- Where a proposed defendant or interested party wishes to seek costs at the permission stage, the acknowledgement of service should include an application for costs and should be accompanied by a schedule setting out the amount claimed.
- The judge refusing permission should include in the refusal a decision whether to award costs in principle, and (if so) an indication of the amount which he proposes to assess summarily.
- The claimant should be given 14 days to respond in writing and should serve a copy on the defendant.
- The defendant should then have seven days to reply in writing to any such response, and to the amount proposed by the judge.
- The judge will then decide and make an award on the papers.

---

333 [2005] EWCA Civ 1583, [2006] 1 WLR 1260, per Carnwath LJ at [47].

18.168 Carnwath LJ said that while the principles established by *Mount Cook*[334] were not in question, they must not be applied in a way that seriously impedes the right of citizens to access to justice, particularly when seeking to protect their environment.[335] In the ordinary case, the court must be particularly careful to ensure that the costs falling on the judicial review claimant are not disproportionately inflated by the involvement of the other parties at the permission stage.[336]

18.169   In relation to the onus on the defendant to file an acknowledgement of service with summary grounds of resistance, neither the rules nor the practice direction explained what was meant by 'summary'. The 'summary' required must, however, be contrasted with the 'detailed grounds for contesting the claim' and the supporting 'written evidence', required following the grant of permission.[337]

> In construing the rule, it is necessary also to have regard to its purpose, and place in the procedural scheme. If the parties have complied with the pre-action protocol, they should be familiar with the general issues between them. The purpose of the 'summary of grounds' is not to provide the basis for full argument of the substantive merits, but rather ... to assist the judge in deciding whether to grant permission, and if so on what terms. If a party's position is sufficiently apparent from the protocol response, it may be appropriate simply to refer to that letter in the acknowledgement of service. In other cases it will be helpful to draw attention to any 'knock-out points' or procedural bars, or the practical or financial consequences for other parties (which may, for example, be relevant to directions for expedition). ... it should be possible to do what is required without incurring 'substantial expense at this stage'.[338]

18.170 Accordingly, if defendants wish to incur greater expense in preparing a document that is more elaborate than the rules require, they should not expect to recover the extra expense from a claimant whose application is dismissed at the permission stage, since they will be doing more than the rules require of them at that stage.[339]

---

334 [2003] EWCA Civ 1346, [2004] CP Rep 12.
335 *Ewing*, per Carnwath LJ at [41].
336 *Ewing*, per Carnwath LJ at [42].
337 CPR r54.14.
338 *Ewing*, per Carnwath LJ at [43].
339 *Ewing*, per Brooke LJ at [53].

Protective costs orders

18.171 The principle of the protective costs order (PCO)[340] was established under the old Rules of the Supreme Court in *R v Lord Chancellor ex p Child Poverty Action Group*,[341] and was affirmed, under the CPR, almost immediately in *R v Hammersmith and Fulham LBC ex p CPRE London Branch*,[342] and *R (Campaign for Nuclear Disarmament) v The Prime Minister and others (Costs)*.[343] The PCO enables a claimant to obtain a protective order, in advance of the determination of the substantive issues in the case and so in advance of any costs order being made against him, limiting the amount of costs he or she would be obliged to pay should the claim fail and a costs order be made against him or her.

18.172 In the *Campaign for Nuclear Disarmament* case,[344] apparently the first case in which the court's jurisdiction was ever exercised, it was said that such an order such an order would only be made in exceptional circumstances.[345] The claimant applied for a PCO limiting the costs it would be obliged to pay if unsuccessful in its judicial review proceedings to £25,000. The application was made prior to consideration of the permission application in a claim for an advisory declaration that UN Resolution 1441 did not authorise the use of military force against the regime of Saddam Hussein in Iraq.

18.173 The claimant contended that the circumstances were exceptional: it was a private company limited by guarantee, it had only modest resources and had not been able to raise money to finance the claim, given the short timescale within which the application had to be made. In the event of a large, adverse costs order, it would run the risk of either being forced into liquidation or at least severely having to curtail its activities. The issues were of undoubted public importance but it would be unable to proceed with the application in the absence of a limitation on its prospective costs liability. £25,000 was an appropriate limit, as that sum would be sufficient to cover its own costs and, if – as the defendant asserted – the claim was found

---

340 The jurisdiction for which appears to arise from the general provisions of CPR r44.3.

341 [1999] 1 WLR 347, QBD. See also *Hodgson v Imperial Tobacco* [1998] 1 WLR 1056 at 1068A.

342 (1999) 26 October, unreported.

343 [2002] EWHC 2712 (Admin), [2003] CP Rep 28. The PCO was referred to as a pre-emptive costs order in this case.

344 [2002] EWHC 2712 (Admin), [2003] CP Rep 28.

345 See *Campaign for Nuclear Disarmament* [2002] EWHC 2712 (Admin), per Simon Brown LJ at [3].

to be without merit and so permission were refused, that sum would surely meet the defendant's entitlement in costs. In any event, if no order were made and the challenge foundered, an alternative claimant would be available, possibly with public funding, in which case the defendant could not hope even to recover £25,000 in costs.

18.174 The court made the order sought, remarking that these arguments were compelling, particularly given that most claimants could usually hope to obtain the court's decision on permission without any adverse costs order at all, and that if permission were refused, the defendant would be unlikely to have incurred more by way of costs than the £25,000 suggested. It was undoubtedly appropriate to make the order sought, which kind of order would be particularly appropriate where such a course would ensure a quick ruling against the claimants if the case were unfounded.[346] Notice of this type of application should be given by the claimant at an early stage, preferably by including it in the claim form.[347]

18.175 In *R (Corner House Research) v Secretary of State for Trade and Industry*,[348] the Court of Appeal reconsidered the principles and practice applicable to the making of PCOs.

- A protective costs order may be made at any stage of proceedings, on such conditions as the court thinks fit, provided that the court is satisfied that:
  - the issues raised are of general public importance;[349]
  - the public interest requires that those issues should be resolved;
  - the applicant has no private interest in the outcome of the case;
  - having regard to the financial resources of the applicant and the respondent(s) and to the amount of costs that are likely to be involved it is fair and just to make the order;
  - if the order is not made the applicant will probably discontinue proceedings and will be acting reasonably in so doing.
- If those acting for the applicant are doing so pro bono this will be likely to enhance the merits of the application for a PCO.

---

346 [2002] EWHC 2712 (Admin), per Simon Brown LJ at [4]–[6].

347 [2002] EWHC 2712 (Admin), per Maurice Kay J at [7].

348 [2005] EWCA Civ 192, [2005] 1 WLR 2600.

349 See, however, *R (Garner) v Elmbridge BC* [2010] EWCA Civ 1006, [2012 PTSR 250, where it was said there was no requirement of 'general public importance' in environmental cases under the Environmental Impact Assessment Directive and Aarhus Convention.

- It is for the court, in its discretion, to decide whether it is fair and just to make the order in the light of the considerations set out above.[350]
- A PCO can take a number of different forms and the choice of the form of the order is an important aspect of the discretion exercised by the judge.[351]
- There is room for considerable variation, depending on what is appropriate and fair in each of the rare cases in which the question may arise. It is likely that a cost capping order for the claimants' costs will be required in all cases other than where their lawyers are acting pro bono.[352]

18.176 The Court of Appeal, in *Corner House*,[353] offered the following additional guidance, derived from *King v Telegraph Group Ltd*.[354]

- When making any PCO where the applicant is seeking an order for costs in its favour if it wins, the court should prescribe by way of a capping order a total amount of the recoverable costs that will be inclusive, so far as a CFA-funded party is concerned, of any additional liability.
- When making any PCO where the applicant is seeking an order for costs in its The purpose of the PCO will be to limit or extinguish the liability of the applicant if it loses, and as a balancing factor the liability of the defendant for the applicant's costs if the defendant loses will thus be restricted to a reasonably modest amount. The applicant should expect the capping order to restrict it to solicitors' fees and a fee for a single advocate of junior counsel status that are no more than modest.
- The overriding purpose of exercising this jurisdiction is to enable the applicant to present its case to the court with a reasonably competent advocate without being exposed to such serious financial risks that would deter it from advancing a case of general public importance at all, where the court considers that it is in the public interest that an order should be made. The beneficiary of a PCO must not expect the capping order that will accompany the PCO to permit anything other than modest representation, and must arrange its legal representation (when its lawyers are not willing to act pro bono) accordingly.[355]

---

350 *Corner House*, per Lord Phillips of Worth Matravers MR at [74].
351 *Corner House*, per Lord Phillips of Worth Matravers MR at [75].
352 *Corner House*, per Lord Phillips of Worth Matravers MR at [76].
353 [2005] EWCA Civ 192, [2005] 1 WLR 2600.
354 [2004] EWCA Civ 613.
355 *Corner House* at [76].

- A PCO should normally be sought on the face of the claim form, supported by evidence, including a schedule of the claimant's future costs of the full judicial review application. If the defendant wishes to resist the application, it should set out its reasons in the acknowledgment of service. The claimant will be liable for the court fee, and for the defendant's proportionate costs if the making of a PCO is successfully resisted, though proportionate costs would not normally exceed £1,000.[356]

- The judge will then consider whether to make the PCO on the papers, at the same time as the permission application and, if he decides to make an order, in what terms, and the size of the cap on the claimant's recoverable costs. If the PCO is refused, any hearing on a renewed application should be limited to an hour and the claimant will face a liability for costs if the PCO is again refused. A defendant's proportionate costs at this stage would be unlikely to exceed £2,500.[357]

- Although CPR r54.13[358] does not in terms apply to the making of a PCO, the defendant will have had the opportunity of providing reasoned written argument before the order is made, and the court should not set a PCO aside unless there is a compelling reason for doing so. The PCO made on paper will provide costs protection if any such application is made. An unmeritorious application to set aside a PCO should be met with an order for indemnity costs, to which any cap imposed by the PCO should not apply.[359]

18.177   There does not need to be anything exceptional about a case in order for a PCO to be made.[360]

18.178   In *Goodson v HM Coroner for Bedfordshire and Luton (Protective Costs)*,[361] the Court of Appeal held that no different principles should apply if an application for a PCO is made at the appellate stage of proceedings. The court rejected an invitation not to apply the requirement that the appellant should have no personal interest in the proceedings.

356 *Corner House* at [78].
357 *Corner House* at [79].
358 No party may apply to set aside a grant of permission.
359 *Corner House* at [79]. If an interested party wishes to oppose the making of a PCO, it will normally be entitled to the proportionate costs of drafting that part of their acknowledgement of service; the court will not generally allow costs to more than one interested party, however, as it will expect such parties to make common cause: at [80].
360 *R (Compton) v Wiltshire Primary Care Trust* [2008] EWCA Civ 749.
361 [2005] EWCA Civ 1172.

18.179   In *R (Ministry of Defence) v Wiltshire and Swindon Coroner*,[362] Collins J stated that there was no reason in principle why a PCO should
not be made in an appropriate case in favour of a defendant. Such
cases would be unusual, but may arise where the defendant had
a public law role but no indemnity for costs from any other body.
This principle was applied in *R (Buglife) v Thurrock Thames Gateway
Development Corporation*,[363] where the Court of Appeal upheld a decision of the High Court to grant a PCO in favour of both the claimant,
Buglife, limiting their costs exposure to £10,000, and also in favour of
the first defendant, so that in the event that the claim was successful,
Buglife would recover no more than £10,000 in costs.

18.180   It was not inevitable that reciprocal PCOs would be made in a
case where the claimant succeeded in obtaining an order; whether
a reciprocal order was appropriate would depend on all the circumstances of the case.[364] If a defendant sought a PCO, it should make
its application in its acknowledgement of service, though the court
would do its utmost to dissuade parties from embarking on expensive satellite litigation over cost-capping orders.[365]

18.181   The 'no personal interest' rule has been the most controversial
condition imposed on the availability of PCOs, and has proved a
significant inhibition on the making of such orders. The Working
Group on Facilitating Public Interest Litigation[366] recommended that
the existence of a private interest should not be a bar to obtaining a
PCO, although it should be a relevant consideration. It also recommended the abandonment of the condition that the party seeking the
order would not proceed with the action if the PCO was refused.

18.182   Such arguments found favour with the Court of Appeal in *R (Derek
England) v Tower Hamlets LBC*.[367] The applicant was a campaigner
opposed to various planned developments in his local area. In particular, he was opposed to the demolition of an historic canal-side
warehouse. He sought judicial review of the decision to proceed with
the demolition. By the time he issued proceedings, the warehouse
had been substantially demolished.

---

362 [2005] EWHC 889 (Admin), [2005] 4 All ER 40.
363 [2008] EWCA Civ 1209.
364 *Buglife* at [26].
365 *Buglife* at [31].
366 Welsh J (Liberty, July 2006): *Litigating the Public Interest, Report of the Working
     Group on Facilitating Public Interest Litigation*, Liberty and the Civil Liberties
     Trust.
367 [2006] EWCA Civ 1742.

18.183   In the Court of Appeal, the issue of a PCO was raised for the first time. It was doubted whether or not the 'no private interest' rule was appropriate and recommended that the report of the working group be incorporated into the CPR. It was also suggested that there might be a difference in approach to cases where the applicant was seeking to protect private interests and interests that he shared with other members of a group, such as the protection of the local environment.[368]

18.184   In *R (Weaver) v London & Quadrant Housing Trust*,[369] in the Court of Appeal, the Legal Services Commission sought a PCO before agreeing to fund the costs of resisting the defendant's appeal. In *R (E) v JFS*,[370] the Supreme Court expressed grave reservations about such an approach.

Judicial review of decisions by the Upper Tribunal

18.185 With effect from 1 October 2012, a new procedure has been introduced for judicial review claims relating to decisions by the Upper Tribunal refusing permission to appeal from a decision of the First-tier Tribunal, or a decision which relates to the decision of the First-tier Tribunal which was the subject of the application for permission to appeal.[371]

18.186   The time limits for seeking judicial review of such a decision have been significantly truncated, with the rules now requiring that the claim form and supporting documents be filed no more than 16 days from the date on which the Upper Tribunal's decision to refuse permission was sent to the applicant.[372]

18.187   The supporting documents which must accompany the claim form are:

---

368 See also *Wilkinson v Kitzinger* [2006] EWHC 835 (Fam) where Sir Mark Potter, President of the Family Division, also doubted the importance of the 'no private interest' rule; *R (Birch) v Barnsley MBC* [2009] EWHC 3561 (Admin), where a PCO was made in favour of both the claimant and defendant, of differing values, despite the claimant's personal interest in bringing the challenge.

369 [2009] EWCA Civ 587, [2010] 1 WLR 363.

370 [2009] UKSC 1.

371 CPR r54.7A(1). This amendment follows the decision in *R (Cart) v The Upper Tribunal* [2011] UKSC 28, [2012] 1 AC 663. See paras 2.50–2.51 and 7.21 above.

372 CPR r54.7A(3). See CPR r54.5 for the normal requirement to act 'promptly' and in any event within three months from the date on which the grounds for challenge first arose.

- the decision of the Upper Tribunal and any document giving reasons for the decision;
- the grounds of appeal to the Upper Tribunal and any documents sent with them;
- the decision of the First-tier Tribunal, the application to that Tribunal for permission to appeal and its reasons for refusing permission; and
- any other documents essential to the claim.[373]

18.188 The applicant must serve the claim form and supporting documents on the Upper Tribunal and any other interested party no later than seven days after the date of issue.[374] The Upper Tribunal and any other interested party who has been served with the claim form and who wishes to take part in the proceedings has 21 days after service of the claim form to file and serve on the applicant and any other party an acknowledgment of service.[375]

18.189 The court will only give permission to apply for judicial review if it considers that there is an arguable case, which has a reasonable prospect of success, that both the decision of the Upper Tribunal refusing permission to appeal and the decision of the First-tier Tribunal against which permission to appeal was sought are wrong in law, and that either the claim raises an important point of principle or practice, or there is some other compelling reason for permission to be given.[376]

18.190 If the application for permission to apply for judicial review is refused, an applicant is not able to renew the application for an oral hearing.[377]

18.191 If permission is granted but the Upper Tribunal or any interested party wants a hearing of the substantive application, it must make a request for such a hearing no later than 14 days after service of the order granting permission. If there is no request for a substantive hearing within the prescribed period, the court will make a final order quashing the refusal of permission without a further hearing.[378] A final order may be made by the Master of the Crown Office or a Master of the Administrative Court.[379]

373 CPR r54.7A(4).
374 CPR r54.7A(5).
375 CPR r54.7A(6).
376 CPR r54.7A(7).
377 CPR r54.7A(8).
378 CPR r54.7A(9).
379 CPR r54.7A(10).

Judicial review in the Upper Tribunal

Introduction

19.1 The Tribunals, Courts and Enforcement Act (TCEA) 2007 transformed the tribunal system in the UK. The structure now consists of a First-tier Tribunal (FTT) and an Upper Tribunal (UT), divided into various chambers according to subject-matter. There are four chambers of the UT: the Administrative Appeals Chamber, the Tax and Chancery Chamber, the Lands Chamber and the Immigration and Asylum Chamber.[1]

19.2 In November 2008, section 31A of the Senior Courts Act (SCA) 1981, came into force,[2] making provision in England and Wales for the mandatory or discretionary transfer of judicial review claims from the High Court to the UT. At the same time, the UT was given jurisdiction to adjudicate on, and grant relief in, certain applications for judicial review under the TCEA 2007.[3] The UT exercises a statutory function of reviewing decisions of public bodies on a point of law but the jurisdiction is restricted by statute and, therefore, its use is not an alternative to bringing a claim in the High Court.

19.3 The UT's procedural rules for judicial review claims are different from those operating in the High Court. We have decided to describe these rules in this separate chapter rather than seek to draw out the differences within the main body of the procedural chapters in this work.

Upper Tribunal's judicial review jurisdiction

19.4 The UT has jurisdiction in an application if four conditions are met.[4]

- The first condition is that the applicant is only seeking relief, or permission to apply for relief, that the UT has power to grant (mandatory, prohibiting and quashing orders, declarations and injunctions),[5] an award of damages, restitution or the recovery of a sum, interest and costs.[6]
- The second condition is that the application is not seeking to challenge anything done by the Crown Court.[7]

---

1 The Immigration and Asylum Chamber was created in February 2010.
2 Amended in August 2011 by Borders, Citizenship and Immigration Act 2009 Pt 4 s53(1)(a), to broaden the range of applications to be transferred to the UT.
3 TCEA 2007 s15(1).
4 TCEA 2007 s18(2).
5 TCEA 2007 s15(1).
6 TCEA 2007 s18(4).
7 TCEA 2007 s18(5).

- The third condition is that the application falls within a class specified for the purposes of TCEA 2007 s18(6), in a direction given in accordance with Pt 1 of Sch 2 to the Constitutional Reform Act 2005.[8]
- The fourth condition is that the judge hearing the application is either a judge of the High Court or the Court of Appeal in England and Wales or Northern Ireland, or a judge of the Court of Session or such other persons as may be agreed between the Lord Chief Justice, the Lord President, or the Lord Chief Justice of Northern Ireland, and the Senior President.[9]

19.5   The circumstances in which the High Court must transfer judicial review applications to the UT are set out at paras 19.10–19.13 below.

19.6   If each of the requisite conditions set out above is not met then, save where the High Court has transferred the application to the UT on the basis that it is just and convenient to do so, even though the third condition is not satisfied (in which case the UT has the function of deciding the case[10]) the UT must transfer the application to the High Court.[11] Where this is done, the application will be treated as if it had originally been made to the High Court seeking the relief sought from the UT.[12] In addition, any steps taken, permission granted or order made prior to transfer by the UT are treated as if taken, granted or made by the High Court.[13]

Specified classes under TCEA 2007 s18(6)

19.7   With effect from 3 November 2008, the Lord Chief Justice directed that the following fall within the specified class:

- any decision of the FTT relating to the Criminal Injuries Compensation Scheme in compliance with section 5(1) of the Criminal Injuries Compensation Act 1995;[14] and

---

8   TCEA 2007 s18(6). The specified classes are set out at paras 19.7–19.9 below.
9   TCEA 2007 s18(8).
10 TCEA 2007 s19(3), (4); SCA 1981 s31A(3)
11 TCEA 2007 s18(3). The UT also cannot hear cases where an injunction is sought to restrain persons from acting in offices in which they are not entitled to act: SCA 1981 s30.
12 TCEA 2007 s18(9)(a).
13 TCEA 2007 s18(9)(b).
14 Review is the only remedy to decisions taken under this Act: Criminal Injuries Compensation Act 1995 s4.

- any decision of the FTT under the Tribunal Procedure Rules or TCEA 2007 s9 where there is no right of appeal to the UT and it is not an excluded decision.[15]

19.8 With effect from 17 October 2011, the Lord Chief Justice issued a direction specifying, for the purposes of TCEA 2007 s18(6), an application ('fresh judicial review claims') that challenged a decision of the Secretary of State not to treat submissions as an asylum claim or a human rights claim within the meaning of Part 5 of the Nationality, Immigration and Asylum Act 2002, wholly or partly, on the basis that they are not significantly different from material that has previously been considered. This specified class also includes an application that challenges a decision to remove, or direct the removal of, the applicant from the UK and/or a failure by the Secretary of State to make a decision on submissions supporting an asylum or human rights claim.

19.9 An application will not fall into the class if it challenges any other decision.[16] An application will not fall into any of the specified classes where an applicant seeks a declaration of incompatibility under HRA 1998 s4 or where he is challenging his detention.

Transfer of applications from the High Court

19.10 Where an application for judicial review, or permission to apply for judicial review, is made to the High Court, then the court must order the transfer of the application to the UT if four conditions are met.[17]

- The first condition is that the applicant is only seeking relief, or permission to apply for relief, that the UT has power to grant, an award of damages, restitution or the recovery of a sum, interest and costs.[18]
- The second condition is that the application is not seeking to call into question anything done by the Crown Court.[19]

---

15 *Practice Direction (Upper Tribunal: Judicial Review Jurisdiction)* [2009] 1 WLR 327. A decision is excluded by virtue of TCEA 2007 s11(5)(b), (c) and (f).

16 *Practice Direction (Upper Tribunal: Judicial Review Jurisdiction No 2)* [2012] 1 WLR 16. See also Borders Citizenship and Immigration Act 2009 s53 – in force from 8 August 2011 – amending the TCEA 2007 and SCA 1981.

17 SCA 1981 ss31A(1) and 31A(2).

18 SCA 1981 s31A(4).

19 SCA 1981 s31A(5).

- The third condition is that the application falls within a class specified in TCEA 2007 s18(6);[20]
- The fourth condition is that the application does not involve a decision made under:
  - the Immigration Acts or the British Nationality Act 1981;
  - any instrument having effect under those Acts or any other provision of law which determines British citizenship, British overseas territories citizenship, the status of the British National overseas or British Overseas citizenship.[21]

19.11   If condition four is not met, but the first three conditions and a fifth condition are met, the High Court must by order transfer the application to the UT.[22]

19.12   The fifth condition is that the application challenges a decision of the Secretary of State not to treat submissions as an asylum claim or a human rights claim within the meaning of Part 5 of the Nationality, Immigration and Asylum Act 2002 wholly or partly on the basis that they are not significantly different from material that has previously been considered (whether or not it calls into question any other decision) (see para 19.8 above).[23]

19.13   If all the conditions except the third condition are met, then the High Court may transfer the matter to the UT, if it considers it just and convenient to do so.[24]

Remedies

19.14   The UT has power, where the conditions are met, or where the High Court has transferred the application to the UT on the basis that it is just and convenient to do so in spite of the third condition not being met,[25] to grant mandatory, prohibiting and quashing orders, declarations and injunctions.[26] The UT must, in deciding whether or not

---

20   SCA 1981 s31A(6).
21   SCA 1981 s31A(7).
22   SCA 1981 s31A(2A).
23   SCA 1981 s31A(8).
24   SCA 1981 s31A(3). For examples of cases that have been transferred under this discretionary power see, *R ((Independent Schools Council) v The Charity Commission for England and Wales* [2010] EWHC 2604, [2011] ACD 2 (transferred so the matter could be heard with related proceedings in the UT); and *R (FZ) v Croydon LBC* [2011] EWCA Civ 59, [2011] HLR 22 (transferred due to fact finding element of claim) (see below).
25   See SCA 1981 s31A(3); TCEA 2007 s19(3), (4).
26   TCEA 2007 s15(1) and (2).

relief should be granted, apply the principles that are applied by the High Court on an application for judicial review.[27] Where the UT is considering granting a declaration or injunction it must also apply the principles that the High Court would apply under SCA 1981 s31(2).[28]

19.15 Any such relief granted by the UT has the same effect as relief granted by the High Court on an application for judicial review and is enforceable as if the High Court had granted the relief.[29] Where the UT quashes a decision it may remit the matter to the decision-maker with a direction that the matter is to be reconsidered so a decision is made that accords with the tribunal's findings or it may substitute its own decision.[30] The UT may, however, only substitute its own decision if the decision-maker was a court or tribunal, the decision was quashed due to an error of law and if the error had not been made, the court or tribunal could only have come to one conclusion.[31]

19.16 The UT may also award damages, restitution or the recovery of a sum due if the application includes such a claim and the tribunal is satisfied that the award would have been made by the High Court.[32] Again, any such award made can be enforced as if it were granted by the High Court.[33]

Requirement for permission

19.17 A substantive application to the UT can only be made if permission has been granted by the tribunal.[34] Permission cannot be granted unless the applicant has sufficient interest in the matter to which the application relates.[35] The UT may refuse to grant permission, or refuse any relief sought, in circumstances where it considers that there has been undue delay in making the application and that the granting of relief would cause substantial hardship to, or substantially

---

27 TCEA 2007 s15(4).
28 TCEA 2007 s15(5).
29 TCEA 2007 s15(3).
30 TCEA 2007 s17(1).
31 TCEA 2007 s17(2). A substituted decision has effect as if it were a decision of the court or tribunal whose decision was quashed (TCEA 2007 s17(3)).
32 TCEA 2007 s16(6).
33 TCEA 2007 s16(7).
34 TCEA 2007 s16(2).
35 TCEA 2007 s16(3).

prejudice the rights of, any person or would be detrimental to good administration.[36]

19.18 Where the UT refuses permission to bring the application for relief, the applicant can appeal against that refusal to the Court of Appeal. Where the Court of Appeal grants permission it may go on to decide the application for relief.[37]

Pre-issue procedure

19.19 In relation to applications concerning criminal injuries compensation, the FTT has issued a practice and guidance statement, which anyone contemplating making application to bring judicial review proceedings should follow. Specifically, the guidance states that, unless the FTT has already provided a written statement of reasons for the decision potentially under challenge, a person must, as soon as possible and in any event no later than one month after notification of the final decision, make a written request for the statement of reasons.[38]

19.20 In addition, a party must, without delay, provide the FTT with written details of the alleged error of law and all facts and matters relied upon in support of the challenge so, where satisfied it is appropriate under the Tribunal Procedure (First-tier Tribunal) (Social Entitlement Chamber) Rules 2008,[39] the FTT's principal judge or nominated tribunal judge can consider whether to correct or set aside the decision.[40]

---

36 TCEA 2007 s16(4) and (5).
37 TCEA 2007 s16(8).
38 Practice and Guidance Statement (CI-6) para 1.
39 SI No 2685.
40 Practice and Guidance Statement (CI-6) para1. The power to correct or set aside a decision is found in Pt 4, Tribunal Procedure (First-tier Tribunal)(Social Entitlement Chamber) Rules 2008 SI No 2685 rr36 and 37. Correction, in r36, extends to any clerical mistake or other accidental slip or omission in a decision. A decision, or part of it, can be set aside if the FTT considers that it is in the interests of justice to do so and at least one of the following apply: a document relating to the proceedings was not sent to, or was not received at an appropriate time by, a party or a party's representative; a document relating to the proceedings was not sent to the FTT at an appropriate time; a party, or a party's representative, was not present at a hearing related to the proceedings; or there has been some other procedural irregularity in the proceedings (r37).

Tribunal procedure

19.21 Generally Part 4 of the Tribunal Procedure (Upper Tribunal) Rules 2008[41] governs the procedure for judicial review proceedings in the UT although reference should also be had to all other parts of the 2008 Rules (especially those sections dealing with case management and sanctions for non-compliance with the Rules), any relevant practice direction or statutory instrument.[42] Broadly, the procedure is the same as that set out in CPR Pt 54.

Applications for permission to apply for judicial review

19.22 An applicant must make a written application to the UT for permission to bring judicial review proceedings.[43] Any such application must be made either:

- promptly and received by the UT no later than three months after the date of the decision, act, or omission to which the application relates; or
- within one month after the date on which the FTT sent the applicant their written reasons for the decision or notification that an application, made in time, for the decision to be set aside was unsuccessful.[44]

19.23 As with judicial proceedings in the High Court, applicants do not have three months in which to bring a claim; the three-month period is a back-stop to the primary requirement of acting promptly. In UT

---

41 SI No 2698.
42 Practice and Guidance Statement (CI-6): Appeals on error of law against final decision of the Tribunal (available at www.justice.gov.uk/downloads/tribunals/criminal-injuries-compensation/FTT_CI_6_PracticeStatement_JRs210509.pdf) and *Practice Direction: Fresh claim judicial review in the Immigration and Asylum Chamber of the Upper Tribunal* (available at www.judiciary.gov.uk/Resources/JCO/Documents/Practice%20Directions/Tribunals/tribunals-practice-direction-fresh-claim-judicial-review-immigration-asylum-chamber.pdf).
43 Tribunal Procedure (Upper Tribunal) Rules 2008 SI No 2698 r28(1). In fresh claims for judicial review, the application must be made on the form displayed on the UT's website (currently form T480): *Practice Direction: Fresh claim judicial review in the Immigration and Asylum Chamber of the Upper Tribunal* para3. Form JRC1 is to be used to start a judicial review case in the UT (Administrative Appeals Chamber) where there is a challenge of a criminal injuries compensation decision (see also JRC 1 Claim Form Notes). For all other applications for judicial review in the UT (Administrative Appeals Chamber) Form JR1 should be used (see also JR 1 Claim Form Notes).
44 Tribunal Procedure (Upper Tribunal) Rules 2008 SI No 2698 r28(2) and (3).

proceedings, however, applicants may be assisted by the alternative time limit – one month after written reasons or notification has been given – especially if the one-month period falls after the three-month back-stop). A failure to act promptly has led to adverse consequences for applicants.[45]

19.24 If the applicant fails to make the application within the time limits prescribed then the UT has power to extend time on application requesting such an extension.[46] The application for an extension of time must include the reasons why the applicant has failed to comply with the rules.[47]

19.25 An application for permission must contain the following information:

- the name and address of the applicant, the respondent and any interested party (if the application relates to a decision of a court or tribunal, the applicant must name each party to the original proceedings as an interested party[48]);
- the name and address of the applicant's representative (if any);
- an address to which documents for the applicant can be sent;
- details of the decision the applicant wishes to challenge, which must include the date, full reference and the identity of the decision-maker;
- that it is an application for permission to bring judicial review proceedings;
- the relief sought; and
- the facts and grounds of review relied upon.[49]

19.26 The applicant must include a written copy of the decision, if available, and copies of any other documents upon which he wishes to rely with his application for permission.[50]

---

45 See, eg, *R (Khan and others) v Secretary of State for the Home Department and Upper Tribunal* [2011] EWHC 2763 (Admin), where the High Court upheld the decision of the UT to refuse permission to bring judicial review proceedings where there had been no proper explanation as to why an application was delayed, with the consequence that the applicant had failed to act promptly (the application was issued on the last day of the three months following the decision subject to the application).

46 Tribunal Procedure (Upper Tribunal) Rules 2008 SI No 2698 rr5(3)(a) and 28(7)(a).

47 Tribunal Procedure (Upper Tribunal) Rules 2008 SI No 2698 r28(7)(a).

48 Tribunal Procedure (Upper Tribunal) Rules 2008 SI No 2698 r28(5).

49 Tribunal Procedure (Upper Tribunal) Rules 2008 SI No 2698 r28(4).

50 Tribunal Procedure (Upper Tribunal) Rules 2008 SI No 2698 r28(6).

19.27   In fresh claims applications, the application must also be accompanied by any written evidence on which it is intended to rely, copies of any relevant statutory material, and a list of essential reading with page references.[51] If the application is verified by a statement of truth, the applicant may rely on the matters set out in the application as evidence.[52] Two copies of a paginated and indexed bundle of documents also need to be provided with the application.[53]

19.28   The UT must not accept an application for permission in a fresh claim for judicial review unless it is either accompanied by any required fee, currently £60,[54] or an undertaking is given and accepted by the UT that the fee will be paid.[55] If an undertaking is given and accepted, a failure to pay will lead to the application being automatically struck out.[56]

19.29   The UT must send a copy of an application and any accompanying documents to each person named in the application as a respondent or interested party upon receipt.[57] This rule does not apply, however, in fresh claim judicial review proceedings; in such applications an applicant must provide a copy of the application and any accompanying documents to each person named in the application as a respondent or an interested party and provide the UT with a written statement confirming how and when the documents were provided, within nine days of making the application.[58]

---

51 *Practice Direction: Fresh claim judicial review in the Immigration and Asylum Chamber of the Upper Tribunal* para 4.1. Applicants should also have regard to Pt 5 of the Practice Direction is the application deals with a challenge to a decision to set removal directions.

52 *Practice Direction: Fresh claim judicial review in the Immigration and Asylum Chamber of the Upper Tribunal* para 4.2.

53 *Practice Direction: Fresh claim judicial review in the Immigration and Asylum Chamber of the Upper Tribunal* para 4.3.

54 Sch 1, Upper Tribunal (Immigration and Asylum Chamber) (Judicial Review) (England and Wales) Fees Order 2011 SI No 2344. Fees are not payable if an applicant is in receipt of certain benefits or his income is below a specified threshold.

55 Tribunal Procedure (Upper Tribunal) Rules 2008 SI No 2698 r28A(1).

56 Tribunal Procedure (Upper Tribunal) Rules 2008 SI No 2698 r8(1)(b).

57 Tribunal Procedure (Upper Tribunal) Rules 2008 SI No 2698 r28(8).

58 Tribunal Procedure (Upper Tribunal) Rules 2008 SI No 2698 r28A(2).

Acknowledgment of service

19.30 A respondent or interested party served with an application for permission to apply for judicial review must, if they wish to take part in the proceedings,[59] provide the UT with an acknowledgment of service no later than 21 days after the date on which the UT sent, or the applicant provided, the application. In fresh claim judicial review proceedings, a person who provides an acknowledgment of service must also, in 21 days or less, provide a copy to the applicant and any interested party.[60] The acknowledgment of service must be in writing and state whether the application for permission is opposed or supported, the grounds of opposition or support, any other submission or information which may assist the tribunal, and, the name and address of any other person not already named in the application whom the person providing the acknowledgment considers to be an interested party.[61]

19 31 If a party does not provide an acknowledgment of service to the UT, they may not take part in the application for permission unless allowed to do so by the UT, but may take part in the subsequent proceedings if permission is granted.[62]

Urgent cases and interim relief

19.32 The UT has power to grant interim relief, although historically there has been no procedure for urgent consideration of interim relief or expedition equivalent to that available in judicial review proceedings in the High Court. Since the UT has had jurisdiction in 'fresh claim' judicial review proceedings, however,[63] a formal procedure has been set down in relation to such applications. It is certainly likely that fresh claim cases will require urgent hearings and interim relief, especially where they involve an applicant's removal.

19.33 In fresh claim judicial review proceedings, therefore, paras 11, 12 and 13, *Practice Direction: Fresh claim judicial review in the Immigration and Asylum Chamber of the Upper Tribunal* make specific provision for urgent consideration.

19.34 Under the procedure specified, an application must be made with a written 'request for urgent consideration' using the specified form

59 Tribunal Procedure (Upper Tribunal) Rules 2008 SI No 2698 r29(1).
60 Tribunal Procedure (Upper Tribunal) Rules 2008 SI No 2698 r29(2A).
61 Tribunal Procedure (Upper Tribunal) Rules 2008 SI No 2698 r29(2).
62 Tribunal Procedure (Upper Tribunal) Rules 2008 SI No 2698 r29(3).
63 Ie since 17 October 2011 (see para 19.8 above).

on the UT's website. The current form is Form T483. The application must state the need for urgency, the timescale within which the applicant seeks consideration of the application and the date by which a substantive hearing should take place.[64] If an injunction is sought, the applicant must also provide a draft order and the grounds for the making of the injunction.[65] The application and the request for urgent consideration – and in injunction cases, the draft order and grounds – must be served (by fax and post) on the defendant and interested parties, advising them of the application and their ability to make any representations.[66] The UT will then consider the application within the timeframe requested and can make any order it considers appropriate.[67] In cases of extreme urgency, applicants should endeavour to check with the Administrative Court Office that there will be an UT judge available to deal with an application. If a judge is not available, an applicant will need to consider making an urgent application in the High Court.

Transfer of applications from the High Court

19.35 When an application is transferred from a court to the UT, the UT must notify each party in writing and give directions as to the future conduct of the proceedings.[68] Where an application is transferred by the High Court it will be treated as if it had been made to the UT and sought relief corresponding to that sought from the High Court.[69] In addition, any permission given, steps taken or orders made by the High Court prior to transfer will be treated as if they had been made by the UT.[70] In cases of discretionary transfer by the High Court[71] the UT will have jurisdiction to adjudicate on the matter even though the

---

64 *Practice Direction: Fresh claim judicial review in the Immigration and Asylum Chamber of the Upper Tribunal* para 11.1.

65 *Practice Direction: Fresh claim judicial review in the Immigration and Asylum Chamber of the Upper Tribunal* para 11.2.

66 *Practice Direction: Fresh claim judicial review in the Immigration and Asylum Chamber of the Upper Tribunal* para 12.

67 *Practice Direction: Fresh claim judicial review in the Immigration and Asylum Chamber of the Upper Tribunal* para 13.1.

68 Tribunal Procedure (Upper Tribunal) Rules 2008 SI No 2698 r27(1).

69 TCEA 2007 s19(3)(a).

70 TCEA 2007 s19(3)(c).

71 Ie under the power contained in s31A(3), that transfer appears to the High Court to be just and convenient even though the case does not fall within a class specified by TCEA 2007 s18(6).

third condition for the UT to have jurisdiction (TCEA 2007 s18(6)) is not satisfied.[72]

19.36   If an application for permission to apply for judicial review is transferred to the UT under SCA 1981 s31A, and the UT grants permission, it also has jurisdiction to decide any subsequent application even if that application does not fall within a specified class.[73]

Permission decision

19.37   The UT must send to the applicant, each respondent and any other person who provided an acknowledgment of service, and may send to any other interested party, written notice of its decision on permission and its reasons if the application is refused or if limitations or conditions have been placed on the grant of permission.[74]

19.38   Where the UT refuses permission, or gives permission on limited grounds or subject to conditions without a hearing, the applicant may apply for the decision to be reconsidered at a hearing.[75] An application for reconsideration of the permission decision must be made in writing and received by the UT within 14 days of the date on which the UT sent written notice of its decision to the applicant. This time requirement is reduced to nine days in fresh claim for judicial review proceedings.[76]

Appeal against refusal of permission

19.39   Where the UT refuses permission to apply for judicial review, permission to appeal against that refusal cannot be sought from the Court of Appeal until the tribunal has given a written statement of reasons for its initial decision and a written application for permission of appeal has been made to and refused by the tribunal.[77]

19.40   When the Court of Appeal grants an application for permission to appeal against the UT's refusal of permission to apply, it is required to hear the substantive appeal against the refusal and, unlike appeals

---

72 TCEA 2007 s19(3)(b).
73 TCEA 2007 s19(4).
74 Tribunal Procedure (Upper Tribunal) Rules 2008 SI No 2698 r30(1).
75 Tribunal Procedure (Upper Tribunal) Rules 2008 SI No 2698 r30(3) and (4).
76 Tribunal Procedure (Upper Tribunal) Rules 2008 SI No 2698 r30(5).
77 TCEA 2007 s13(5) and Tribunal Procedure (Upper Tribunal) Rules 2008 SI No 2698 rr40(1)(2) and 44(4).

following refusal of permission in the High Court,[78] cannot, simply, grant permission to apply for judicial review.

19.41   In *R (NB (Algeria)) v Secretary of State for the Home Department,*[79] the Court of Appeal considered its powers and jurisdiction in relation to appeals against refusals of the UT to grant permission to seek judicial review. The Court of Appeal urged that certain changes be made to the Tribunal Procedure (Upper Tribunal) Rules 2008 and CPR Pt 52. The changes sought by the Court were as follows:

- the rules should provide that, at least in cases where a stay pending appeal may be sought, an applicant can apply to the UT for permission to appeal as soon as his application for permission to apply for judicial review is refused. This would facilitate an applicant being able to make an application for a stay with an application to the Court of Appeal for permission to appeal.
- CPR r52.15(3) should be amended so as to also apply to appeals from the UT, enabling the Court of Appeal to grant the applicant permission to apply for judicial review.[80]

Response to the grant of permission

19.42   Where the UT grants permission to apply for judicial review, any person who receives notification and wishes to contest, or support on additional grounds, the application for judicial review, must provide detailed grounds for contesting or supporting the application so that they are received by the UT not more than 35 days after the tribunal sent notice of the grant of permission.[81]

Amendment and additional grounds

19.43   Where permission has been granted, the applicant may not rely on any other grounds of review without the consent of the UT.[82] The power to allow, or indeed require, an applicant to amend a document is contained within r5 of the Tribunal Procedure (Upper Tribunal) Rules 2008 that deal with the tribunal's general case management powers.[83] This power allows the UT to permit or require an amend-

---

78 See CPR r52.15(3).
79 [2012] EWCA Civ 1050, [2013] 1 WLR 31.
80 [2012] EWCA Civ 1050, [2013] 1 WLR 31 at paras 36, 37, 42, 43.
81 Tribunal Procedure (Upper Tribunal) Rules 2008 SI No 2698 r31.
82 Tribunal Procedure (Upper Tribunal) Rules 2008 SI No 2698 r32.
83 Tribunal Procedure (Upper Tribunal) Rules 2008 SI No 2698 r5(3)(c).

ment that would lead to the tribunal having to, or having the option to, exercise the power to transfer the proceedings to the High Court.[84]

19.44　Additional grounds may not be advanced without the permission of the UT, if they would give rise to an obligation or power to transfer the proceedings to the High Court in circumstances where the requisite conditions were not met under section 18(3) of the TCEA 2007.[85]

19.45　Where the High Court has already transferred the proceedings to the UT and the proceedings are amended or any party advances additional grounds meaning that the proceedings could not have been transferred to the tribunal had they been in that form at the time of the transfer, the UT must transfer the proceedings back to the High Court.[86] Where the proceedings were transferred to the UT using the discretionary power to transfer proceedings under SCA 1981 s31A(3), the tribunal may transfer proceedings back to the High Court if it appears just and convenient to do so.[87]

19.46　There is an additional requirement in relation to fresh claims for judicial review: where an applicant intends to apply to rely on additional grounds at the substantive hearing, the applicant must give written notice to the UT and to any other person served with the application, not later than seven working days before the hearing.[88]

Fees

19.47　Once permission has been granted in a fresh claim for judicial review, the applicant must pay, within seven days of service on him of the order granting permission, a fee of £215.[89]

Substantive hearing

19.48　Procedurally, the UT has a variety of case management powers under r5 of the Tribunal Procedure (Upper Tribunal) Rules 2008 that it can utilise prior to the substantive hearing.

84　Tribunal Procedure (Upper Tribunal) Rules 2008 SI No 2698 r33A(2)(a).
85　Tribunal Procedure (Upper Tribunal) Rules 2008 SI No 2698 r33A(2)(b).
86　Tribunal Procedure (Upper Tribunal) Rules 2008 SI No 2698 r33A(3)(a).
87　Tribunal Procedure (Upper Tribunal) Rules 2008 SI No 2698 r33A(3)(b).
88　*Practice Direction: Fresh claim judicial review in the Immigration and Asylum Chamber of the Upper Tribunal* para 7.1.
89　Upper Tribunal (Immigration and Asylum Chamber) (Judicial Review) (England and Wales) Fees Order 2011 SI No 2344 Sch 1. If the claim for judicial review was started otherwise than by using the judicial review procedure then the fee payable prior to a substantive hearing is £60.

19.49   In relation to fresh claims for judicial review, however, the Practice Direction: *Fresh claims for judicial review in the Immigration and Asylum Chamber of the Upper Tribunal*, provides specific rules in relation to skeleton arguments, bundles and agreed final orders.[90] The applicant must serve a skeleton argument on the UT and any other person served with the application, not later than 21 days before the substantive hearing. The respondent and any other party wishing to make representations must file and serve their skeleton arguments not later than 14 days before the hearing.

19.50   The skeleton argument must include the following matters:

- a time estimate for the entire hearing including judgment;
- a list of issues;
- a list of the legal points being raised (citing authorities with page references to the passages relied upon);
- a chronology of events including page references to the bundle of documents;
- a list of essential reading and a time estimate for that reading; and
- a list of persons referred to.[91]

19.51   The applicant must also serve, with the skeleton argument, a paginated and indexed bundle of all relevant documents, including any documents relied upon by any other party, on the UT and any other person served with the application.[92]

19.52   Finally, if the parties agree about the final order to be made, the applicant must file at the UT a document, with two copies, signed by all the parties setting out the terms of the proposed agreed order, together with a short statement of the matters relied on as justifying the proposed agreed order and copies of any authorities or statutory provisions relied on. If the UT is satisfied the order should be made, it will make the order in the terms sought. If the UT is not so satisfied, it will set a date for the substantive hearing.[93]

---

90 See Practice Direction paras 8–10.
91 Practice Direction para 8.
92 Practice Direction para 9.
93 Practice Direction para 10.

Costs

19.53 The UT has a power to award costs in judicial review claims,[94] any application for which must be made in writing.[95] Although s15 of the TCEA 2007, requires the UT, when considering whether to grant relief, to apply the principles that are applied by the High Court on an application for judicial review, it would appear that this requirement does not apply to the question of costs. It seems, however, that the UT is likely to use the principles developed by the High Court in judicial review claims when deciding the questions of whether costs are payable and, if so, by whom they are payable, at all stages of the proceedings.

Possible future developments

19.54 In 2011, the Tribunal Procedure Committee carried out two consultations regarding judicial review in the UT. The reply to the consultation responses by the Tribunal Procedure Committee[96] commented on whether age assessment[97] judicial review claims should also be a specified class following the Court of Appeal's decision in *R (FZ) v Croydon LBC*[98] where it was highlighted there was a discretionary

---

94 Tribunal Procedure (Upper Tribunal) Rules 2008 SI No 2698 r10(3)(a).

95 Tribunal Procedure (Upper Tribunal) Rules 2008 SI No 2698 r10(5).

96 Available at www.justice.gov.uk/downloads/about/moj/advisory-groups/fresh-claim-upper-tribunal-judicial-review-consultation-reply.pdf.

97 Immigration and Asylum Act 1999 Pt 6 makes provision for the support of asylum-seekers by the Secretary of State for the Home Department who may, provide, or arrange for provision of, support for asylum-seekers who appear to him to be destitute or likely to become destitute (s59(1)). Such support may include the provision of accommodation (s96(1)(a)) but can only be provided to an asylum-seeker who is over the age of 18 (s94(1)). Under CA 1989 s20, authorities must provide accommodation for any child in need in their area who appears to them to require accommodation as a result of, *inter alia*, there being no person who has parental responsibility for him. By CA 1989 s105(1), a person is a child if he is under the age of 18 and, therefore, an authority may have to decide an asylum-seeker's age to determine whether he is a child and, if so, for how long they may have to provide him with accommodation.

98 [2011] EWCA Civ 59, [2011] HLR 22.

power to transfer these claims from the High Court so long as the other requisite conditions (discussed above) were met.[99]

19.55   Age assessment judicial reviews, unlike the majority of judicial review claims, are concerned with an objective question of fact.[100] Where there is a challenge to an authority's decision, therefore, it may be necessary for the court to hear evidence in order to decide the question of the applicant's age.[101] This element of age assessment judicial reviews, led to the Court of Appeal to indicate that the UT may well be the most appropriate venue:[102]

> The Administrative Court does not habitually decide questions of fact on contested evidence and is not generally equipped to do so. Oral evidence is not normally a feature of judicial review proceedings or statutory appeals. We would therefore draw attention to the power which there now is to transfer age assessment cases where permission is given for the factual determination of the claimant's age to the Upper Tribunal under s.31A(3) of the SCA 1981, as inserted by s.19 of the TCEA 2007. The Upper Tribunal has a sufficient judicial review jurisdiction for this purpose under s.15 of the 2007 Act ... Transfer to the Upper Tribunal is appropriate because the judges there have experience of assessing the ages of children from abroad in the context of disputed asylum claims.

19.56   In light of such comments, it may well be that, in the future, age assessment judicial review application will become another specified class. For the time being, however, they are claims that the High Court is likely to consider transferring to the UT using its discretionary power.

19.57   In addition, the Crime and Courts Bill 2012–13, which completed its House of Lords stages on 18 December 2012, and is currently awaiting further consideration in the House of Commons, at clause 20, proposes to remove the restriction on the power of the High Court[103] to transfer immigration and nationality claims for judicial review to the UT and will allow, therefore, for a direction that all, or, at least, additional classes of, immigration and nationality claims will become a specified class that must be transferred to the UT.

---

99 See also, First-tier Tribunal and Upper Tribunal (Chambers) Order 2010 SI No 2655 art 11(c)(ii), which allocates the function of determining an application for judicial review which 'is made by a person who claims to be a minor from outside the United Kingdom challenging a defendant's assessment of that person's age' to the UT.

100 *R (A) v Croydon LBC* [2009] UKSC 8, [2009] 1 WLR 2557.

101 *R (A) v Croydon LBC* [2009] UKSC 8, [2009] 1 WLR 2557.

102 *R (FZ) v Croydon LBC* [2011] EWCA Civ 59, [2011] HLR 22 at [31].

103 SCA 1981 s31A(7) 'condition 4'.

CHAPTER 20

The post-permission procedure

No requirement of service

20.1 There is no requirement on claimants who have been granted permission to serve notice or documents on the defendant and interested parties. Service now takes place prior to the application for permission.[1] Even where the urgency procedure for seeking permission is invoked, it is still necessary to send the claim form by e-mail or fax to the defendant and interested parties prior to issuing the proceedings, and the urgency form (N463) requires the claimant's advocate personally to confirm the date and time that this was done.[2]

20.2 Accordingly, the time for the respondent's response, following the grant of permission, no longer starts to run from the date of service of a notice of motion by the claimant (as it used to under the old rules),[3] but instead from the date of service by the court of the order granting permission.[4]

Fees

20.3 On the grant of permission, an additional fee of £215 becomes payable.[5] The fee must be paid within seven days of service on the claimant of the order granting permission.[6] If the proceedings were commenced otherwise than by the judicial review procedure, the additional fee on the grant of permission is only £60.[7] This would presumably apply where an ordinary claim had been brought (and

---

1 CPR r54.7.
2 See appendix A, p645 below. See also paras 18.95–18.102 above.
3 RSC Ord 53 r14(1).
4 CPR r54.14.
5 At the time of writing, the Government is consulting on increasing this fee to £235 (*Fees in the High Court and Court of Appeal*, CP 15/2011, Ministry of Justice, November 2011). The Government has announced in *Reform of Judicial Review: the Government response*, Cm 8611, Ministry of Justice, April 2013 (Response), (its response to a consultation exercise carried out in December 2012 and January 2013) that it proposes to introduce a fee of £215 for an oral renewal of the permission application. The fee will rise to £235 if the consultation on fees results in the increase of fees generally to that level but at the time of writing the response to that consultation has not been published. Should permission be granted on the renewed application, no further fee will be payable (ie the fee referred to at para 18.73, above, will not be required).
6 Civil Proceedings Fees Order 2008 SI No 1053, as amended, Sch 1 para 1.9(b).
7 Civil Proceedings Fees Order 2008 SI No 1053 Sch 1 para 1.9(c).

the £175 issue fee paid)[8] but was then transferred into the Administrative Court under CPR r54.20,[9] so that the claimant would not be obliged to pay double fees.

20.4   A failure to pay the fees referred to above gives rise to the sanctions provided by CPR r3.7.[10] If the fee has not been paid within the seven-day period referred to above, and no application for exemption or remission has been made, the court will initially serve a notice on the claimant requiring payment of the fee by a date specified in the notice.[11] If the fee is not paid by that date (and no application for exemption from or remission of the fee has been made) the claim will be struck out and the claimant will become liable for any costs incurred by the defendant, unless the court orders otherwise.[12]

20.5   If the claimant applies to be relieved from this sanction,[13] and to have the claim reinstated, any such reinstatement will be conditional on the claimant either paying the fee or filing evidence of exemption from or remission of the fee within two days of the date of the order reinstating the claim.[14]

Setting aside permission

CPR rule 54.13

20.6   CPR r54.13 provides that 'neither the defendant nor any other person served with the claim form may apply to set aside an order giving permission to proceed'. This is the logical consequence of service of the proceedings on the defendant and all interested parties taking place prior to the permission application being dealt with, enabling those parties to put their arguments before the judge considering the permission application by means of the acknowledgement of service

---

8   General county court issue fee for a non-money claim. For other issue fees, and civil court fees generally, see Civil and Family Court Fees: High Court and County Court – From April 2011, Form EX50.

9   See paras 18.73 above and note 112.

10 See CPR r3.7(1)(d).

11 CPR r3.7(2) and (3). The notice is in form N173.

12 CPR r3.7(4). CPR r3.7(5) and (6) deal with the effect of an application for an exemption from or remission of the fee. If the application is refused, the court will serve a notice requiring payment by a specified date. If payment is not made by that date, the claim will be struck out and the claimant becomes liable for the defendant's costs unless the court orders otherwise.

13 Under CPR r3.9.

14 CPR r3.7(7); SCA 1981 s19(2).

and, if there is an oral hearing, by attending that hearing. This procedure is designed to ensure that all relevant information from all parties is before the judge when the permission decision is made, rendering it unnecessary – and indeed undesirable – for defendants to have a second chance to prevent the application proceeding to a full hearing under the guise of a set-aside application.

Inherent jurisdiction

20.7   In *R (Webb) v Bristol CC*,[15] the Administrative Court held that, notwithstanding CPR r54.13, it retains an inherent jurisdiction to set aside an order granting permission. In *Webb*, permission had been granted on a paper application prior to the expiry of the time for filing the defendants' acknowledgement of service. Accordingly, the defendants had not had an opportunity to put their case to the judge granting permission. There was no suggestion of bad faith on the part of the claimant's advisers, who had genuinely considered the case to be urgent.

20.8   Turner J held that the power to set aside an order made where one party had not had the opportunity to put its case as to why the order should not be made was part of the court's inherent jurisdiction which had been expressly preserved by SCA 1981 s19(2). There was no satisfactory juridical basis for such a power, expressly preserved by statute, being removed by delegated legislation such as the CPR, notwithstanding the apparently express terms of CPR r54.13.

20.9   CPR Pt 54 contemplated that the consideration of an application for permission would not take place prior to the filing of the defendant's acknowledgement of service, including its arguments why permission should not be granted, save in 'circumstances of high exception'.[16] Accordingly, CPR r54.13 had to be read down 'in the context of the pre-existing power of this court to exercise its inherent jurisdiction'[17] and *Webb* was one of the rare cases in which it was appropriate to exercise that power to set the grant of permission aside.

---

15 [2001] EWHC 696 (Admin).
16 [2001] EWHC 696 (Admin) at [13].
17 [2001] EWHC 696 (Admin) at [15].

20.10   In *R (Enfield LBC) v Secretary of State for Health*,[18] the deputy High Court judge said that the jurisdiction to set aside the grant of permission:[19]

> is an exceptional one and should be exercised sparingly, in an obvious case. It seems to me that I should only set aside the Order if, on consideration of all the material that has now been put before the Court, I would not be prepared to grant permission.

Principles applicable

20.11   Under the old rules,[20] which may still be instructive on the procedure for making of such applications, the application to set aside had to be made promptly and, if possible, to the same judge who granted permission. Moreover, the court indicated on numerous occasions that set-aside applications should only be made in exceptional circumstances.

20.12   The court did not approve of applications to set aside based on objections that could more properly be dealt with at the substantive hearing. Those based, for instance, on contentions that were in reality no more than a substantive defence to the claimant's allegations would be regarded by the court as an unacceptable attempt to 'jump the queue' of cases waiting to be heard. Accordingly, permission would be set aside only 'where the respondent could show that the substantive application would clearly fail.[21]

20.13   Grounds upon which it was been held proper to apply to set aside under the old rules must now be treated with considerable caution in the light of CPR r54.13. Nonetheless, even since the introduction of the CPR, the courts have suggested that a set-aside application may be permissible where, for example, the application was fundamentally misconceived, where the applicant had failed to identify a proper point of law for review, where the permission was granted in error or where there had been fraud or material non-disclosure in obtaining permission.[22]

---

18   [2009] EWHC 743 (Admin).

19   At [11].

20   RSC Ord 32 r6 (power to set aside without notice orders).

21   This statement was contained in *Supreme Court Practice* (1993) Vol 1 p841 53/1–14/1 para 3.

22   *R v Chief Constable of West Yorkshire ex p Wilkinson* [2002] EWHC 2353 (Admin), *R (Tataw) v Immigration Appeal Tribunal* [2003] EWCA Civ 925, [2003] INLR 585; *R (Khan) v Secretary of State for the Home Department* [2008] EWHC 1367 (Admin); and *R (Enfield LBC) v Secretary of State for Health* [2009] EWHC 743 (Admin).

20.14   The court has set aside permission where the claim had been served on the incorrect part of a department, where permission had been granted prior to the expiry of the time period for filing an acknowledgment of service and the defendants were able to demonstrate the claim was neither prompt nor arguable, and where the acknowledgment of service from an interested party had not been brought to the judge's attention due to an administrative error.[23]

20.15   The grounds upon which it is sought to set aside permission must be specified with particularity.[24] Any prejudice which may be suffered by the defendant should the matter proceed to the full hearing should be set out in the application (although such an argument should generally be accompanied by an application, in the alternative, for expedition).

20.16   The test on an application to set aside is the same as that on an application for permission: does the applicant have an arguable case, or a case fit for further consideration?[25] The court should be wary of going too deeply into the substance of the matter, although in some cases it has been prepared to do so.[26]

Appeals from decision to set aside

20.17   If permission is set aside, there seems to be no reason why the claimant may not appeal, with permission.[27]

20.18   Under CPR r52.15(1), the procedure for challenging a refusal of permission is to appeal to the Court of Appeal. It would seem logical to assume that the same procedure is to be followed where the claimant wishes the Court of Appeal to consider whether permission ought to have been set aside.

20.19   Where the court refuses to set aside permission, the defendant may appeal, again with permission, to the Court of Appeal.[28] The

---

23   *R (Candish) v Hastings BC* [2005] EWHC 1539 (Admin), [2006] Env LR 13; *R (Enfield LBC) v Secretary of State for Health* [2009] EWHC 743 (Admin); and *R (Valentines Homes and Construction Ltd) v Revenue and Customs Commissioners* [2010] EWCA Civ 345 (at [17]).

24   *R v Lloyd's of London ex p Briggs* [1992] COD 456, DC.

25   *R v Secretary of State for the Home Department ex p Rukshanda Begum* [1990] COD 109, CA. See also *R (Enfield LBC) v Secretary of State for Health* [2009] EWHC 743 (Admin) at [11].

26   See also *R v Darlington BC ex p Association of Darlington Taxi Owners* [1994] COD 424, QBD (see para 4.9 above): permission set aside (probably wrongly) because of lack of capacity.

27   CPR r52.3.

28   See para 20.52 below.

court has indicated, however, that where a judge has been satisfied, after hearing argument from both parties, that there is a case meriting further consideration, only rarely would an appeal be likely to succeed, and it would be necessary to establish that the judge's decision had been plainly wrong.[29]

The defendant's response

20.20 The requirements imposed on a defendant, or interested party, who wishes either to contest or support the claim on additional grounds, are contained in CPR Pt 54, r54.14. Detailed grounds for defending (or supporting on additional grounds) the claim must be filed and served, along with any written evidence within 35 days from service of the order containing the grant of permission[30] (the defendant will already have had 21 days prior to the permission decision in which to summarise the grounds of defence).[31]

20.21 It is not entirely clear what the requirement under CPR r54.14, for detailed grounds of resistance, adds, given the requirement for skeleton arguments,[32] but it is consistent with the approach to judicial review discernible from the provisions of CPR Pt 54 as a whole, that the intention is to inform all parties, as early in the proceedings as possible, of the detail of each party's contentions, in order to facilitate dealing with the proceedings more efficiently and cost-effectively.

20.22 This is not to say that the proliferation of documentation for the hearing is desirable for its own sake. If the defendant has filed a full statement of defence in the acknowledgement of service[33] and genuinely has nothing additional to say, it may be that there is nothing to be gained by filing and serving a repetitive document and that the preferable course would be simply to prepare a document making it clear that the summary grounds contained in the acknowledgement of service will be relied upon. Of course, defendants should be very careful to ensure, if adopting such an approach, that the contents of the summary grounds do in fact cover all the arguments to be raised at the hearing in sufficient detail to comply with the requirements of CPR r54.14(1)(a).

29 *R v Secretary of State for the Home Department ex p Rukshanda Begum* [1990] COD 109, CA.
30 CPR r54.14.
31 CPR r54.8(2)(a).
32 CPR PD 54A para 15.
33 See paras 18.129–18.133 above.

20.23 Written evidence may not be relied on unless it has been served in accordance with the provisions of CPR Pt 54, or the court directs or permits otherwise.[34]

20.24 The contents of the defendant's detailed grounds and witness statements are as important as the grounds and evidence of the claimant, since this is the defendant's only opportunity to explain the decision challenged, how and why it was reached and its legality and reasonableness. Much of the hearing is likely to turn on the defendant's explanations as set out in these documents,[35] and so it is worthwhile to devote careful attention to their drafting.

20.25 The witness statement is also the appropriate means by which the defendant can take issue with the claimant's version of events. The witness statement, rather than the detailed grounds, is the more appropriate vehicle to raise such disputes. Issues such as delay and the failure to exhaust other remedies, together with the prejudice/hardship/detriment to good administration that such matters will cause should also be addressed in the documentation. Likewise, factual matters would generally be more suitable for inclusion in the witness statement and matters of law in the detailed grounds.

Defendant's duty of candour

20.26 When formulating its response and the evidence to be filed and served under CPR r54.14, a public authority must remember the duty of candour that attaches to judicial review proceedings.[36] The very high duty on public authorities to assist the court with full and accurate explanations of all the facts relevant to this issues,[37] appears to involve the disclosure of such materials that are reasonably required for the court to uphold decisions that are lawful and correct those that are not.[38]

---

34 CPR r54.16.
35 But see below regarding supplementing statutorily-required reasons, paras 20.29–20.34.
36 See *R v Lancashire CC ex p Huddleston* [1986] 2 AER 941; *Tweed v Parades Commission for Northern Ireland* [2007] 1 AC 650 at [31] and [54]. See also, generally as a useful guide, *Treasury Solicitor's Department: Guidance on discharging the duty of candour and disclosure in judicial review proceedings* [2010] JR 177 15(3) pp177–200.
37 *R (Quark Fishing Ltd) v Secretary of State for Foreign & Commonwealth Affairs (No 1)* [2002] EWCA Civ 1409, per Laws LJ at [50].
38 *Graham v Police Service Commission* [2011] UKPC 46 at [19].

20.27   In *R (AKH & Others) v Secretary of State for the Home Department*,[39] the duty was described as follows.[40]

> The [defendant] is also subject to the duty of candour in judicial review proceedings: the duty on the defendant public authority to explain the full facts and reasoning underlying the decision challenged, and to disclose the relevant documents, unless in the particular circumstances of the case, other factors, including those which may fall short of requiring public interest immunity, may exclude their disclosure.

20.28   In *R (Al-Sweady) v Secretary of State for Defence*,[41] it was held that the duty was heightened where the case raised some of the most basic human rights issues under the Convention.[42] A lawyer or other suitably experienced person should either carry out or supervise the exercise to comply with this duty.[43]

Supplementary reasons

20.29   In some cases, the defendant is entitled to amplify the reasons for his or her decision in the evidence in response.[44] In *Re C and P*,[45] Simon Brown J set out the types of case in which this was possible. No evidence, even to supplement and explain the reasons, would be admitted in relation to arbitrators' awards and the decisions of statutory medical boards, decisions of certain tribunals, such as employment tribunals, or where the decision can be set aside for mere inadequacy of reasoning, such as planning cases and cases where the reasoning is made fundamental to the decision.

20.30   In *R v Westminster CC ex p Ermakov*,[46] the Court of Appeal stated that in the context of a statutory requirement for reasons to be given for decisions, deficiencies in the decision letter cannot be rectified by evidence to explain the 'real' basis for the decision given in the

---

39 [2012] EWHC 1117 (Admin), [2012] ACD 66.
40 [2012] EWHC 1117 (Admin), per Ouseley J at [22].
41 [2009] EWHC 2387 (Admin), [2010] HRLR 2.
42 [2010] HRLR 2 at [25]–[26]. The Secretary of State was criticised for his consistent and repeated failure to comply with the duty. See also, *R (I) v Secretary of State for the Home Department* [2010] EWCA Civ 727 at [50], where it was held that once permission has been granted there is an obligation on the Secretary of State to make proper disclosure.
43 See, *R (DL) v Newham LBC* [2011] EWHC 1127 (Admin), [2011] 2 FLR 1033.
44 See chapter 6 above.
45 [1992] COD 29, QBD.
46 [1996] 2 All ER 302, (1996) 28 HLR 819. See also *R v Secretary of State for the Home Department ex p Lillycrop* (1996) *Times* 13 December; *R (McGowan) v Brent Justices* [2001] EWHC 814 (Admin), [2002] HLR 55.

course of proceedings. The court would permit evidence to elucidate[47] or, exceptionally, correct or add to the reasons already given, such as where a word was inadvertently omitted in the original decision, or there was a mistake in transcription, but would be very cautious about doing so and would not generally allow written evidence the purpose of which was to show that the reasons previously stated were not in fact the true basis of the decision, or to provide some '*ex post facto* rationalisation'.[48]

20.31　The evidence, if it does elucidate, must not contradict the reasons given at the time. If there is no inconsistency between the evidence and the contemporaneous documents, then there is no reason to discount a later witness statement.[49]

20.32　Although the court has to be cautious, where the evidence is seeking to respond to something raised for the first time on review, it has been held that the court should take that evidence into account.[50] It will also be appropriate for the court to take such evidence into account to enable the amplification of reasons,[51] where it is the best evidence of what was in the decision-maker's mind at the time,[52] and/ or to illustrate how the decision-maker's approach was flawed.[53]

20.33　In other cases, particularly where reasons were not given at the time, it has been held that it is the duty of the defendant to give sufficient explanation of the decision taken that the court can properly adjudicate on the claim.[54] It was also held that in the absence of an

---

47　See, eg, *Hijazi v Kensington and Chelsea RLBC* [2003] EWCA Civ 692, [2003] HLR 72.

48　*R v Westminster CC ex p Ermakov* [1996] 2 All ER 302, per Hutchison LJ at 315F–317C. See also, as to the caution with which *ex post facto* evidence should be treated, eg, *R (Mavalon Care Ltd) v Pembrokeshire County Council* [2011] EWHC 3371 (Admin), (2012) 15 CCLR 229; *R (M) v Haringey Independent Appeal Panel* [2010] EWCA Civ 1103; and *R (Macrae) v Herefordshire DC* [2012] EWCA Civ 457. In *Macrae*, Pill LJ commented that *ex post facto* reasoning was inevitably suspect and what was important was how the statutory duty was discharged at the time of the decision under challenge (at [40]–[41]). See also the discussion at paras 6.218–6.219 below.

49　*R (LE (Jamaica)) v Secretary of State for the Home Department* [2012] EWCA Civ 597 at [22].

50　*Keane v Law Society* [2009] EWHC 783 (Admin).

51　*R (KM) v Cambridgeshire County Council* [2012] UKSC 23.

52　*R (Hewitson) v Guildford BC* [2011] EWHC 3440 (Admin).

53　See, eg, *R (London Fire and Emergency Planning Authority) v Secretary of State for Communities and Local Government* [2007] EWHC 1176 (Admin), [2007] LGR 591; and *R (Nash) v Chelsea College of Art and Design* [2001] EWHC 538 (Admin).

54　See para 20.26 above.

explanation for a decision, the court may have to conclude that there was no good reason for having taken it.[55] These cases predated the coming into force of the HRA 1998, and the more general acceptance of the need to explain decisions.[56]

20.34   While, therefore, the content of the defendant's evidence and detailed grounds is a matter to be decided in each individual case, and such evidence/grounds should plainly deal fully with all matters to be advanced at the hearing, and which may assist the court, the case-law does limit the ability of public authorities to introduce extensive restatements of the decision and/or the reasons for it, whether in a witness statement or in the detailed grounds of defence, especially where reasons were given at the time.

Receipt of defendant's response

20.35   On receipt of the defendant's evidence and detailed grounds, the claimant's legal representatives are under a professional obligation to reconsider the merits of the application and to withdraw it if it appears that there are no longer reasonable prospects of success. This obligation arises in all cases, regardless of whether or not the applicant is publicly funded. It is separate from any duty to report to the Legal Aid Agency, which, of course, only arises in legally aided applications.

20.36   If the court takes the view at the full hearing that the application should not have been continued, there may be costs consequences, whether for the applicant or even for the legal representative(s) concerned.[57]

Additional grounds or evidence

20.37   If either party wishes to rely on evidence which has not been served in accordance with the provisions of CPR Pt 54, the permission of the court will be required.[58] Thus, a claimant may wish to reply to the evidence filed by the defendant, or simply update the court as to his or her current circumstances, or exhibit a new document or report,

55 See *R v Lancashire CC ex p Huddleston* [1986] 2 All ER 941, CA. See also *Padfield v Minister of Agriculture, Fisheries and Food* [1968] AC 997, HL.

56 HRA 1998 Sch 1 art 6.

57 See SCA 1981 s51(6), CPR Pt 43, and *R v Horsham DC ex p Wenman* (1992) 24 HLR 669, and [1994] 4 All ER 681, QBD.

58 CPR r54.16(2)(b).

etc. Permission to rely on such evidence can be granted at any stage, either on an interim application or at the full hearing.

20.38   If it is intended to seek to rely on additional evidence, a copy of the evidence should be sent to the other parties with a request that they consent. If consent is not received, an application should be made to the court in the normal way. It will usually be sensible for such an application to be made, returnable at the substantive hearing, unless the party wishing to rely on the evidence will wish to take some other action if permission is not granted. Generally, so long as the other parties have sufficient time to deal with the new evidence before the hearing (including filing fresh evidence themselves) permission will be granted.

20.39   A claimant will also require permission to rely on any grounds at the substantive hearing other than those for which he was given permission.[59] The procedure for obtaining permission is generally the same as that referred to above in relation to additional evidence, save that notice must be given to the court and the other parties served with the claim form no later than seven clear days before the date of the hearing (or the warned date, where appropriate).[60]

20.40   The position is different where an additional ground sought to be relied on was included in the claim form, but permission on that ground was refused (though permission was granted on other grounds). In *R (Opoku) v Southwark College Principal*,[61] where permission had been granted but not on all the pleaded grounds, the claimant sought to rely at the substantive hearing on the ground for which permission had been refused. It would have been open to him to have appealed the refusal of permission in relation to that ground, but no such appeal had been brought.

20.41   The court held that the appropriate procedure would have been to have brought an appeal, but that the failure to have done so did not deprive the court of its powers to permit the additional ground to be raised. In such a situation, however, the court should only exercise its powers in limited circumstances, namely:

• where the claimant established a significant change of circumstances since the permission decision;
• where there were significant new facts; or

59   CPR r54.15.
60   CPR PD 54 para 11.1.
61   [2002] EWHC 2092 (Admin), [2003] 1 WLR 234.

- where a proposition of law, not available at the time permission was considered, was now available.[62]

20.42 In *R (Smith) v Parole Board*,[63] the Court of Appeal, however, held that this approach was too restrictive. Although the judge at the full hearing would require justification before taking a different view from that of a permission judge who had heard full argument at that stage, if the judge concluded that there was good reason – and there would need to be a real justification – to allow argument on an additional ground, permission should be granted. Each case should be considered in relation to its own circumstances, but the judge should bear in mind that if permission to rely on an additional ground was refused, the Court of Appeal would be prevented from considering it should there be an appeal from the first instance decision.

Other interim applications

20.43 The Administrative Court has power to grant broadly the same forms of interim relief as any other court.[64] Abridgement of time for the defendant to file and serve its response, and expedition of the substantive hearing are commonly granted, even though the time allowed by the rules is 35 days. Injunctions and stays are equally common.

20.44   Disclosure is not required unless ordered by the court,[65] and is not generally ordered, unless there is a specific reason for so doing.[66] Disclosure has been ordered where it is necessary and so far as it is relevant.[67] In many cases, however, claimants will have the right to see information held by the defendant concerning their case[68] and a public authority should remember its duty of candour.[69]

20.45   Oral evidence and cross-examination may still be ordered by the court, in appropriate cases. The Administrative Court so held in *R*

---

62 [2002] EWHC 2092 (Admin) at [16].

63 [2003] EWCA Civ 1014, [2003] 1 WLR 2548.

64 See 'Directions and orders on the grant of permission' at paras 18.158–18.161 above. See also 'Remedies' at chapter 5 above.

65 CPR PD 54A para 12.1.

66 See 'Interim relief' at paras 5.53–5.71 above.

67 See, eg, *Tweed v Parades Commission for Northern Ireland* [2006] UKHL 53, [2007] 1 AC 650; and *R (Corner House Research) v Director of Serious Fraud Office* [2008] EWHC 71 (Admin), where disclosure of letters was ordered.

68 See 'Pre-application procedure' at chapter 7 above, but see also, generally chapter 14.

69 See paras 20.26–20.28 above.

(PG) v Ealing LBC,[70] in spite of the indication to the contrary contained in CPR r54.16(1) as originally enacted.

20.46   It was argued that the disapplication of CPR r8.6, by CPR r54.16 (including the power contained in CPR r8.6(2) to call oral evidence) had the effect of excluding the court's power to order oral cross-examination. This argument was rejected. CPR r54.16 was amended so that the disapplication now applies to CPR r8.6(1) alone.[71] Since this change in rules, it has been confirmed that although they rarely arise, where there are factual disputes the permission stage gives the court full control of the proceedings and it may give any necessary directions for the attendance of witnesses and cross-examination.[72]

20.47   The courts have shown themselves to be far more willing to order oral evidence and cross-examination in claims involving fundamental rights than in other cases,[73] and have indicated that a similar approach may be adopted in relation to disclosure.[74]

20.48   In *Bubb v Wandsworth LBC*,[75] a case concerning a homelessness appeal under statutory provisions akin to judicial review proceedings, Lord Neuberger MR accepted that:[76]

> ... it is, as a matter of principle, open to a judge, hearing a judicial review application, to permit one or more parties to adduce oral evidence ... However, for reasons of both principle and practice, such a course should only be taken in the most exceptional case. As its name suggests, judicial review involves a judge reviewing a decision, not making it; if the judge receives evidence so as to make fresh findings of fact for himself, he is likely to make his own decision rather than to review the original decision. Also, if judges regularly allow witnesses and cross-examination in judicial review cases, the court time and legal costs involved in such cases will spiral. In the overwhelming majority of judicial review cases ... there should be no question of

---

70 [2002] EWHC 250 (Admin), (2002) *Times* 18 March.

71 Civil Procedure (Amendment) Rules 2002 SI No 2058 (in force from 2 December 2002).

72 *Trim v North Dorset DC* [2010] EWCA Civ 1446, [2011] 1 WLR 1901 at [24].

73 See, eg, *R (Wilkinson) v Broadmoor Special Hospital Authority* [2001] EWCA Civ 1545, [2002] 1 WLR 419; *S v Airedale NHS Trust* [2002] EWHC 1780 (Admin); (2002) *Times* 5 September; *R (PG) v Ealing LBC* [2002] EWHC 250 (Admin); *R (Mullen) v Secretary of State for the Home Department* [2002] EWHC 230 (Admin), [2002] 1 WLR 1857; *R (B) v Haddock* [2006] EWCA Civ 961, [2006] HRLR 1237.

74 See, eg, *R v Ministry of Defence ex p Smith* [1996] QB 517, CA, per Henry LJ at 543; and, *R (Al Sweady) v Secretary of State for Defence* [2009] EWHC 2387 (Admin), [2010] HRLR 12.

75 [2011] EWCA Civ 1285, [2012] HLR 13.

76 [2012] HLR 13 at [24]–[25].

live witnesses. Even the provision of further documentary evidence which was not before the original decision-maker must often be questionable.

20.49 Cross-examination can be ordered where it is necessary for the claim to be fairly and justly adjudicated. It has been ordered, for example, where the court has to consider a challenge of improper motive.[77] Evidence is also frequently heard in age-assessment cases. The latter are now routinely transferred to the Upper Tribunal because it is considered to be better equipped to deal with questions of fact.[78]

20.50 Nevertheless, the scope for these forms of interim relief is more limited in a public law context than in private law actions. As regards cross-examination, this is because, ordinarily, there has already been a determination of fact with which the court will interfere only reluctantly. In *O'Reilly v Mackman*,[79] Lord Diplock expressed the fear echoed by Lord Neuberger in *Bubb*,[80] that hearing oral evidence may present the court with a temptation, not always easily resisted, to substitute its own view of the facts.

Making interim applications

20.51 Under the CPR, applications following the permission stage (which can be included in the claim form) are made in the same way as in any other civil litigation, namely by means of an application notice and evidence, whether contained in a separate witness statement or in the application form itself.[81] In relation to many types of applications, however, the Administrative Court's practice is to require only a letter setting out the basis of the application. The Administrative Court's Guidance however, indicates that the CPR Pt 23 procedure should be used, once the permission decision has been made.[82] If in doubt, advisers should contact the Administrative Court Office.

---

77 *R (Bancoult) v Secretary of State for the Foreign and Commonwealth Office* [2012] EWHC 2115 (Admin).

78 See para 19.55 above.

79 [1983] 2 AC 237, HL.

80 [2012] HLR 13 at [24]–[25].

81 See CPR Pts 23 and 25; Form N244 and Form PF244.

82 *Administrative Court Guidance Notes for guidance on applying for Judicial Review* (1 April 2011) para 14.1. An application should be made using Form PR244 with the appropriate fee (currently £80 – or £45.00 where the parties provide their written consent for the order to be made – unless a party is entitled to a fee remission).

Appeals from interim orders

20.52   In non-criminal cases, there is a right of appeal to the Court of Appeal, but permission is required.[83] In criminal cases, it appears that interim judgments may only be appealed to the Supreme Court, by virtue of the Administration of Justice Act 1960.[84]

---

83   CPR r52.3(1). In relation to an appeal concerning a case management decision (including decisions concerning disclosure, filing statements, timetable, etc), the court considering the application for permission to appeal may take into account whether the issues are of sufficient importance to justify an appeal; whether the procedural consequences of an appeal (eg loss of trial date) outweigh the significance of the decision appealed; and whether it would be more convenient to determine the issue at or after trial: CPR PD 52 paras 4.4–4.5.

84   Section 1. See Senior Courts Act 1981 s18(1)(a).

CHAPTER 21

The hearing

continued

Discontinuance and settlement

Discontinuance

21.1   The rules on discontinuance are generally governed by CPR Pt 38. Discontinuance has a special significance in judicial review proceedings given the obligation on the claimant to reconsider the merits of the claim on receipt of the defendant's (and any interested party's) evidence and detailed grounds for contesting the claim. On the other hand, given the unfavourable costs consequences of discontinuance (and limitations on its availability where interim relief has been granted) claimants may find it preferable to seek to negotiate the consensual withdrawal or dismissal of the claim, in circumstances where they consider it inappropriate, for whatever reason, to continue to the full hearing.

21.2   The claimant has a right to discontinue a claim, or any part of a claim, at any time,[1] save in certain circumstances that include the situations where an interim injunction has been granted (or an undertaking to the court given) and where there is more than one claimant. In the first of these situations, the permission of the court will be required. In the second, either every other claimant must consent or the permission of the court must be obtained.[2]

21.3   Subject to the matters noted above, the procedure for discontinuing a claim is, in summary, as follows. The claimant must file a notice of discontinuance at the Administrative Court Office, and serve a copy of the notice on every other party.[3] The defendant may apply to have the notice of discontinuance set aside, provided such an application is made not more than 28 days after the notice of discontinuance was served on him.[4]

21.4   Discontinuance takes effect on the date of the service of the notice and the proceedings come to an end on that date, subject to any application to set aside the notice, though proceedings to deal with any question of costs may still continue.[5]

---

1   CPR r38.2(1).
2   CPR r38.2(2).
3   CPR r38.3(1).
4   CPR r38.4. This provision appears to be aimed at the prevention of the abuse of the discontinuance procedure, or its use for the purpose of gaining some tactical or other advantage. The court may impose conditions for the discontinuance of the proceedings.
5   CPR r38.5.

21.5   The claimant who discontinues proceedings is liable for the costs of the defendant up to the date of the discontinuance unless the court orders otherwise.[6] If the proceedings are only partly discontinued, then the claimant will be liable for the costs of that part and such costs will normally be assessed at the conclusion of the proceedings.[7] The permission of the court will be required to bring a further claim against the same defendant based on substantially the same facts if the claim was discontinued after a defence was filed.[8] In relation to judicial review proceedings, it is not entirely clear what is the equivalent stage to the filing of a defence, though the nearest equivalent would seem to be the lodging of the acknowledgement of service.[9] Given that permission would in any event be required for any future claim brought by the claimant, this provision is probably of less significance in the context of the CPR Pt 54 procedure, however, than it is in the context of civil proceedings generally.

Settlement and consent orders

21.6   If the parties agree on the final order that should be made, they must submit a draft of terms of the proposed agreed order (with two copies), signed by all the parties, together with a short statement of the reasons justifying the proposed agreed order and copies of any authorities or statutory provisions relied on.[10] If the proposed order only relates to the question of costs, however, it is not necessary to include a statement of reasons or to attach any documents.[11]

21.7   The court will consider the reasons and documents, if any, and decide whether to grant the agreed order or whether, if it is not satisfied that the order should be made, to list the matter for hearing.[12]

21.8   It appears that even if the defendant capitulates before the full hearing, the claimant may be entitled to proceed in order to obtain a declaration, if it is necessary to do so in order to proceed with a claim for damages that has been pursued in the application. Without a determination of the applicant's rights, it may be that no claim for

---

6   CPR r38.6(1).
7   CPR r38.6(2).
8   CPR r38.7.
9   CPR r54.8.
10   PD 54A para 17.1.
11   PD 54A para 17.4.
12   PD 54A paras 17.2–17.3.

damages could be brought and, where this is so, it seems that a declaration may be awarded.[13]

Decision without a hearing

21.9 The court may decide the claim without a hearing where all the parties agree.[14] This is most likely to happen where the parties are agreed as to the final order, having compromised the action, but the rules do not so limit the ability of the parties to consent. It is now becoming common for questions of costs to be dealt with in this manner where the claim has not been contested, or following a 'handed-down' judgment. The parties put in written representations on costs, following which a decision is made.

Listing

21.10 Assuming a hearing is to take place, the Administrative Court's listing policy is summarised in the *Notes for Guidance on Applying for Judicial Review*[15] and on the Ministry of Justice website.[16] Once the case is ready for a substantive hearing (ie once the defendant and any interested party has filed its evidence and detailed grounds of defence, or the time for doing so has elapsed), it will enter the warned list and all parties will be informed of this.[17]

Expedited warned list

21.11 There are, in effect, three parts to the warned list. The first is the 'expedited warned list'. This contains cases where an expedited, or early, hearing has been ordered. Cases in this list take priority over others waiting to be fixed.

---

13 *R v Northavon District Council ex p Palmer* (1993) 25 HLR 674, QBD.
14 CPR r54.18.
15 1 April 2011, section 13 at paras 13.3–13.6.
16 The listing policy can be found at www.justice.gov.uk/courts/rcj-rolls-building/administrative-court/listing-policy. See also, Annex C to *Practice Statement*, Scott Baker J, 1 February 2002, [2002] 1 All ER 633.
17 *Administrative Court Guidance, Notes for applying for judicial review* (1 April 2011) section 13 at para 13.1.

Short warned list

21.12 Secondly, there is the 'short warned list'. This contains cases that may come on at any time during a specified period. Parties will be informed that their case may be listed from a certain date on less than a day's notice. Around six cases will be warned for any particular week. The reason for short warning is stated to be the need to provide cover for the large number of settlements that occur in the Administrative Court.[18] In other words, if some cases could not be called on at very short notice, Administrative Court judges may be left with no cases to hear.

21.13 The criteria for short warning are not spelt out, but the general philosophy of short warned lists is that they should contain the more straightforward cases, given that they are listed without consultation with the parties. A new advocate may be required to pick up a short warned case at, by definition, less than a day's notice if the advocate previously instructed is not available.

21.14 If the case does not come into the list in the period during which it is short warned, the parties will be consulted on the listing, which will be as soon as possible after the short warned period.

Warned list

21.15 The rest of the cases in the warned list are listed by consultation with the parties. A range of dates is offered to the advocates whose names appear on the court record, and they are given 48 hours to accept one of them. If the list office is not contacted within that 48-hour period, it will fix the case for hearing on one of the offered dates, without further consultation with the parties, who will be informed of the hearing date by letter.

21.16 Where listing occurs in this fashion, the Administrative Court Office will only vacate the hearing date by the consent of both parties. If consent cannot be achieved, a formal application for an adjournment must be made to the court on notice to all parties.[19]

---

18 *Administrative Court Guidance, Notes for applying for judicial review* (1 April 2011) section 13 at para 13.7.

19 The same procedure applies where the claimant is a self-represented litigant, ie acting in person.

Vacating hearings

21.17　The court may vacate hearings at very short notice. The *Notes for Guidance* confirm that this may occur as late as 4.30 pm on the day before the hearing, suggesting that this may be necessary for example where a case unexpectedly overruns or a judge becomes unavailable.[20] It may also occur where a very urgent case comes into the list and must be heard immediately.

21.18　　If a hearing has to be vacated, the List Office will endeavour to refix the case on the next available date convenient to the parties. Once a decision has been taken, the parties concerned will be informed. It will be noted on the case record that it is not to be adjourned again by the court.

Documentation for the hearing

21.19　The claimant must file and serve a skeleton argument and a bundle of documents for the hearing not less than 21 working days (ie just over four weeks) prior to the date of the hearing, or the warned date.[21] Defendants and other persons wishing to make representations at the hearing must file and serve a skeleton argument not less than 14 working days before the hearing date (or warned date).[22]

The skeleton argument

21.20　The skeleton argument must contain:

- the time estimate for the complete hearing (including judgment);
- a list of issues;
- a list of the propositions of law to be advanced at the hearing;
- the authorities relied on in support of each such proposition of law, with page references to passages relied on;
- a chronology of events (with page references to the paginated bundle);
- a list of the essential documents for advance reading by the court, with page references to the passages relied on (if different from

20　*Administrative Court Guidance, Notes for applying for judicial review* (1 April 2011) section 13 at para 13.6

21　CPR PD 54A paras 15.1 and 16.1.

22　CPR PD 54A para 15.2.

those included in the claim form) and a time estimate for that advance reading; and

• a list of persons referred to.[23]

The bundle

21.21   One copy of the bundle must be filed, unless the matter is to be heard by a Divisional Court instead of the single judge, in which case two copies will be required.[24]

21.22   A bundle must be filed whether or not a skeleton argument is filed.[25] The bundle must be paginated and indexed, and must contain all relevant documents required for the hearing, including those documents required by the defendant(s) and any other party taking part in the hearing.[26] It is clear, therefore, that the compiling of the bundle is intended to be a matter of co-operation between the parties. In the light of the time limits, consideration of the contents of the bundle may need to begin early, especially where it appears that there may be disagreement.[27]

21.23   This could be important as, given the requirement to give a time estimate for the court's pre-reading of the bundle, it is necessary to be able to assess accurately what the court does need to have read before the hearing. If a large number of documents is included (particularly if listed as essential pre-reading) that the court considers irrelevant, there may be costs consequences for the party or parties which required their inclusion.[28]

21.24   CPR r39.5 and PD 39A contain more detailed provisions regarding the contents of bundles and the manner in which they should be compiled (although these general requirements will give way to the provisions of CPR Pt 54 itself where there is any conflict).[29]

21.25   The preparation and production of the bundle is the responsibility of the legal representative who has conduct of the case for the

---

23 CPR PD 54A para 15.3.
24 See the *Administrative Court Guidance, Notes for applying for judicial review* (1 April 2011) section 13 para 13.13.
25 *Administrative Court Guidance, Notes for applying for judicial review* (1 April 2011) section 13 para 13.13.
26 CPR PD 54A para 16.1–16.2.
27 See para 21.26 below.
28 See eg *R (Cowl) v Plymouth CC* [2001] EWCA Civ 1935, [2002] 1 WLR 803 at [20]; *Anufrijeva v Southwark LBC* [2003] EWCA Civ 1406, [2004] QB 1124 at [81].
29 See CPR PD 39A paras 3.1–3.2.

claimant, even where the work is delegated to another person.[30] A copy of the bundle, identical with that which has been filed, should be supplied to each of the parties, including any interested parties.[31]

21.26 The parties should agree the bundle where possible (as stated above) and also agree that the documents it contains are authentic (whether or not they have been disclosed under CPR Pt 31) and that they may be taken as evidence of the facts stated in them (whether or not a notice under the Civil Evidence Act 1995 has been served). If such agreement is not possible, a summary of the points in dispute should be included.[32]

21.27 Where a document included in a bundle is illegible, a typescript of it should be included, next to it in the bundle, with appropriate cross-referencing.[33] The originals of documents included in the bundle should be available at the hearing.[34] If applicable, experts' reports may be contained in a separate bundle with cross-references to them included in the main bundle.[35]

21.28 In general, bundles must be paginated continuously throughout. If it contains more than 100 pages, numbered page-dividers should be placed at intervals between groups of documents. The bundle must also be indexed with the index including a description of each document and giving its page number.[36]

21.29 The bundle should usually be contained in a ring-binder or lever-arch file. If it is in more than one volume, each volume must be clearly distinguishable, for example, by the use of numbers or letters (or colours). If there are numerous volumes, a core bundle should be prepared including only the essential documents, with references to the supplementary documents in the other volumes.[37]

21.30 In *R v Humberside CC ex p Bogdal*,[38] it was held that the claimant could not pick and choose the documents to be put before the court where they were relevant to issues raised in the claim. Accordingly, an attempt to strike out certain documents included by the defendant in its bundle was unsuccessful. Once the claimant sought to quash a decision, the court should not be excluded from having before it

30 CPR PD 39A para 3.4.
31 CPR PD 39A para 3.10.
32 CPR PD 39A para 3.9.
33 CPR PD 39A para 3.7.
34 CPR PD 39A para 3.3.
35 CPR PD 39A para 3.7.
36 CPR PD 39A para 3.5.
37 CPR PD 39A para 3.6.
38 [1991] COD 66, QBD.

the relevant background documents. All documents before the court, however, must be relevant, on the ordinary principles of litigation.

Power to hear any person

21.31 Even if not served as an interested party, any person may apply for permission to file evidence and/or be heard at the full hearing. Such an application must be made promptly.[39] Where the court gives permission, it may do so on conditions and may give case management directions.

The hearing

21.32 The hearing generally takes place before a single judge assigned to the Administrative Court, although the court may direct that a Divisional Court should hear the claim. The hearing will generally take place at the Royal Courts of Justice in London or at the District Registry of the High Court at Birmingham, Bristol,[40] Cardiff, Leeds or Manchester. Claims against the Welsh Government are now heard in Cardiff. In urgent cases, it may be possible to list hearings in other locations. Urgent applications made during court hours, to the court outside London, must be made to the judge designated to deal with urgent applications in the relevant District Registry. Outside court hours, urgent applications must be made to the duty out of hours judge.[41]

Remedies

21.33 The grant of relief is at the discretion of the court. The principles on which such discretion will be exercised and the types of remedy available are discussed elsewhere.[42]

---

39 CPR r54.17.
40 Since 5 November 2012. The Administrative Court Office in Cardiff deals with the administration for Bristol cases and so cases to be heard in Bristol will need, it appears to be issued in Cardiff. See Judicial Office News Release, 31/10/12, to be found at www.judiciary.gov.uk/media/media-releases/2012/admin-court-to-sit-in-bristol-31102012 (accessed on 28 March 2013).
41 See CPR PD 54D and para 18.101 above.
42 Remedies are dealt with in paras 5.1–5.52; the principles of discretion are dealt with in paras 7.1–7.36.

Costs

General principles

21.34　The court has a broad discretion to determine the issue of costs,[43] and it has been said that the fundamental rule in questions of costs is that there are no rules.[44] The question of costs is very much a matter for the first instance tribunal and is highly fact-sensitive.[45] It has been recognised, however, that there are features of public law that distinguish it from private law civil and family litigation and that, therefore, it should not necessarily be expected that the same principles will govern the question of costs in public law cases.[46] That said, there are general principles that the court should apply when making a decision as to who should pay the costs and to what extent costs are paid.[47] It is also important to note that the fact that a party is in receipt of Legal Aid should not affect the rights or liabilities of other parties to proceedings or the principles upon which the court should exercise its discretion;[48] costs orders often being vital to the sustainability of legal aid practices.[49]

21.35　The general costs provisions of CPR Pt 44 are applicable to judicial review proceedings. Accordingly, the court will be obliged, in exercising its discretion regarding the award of costs, to take account of the factors in CPR r44.3.[50] The starting point is that costs will generally follow the event,[51] but the court may make a different order, and will be likely to do so in the following situations.

43　SCA 1981 s51.

44　*Bolton Metropolitan District Council v Secretary of State for the Environment (Practice Note)* [1995] 1 WLR 1776, per Lord Lloyd at 1178F.

45　*R (M) v Croydon LBC* [2012] EWCA Civ 595, [2012] 1 WLR 2607, per Lord Neuberger MR at [1] and [65].

46　*R (Corner House Research) v Secretary of State for Trade and Industry* [2005] 1 WLR 2600 at [69]–[70].

47　SCA 1981 s51(3).

48　Legal Aid, Sentencing and Punishment of Offenders Act 2012 s30.

49　See, eg *Re appeals by Governing Body of JFS* [2009] UKSC 1, [2009] 1 WLR 2353 and *R (Bahta) v Secretary of State for the Home Department* [2011] EWCA Civ 895, [2011] CP Rep 43.

50　See, in particular, CPR r44.3(2)–(7).

51　See CPR r44.3(2)(a), and *R (Smeaton) v Secretary of State for Health* [2002] EWHC 886 (Admin), [2002] 2 FLR 146 at [406], in which it was held that the starting point in judicial review proceedings is the same as in other types of cases. See also, however, *R (M) v Croydon LBC* [2012] EWCA Civ 595, [2012] 1 WLR 2607, per Lord Neuberger MR at [49] and [52]–[58].

21.36   If the decision-maker does not appear, it is unusual for costs to be awarded against him. The situation may be different if the court considers that the decision-maker's error calls for the court's disapproval to be shown (eg bad faith).[52] In *R v Huntingdon Magistrates' Court ex p Percy*,[53] the court, exceptionally, ordered the justices to pay the applicant's costs of the judicial review proceedings where they had refused to state a case on the ground that the application for them to do so was 'frivolous'. Their refusal was maintained even after they were informed that leave to move for judicial review of their decision had been granted, a stance that the Divisional Court found 'surprising, to put it mildly'.[54]

21.37   In *R (Davies) v Birmingham Deputy Coroner*,[55] the Court of Appeal considered this practice, in relation to courts and tribunals. In that case, the claimant was publicly funded and challenged a decision by the coroner. The claimant was unsuccessful in the Administrative Court but by the time the case came to appeal the law had changed and the claimant succeeded. The coroner had chosen to appear at all stages of the proceedings. The court awarded the claimant the costs of appeal and, although it considered it an unsatisfactory outcome, made the following rulings concerning costs against courts and tribunals:

- the established practice of the courts was to treat an inferior court or tribunal that resisted an application actively by way of argument in such a way that it made itself an active party to the litigation, as if it was such a party, so that in the normal course of things costs would follow the event;
- if an inferior court or tribunal appeared in the proceedings in order to assist the court neutrally on questions of jurisdiction, procedure, specialist case-law and such like, the established practice of the courts was to treat it as a neutral party, so that it would not make an order for costs in its favour or an order for costs against it whatever the outcome of the application;
- there are a number of important considerations that might tend to make the courts exercise their discretion in a different way today, so that a successful applicant, who has to finance his own

---

52 *R v West Yorkshire Coroner* (1984) *Times* 11 April.

53 [1994] COD 323, DC.

54 See also *R v Maidstone Coroner ex p Johnstone* (1994) *Times* 19 October, DC, where the coroner was ordered to pay the applicant's costs even though no strong disapproval was shown.

55 [2004] EWCA Civ 207, [2004] 1 WLR 2739.

litigation without external funding, may be fairly compensated out of a source of public funds and not be put to irrecoverable expense in asserting his rights after a coroner, or other inferior tribunal, has gone wrong in law, and where there is no other very obvious candidate available to pay his costs;

• costs could be avoided by submitting a written statement setting out all relevant facts and dealing with any questions from a claimant but the court may then feel compelled to seek the assistance of an advocate.[56]

21.38 Where a person who was not served is heard by virtue of CPR r54.17, it is rare for that person to be awarded costs. The same appears to be the case where a party who has been served has appeared in support of the application. For instance, in *R v Secretary of State for Social Security ex p Association of Metropolitan Authorities*,[57] Hackney LBC appeared but was not awarded costs, even though the claim succeeded. This is an application of the principle that two or more parties with the same interest will not each be granted their costs. The court is reluctant to award more than one set of costs,[58] but there is no inflexible rule to this effect;[59] the court will be able to depart from the principle if it thinks it fair, just and appropriate to do so.[60]

Conduct of the parties

21.39 More significant, however, is the willingness of the courts to take into account the conduct of the parties in such a way as to deprive successful claimants of their costs, or part of them, on the basis that they prolonged the proceedings unreasonably, thereby causing the unnecessary or unreasonable incurring of additional costs. The availability of this basis for refusing a costs order in favour of a successful party is founded on the provisions of CPR r44.3(4), (5) and (6).

21.40 CPR r44.3(4)(a) requires the court to have regard, when making a costs decision, to the conduct of the parties, which includes the question of conduct before as well as during proceedings, including

---

56 Ibid, at [47]–[49].
57 (1993) 25 HLR 131, QBD.
58 See *R v Industrial Disputes Tribunal ex p American Express Co Ltd* [1954] 1 WLR 1118
59 *R v Registrar of Companies ex p Central Bank of India* [1986] QB 1114 at 1162; *R v HM Inspectorate of Pollution and the Ministry of Agriculture, Fisheries and Food ex p Greenpeace Ltd* [1994] COD 116, QBD.
60 *R (A) v East Sussex County Council* [2005] EWHC 585 (Admin), (2005) 8 CCLR 228 at [47].

compliance with the pre-action protocol; whether it was reasonable to raise, pursue or contest a particular allegation or issue; the manner in which a party has pursued or defended his case or a particular allegation or issue; and whether a successful (whether wholly or in part) claimant has exaggerated the claim.[61] CPR r44.3(4)(b) requires the court to take account of whether a party has succeeded on part of his case, even if not wholly successful. Offers of settlement also fall to be considered.[62]

21.41   In relation to pre-action conduct, in *Aegis Group plc v Commissioners of Inland Revenue*,[63] the claimant discontinued judicial review proceedings and the defendant sought costs under CPR r38.6. The defendant was awarded 85 per cent of its costs due to an unexplained, late response to the pre-action protocol letter and its failure to make any attempt to comply with the terms, or even with the spirit, of the judicial review pre-action protocol until an unacceptably late stage. In such circumstances, the court held that it would be wrong for the defendant to receive the whole of their assessed procedural costs of the discontinued claim, though it would be 'an unjustified overreaction' to deprive them of the majority of their costs or to order them to pay any part of the claimant's costs.[64]

21.42   The court will also take into account, in determining the appropriate costs order, a party's refusal to engage with an offer of ADR,[65] although the unsuccessful party will need to show that the successful party was unreasonable in its refusal to agree to ADR.[66]

21.43   A failure to give proper disclosure may result in adverse costs consequences even where a party has been successful. A stark application of this principle arose in *R (Al-Sweady) v Secretary of State for Defence*.[67] The Secretary of State's failure to provide proper disclosure was described as 'lamentable' and resulted in an interim costs order being made against him.[68]

61 CPR r44.3(5)(a)–(d).
62 CPR r44.3(4)(c).
63 [2005] EWHC 1468 (Ch), [2006] STC 23.
64 [2005] EWHC 1468 (Ch), [2006] STC 23 at [36] and [45].
65 See *R (Nurse Prescribers Ltd) v Secretary of State for Health* [2004] EWHC 403 (Admin)
66 See *Halsey v Milton Keynes General NHS Trust* [2004] EWCA Civ 576, [2004] 4 All ER 920, *R (Johnson) v Reading BC* [2004] EWHC 765 (Admin) and *R (A) v East Sussex County Council* [2005] EWHC 585 (Admin), (2005) 8 CCLR 228; *R (Rodriguez-Bannister) v Somerset Partnership NHS and Social Case Trust* [2003] EWHC 2184 (Admin).
67 [2009] EWHC 2387 (Admin), [2010] HRLR 2.
68 [2010] HRLR 2 at [13].

21.44   The court may make costs orders that require a party to pay a proportion only of another party's costs or that relate only to a distinct part of the proceedings.[69]

21.45   The courts have also used their powers under these rules to make orders for costs based on success or failure on individual issues rather than overall success or failure, particularly where the winning party raised an issue or issues on which he or she was unsuccessful but which took up a significant part of the hearing. In *AEI Rediffusion Music v Phonographic Performance Ltd*,[70] for example, Lord Woolf MR described the 'costs follow the event' principle as a 'starting point from which a court can readily depart'. In numerous subsequent cases, the courts have made costs orders that do not follow the event where they considered it appropriate to do so. The Master of the Rolls continued that '... it is no longer necessary for a party to have acted unreasonably or improperly to be deprived of his costs of a particular issue on which he has failed'.[71]

21.46   Specifically, in relation to judicial review proceedings, attention must be drawn to the decision of Munby J in *R (Bateman) v Legal Services Commission*.[72] In that case, the claimants, though successful in their challenge to the LSC's decision to revoke their funding certificates, were deprived of a proportion of their costs on the basis of their conduct of the proceedings; in particular, their persisting in a number of grounds of challenge which the court considered to have been always doomed to failure. It is noteworthy that the fact that permission had been granted to pursue these grounds did not dissuade the judge from penalising the claimants in costs for arguing them,

---

69 CPR r44.3(6).See also, eg, *R (Essex County Council) v Secretary of State for Education* [2012] EWHC 1460 (Admin), [2012] ACD 93; and *R (Hillingdon LBC) v Secretary of State for Transport* [2010] EWHC 1001 (Admin). In *Essex CC*, the claimant was awarded 50 per cent of its costs because they won on a significant ground but lost on the grounds which had taken the majority of the effort (at [95]).

70 [1999] 1 WLR 1507, CA, at 1523H.

71 See also, eg, *Summit Property Ltd v Pitmans* [2001] EWCA Civ 2020; *Kastor Navigation Ltd v AGF MAT* [2003] EWHC 472 (Comm); *Stena Rederi Aktiebolag v Irish Ferries Ltd* [2003] EWCA Civ 214; and *R (Luton BC) v Secretary of State for Education* [2011] EWHC 556 (Admin). In *Kastor* at [18], the rejection of a CPR Pt 36 payment did not prevent the court from departing from the usual rules relating to the rejection of a payment by a party who then failed to beat it. In *Luton* at [358], the claimant local authorities were awarded all of their costs despite failing on some of their grounds of challenge on the basis the hearing would have taken approximately the same amount of court time and there had been no flexibility from the defendant.

72 [2001] EWHC 797 (Admin), [2002] ACD 29.

for two related reasons. The first was that '... it is only comparatively infrequently that the judge who grants permission will be in any effective position to limit the ambit of the subsequent application for which he has granted permission'[73] and that:[74]

> ... [t]he fact that the judge who grants permission has not made adverse comment on some part of the claimant's case is not, in my judgment, to be taken as any judicial acknowledgment of the appropriateness of pursuing that particular point further.

21.47 The second reason was that the claimants' legal advisers were under a duty to consider with care, even where permission had been granted, which arguments should and which should not be pursued at the full hearing. This is why the form used by the court on the grant of permission includes the words:

> Where permission to apply has been granted, claimants and their legal advisers are reminded of their obligation to reconsider the merits of their application in the light of the defendant's evidence.

21.48 Munby J went on to say:[75]

> The need for conscientious performance of this obligation has been pointed out on previous occasions: see for example Brooke J in *R v Horsham D ex p Wenman* [1995] 1 WLR 680 at p 701A referring to what Hodgson J had earlier said in *R v Secretary of State for the Home Department ex p Brown* (1984) *Times* 6 February. People must appreciate that failure in this regard may be visited with adverse costs orders.

21.49 In reducing the costs awarded to Mrs Bateman and Mr Bateman, who had claimed separately, by 15 per cent and 25 per cent respectively, the court took account of the following factors:

- that the case was one of the utmost gravity to both claimants;
- that the penalty which had been inflicted on them by the Legal Services Commission and which they sought to challenge was a draconian one;
- that no allegation of dishonesty or deliberate concealment had been made against Mrs Bateman and that the allegation which had been made against Mr Bateman had been introduced in a profoundly unsatisfactory manner;

---

73 [2001] EWHC 797 (Admin) at [19].
74 [2001] EWHC 797 (Admin) at [20].
75 [2001] EWHC 797 (Admin) at [21].

- that the judge had granted permission and had expressly regarded as arguable one of the points on which the claimants ultimately lost;
- that the defendant had rejected an offer of settlement made by Mrs Bateman; and
- that the claimants had succeeded in overturning the defendant's decision not just on one but on a number of grounds.

21.50   In spite of these factors however:[76]

> ... the stark fact nevertheless remains that both claimants, and Mr Bateman to a greater extent than Mrs Bateman, pursued, at no little expenditure of time and money, a great number of points on which they ultimately failed, many of them, I have to say, in circumstances where the prospects of success were from the outset exiguous or worse ... Mrs Bateman showed somewhat more restraint, but Mr Bateman, in effect, took virtually every point that could possibly have been taken without going beyond the limits of what is proper.

21.51   At one level, the *Bateman* decision is simply a decision on its own facts that states no more than that where 'unmeritorious points [are] vigorously pursued ... [t]hat, in my judgment, is something which ought fairly to be reflected in my order as to costs'.[77]

21.52   Decisions of this sort do, however, leave the parties, and particularly those advising claimants, in an unfortunately difficult and uncertain position. This was recognised by the judge, who referred to the tension, which had existed for as long as there had been professional advocates, between the pursuit of forensic brevity and the fear of betraying the client's interests by not raising every possible point.[78]

21.53   Nevertheless, if even an express ruling at the permission stage that a ground is arguable, and an express ruling in the judgment following the full hearing that it was entirely proper to raise it, does not necessarily protect the party advancing that ground from a retrospective judicial re-evaluation of its arguability for the purposes of a costs decision, then it is difficult to know by what yardstick legal representatives are meant to comply with their obligation to reconsider the merits of their case on receipt of the defendant's grounds for contesting it, or to consider which grounds ought to be pursued and which abandoned.

---

76 [2001] EWHC 797 (Admin) at [25].
77 [2001] EWHC 797 (Admin) at [26].
78 [2001] EWHC 797 (Admin) at [17] referring to an exchange between Pliny and Regulus, later recounted by Pliny in a letter to Tacitus (Ep I, xx, 14).

21.54   What is clear, however, is that these issues are firmly on the agenda for all parties and that it is the responsibility of legal representatives to give effect to their obligations as best they can. The High Court has held that practitioners should not expect the court to adopt a laid-back approach but to take a robust approach to ensuring that claimants are using judicial review proceedings appropriately as a means of monitoring and regulating the performance of public authorities in carrying out their duties.[79] Parties and, importantly, the practitioners that find themselves at fault in proceedings can expect to have their claims summarily dismissed with lawyers at risk of an application for wasted costs.[80]

21.55   On a related issue, legal representatives must be diligent and make appropriate amendments to the pleadings in order to reflect changes in the case actually being advanced and to cure original defective grounds. Failure to do so is likely to attract criticism from the court and may also be reflected in the costs order that is ultimately made.[81]

Failure to withdraw applications

21.56   If the claimant ought to have withdrawn his or her application because of the defendant's conduct (such as offering a reconsideration upon the grant of permission) or for any other reason (such as a decision of the court in another matter that effectively decides the issue in the case, or the defendant's evidence disclosing that the decision complained of was lawful), then the defendant may recover his or her costs from the date on which the claimant ought to have withdrawn.[82] There is also the danger of a wasted costs order being made against the claimant's legal representative(s).[83]

21.57   There is another possible danger, where claimants proceed with cases that ought to have been withdrawn. In the case of legally aided parties, the defendant may object to the claimant being granted a detailed assessment of his or her legally aided costs (see below),

---

79 See *R (P) v Essex CC* [2004] EWHC 2027 (Admin) at [30]–[39].

80 See *R (P) v Essex CC* [2004] EWHC 2027 (Admin) at [40] and *R (B) v Lambeth LBC* [2006] EWHC 639 (Admin), [2007] 1 FLR 2091 at [42].

81 See, for example, *R (B) v Lambeth LBC* [2006] EWHC 639 (Admin), [2007] 1 FLR 2091.

82 See *R v Warley Justices ex p Callis* [1994] COD 240, QBD. See also *R v Liverpool CC ex p Newman* [1993] COD 65, QBD.

83 *R v Horsham DC and another ex p Wenman* (1992) 24 HLR 669 and [1994] 4 All ER 681, QBD.

rather than applying for a personal costs order against the claimant's legal representative.

21.58   Alternatively, the court may order that, on a detailed assessment of publicly funded costs, the costs of certain matters or procedural steps, etc, should be disallowed. Either course, from the defendant's point of view, has a severe deterrent effect upon the bringing of applications while not involving the time and expense of the kind occasioned by an application for a wasted costs order, where notice to show cause must be given and the matter further investigated by the court, usually at a further hearing.[84]

Costs following settlement

21.59   In *R (Boxall) v Waltham Forest LBC*,[85] Scott-Baker J suggested that the following principles would apply where the dispute has been settled but no agreement has been reached about costs:

- the court has power to make a costs order when the substantive proceedings have been resolved without a trial but the parties have not agreed about costs;
- it will ordinarily be irrelevant that the claimant is legally aided;
- the overriding objective is to do justice between the parties without incurring unnecessary court time and consequently additional cost;
- at each end of the spectrum there will be cases where it is obvious which side would have won had the substantive issues been fought to a conclusion. In between, the position will, in differing degrees, be less clear. How far the court will be prepared to look into the previously unresolved substantive issues will depend on the circumstances of the particular case, not least the amount of costs at stake and the conduct of the parties;
- in the absence of a good reason to make any other order the fallback is to make no order as to costs;
- the court should take care to ensure that it does not discourage parties from settling judicial review proceedings, for example by a local authority making a concession at an early stage.

21.60   *Boxall* was approved and adopted by the Court of Appeal in *R (Kuzeva) v Southwark LBC*,[86] and *Dearling v Foregate Developments (Chester)*

---

84   SCA 1981 s51; CPR r48.7.
85   (2001) 4 CCLR 258 at [22]. See also *R v Liverpool CC ex p Newman* [1993] COD 65, QBD.
86   [2002] EWCA Civ 781 CA, per Schiemann LJ at [18].

Ltd,[87] and followed in *Rambus Inc v Hynix Semiconductor UK Ltd,*[88] and *Brawley v Marczynski.*[89]

21.61   In *R (DG) v Worcestershire County Council,*[90] Collins J, having referred to *Boxall,* cited with approval[91] the following statement from *R (Kaya) v AIT:*[92]

> It is not for me, at this stage, in effect, to rehear a substantive challenge. That would be time-consuming, costly and wholly disproportionate to the amount of costs at stake. It seems to me that I have to approach it on this basis: does a comparatively cursory reading of the papers, albeit a reading which is intended to be informed, demonstrate to me, clearly, that the Secretary of State was very likely to lose and the claimant very likely to succeed as at the permission stage? I do not think I could possibly reach such a conclusion applying that test. In the absence of a good reason the normal order is that there should be no order as to costs. I have been unable to discern the good reason why I should depart from what is normally done in this court.

21.62   What may sometimes be lost from the judgment in *Boxall* is Scott-Baker J's warning as to the danger of judges being tempted too readily to adopt the fallback position and making no award as to costs. More recently, however, the courts have considered critically the *Boxall* approach. In *R (Bahta) v Secretary of State for the Home Department,*[93] Pill LJ said:

> 59. What is not acceptable is a state of mind in which the issues are not addressed by a defendant once an adequately formulated letter of claim is received by the defendant. In the absence of an adequate response, a claimant is entitled to proceed to institute proceedings. If the claimant then obtains the relief sought, or substantially similar relief, the claimant can expect to be awarded costs against the defendant ...
> ...
> 64. In addition to those general statements, what needs to be underlined is the starting point in the CPR that a successful claimant is entitled to his costs and the now recognised importance of complying with Pre-Action Protocols. These are intended to prevent litigation and facilitate and encourage parties to settle proceedings, including judicial review proceedings, if at all possible. That should be the stage

---

87 [2003] EWCA Civ 913.
88 [2004] EWHC 2313 (Pat).
89 [2002] EWCA Civ 756, [2002] 4 All ER 1060.
90 [2005] EWHC 2332 (Admin).
91 *R (DG) v Worcestershire County Council* [2005] EWHC 2332 (Admin) at [21].
92 [2003] EWHC 2716 (Admin), per Mr Williams QC.
93 [2011] EWCA Civ 895.

at which the concessions contemplated in *Boxall* principle (vi) are normally made. It would be a distortion of the procedure for awarding costs if a defendant who has not complied with a Pre-Action Protocol can invoke *Boxall* principle (vi) in his favour when making a concession which should have been made at an earlier stage. If concessions are due, public authorities should not require the incentive contemplated by principle (vi) to make them ....

21.63   The approach in *Bahta* was affirmed in *M v Croydon LBC*,[94] where the position was reiterated that cases that settle in the Administrative Court should be no different from those that settle in general civil litigation and, therefore, where a claimant obtains all the relief he has sought, even if by consent, he is the successful party who is entitled to his costs, in the absence of a good reason to the contrary.[95]

21.64   Despite the qualifications applied to the *Boxall* principles in *Bahta* and *M*, and although those principles have been deemed inappropriate for use in control order cases,[96] *Boxall* is still highly relevant to the starting position of costs when cases settle; especially where the claimant has agreed a settlement containing only some of the relief originally sought in the claim. In such cases, it will be somewhat easier for a defendant to justify a departure from the principle that costs follow the event.

Central funds

21.65   In criminal cases, there is power to award costs (either in whole or in such part as is just and reasonable and subject to certain conditions) to any party to be paid out of central funds, except for a prosecutor who is also, or is appointed by or acting on behalf of, a public authority.[97]

Publicly funded cases

21.66   Funded parties should remember to request a detailed assessment of their publicly funded costs.

94 [2012] EWCA Civ 595, [2012] 1 WLR 2607.
95 [2012] 1 WLR 2607 at [49].
96 *R (Secretary of State for the Home Department) v E* [2009] EWHC 597 (Admin) at [17]–[18]: the appropriate test in control order cases was whether it was more likely than not that the decision to make or maintain the control order or an individual obligation would have been held to have been flawed and so have been quashed. The default position on costs, in the absence of material either way, was for there to be no order for costs.
97 Prosecution of Offences Act 1985 ss16, 16A and 17.

Appeal to the Court of Appeal

21.67 In civil matters, an appeal to the Court of Appeal lies, with permission, from the refusal of an application for judicial review, or from the refusal of relief. Permission, if not obtained from the Administrative Court judge at the conclusion of the case, must be sought from the Court of Appeal within 21 days of judgment.[98]

21.68 CPR r52.15 provides that an application for permission to appeal to the Court of Appeal may be made

- where permission to apply for judicial review has been refused at a hearing in the High Court; or
- where permission to apply for judicial review of a decision of the Upper Tribunal has been refused.

Any application under the second head will be determined on paper without an oral hearing. An application under CPR r52.15 must be made within seven days of the decision of the High Court to refuse permission to apply for judicial review. The Court of Appeal may give permission to apply for judicial review rather than grant permission to appeal and, where this occurs, the case will proceed in the High Court unless the Court of Appeal orders otherwise.[99]

Appeal to the Supreme Court

Civil matters

21.69 A further appeal, from an order of the Court of Appeal, lies to the Supreme Court. This requires the permission of the Court of Appeal or of the Supreme Court itself.[100] The Supreme Court will granted permission for applications that, in the opinion of an Appeal Panel, raise an arguable point of law of general public importance.[101] Generally,

---

98 See generally, CPR rr52.3, 52.4, PD 52 para 4 and *Administrative Court Guidance, Notes for applying for judicial review* (1 April 2011) section 19 para 19.2.

99 See generally, CPR r52.15 and *Administrative Court Guidance, Notes for applying for judicial review* (1 April 2011) section 19 para 19.1.

100 Constitutional Reform Act 2005 s40(6). See also generally UKSC PD 1, section 2.

101 See generally, Supreme Court Rules 2009 SI No 1603 and UKSC PD 1 (General Note and the Jurisdiction of the Supreme Court) and UKSC PD 3 (Applications for Permission to Appeal).

an application for permission to appeal must be filed within 28 days from the date of the order or decision of the court below.[102]

Criminal matters

21.70 There is no right of appeal if the Administrative Court has refused permission to apply for judicial review and, more generally, there is no right of appeal to the Court of Appeal in criminal matters.[103] Instead, after a substantive judicial review hearing, an appeal lies direct to the Supreme Court. Permission is required, and may be granted by the Administrative Court (a Divisional Court) or the Supreme Court. Permission to appeal may only be granted where the Administrative Court certifies that the case involves a point of law of general public importance and either the Administrative Court or the Supreme Court consider the matter suitable for consideration by the Appeal Panel.[104] Generally, an application for permission to appeal must be made within 28 days beginning on the date on which the application for permission was refused by the court below.[105]

Fresh evidence

First instance

21.71 As discussed above,[106] evidence in judicial review proceedings is not restricted solely to evidence that was before the decision-maker,[107] although the court will exercise caution in relation to the reception of fresh evidence as this may well lead to the court being asked to

---

102 Supreme Court Rules 2009 SI No 1603 r11 and UKSC PD 1 para1.2.9. Where a legally aided party is awaiting a decision on the extension of legal aid to permit an application for permission to the Supreme Court, the practise of the court is to grant an extension of the time for applying for permission so that the appellant has 28 days from the grant of funding.

103 SCA 1981 s18(1)(a).

104 Administration of Justice Act 1960 s1.

105 See Criminal Appeal Act 1968 s34(1) and Administration of Justice Act 1960 s2(1).

106 Paras 6.23 and 6.49.

107 See *R v Secretary of State for the Home Department ex p Launder* [1997] 1 WLR 839 at 860H–861B and *R v Secretary of State for the Home Department ex p Turgut* [2001] 1 All ER 729 at 735g.

consider the merits of the case rather than reviewing the decision already made.[108]

21.72 The court will admit evidence that was not before the decision-maker in certain situations. It may receive such evidence to show what materials were before the decision-maker. In addition, where the question before the court is one of jurisdictional fact or whether essential procedural requirements were observed, the court may consider additional evidence to determine that jurisdictional fact or procedural error.[109]

21.73 Fresh evidence is also admissible where the decision-maker or another party has been guilty of misconduct, to prove the misconduct alleged (eg bias, perjury, fraud, etc).[110]

21.74 More recently, the court has enunciated the basis of a right to entertain consideration of the merits, and thus admit fresh evidence, in cases where a litigant's fundamental rights are at stake, such as where the rights of compulsorily detained patients are involved.[111]

On appeal

21.75 The principles of *Ladd v Marshall*,[112] which usually govern the admissibility of fresh evidence on appeal, do not strictly apply.[113] They are that:

- the evidence could not have been obtained with reasonable diligence for use at the trial;
- the evidence would have an important (though not necessarily decisive) influence on the result of the case; and
- the evidence is apparently credible, though it need not be incontrovertible.

21.76 In the interests of finality of litigation, the Court of Appeal will generally, in judicial review proceedings, adopt a similar approach to that

108 *R (YH) v Secretary of State for the Home Department* [2010] EWCA Civ 116, [2010] 4 All ER 448 at [21].

109 *R v Secretary of State for the Home Department ex p Khawaja* [1984] AC 74, HL.

110 See *R v Secretary of State for the Environment ex p Powis* [1981] 1 WLR 584

111 See, for example, *R (BBC) v Secretary of State for Justice* [2012] EWHC 13 (Admin), [2012] 2 All ER 1089 at [27]; *R (Middlebrook Mushrooms Ltd) v Agricultural Wages Board for England and Wales* [2004] EWHC 1447 (Admin) at [84]; *R (Wilkinson) v Broadmoor Special Hospital Authority* [2001] EWCA Civ 1545, [2002] 1 WLR 419, per Simon Brown LJ at [36], [83].

112 [1954] 1 WLR 1489.

113 *Ladd v Marshall* principles still apply but there is flexibility: *E v Secretary of State for the Home Department* [2004] EWCA Civ 49, [2004] QB 1044 at [81].

set out in *Ladd v Marshall*,[114] but it does have a wider discretion to receive fresh evidence, and will do so if the wider interests of justice so require.[115]

114 It should be noted that the Supreme Court has also utilised the *Ladd v Marshall* principles to exclude the use of fresh evidence in a planning appeal: *Welwyn BC v Secretary of State for Communities and Local Government* [2011] UKSC 15, [2011] 2 AC 304.

115 See, eg *E v Secretary of State for the Home Department* [2004] EWCA Civ 49, [2004] QB 1044; and *Momin Ali v Secretary of State for the Home Department* [1984] 1 WLR 663, CA.

APPENDICES

continued

Precedents

1 LETTER BEFORE CLAIM

[D Pechmoad Solicitors]
[12 High Street]
[London SE1 1HT]

[Tel: 020 7833 1111]
[Fax: 020 7833 1222]

[Our ref: DP/tt/BS.002]

[14 July 2013]

[Mrs Paula Ford]
[Pawlard Castle District Council]
[1 The Rectory]
[Northamptonshire NN19 0MD]

Dear [Mrs Ford]

Our client: [Bea Steadman, 6 Belmont Road, Uxbridge, UB40 4LM]
Our ref: [DP/tt/Steadman.002]
Your reference: [VOID/137-1]

Proposed claim for judicial review
1. We are instructed by [Ms Steadman] who yesterday received notice from the County Court Bailiffs, dated 10 July, 2013, that a warrant for possession of her home at [6 Belmont Road] (the 'house') will be executed on 21 July 2013.

2. This letter is sent to you in accordance with the judicial review pre-action protocol. In accordance with that protocol, a copy of this letter has been sent to [Mr Manly].

Background
3. Briefly, the background to this matter is as follows. On 16 October 2012, Ms Steadman was granted by your authority an introductory tenancy of the house. On 21 February 2013, you served a notice of proceedings on her under section 128 of the Housing Act 1996 (the '1996 Act'), stating that you intended to bring possession proceedings against her on the basis that she was in arrears with her rent in the sum of £1,560.36.

4. Our client requested a review of the decision pursuant to section 129 of the 1996 Act by letter of 23 February 2013. The grounds for the review were that the rent arrears were caused entirely by failures on the part of your authority's housing benefit department. The review was unsuccessful and proceedings were issued on 24 March 2013. Our client attended the hearing on 12 May 2013, but the judge informed her that he had no power to refuse your authority a possession order.

5. On 3 July 2013, housing benefit was finally paid into our client's rent account, paying off the arrears in full.

6. By letter of yesterday's date, we requested that the authority reconsider the decision to evict in the light of the payment of the arrears, the medical

evidence concerning our client's mental health and vulnerability which we enclosed with the letter and the effect of the decision on our client's three children who are currently looked after by your authority's social services department but who had been expected to return to live with our client in a few weeks' time. We asked you to agree to withdraw the warrant in order to facilitate your reconsideration.

7. In response, we were telephoned this morning by a Mr Hugh Manly, who we understand is your authority's housing department evictions Team Leader. He informed me that in spite of the fact that our client's rent account is now clear, and in spite of the effect on her health and her children which would be caused by an eviction, he intended to evict our client in any event, on the basis that she is not suitable to be a council tenant, and that she has already had her 'day in court' before the review panel and in the court proceedings, and that the law was 'on the council's side'. He stated that he would not reconsider this decision and would not withdraw the warrant. He confirmed this to us in writing in a letter he faxed to our offices this afternoon.

Details of the proposed challenged

8. The proposed claimant is challenging the decisions of your authority:
(i) notified to our client only by way of the notice of eviction referred to above, to evict her from the house in spite of the fact that the only reason for her rent arrears was a failure by your authority to pay her housing benefit to which she was entitled and which has now been paid;
(ii) notified to us by a letter from Mr Manly of today's date, refusing to reconsider the decision to evict; and
(iii) also notified to us by the letter of today's date, to refuse to withdraw the warrant.

9. We consider the above decisions to be unlawful for the reasons set out below, namely, in summary, that they:
(i) were taken without any proper consideration being given to relevant matters and taking account of irrelevancies; and
(ii) constitute a disproportionate interference with her Article 8 right to respect for her home and private and family life;
(iii) were taken in breach of the public sector equality duty (PSED) under section 149 of the Equality Act (EA) 2010.

10. We have public funding, to commence judicial review proceedings against you, including a claim for interim relief to stay the warrant, unless by 4.00 pm on 18 July 2013, we have received your agreement to the proposals which we set out below. In *Ngessa v Crawley BC* [2011] EWCA Civ 1291, the Court of Appeal held that applications made more than six weeks after the date of the possession order must be made by way of judicial review, because the County Court has no jurisdiction to deal with the application in the light of section 89 of the Housing Act 1980.

11. For your convenience, we enclose with this letter a copy of the warrant for possession referred to above, together with a copy of our letter of yesterday's date and the medical evidence included with it, and a copy of Mr Manly's reply.

Grounds for review

12. We believe these decisions to be unlawful for the following, principal reasons.

Relevant considerations

13. You have failed to take account of relevant considerations, in relation to your decision to evict, to refuse to reconsider and to refuse to withdraw the current warrant, namely:

(i) the cause of the arrears being entirely due to your housing benefit department's unlawful refusal of benefit, our client's request for a revision of which decision was still under consideration at the date proceedings were issued;

(ii) the proportionality of any eviction under Article 8, Schedule 1 to the Human Rights Act 1998;

(iii) the effect of the Equality Act 2010 Part 3 (which prohibits discrimination in relation to the provision of a service to the public- see section 9(2)) and/or Part 4 of which prohibits discriminatory conduct in relation to management of premises (see section 35(1));

(iv) the effect on our client's children of their mother being evicted;

(v) the authority's awareness at all times of our client's mental health problems, difficulties with her children, and housing benefit problems;

(vi) the authority's failure to offer our client any support for her tenancy at any time prior to the service of the section 128 notice;

(vii) the fundamental change in our client's circumstances arising from the payment of all the arrears;

(viii) the fact that the grant of full benefit on revision by your authority indicates that benefit ought not to have been refused – and so the arrears ought not to have arisen – in the first place, and that our client was not at fault in relation to her rent arrears;

(ix) that in the light of these factors, your conclusion that our client is 'an unsuitable tenant' is clearly unsubstantiated and wrong; and

(x) the medical evidence concerning our client's mental health and vulnerability which you now have;

(xi) due regard to the matters referred to in EA 2010 s149.

Irrelevant considerations

14. You had regard, in refusing to reconsider the decision to evict, to irrelevant matters, and erred in law, namely:

(i) that our client had already had her 'day in court';

(ii) that our client was an 'unsuitable tenant'; and

(iii) that the authority had the law on its side.

15. Apart from anything else, these comments all demonstrate that no proper account has been taken of the matters referred to at paragraph 13 above.

Proportionality

16. Irrespective of the matters referred to above, the decision to evict our client in all the circumstances breached her rights under Article 8 of Schedule 1 to the Human Rights Act 1998, and were disproportionate, *Wednesbury* unreasonable and unfair.

17. We rely on the decisions of the Supreme Court in *Manchester CC v Pinnock* [2010] UKSC 45 and *Hounslow LBC v Powell* [2011] UKSC 6 and *R (JL) v Secretary of State for Defence* [2013] EWCA Civ 449, to the effect that:
> (i) Article 8 may provide a basis for challenging a decision to evict an introductory tenant;
> (ii) the issue of proportionality arises at each stage of possession proceeding and while the tenant's entitlement to consideration of her Article 8 rights by an independent and impartial tribunal will normally be satisfied by consideration at the hearing of the possession claim, such a challenge may also be raised at the eviction stage, particularly where there has been a significant change of circumstances between the making of the possession order and the warrant stage.

18. We also rely on *Southend-on-Sea BC v Armour* [2012] EWHC 3361 (QB), the court confirmed that matters which have taken place up to the date of the hearing fall to be considered by the court.

19. In any event, the principles of domestic administrative law form part of the relevant domestic law in relation to consideration of whether or not the proposed eviction of an introductory tenant is lawful (*Wandsworth LBC v Winder* [1985] AC 461, *Kay v Lambeth LBC* [2006] 2 AC 465, HL, and *Pinnock/Powell* (above)). It is clear that the decisions challenged are unlawful as a matter of domestic public law for the reasons set out above at paras 13–14 and because the decisions were, in all the circumstances, perverse in the *Wednesbury* sense.

Public Sector Equality Duty

20. The decision to evict was also contrary to the Equality Act 2010, in that your client has failed to perform its Public Sector Equality Duty under section 149 of the 2010 Act. Section 149(1) requires local authorities, in the exercise of their functions, to have 'due regard' to the need to eliminate unlawful discrimination, harassment and victimisation and to advance equality of opportunity and foster good relations between persons with 'protected characteristics' and others. The 'protected characteristics' for the purposes of the equality duty include disability (s149(7)).

21. Having due regard to the need to advance equality of opportunity involves, inter alia, having due regard, in particular, to the need to remove or minimise disadvantages suffered by persons who share a relevant protected characteristic that are connected to that characteristic, and taking steps to meet the needs of persons who share a relevant protected characteristic that are different from the needs of persons who do not share it (s149(3)).

22. The steps involved in meeting the needs of disabled persons that are different from the needs of persons who are not disabled include, in particular, steps to take account of disabled persons' disabilities (s149(4)). Compliance with the section 149 duties may involve treating some persons more favourably than others (s149(6)).

Due regard

23. The duty to have 'due regard' applies not only to the formulation of policies, but also to the application of those policies in individual cases (*Pieretti v*

Enfield LBC [2010] EWCA Civ 1104; [2011] HLR 3. See also, *Barnsley MBC v Norton* [2011] EWCA Civ 834, at [15]). Due regard is the regard that is appropriate in all the circumstances; the question in every case is whether the decision-maker has *in substance* had due regard to the relevant statutory need: *R (Baker) v Secretary of State for Communities and Local Government* [2008] EWCA Civ 141, [2009] PTSR 809, at [31], [37].

24. Compliance is important 'not as a rearguard action following a concluded decision but as an essential preliminary to any such decision. Inattention to it is both unlawful and bad government': (*R (BAPIO) v Secretary of State for the Home Department* [2007] EWCA Civ 1139 at [3]).

25. While section 149 imposes no specific duty to undertake a formal equality impact assessment, the authority must be able to demonstrate in some way that it has fulfilled the substantive requirements of the duty during the decision-making process in issue: *R (Brown) v Work and Pensions Secretary* [2008] EWHC 3158 (Admin), [2009] PTSR 1506 at [89].

26. Your authority undertook no assessment of, and had no regard to, the impact of your decision to evict our client, given her status as a person with the protected characteristic of disability. You have failed, therefore to comply with the requirements of the PSED and have also failed to have regard to a relevant consideration when deciding to evict our client.

Action to be taken

27. We shall issue an application for judicial review without further notice to you unless, by 4.00 pm on 16 July 2013, you have confirmed to us that you will withdraw the current warrant (and so the urgency of the threat of eviction) in order that we may negotiate further. It is the imminent threat of eviction which causes us to threaten judicial review at this stage.

28. We are mindful of our obligations to attempt to resolve this dispute without the need to involve the court (see eg *R (Cowl) v Plymouth CC* [2001] EWCA Civ 1935, [2002] 1 WLR 803). Accordingly, if you will withdraw the warrant, we are willing to discuss with you ways in which this matter may be resolved. To that end, we would inform you that the substance of our client's case is that the possession proceedings were unlawfully brought, and that the possession order itself ought to be set aside and our client's introductory tenancy revived. At the very least, however, it is quite clear to us that your decision to execute the possession order and refusal to reconsider that decision need to be reconsidered.

29. We are willing to hold off issuing proceedings for a reasonable time in order to discuss these issues with you in more detail but, as stated above, we cannot hold off while our client is threatened with eviction in just a few days' time.

Claimant's legal advisers

30. The solicitor with conduct of this case on behalf of the claimant is Ms D Pechmoad who can be contacted using the details at the head of this letter. Please use our reference at set out above.

Interested parties

31. If proceedings are issued, we shall seek a direction, should permission be granted, as to whether it is necessary to join Pawlard Castle County Court to these proceedings for the purpose of seeking to quash the possession order.

Information sought

32. Please supply, pursuant to section 7 of the Data Protection Act 1998, a copy of our client's housing file. We enclose a signed permission from our client for this purpose, and enclose a cheque to cover your fee.

Yours sincerely,

D Pechmoad Solicitors
cc Mr Hugh Manly, Housing Department Evictions Team Leader.

2   RESPONSE TO LETTER BEFORE CLAIM

[Mrs Paula Ford]
[Pawlard Castle District Council]
[Northamptonshire NN19 0MD]
Tel: 01933 111222
Fax: 01933 333444
email: P.Ford@pawlardcastle.gov.uk

[Our ref: VOID/137-1]

16 July 2013

[D Pechmoad Solicitors]
[12 High Street]
[London SE1 1HT]

Your ref: DP/tt/BS.002

Dear Ms Pechmoad,

Re Bea Steadman, 6 Belmont Road, Uxbridge, UB40 4LM

Thank you for your letter of 14 July 2013. It seemed to raise very serious issues for this Authority with its commitment to renewal and best value, and I called in Mr Manly to discuss its contents with me. This we did at some considerable length, and I am now in a position to reply to the detailed points you raise. This reply constitutes the authority's response to your letter before claim for the purposes of the Judicial Review Pre-Action Protocol.

Details of challenge

I have considered the proposed grounds of challenge set out in your letter before claim. I should like to make the following preliminary comments. I must admit that I was initially troubled by your claim, in particular the grounds concerning relevant and irrelevant considerations and perversity. If it were the case that the Authority had failed in the manner you allege, I should be able to see the force of your arguments. Mr Manly, however, has assured me that all relevant matters known to the Authority were taken into account at the appropriate stages to which you refer. He has also persuaded me that there is no merit in your arguments for the following main reasons (in no particular order):

(i) it does not follow from the award of housing benefit on revision that the initial refusal was wrong. Your client gave information to the benefits department on the revision that was absent from her original claim;

(ii) it is the tenant's responsibility to pay the rent;

(iii) no rent was paid for the first six months of the tenancy;

(iv) it is not this authority's responsibility to 'support' your client in the sense of giving her benefit to which she was not entitled on the basis of the claim form she submitted;

(v) contrary to your assertions, we did not know about your client's ill health or her children until your letter before claim. We therefore could not have taken them into account when issuing proceedings. By the time of the letter before claim, other factors were considered to outweigh them;

(vi) although Mr Manly's reasons may have been expressed in a less than sophisticated way, in essence he was right – your client has already had two bites at the cherry of retaining her tenancy: in the review of the decision to serve the section 128 notice and at court on the possession proceeding when she could have applied for an adjournment to seek judicial review but did not (for whatever reason);

(viii) your client is an unsuitable tenant because she did not pay her rent, did not efficiently process her benefit claim so that her rent was not paid for her; and has been guilty of anti-social behaviour through her children while they were being looked after by this authority;

(ix) the fact that the arrears have now been paid is not the only issue; we are entitled to consider your client unsuitable taking account of her history of persistent non-payment and her children's bad behaviour while in our care;

(x) your human rights and disability discrimination claims are unarguable and nonsensical; *Pinnock et al* make it quite clear that proportionality will only amount even to an arguable defence in highly exceptional circumstances; the circumstances of your client's case are not exceptional and your suggested proportionality defence is not arguable

(xi) in summary, then, although perhaps inelegantly expressed, Mr Manly seems to me to have been quite right in substance to the effect that the authority has the law on its side.

Response to the proposed claim

I have made this Authority's position clear above. I am not prepared to stay the eviction currently planned for 21 July 2013. That eviction will go ahead.

In addition, I would point out that it is wholly inappropriate to seek to derail the eviction proceedings in this way. Your client ought to have raised the substance of these arguments at the possession hearing and not now seek to do so for the first time at warrant stage. Moreover, your application is misconceived unless you seek to set aside the possession order itself, which you are:

(i) out of time to do as you have not acted promptly for the purposes of CPR rule 54.5 and

(ii) unable to do as you did not challenge the making of the possession order at the time.

Leaving aside, however, the Authority's formal position as a matter of law, I would make you the following proposal in the hope of being able to short-circuit this dispute, especially given that public funds on both sides will bear the costs of any legal proceedings.

Although I am not prepared to stay the eviction, I am prepared to treat your letter before claim as a complaint within the authority's corporate complaint's service. The complaint would be dealt with by our dedicated Complaints Service and not by Mr Manly or myself. The procedure is in four stages, ultimately being dealt with by the Chief Executive personally. If your client's case is accepted, we would be willing to arrange bed and breakfast accommodation for your client until she finds somewhere for herself to live in the private sector. Seeing as she now understands the benefit system, this should not take her too long. The average length of time it takes a complaint to complete the four stages of our procedure is two years, but this is only because of our commitment to considering complaints carefully and thoroughly.

If you can demonstrate exceptional hardship on the part of your client, I would be prepared to recommend to the Complaints Service that such accommodation be made available pending the outcome of the complaint. Your client may even be able to have her children live with her, although not if they continue to behave badly.

This seems to me to be by far the most sensible way forward for your client, and I would remind you that if you do issue judicial review proceedings, you must include a copy of this letter in the bundle placed before the court.

Other interested parties

None, but I note your comments about the County Court.

Address for correspondence/service of documents

Please use the address at the head of this letter, quoting our reference. We do not accept service by fax, e-mail or on our e-community notice board.

If you do issue proceedings in this matter, we shall instruct our external solicitors to defend them vigorously on our behalf. Their details are as follows:

Mitchell and Clifford
Cosgrove House
1 High Street
Northampton NN19 1XD

Tel: 01933 232425
Fax: 01933 243546
E-mail: info@ mitchellclifford.com

Yours sincerely,

Paula Ford

cc. Mr Hugh Manly, Housing Department Evictions Team Leader.

3 JUDICIAL REVIEW CLAIM FORM N461

| Click here to reset form | Click here to print form |

Judicial Review
Claim Form

In the High Court of Justice
Administrative Court

**Notes for guidance are available which explain
how to complete the judicial review claim
form. Please read them carefully before you
complete the form.**

For Court use only

| Administrative Court Reference No. | |
| Date filed | |

Seal

SECTION 1 Details of the claimant(s) and defendant(s)

Claimant(s) name and address(es)

name

Ms Bea Steadman

address

6 Belmont Road
Uxbridge
UB40 4LM

Telephone no.

Fax no.

E-mail address

Claimant's or claimant's solicitors' address to which
documents should be sent.

name

D Pechmoad Solicitors

address

12 High Street
London SE1 1HT

Telephone no.
01010 666999

Fax no.
020 7833 1111

E-mail address
help@dpechmoad.com

Claimant's Counsel's details

name

Guy Salmon

address

St John's Chambers
London
EC4A 6LF

Telephone no.
020 7111 2233

Fax no.
020 7 111

E-mail address
clerks@stjohnschamber.com

1st Defendant

name

Pawlard Castle District Council

Defendant's or (where known) Defendant's solicitors'
address to which documents should be sent.

name

Mrs Paula Ford

address

Pawlard Castle District Council
Northamptonshire
NN19 0MD

Telephone no.
01933 111222

Fax no.
01933 333444

E-mail address
P.Ford@pawlardcastle.gov.uk

2nd Defendant

name

Defendant's or (where known) Defendant's solicitors'
address to which documents should be sent.

name

address

Telephone no.

Fax no.

E-mail address

N461 Judicial review claim form (04.13)

1 of 6

© Crown copyright 2013

SECTION 2 Details of other interested parties

Include name and address and, if appropriate, details of DX, telephone or fax numbers and e-mail

┌─name────────────────────────────┐   ┌─name────────────────────────────┐
│ See section 7 below   │   │   │

┌─address─────────────────────────┐   ┌─address─────────────────────────┐
│   │   │   │
│   │   │   │
│   │   │   │

┌─Telephone no.──┐ ┌─Fax no.──────┐   ┌─Telephone no.──┐ ┌─Fax no.──────┐

┌─E-mail address──────────────────┐   ┌─E-mail address──────────────────┐

SECTION 3 Details of the decision to be judicially reviewed

┌─Decision:──┐
│ (1) Decision to apply for a warrant for possession on or about 10 July 2013; (2) to refuse to reconsider the
│ decision referred to at (1) above; and (3) to refuse to withdraw

┌─Date of decision:───┐
│ (1) not known but around 10/7/13; (2) 14/07/13; (3) 16/07/13

Name and address of the court, tribunal, person or body who made the decision to be reviewed.

┌─name─────────────────────────────┐   ┌─address──────────────────────────┐
│ Mr H Manly, Housing Evictions Team Leader │   │ Pawlard Castle District Council, NN19 0MD │

SECTION 4 Permission to proceed with a claim for judicial review

I am seeking permission to proceed with my claim for Judicial Review.

Is this application being made under the terms of Section 18 Practice
Direction 54 (Challenging removal)?   ☒ Yes ☐ No

Are you making any other applications? If Yes, complete Section 8.   ☒ Yes ☐ No

Is the claimant in receipt of a Community Legal Service Fund (CLSF)
certificate?   ☒ Yes ☐ No

Are you claiming exceptional urgency, or do you need this application
determined within a certain time scale? If Yes, complete Form N463 and   ☒ Yes ☐ No
file this with your application.

Have you complied with the pre-action protocol? If No, give reasons for   ☒ Yes ☐ No
non-compliance in the box below.

┌──┐
│ A letter before claim was sent to the Defendant's Director of legal services dated 14 July 2013. The Defendant
│ was only given until 4.00 pm on 16 July 2013, to respond (i.e. less than the suggested period of 14 days) due to
│ the urgency of the case. A fully considered response was given by the Defendant, however, within the timescale
│ referred to above.

Have you issued this claim in the region with which you have the closest
connection? (Give any additional reasons for wanting it to be dealt with in   ☒ Yes ☐ No
this region in the box below). If No, give reasons in the box below.

┌──┐
│   │
│   │

Does the claim include any issues arising from the Human Rights Act 1998?
If Yes, state the articles which you contend have been breached in the box below.   ☒ Yes   ☐ No

> Article 8.

SECTION 5 Detailed statement of grounds

☐ set out below   ☒ attached

> Please see attached Statement of Facts and Grounds.

SECTION 6 Aarhus Convention claim

I contend that this claim is an Aarhus Convention claim   ☐ Yes   ☐ No

If Yes, indicate in the following box if you do not wish the costs limits under CPR 45.43 to apply.

If you have indicated that the claim is an Aarhus claim set out the grounds below

SECTION 7 Details of remedy (including any interim remedy) being sought

1. A quashing order, quashing the decisions referred to under Section 3 above.
2. Further or alternatively, a quashing order quashing the possession order granted by the Pawlard Castle County Court on 12 May 2013.
3. Further or alternatively, a mandatory order, requiring the Defendant to reconsider its decision to apply for a warrant for possession to evict the Claimant.
4. Further or alternatively, a declaration that the said decisions were unlawful and must be reconsidered.
5. Interim relief in the form of a stay on the warrant for possession due to be executed on 21 August 2003.
6. An order that this claim is suitable to be expedited and abridging the time for the filing and service of the Defendant's evidence and detailed grounds of resisting this claim to 21 days.
7. Further or other relief.
8. Costs

SECTION 8 Other applications

I wish to make an application for:-

1. An order, should permission be granted, that the hearing of this application be expedited and that the time for filing and service of the Defendant's evidence and detailed grounds of resisting this claim be abridged to 21 days.

2. A direction whether it is necessary to serve the Pawlard Castle County Court, which made the possession order the Claimant seeks to quash, as an interested party, or to join it as a Defendant.

SECTION 9 Statement of facts relied on

Please see attached Statement of Facts and Grounds.

Statement of Truth

I believe (The claimant believes) that the facts stated in this claim form are true.

Full name_____

Name of claimant's solicitor's firm _____

Signed_____ Position or office held_____

      Claimant ('s solicitor)   (if signing on behalf of firm or company)

SECTION 10 Supporting documents

If you do not have a document that you intend to use to support your claim, identify it, give the date when you expect it to be available and give reasons why it is not currently available in the box below.

Please tick the papers you are filing with this claim form and any you will be filing later.

[×] Statement of grounds   [ ] included   [×] attached

[ ] Statement of the facts relied on   [ ] included   [×] attached

[ ] Application to extend the time limit for filing the claim form   [ ] included   [ ] attached

[ ] Application for directions   [×] included   [ ] attached

[×] Any written evidence in support of the claim or
application to extend time

[ ] Where the claim for judicial review relates to a decision of
a court or tribunal, an approved copy of the reasons for
reaching that decision

[×] Copies of any documents on which the claimant
proposes to rely

[×] A copy of the legal aid or CSLF certificate *(if legally represented)*

[×] Copies of any relevant statutory material

[×] A list of essential documents for advance reading by
the court *(with page references to the passages relied upon)*

If Section 18 Practice Direction 54 applies, please tick the relevant box(es) below to indicate which papers you are filing with this claim form:

[ ] a copy of the removal directions and the decision to which
the application relates   [ ] included   [ ] attached

[ ] a copy of the documents served with the removal directions
including any documents which contains the Immigration and   [ ] included   [ ] attached
Nationality Directorate's factual summary of the case

[ ] a detailed statement of the grounds   [ ] included   [ ] attached

Reasons why you have not supplied a document and date when you expect it to be available:-

Signed _____ Claimant ('s Solicitor)_____

Click here to print form

4 ATTACHED STATEMENT OF FACTS AND GROUNDS FOR REVIEW

R (Steadman) v Pawlard Castle District Council
N461 Sections 5 and 8

STATEMENT OF FACTS AND GROUNDS FOR REVIEW

FACTS

Introduction

1. The claimant is a single woman with three daughters: Isabel (dob 12 November 2001); Freya (dob 23 July 2003); and Emma (dob 4 June 2005). She has a history of mental health problems including severe depression and has suffered repeated breakdowns in her mental health, requiring hospitalisation.

2. On 16 October 2012, following a period of homelessness during which she suffered severe mental health problems and was hospitalised for three weeks, the claimant was granted by the defendant an introductory tenancy of a house at 6 Belmont Road, Uxbridge, UB40 4LM (the 'house'). On the same date she made an application for housing benefit.

3. The claimant's benefit application was not processed. The claimant chased up the defendant's housing benefit department as best she should but given her state of health, she was not able to do so as proactively as she would have liked. In January 2013, the defendant's social services department agreed to look after the claimant's children for a short period while the claimant attempted to recover her health.

The benefit application

4. By letter of 16 January 2013 (**bundle 34**), the defendant's housing benefit department demanded, pursuant to Regulation 86 of the Housing Benefit Regulations 2006 SI No 213, as amended, (the 'Benefit Regulations') that the claimant produce details of her bank account and two recent utility bills to establish her residence at the house. The claimant provided her most recent water and gas bills but informed the benefit office that she did not have a bank account. Instead, she provided a copy of her building society passbook (**bundle 35–39**).

5. By letter of 23 March 2003 (**bundle 40–41**), the benefits department informed her that her claim for benefit was refused as she had failed to comply with their reasonable request for information. Although two utility bills had been provided, one of these was a water bill which was not satisfactory and no bank statements had been provided. The building society passbook was 'insufficient' to award benefit because there was less than £25 in the account, which was 'not enough to live on', and it was 'not considered credible' that the claimant did not have a bank account.

6. The claimant requested a revision of this decision (under regulation 4 of the Housing Benefit and Council Tax Benefit (Decisions and Appeals) Regulations 2001 SI No 1002) by letter of 28 March 2003 (**bundle 42**).

The decision to evict the claimant

7. On 21 February 2013, the defendant served a notice on the claimant under section 128 of the Housing Act 1996 (the '1996 Act'), informing her that they intended to issue proceedings to recover possession of her home. The reason given for this decision was that she was in arrears with her rent in the sum of £1,560.36. The letter informed her that proceedings would not be commenced before 24 March, 2013, and of her right to request a review of the decision to take proceedings under section 129 of the 1996 Act (**bundle 43–45**).

8. The claimant, without seeking legal advice, did request a review of the decision by letter of 23 February 2013. The grounds for the review were that the rent arrears were caused entirely by failures on the part of the defendant's housing benefit department, in that they had wrongly refused her benefit, which decision she had sought to get revised, a decision on which was still outstanding. She told them that she felt very low and was recovering from a mental health breakdown. She also told them that her children were currently being looked after by the defendant's social services department but that it had been suggested to her that they ought to return to her within the following eight weeks. She requested the defendant to decide not to take any steps to evict her until their own benefit department had completed the revision process. (**bundle 46–47**).

9. The decision on review, given on 14 March, 2013, was to confirm the original decision to recover possession of the house. The reasons given for this was that the rent arrears, now £1,665.49, were significant, there had been a long history of non-payment, and the tenant was 'deemed responsible' for either paying the rent personally or else arranging for housing benefit. The claimant had done neither and so was not 'deemed suitable to be a Pawlard Castle tenant' (**bundle 48**).

10. Possession proceedings were issued on 24 March, 2013. At the first hearing on 12 May, 2013, the claimant attended in person – still without the benefit of legal advice – and asked the Judge to allow her to defend the proceedings on the basis of her still outstanding request for a revision of the original refusal of housing benefit. The Judge informed her that under the scheme of Part 5 of the 1996 Act for the recovery of possession of premises let under introductory tenancies, so long as he was satisfied that the section 128 notice was valid and the review had been lawfully carried out, which he was, he had no discretion to do anything other than make an order for possession. The Judge ordered that the claimant must give up possession by 23 June, 2013, ie six weeks from the date of the hearing (Housing Act 1980 s89). (**bundle 49**).

11. By a letter of 3 July 2013, the claimant was informed that her request for a revision of the refusal of housing benefit had succeeded and that the benefit had been credited to her rent account (**bundle 50**). This had the effect of paying off her arrears of rent in full, as she had been paying the water rates element personally since the beginning of the tenancy.

12. On 10 July 2013, the defendant applied for a warrant for possession of the house. The warrant was issued the same day and notification was delivered by hand to the claimant informing her that a date for eviction of 21 July had

been set **(bundle 51)**. At this point, the claimant sought legal advice for the first time, from the solicitors she has now instructed in this claim.

13. By letter of 13 July 2013, the claimant's solicitor requested the defendant to reconsider the decision to evict in the light of the payment off of the arrears. They enclosed medical evidence which the claimant had obtained via social services setting out the claimant's history of mental health problems and continuing vulnerabilities. They further informed the defendant of the effect of the decision to evict the claimant on her 3 children who had been expected to return to live with the claimant within a very few weeks' time. The claimant's solicitor's letter requested the defendant at the very least to agree to withdraw the warrant in order to facilitate a proper reconsideration of the position **(bundle 52–56)**.

14. In response to this letter, the claimant's solicitor was telephoned on 14 July 2013, by the defendant's Housing Department Evictions Team Leader, Mr Hugh Manly. Mr Manly informed the claimant's solicitor that despite the fact that the claimant's rent account was now clear, and in spite of the effect on her health and her children which would be caused by an eviction, he intended to evict the claimant in any event, on the basis that she was not suitable to be a council tenant, and that she had already had her 'day in court' before the review panel and in the court proceedings, and that the law was 'on the council's side'. He stated that he would not reconsider this decision and would not withdraw the warrant. He confirmed this decision in a letter of 14 July, faxed to the solicitor's offices that same day **(bundle 57–58)**.

15. The material part of the letter states:
> As far as I am concerned, your client has already had her chance to be a council tenant but she blew it big time by not paying any rent (until the 11th hour before eviction). She has also already had her 'day in court' both at the review stage and in the county court but the fact remains that the law is on the council's side. I have no cause to reconsider the fair and reasonable position which this Authority has adopted in relation to your client. A person who does not pay the rent and does not arrange for housing benefit in due time is not suitable to be a council tenant, certainly not of this authority. The order will be executed as planned. She will be evicted. I trust this answers your query.

16. By letter before claim of 14 July, 2013, the claimant's solicitor informed the defendant that these proceedings would be issued unless the defendant agreed to withdraw the current warrant by 4.00 pm on 16 July 2013, in order to remove the imminent threat of eviction and facilitate further discussion **(bundle 59–65)**.

17. The defendant responded by letter of 16 July 2013 **(bundle 66–70)**, refusing to withdraw the warrant or postpone the eviction, and raising for the very first time an allegation that the claimant had been 'guilty of anti-social behaviour' through her children 'while they were being looked after' by the defendant.

18. The letter offered, purportedly as a means of resolving the dispute without recourse to the courts, to treat the claimant's letter before claim as a complaint, to be referred to the defendant's 4-stage corporate complaints service. The average time it took for a complaint to complete all 4 stages was 2 years.

In the interim, the eviction would go ahead so that the claimant would lose her home even if her complaint succeeded. She would only be accommodated while the complaint was pending if she could demonstrate 'exceptional hardship' and even then only in bed and breakfast accommodation where it was far from clear whether her children would be able to join her. If the complaint did succeed, it would only result in the defendant making bed and breakfast accommodation available until the claimant could make her own arrangements. This is even less than the claimant could achieve if she presented herself to the defendant as homeless (1996 Act, Part 7), as she is entitled to do, and was found to be intentionally homeless. It would be wholly unreasonable to expect the claimant to accept this offer.

19. The claimant's eviction is still scheduled for 21 July 2013.

Legal framework

20. Part 5 of the 1996 Act governs Introductory Tenancies. By sections 124 and 125, where a local authority elect to operate an introductory tenancy regime, a tenancy granted by the authority will take effect as an introductory tenancy (with certain exceptions not here relevant), and therefore without security of tenure, for the first twelve months of its existence.

23. By section 127 of the 1996 Act:

127 (1) The landlord may only bring an introductory tenancy to an end by obtaining an order of the court for the possession of the dwelling-house.

(2) The court shall make such an order unless the provisions of section 128 apply.

(3) Where the court makes such an order, the tenancy comes to an end on the date on which the tenant is to give up possession in pursuance of the order.

22. By section 128 of the 1996 Act:

128 (1) The court shall not entertain proceedings for the possession of a dwelling-house let under an introductory tenancy unless the landlord has served on the tenant a notice of proceedings complying with this section.

(2) The notice shall state that the court will be asked to make an order for the possession of the dwelling-house.

(3) The notice shall set out the reasons for the landlord's decision to apply for such an order.

(4) The notice shall specify a date after which proceedings for the possession of the dwelling-house may be begun.

'The date so specified must not be earlier than the date on which the tenancy could, apart from this Chapter, be brought to an end by notice to quit given by the landlord on the same date as the notice of proceedings.

(5) The court shall not entertain any proceedings for possession of the dwelling-house unless they are begun after the date specified in the notice of proceedings.

(6) The notice shall inform the tenant of his right to request a review of the landlord's decision to seek an order for possession and of the time within which such a request must be made.

(7) The notice shall also inform the tenant that if he needs help or advice about the notice, and what to do about it, he should take it immediately to a Citizens' Advice Bureau, a housing aid centre, a law centre or a solicitor.

23. Section 129 of the 1996 Act makes provision for the conduct of the review referred to in section 128(6):

129 (1) A request for review of the landlord's decision to seek an order for possession of a dwelling-house let under an introductory tenancy must be made before the end of the period of 14 days beginning with the day on which the notice of proceedings is served.

(2) On a request being duly made to it, the landlord shall review its decision.

(3) The Secretary of State may make provision by regulations as to the procedure to be followed in connection with a review under this section. Nothing in the following provisions affects the generality of this power.

(4) Provision may be made by regulations-

(a) requiring the decision on review to be made by a person of appropriate seniority who was not involved in the original decision, and

(b) as to the circumstances in which the person concerned is entitled to an oral hearing, and whether and by whom he may be represented at such a hearing.

(5) The landlord shall notify the person concerned of the decision on the review. If the decision is to confirm the original decision, the landlord shall also notify him of the reasons for the decision.

(6) The review shall be carried out and the tenant notified before the date specified in the notice of proceedings as the date after which proceedings for the possession of the dwelling-house may be begun.

24. The Introductory Tenants (Review) Regulations 1997, SI No 72 makes detailed provision for the conduct of reviews under section 129 of the 1996 Act.

25. In addition, the Secretary of State has given guidance to local authorities as to the operation of introductory tenancies and decisions to evict introductory tenants (Department of the Environment Circular 2/97).

26. In *Hounslow LBC v Powell* [2011] UKSC 8, Lord Hope said, at [56]:

The fact that there is no mention in section 127(2) of the review procedure under section 129 can be seen to be of no consequence, in view of the direction in section 128(6) that the tenant must be informed of his right to request a review. The fact that there is no demotion stage in the case of an introductory tenancy does not affect the reasoning on which the decision in *Pinnock* was based. It was that, as lawfulness must be an inherent requirement of the procedure for seeking a possession order, it must equally be open to the court to consider whether that procedure has been lawfully followed having regard to the defendant's Article 8 Convention rights: para 77. It was by this route, and by the application of sections 3(1) and 7(1)(b) of the 1998 Act, that the Court held that section 143D(2) could be read and given effect to enable the county court judge to deal with a defence that relies on an alleged breach of the defendant's rights under Article 8. There is a sufficient similarity between section 127(2) and section 143D(2) to apply the reasoning in *Pinnock* to introductory tenancies also. Although the word 'procedure' is not used in section 127(2), it does refer to the procedural requirements in section 128. So it should be read and given effect in the same way, and it is not necessary to resort to the making of a declaration of incompatibility.

Proportionality

27. Article 8(1) of Schedule 1 to the Human Rights Act 1998 entitles a person to respect for, amongst other things, his home, private and family life. An eviction is so serious an interference with art 8(1) rights that a person is entitled to a determination by an independent tribunal of the justification, and proportionality, for such treatment: see *Manchester CC v Pinnock* [2010] UKSC 45 at [77].

28. Where there has been a change of circumstances since the hearing of the possession claim and/or in other exceptional circumstances, an occupier of land is entitled to challenge the proportionality of her eviction at execution of the warrant stage: *Pinnock* (above) at [72]; *R (JL) v Secretary of State for Defence* [2013] EWCA Civ 449 at [38]–[42].

Public Sector Equality Duty

29. Section 149(1) of Equality Act (EA) 2010, provides that local authorities, amongst others, must, in the exercise of their functions, have 'due regard' to the need to eliminate unlawful discrimination, harassment and victimisation and to advance equality of opportunity and foster good relations between persons with 'protected characteristics' and others. The 'protected characteristics' for the purposes of the equality duty are (s149(7)):

  (i) age,
  (ii) disability,
  (iii) gender reassignment,
  (iv) pregnancy and maternity,
  (v) race,
  (vi) religion or belief,
  (vii) sex, and
  (viii) sexual orientation

30. Having due regard to the need to advance equality of opportunity involves, *inter alia*, having due regard, in particular, to the need to remove or minimise disadvantages suffered by persons who share a relevant protected characteristic that are connected to that characteristic, and taking steps to meet the needs of persons who share a relevant protected characteristic that are different from the needs of persons who do not share it (s149(3)).

31. The steps involved in meeting the needs of disabled persons that are different from the needs of persons who are not disabled include, in particular, steps to take account of disabled persons' disabilities (s149(4)). Compliance with the section 149 duties may involve treating some persons more favourably than others (s149(6)).

Due regard

32. The duty to have 'due regard' is unqualified: *R (Meany) v Harlow DC* [2009] EWHC 559 (Admin) at [61]. It applies not only to formulation of policies, but also to the application of those policies in individual cases: *Pieretti v Enfield LBC* [2010] EWCA Civ 1104, [2011] HLR 3; and *Barnsley MBC v Norton* [2011] EWCA Civ 834 at [15].

33. Due regard is the regard that is appropriate in all the circumstances: *R (Baker) v Secretary of State for Communities and Local Government* [2008] EWCA Civ 141, [2009] PTSR 809 at [31]. In *Baker*, Dyson LJ said at [37] that:

[t]he question in every case is whether the decision-maker has *in substance* had due regard to the relevant statutory need. Just as the use of a mantra referring to the statutory provision does not of itself show that the duty has been performed, so too a failure to refer expressly to the statute does not of itself show that the duty has *not* been performed. ... To see whether the duty has been performed, it is necessary to turn to the substance of the decision and its reasoning. (emphases in original)

34. Compliance is important 'not as a rearguard action following a concluded decision but as an essential preliminary to any such decision. Inattention to it is both unlawful and bad government': *R (BAPIO) v Secretary of State for the Home Department* [2007] EWCA Civ 1139 at [3] (concerning section 71 of the Race Relations Act 1976).

35. While section 149 of the Equality Act 2010 imposes no specific duty to undertake a formal equality impact assessment (*R (Brown) v Work and Pensions Secretary* [2008] EWHC 3158 (Admin), [2009] PTSR 1506 at [89]), the authority must be able to demonstrate in some way that it has fulfilled the substantive requirements of the duty during the decision-making process in issue. In *Brown* (above) the Divisional Court laid down six general principles as to how a public authority may demonstrate that it has done so:

90. ... First, those in the public authority who have to take decisions that do or might affect disabled people must be made aware of their duty to have 'due regard' to the identified goals... Thus, an incomplete or erroneous appreciation of the duties will mean that 'due regard' has not been given to them...

91. Secondly, the 'due regard' duty must be fulfilled before and at the time that a particular policy that will or might affect disabled people is being considered by the public authority in question. It involves a conscious approach and state of mind. ... Attempts to justify a decision as being consistent with the exercise of the duty when it was not, in fact, considered before the decision, are not enough to discharge the duty...

92. Thirdly, the duty must be exercised in substance, with rigour and with an open mind. The duty has to be integrated within the discharge of the public functions of the authority. It is not a question of 'ticking boxes'...

93. ...it is good practice for the policy or decision maker to make reference to the provision and any code or other non-statutory guidance in all cases where [the duty] is in play. ...

94. Fourthly, the duty... is a non-delegable duty. The duty will always remain on the public authority charged with it. ...

95. Fifthly, and obviously, the duty is a continuing one.

96. Sixthly, it is good practice for those exercising public functions in public authorities to keep an adequate record showing that they had actually considered their disability equality duties and pondered relevant questions. Proper record-keeping encourages transparency and will discipline those carrying out the relevant function to undertake their disability equality duties conscientiously. If records are not kept it may make it more difficult, evidentially, for a public authority to persuade a court that it has fulfilled the duty imposed by section 49A(1)...

36. In _R (Harris) v Haringey LBC_ [2010] EWCA Civ 703, [2011] PTSR 931, the Court of Appeal rejected an argument by the local authority that equality duty considerations were effectively built into the decision-making process because the development brief for the area and the relevant planning policies themselves reflected those considerations. The Court emphasised the need for the authority to consider actively _in the context of the PSED_ the material that was before it.

Grounds for seeking judicial review

Ground 1 – failure to take account of relevant considerations

37. The defendant's decision to proceed with the possession proceedings against the claimant to eviction failed to take account of relevant considerations, namely:

(i) the fact that the claimant's rent arrears, said to form the basis for the decision to recover possession, were caused entirely by the wrong and unlawful refusal of housing benefit to the claimant by the defendant's own housing benefit department. The claimant's request for a revision of that refusal was still being considered by the defendant's housing benefit department at the date proceedings were issued;

(ii) the fact that the defendant's own housing benefit department has, by revising its decision to refuse benefit to the claimant and paying all benefit due to her since the commencement of the tenancy, accepted that the claimant was not responsible for or at fault in relation to her rent arrears;

(iii) the severely detrimental effect to the claimant and her children of losing her accommodation, given the unlikelihood of her being able to have her children returned to her without accommodation;

(iv) the claimant's health problems, difficulties with her children, and housing benefit problems, of which the defendant was, at all times, including when granting the tenancy, aware;

(v) the defendant's failure to offer the claimant any assistance or support for her tenancy at any time prior to the decision to commence proceedings against the claimant;

(vi) the proportionality of evicting the claimant in all the circumstances;

(vii) the PSED under the EA 2010 s149;

(viii) the Secretary of State's guidance (Circular 2/97), in particular paragraphs 11.1–11.9;

Ground 2 – taking account of irrelevant matters

38. The defendant has taken account of irrelevant considerations, namely:

(i) the allegations of anti-social behaviour made against the claimant's children. This factor could have no possible relevance to the issues before the defendant for the following reasons:

(a) they are wholly unparticularised, unsubstantiated and raised for the first time in the response to the claimant's pre-claim letter;

(b) they concern the behaviour of the children while they have been looked after by, and living in accommodation provided by, the defendant. Even if true, therefore, the behaviour was

– entirely outside the control of the claimant – and within the control of the defendant

- wholly unrelated to the occupation of the house (having occurred nowhere near it), and
- cannot have any relevance to the question of whether the claimant has acted in such a way as to render it lawful for the defendant to conclude that she should not be entitled to remain as a tenant of her home;

(ii) the views of Mr Manly that the claimant was 'unsuitable' as a tenant, and had 'had her day in court', and that the law was on the defendant's side.

Ground 3 – disproportionality and perversity

39. The decision to evict the claimant, and the refusal to reconsider that decision in the light of the evidence and submissions of the claimant's solicitors on 13 and 14 July 2013 was a disproportionate infringement of the Article 8 rights of the claimant and her children, and was perverse in the *Wednesbury* sense.

(i) The decision to recover possession against the claimant was taken on the basis of rent arrears, caused solely by the defendant's refusal to pay housing benefit to the claimant. Even at the time of taking that decision it was known that the claimant had sought a revision of that decision. It was also known that the claimant was paying the part of the rent ineligible for housing benefit personally and on time.

(ii) By the time of the decision to evict, it was known that the revision application had been successful and all arrears had been cleared.

(iii) It was not necessary for the defendant to commence such proceedings in order to preserve its position in the event that the housing benefit decision was adverse to the claimant, because the claimant's introductory tenancy 'trial period' (ie 12 months after it was first granted) will not expire until 15 October 2013 – even now it still has three months to run.

(iv) Conversely, the effect of eviction on the claimant and on her children will seriously interfere with their right to respect for their private and family life and for their home. As set out above, it will render them without any accommodation, prevent them from reuniting as a family, and seriously affect the claimant's mental health which may well, itself, set back the family's ability to live together.

(v) In all the circumstances, including those set out at para 37, above, while the eviction meets a legitimate aim, it is, because it is *Wednesbury* unreasonable, not lawful in domestic law and it is, in any event, a grossly disproportionate response to that aim.

40. Further or alternatively, the decision to apply for and execute the warrant for possession obtained by the defendant was perverse. In addition, the defendant has perversely refused:

(i) to reconsider, properly or at all, its decision to evict the claimant from her home in the light of the fundamental change in the claimant's circumstances, brought about by her repayment of all of her rent arrears; and

(ii) to withdraw the warrant to evict the claimant, due to be executed on 21 July 2013, pending further negotiations or pending the outcome of these proceedings.

41. The repayment of the rent arrears in full, following the defendant's housing benefit department's decision to accede to the claimant's request for a revision of their original decision, taken into account with the matters referred to at para 37, above, render it perverse and unlawful for the defendant to have refused to reconsider its position concerning the claimant's eviction or to withdraw the warrant referred to above.

42. The only written response to the claimant's solicitor's letters, explaining this decision, has been the letter of 14 July 2013 set out at paragraph 15 above, which did not deal with these points, and the response to the claimant's letter before claim, which confirmed that the defendant considered that it had the law on its side, while denying knowledge of the claimant's personal problems (of which it was clearly aware, see e.g. **bundle 79–80; 84–85 and 92** – extracts from the claimant's housing file case record); made new, unsubstantiated and wholly irrelevant allegations of anti-social behaviour against the claimant's children who are being looked after by the defendant itself, and held against the claimant that fact that her rent had not been paid notwithstanding the matters referred to above, concluding that she was not a 'suitable tenant'.

43. In the circumstances, the defendant's decision not to carry out any or any proper reconsideration of the claimant's case is irrational and unfair. In the alternative, any reconsideration which has taken place by way of the letters of 14 and 16 July 2013, referred to above, was likewise irrational for the reasons set out above, has failed to take account of relevant considerations (Ground 1, above) and has considered irrelevant matters (ground 2, above).

Ground 4 – PSED
44. The defendant has failed to have any or any due regard to the matters to which it is obliged to give due regard by EA 2010 s149. It has given no explanation, and disclosed no record, of any such consideration. Accordingly, the claimant cannot (and does not need to) plead this ground in any detail. The defendant has at all times been aware of the claimant's disabilities. Accordingly, it has failed to comply with its statutory obligations and has failed to have regard to a relevant consideration (ie its obligation to do so).

Guy Salmon

5 CLAIMANT'S WITNESS STATEMENT (OPTIONAL)

Claimant
1st statement
B. Steadman
Date: 17.07.13
Filed: 17.07.13
Exhibits: 'BS-1' – 'BS-2'

CO/......./2013

IN THE HIGH COURT OF JUSTICE
QUEEN'S BENCH DIVISION
ADMINISTRATIVE COURT

THE QUEEN

on the application of BEA STEADMAN

Claimant

and

PAWLARD CASTLE DISTRICT COUNCIL

Defendant

WITNESS STATEMENT OF THE CLAIMANT

I, BEA STEADMAN, of 6 Belmont Road, Uxbridge UB40 4LM (the 'house'), unemployed, WILL SAY as follows:

INTRODUCTION

1. I am the claimant, and I make this statement in support of my claim for judicial review of the decisions of Pawlard Castle District Council referred to in my Claim Form. I have read the statement of facts attached to the Claim Form and so far as they are within my knowledge, they are true. The purpose of this statement is not to repeat what has been said there but to give the court some further information about the events which caused me to be unable to pay my rent and about the course of the possession proceedings which were taken against me.

2. The facts contained in this statement are either within my own knowledge, in which case they are true, or I have obtained them from an outside source, in which case the source is indicated and they are true to the best of my knowledge and belief.

3. I have suffered from depression and other mental health problems since I was a child. I now produce, marked 'BS-1', a copy of the latest medical report which I have recently obtained and which my solicitor tells me she sent to the defendant on 11 July 2013. This explains my problems in detail.

MY BENEFIT CLAIM

4. I was granted an introductory tenancy of the property on 16 October 2012, and I applied for housing benefit by filling in a claim at the defendant's housing benefit office on the same day. I did not keep a copy of the claim form because the officer who I gave it to said that the department's copiers could not be used by members of the public and, as she put it, did I want to make my claim or didn't I?

5. On the claim form, however, I put the house down as my home address and that of my children.

6. I did not hear anything. I would normally have been far more proactive in chasing it up, because I have been a tenant all my adult life and I am aware of the importance of paying my rent on time. I was, however, very unwell at the time. I had split with my partner as a result of domestic violence and was homeless for about six months, during which time everything became too much for me and I suffered a breakdown.

7. In November 2002, I went into my local housing office to explain to them that I had applied for benefit but had not heard anything back, and that I was worried about my rent. No-one seemed very interested and they just told me I had to wait till the benefit came through. I asked if they could ring the benefit office for me, but they said they the Benefit Office were having their Christmas party that day and I would not get any sense out of them.

8. I telephoned the benefit office in early January about 10 times, but I just got an answer phone message which said that they could not come to the phone because they were training staff and I could not leave a message because the mailbox was full.

9. Then I got a letter from the benefit office dated 16 January 2013 demanding that I provide evidence that I lived at the house. They said I had to give them copies of my bank statements and two recent utility bills to prove that I lived there. They did not explain why they thought I might not live there.

10. I took in to the benefit office a copy of my most recent water and gas bills. Because I had only moved in to the property so recently, they were the first bills I had received. I also told the receptionist that I did not have any bank statements because I do not have a bank account. I showed her my building society pass book, which is the only account I have. She took a copy of it but said it would be no good because it was not a bank statement.

11. Again, I heard nothing. Then, I got a letter dated 23 February 2013 in which the benefits manager stated that my benefit claim had been refused because I had not provided the information they had reasonably requested. Although two utility bills had been provided, one of these was a water bill which was not satisfactory and no bank statements had been provided. The letter went on that the building society passbook was 'insufficient' to award benefit because there was less than £25.00 in the account, which was 'not enough to live on', that it was 'not considered credible' that I did not have a bank account in the twenty-first century.

12. I was so cross that I wrote back stating that I did not consider it credible that the benefits office could employ such an idiot in the twenty-first century, but I then regretted having been so rude and I wrote a letter of apology.

13. I should say that all this time, I had been paying £5.00 a week in cash at the housing office which was what I was told I would have to pay for my water rates.

14. I went to my local CAB and they told me that I had the right to ask for a revision of the benefit decision, and they explained how I could do this and helped me to write my request, which I sent off on 28 March 2013.

15. Eventually, after all the possession proceedings had taken place, I heard from the benefit office on 3 July 2013 saying that they had decide to accept my case and that they had paid all the outstanding benefit into my rent account. The letter said that they would agree to work on the basis of the information that I had provided, given that they were not actually disputing that I lived at the property but were just saying that they needed evidence of it for their records.

16. I could not understand why this issue had caused so much fuss at all, but I was relieved, because I thought that at least now the defendant would not evict me from the property.

SOCIAL SERVICES

17. Going back to January, when I could not get any answer from the benefit office everything started getting too much for me again and so I asked the defendant's social services department to look after my children for me for a little while so that I could try and sort things out.

18. I was just worried and depressed for most of this year, about my benefit and not having the children, and breaking up with my partner. Then the possession notice came through the door in February and that just made everything worse. I asked for a review of that decision, and I told them that the benefit office's decision was wrong and that I had asked them to review it. I told them about my depression and my children, but I was not surprised that it went against me. The social worker had started saying that I must start thinking about having my children back because she thought that they were suffering from being away from their mother and that I was suffering too, but I did not feel able to cope. Anyway, it looked like I was going to be evicted so there did not seem any point in trying to make arrangements for their return.

19. Winning my benefit was such a relief, that I started to believe I could cope looking after my children – and I thought that the eviction would be called off now that the rent had been paid off. I agreed with social services that my children would come and stay the weekend with me to start with so we could all get used to each other again.

20. They did come home on the weekend of 6–7 July, and it went so well that the social worker said that they should come back to me permanently really soon. I was so excited about the thought of them coming home, and I was just about to sort out the arrangements for this when I got the eviction notice from the court. I was devastated.

21. I had not sought legal advice before (other than going to the CAB about my benefit) because I was told by the housing officer that I did not have a leg to stand on and that the defendant 'had the law on their side'. The housing officers all kept saying this whenever I saw them at court or when I went to the housing office or pay my water rates and asked them about what was going on.

22. I was so devastated at the thought that my children might not come home to me after all that I went to see my solicitor, and she got in touch with the defendant and wrote to them and advised me that I had a good case for judicial review.

23. I now produce a bundle of documents containing all the correspondence I have referred to in this statement, marked 'BS-2'.

CONCLUSION

24. I do not understand why the defendant still wants to evict me. All the rent has been paid off and it is their fault that it wasn't paid in the first place because of the ridiculous stance they took up about the information I had provided. The fact that it was their fault is confirmed by the fact that on review, the review officer said that he agreed with me that the information I had provided was adequate for the purpose.

25. If I lose my home now I will not be able to have my children live with me, which will devastate me and them, and for no good reason. I will also be homeless and I am afraid that because the possession order was made because the rent did not get paid, the homelessness department might say that I am intentionally homeless and refuse to find me anywhere to go. I have no deposit for a private sector tenancy and no confidence in the benefit office to pay me benefit in time to stop me being evicted again even if I did find somewhere to go.

26. Even if an intentional homeless decision would be challengeable, I am advised by my solicitor that the council do not have to provide me with accommodation while I challenge it. I do not know where I could go if I were evicted from the property. I have no family or friends I could stay with. I would have to sleep on the street or try to go back to live with my ex-partner, but I do not feel I can do that bearing in mind the violence I suffered from him, which caused me to leave in the first place.

27. There are no rent arrears, the benefit is now being paid, and it was entirely the defendant's fault that the benefit and so the rent were not paid to start with. There is therefore no prejudice to the defendant in letting me stay in the property, at least on a temporary basis while this claim is being dealt with. For all of these reasons, I would respectfully request the court to allow my claim for judicial review and grant me the interim relief I seek.

STATEMENT OF TRUTH
I believe that the facts stated in this witness statement are true

Signed: Bea Steadman
           (Claimant)
Date: 17/7/13
Dated the 17 July 2013.

6 URGENCY FORM N463

	Click here to reset form || Click here to print form

Judicial Review
Application for urgent consideration

In the High Court of Justice
Administrative Court

This form must be completed by the Claimant or the Claimant's advocate if exceptional urgency is being claimed and the application needs to be determined within a certain time scale.

Claim No.	CO/....../2013
Claimant(s) *(including ref.)*	Ms Bea Steadman

The claimant, or the claimant's solicitors must serve this form on the defendant(s) and any interested parties with the N461 Judicial review claim form.

Defendant(s)	Pawlard Castle District Council

To the Defendant(s) and Interested Party(ies)
Representations as to the urgency of the claim may be made by defendants or interested parties to the relevant Administrative Court Office by fax or email:-

Interested Party(ies)	

For cases proceeding in

London
Fax: 020 7947 6802   email: administrativecourtoffice.generaloffice@hmcts.x.gsi.gov.uk

Birmingham
Fax: 0121 250 6730   email: administrativecourtoffice.birmingham@hmcts.x.gsi.gov.uk

Cardiff
Fax: 02920 376461   email: administrativecourtoffice.cardiff@hmcts.x.gsi.gov.uk

Leeds
Fax: 0113 306 2581   email: administrativecourtoffice.leeds@hmcts.x.gsi.gov.uk

Manchester
Fax: 0161 240 5315   email: administrativecourtoffice.manchester@hmcts.x.gsi.gov.uk

---

SECTION 1 Reasons for urgency

1. This challenge concerns the Defendant's decision to evict the Claimant from her home.

2. The urgency arises from the fact that the eviction is currently scheduled to take place on 21 July 2013. The Defendant has refused to postpone it pending the resolution of these proceedings. Accordingly, the Claimant requires interim relief to stay the eviction on that date, pending the outcome of these proceedings.

SECTION 2 Proposed timetable *(tick the boxes and complete the following statements that apply)*

[x] a) The N461 application for permission should be considered within By 4.00 pm on 19/7/13 hours/days

   If consideration is sought within 48 hours, you must complete Section 3 below

[ ] b) Abridgement of time is sought for the lodging of acknowledgments of service

[ ] c) If permission for judicial review is granted, a substantive hearing is sought by _____ (date)

SECTION 3 Justification for request for immediate consideration

Date and time when it was first appreciated that an immediate application might be necessary.

Date
16/7/2013

Time
17.15

Please provide reasons for any delay in making the application.

What efforts have been made to put the defendant and any interested party on notice of the application?

Letter before action and see section 5 below. The defendant's solicitors were informed of this application by email on 16/7/2013 at 17.30

SECTION 4 Interim relief *(state what interim relief is sought and why in the box below)*

A draft order must be attached.

1. The Claimant seeks an interim order staying the proposed eviction of the Claimant from her home on 21 July 2013, and forbidding the Defendant from executing the possession order it obtained against her dated 12 May, 2013, pending the resolution of these proceedings.

2. The Claimant is an introductory tenant against whom an order for possession has been made. The Claimant challenges the Defendant's decision to continue the proceedings against her by applying for a warrant of possession and refusing to reconsider or to withdraw the warrant. If interim relief is not granted, the warrant will be executed before this claim has been resolved, leaving the Claimant homeless and rendering this claim academic even if well founded.

3. Accordingly, the Claimant seeks the orders referred to at paragraph 1 above, in order to preserve her position pending the resolution of these proceedings.

SECTION 5 Service

A copy of this form of application was served on the defendant(s) and interested parties as follows:

Defendant		**Interested party**	
☒ by fax machine to	time sent	☐ by fax machine to	time sent
Fax no. 01010 333444	time 09.28	Fax no.	time
☐ by handing it to or leaving it with		☐ by handing it to or leaving it with	
name		name	
☐ by e-mail to		☐ by e-mail to	
e-mail address		e-mail address	
Date served		Date served	
Date		Date	

I confirm that all relevant facts have been disclosed in this application

Name of claimant's advocate

name
Guy Salmon

Claimant (claimant's advocate)

Signed

7 DRAFT ORDER

IN THE HIGH COURT OF JUSTICE
QUEEN'S BENCH DIVISION
ADMINISTRATIVE COURT

THE QUEEN

On the application of BEA STEADMAN

Claimant

and

PAWLARD CASTLE DISTRICT COUNCIL

Defendant

---

draft/ORDER

ON reading the claimant's Claim Form, Application for Urgent Consideration and Witness Statement, all dated 17 July 2013.

IT IS ORDERED THAT

1. the warrant for possession of 6 Belmont Road, Uxbridge, UB40 4LM (the 'house'), due to be executed on 21 July 2013, be stayed until the final resolution of these proceedings or further order of this Court;

2. the defendant be prohibited from executing the order for possession of the property, dated 12 May, 2013, until the final resolution of these proceedings or the further order of this Court;

3. the defendant has permission to apply to the court for the variation or discharge of this order on 48 hours written notice to the claimant's solicitor.

8 ACKNOWLEDGEMENT OF SERVICE N462

Click here to reset form	**Click here to print form**

Judicial Review
Acknowledgment of Service

In the High Court of Justice
Administrative Court

Name and address of person to be served

name
Bea Steadman

address
C/O D Pechmoad Solicitors
12 High Street
London SE1 1HT

Claim No.	CO/5823/2013
Claimant(s) *(including ref.)*	Ms Bea Steadman
Defendant(s)	Pawlard Castle District Council
Interested Parties	

SECTION A
Tick the appropriate box

1. I intend to contest all of the claim ☒
2. I intend to contest part of the claim ☐ } complete sections B, C, D and F

3. I do not intend to contest the claim ☐ complete section F

4. The defendant (interested party) is a court or tribunal and **intends** to make a submission. ☐ complete sections B, C and F

5. The defendant (interested party) is a court or tribunal and **does not intend** to make a submission. ☐ complete sections B and F

6. The applicant has indicated that this is a claim to which the Aarhus Convention applies. ☐ complete sections E and F

Note: If the application seeks to judicially review the decision of a court or tribunal, the court or tribunal need only provide the Administrative Court with as much evidence as it can about the decision to help the Administrative Court perform its judicial function.

SECTION B
Insert the name and address of any person you consider should be added as an interested party.

name

address

Telephone no.   Fax no.

E-mail address

name

address

Telephone no.   Fax no.

E-mail address

SECTION C

Summary of grounds for contesting the claim. If you are contesting only part of the claim, set out which part before you give your grounds for contesting it. If you are a court or tribunal filing a submission, please indicate that this is the case.

1. The Claimant's grounds are hopeless, for the following reasons.

2. The Defendant was entitled to conclude that the Claimant was not a suitable tenant, to issue proceedings against her and to enforce the possession order obtained (including to refuse to stay the execution of the warrant pending the outcome of these proceedings, on the basis that for a period of more than 9 months, she did not pay any rent due on her introductory tenancy

3. The fact that the Claimant was eventually awarded housing benefit does not affect this. It does not follow from the award of housing benefit on revision that the initial refusal of benefit was wrong, because the Claimant gave additional information to the benefits department on her request for the revision that she had not given when making her original claim.

4. In any event:
    (i) it is the tenant's responsibility to pay the rent;
    (ii) it is not the Defendant's responsibility to "support" the Claimant in her tenancy in the sense of awarding her benefit to which she was not entitled on the basis of the claim form she submitted or applying for housing benefit for her.

5. At no time prior to the letter before claim did the Claimant inform the Defendant of her ill health or of her children being looked after by the Defendant. The Defendant could not, therefore, have taken such considerations into account when issuing proceedings. By the time of the letter before claim, other factors outweighed them, including
    (i) the Claimant's failure to mention them until the eleventh hour before her eviction;
    (ii) the Claimant's failure to challenge the decisions at the time of the possession hearing (by seeking to defend the proceedings). It is an abuse of the process of the court for the Claimant to seek to delay her eviction by bringing proceedings at this eleventh hour which could and should have been brought months' earlier.

6. The claimant's human rights and PSED claims are unarguable and nonsensical. The decision of the Supreme Court in *Hounslow LBC v Powell* [2011] UKSC 8, at [92] that only in a very highly exceptional case would an Article 8 defence avail an introductory tenant and that of the Court of Appeal in *Corby BC v Scott* [2012] EWCA Civ 269 at [25] that it was fanciful to think that the payment of rent arrears that were owed to the landlord could take an introductory tenant over the arguability threshold for such a defence, demonstrate that the claim on these grounds is hopeless. Moreover, as the Court of Appeal held in *R (JL) v Secretary of State for Defence* [2013] EWCA Civ 449.

7. As to the PSED claim, the Claimant had not informed the Defendant of her disability; there was therefore nothing substantive to which the Defendant was obliged or could have due regard: see *R (Greenwich Community Law Centre) v Greenwich LBC* [2012] EWCA Civ 496, at [30].

8. The purpose of the introductory tenancy regime was to permit local authorities to evict unsuitable tenants without the need for lengthy and expensive legal procedures. The judicial review court should not be used as a substitute for the county court in this type of case, where Parliament has expressly legislated to the contrary.

9. The Defendant was entitled to make the decisions it did and permission to proceed with this claim should be refused.

TOM SUMMER

SECTION D

Give details of any directions you will be asking the court to make, or tick the box to indicate that a separate application notice is attached.

If you are seeking a direction that this matter be heard at an Administrative Court venue other than that at which this claim was issued, you should complete, lodge and serve on all other parties Form N464 with this acknowledgment of service.

SECTION E

Response to the claimant's contention that the claim is an Aarhus claim

Do you deny that the claim is an Aarhus Convention claim? ☐ Yes ☐ No

If Yes, please set out your grounds for denial in the box below.

SECTION F

*delete as appropriate

*(I believe)(The defendant believes) that the facts stated in this form are true.

*I am duly authorised by the defendant to sign this statement.

(If signing on behalf of firm or company, court or tribunal)

Position or office held

(To be signed by you or by your solicitor or litigation friend)

Signed

Date

Give an address to which notices about this case can be sent to you

name

address

Telephone no.

Fax no.

E-mail address

If you have instructed counsel, please give their name address and contact details below.

name

address

Telephone no.

Fax no.

E-mail address

Completed forms, together with a copy, should be lodged with the Administrative Court Office (court address, over the page), at which this claim was issued within 21 days of service of the claim upon you, and further copies should be served on the Claimant(s), any other Defendant(s) and any interested parties within 7 days of lodgement with the Court.

Click here to print form

3 of 4

Administrative Court addresses

- Administrative Court in **London**

  Administrative Court Office, Room C315, Royal Courts of Justice, Strand, London, WC2A 2LL.

- Administrative Court in **Birmingham**

  Administrative Court Office, Birmingham Civil Justice Centre, Priory Courts, 33 Bull Street, Birmingham B4 6DS.

- Administrative Court in **Wales**

  Administrative Court Office, Cardiff Civil Justice Centre, 2 Park Street, Cardiff, CF10 1ET.

- Administrative Court in **Leeds**

  Administrative Court Office, Leeds Combined Court Centre, 1 Oxford Row, Leeds, LS1 3BG.

- Administrative Court in **Manchester**

  Administrative Court Office, Manchester Civil Justice Centre, 1 Bridge Street West, Manchester, M3 3FX.

9   RENEWAL OF CLAIM (FORM 86B)

CO Ref No: CO/5823/2013

IN THE HIGH COURT OF JUSTICE
QUEEN'S BENCH DIVISION
ADMINISTRATIVE COURT

In the matter of a claim for judicial review

The Queen on the application of

BEA STEADMAN

v

PAWLARD CASTLE DISTRICT COUNCIL

Notice of RENEWAL of claim for permission to apply for Judicial Review
(CPR 54.12).

1. *This notice must be lodged in the Administrative Court Office and served upon the defendant (and interested parties who were served with the claim form) within 7 days of the service on the claimant or his solicitor of the notice that the claim for permission has been refused.*

2. *If this form has not been lodged within 7 days of service (para 1 above) please set out the **reasons for delay**:*

3. *Set out below the grounds for renewing the application:*

1. The learned Judge wrongly concluded that the claimant's claim was wholly misconceived. The claimant repeats her pleaded grounds for review and the matters and her witness statement.

2. The learned Judge was also wrong to state that the claimant had delayed because she had not sought to defend her possession proceedings at the time of the hearing of the possession claim, on 12 May 2013. At the date of the hearing, the claimant was in an entirely different situation:
(i) she had no legal advice or representation;
(ii) and her housing benefit was still in dispute with the defendant asserting that she was not entitled to any housing benefit, and her rent account was therefore considerably in arrears (see **bundle 71–76**).

3. In any event, it is not suggested that the rights of any third parties are in any way affected by these proceedings, so as to call for particular or unusual promptness in bringing a claim. The claimant is aware of the primary obligation to act promptly, but she is still within the backstop period of 3 months for an application and the facts of this matter are such that she should be considered to have acted promptly.

4. Please supply

COUNSEL'S NAME: GUY SALMON

COUNSEL'S TELEPHONE NUMBER: 020 7811 1234

Signed

Dated   20/7/13

Claimant's Ref No.   DP/tt/Steadman.002

Tel No.   020 7833 1111

Fax No.   020 7833 1222

To the Master of the Administrative Court, Royal Courts of Justice, Strand, London, WC2A 2LL

Form 86B

10 DETAILED GROUNDS FOR DEFENDING CLAIM

CO/5823/2013

IN THE HIGH COURT OF JUSTICE
QUEEN'S BENCH DIVISION
ADMINISTRATIVE COURT

THE QUEEN

On the application of BEA STEADMAN

Claimant

and

PAWLARD CASTLE DISTRICT COUNCIL

Defendant

DETAILED GROUNDS FOR DEFENDING THE CLAIM

Housing benefit

1. The claimant's case depends on the twin propositions that the payment of her housing benefit on review, reducing her arrears to nothing:

(a) must necessarily mean that the defendant was wrong to have refused it initially; and

(b) must necessarily render it now unreasonable to continue with her eviction.

2. Neither of these propositions is correct. The mere fact that, on review the defendant's housing benefit review officer was prepared to waive the requirements originally imposed by the benefits manager in no way indicates that those original requirements were unreasonable or impossible for the claimant to have complied with. It simply means that the reviews officer considered it appropriate to waive them in the circumstances of this particular review.

Public law challenge

3. Nor is the decision whether or not to evict limited to consideration of only the identical circumstances to those which formed the subject of the housing benefit review. The introductory tenancy regime left it to the landlord to decide whether or not it wished to continue with a person as its tenant. Even following *Manchester CC v Pinnock* [2010] UKSC 45 and *Hounslow LBC v Powell* [2011] UKSC 8, the jurisdiction of the county court judge to interfere with that decision on the grounds of proportionality or of a public law defence are extremely limited, or, as stated by Lord Phillips PSC, in *Powell*, only to be exercised in 'very highly exceptional' cases (at [92]).

4. While it is not suggested that this excludes the jurisdiction of the court on judicial review, it is not for this court to second guess the decision of the local authority on the merits. Indeed, it is suggested that the court should only

interfere with such decisions extremely sparingly, by reference to *Powell*, and in accordance with the well-known line of public law authorities beginning with the speech of Lord Brightman in *R v Hillingdon LBC ex p Puhlhofer* [1986] AC 484.

Relevant considerations

5. As can be seen from the witness statement of Mr Hugh Manly, the defendant took account only of relevant matters and considered all relevant matters known to it at the time. The claimant can hardly claim, in a public law challenge, that the defendant was somehow obliged to take account of matters she never put before them. It can be seen from the tenancy file exhibited to Mr Manly's statement that none of the matters now complained of relating to the claimant's mental health and her children were before the defendant at the relevant time. When they were put before Mr Manly at the 11th hour, he was entitled to refuse to change his mind.

Decision to proceed with eviction

6. It is the tenant's responsibility to ensure the rent is paid, and properly to process any benefit claim she may make. The claimant did not do so. Nor did she persuade a review panel that she should not be evicted. Critically, she is not seeking to challenge the panel's decision. Once it is accepted that the panel was entitled to reach the decision it did (as the claimant must be taken to accept in the absence of challenge), the decision to issue proceedings resultant on the decision of the review panel must be unchallengeable, and so must be the decision to evict, absent the most marked change of circumstances: *Pinnock* at [71].

7. Parliament did not set up a review procedure only to require officers to reconsider the review which had just happened before proceedings could be validly brought. To impute such an intention to Parliament is absurd. Nor is there any marked change of circumstances. The review panel and the county court judge granting the possession order were well aware of the possibility that the revision application made by the claimant in respect of the original housing benefit decision might succeed, and, if it did, would lead to the payment of the arrears of rent. They must be taken to have taken that possibility into account, yet decided that eviction was appropriate. The fact that that possibility has now eventuated, does not amount to a change of circumstances at all, let alone a marked change.

Proportionality/Perversity/PSED

Proportionality

8. The claimant's Article 8 point is unarguable for the reasons set out above. The tenancy was introductory, to assess the suitability of the claimant to be a tenant. She did not arrange for housing benefit to pay her rent, nor did she pay it herself. In the context of Parliament's decision to withhold security of tenure for a period of time from persons in the claimant's position, there is nothing exceptional about the claimant's circumstances to suggest that her eviction would be disproportionate.

9. Moreover, in *Corby BC v Scott* [2012] EWCA Civ 276, Lord Neuberger said, at [25]:

The only other fact relied on...was that the rent arrears were cleared the day before the hearing. I do not think that that is an impressive point at all. I suppose that it is just about conceivable that it might provide a little support for a proportionality argument, based on other, much stronger points. However, I find it difficult to think of circumstances where the fact that the tenant...paid off the rent arrears at the last minute could carry significant weight in the Article 8 proportionality argument. In the absence of extraordinary facts, it seems to me fanciful to suggest that a residential occupier should be able to pray in aid the fact that she has paid the landlord money which she owed him, as a significant factor, which enables her to cross the high threshold identified in the two Supreme Court cases, when invoking Article 8.

Perversity

10   For the reasons already stated, there is nothing perverse about the defendant's decision.

PSED

11. If the claimant did not alert the defendant to her disability it can hardly be said as a matter of logical possibility that the defendant ought to have conducted a detailed PSED assessment. Nor does the case law establish any obligation to do so. To the contrary, in *R (Greenwich Community Law Centre) v Greenwich LBC* [2012] EWCA Civ 496, Elias LJ said, at [30]:

> Furthermore, as Pill LJ observed in *R (Bailey) v Brent London Borough Council* [2011] EWCA Civ 1586 para 83, it is only if a characteristic or combination of characteristics is likely to arise in the exercise of the public function that they need be taken into consideration. I would only add the qualification that there may be cases where that possibility exists in which case there may be a need for further investigation before that characteristic can be ignored: see the observations of Elias LJ in *Hurley and Moore* para 96. (Perhaps more accurately it may be said that whilst the Council has to have due regard to all aspects of the duty, some of them may immediately be rejected as plainly irrelevant to the exercise of the function under consideration – no doubt often subliminally and without being consciously addressed. As Davis LJ observed in *Bailey*, para 91, it is then a matter of semantics whether one says that the duty is not engaged or that it is engaged but the matter is ruled out as irrelevant or insignificant).

12. In the absence of any suggestion that the claimant had any protected characteristic, that was the approach that the defendant in the present case was entitled to take.

Relief

13. In any event, the Court should in its discretion refuse any relief to the claimant on the grounds of her delay. The correct time for her to have challenged the decisions of which she now complains was at the time of the possession order being made. She could and should have sought to defend the proceedings on the basis of the arguments she now raises. Having not done so, she should not be permitted to raise those arguments now (see *R (JL) v Secretary of State for Defence* [2013] EWCA Civ 449 at [38]–[42]).

14. No proper reasons have been advanced to explain why this was not done, other than a bald assertion that the claimant was not legally represented. That was the claimant's choice. It did not prevent her from challenging the defendant at the appropriate time and she should not now be permitted to do so some 2 months later, given the prejudice and detriment to good administration it will cause: namely the defendant will lose this unit of accommodation which it could otherwise have offered to one of the 312 families waiting for accommodation of this sort on its waiting list.

15 For these reasons, this claim should be dismissed.

Tom Summer
28 August 2013

11 DEFENDANT'S EVIDENCE

Defendant
1st statement
H Manly
Date: 15.08.13
Filed: 15.08.13
Exhibit 'HM-1'

CO/5823/2013

IN THE HIGH COURT OF JUSTICE
QUEEN'S BENCH DIVISION
ADMINISTRATIVE COURT

THE QUEEN

On the application of BEA STEADMAN

Claimant

and

PAWLARD CASTLE DISTRICT COUNCIL

Defendant

WITNESS STATEMENT OF HUGH MANLY

I, HUGH MANLY, of Pawlard Castle District Council, Northamptonshire NN19 0MD, Local Government Officer, WILL SAY as follows.

1. I am the defendant's Housing Department Evictions Team Leader and I am authorised to make this witness statement on behalf of the defendant, resisting this application for judicial review. I have been employed in my current post for five years, before which I was the manager of the Pawlard Castle Civic Amenity Dump for seven years. In many ways, the two jobs are quite similar – I am responsible for getting rid of the community's trash.

2. Edgy comedy aside, I made all the decisions challenged in this case, and so the facts stated in this witness statement are within my own knowledge and are true. I now produce, marked 'HM-1' a true copy of the claimant's tenancy file.

Decision to take proceedings

3. I took the decision in March 2013 to issue proceedings for possession against the claimant, she having already been served with a notice of proceedings under section 128 of the Housing Act 1996, and having fought and lost a review under section 129 of the same Act. I took no part in the review, but a panel of elected members decided to uphold the section 128 notice. This made it practically inevitable that proceedings would be issued.

4.   I have to say that this was one of the factors I took into account when deciding to issue proceedings. It seemed to me that, Parliament having provided for a review procedure under section 129 which must be completed before the date specified in the section 128 notice as the date after which possession proceedings may be begun (s129(6)), it must have been Parliament's intention that the decision on the review will be influential in the decision whether or not to issue proceedings. I am not saying it is the only relevant factor, but it was a strong indication to me that proceedings should be issued.

5.   What was there to set against that? Not very much. The claimant was more than £1,600 in arrears with her rent; she had been refused housing benefit on the basis of her own default in supplying information requested by the housing benefits department. The only matter to counter all of that was the fact that she had put in a request for a revision of the refusal of her housing benefit. I did not know about her children, nor about her depression because she had never put this information before the defendant.

6.   Revision applications are extremely common, however, and do not indicate without more that the application has any merit. I thought this application stood very little chance of success. Although with hindsight, that turned out not to be so, and the revision was made, I cannot be criticised for not being able to foresee that happening. It had not happened when I made my decision so I could not have considered it. Weighing up all these factors, I decided that we should issue proceedings. There was no material before me to indicate the contrary.

Decision to issue warrant/refusal to withdraw warrant

7.   I now turn to explain the decision to request the warrant and my refusal to withdraw it. Pawlard Castle District Council obtained a possession order from the Judge. There was no reason why I should not enforce it. The fact that the housing benefit had finally been paid did not alter the fact that the defendant had been kept out its money for some nine months by the time of that payment. The defendant is a local authority not a bank giving interest-free loans. Paying the rent in full and on time is the tenant's responsibility. I am of course sympathetic to anyone who has difficulties claiming housing benefit, but the fact remains that if the claimant had produced the information requested in January 2013, when it was requested, none of this would ever have happened.

8.   Moreover, it does not follow from the award of housing benefit on revision that the initial refusal was wrong. The decision on revision was, as I read it, made as a concession to the claimant, not by way of a strict application of the Housing Benefit Regulations. In any event, I cannot be bound by a decision of a housing benefit officer. Our roles are entirely different, as are the considerations to be taken into account.

9.   The claimant, by this time, had already had two bites at the cherry of retaining her tenancy: in the review of the decision to serve the section 128 notice and at court on the possession proceeding when she could filed a defence raising the arguments that are now put forward on her behalf, but did not (for whatever reason);

10. For all these reasons, I took the view, as I believe I was entitled to, that the claimant was an unsuitable tenant. because persistently she did not pay her rent, did not organise her housing benefit, and did not, therefore, behave in a tenant-like manner. Nor did she challenge the making of a possession order at the appropriate time. In fact she did nothing at all until the eleventh hour, at which point she suddenly announced a number of additional problems never previously raised.

11. I do not believe, in the circumstances, that those matters – at this stage – oblige me to change my mind. Pawlard Castle District Council does not want the claimant as its tenant. That decision is reasonable and supportable. The implementation of it is the very purpose of the introductory tenancy regime.

12. For these reasons, I would ask the court to refuse this application.

STATEMENT OF TRUTH
I believe the facts contained in this witness statement to be true

Signed: Hugh Manly
Date: 15/08/13

Dated this 15ᵗʰ day of August 2013.

13 CONSENT ORDER

C0/5823/2013

IN THE HIGH COURT OF JUSTICE
QUEEN'S BENCH DIVISION
ADMINISTRATIVE COURT

THE QUEEN

On the application of BEA STEADMAN

Claimant

and

PAWLARD CASTLE DISTRICT COUNCIL

Defendant

CONSENT ORDER

ON the parties coming to terms in this application

BY CONSENT, IT IS ORDERED:

1. that the claimant's application for judicial review be dismissed;

2. that the defendant shall pay the claimant's costs of and incidental to this application, to be subject to detailed assessment if not agreed.

3. that there be a detailed assessment of the claimant's publicly funded costs.

The reason for the making of this order is that the defendant has agreed that the possession order obtained by the defendant from the Pawlard Castle County Court on 12th May 2013 (copy attached) should be set aside and that the possession proceedings within which they were made should be dismissed by consent. Accordingly, this claim is now rendered academic, and there is no need for the court to adjudicate on it.

Signed   Signed
Guy Salmon   Tom Summer
Counsel for the claimant   Counsel for the defendant
4 November 2013.   4 November 2013.

Legislation[1]

SENIOR COURTS ACT 1981

Restrictions on appeals to Court of Appeal

18 (1) No appeal shall lie to the Court of Appeal–

    (a) except as provided by the Administration of Justice Act 1960, from any judgment of the High Court in any criminal cause or matter;

    (b) from any order of the High Court or any other court or tribunal allowing an extension of time for appealing from a judgment or order;

    (c) from any order, judgment or decision of the High Court or any other court or tribunal which, by virtue of any provision (however expressed) of this or any other Act, is final;

    (d) from a decree absolute of [divorce or]² nullity of marriage, by a party who, having had time and opportunity to appeal from the decree nisi on which that decree was founded, has not appealed from the decree nisi;

    (dd) *from a divorce order;*³

    (e), (f) ...

    (fa) from a dissolution order, nullity order or presumption of death order under Chapter 2 of Part 2 of the Civil Partnership Act 2004 that has been made final, by a party who, having had time and opportunity to appeal from the conditional order on which that final order was founded, has not appealed from the conditional order;

    (g) except as provided by Part I of the Arbitration Act 1996, from any decision of the High Court under that Part;

    (h) ...

(1A), (1B), (2) ...

Appeals from Crown Court and inferior courts

28 (1) Subject to subsection (2), any order, judgment or other decision of the Crown Court may be questioned by any party to the proceedings, on the ground that it is wrong in law or is in excess of jurisdiction, by applying to the Crown Court to have a case stated by that court for the opinion of the High Court.

  (2) Subsection (1) shall not apply to–

    (a) a judgment or other decision of the Crown Court relating to trial on indictment; or

    (b) any decision of that court under the Local Government (Miscellaneous Provisions) Act 1982 which, by any provision of any of those Acts, is to be final.

  (3) Subject to the provisions of this Act and to rules of court, the High Court shall, in accordance with section 19(2), have jurisdiction to hear and determine–

    (a) any application, or any appeal (whether by way of case stated or otherwise), which it has power to hear and determine under or by virtue of this or any other Act; and

    (b) all such other appeals as it had jurisdiction to hear and determine immediately before the commencement of this Act.

  (4) In subsection (2)(a) the reference to a decision of the Crown Court relating to trial on indictment does not include a decision relating to [an order under

---

2 Words in square brackets prospectively repealed by Family Law Act 1996. See s66 and Sch 8.

3 Words in italics prospectively inserted by Family Law Act 1996. See s66 and Sch 8.

section 17 of the Access to Justice Act 1999] *a requirement to make a payment under regulations under section 23 or 24 of the Legal Aid, Sentencing and Punishment of Offenders Act 2012.*[4]

Proceedings on case stated by magistrates' court or Crown Court]

28A (1)This section applies where a case is stated for the opinion of the High Court–

(a) by a magistrates' court under section 111 of the Magistrates' Courts Act 1980; or

(b) by the Crown Court under section 28(1) of this Act.

(2) The High Court may, if it thinks fit, cause the case to be sent back for amendment and, where it does so, the case shall be amended accordingly.

(3) The High Court shall hear and determine the question arising on the case (or the case as amended) and shall--

(a) reverse, affirm or amend the determination in respect of which the case has been stated; or

(b) remit the matter to the magistrates' court, or the Crown Court, with the opinion of the High Court,

and may make such other order in relation to the matter (including as to costs) as it thinks fit.

(4) Except as provided by the Administration of Justice Act 1960 (right of appeal to Supreme Court in criminal cases), a decision of the High Court under this section is final.

Mandatory, prohibiting and quashing orders

29 (1) The orders of mandamus, prohibition and certiorari shall be known instead as mandatory, prohibiting and quashing orders respectively.

(1A) The High Court shall have jurisdiction to make mandatory, prohibiting and quashing orders in those classes of case in which , immediately before 1 May 2004, it had jurisdiction to make orders of mandamus, prohibition and certiorari respectively.

(2) Every such order shall be final, subject to any right of appeal therefrom.

(3) In relation to the jurisdiction of the Crown Court, other than its jurisdiction in matters relating to trial on indictment, the High Court shall have all such jurisdiction to make mandatory, prohibiting or quashing orders as the High Court possesses in relation to the jurisdiction of an inferior court.

(3A) The High Court shall have no jurisdiction to make mandatory, prohibiting or quashing orders in relation to the jurisdiction of the Court Martial in matters relating to–

(a) trial by the Court Martial for an offence; or

(b) appeals from the Service Civilian Court.

(4) The power of the High Court under any enactment to require justices of the peace or a judge or officer of a county court to do any act relating to the duties of their respective offices, or to require a magistrates' court to state a case for the opinion of the High Court, in any case where the High Court formerly had by virtue of any enactment jurisdiction to make a rule absolute, or an order, for any of those purposes, shall be exercisable by mandatory order.

---

4 Words in square brackets repealed, and words in italics substituted, by LASPO 2012 s39, Sch 5. Not yet in force, see LASPO 2012 s151.

(5) In any statutory provision–
  (a) references to mandamus or to a writ or order of mandamus shall be read as references to a mandatory order;
  (b) references to prohibition or to a writ or order of prohibition shall be read as references to a prohibiting order;
  (c) references to certiorari or to a writ or order of certiorari shall be read as references to a quashing order; and
  (d) references to the issue or award of a writ of mandamus, prohibition or certiorari shall be read as references to the making of the corresponding mandatory, prohibiting or quashing order.
(6) In subsection (3) the reference to the Crown Court's jurisdiction in matters relating to trial on indictment does not include its jurisdiction relating to [orders under section 17 of the Access to Justice Act 1999] *requirements to make payments under regulations under section 23 or 24 of the Legal Aid, Sentencing and Punishment of Offenders Act 2012.*[5]

Injunctions to restrain persons from acting in offices in which they are not entitled to act

30 (1) Where a person not entitled to do so acts in an office to which this section applies, the High Court may–
  (a) grant an injunction restraining him from so acting; and
  (b) if the case so requires, declare the office to be vacant.
(2) This section applies to any substantive office of a public nature and permanent character which is held under the Crown or which has been created by any statutory provision or royal charter.

Application for judicial review

31 (1) An application to the High Court for one or more of the following forms of relief, namely–
  (a) a mandatory, prohibiting or quashing order;
  (b) a declaration or injunction under subsection (2); or
  (c) an injunction under section 30 restraining a person not entitled to do so from acting in an office to which that section applies,
  shall be made in accordance with rules of court by a procedure to be known as an application for judicial review.
(2) A declaration may be made or an injunction granted under this subsection in any case where an application for judicial review, seeking that relief, has been made and the High Court considers that, having regard to–
  (a) the nature of the matters in respect of which relief may be granted by mandatory, prohibiting or quashing orders;
  (b) the nature of the persons and bodies against whom relief may be granted by such orders; and
  (c) all the circumstances of the case,
  it would be just and convenient for the declaration to be made or of the injunction to be granted, as the case may be.
(3) No application for judicial review shall be made unless the leave of the High

---

5 Words in square brackets repealed, and words in italics substituted, by LASPO 2012 s39, Sch 5. Not yet in force, see LASPO 2012 s151.

Court has been obtained in accordance with rules of court; and the court shall not grant leave to make such an application unless it considers that the applicant has a sufficient interest in the matter to which the application relates.

(4) On an application for judicial review the High Court may award damages to the applicant if–
   (a) the application includes a claim for such an award arising from any matter to which the application relates; and
   (b) the court is satisfied that such an award would have been made if the claim had been made in an action begin by the applicant at the time of making the application.

(5) If, on an application for judicial review, the High Court quashes the decision to which the application relates, it may in addition–
   (a) remit the matter to the court, tribunal or authority which made the decision, with a direction to reconsider the matter and reach a decision in accordance with the findings of the High Court, or
   (b) substitute its own decision for the decision in question.

(5A) But the power conferred by subsection (5)(b) is exercisable only if–
   (a) the decision in question was made by a court or tribunal,
   (b) the decision is quashed on the ground that there has been an error of law, and
   (c) without the error, there would have been only one decision which the court or tribunal could have reached.

(5B) Unless the High Court otherwise directs, a decision substituted by it under subsection (5)(b) has effect as if it were a decision of the relevant court or tribunal.

(6) Where the High Court considers that there has been undue delay in making an application for judicial review, the court may refuse to grant–
   (a) leave for the making of the application; or
   (b) any relief sought on the application,
   if it considers that the granting of the relief sought would be likely to cause substantial hardship to, or substantially prejudice the rights of, any person or would be detrimental to good administration.

(7) Subsection (6) is without prejudice to any enactment or rule of court which has the effect of limiting the time within which an application for judicial review may be made.

Transfer of judicial review applications to Upper Tribunal

31A (1)This section applies where an application is made to the High Court–
   (a) for judicial review, or
   (b) for permission to apply for judicial review.

(2) If Conditions 1, 2, 3 and 4 are met, the High Court must by order transfer the application to the Upper Tribunal.

(2A) If Conditions 1, 2, 3 and 5 are met, but Condition 4 is not, the High Court must by order transfer the application to the Upper Tribunal.

(3) If Conditions 1, 2 and 4 are met, but Condition 3 is not, the High Court may by order transfer the application to the Upper Tribunal if it appears to the High Court to be just and convenient to do so.

(4) Condition 1 is that the application does not seek anything other than–
   (a) relief under section 31(1)(a) and (b);

(b) permission to apply for relief under section 31(1)(a) and (b);

(c) an award under section 31(4);

(d) interest;

(e) costs.

(5) Condition 2 is that the application does not call into question anything done by the Crown Court.

(6) Condition 3 is that the application falls within a class specified under section 18(6) of the Tribunals, Courts and Enforcement Act 2007.

(7) Condition 4 is that the application does not call into question any decision made under–

(a) the Immigration Acts,

(b) the British Nationality Act 1981,

(c) any instrument having effect under an enactment within paragraph (a) or (b), or

(d) any other provision of law for the time being in force which determines British citizenship, British overseas territories citizenship, the status of a British National (Overseas) or British Overseas citizenship.

(8) Condition 5 is that the application calls into question a decision of the Secretary of State not to treat submissions as an asylum claim or a human rights claim within the meaning of Part 5 of the Nationality, Immigration and Asylum Act 2002 wholly or partly on the basis that they are not significantly different from material that has previously been considered (whether or not it calls into question any other decision).

Power of High Court to vary sentence on certiorari

43 (1) Where a person who has been sentenced for an offence–

(a) by a magistrates' court; or

(b) by the Crown Court after being convicted of the offence by a magistrates' court and committed to the Crown Court for sentence; or

(c) by the Crown Court on appeal against conviction or sentence,

applies to the High Court in accordance with section 31 for an order of certiorari to remove the proceedings of the magistrates' court or the Crown Court into the High Court, then, if the High Court determines that the magistrates' court or the Crown Court had no power to pass the sentence, the High Court may, instead of quashing the conviction, amend it by substituting for the sentence passed any sentence which the magistrates' court or, in a case within paragraph (b), the Crown Court had power to impose.

(2) Any sentence passed by the High Court by virtue of this section in substitution for the sentence passed in the proceedings of the magistrates' court or the Crown Court shall, unless the High Court otherwise directs, begin to run from the time when it would have begun to run if passed in those proceedings; but in computing the term of the sentence, any time during which the offender was released on bail in pursuance of section 37(1)(d) of the Criminal Justice Act 1948 shall be disregarded.

(3) Subsections (1) and (2) shall, with the necessary modifications, apply in relation to any order of a magistrates' court or the Crown Court which is made on, but does not form part of, the conviction of an offender as they apply in relation to a conviction and sentence.

TRIBUNALS, COURTS AND ENFORCEMENT ACT 2007

Judicial review

Upper Tribunal's 'judicial review' jurisdiction

15 (1) The Upper Tribunal has power, in cases arising under the law of England and Wales or under the law of Northern Ireland, to grant the following kinds of relief–

(a) a mandatory order;

(b) a prohibiting order;

(c) a quashing order;

(d) a declaration;

(e) an injunction.

(2) The power under subsection (1) may be exercised by the Upper Tribunal if–

(a) certain conditions are met (see section 18), or

(b) the tribunal is authorised to proceed even though not all of those conditions are met (see section 19(3) and (4)).

(3) Relief under subsection (1) granted by the Upper Tribunal–

(a) has the same effect as the corresponding relief granted by the High Court on an application for judicial review, and

(b) is enforceable as if it were relief granted by the High Court on an application for judicial review.

(4) In deciding whether to grant relief under subsection (1)(a), (b) or (c), the Upper Tribunal must apply the principles that the High Court would apply in deciding whether to grant that relief on an application for judicial review.

(5) In deciding whether to grant relief under subsection (1)(d) or (e), the Upper Tribunal must–

(a) in cases arising under the law of England and Wales apply the principles that the High Court would apply in deciding whether to grant that relief under section 31(2) of the Senior Courts Act 1981 on an application for judicial review, and

(b) in cases arising under the law of Northern Ireland apply the principles that the High Court would apply in deciding whether to grant that relief on an application for judicial review.

(6) For the purposes of the application of subsection (3)(a) in relation to cases arising under the law of Northern Ireland–

(a) a mandatory order under subsection (1)(a) shall be taken to correspond to an order of mandamus,

(b) a prohibiting order under subsection (1)(b) shall be taken to correspond to an order of prohibition, and

(c) a quashing order under subsection (1)(c) shall be taken to correspond to an order of certiorari.

Application for relief under section 15(1)

16 (1) This section applies in relation to an application to the Upper Tribunal for relief under section 15(1).

(2) The application may be made only if permission (or, in a case arising under the law of Northern Ireland, leave) to make it has been obtained from the tribunal.

(3) The tribunal may not grant permission (or leave) to make the application

unless it considers that the applicant has a sufficient interest in the matter to which the application relates.

(4) Subsection (5) applies where the tribunal considers–
  (a) that there has been undue delay in making the application, and
  (b) that granting the relief sought on the application would be likely to cause substantial hardship to, or substantially prejudice the rights of, any person or would be detrimental to good administration.

(5) The tribunal may–
  (a) refuse to grant permission (or leave) for the making of the application;
  (b) refuse to grant any relief sought on the application.

(6) The tribunal may award to the applicant damages, restitution or the recovery of a sum due if–
  (a) the application includes a claim for such an award arising from any matter to which the application relates, and
  (b) the tribunal is satisfied that such an award would have been made by the High Court if the claim had been made in an action begun in the High Court by the applicant at the time of making the application.

(7) An award under subsection (6) may be enforced as if it were an award of the High Court.

(8) Where–
  (a) the tribunal refuses to grant permission (or leave) to apply for relief under section 15(1),
  (b) the applicant appeals against that refusal, and
  (c) the Court of Appeal grants the permission (or leave),
  the Court of Appeal may go on to decide the application for relief under section 15(1).

(9) Subsections (4) and (5) do not prevent Tribunal Procedure Rules from limiting the time within which applications may be made.

Quashing orders under section 15(1): supplementary provision

17 (1) If the Upper Tribunal makes a quashing order under section 15(1)(c) in respect of a decision, it may in addition–
  (a) remit the matter concerned to the court, tribunal or authority that made the decision, with a direction to reconsider the matter and reach a decision in accordance with the findings of the Upper Tribunal, or
  (b) substitute its own decision for the decision in question.

(2) The power conferred by subsection (1)(b) is exercisable only if–
  (a) the decision in question was made by a court or tribunal,
  (b) the decision is quashed on the ground that there has been an error of law, and
  (c) without the error, there would have been only one decision that the court or tribunal could have reached.

(3) Unless the Upper Tribunal otherwise directs, a decision substituted by it under subsection (1)(b) has effect as if it were a decision of the relevant court or tribunal.

Limits of jurisdiction under section 15(1)

18 (1) This section applies where an application made to the Upper Tribunal seeks (whether or not alone)–
  (a) relief under section 15(1), or

(b) permission (or, in a case arising under the law of Northern Ireland, leave) to apply for relief under section 15(1).

(2) If Conditions 1 to 4 are met, the tribunal has the function of deciding the application.

(3) If the tribunal does not have the function of deciding the application, it must by order transfer the application to the High Court.

(4) Condition 1 is that the application does not seek anything other than–
   (a) relief under section 15(1);
   (b) permission (or, in a case arising under the law of Northern Ireland, leave) to apply for relief under section 15(1);
   (c) an award under section 16(6);
   (d) interest;
   (e) costs.

(5) Condition 2 is that the application does not call into question anything done by the Crown Court.

(6) Condition 3 is that the application falls within a class specified for the purposes of this subsection in a direction given in accordance with Part 1 of Schedule 2 to the Constitutional Reform Act 2005 (c 4).

(7) The power to give directions under subsection (6) includes–
   (a) power to vary or revoke directions made in exercise of the power, and
   (b) power to make different provision for different purposes.

(8) Condition 4 is that the judge presiding at the hearing of the application is either–
   (a) a judge of the High Court or the Court of Appeal in England and Wales or Northern Ireland, or a judge of the Court of Session, or
   (b) such other persons as may be agreed from time to time between the Lord Chief Justice, the Lord President, or the Lord Chief Justice of Northern Ireland, as the case may be, and the Senior President of Tribunals.

(9) Where the application is transferred to the High Court under subsection (3)–
   (a) the application is to be treated for all purposes as if it–
      (i) had been made to the High Court, and
      (ii) sought things corresponding to those sought from the tribunal, and
   (b) any steps taken, permission (or leave) given or orders made by the tribunal in relation to the application are to be treated as taken, given or made by the High Court.

(10) Rules of court may make provision for the purpose of supplementing subsection (9).

(11) The provision that may be made by Tribunal Procedure Rules about amendment of an application for relief under section 15(1) includes, in particular, provision about amendments that would cause the application to become transferrable under subsection (3).

(12) For the purposes of subsection (9)(a)(ii), in relation to an application transferred to the High Court in Northern Ireland–
   (a) an order of mandamus shall be taken to correspond to a mandatory order under section 15(1)(a),
   (b) an order of prohibition shall be taken to correspond to a prohibiting order under section 15(1)(b), and
   (c) an order of certiorari shall be taken to correspond to a quashing order under section 15(1)(c).

Transfer of judicial review applications from High Court

19 (1) In the Senior Courts Act 1981, after section 31 insert–

'**31A   Transfer of judicial review applications to Upper Tribunal**

(1) This section applies where an application is made to the High Court–
   (a) for judicial review, or
   (b) for permission to apply for judicial review.

(2) If Conditions 1, 2, 3 and 4 are met, the High Court must by order transfer the application to the Upper Tribunal.

(3) If Conditions 1, 2 and 4 are met, but Condition 3 is not, the High Court may by order transfer the application to the Upper Tribunal if it appears to the High Court to be just and convenient to do so.

(4) Condition 1 is that the application does not seek anything other than–
   (a) relief under section 31(1)(a) and (b);
   (b) permission to apply for relief under section 31(1)(a) and (b);
   (c) an award under section 31(4);
   (d) interest;
   (e) costs.

(5) Condition 2 is that the application does not call into question anything done by the Crown Court.

(6) Condition 3 is that the application falls within a class specified under section 18(6) of the Tribunals, Courts and Enforcement Act 2007.

(7) Condition 4 is that the application does not call into question any decision made under–
   (a) the Immigration Acts,
   (b) the British Nationality Act 1981,
   (c) any instrument having effect under an enactment within paragraph (a) or (b), or
   (d) any other provision of law for the time being in force which determines British citizenship, British overseas territories citizenship, the status of a British National (Overseas) or British Overseas citizenship.'

(2) In the Judicature (Northern Ireland) Act 1978, after section 25 insert–

'**25A   Transfer of judicial review applications to Upper Tribunal**

(1) This section applies where an application is made to the High Court–
   (a) for judicial review, or
   (b) for leave to apply for judicial review.

(2) If Conditions 1, 2, 3 and 4 are met, the High Court must by order transfer the application to the Upper Tribunal.

(3) If Conditions 1, 2 and 4 are met, but Condition 3 is not, the High Court may by order transfer the application to the Upper Tribunal if it appears to the High Court to be just and convenient to do so.

(4) Condition 1 is that the application does not seek anything other than–
   (a) relief under section 18(1)(a) to (e);
   (b) leave to apply for relief under section 18(1)(a) to (e);
   (c) an award under section 20;
   (d) interest;
   (e) costs.

(5) Condition 2 is that the application does not call into question anything done by the Crown Court.

(6) Condition 3 is that the application falls within a class specified under section 18(6) of the Tribunals, Courts and Enforcement Act 2007.

(7) Condition 4 is that the application does not call into question any decision made under–

(a) the Immigration Acts,

(b) the British Nationality Act 1981,

(c) any instrument having effect under an enactment within paragraph (a) or (b), or

(d) any other provision of law for the time being in force which determines British citizenship, British overseas territories citizenship, the status of a British National (Overseas) or British Overseas citizenship.'

(3) Where an application is transferred to the Upper Tribunal under 31A of the Senior Courts Act 1981 or section 25A of the Judicature (Northern Ireland) Act 1978 (transfer from the High Court of judicial review applications)–

(a) the application is to be treated for all purposes as if it–

(i) had been made to the tribunal, and

(ii) sought things corresponding to those sought from the High Court,

(b) the tribunal has the function of deciding the application, even if it does not fall within a class specified under section 18(6), and

(c) any steps taken, permission given, leave given or orders made by the High Court in relation to the application are to be treated as taken, given or made by the tribunal.

(4) Where–

(a) an application for permission is transferred to the Upper Tribunal under section 31A of the Senior Courts Act 1981 and the tribunal grants permission, or

(b) an application for leave is transferred to the Upper Tribunal under section 25A of the Judicature (Northern Ireland) Act 1978 and the tribunal grants leave,

the tribunal has the function of deciding any subsequent application brought under the permission or leave, even if the subsequent application does not fall within a class specified under section 18(6).

(5) Tribunal Procedure Rules may make further provision for the purposes of supplementing subsections (3) and (4).

(6) For the purposes of subsection (3)(a)(ii), in relation to an application transferred to the Upper Tribunal under section 25A of the Judicature (Northern Ireland) Act 1978–

(a) a mandatory order under section 15(1)(a) shall be taken to correspond to an order of mandamus,

(b) a prohibiting order under section 15(1)(b) shall be taken to correspond to an order of prohibition, and

(c) a quashing order under section 15(1)(c) shall be taken to correspond to an order of certiorari.

Transfer of judicial review applications from the Court of Session

20 (1) Where an application is made to the supervisory jurisdiction of the Court of Session, the Court–
- (a) must, if Conditions 1, 2 and 4 are met,
- (aa) must, if Conditions 1, 2 and 5 are met, but Condition 4 is not, and
- (b) may, if Conditions 1, 3 and 4 are met, but Condition 2 is not,

by order transfer the application to the Upper Tribunal.

(2) Condition 1 is that the application does not seek anything other than an exercise of the supervisory jurisdiction of the Court of Session.

(3) Condition 2 is that the application falls within a class specified for the purposes of this subsection by act of sederunt made with the consent of the Lord Chancellor.

(4) Condition 3 is that the subject matter of the application is not a devolved Scottish matter.

(5) Condition 4 is that the application does not call into question any decision made under–
- (a) the Immigration Acts,
- (b) the British Nationality Act 1981 (c 61),
- (c) any instrument having effect under an enactment within paragraph (a) or (b), or
- (d) any other provision of law for the time being in force which determines British citizenship, British overseas territories citizenship, the status of a British National (Overseas) or British Overseas citizenship.

(5A) Condition 5 is that the application calls into question a decision of the Secretary of State not to treat submissions as an asylum claim or a human rights claim within the meaning of Part 5 of the Nationality, Immigration and Asylum Act 2002 wholly or partly on the basis that they are not significantly different from material that has previously been considered (whether or not it calls into question any other decision).

(6) There may not be specified under subsection (3) any class of application which includes an application the subject matter of which is a devolved Scottish matter.

(7) For the purposes of this section, the subject matter of an application is a devolved Scottish matter if it–
- (a) concerns the exercise of functions in or as regards Scotland, and
- (b) does not relate to a reserved matter within the meaning of the Scotland Act 1998 (c 46).

(8) In subsection (2), the reference to the exercise of the supervisory jurisdiction of the Court of Session includes a reference to the making of any order in connection with or in consequence of the exercise of that jurisdiction.

Civil Procedure Rules and Practice Directions

PART 8: ALTERNATIVE PROCEDURE FOR CLAIMS

Contents of this part

Types of claim in which part 8 procedure may be followed

8.1 (1) The Part 8 procedure is the procedure set out in this Part.

(2) A claimant may use the Part 8 procedure where–

(a) he seeks the court's decision on a question which is unlikely to involve a substantial dispute of fact; or

(b) paragraph (6) applies.

(3) The court may at any stage order the claim to continue as if the claimant had not used the Part 8 procedure and, if it does so, the court may give any directions it considers appropriate.

(4) Paragraph (2) does not apply if a practice direction provides that the Part 8 procedure may not be used in relation to the type of claim in question.

(5) Where the claimant uses the Part 8 procedure he may not obtain default judgment under Part 12.

(6) A rule or practice direction may, in relation to a specified type of proceedings–

(a) require or permit the use of the Part 8 procedure; and

(b) disapply or modify any of the rules set out in this Part as they apply to those proceedings.

(Rule 8.9 provides for other modifications to the general rules where the Part 8 procedure is being used)

(Part 78 provides procedures for European orders for payment and for the European small claims procedure. It also provides procedures for applications for mediation settlement enforcement orders in relation to certain cross-border disputes.)

Contents of the claim form

8.2 Where the claimant uses the Part 8 procedure the claim form must state –

(a) that this Part applies;

(b) (i) the question which the claimant wants the court to decide; or

(ii) the remedy which the claimant is seeking and the legal basis for the claim to that remedy;

(c) if the claim is being made under an enactment, what that enactment is;

(d) if the claimant is claiming in a representative capacity, what that capacity is; and

(e) if the defendant is sued in a representative capacity, what that capacity is.

(Part 22 provides for the claim form to be verified by a statement of truth)

(Rule 7.5 provides for service of the claim form)

(The costs practice direction sets out the information about a funding arrangement to be provided with the claim form where the claimant intends to seek to recover an additional liability)

('Funding arrangement' and 'additional liability' are defined in rule 43.2)

Issue of claim form without naming defendants

8.2A(1)A practice direction may set out circumstances in which a claim form may be issued under this Part without naming a defendant.

(2) The practice direction may set out those cases in which an application for permission must be made by application notice before the claim form is issued.

(3) The application notice for permission–
- (a) need not be served on any other person; and
- (b) must be accompanied by a copy of the claim form that the applicant proposes to issue.

(4) Where the court gives permission it will give directions about the future management of the claim.

Acknowledgment of service

8.3 (1)The defendant must–
- (a) file an acknowledgment of service in the relevant practice form not more than 14 days after service of the claim form; and
- (b) serve the acknowledgment of service on the claimant and any other party.

(2) The acknowledgment of service must state–
- (a) whether the defendant contests the claim; and
- (b) if the defendant seeks a different remedy from that set out in the claim form, what that remedy is.

(3) The following rules of Part 10 (acknowledgment of service) apply–
- (a) rule 10.3(2) (exceptions to the period for filing an acknowledgment of service); and
- (b) rule 10.5 (contents of acknowledgment of service).

(4) Omitted.

(The costs practice direction sets out the information about a funding arrangement to be provided with the acknowledgment of service where the defendant intends to seek to recover an additional liability)

('Funding arrangement' and 'additional liability' are defined in rule 43.2)

Consequence of not filing an acknowledgment of service

8.4 (1)This rule applies where–
- (a) the defendant has failed to file an acknowledgment of service; and
- (b) the time period for doing so has expired.

(2) The defendant may attend the hearing of the claim but may not take part in the hearing unless the court gives permission.

Filing and serving written evidence

8.5 (1)The claimant must file any written evidence on which he intends to rely when he files his claim form.

(2) The claimant's evidence must be served on the defendant with the claim form.

(3) A defendant who wishes to rely on written evidence must file it when he files his acknowledgment of service.

(4) If he does so, he must also, at the same time, serve a copy of his evidence on the other parties.

(5) The claimant may, within 14 days of service of the defendant's evidence on him, file further written evidence in reply.

(6) If he does so, he must also, within the same time limit, serve a copy of his evidence on the other parties.

(7) The claimant may rely on the matters set out in his claim form as evidence under this rule if the claim form is verified by a statement of truth.

Evidence – general

8.6(1) No written evidence may be relied on at the hearing of the claim unless–

(a) it has been served in accordance with rule 8.5; or

(b) the court gives permission.

(2) The court may require or permit a party to give oral evidence at the hearing.

(3) The court may give directions requiring the attendance for cross-examination of a witness who has given written evidence.

(Rule 32.1 contains a general power for the court to control evidence)

Part 20 claims

8.7 Where the Part 8 procedure is used, Part 20 (counterclaims and other additional claims) applies except that a party may not make a Part 20 claim (as defined by rule 20.2) without the court's permission.

Procedure where defendant objects to use of the part 8 procedure

8.8 (1) Where the defendant contends that the Part 8 procedure should not be used because–

(a) there is a substantial dispute of fact; and

(b) the use of the Part 8 procedure is not required or permitted by a rule or practice direction,

he must state his reasons when he files his acknowledgment of service.

(Rule 8.5 requires a defendant who wishes to rely on written evidence to file it when he files his acknowledgment of service)

(2) When the court receives the acknowledgment of service and any written evidence it will give directions as to the future management of the case.

(Rule 8.1(3) allows the court to make an order that the claim continue as if the claimant had not used the Part 8 procedure)

Modifications to the general rules

8.9 Where the Part 8 procedure is followed–

(a) provision is made in this Part for the matters which must be stated in the claim form and the defendant is not required to file a defence and therefore–

(i) Part 16 (statements of case) does not apply;

(ii) Part 15 (defence and reply) does not apply;

(iii) any time limit in these Rules which prevents the parties from taking a step before a defence is filed does not apply;

(iv) the requirement under rule 7.8 to serve on the defendant a form for defending the claim does not apply;

(b) the claimant may not obtain judgment by request on an admission and therefore–
  (i)   rules 14.4 to 14.7 do not apply; and
  (ii) the requirement under rule 7.8 to serve on the defendant a form for admitting the claim does not apply; and
(c) the claim shall be treated as allocated to the multi-track and therefore Part 26 does not apply.

PRACTICE DIRECTION 8A – ALTERNATIVE PROCEDURE FOR CLAIMS

THIS PRACTICE DIRECTION SUPPLEMENTS CPR PART 8 AND SCHEDULE 1 & SCHEDULE 2 TO THE CPR

TERMINOLOGY

1.1 In this Practice Direction, 'Schedule rules' means provisions contained in the Schedules to the CPR, which were previously contained in the Rules of the Supreme Court (1965) or the County Court Rules (1981).

APPLICATION OF THIS PRACTICE DIRECTION

2.1 Section A contains general provisions about claims and applications to which Part 8 applies. Section B comprises a table listing claims, petitions and applications under various enactments which must be made under Part 8. Section C contains certain additions and modifications to the Part 8 procedure that apply to the particular claims and applications identified.

2.2 Some of the claims and applications listed in the table in Section B are dealt with in the Schedule Rules in the CPR. The table in Section B contains cross-reference to the relevant Schedule Rules.

SECTION A: GENERAL PROVISIONS APPLICABLE TO PART 8 CLAIMS

Types of claim in which the Part 8 procedure may be used

3.1 The types of claim for which the Part 8 procedure may be used include –

(1) a claim by or against a child or protected party, as defined in rule 21.1(2), which has been settled before the commencement of proceedings and the sole purpose of the claim is to obtain the approval of the court to the settlement; or

(2) a claim for provisional damages which has been settled before the commencement of proceedings and the sole purpose of the claim is to obtain a consent judgment.

3.2 (1) The Part 8 procedure must be used for those claims, petitions and applications listed in the table in Section B.

(2) Where a claim is listed in the table in Section B and is identified as a claim to which particular provisions of Section C apply, the Part 8 procedure shall apply subject to the additions and modifications set out in the relevant paragraphs in Section C.

3.3 The Part 8 procedure must also be used for any claim or application in relation to which an Act, rule or practice direction provides that the claim or application is brought by originating summons, originating motion or originating application.

3.4 Where it appears to a court officer that a claimant is using the Part 8 procedure inappropriately, he may refer the claim to a judge for the judge to consider the point.

3.5 The court may at any stage order the claim to continue as if the claimant had not used the Part 8 procedure and, if it does so, the court will allocate the claim to a track and give such directions as it considers appropriate.

Issuing the claim

4.1 Part 7 and Practice Direction 7A contain a number of rules and directions applicable to all claims, including those to which Part 8 applies. Those rules and directions should be applied where appropriate.

4.2 Where a claimant uses the Part 8 procedure, the claim form (practice form N208) should be used and must state the matters set out in rule 8.2 and, if rule 8.1(6) applies, must comply with the requirements of the rule or practice direction in question. In particular, the claim form must state that Part 8 applies; a Part 8 claim form means a claim form which so states.

(The Costs Practice Direction supplementing Parts 43 to 48 contains details of the information required to be filed with a claim form to comply with rule 44.15 (providing information about funding arrangements))

Responding to the claim

5.1 The provisions of Part 15 (defence and reply) do not apply where the claim form is a Part 8 claim form.

5.2 Where a defendant who wishes to respond to a Part 8 claim form is required to file an acknowledgment of service, that acknowledgment of service should be in practice form N210.

5.3 Where a defendant objects to the use of the Part 8 procedure, and his statement of reasons includes matters of evidence, the acknowledgment of service must be verified by a statement of truth.

Managing the claim

6.1 The court may give directions immediately a Part 8 claim form is issued either on the application of a party or on its own initiative. The directions may include fixing a hearing date where–

(1) there is no dispute, such as in child and protected party settlements; or

(2) where there may be a dispute, but a hearing date could conveniently be given.

6.2 Where the court does not fix a hearing date when the claim form is issued, it will give directions for the disposal of the claim as soon as practicable after the defendant has acknowledged service of the claim form or, as the case may be, after the period for acknowledging service has expired.

6.3 Certain applications may not require a hearing.

6.4 The court may convene a directions hearing before giving directions.

Evidence

7.1 A claimant must file the written evidence on which he relies when his Part 8 claim form is issued (unless the evidence is contained in the claim form itself).

7.2 Evidence will normally be in the form of a witness statement or an affidavit but a claimant may rely on the matters set out in his claim form provided that it has been verified by a statement of truth.

(For information about (1) statements of truth see Part 22 and Practice Direction 22, and (2) written evidence see Part 32 and Practice Direction 32.)

7.3 A defendant wishing to rely on written evidence, must file it with his acknowledgment of service.

7.4 A party may apply to the court for an extension of time to serve and file evidence under rule 8.5 or for permission to serve and file additional evidence under rule 8.6(1).

(For information about applications see Part 23 and Practice Direction 23A.)

7.5 (1) The parties may, subject to the following provisions, agree in writing on an extension of time for serving and filing evidence under rule 8.5(3) or rule 8.5(5).

(2) An agreement extending time for a defendant to file evidence under rule 8.5(3)–

    (a) must be filed by the defendant at the same time as he files his acknowledgement of service; and

    (b) must not extend time by more than 14 days after the defendant files his acknowledgement of service.

(3) An agreement extending time for a claimant to file evidence in reply under rule 8.5(5) must not extend time to more than 28 days after service of the defendant's evidence on the claimant.

Hearing

8.1 The court may on the hearing date –

(1) proceed to hear the case and dispose of the claim;

(2) give case management directions.

8.2 Case management directions may include the specific allocation of a case to a track.

8.3 CPR rules 26.5(3) to (5) and rules 26.6 to 26.10 apply to the allocation of a claim under paragraph 8.2.

SECTION B: CLAIMS AND APPLICATIONS THAT MUST BE MADE UNDER PART 8

9.1 The claimant must use the Part 8 procedure if the claim is listed in the table below.

9.2 Section C of this Practice Direction contains special provisions modifying the Part 8 procedure, and where it does so, those provisions should be followed. The table below refers to the relevant paragraph of Section C where it applies.

9.3 Some of the claims and applications listed in the table below are dealt with in the Schedule Rules, and those rules modify the Part 8 procedure. A cross-reference to the relevant Schedule Rule is contained in the table below.

9.4 For applications that may or must be brought in the High Court, where no other rule or practice direction assigns the application to a Division of the court, the table specifies the Division to which the application is assigned.

Type of claim or application	Paragraph of Section C	Division	Schedule Rule
Application under section 14 of the Bills of Sale Act 1878 (Rectification of register)	Paragraph 10A	Queen's Bench Central Office	
Application under section 15 of the Bills of Sale Act 1878 (Entry of satisfaction)	Paragraph 11	Queen's Bench Central Office	

Type of claim or application	Paragraph of Section C	Division	Schedule Rule
Application under section 16 of the Bills of Sale Act 1878 (Search of the bills of sale register)	Paragraph 11A	Queen's Bench Central Office	
Application under the proviso to section 7 of the Bills of Sale Act (1878) Amendment Act 1882 (Restraining removal or sale of goods seized)		Queen's Bench Central Office	
Application under the Public Trustee Act 1906 (free-standing proceedings)	Paragraph 12	Chancery	
Application under section 7 of the Deeds of Arrangement Act 1914 (Rectification of register)	Paragraph 12A	Queen's Bench Central Office	
Proceedings under the Trustee Act 1925		Chancery	
Applications under section 2(3) of the Public Order Act 1936	Paragraph 13	Chancery	
Proceedings under jurisdiction conferred by section 1 of the Railway and Canal Commission (Abolition) Act 1949	Paragraph 14	Chancery	
Administration of Justice Act 1960 (Applications under the Act)		Divisional Court	RSC Ord 109, r1(3)
Administration of Justice Act 1960 (Appeals under section 13 of the Act)		Divisional Court	RSC Ord 109, r2(4)
Proceedings under section 14 of the Commons Registration Act 1965		Chancery	
Application under the Mines (Working Facilities and Support) Act 1966	Paragraph 15	Chancery	
Proceedings under section 21 or 25 of the Law of Property Act 1969		Chancery	

Type of claim or application	Paragraph of Section C	Division	Schedule Rule
Local Government Act 1972 (claims under section 92 – proceedings for disqualification)		Queen's Bench Central Office	
Application under article 10 of the Mortgaging of Aircraft Order 1972 (Rectification of register)	Paragraph 15A	Chancery	
Application to register an assignment of book debts (section 344 of the Insolvency Act 1986)	Paragraph 15B	Queen's Bench Central Office	
Proceedings under the Control of Misleading Advertisements Regulations 1988		Chancery	
Application under section 42 of the Senior Courts Act 1981	Paragraph 16	Administrative Court	
Proceedings in the High Court under the Representation of the People Acts	Paragraph 17A	Queen's Bench Central Office	
Applications under Part II of the Mental Health Act 1983	Paragraph 18	Administrative Court	
Applications under section 13 of the Coroners Act 1988	Paragraph 19	Administrative Court	
Application for an injunction to prevent environmental harm under section 187B or 214A of the Town and Country Planning Act 1990; section 44A of the Planning (Listed Buildings and Conservation Areas) Act 1990; or section 26AA of the Planning (Hazardous Substances) Act 1990	Paragraph 20	Queen's Bench	
Confiscation and forfeiture in connection with criminal proceedings (I. Drug Trafficking Act 1994 and Criminal Justice (International Co-operation) Act 1990 – Application for a confiscation order)		Queen's Bench	RSC Ord 115, r2B(1)

Type of claim or application	Paragraph of Section C	Division	Schedule Rule
Confiscation and forfeiture in connection with criminal proceedings (I. Drug Trafficking Act 1994 and Criminal Justice (International Co-operation) Act 1990 – Application for a restraint order or charging order)		Queen's Bench	RSC Ord 115, r3(1)
Confiscation and forfeiture in connection with criminal proceedings (I. Drug Trafficking Act 1994 and Criminal Justice (International Co-operation) Act 1990 – Realisation of property)		Queen's Bench	RSC Ord 115, r7(1)
Criminal Procedure and Investigations Act 1996 (Application under section 54(3))		Administrative Court	
Confiscation and forfeiture in connection with criminal proceedings (III. Terrorism Act 2000 – Application for a restraint order)		Queen's Bench	RSC Ord 115, r26(1)
Proceedings under the Financial Services and Markets Act 2000	Paragraph 21	Chancery	
Application for an injunction under section 12 or 26 of the Energy Act 2008	Paragraph 20	Queen's Bench	
Interpleader (Mode of application)		Chancery or Queen's Bench	RSC Ord 17, r3(1)
Criminal proceedings (estreat of recognizances)		Queen's Bench	RSC Ord 79, r8(2
Criminal proceedings (bail)		Queen's Bench	RSC Ord 79, r9(2)

Type of claim or application	Paragraph of Section C	Division	Schedule Rule
Application under an enactment giving the High Court jurisdiction to quash or prohibit any order, scheme, certificate or plan, any amendment or approval of a plan, any decision of a Minister or government department or any action on the part of a Minister or government department	Paragraph 22	Administrative Court	

SECTION C: SPECIAL PROVISIONS

10.1 The following special provisions apply to the applications indicated.

Applications under section 14 of the Bills of Sale Act 1878

10A.1 This paragraph applies to an application under section 14 of the Bills of Sale Act 1878 for an order to rectify an omission or mis-statement in relation to the registration, or renewal of the registration, of a bill of sale –

(1) by inserting in the register the true name, residence or occupation of a person; or

(2) by extending the time for registration of the bill of sale or an affidavit of its renewal.

10A.2 The application must be made –

(1) by claim form under Part 8; or

(2) by witness statement.

10A.3 Where the application is made by witness statement –

(1) Part 23 applies to the application;

(2) the witness statement constitutes the application notice under that Part;

(3) the witness statement does not need to be served on any other person; and

(4) the application will normally be dealt with without a hearing.

10A.4 The application must set out –

(1) the particulars of the bill of sale and of the omission or mis-statement; and

(2) the grounds on which the application is made.

10A.5 The application must be made to a Master of the Queen's Bench Division and accompanied by payment of the prescribed fee.

Applications under Section 15 of the Bills of Sale Act 1878

11.1 This paragraph applies where an application is made under section 15 of the Bills of Sale Act 1878 for an order that a memorandum of satisfaction be written on a registered copy of a bill of sale.

11.2 If the person entitled to the benefit of the bill of sale has not consented to the satisfaction, the claim form –

(1) must be served on that person; and

(2) must be supported by evidence that the debt (if any) for which the bill of sale was made has been satisfied or discharged.

11.3 If the person entitled to the benefit of the bill of sale has consented to the satisfaction, the application may be made by –
(1) claim form under Part 8; or
(2) witness statement.

11.4 Where paragraph 11.3 applies and the application is made by Part 8 claim form, the claim form –
(1) must contain details of the consent;
(2) must be supported by a witness statement by a person who witnessed the consent verifying the signature on it; and
(3) must not be served on any person other than the person entitled to the benefit of the bill of sale.

11.5 Where paragraph 11.3 applies and the application is made by witness statement –
(1) Part 23 will apply to the application;
(2) the witness statement will constitute the application notice under that Part;
(3) the witness statement does not need to be served on any other person; and
(4) the application will normally be dealt with without a hearing.

Applications under section 16 of the Bills of Sale Act 1878

11A.1 This paragraph applies to an application under section 16 of the Bills of Sale Act 1878 for a search of the bills of sale register and for a certificate of the results of the search.

11A.2 The application must be made –
(1) by claim form under Part 8; or
(2) by written request.

11A.3 The application must give sufficient information to enable the relevant bill of sale to be identified.

11A.4 The application must be made to a Master of the Queen's Bench Division and accompanied by payment of the prescribed fee.

Application under the Public Trustee Act 1906

12.1 An application under the Public Trustee Act 1906 must be made –
(1) where no proceedings have been issued, by a Part 8 claim;
(2) in existing proceedings, by a Part 23 application.

12.2 Without prejudice to sections 10(2) and 13(7) of the Public Trustee Act 1906, the jurisdiction of the High Court under the Act is exercised by a single judge of the Chancery Division sitting in private.

Applications under section 7 of the Deeds of Arrangement Act 1914

12A.1 This paragraph applies to an application under section 7 of the Deeds of Arrangement Act 1914 for an order to rectify an omission or mis-statement in relation to the registration of a deed of arrangement –
(1) by inserting in the register the true name, residence or description of a person; or
(2) by extending the time for registration.

12A.2 The application must be made –
(1) by claim form under Part 8; or
(2) by witness statement.

12A.3 Where the application is made by witness statement –
(1) Part 23 applies to the application;
(2) the witness statement constitutes the application notice under that Part;
(3) the witness statement does not need to be served on any other person; and
(4) the application will normally be dealt with without a hearing.

12A.4 The application must set out –
(1) the particulars of the deed of arrangement and of the omission or misstatement; and
(2) the grounds on which the application is made.

12A.5 The application must be made to a Master of the Queen's Bench Division and accompanied by payment of the prescribed fee.

Application under section 2(3) of the Public Order Act 1936

13.1 The Attorney General may determine the persons who should be made defendants to an application under section 2(3) of the Public Order Act 1936.

13.2 If the court directs an inquiry under section 2(3), it may appoint the Official Solicitor to represent any interests it considers are not sufficiently represented and ought to be represented.

Proceedings under section 1 of the Railway and Canal Commission (Abolition) Act 1949

14.1 Paragraphs 15.3 to 15.14 apply, with appropriate modifications, to proceedings in which jurisdiction has been conferred on the High Court by section 1 of the Railway and Canal Commission (Abolition) Act 1949, except to the extent that –
(1) an Act;
(2) a rule;
(3) a practice direction,
provides otherwise.

Application under the Mines (Working Facilities and Support) Act 1966

15.1 In this paragraph –
(1) 'the Act' means the Mines (Working Facilities and Support) Act 1966;
(2) 'the applicant' means the person who has applied for the grant of a right under the Act.

15.2 This paragraph applies where the Secretary of State refers an application to the High Court under any provision of the Act.

15.3 The Secretary of State must –
(1) file a reference signed by him or a person authorised to sign on his behalf in the Chancery Division of the High Court;
(2) file, along with the reference, any documents and plans deposited with him by the applicant in support of his application; and
(3) within 3 days of filing the reference, give notice to the applicant that the reference has been filed.

15.4 Within 10 days of receiving the notice referred to in paragraph 15.3(3), the applicant must issue a claim form.

15.5 The claim form –
(1) must identify the application under the Act and the remedy sought; and
(2) need not be served on any other party.

15.6 Within 7 days of the claim form being issued, the applicant must –

(1) apply for the claim to be listed for a hearing before a Master; and

(2) give notice of the hearing date to the Secretary of State.

15.7 The applicant must, not less than 2 days before the date fixed for a hearing, file at court –

(1) a witness statement in support of the claim, giving details of all persons known to the applicant to be interested in, or affected by, the application; and

(2) a draft of any proposed advertisement or notice of the application.

15.8 At the hearing, the Master will –

(1) fix a date by which any notice of objection under paragraph 15.9 must be filed;

(2) fix a date for a further hearing of the claim; and

(3) give directions about –

(a) any advertisement that is to be inserted or notice of the application and hearing date that is to be given; and

(b) what persons are to be served with a copy of the application or any other document in the proceedings.

15.9 Any person who wishes to oppose the application must, within the time fixed by the court under paragraph 15.8, serve notice of objection on the applicant, stating –

(a) his name and address;

(b) the name and address of his solicitor, if any;

(c) the grounds of his objection;

(d) any alternative method for effecting the objects of the application that he alleges may be used; and

(e) the facts on which he relies.

15.10 Any document that is required to be served on the person who has given notice of objection ('the objector') may be served by posting it to the following address –

(1) where the notice of objection gives the name and address of a solicitor, to the solicitor;

(2) in any other case, to the objector at the address stated in the notice of objection.

15.11 The objector may appear, or be represented at any further hearing, and may take such part in the proceedings as the court allows.

15.12 The applicant must, not less than two days before the date set for the further hearing, file at court –

(1) any notices of objection served on him;

(2) a list of objectors, together with –

(a) their names and addresses;

(b) the names and addresses of their solicitors, if any; and

(c) a summary of their respective grounds of objection.

15.13 If the objector does not appear, or is not represented, at the further hearing –

(1) his notice of objection will have no effect; and

(2) he will not be entitled to take any further part in the proceedings unless the court orders otherwise.

15.14 At the further hearing, the court will –

(1) give directions about the future conduct of the claim, including –

(a) any further information the applicant is required to give in relation to any of the grounds or facts relied on in support of the application;
(b) any further information the objector is required to give in relation to any of the grounds or facts relied on in opposition to the application;
(c) whether the applicant may serve a reply to any notice of objection;
(d) whether any particular fact should be proved by a witness statement;
(e) whether any statements of case or points of claim or defence are to be served; and

(2) adjourn the claim for hearing before a judge.

Applications under article 10 of the Mortgaging of Aircraft Order 1972

15A.1 This paragraph applies to an application under article 10 of the Mortgaging of Aircraft Order 1972 for an order to amend the Register of Aircraft Mortgages.

15A.2 The application must be made by claim form under Part 8.

15A.3 Every person (other than the claimant) who appears in the register as mortgagor or mortgagee of the aircraft concerned must be made a defendant to the claim.

15A.4 A copy of the claim form must be sent to the Civil Aviation Authority.

15A.5 The application will be assigned to the Chancery Division.

15A.6 The Civil Aviation Authority is entitled to be heard in the proceedings.

Applications under section 344 of the Insolvency Act 1986 for registration of assignments of book debts

15B.1 This paragraph applies to an application under section 344 of the Insolvency Act 1986 to register an assignment of book debts.

15B.2 The application must be made –
(1) by claim form under Part 8; or
(2) by witness statement.

15B.3 The application must be made to a Master of the Queen's Bench Division and accompanied by payment of the prescribed fee.

15B.4 Where the application is made by witness statement –
(1) Part 23 applies to the application;
(2) the witness statement constitutes the application notice under that Part;
(3) the witness statement does not need to be served on any other person; and
(4) the application will normally be dealt with without a hearing.

15B.5 The application –
(1) must have exhibited to it a true copy of the assignment and of every schedule to it;
(2) must set out the particulars of the assignment and the parties to it; and
(3) must verify the date and time of the execution of the assignment, and its execution in the presence of a witness.

15B.6 Upon the court being satisfied, the documents so exhibited will be filed and the particulars of the assignment and of the parties to it entered in the register.

Application under section 42 of the Senior Courts Act 1981

16.1 An application under section 42 of the Senior Courts Act 1981 is heard and determined by a Divisional Court.

16.2 The claim form must be filed at the Administrative Court and –

(1) be accompanied by a witness statement in support; and

(2) be served on the person against whom the order is sought.

Application for detailed assessment of a returning officer's account

17.1 An application by the Secretary of State under section 30 of the Representation of the People Act 1983 for the detailed assessment of a returning officer's account must be made by claim form.

17.2 When it issues the claim form, the court will fix a date for the hearing of the detailed assessment to be dealt with if the application is granted.

17.3 The returning officer may, on the application, apply to the court to examine any claim made against him in respect of matters charged in the account.

17.4 To make an application under paragraph 17.3, the returning officer must file an application within 7 days of being served with a copy of the application for detailed assessment.

17.5 When an application is filed under paragraph 17.3, the court will –

(a) fix a date for the hearing;

(b) give notice of the hearing date to the returning officer; and

(c) serve a copy of the application and notice of hearing on the claimant.

17.6 The examination and detailed assessment may take place on the same day, provided that the examination is determined before the detailed assessment is concluded.

17.7 The district judge may hear and determine –

(a) an application for detailed assessment;

(b) any application under paragraph 17.3.

17.8 The court will serve a copy of the order made in the application on –

(a) the Secretary of State;

(b) the returning officer; and

(c) in an application under paragraph 17.3, the claimant.

Other proceedings under the Representation of the People Acts

17A.1 (1) This paragraph applies to proceedings under the Representation of the People Acts (other than proceedings under section 30 of the Representation of the People Act 1983).

(2) The jurisdiction of the High Court under those Acts in matters relating to Parliamentary and local government elections will be exercised by a Divisional Court except that –

(a) any jurisdiction, under a provision of any of those Acts, exercisable by a single judge will be exercised by a single judge;

(b) any jurisdiction, under any such provision, exercisable by a Master will be exercised by a Master; and

(c) where the court's jurisdiction in matters relating to Parliamentary elections is exercisable by a single judge, that jurisdiction in matters relating to local government elections is also exercisable by a single judge.

Application under Mental Health Act 1983

18.1 In this paragraph –

(1) a section referred to by a number refers to the section so numbered in the Mental Health Act 1983 and 'Part II' means Part II of that Act;

(2) 'hospital manager' means the manager of a hospital as defined in section 145(1) of the Act; and

(3) 'place of residence' means, in relation to a patient who is receiving treatment as an in-patient in a hospital or other institution, that hospital or institution.

18.2 The claim form must be filed –

(1) in the court for the district in which the patient's place of residence is situated; or

(2) in the case of an application under section 30, in the court that made the order under section 29 which the application seeks to discharge or vary.

18.3 Where an application is made under section 29 for an order that the functions of the nearest relative of the patient are to be exercisable by some other person –

(1) the nearest relative must be made a respondent, unless –

(a) the application is made on the grounds that the patient has no nearest relative or that it is not reasonably practicable to ascertain whether he has a nearest relative; or

(b) the court orders otherwise; and

(2) the court may order that any other person shall be made a respondent.

18.4 Subject to paragraph 18.5, the court may accept as evidence of the facts relied upon in support of the application, any report made –

(1) by a medical practitioner; or

(2) by any of the following acting in the course of their official duties –

(a) a probation officer;

(b) an officer of a local authority;

(c) an officer of a voluntary body exercising statutory functions on behalf of a local authority; or

(d) an officer of a hospital manager.

18.5 The respondent must be informed of the substance of any part of the report dealing with his fitness or conduct that the court considers to be material to the determination of the claim.

18.6 An application under Part II shall be heard in private unless the court orders otherwise.

18.7 The judge may, for the purpose of determining the application, interview the patient. The interview may take place in the presence of, or separately from, the parties. The interview may be conducted elsewhere than at the court. Alternatively, the judge may direct the district judge to interview the patient and report to the judge in writing.

Applications under section 13 of the Coroners Act 1988

19.1 An application under section 13 of the Coroners Act 1988 is heard and determined by a Divisional Court.

19.2 The application must, unless made by the Attorney General, be accompanied by the Attorney General's fiat.

19.3 The claim form must –

(1) state the grounds for the application;

(2) be filed at the Administrative Court; and

(3) be served upon all persons directly affected by the application within six weeks of the grant of the Attorney General's fiat.

Application for injunction to prevent environmental harm or unlicensed activities

20.1 This paragraph relates to applications under –
    (1) section 187B or 214A of the Town and Country Planning Act 1990;
    (2) section 44A of the Planning (Listed Buildings and Conservation Areas) Act 1990;
    (3) section 26AA of the Planning (Hazardous Substances) Act 1990; or
    (4) section 12 or 26 of the Energy Act 2008.

20.2 An injunction may be granted under those sections against a person whose identity is unknown to the applicant.

20.3 In this paragraph, an injunction refers to an injunction under one of those sections and 'the defendant' is the person against whom the injunction is sought.

20.4 In the claim form, the applicant must describe the defendant by reference to –
    (1) a photograph;
    (2) a thing belonging to or in the possession of the defendant; or
    (3) any other evidence.

20.5 The description of the defendant under paragraph 20.4 must be sufficiently clear to enable the defendant to be served with the proceedings.
(The court has power under Part 6 to dispense with service or make an order permitting service by an alternative method or at an alternative place).

20.6 The application must be accompanied by a witness statement. The witness statement must state –
    (1) that the applicant was unable to ascertain the defendant's identity within the time reasonably available to him;
    (2) the steps taken by him to ascertain the defendant's identity;
    (3) the means by which the defendant has been described in the claim form; and
    (4) that the description is the best the applicant is able to provide.

20.7 When the court issues the claim form it will –
    (1) fix a date for the hearing; and
    (2) prepare a notice of the hearing date for each party.

20.8 The claim form must be served not less than 21 days before the hearing date.

20.9 Where the claimant serves the claim form, he must serve notice of the hearing date at the same time, unless the hearing date is specified in the claim form.
(CPR rules 3.1(2) (a) and (b) provide for the court to extend or shorten the time for compliance with any rule or practice direction, and to adjourn or bring forward a hearing)

20.10 The court may on the hearing date –
    (1) proceed to hear the case and dispose of the claim; or
    (2) give case management directions.

Proceedings under the Financial Services and Markets Act 2000

21.1 This paragraph applies to proceedings in the High Court under the Financial Services and Markets Act 2000.

21.2 Proceedings in the High Court under the Act (other than applications for a mandatory order) and actions for damages for breach of a statutory duty imposed by the Act shall be assigned to the Chancery Division.

21.3 Such proceedings and actions must be begun by claim form (except for applications by petition by the Financial Services Authority under section 367 of the Act).

21.4 The Financial Services Authority may make representations to the court where there is a question about the meaning of any rule or other instrument made by, or with the approval or consent of, the Financial Services Authority.

Application to quash certain orders, schemes, etc

22.1 This paragraph applies where the High Court has jurisdiction under any enactment, on the application of any person to quash or prohibit any –

(1) order, scheme, certificate or plan of;

(2) amendment or approval of a plan of;

(3) decision of;

(4) action on the part of,

a Minister or government department.

22.2 The jurisdiction shall be exercisable by a single judge of the Queen's Bench Division.

22.3 The claim form must be filed at the Administrative Court and served within the time limited by the relevant enactment for making the application. Practice Direction 54D applies to applications under this paragraph.

22.4 Subject to paragraph 22.6, the claim form must be served on the appropriate Minister or government department and on the person indicated in the following table.

If the application relates to – 1) a compulsory purchase order made by an authority other than the appropriate Minister or government department; or 2) a clearance order under the Housing Act 1985.	The authority that made the order.
If the application relates to a scheme or order – 1) to which Section 2 of the Highways Act 1980 applies; and 2) which was made by an authority other than the Secretary of State	The authority that made the scheme or order.
If the application relates to a structure plan, local plan or other development plan within the meaning of the Town and Country Planning Act 1990	The local planning authority who prepared the plan.

If the application relates to any decision or order, or any action on the part of a Minister of the Crown to which – 1) section 21 of the Land Compensation Act 1961; or 2) section 288 of the Town and Country Planning Act 1990, applies.	a) The authority directly concerned with such decision, order or action; or b) if that authority is the applicant, on every person who would, if he were aggrieved by the decision, order or action, be entitled to apply to the High Court under section 21 of the Land Compensation Act or section 288 of the Town and Country Planning Act, as the case may be.
If the application relates to a scheme to which Schedule 32 of the Local Government, Planning and Land Act 1980 applies	The body which adopted the scheme.

22.5 In paragraph 22.4, 'the appropriate Minister or government department' means the Minister of the Crown or government department –
   (1) by whom the order, scheme, certificate, plan, amendment, approval or decision in question was or may be made, authorised, confirmed, approved or given;
   (2) on whose part the action in question was or may be taken.

22.6 Where the application relates to an order made under the Road Traffic Regulation Act 1984, the claim form must be served –
   (1) if the order was made by a Minister of the Crown, on that Minister;
   (2) if the order was made by a local authority with the consent, or following a direction, of a Minister of the Crown, on that authority and also on that Minister;
   (3) in any other case, on the local authority by whom the order was made.

22.7 Evidence at the hearing of an application under this paragraph is by witness statement.

22.8 The applicant must –
   (1) file a witness statement in support of the application in the Administrative Court within 14 days after service of the claim form; and
   (2) serve a copy of the witness statement and of any exhibit on the respondent at the time of filing.

22.9 The respondent must –
   (1) file any witness statement in opposition to the application in the Administrative Court within 21 days after service on him of the applicant's witness statement; and
   (2) serve a copy of his witness statement and of any exhibit on the applicant at the time of filing.

22.10 A party must, when filing a witness statement, file a further copy of the witness statement, including exhibits, for the use of the court.

22.11 Unless the court otherwise orders, the application will not be heard earlier than 14 days after the time for filing a witness statement by the respondent has expired.

PART 19: PARTIES AND GROUP LITIGATION

ADDITION AND SUBSTITUTION OF PARTIES

Human rights

19.4A Section 4 of the Human Rights Act 1998

(1) The court may not make a declaration of incompatibility in accordance with section 4 of the Human Rights Act 1998 unless 21 days' notice, or such other period of notice as the court directs, has been given to the Crown.

(2) Where notice has been given to the Crown a Minister, or other person permitted by that Act, shall be joined as a party on giving notice to the court.

(Only courts specified in section 4 of the Human Rights Act 1998 can make a declaration of incompatibility)

Section 9 of the Human Rights Act 1998

(3) Where a claim is made under that Act for damages in respect of a judicial act–

(a) that claim must be set out in the statement of case or the appeal notice; and

(b) notice must be given to the Crown.

(4) Where paragraph (3) applies and the appropriate person has not applied to be joined as a party within 21 days, or such other period as the court directs, after the notice is served, the court may join the appropriate person as a party.

(Practice Direction 19A makes provision for these notices).

PART 19A PRACTICE DIRECTION – ADDITION AND SUBSTITUTION OF PARTIES

THIS PRACTICE DIRECTION SUPPLEMENTS CPR PART 19

A party applying for an amendment will usually be responsible for the costs of and arising from the amendment.

CHANGES OF PARTIES

General

1.1 Parties may be removed, added or substituted in existing proceedings either on the court's own initiative or on the application of either an existing party or a person who wishes to become a party.

1.2 The application may be dealt with without a hearing where all the existing parties and the proposed new party are in agreement.

1.3 The application to add or substitute a new party should be supported by evidence setting out the proposed new party's interest in or connection with the claim.

1.4 The application notice should be filed in accordance with rule 23.3 and, unless the application is made under rule 19.2(4),1 be served in accordance with rule 23.4.

1.5 An order giving permission to amend will, unless the court orders otherwise, be drawn up. It will be served by the court unless the parties wish to serve it or the court orders them to do so.

Addition or substitution of claimant

2.1 Where an application is made to the court to add or to substitute a new party to the proceedings as claimant, the party applying must file:

(1) the application notice,

(2) the proposed amended claim form and particulars of claim, and

(3) the signed, written consent of the new claimant to be so added or substituted.

2.2 Where the court makes an order adding or substituting a party as claimant but the signed, written consent of the new claimant has not been filed:

(1) the order, and

(2) the addition or substitution of the new party as claimant,

will not take effect until the signed, written consent of the new claimant is filed.

2.3 Where the court has made an order adding or substituting a new claimant, the court may direct:

(1) a copy of the order to be served on every party to the proceedings and any other person affected by the order,

(2) copies of the statements of case and of documents referred to in any statement of case to be served on the new party,

(3) the party who made the application to file within 14 days an amended claim form and particulars of claim.

Addition or substitution of defendant

3.1 The Civil Procedure Rules apply to a new defendant who has been added or

---

1   See rule 19.4(3)(a).

substituted as they apply to any other defendant (see in particular the provisions of Parts 9, 10, 11 and 15).

3.2 Where the court has made an order adding or substituting a defendant whether on its own initiative or on an application, the court may direct:

(1) the claimant to file with the court within 14 days (or as ordered) an amended claim form and particulars of claim for the court file,

(2) a copy of the order to be served on all parties to the proceedings and any other person affected by it,

(3) the amended claim form and particulars of claim, forms for admitting, defending and acknowledging the claim and copies of the statements of case and any other documents referred to in any statement of case to be served on the new defendant.

(4) unless the court orders otherwise, the amended claim form and particulars of claim to be served on any other defendants.

3.3 A new defendant does not become a party to the proceedings until the amended claim form has been served on him.[2]

Removal of party

4 Where the court makes an order for the removal of a party from the proceedings:

(1) the claimant must file with the court an amended claim form and particulars of claim, and

(2) a copy of the order must be served on every party to the proceedings and on any other person affected by the order.

Transfer of interest or liability

5.1 Where the interest or liability of an existing party has passed to some other person, application should be made to the court to add or substitute that person.[3]

5.2 The application must be supported by evidence showing the stage the proceedings have reached and what change has occurred to cause the transfer of interest or liability.

(For information about making amendments generally, see the practice direction supplementing Part 17.)

HUMAN RIGHTS, JOINING THE CROWN
Section 4 of the Human Rights Act 1998

6.1 Where a party has included in his statement of case–

(1) a claim for a declaration of incompatibility in accordance with section 4 of the Human Rights Act 1998, or

(2) an issue for the court to decide which may lead to the court considering making a declaration,

then the court may at any time consider whether notice should be given to the Crown as required by that Act and give directions for the content and service of the notice. The rule allows a period of 21 days before the court will make the declaration but the court may vary this period of time.

---

2   *Kettleman v Hansel Properties Ltd* (1987) AC 189, HL.

3   See rule 19.2(4).

6.2 The court will normally consider the issues and give the directions referred to in paragraph 6.1 at the case management conference.

6.3 Where a party amends his statement of case to include any matter referred to in paragraph 6.1, then the court will consider whether notice should be given to the Crown and give directions for the content and service of the notice.
(The practice direction to CPR Part 16 requires a party to include issues under the Human Rights Act 1998 in his statement of case)

6.4 (1) The notice given under rule 19.4A must be served on the person named in the list published under section 17 of the Crown Proceedings Act 1947.
(The list, made by the Minister for the Civil Service, is annexed to this practice direction)

(2) The notice will be in the form directed by the court but will normally include the directions given by the court and all the statements of case in the claim. The notice will also be served on all the parties.

(3) The court may require the parties to assist in the preparation of the notice.

(4) In the circumstances described in the National Assembly for Wales (Transfer of Functions)(No 2) Order 2000 the notice must also be served on the National Assembly for Wales.

(Section 5(3) of the Human Rights Act 1998 provides that the Crown may give notice that it intends to become a party at any stage in the proceedings once notice has been given)

6.5 Unless the court orders otherwise, the Minister or other person permitted by the Human Rights Act 1998 to be joined as a party must, if he wishes to be joined, give notice of his intention to be joined as a party to the court and every other party. Where the Minister has nominated a person to be joined as a party the notice must be accompanied by the written nomination.
(Section 5(2)(a) of the Human Rights Act 1998 permits a person nominated by a Minister of the Crown to be joined as a party. The nomination may be signed on behalf of the Minister)

Section 9 of the Human Rights Act 1998

6.6 (1) The procedure in paragraphs 6.1 to 6.5 also applies where a claim is made under sections 7(1)(a) and 9(3) of the Human Rights Act 1998 for damages in respect of a judicial act.

(2) Notice must be given to the Lord Chancellor and should be served on the Treasury Solicitor on his behalf, except where the judicial act is of a Court-Martial when the appropriate person is the Secretary of State for Defence and the notice must be served on the Treasury Solicitor on his behalf.

(3) The notice will also give details of the judicial act, which is the subject of the claim for damages, and of the court or tribunal that made it.

(Section 9(4) of the Human Rights Act 1998 provides that no award of damages may be made against the Crown as provided for in section 9(3) unless the appropriate person is joined in the proceedings. The appropriate person is the Minister responsible for the court concerned or a person or department nominated by him (section 9(5) of the Act))

PART 23: GENERAL RULES ABOUT APPLICATIONS FOR COURT ORDERS

Contents of this part

Meaning of 'application notice' and 'respondent'

23.1 In this Part–

'application notice' means a document in which the applicant states his intention to seek a court order; and

'respondent' means–

(a) the person against whom the order is sought; and

(b) such other person as the court may direct.

Where to make an application

23.2 (1) The general rule is that an application must be made to the court where the claim was started.

(2) If a claim has been transferred to another court since it was started, an application must be made to the court to which the claim has been transferred.

(3) If the parties have been notified of a fixed date for the trial, an application must be made to the court where the trial is to take place.

(4) Subject to paragraph (4A), if an application is made before a claim has been started, it must be made to the court where it is likely that the claim to which the application relates will be started unless there is good reason to make the application to a different court.

(4A) If –

(a) an application is made before a claim has been started; and

(b) the claim is a designated money claim;

the application made be made in any county court.

(5) If an application is made after proceedings to enforce judgment have begun, it must be made to any court which is dealing with the enforcement of the judgment unless any rule or practice direction provides otherwise.

Application notice to be filed

23.3 (1) The general rule is that an applicant must file an application notice.

(2) An applicant may make an application without filing an application notice if–

(a) this is permitted by a rule or practice direction; or

(b) the court dispenses with the requirement for an application notice.

Notice of an application

23.4 (1) The general rule is that a copy of the application notice must be served on each respondent.

(2) An application may be made without serving a copy of the application notice if this is permitted by–

(a) a rule;
(b) a practice direction; or
(c) a court order.

(Rule 23.7 deals with service of a copy of the application notice)

Time when an application is made

23.5 Where an application must be made within a specified time, it is so made if the application notice is received by the court within that time.

What an application notice must include

23.6 An application notice must state–

(a) what order the applicant is seeking; and
(b) briefly, why the applicant is seeking the order.

(Part 22 requires an application notice to be verified by a statement of truth if the applicant wishes to rely on matters set out in his application notice as evidence)

Service of a copy of an application notice

23.7 (1) A copy of the application notice–

(a) must be served as soon as practicable after it is filed; and
(b) except where another time limit is specified in these Rules or a practice direction, must in any event be served at least 3 days before the court is to deal with the application.

(2) If a copy of the application notice is to be served by the court, the applicant must, when he files the application notice, file a copy of any written evidence in support.

(3) When a copy of an application notice is served it must be accompanied by–

(a) a copy of any written evidence in support; and
(b) a copy of any draft order which the applicant has attached to his application.

(4) If–

(a) an application notice is served; but
(b) the period of notice is shorter than the period required by these Rules or a practice direction,

the court may direct that, in the circumstances of the case, sufficient notice has been given and hear the application.

(5) This rule does not require written evidence–

(a) to be filed if it has already been filed; or
(b) to be served on a party on whom it has already been served.

(Part 6 contains the general rules about service of documents including who must serve a copy of the application notice)

Applications which may be dealt with without a hearing

23.8 The court may deal with an application without a hearing if–

(a) the parties agree as to the terms of the order sought;
(b) the parties agree that the court should dispose of the application without a hearing, or
(c) the court does not consider that a hearing would be appropriate.

Service of application where application made without notice

23.9 (1) This rule applies where the court has disposed of an application which it permitted to be made without service of a copy of the application notice.

(2) Where the court makes an order, whether granting or dismissing the application, a copy of the application notice and any evidence in support must, unless the court orders otherwise, be served with the order on any party or other person–

(a) against whom the order was made; and
(b) against whom the order was sought.

(3) The order must contain a statement of the right to make an application to set aside or vary the order under rule 23.10.

Application to set aside or vary order made without notice

23.10 (1) A person who was not served with a copy of the application notice before an order was made under rule 23.9, may apply to have the order set aside or varied.

(2) An application under this rule must be made within 7 days after the date on which the order was served on the person making the application.

Power of the court to proceed in the absence of a party

23.11 (1) Where the applicant or any respondent fails to attend the hearing of an application, the court may proceed in his absence.

(2) Where–

(a) the applicant or any respondent fails to attend the hearing of an application; and
(b) the court makes an order at the hearing,

the court may, on application or of its own initiative, re-list the application.

(Part 40 deals with service of orders)

Dismissal of totally without merit applications

23.12 If the court dismisses an application (including an application for permission to appeal or for permission to apply for judicial review) and it considers that the application is totally without merit –

(a) the court's order must record that fact; and
(b) the court must at the same time consider whether it is appropriate to make a civil restraint order.

PART 23A PRACTICE DIRECTION – APPLICATIONS

THIS PRACTICE DIRECTION SUPPLEMENTS CPR PART 23

Reference to a judge

1 A Master or district judge may refer to a judge any matter which he thinks should properly be decided by a judge, and the judge may either dispose of the matter or refer it back to the Master or district judge.

Application notices

2.1 An application notice must, in addition to the matters set out in rule 23.6, be signed and include:

(1) the title of the claim,

(2) the reference number of the claim,

(3) the full name of the applicant,

(4) where the applicant is not already a party, his address for service, including a postcode. Postcode information may be obtained from www.royal-mail.com or the Royal Mail Address Management Guide, and

(5) either a request for a hearing or a request that the application be dealt with without a hearing.

(Practice Form N244 may be used.)

2.2 On receipt of an application notice containing a request for a hearing the court will notify the applicant of the time and date for the hearing of the application.

2.3 On receipt of an application notice containing a request that the application be dealt with without a hearing, the application notice will be sent to a Master or district judge so that he may decide whether the application is suitable for consideration without a hearing.

2.4 Where the Master or district judge agrees that the application is suitable for consideration without a hearing, the court will so inform the applicant and the respondent and may give directions for the filing of evidence. (Rules 23.9 and 23.10 enable a party to apply for an order made without a hearing to be set aside or varied.)

2.5 Where the Master or district judge does not agree that the application is suitable for consideration without a hearing, the court will notify the applicant and the respondent of the time, date and place for the hearing of the application and may at the same time give directions as to the filing of evidence.

2.6 If the application is intended to be made to a judge, the application notice should so state. In that case, paragraphs 2.3, 2.4 and 2.5 will apply as though references to the Master or district judge were references to a judge.

2.7 Every application should be made as soon as it becomes apparent that it is necessary or desirable to make it.

2.8 Applications should wherever possible be made so that they can be considered at any other hearing for which a date has already been fixed or for which a date is about to be fixed. This is particularly so in relation to case management conferences, allocation and listing hearings and pre-trial reviews fixed by the court.

2.9 The parties must anticipate that at any hearing the court may wish to review the conduct of the case as a whole and give any necessary case management directions. They should be ready to assist the court in doing so and to answer questions the court may ask for this purpose.

2.10 Where a date for a hearing has been fixed and a party wishes to make an application at that hearing but he does not have sufficient time to serve an application notice he should inform the other party and the court (if possible in writing) as soon as he can of the nature of the application and the reason for it. He should then make the application orally at the hearing.

Applications without service of application notice

3 An application may be made without serving an application notice only:
(1) where there is exceptional urgency,
(2) where the overriding objective is best furthered by doing so,
(3) by consent of all parties,
(4) with the permission of the court,
(5) where paragraph 2.10 above applies, or
(6) where a court order, rule or practice direction permits.

Giving notice of an application

4.1 Unless the court otherwise directs or paragraph 3 of this practice direction applies the application notice must be served as soon as practicable after it has been issued and, if there is to be a hearing, at least 3 clear days before the hearing date (rule 23.7(1)(b)).

4.1A Where there is to be a telephone hearing the application notice must be served as soon as practicable after it has been issued and in any event at least 5 days before the date of the hearing.

4.2 Where an application notice should be served but there is not sufficient time to do so, informal notification of the application should be given unless the circumstances of the application require secrecy.

(Rule 2.8 explains how to calculate periods of time expressed in terms of days.)

Pre-action applications

5 All applications made before a claim is commenced should be made under Part 23 of the Civil Procedure Rules. Attention is drawn in particular to rule 23.2(4).

Telephone hearings

Interpretation

6.1 In this paragraph –
(a) 'designated legal representative' means the applicant's legal representative (if any), or the legal representative of such other party as the court directs to arrange the telephone hearing; and
(b) 'telephone conference enabled court' means –
(i) a district registry of the High Court; or
(ii) a county court,
in which telephone conferencing facilities are available.

When a hearing is to be conducted by telephone

6.2 Subject to paragraph 6.3, at a telephone conference enabled court the following hearings will be conducted by telephone unless the court otherwise orders –

(a) allocation hearings;

(b) listing hearings; and

(c) interim applications, case management conferences and pre-trial reviews with a time estimate of no more than one hour.

6.3 Paragraph 6.2 does not apply where –

(a) the hearing is of an application made without notice to the other party;

(b) all the parties are unrepresented; or

(c) more than four parties wish to make representations at the hearing (for this purpose where two or more parties are represented by the same person, they are to be treated as one party).

6.4 A request for a direction that a hearing under paragraph 6.2 should not be conducted by telephone –

(a) must be made at least 7 days before the hearing or such shorter time as the court may permit; and

(b) may be made by letter,

and the court shall determine such request without requiring the attendance of the parties.

6.5 The court may order that an application, or part of an application, to which paragraph 6.2 does not apply be dealt with by a telephone hearing. The court may make such order –

(a) of its own initiative; or

(b) at the request of the parties.

6.6 The applicant should indicate on his application notice if he seeks a court order under paragraph 6.5. Where he has not done so but nevertheless wishes to seek an order, the request should be made as early as possible.

6.7 An order under paragraph 6.5 will not normally be made unless every party entitled to be given notice of the application and to be heard at the hearing has consented to the order.

6.8 If the court makes an order under paragraph 6.5 it will give any directions necessary for the telephone hearing.

Conduct of the telephone hearing

6.9 No party, or representative of a party, to an application being heard by telephone may attend the judge in person while the application is being heard unless every other party to the application has agreed that he may do so.

6.10 If an application is to be heard by telephone the following directions will apply, subject to any direction to the contrary –

(1) The designated legal representative is responsible for arranging the telephone conference for precisely the time fixed by the court. The telecommunications provider used must be one on the approved panel of service providers (see Her Majesty's Courts and Tribunals Service website)

(2) The designated legal representative must tell the operator the telephone numbers of all those participating in the conference call and the sequence in which they are to be called.

(3) It is the responsibility of the designated legal representative to ascertain from all the other parties whether they have instructed counsel and, if so, the identity of counsel, and whether the legal representative and counsel will be on the same or different telephone numbers.

(4) The sequence in which they are to be called will be –

(a) the designated legal representative and (if on a different number) his counsel;

(b) the legal representative (and counsel) for all other parties; and

(c) the judge.

(5) Each speaker is to remain on the line after being called by the operator setting up the conference call. The call shall be connected at least ten minutes before the time fixed for the hearing.

(6) When the judge has been connected the designated legal representative (or his counsel) will introduce the parties in the usual way.

(7) If the use of a 'speakerphone' by any party causes the judge or any other party any difficulty in hearing what is said the judge may require that party to use a hand held telephone.

(8) The telephone charges debited to the account of the party initiating the conference call will be treated as part of the costs of the application.

Documents

6.11 Where a document is required to be filed and served the party or the designated legal representative must do so no later than 4pm at least 2 days before the hearing.

6.12 A case summary and draft order must be filed and served in –

(a) multi-track cases; and

(b) small and fast track cases if the court so directs.

6.13 Any other document upon which a party seeks to rely must be filed and served in accordance with the period specified in paragraph 6.11.

(Rule 2.8 explains how to calculate period of time expressed in terms of days.)

Video conferencing

7 Where the parties to a matter wish to use video conferencing facilities, and those facilities are available in the relevant court, they should apply to the Master or district judge for directions.

(Paragraph 29 and Annex 3 of Practice Direction 32 provide guidance on the use of video conferencing in the civil courts)

Note of proceedings

8 The procedural judge should keep, either by way of a note or a tape recording, brief details of all proceedings before him, including the dates of the proceedings and a short statement of the decision taken at each hearing.

Evidence

9.1 The requirement for evidence in certain types of applications is set out in some of the rules and practice directions. Where there is no specific requirement to provide evidence it should be borne in mind that, as a practical matter, the court will often need to be satisfied by evidence of the facts that are relied on in support of or for opposing the application.

9.2 The court may give directions for the filing of evidence in support of or opposing a particular application. The court may also give directions for the filing of evidence in relation to any hearing that it fixes on its own initiative. The directions may specify the form that evidence is to take and when it is to be served.

9.3 Where it is intended to rely on evidence which is not contained in the application itself, the evidence, if it has not already been served, should be served with the application.

9.4 Where a respondent to an application wishes to rely on evidence which has not yet been served he should serve it as soon as possible and in any event in accordance with any directions the court may have given.

9.5 If it is necessary for the applicant to serve any evidence in reply it should be served as soon as possible and in any event in accordance with any directions the court may have given.

9.6 Evidence must be filed with the court as well as served on the parties. Exhibits should not be filed unless the court otherwise directs.

9.7 The contents of an application notice may be used as evidence (otherwise than at trial) provided the contents have been verified by a statement of truth.[4]

Consent orders

10.1 Rule 40.6 sets out the circumstances where an agreed judgment or order may be entered and sealed.

10.2 Where all parties affected by an order have written to the court consenting to the making of the order a draft of which has been filed with the court, the court will treat the draft as having been signed in accordance with rule 40.6(7).

10.3 Where a consent order must be made by a judge (i.e. rule 40.6(2) does not apply) the order must be drawn so that the judge's name and judicial title can be inserted.

10.4 The parties to an application for a consent order must ensure that they provide the court with any material it needs to be satisfied that it is appropriate to make the order. Subject to any rule or practice direction a letter will generally be acceptable for this purpose.

10.5 Where a judgment or order has been agreed in respect of an application or claim where a hearing date has been fixed, the parties must inform the court immediately. (note that parties are reminded that under rules 28.4 and 29.5 the case management timetable cannot be varied by written agreement of the parties.)

Other applications considered without a hearing

11.1 Where rule 23.8(b) applies the parties should so inform the court in writing and each should confirm that all evidence and other material on which he relies has been disclosed to the other parties to the application.

11.2 Where rule 23.8(c) applies the court will treat the application as if it were proposing to make an order on its own initiative.

Applications to stay claim where related criminal proceedings

11A.1 An application for the stay of civil proceedings pending the determination of related criminal proceedings may be made by any party to the civil proceedings or by the prosecutor or any defendant in the criminal proceedings.

11A.2 Every party to the civil proceedings must, unless he is the applicant, be made a respondent to the application.

11A.3 The evidence in support of the application must contain an estimate of the

---

4   See Part 22.

expected duration of the stay and must identify the respects in which the continuance of the civil proceedings may prejudice the criminal trial.

11A.4 In order to make an application under paragraph 11A.1, it is not necessary for the prosecutor or defendant in the criminal proceedings to be joined as a party to the civil proceedings.

Miscellaneous

12.1 Except in the most simple application the applicant should bring to any hearing a draft of the order sought. If the case is proceeding in the Royal Courts of Justice and the order is unusually long or complex it should also be supplied on disk for use by the court office.

12.2 Where rule 23.11 applies, the power to re-list the application in rule 23.11(2) is in addition to any other powers of the court with regard to the order (for example to set aside, vary, discharge or suspend the order).

Costs

13.1 Attention is drawn to the costs practice direction and, in particular, to the court's power to make a summary assessment of costs.

13.2 Attention is also drawn to rule 44.13(i) which provides that if an order makes no mention of costs, none are payable in respect of the proceedings to which it relates.

PART 30: TRANSFER

Transfer between divisions and to and from a specialist list

30.5 (1) The High Court may order proceedings in any Division of the High Court to be transferred to another Division.

(2) The court may order proceedings to be transferred to or from a specialist list.

(3) An application for the transfer of proceedings to or from a specialist list.

PRACTICE DIRECTION 30 – TRANSFER

THIS PRACTICE DIRECTION SUPPLEMENTS CPR PART 30

VALUE OF A CASE AND TRANSFER

1 In addition to the criteria set out in Rule 30.3(2) attention is drawn to the financial limits set out in the High Court and County Courts Jurisdiction Order 1991, as amended.

2 Attention is also drawn to paragraph 2 of the Practice Direction 29.

DATE OF TRANSFER

3 Where the court orders proceedings to be transferred, the order will take effect from the date it is made by the court.

PROCEDURE ON TRANSFER

4.1 Where an order for transfer has been made the transferring court will immediately send notice of the transfer to the receiving court. The notice will contain:

(1) the name of the case, and

(2) the number of the case.

4.2 At the same time as the transferring court notifies the receiving court it will also notify the parties of the transfer under rule 30.4(1).

PROCEDURE FOR AN APPEAL AGAINST ORDER OF TRANSFER

5.1 Where a district judge orders proceedings to be transferred and both the transferring and receiving courts are county courts, any appeal against that order should be made in the receiving court.

5.2 The receiving court may, if it is more convenient for the parties, remit the appeal to the transferring court to be dealt with there.

APPLICATIONS TO SET ASIDE

6.1 Where a party may apply to set aside an order for transfer (e.g. under rule 23.10) the application should be made to the court which made the order.

6.2 Such application should be made in accordance with Part 23 of the Rules and Practice Direction 23A.

TRANSFER ON THE CRITERION IN RULE 30.3(2)(g)

7 A transfer should only be made on the basis of the criterion in rule 30.3(2)(g) where there is a real prospect that a declaration of incompatibility will be made.

ENTERPRISE ACT 2002

8.1 In this paragraph –

(1) 'the 1998 Act' means the Competition Act 1998;

(2) 'the 2002 Act' means the Enterprise Act 2002; and

(3) 'the CAT' means the Competition Appeal Tribunal.

8.2 Rules 30.1, 30.4 and 30.5 and paragraphs 3 and 6 apply.

Transfer from the High Court or a county court to the Competition Appeal Tribunal under section 16(4) of the Enterprise Act 2002

8.3 The High Court or a county court may pursuant to section 16(4) of the 2002 Act, on its own initiative or on application by the claimant or defendant, order the transfer of any part of the proceedings before it, which relates to a claim to which section 47A of the 1998 Act applies, to the CAT.

8.4 When considering whether to make an order under paragraph 8.3 the court shall take into account whether –

(1) there is a similar claim under section 47A of the 1998 Act based on the same infringement currently before the CAT;

(2) the CAT has previously made a decision on a similar claim under section 47A of the 1998 Act based on the same infringement; or

(3) the CAT has developed considerable expertise by previously dealing with a significant number of cases arising from the same or similar infringements.

8.5 Where the court orders a transfer under paragraph 8.3 it will immediately –

(1) send to the CAT –

(a) a notice of the transfer containing the name of the case; and

(b) all papers relating to the case; and

(2) notify the parties of the transfer.

8.6 An appeal against a transfer order made under paragraph 8.3 must be brought in the court which made the transfer order.

Transfer from the Competition Appeal Tribunal to the High Court under section 16(5) of the Enterprise Act 2002

8.7 Where the CAT pursuant to section 16(5) of the 2002 Act directs transfer of a claim made in proceedings under section 47A of the 1998 Act to the High Court, the claim should be transferred to the Chancery Division of the High Court at the Royal Courts of Justice.

8.8 As soon as a claim has been transferred under paragraph 8.7, the High Court must –

(1) allocate a case number; and

(2) list the case for a case management hearing before a judge.

8.9 A party to a claim which has been transferred under paragraph 8.7 may apply to transfer it to the Commercial Court if it otherwise falls within the scope of rule 58.2(1), in accordance with the procedure set out in rules 58.4(2) and 30.5(3).

TRANSFER TO OR FROM A PATENTS COUNTY COURT (RULE 63.18)

9.1 When deciding whether to order a transfer of proceedings to or from a patents county court the court will consider whether –

(1) a party can only afford to bring or defend the claim in a patents county court; and

(2) the claim is appropriate to be determined by a patents county court having regard in particular to –

(a) the value of the claim (including the value of an injunction);

(b) the complexity of the issues; and

(c) the estimated length of the trial.

9.2 Where the court orders proceedings to be transferred to or from a patents county court it may –

(1) specify terms for such a transfer; and

(2) award reduced or no costs where it allows the claimant to withdraw the claim.

PART 32: EVIDENCE

Contents of this part

Power of court to control evidence

32.1 (1) The court may control the evidence by giving directions as to–

(a) the issues on which it requires evidence;

(b) the nature of the evidence which it requires to decide those issues; and

(c) the way in which the evidence is to be placed before the court.

(2) The court may use its power under this rule to exclude evidence that would otherwise be admissible.

(3) The court may limit cross-examination.[GL]

Evidence of witnesses – general rule

32.2 (1) The general rule is that any fact which needs to be proved by the evidence of witnesses is to be proved–

(a) at trial, by their oral evidence given in public; and

(b) at any other hearing, by their evidence in writing.

(2) This is subject–

(a) to any provision to the contrary contained in these Rules or elsewhere; or

(b) to any order of the court.

(3) The court may give directions–

(a) identifying or limiting the issues to which factual evidence may be directed;

(b) identifying the witnesses who may be called or whose evidence may be read; or

(c) limiting the length or format of witness statements.

Evidence by video link or other means

32.3 The court may allow a witness to give evidence through a video link or by other means.

Requirement to serve witness statements for use at trial

32.4 (1) A witness statement is a written statement signed by a person which contains the evidence which that person would be allowed to give orally.

(2) The court will order a party to serve on the other parties any witness statement of the oral evidence which the party serving the statement intends to rely on in relation to any issues of fact to be decided at the trial.

(3) The court may give directions as to—
   (a) the order in which witness statements are to be served; and
   (b) whether or not the witness statements are to be filed.

Use at trial of witness statements which have been served

32.5 (1) If—
   (a) a party has served a witness statement; and
   (b) he wishes to rely at trial on the evidence of the witness who made the statement,

he must call the witness to give oral evidence unless the court orders otherwise or he puts the statement in as hearsay evidence.

(Part 33 contains provisions about hearsay evidence)

(2) Where a witness is called to give oral evidence under paragraph (1), his witness statement shall stand as his evidence in chief unless the court orders otherwise.

(3) A witness giving oral evidence at trial may with the permission of the court—
   (a) amplify his witness statement; and
   (b) give evidence in relation to new matters which have arisen since the witness statement was served on the other parties.

(4) The court will give permission under paragraph (3) only if it considers that there is good reason not to confine the evidence of the witness to the contents of his witness statement.

(5) If a party who has served a witness statement does not—
   (a) call the witness to give evidence at trial; or
   (b) put the witness statement in as hearsay evidence, any other party may put the witness statement in as hearsay evidence.

Evidence in proceedings other than at trial

32.6 (1) Subject to paragraph (2), the general rule is that evidence at hearings other than the trial is to be by witness statement unless the court, a practice direction or any other enactment requires otherwise.

(2) At hearings other than the trial, a party may, rely on the matters set out in—
   (a) his statement of case; or
   (b) his application notice, if the statement of case or application notice is verified by a statement of truth.

Order for cross-examination

32.7 (1) Where, at a hearing other than the trial, evidence is given in writing, any party may apply to the court for permission to cross-examine the person giving the evidence.

(2) If the court gives permission under paragraph (1) but the person in question does not attend as required by the order, his evidence may not be used unless the court gives permission.

(Rules 78.26 to 78.28 contain rules in relation to evidence arising out of mediation of certain cross-border disputes. Rule 78.27(1)(b) relates specifically to this rule.

Form of witness statement

32.8 A witness statement must comply with the requirements set out in the relevant practice direction.

(Part 22 requires a witness statement to be verified by a statement of truth)

Witness summaries

32.9 (1) A party who–
  (a) is required to serve a witness statement for use at trial; but
  (b) is unable to obtain one, may apply, without notice, for permission to serve a witness summary instead.
(2) A witness summary is a summary of–
  (a) the evidence, if known, which would otherwise be included in a witness statement; or
  (b) if the evidence is not known, the matters about which the party serving the witness summary proposes to question the witness.
(3) Unless the court orders otherwise, a witness summary must include the name and address of the intended witness.
(4) Unless the court orders otherwise, a witness summary must be served within the period in which a witness statement would have had to be served.
(5) Where a party serves a witness summary, so far as practicable rules 32.4 (requirement to serve witness statements for use at trial), 32.5(3) (amplifying witness statements), and 32.8 (form of witness statement) shall apply to the summary.

Consequence of failure to serve witness statement or summary

32.10 If a witness statement or a witness summary for use at trial is not served in respect of an intended witness within the time specified by the court, then the witness may not be called to give oral evidence unless the court gives permission.

Cross-examination on a witness statement

32.11 Where a witness is called to give evidence at trial, he may be cross- examined on his witness statement whether or not the statement or any part of it was referred to during the witness's evidence in chief.

Use of witness statements for other purposes

32.12 (1) Except as provided by this rule, a witness statement may be used only for the purpose of the proceedings in which it is served.
(2) Paragraph (1) does not apply if and to the extent that–
  (a) he witness gives consent in writing to some other use of it;
  (b) the court gives permission for some other use; or

(c) the witness statement has been put in evidence at a hearing held in public.

Availability of witness statements for inspection

32.13 (1) A witness statement which stands as evidence in chief is open to inspection during the course of the trial unless the court otherwise directs.

(2) Any person may ask for a direction that a witness statement is not open to inspection.

(3) The court will not make a direction under paragraph (2) unless it is satisfied that a witness statement should not be open to inspection because of–

(a) the interests of justice;

(b) the public interest;

(c) the nature of any expert medical evidence in the statement;

(d) the nature of any confidential information (including information relating to personal financial matters) in the statement; or

(e) the need to protect the interests of any child or protected party.

(4) The court may exclude from inspection words or passages in the statement.

False statements

32.14 (1) Proceedings for contempt of court may be brought against a person if he makes, or causes to be made, a false statement in a document verified by a statement of truth without an honest belief in its truth.

(Part 22 makes provision for a statement of truth)

(Section 6 of Part 81 contains provisions in relation to committal for making a false statement of truth)

Affidavit evidence

32.15 (1) Evidence must be given by affidavit instead of or in addition to a witness statement if this is required by the court, a provision contained in any other rule, a practice direction or any other enactment.

(2) Nothing in these Rules prevents a witness giving evidence by affidavit at a hearing other than the trial if he chooses to do so in a case where paragraph (1) does not apply, but the party putting forward the affidavit may not recover the additional cost of making it from any other party unless the court orders otherwise.

Form of affidavit

32.16 An affidavit must comply with the requirements set out in the relevant practice direction.

Evidence affidavit made outside the jurisdiction

32.17 A person may make an affidavit outside the jurisdiction in accordance with–

(a) this Part; or

(b) the law of the place where he makes the affidavit.

Notice to admit facts

32.18 (1) A party may serve notice on another party requiring him to admit the facts, or the part of the case of the serving party, specified in the notice.

(2) A notice to admit facts must be served no later than 21 days before the trial.

(3) Where the other party makes any admission in response to the notice, the admission may be used against him only–
   (a) in the proceedings in which the notice to admit is served; and
   (b) by the party who served the notice.

(4) The court may allow a party to amend or withdraw any admission made by him on such terms as it thinks just.

Notice to admit or produce documents

32.19 (1) A party shall be deemed to admit the authenticity of a document disclosed to him under Part 31 (disclosure and inspection of documents) unless he serves notice that he wishes the document to be proved at trial.

(2) A notice to prove a document must be served–
   (a) by the latest date for serving witness statements; or
   (b) within 7 days of disclosure of the document, whichever is later.

Notarial acts and instruments

32.20 A notarial act or instrument may be received in evidence without further proof as duly authenticated in accordance with the requirements of law unless the contrary is provide.

PART 32 PRACTICE DIRECTION – WRITTEN EVIDENCE

THIS PRACTICE DIRECTION SUPPLEMENTS CPR PART 32

EVIDENCE IN GENERAL

1.1 Rule 32.2 sets out how evidence is to be given and facts are to be proved.

1.2 Evidence at a hearing other than the trial should normally be given by witness statement[5] (see paragraph 17 onwards). However a witness may give evidence by affidavit if he wishes to do so[6] (and see paragraph 1.4 below).

1.3 Statements of case (see paragraph 26 onwards) and application notices[7] may also be used as evidence provided that their contents have been verified by a statement of truth.[8]

(For information regarding evidence by deposition see Part 34 and Practice Direction 34A.)

1.4 Affidavits must be used as evidence in the following instances:

(1) where sworn evidence is required by an enactment;[9] rule, order or practice direction,

(2) in any application for a search order, a freezing injunction, or an order requiring an occupier to permit another to enter his land, and

(3) in any application for an order against anyone for alleged contempt of court.

1.5 If a party believes that sworn evidence is required by a court in another jurisdiction for any purpose connected with the proceedings, he may apply to the court for a direction that evidence shall be given only by affidavit on any pre-trial applications.

1.6 The court may give a direction under rule 32.15 that evidence shall be given by affidavit instead of or in addition to a witness statement or statement of case:

(1) on its own initiative, or

(2) after any party has applied to the court for such a direction.

1.7 An affidavit, where referred to in the Civil Procedure Rules or a practice direction, also means an affirmation unless the context requires otherwise.

AFFIDAVITS

Deponent

2 A deponent is a person who gives evidence by affidavit or affirmation.

Heading

3.1 The affidavit should be headed with the title of the proceedings (see paragraph 4 of Practice Direction 7A and paragraph 7 of Practice Direction 20); where the proceedings are between several parties with the same status it is sufficient to identify the parties as follows:

	Number:
A.B. (and others)	Claimants/Applicants
C.D. (and others)	Defendants/Respondents
	(as appropriate)

---

5 See rule 35.6(1).

6 See rule 32.15(2).

7 See Part 23 for information about making an application.

8 Rule 32.6(2) and see Part 22 for information about the statement of truth.

9 See, eg, Protection from Harassment Act 1997 s3(5)(a).

3.2 At the top right hand corner of the first page (and on the backsheet) there should be clearly written:

(1) the party on whose behalf it is made,

(2) the initials and surname of the deponent,

(3) the number of the affidavit in relation to that deponent,

(4) the identifying initials and number of each exhibit referred to, and

(5) the date sworn.

Body of affidavit

4.1 The affidavit must, if practicable, be in the deponent's own words, the affidavit should be expressed in the first person and the deponent should:

(1) commence 'I (*full name*)of (*address*) state on oath ... ',

(2) if giving evidence in his professional, business or other occupational capacity, give the address at which he works in (1) above, the position he holds and the name of his firm or employer,

(3) give his occupation or, if he has none, his description, and

(4) state if he is a party to the proceedings or employed by a party to the proceedings, if it be the case.

4.2 An affidavit must indicate:

(1) which of the statements in it are made from the deponent's own knowledge and which are matters of information or belief, and

(2) the source for any matters of information or belief.

4.3 Where a deponent:

(1) refers to an exhibit or exhibits, he should state 'there is now shown to me marked ' ... ' the (*description of exhibit*)', and

(2) makes more than one affidavit (to which there are exhibits) in the same proceedings, the numbering of the exhibits should run consecutively throughout and not start again with each affidavit.

Jurat

5.1 The jurat of an affidavit is a statement set out at the end of the document which authenticates the affidavit.

5.2 It must:

(1) be signed by all deponents,

(2) be completed and signed by the person before whom the affidavit was sworn whose name and qualification must be printed beneath his signature,

(3) contain the full address of the person before whom the affidavit was sworn, and

(4) follow immediately on from the text and not be put on a separate page.

Format of affidavits

6.1 An affidavit should:

(1) be produced on durable quality A4 paper with a 3.5cm margin,

(2) be fully legible and should normally be typed on one side of the paper only,

(3) where possible, be bound securely in a manner which would not hamper filing, or otherwise each page should be endorsed with the case number and should bear the initials of the deponent and of the person before whom it was sworn,

(4) have the pages numbered consecutively as a separate document (or as one of several documents contained in a file),

(5) be divided into numbered paragraphs,

(6) have all numbers, including dates, expressed in figures, and

(7) give the reference to any document or documents mentioned either in the margin or in bold text in the body of the affidavit.

6.2 It is usually convenient for an affidavit to follow the chronological sequence of events or matters dealt with; each paragraph of an affidavit should as far as possible be confined to a distinct portion of the subject.

Inability of deponent to read or sign affidavit

7.1 Where an affidavit is sworn by a person who is unable to read or sign it, the person before whom the affidavit is sworn must certify in the jurat that:

(1) he read the affidavit to the deponent,

(2) the deponent appeared to understand it, and

(3) the deponent signed or made his mark, in his presence.

7.2 If that certificate is not included in the jurat, the affidavit may not be used in evidence unless the court is satisfied that it was read to the deponent and that he appeared to understand it. Two versions of the form of jurat with the certificate are set out at Annex 1 to this practice direction.

Alterations to affidavits

8.1 Any alteration to an affidavit must be initialled by both the deponent and the person before whom the affidavit was sworn.

8.2 An affidavit which contains an alteration that has not been initialled may be filed or used in evidence only with the permission of the court.

Who may administer oaths and take affidavits

9.1 Only the following may administer oaths and take affidavits:

(1) Commissioners for oaths,[10]

(2) omitted

(3) other persons specified by statute,[11]

(4) certain officials of the Supreme Court,[12]

(5) a circuit judge or district judge,[13]

(6) any justice of the peace,[14] and

(7) certain officials of any county court appointed by the judge of that court for the purpose.[15]

9.2 An affidavit must be sworn before a person independent of the parties or their representatives.

Filing of affidavits

10.1 If the court directs that an affidavit is to be filed,[16] it must be filed in the court

---

10 Commissioner for Oaths 1889 and 1891.

11 Legal Services Act 2007 ss12, 18, Schs 2–4.

12 Commissioners for Oaths Act 1889 s2.

13 County Courts Act 1984 s58.

14 County Courts Act 1984 s58.

15 County Courts Act 1984 s58.

16 Rules 32.1(3) and 32.4(3)(b).

or Division, or Office or Registry of the court or Division where the action in which it was or is to be used, is proceeding or will proceed.

10.2 Where an affidavit is in a foreign language:

(1) the party wishing to rely on it–

(a) must have it translated, and

(b) must file the foreign language affidavit with the court, and

(2) the translator must make and file with the court an affidavit verifying the translation and exhibiting both the translation and a copy of the foreign language affidavit.

EXHIBITS

Manner of exhibiting documents

11.1 A document used in conjunction with an affidavit should be:

(1) produced to and verified by the deponent, and remain separate from the affidavit, and

(2) identified by a declaration of the person before whom the affidavit was sworn.

11.2 The declaration should be headed with the name of the proceedings in the same way as the affidavit.

11.3 The first page of each exhibit should be marked:

(1) as in paragraph 3.2 above, and

(2) with the exhibit mark referred to in the affidavit.

Letters

12.1 Copies of individual letters should be collected together and exhibited in a bundle or bundles. They should be arranged in chronological order with the earliest at the top, and firmly secured.

12.2 When a bundle of correspondence is exhibited, the exhibit should have a front page attached stating that the bundle consists of original letters and copies. They should be arranged and secured as above and numbered consecutively.

Other documents

13.1 Photocopies instead of original documents may be exhibited provided the originals are made available for inspection by the other parties before the hearing and by the judge at the hearing.

13.2 Court documents must not be exhibited (official copies of such documents prove themselves).

13.3 Where an exhibit contains more than one document, a front page should be attached setting out a list of the documents contained in the exhibit; the list should contain the dates of the documents.

Exhibits other than documents

14.1 Items other than documents should be clearly marked with an exhibit number or letter in such a manner that the mark cannot become detached from the exhibit.

14.2 Small items may be placed in a container and the container appropriately marked.

General provisions

15.1 Where an exhibit contains more than one document:

(1) the bundle should not be stapled but should be securely fastened in a way that does not hinder the reading of the documents, and

(2) the pages should be numbered consecutively at bottom centre.

15.2 Every page of an exhibit should be clearly legible; typed copies of illegible documents should be included, paginated with 'a' numbers.

15.3 Where affidavits and exhibits have become numerous, they should be put into separate bundles and the pages numbered consecutively throughout.

15.4 Where on account of their bulk the service of exhibits or copies of exhibits on the other parties would be difficult or impracticable, the directions of the court should be sought as to arrangements for bringing the exhibits to the attention of the other parties and as to their custody pending trial.

Affirmations

16 All provisions in this or any other practice direction relating to affidavits apply to affirmations with the following exceptions:

(1) the deponent should commence 'I (*name*)of (*address*) do solemnly and sincerely affirm ...', and

(2) in the jurat the word 'sworn' is replaced by the word 'affirmed'.

WITNESS STATEMENTS

Heading

17.1 The witness statement should be headed with the title of the proceedings (see paragraph 4 of Practice Direction 7A and paragraph 7 of Practice Direction 20); where the proceedings are between several parties with the same status it is sufficient to identify the parties as follows:

	Number:
A.B. (and others)	Claimants/Applicants
C.D. (and others)	Defendants/Respondents
	(as appropriate)

17.2 At the top right hand corner of the first page there should be clearly written:

(1) the party on whose behalf it is made,

(2) the initials and surname of the witness,

(3) the number of the statement in relation to that witness,

(4) the identifying initials and number of each exhibit referred to, and

(5) the date the statement was made.

Body of witness statement

18.1 The witness statement must, if practicable, be in the intended witness's own words, the statement should be expressed in the first person and should also state:

(1) the full name of the witness,

(2) his place of residence or, if he is making the statement in his professional, business or other occupational capacity, the address at which he works, the position he holds and the name of his firm or employer,

(3) his occupation, or if he has none, his description, and

(4) the fact that he is a party to the proceedings or is the employee of such a party if it be the case.

18.2 A witness statement must indicate:

(1) which of the statements in it are made from the witness's own knowledge and which are matters of information or belief, and

(2) the source for any matters of information or belief.

18.3 An exhibit used in conjunction with a witness statement should be verified and identified by the witness and remain separate from the witness statement.

18.4 Where a witness refers to an exhibit or exhibits, he should state 'I refer to the (description of exhibit) marked ' ... '.

18.5 The provisions of paragraphs 11.3 to 15.4 (exhibits) apply similarly to witness statements as they do to affidavits.

18.6 Where a witness makes more than one witness statement to which there are exhibits, in the same proceedings, the numbering of the exhibits should run consecutively throughout and not start again with each witness statement.

Format of witness statement

19.1 A witness statement should:

(1) be produced on durable quality A4 paper with a 3.5cm margin,

(2) be fully legible and should normally be typed on one side of the paper only,

(3) where possible, be bound securely in a manner which would not hamper filing, or otherwise each page should be endorsed with the case number and should bear the initials of the witness,

(4) have the pages numbered consecutively as a separate statement (or as one of several statements contained in a file),

(5) be divided into numbered paragraphs,

(6) have all numbers, including dates, expressed in figures, and

(7) give the reference to any document or documents mentioned either in the margin or in bold text in the body of the statement.

19.2 It is usually convenient for a witness statement to follow the chronological sequence of the events or matters dealt with, each paragraph of a witness statement should as far as possible be confined to a distinct portion of the subject.

Statement of truth

20.1 A witness statement is the equivalent of the oral evidence which that witness would, if called, give in evidence; it must include a statement by the intended witness that he believes the facts in it are true.[17]

20.2 To verify a witness statement the statement of truth is as follows:
'I believe that the facts stated in this witness statement are true'

20.3 Attention is drawn to rule 32.14 which sets out the consequences of verifying a witness statement containing a false statement without an honest belief in its truth.

21 Omitted

Alterations to witness statements

22.1 Any alteration to a witness statement must be initialled by the person making the statement or by the authorised person where appropriate (see paragraph 21).

22.2 A witness statement which contains an alteration that has not been initialled may be used in evidence only with the permission of the court.

---

17 See Part 22 for information about the statement of truth.

Filing of witness statements

23.1 If the court directs that a witness statement is to be filed,[18] it must be filed in the court or Division, or Office or Registry of the court or Division where the action in which it was or is to be used, is proceeding or will proceed.

23.2 Where the court has directed that a witness statement in a foreign language is to be filed:

(1) the party wishing to rely on it must–
   (a) have it translated, and
   (b) file the foreign language witness statement with the court, and
(2) the translator must make and file with the court an affidavit verifying the translation and exhibiting both the translation and a copy of the foreign language witness statement.

Certificate of court officer

24.1 Where the court has ordered that a witness statement is not to be open to inspection by the public[19] or that words or passages in the statement are not to be open to inspection[20] the court officer will so certify on the statement and make any deletions directed by the court under rule 32.13(4).

Defects in affidavits, witness statements and exhibits

25.1 Where:

(1) an affidavit,
(2) a witness statement, or
(3) an exhibit to either an affidavit or a witness statement,

does not comply with Part 32 or this practice direction in relation to its form, the court may refuse to admit it as evidence and may refuse to allow the costs arising from its preparation.

25.2 Permission to file a defective affidavit or witness statement or to use a defective exhibit may be obtained from a judge[21] in the court where the case is proceeding.

STATEMENTS OF CASE

26.1 A statement of case may be used as evidence in an interim application provided it is verified by a statement of truth.[22]

26.2 To verify a statement of case the statement of truth should be set out as follows:

'[I believe][the (*party on whose behalf the statement of case is being signed*) believes] that the facts stated in the statement of case are true'.

26.3 Attention is drawn to rule 32.14 which sets out the consequences of verifying a witness statement containing a false statement without an honest belief in its truth.

(For information regarding statements of truth see Part 22 and Practice Direction 22.)

18 Rule 32.4(3)(b).
19 Rule 32.13(2).
20 Rule 32.13(4).
21 Rule 2.3(1); definition of judge.
22 See rule 32.6(2)(a).

(Practice Directions 7A and 17 provide further information concerning statements of case.)

AGREED BUNDLES FOR HEARINGS

27.1 The court may give directions requiring the parties to use their best endeavours to agree a bundle or bundles of documents for use at any hearing.

27.2 All documents contained in bundles which have been agreed for use at a hearing shall be admissible at that hearing as evidence of their contents, unless–
(1) the court orders otherwise; or
(2) a party gives written notice of objection to the admissibility of particular documents.

PENALTY

28.1 (1) Where a party alleges that a statement of truth or a disclosure statement is false the party shall refer that allegation to the court dealing with the claim in which the statement of truth or disclosure statement has been made.
(2) the court may–
(a) exercise any of its powers under the rules;
(b) initiate steps to consider if there is a contempt of court and, where there is, to punish it;

(Practice Direction RSC 52 and CCR 29 makes provision where committal to prison is a possibility if contempt is proved)

(c) direct the party making the allegation to refer the matter to the Attorney General with a request to him to consider whether he wishes to bring proceedings for contempt of court.

28.2 (1) An request to the Attorney General must be made in writing and sent to the Attorney General's Office at 20 Victoria Street, London SW1H 0NF. The request must be accompanied by a copy of the order directing that the matter be referred to the Attorney General and must
(a) identify the statement said to be false;
(b) explain–
(i) why it is false, and
(ii) why the maker knew it to be false at the time it was made ; and
(c) explain why contempt proceedings would be appropriate in the light of the overriding objective in Part 1.
(2) The practice of the Attorney General is to prefer an application that comes from the court, and so has received preliminary consideration by a judge, to one made direct to him by a party to the claim in which the alleged contempt occurred without prior consideration by the court. An application to the Attorney General is not a way of appealing against, or reviewing, the decision of the judge.

28.3 Where a party makes an application to the court for permission for that party to commence proceedings for contempt of court, it must be supported by written evidence containing the information specified in paragraph 28.2(1) and the result of the application to the Attorney General made by the applicant.

28.4 The rules do not change the law of contempt or introduce new categories of contempt. A person applying to commence such proceedings should consider whether the incident complained of does amount to contempt of court and whether such proceedings would further the overriding objective in Part 1 of the Civil Procedure Rules.

VIDEO CONFERENCING

29.1 Guidance on the use of video conferencing in the civil courts is set out at Annex 3 to this practice direction.

A list of the sites which are available for video conferencing can be found n Her Majesty's Courts and Tribunals Service website.

ANNEX 1

CERTIFICATE TO BE USEDWHEREA DEPONENT TO AN AFFIDAVIT IS UNABLE TO READ OR SIGN IT

Sworn at . . . . this . . . . . . day of . . . . Before me, I having first read over the contents of this affidavit to the deponent [*if there are exhibits, add* 'and explained the nature and effect of the exhibits referred to in it'] who appeared to understand it and approved its content as accurate, and made his mark on the affidavit in my presence.

Or, (after, Before me) the witness to the mark of the deponent having been first sworn that he had read over etc. (*as above*) and that he saw him make his mark on the affidavit. (*Witness must sign*).

CERTIFICATE TO BE USEDWHERE A DEPONENT TO AN AFFIRMATION IS UNABLE TO READ OR SIGN IT

Affirmed at . . . . this . . . . . . day of . . . . Before me, I having first read over the contents of this affirmation to the deponent [*if there are exhibits, add* 'and explained the nature and effect of the exhibits referred to in it'] who appeared to understand it and approved its content as accurate, and made his mark on the affirmation in my presence.

Or, (after, Before me) the witness to the mark of the deponent having been first sworn that he had read over etc. (*as above*) and that he saw him make his mark on the affirmation. (*Witness must sign*).

ANNEX 2

Omitted

ANNEX 3

VIDEO CONFERENCING GUIDANCE
This guidance is for the use of video conferencing (VCF) in civil proceedings. It is in part based, with permission, upon the protocol of the Federal Court of Australia. It is intended to provide a guide to all persons involved in the use of VCF, although it does not attempt to cover all the practical questions which might arise.

Video conferencing generally

1. The guidance covers the use of VCF equipment both (a) in a courtroom, whether via equipment which is permanently placed there or via a mobile unit, and (b) in a separate studio or conference room. In either case, the location at which the judge sits is referred to as the 'local site'. The other site or sites to and from which transmission is made are referred to as 'the remote site' and in any particular case any such site may be another courtroom. The

guidance applies to cases where VCF is used for the taking of evidence and also to its use for other parts of any legal proceedings (for example, interim applications, case management conferences, pre-trial reviews).

2. VCF may be a convenient way of dealing with any part of proceedings: it can involve considerable savings in time and cost. Its use for the taking of evidence from overseas witnesses will, in particular, be likely to achieve a material saving of costs, and such savings may also be achieved by its use for taking domestic evidence. It is, however, inevitably not as ideal as having the witness physically present in court. Its convenience should not therefore be allowed to dictate its use. A judgment must be made in every case in which the use of VCF is being considered not only as to whether it will achieve an overall cost saving but as to whether its use will be likely to be beneficial to the efficient, fair and economic disposal of the litigation. In particular, it needs to be recognised that the degree of control a court can exercise over a witness at the remote site is or may be more limited than it can exercise over a witness physically before it.

3. When used for the taking of evidence, the objective should be to make the VCF session as close as possible to the usual practice in a trial court where evidence is taken in open court. To gain the maximum benefit, several differences have to be taken into account. Some matters, which are taken or granted when evidence is taken in the conventional way, take on a different dimension when it is taken by VCF: for example, the administration of the oath, ensuring that the witness understands who is at the local site and what their various roles are, the raising of any objections to the evidence and the use of documents.

4. It should not be presumed that all foreign governments are willing to allow their nationals or others within their jurisdiction to be examined before a court in England or Wales by means of VCF. If there is any doubt about this, enquiries should be directed to the Foreign and Commonwealth Office (International Legal Matters Unit, Consular Division) with a view to ensuring that the country from which the evidence is to be taken raises no objection to it at diplomatic level. The party who is directed to be responsible for arranging the VCF (see paragraph 8 below) will be required to make all necessary inquiries about this well in advance of the VCF and must be able to inform the court what those inquiries were and of their outcome.

5. Time zone differences need to be considered when a witness abroad is to be examined in England or Wales by VCF. The convenience of the witness, the parties, their representatives and the court must all be taken into account. The cost of the use of a commercial studio is usually greater outside normal business hours.

6. Those involved with VCF need to be aware that, even with the most advanced systems currently available, there are the briefest of delays between the receipt of the picture and that of the accompanying sound. If due allowance is not made for this, there will be a tendency to 'speak over' the witness, whose voice will continue to be heard for a millisecond or so after he or she appears on the screen to have finished speaking.

7. With current technology, picture quality is good, but not as good as a television picture. The quality of the picture is enhanced if those appearing on VCF monitors keep their movements to a minimum.

Preliminary arrangements

8. The court's permission is required for any part of any proceedings to be dealt with by means of VCF. Before seeking a direction, the applicant should notify the listing officer, diary manager or other appropriate court officer of the intention to seek it, and should enquire as to the availability of court VCF equipment for the day or days of the proposed VCF. The application for a direction should be made to the Master, District Judge or Judge, as may be appropriate. If all parties consent to a direction, permission can be sought by letter, fax or e-mail, although the court may still require an oral hearing. All parties are entitled to be heard on whether or not such a direction should be given and as to its terms. If a witness at a remote site is to give evidence by an interpreter, consideration should be given at this stage as to whether the interpreter should be at the local site or the remote site. If a VCF direction is given, arrangements for the transmission will then need to be made. The court will ordinarily direct that the party seeking permission to use VCF is to be responsible for this. That party is hereafter referred to as 'the VCF arranging party'.

9. Subject to any order to the contrary, all costs of the transmission, including the costs of hiring equipment and technical personnel to operate it, will initially be the responsibility of, and must be met by, the VCF arranging party. All reasonable efforts should be made to keep the transmission to a minimum and so keep the costs down. All such costs will be considered to be part of the costs of the proceedings and the court will determine at such subsequent time as is convenient or appropriate who, as between the parties, should be responsible for them and (if appropriate) in what proportions.

10. The local site will, if practicable, be a courtroom but it may instead be an appropriate studio or conference room. The VCF arranging party must contact the listing officer, diary manager or other appropriate officer of the court which made the VCF direction and make arrangements for the VCF transmission. Details of the remote site, and of the equipment to be used both at the local site (if not being supplied by the court) and the remote site (including the number of ISDN lines and connection speed), together with all necessary contact names and telephone numbers, will have to be provided to the listing officer, diary manager or other court officer. The court will need to be satisfied that any equipment provided by the parties for use at the local site and also that at the remote site is of sufficient quality for a satisfactory transmission. The VCF arranging party must ensure that an appropriate person will be present at the local site to supervise the operation of the VCF throughout the transmission in order to deal with any technical problems. That party must also arrange for a technical assistant to be similarly present at the remote site for like purposes.

11. It is recommended that the judge, practitioners and witness should arrive at their respective VCF sites about 20 minutes prior to the scheduled commencement of the transmission.

12. If the local site is not a courtroom, but a conference room or studio, the judge will need to determine who is to sit where. The VCF arranging party must take care to ensure that the number of microphones is adequate for the speakers and that the panning of the camera for the practitioners' table encompasses all legal representatives so that the viewer can see everyone seated there.

13. The proceedings, wherever they may take place, form part of a trial to which the public is entitled to have access (unless the court has determined that they should be heard in private). If the local site is to be a studio or conference room, the VCF arranging party must ensure that it provides sufficient accommodation to enable a reasonable number of members of the public to attend.

14. In cases where the local site is a studio or conference room, the VCF arranging party should make arrangements, if practicable, for the royal coat of arms to be placed above the judge's seat.

15. In cases in which the VCF is to be used for the taking of evidence, the VCF arranging party must arrange for recording equipment to be provided by the court which made the VCF direction so that the evidence can be recorded. An associate will normally be present to operate the recording equipment when the local site is a courtroom. The VCF arranging party should take steps to ensure that an associate is present to do likewise when it is a studio or conference room. The equipment should be set up and tested before the VCF transmission. It will often be a valuable safeguard for the VCF arranging party also to arrange for the provision of recording equipment at the remote site. This will provide a useful back-up if there is any reduction in sound quality during the transmission. A direction from the court for the making of such a back-up recording must, however, be obtained first. This is because the proceedings are court proceedings and, save as directed by the court, no other recording of them must be made. The court will direct what is to happen to the back-up recording.

16. Some countries may require that any oath or affirmation to be taken by a witness accord with local custom rather than the usual form of oath or affirmation used in England and Wales. The VCF arranging party must make all appropriate prior inquiries and put in place all arrangements necessary to enable the oath or affirmation to be taken in accordance with any local custom. That party must be in a position to inform the court what those inquiries were, what their outcome was and what arrangements have been made. If the oath or affirmation can be administered in the manner normal in England and Wales, the VCF arranging party must arrange in advance to have the appropriate holy book at the remote site. The associate will normally administer the oath.

17. Consideration will need to be given in advance to the documents to which the witness is likely to be referred. The parties should endeavour to agree on this. It will usually be most convenient for a bundle of the copy documents to be prepared in advance, which the VCF arranging party should then send to the remote site.

18. Additional documents are sometimes quite properly introduced during the course of a witness's evidence. To cater for this, the VCF arranging party should ensure that equipment is available to enable documents to be transmitted between sites during the course of the VCF transmission. Consideration should be given to whether to use a document camera. If it is decided to use one, arrangements for its use will need to be established in advance. The panel operator will need to know the number and size of documents or objects if their images are to be sent by document camera. In many cases, a simpler and sufficient alternative will be to ensure that there are fax transmission and reception facilities at the participating sites.

The hearing

19. The procedure for conducting the transmission will be determined by the judge. He will determine who is to control the cameras. In cases where the VCF is being used for an application in the course of the proceedings, the judge will ordinarily not enter the local site until both sites are on line. Similarly, at the conclusion of the hearing, he will ordinarily leave the local site while both sites are still on line. The following paragraphs apply primarily to cases where the VCF is being used for the taking of the evidence of a witness at a remote site. In all cases, the judge will need to decide whether court dress is appropriate when using VCF facilities. It might be appropriate when transmitting from courtroom to courtroom. It might not be when a commercial facility is being used.

20. At the beginning of the transmission, the judge will probably wish to introduce himself and the advocates to the witness. He will probably want to know who is at the remote site and will invite the witness to introduce himself and anyone else who is with him. He may wish to give directions as to the seating arrangements at the remote site so that those present are visible at the local site during the taking of the evidence. He will probably wish to explain to the witness the method of taking the oath or of affirming, the manner in which the evidence will be taken, and who will be conducting the examination and cross-examination. He will probably also wish to inform the witness of the matters referred to in paragraphs 6 and 7 above (co-ordination of picture with sound, and picture quality).

21. The examination of the witness at the remote site should follow as closely as possible the practice adopted when a witness is in the courtroom. During examination, cross-examination and re-examination, the witness must be able to see the legal representative asking the question and also any other person (whether another legal representative or the judge) making any statements in regard to the witness's evidence. It will in practice be most convenient if everyone remains seated throughout the transmission.

PART 52: JUDICIAL REVIEW APPEALS

52.15 (1) Where permission to apply for judicial review has been refused at a hearing in the High Court, the person seeking that permission may apply to the Court of Appeal for permission to appeal.

(1A) Where permission to apply for judicial review of a decision in the Upper Tribunal has been refused by the High Court

   (a) the applicant may apply to the Court of Appeal for permission to appeal;

   (b) the application will be determined on paper without an oral hearing.

(2) An application in accordance with paragraphs (1) and (1A) must be made within 7 days of the decision of the High Court to refuse to give permission to apply for judicial review.

(3) On an application under paragraph (1), the Court of Appeal may, instead of giving permission to appeal, give permission to apply for judicial review.

(4) Where the Court of Appeal gives permission to apply for judicial review in accordance with paragraph (3), the case will proceed in the High Court unless the Court of Appeal orders otherwise.

PRACTICE DIRECTION 52A – APPEALS

GENERAL PROVISIONS

This Practice Direction supplements CPR Part 52

Contents of this Practice Direction
This Practice Direction is divided into the following sections –
Section I – Practice Directions supplementing Part 52
Section II –Introduction
Section III – Destinations of Appeal
Section IV – Obtaining permission to appeal
Section V – Skeleton arguments
Section VI – Disposing of applications and appeals by consent
Section VII – Reopening appeals
Section VIII – Transitional provisions

SECTION I – PRACTICE DIRECTIONS SUPPLEMENTING PART 52

1.1 There are five Practice Directions supplementing Part 52 –
PD 52A – Appeals: general provisions
PD 52B – Appeals in the county courts and the High Court
PD 52C – Appeals to the Court of Appeal
PD 52D – Statutory appeals and appeals subject to special provision
PD 52E – Appeals by way of case stated

SECTION II – INTRODUCTION

2.1 These Practice Directions apply to all appeals to which Part 52 applies.

2.2 Part 52 complements the provisions of sections 54 to 57 of the Access to Justice Act 1999 and provides a uniform procedure for appeals in the county courts and the High Court and a modified procedure for the Civil Division of the Court of Appeal. Part 52 does not apply to –

(a) family proceedings in the High Court or county courts but does apply to appeals to the Court of Appeal from decisions made in family proceedings with such modifications as may be required;

(b) appeals in detailed assessment proceedings against the decision of an authorised court officer.

SECTION III – DESTINATIONS OF APPEAL

3.1 Section 56 of the Access to Justice Act 1999 enables the Lord Chancellor by Order to specify the destinations of appeal in different cases. The Access to Justice Act 1999 (Destination of Appeals) Order 2000, SI 2000/1071 made under section 56, specifies the general destinations of appeal which apply subject to any statutory provision to the contrary. The destinations of appeal provided by that Order are explained in the following paragraphs of this section of this Practice Direction.

3.2 'Statutory appeals' and 'Appeals by way of case stated' are dealt with in PD52D – refer to those provisions for the appropriate court to which such an appeal may lie.

3.3 The court or judge to which an appeal is to be made (subject to obtaining any necessary permission) is set out in the tables below–

Table 1 deals with appeals in proceedings other than family and insolvency proceedings;

Table 2 deals with appeals in insolvency proceedings; and

Table 3 deals with appeals in family proceedings which may be heard in the Family Division and to which the CPR may apply.

3.4 Definitions of terms and abbreviations used in Tables 1, 2 and 3 –

'Destination': the court to which the appeal lies.

'Pt 7 Claim (not MT)': Part 7 Claim, other than a claim allocated to the multi-track.

'Pt 7 Claim (MT)': Part 7 Claim, allocated to the multi-track.

'Pt 8 Claim (not MT)': Part 8 Claim, other than a claim allocated to the multi-track.

'Pt 8 Claim (MT)': Part 8 Claim, allocated to the multi-track.

'DJ': District judge.

'CJ': Circuit judge including a recorder or a district judge who is exercising the jurisdiction of a Circuit judge with the permission of the Designated Civil Judge in respect of the case.

'CJ (CC)': Circuit judge in the county court.

'Master': Master, district judge sitting in a district registry or any other judge referred to in article 2 of the Destination of Appeals Order.

'Final': A final decision within the meaning of paragraphs 3.6 to 3.8 of this Practice Direction.

'Interim': A decision that is not a final decision within the meaning of paragraphs 3.6 to 3.8 of this Practice Direction.

'HCJ': single judge of the High Court.

'HCJ(FD)': single judge of the family Division of the High Court.

'CA': Court of Appeal.

'Other': Claims or originating or pre-action applications started otherwise than by a Part 7 or Part 8 claim (for example an application under Part 23).

'Specialist': Specialist proceedings (under the Companies Act 1985 or the Companies Act 1989 or to which Sections I, II or III of Part 57 or any of Parts 58,59,60, 62 or 63 apply).

(Note: Tables 1, 2 and 3 do not include so-called 'leap frog' appeals either to the Court of Appeal pursuant to section 57 of the Access to Justice Act 1999 or to the Supreme Court pursuant to section 13 of the Administration of Justice Act 1969.)

3.5 The destinations in the tables set out below apply whether the decision is interim or final. For the meaning of 'final decision' for the purposes of this table see paragraphs 3.6 to 3.8 below.

Table 1 – Proceedings other than family or insolvency proceedings				
Court	Deciding judge	Nature of claim	Interim / final	Destination
County	DJ	Pt 7 Claim	Interim	CJ (CC)
		Pt 7 Claim (not MT)	Final	
		Pt 7 Claim (MT)	Final	CA
		Pt 8 Claim	Interim / final	CJ (CC)
		Other	Interim / final	
		Specialist	Interim	
			Final	CA
	CJ	Pt 7 Claim	Interim	HCJ
		Pt 7 Claim (not MT)	Final	
		Pt 7 Claim (MT)	Final	CA
		Pt 8 Claim	Interim / final	HCJ
		Other	Interim / final	
		Specialist	Interim	
			Final	CA
High	Master	Pt 7 Claim	Interim	HCJ
		Pt 7 Claim (not MT)	Final	
		Pt 7 Claim (MT)	Final	CA
		Pt 8 Claim	Interim / final	HCJ
		Other	Interim / final	
		Specialist	Interim	
			Final	CA
	HCJ	Any	Interim / final	CA

Table 2 – Insolvency proceedings		
Court	Deciding judge	Destination
County	DJ or CJ	HCJ
High	Registrar	
	HCJ	CA

Table 3 – Family proceedings in the Principal Registry of the Family Division and to which the CPR will apply			
The proceedings to which this table applies include proceedings under the Inheritance (Provision for Family and Dependants) Act 1975 and proceedings under the Trusts of Land and Appointment of Trustees Act 1996.			
Deciding judge	Nature of claim	Decision under appeal	Destination
DJ	Part 7 Claim (not MT)	Any decision other than a final decision	HCJ(FD)
	Pt 7 Claim (MT)	Final decision	CA
	Part 8 Claim (not MT)	Any decision	HCJ(FD)
	Part 8 Claim (MT)		
HCJ(FD)	Any	Any decision	CA

3.6 A 'final decision' is a decision of a court that would finally determine (subject to any possible appeal or detailed assessment of costs) the entire proceedings whichever way the court decided the issues before it.

3.7 A decision is to be treated as a final decision for destination of appeal purposes where it –

    (a) is made at the conclusion of part of a hearing or trial which has been split into parts; and

    (b) would, if it had been made at the conclusion of that hearing or trial, have been a final decision.

3.8 (1) The following are examples of final decisions –

    • a judgment on liability at the end of a split trial;

    • a judgment at the conclusion of an assessment of damages following a judgment on liability.

    (2) The following are examples of decisions that are not final –

    • a case management decision (within the meaning of paragraph 4.6);

    • a grant or refusal of interim relief;

    • summary judgment;

    • striking out a claim or statement of case;

    • a summary or detailed assessment of costs;

    • an order for the enforcement of a final decision.

Filing appellant's notice in wrong court

3.9 (1) Where a party attempts to file an appellant's notice in a court which does not have jurisdiction to issue the notice, a court officer may notify that party in writing that the appeal court does not have jurisdiction in respect of the notice.

    (2) Before notifying a person under paragraph (1) the court officer must confer–

    (a) with a judge of the appeal court; or

    (b) where the Court of Appeal is the appeal court, with a court officer who exercises the jurisdiction of that Court under rule 52.16.

(3) Where a court officer, in the Court of Appeal, notifies a person under paragraph (1), rule 52.16(5) and (6) shall not apply.

SECTION IV – OBTAINING PERMISSION TO APPEAL

Where to apply for permission

4.1 An application for permission to appeal may be made–
  (a) to the lower court at the hearing at which the decision to be appealed against is given (in which case the lower court may adjourn the hearing to give a party an opportunity to apply for permission to appeal); or
  (b) where the lower court refuses permission to appeal or where no application is made to the lower court, to the appeal court in accordance with rule 52.4.

Form

4.2 An application for permission to appeal to the appeal court must be made using an appellant's notice (form N161 or N164 (small claims track)).

Appeals from Masters and district judges of High Court

4.3 In relation to appeals from Masters or district judges of the High Court: appeals, applications for permission and any other applications in the appeal may be heard and directions in the appeal may be given by a High Court Judge or by any person authorised under section 9 of the Senior Courts Act 1981 to act as a judge of the High Court.

Where the lower court is a county court

4.4 Where the lower court is a county court –
  (a) subject to sub-paragraph (b), appeals and applications for permission to appeal will be heard by a High Court Judge or by a person authorised under paragraphs (1), (2) or (4) of the Table in section 9(1) of the Senior Courts Act 1981 to act as a judge of the High Court;
  (b) an appeal or application for permission to appeal from the decision of a recorder may be heard by a Designated Civil Judge who is authorised under paragraph (5) of the Table in section 9(1) of the Senior Courts Act 1981 to act as a judge of the High Court; and
  (c) other applications in the appeal may be heard and directions in the appeal may be given either by a High Court Judge or by any person authorised under section 9 of the Senior Courts Act 1981 to act as a judge of the High Court.

4.5 The Designated Civil Judge in consultation with the Presiding Judge has responsibility for allocating appeals from decisions of district judges to circuit judges.

Appeal in relation to case management decision

4.6 Where the application is for permission to appeal from a case management decision, the court dealing with the application may take into account whether–
  (a) the issue is of sufficient significance to justify the costs of an appeal;
  (b) the procedural consequences of an appeal (e.g. loss of trial date) outweigh the significance of the case management decision;
  (c) it would be more convenient to determine the issue at or after trial.
Case management decisions include decisions made under rule 3.1(2) and

decisions about disclosure, filing of witness statements or experts' reports, directions about the timetable of the claim, adding a party to a claim and security for costs.

Second appeal

4.7 An application for permission to appeal from a decision of the High Court or a county court which was itself made on appeal is a second appeal and must be made to the Court of Appeal. If permission to appeal is granted the appeal will be heard by the Court of Appeal.

SECTION V – SKELETON ARGUMENTS

5.1 (1) The purpose of a skeleton argument is to assist the court by setting out as concisely as practicable the arguments upon which a party intends to rely.

(2) A skeleton argument must–
- be concise;
- both define and confine the areas of controversy;
- be set out in numbered paragraphs;
- be cross-referenced to any relevant document in the bundle;
- be self-contained and not incorporate by reference material from previous skeleton arguments;
  - not include extensive quotations from documents or authorities.

(3) Documents to be relied on must be identified.

(4) Where it is necessary to refer to an authority, a skeleton argument must –
   (a) state the proposition of law the authority demonstrates; and
   (b) identify the parts of the authority that support the proposition.
   If more than one authority is cited in support of a given proposition, the skeleton argument must briefly state why.

(5) The cost of preparing a skeleton argument which –
   (a) does not comply with the requirements set out in this paragraph; or
   (b) was not filed within the time limits provided by this Practice Direction (or any further time granted by the court),
   will not be allowed on assessment except as directed by the court.

5.2 The appellant should consider what other information the appeal court will need. This may include a list of persons who feature in the case or glossaries of technical terms. A chronology of relevant events will be necessary in most appeals.

5.3 Any statement of costs must show the amount claimed for the skeleton argument separately.

SECTION VI – DISPOSING OF APPLICATIONS AND APPEALS BY CONSENT

Dismissal of applications or appeals by consent

6.1 An appellant who does not wish to pursue an application or appeal may request the appeal court to dismiss the application or the appeal. If such a request is granted it will usually be subject to an order that the appellant pays the costs of the application or appeal.

6.2 If the appellant wishes to have the application or appeal dismissed without costs, his request must be accompanied by a letter signed by the respondent stating that the respondent so consents.

6.3 Where a settlement has been reached disposing of the application or appeal, the parties may make a joint request to the court for the application or appeal to be dismissed by consent. If the request is granted the application or appeal will be dismissed.

Allowing unopposed appeals or applications on paper

6.4 The appeal court will not normally make an order allowing an appeal unless satisfied that the decision of the lower court was wrong or unjust because of a serious procedural or other irregularity. The appeal court may, however, set aside or vary the order of the lower court by consent and without determining the merits of the appeal if it is satisfied that there are good and sufficient reasons for so doing. Where the appeal court is requested by all parties to allow an application or an appeal the court may consider the request on the papers. The request should set out the relevant history of the proceedings and the matters relied on as justifying the order and be accompanied by a draft order.

Disposal of applications and appeals involving children or protected parties

6.5 Where one of the parties is a child or protected party, any disposal of an application or the appeal requires the court's approval. A draft order signed by the parties' solicitors should be sent to the appeal court, together with an opinion from the advocate acting on behalf of the child or protected party and, in the case of a protected party, any relevant documents prepared for the Court of Protection.

SECTION VII – REOPENING APPEALS (RULE 52.17)

7.1 A party applying for permission to reopen an appeal or an application for permission to appeal must apply for such permission from the court whose decision the party wishes to reopen.

7.2 The application for permission must be made by application notice and be supported by written evidence, verified by a statement of truth. A copy of the application for permission must not be served on any other party to the original appeal unless the court so directs.

7.3 Where the court directs that the application for permission is to be served on another party, that party may, within 14 days of the service on him of the copy of the application, file and serve a written statement either supporting or opposing the application.

7.4 The application for permission will be considered on paper by a single judge.

SECTION VIII – TRANSITIONAL PROVISIONS

8.1 This Practice Direction and Practice Directions 52B, 52C, 52D and 52E shall come into force on 1 October 2012 and shall apply to all appeals where –
(a) the appeal notice was filed; or
(b) permission to appeal was given
on or after that date.

8.2 The appeal court may at any time direct that, in relation to any appeal, one or more of Practice Directions 52A, 52B, 52C, 52D or 52E shall apply irrespective of the date on which the appeal notice was filed or permission to appeal was given.

PRACTICE DIRECTION 52C – APPEALS TO THE COURT OF APPEAL

THIS PRACTICE DIRECTION SUPPLEMENTS CPR PART 52

Contents of this Practice Direction

This Practice Direction is divided into the following sections –

Section I – Introduction and interpretation

Section II – Starting an appeal to the Court of Appeal, Grounds of Appeal and Skeleton Arguments

Section III –Respondent's notice and respondent's skeleton argument

Section IV – Procedure where permission to appeal is sought from the Court of Appeal

Section V –Timetable

Section VI – Management of the appeal

Section VII – Bundles, amendment and supplementary skeleton arguments

SECTION I – INTRODUCTION AND INTERPRETATION

1. In this Practice Direction –

    'appeal notice' means either an appellant's notice in form N161 or a respondent's notice in form N162 ;

    'appellant's notice' means an appeal notice filed by an appellant and a 'respondent's notice' means an appeal notice filed by a respondent;

    'hearing date' means the date on which the appeal is listed to be heard, including a'floating' date over two or more days;

    'listing window notification' means the letter sent by the Civil Appeals Office in accordance with Section 5: Timetable Part 1 notifying the parties of the window within which the appeal is likely to be heard; and 'date of the listing window notification' means the date of such letter;

    'replacement skeleton argument' means a skeleton argument which has been amended in order to include cross references to the appeal bundle and is lodged and served in accordance with the timetable at Section 5 Part 2.

2. The court may make such directions as the case may require and such directions will prevail over any provision of this practice direction.

SECTION II – STARTING AN APPEAL TO THE COURT OF APPEAL

Filing the Appellant's Notice and accompanying documents

3. (1) An appellant's notice (Form N161) must be filed and served in all cases. The appellant's notice must be accompanied by the appropriate fee or, if appropriate, a fee remission certificate.

    (2) The appellant's notice and accompanying documents must be filed in the Civil Appeals Office Registry, Room E307, Royal Courts of Justice, Strand, London, WC2A 2LL.

    (3) At the same time as filing an appellant's notice, the appellant must provide for the use of the court three copies of the appellant's notice and one copy of each of the following –

    (a) the sealed order or tribunal determination being appealed;

    (b) any order granting or refusing permission to appeal, together with a copy of the judge's or tribunal's reasons for granting or refusing permission to appeal;

(c) any witness statements or affidavits relied on in support of any application included in the appellant's notice;

(d) in cases where the decision of the lower court was itself made on appeal, the first order, the reasons given by the judge who made it, and the appellant's notice of appeal against that order;

(e) in a claim for judicial review or a statutory appeal, the original decision which was the subject of the application to the lower court;

(f) the order allocating the case to a track (if any);

(g) the appellant's skeleton argument in support of the appeal;

(h) the approved transcript of the judgment.

(4) The appellant must also provide to the court one copy of the appellant's notice for each respondent for sealing by the court and return to the appellant for service.

(5) Where the appellant applies for permission to appeal, additional documents are required: see Section 4 of this Practice Direction.

(5) Provisions in relation to the skeleton argument are set out in paragraph 31.

Extension of time for filing appellant's notice

4. (1) Where the time for filing an appellant's notice has expired, the appellant must –

(a) file the appellant's notice; and

(b) include in that appellant's notice an application for an extension of time.

(2) The appellant's notice must state the reason for the delay and the steps taken prior to the application being made.

(3) Where the appellant's notice includes an application for an extension of time and permission to appeal has been given or is not required, the respondent has the right to oppose that application and to be heard at any hearing of that application. In respect of any application to extend time –

(a) The respondent must–

(i) be served with a copy of any evidence filed in support of the application; and

(ii) inform the court in writing of any objections to the grant of the extension of time within 7 days of being served with the appellant's notice.

(b) A respondent who unreasonably opposes an application for an extension of time may be ordered to pay the costs of the application.

(c) An application for an extension of time will normally be determined without a hearing unless the court directs otherwise.

Grounds of Appeal

5. (1) The grounds of appeal must identify as concisely as possible the respects in which the judgment of the court below is –

(a) wrong; or

(b) unjust because of a serious procedural or other irregularity,

as required by rule 52.11(3).

(2) The reasons why the decision under appeal is wrong or unjust must not be included in the grounds of appeal and must be confined to the skeleton argument.

Second appeals

5A An application to make a second appeal must identify in the grounds of
appeal –
(1) the important point of principle or practice, or
(2) the compelling reason
which is said to justify the grant of permission to appeal.

Non-availability of documents

6. If the appellant is unable to provide any of the necessary documents in time,
the appellant must complete the appeal notice on the basis of the available
documents. The notice may be amended subsequently with the permission of
the court (see paragraph 30).

Service of appellant's notice on the respondent

7.1 The Civil Appeals Office will not serve documents. Where service is required
by the Rules or this Practice Direction, it must be effected by the parties.

7.2 The evidence in support of any application made in an appellant's notice must
be filed and served with the appellant's notice.

7.3 An application for an order to dispense with service of the appellant's notice
under rule 6.28 must be made in the appeal notice or, thereafter, by application notice under Part 23.

SECTION III – RESPONDENT'S NOTICE (RULE 52.5) AND RESPONDENT'S SKELETON ARGUMENT

Respondent's notice

8. (1) A respondent who seeks to appeal against any part of the order made by
the court below must file an appeal notice.
(2) A respondent who seeks a variation of the order of the lower court must
file an appeal notice and must obtain permission to appeal.
(3) A respondent who seeks to contend that the order of the court below
should be upheld for reasons other than those given by that court must
file a respondent's notice.
(4) The notice may be amended subsequently with the permission of the
court (see paragraph 30).

Skeleton argument to be lodged with the respondent's notice

9. A respondent who files a respondent's notice must, within 14 days of filing
the notice, lodge a skeleton argument with the court and serve a copy of the
skeleton argument on every other party to the appeal.
(Provisions in relation to the skeleton argument are set out in paragraph 31.)

Documents to be filed with respondent's notice

10. The respondent must file the following documents with the respondent's
notice –
(a) two additional copies of the respondent's notice for the court; and
(b) one copy each for the appellant and any other respondents.

Applications within respondent's notice

11. (1) A respondent may include an application within a respondent's notice.
(2) The parties must consider whether it would be more convenient for any

application to be listed with the appeal or whether the application needs to be considered in advance.

(3) Where parties consider that the time estimate for the appeal will be affected by listing the application with the appeal, they must inform the court without delay.

Time limits: rule 52.5(4) and (5)

12. Where an extension of time is required, the respondent must apply in the respondent's notice and explain the delay.

Respondent's skeleton argument (where no respondent's notice filed)

13. (1) In all cases where the respondent is legally represented and proposes to address the court, the respondent must lodge and serve a skeleton argument.

(2) A respondent's skeleton argument must be lodged and served in accordance with Part 1 of the Timetable in Section 5.

(Provisions in relation to the skeleton argument are set out in paragraph 31.)

SECTION IV – PROCEDURE WHERE PERMISSION TO APPEAL IS SOUGHT FROM THE COURT OF APPEAL

Documents for use on an application for permission

14. (1) Within 14 days of filing the appeal notice the appellant must lodge a bundle containing only those documents which are necessary for the court to determine that application.

(2) The bundle of documents must–
   (a) be paginated and in chronological order;
   (b) contain an index at the front.

Determination of applications for permission to appeal

15. (1) Applications for permission to appeal will generally be considered by the court without a hearing in the first instance. The court will notify the parties of the decision and the reasons for it.

(2) If permission is refused the appellant is entitled to have the decision reconsidered at an oral hearing, except where rule 52.3(4A) (applications totally without merit) applies. The hearing may be before the same judge.

(3) A request for the decision to be reconsidered at an oral hearing must be filed within 7 days after service of the letter giving notice that permission has been refused. A copy of the request must be served by the appellant on the respondent at the same time.

Permission hearing

16. (1) Where an appellant who is represented makes a request for a decision to be reconsidered at an oral hearing, the appellant's advocate must at least 4 days before the hearing file a brief written statement –
   (a) informing the court and the respondent of the points which are to be raised at the hearing; and
   (b) setting out the reasons why permission should be granted notwithstanding the reasons given for the refusal of permission.

(2) The court will notify the respondent of the hearing but the respondent is not expected to attend unless the court so directs.

(3) If the court directs the respondent to attend the permission hearing, the appellant must supply the respondent with a copy of the skeleton argument and any documents to which the appellant intends to refer.

Appellant in receipt of services funded by the Legal Services Commission applying for permission to appeal

17. Where the appellant is in receipt of services funded by the Legal Services Commission and permission to appeal has been refused by the court without a hearing, the appellant must send a copy of the court's reasons for refusing permission to the Legal Services Commission as soon as it has been received. The court will require confirmation that this has been done if a hearing is requested to re-consider the application.

Limited permission: rule 52.3

18. (1) If, under rule 52.3(7), the court grants permission to appeal on some issues only, it will –

   (a) refuse permission on any remaining issues; or

   (b) adjourn the application in respect of those issues to the hearing of the appeal.

(2) If the court adjourns the application under sub-paragraph (1)(b), the appellant must inform the court and the respondent in writing, within 14 days after the date of the court's order, whether the appellant intends to pursue the application. If the appellant intends to pursue the application, the parties must include in any time estimate for the appeal hearing an allowance for the adjourned application.

(3) If the court refuses permission to appeal on the remaining issues without a hearing and the applicant wishes to have that decision reconsidered at an oral hearing, the time limit in rule 52.3(5) applies. Any application for an extension of this time should be made promptly. When hearing the appeal on the issues for which permission has been given the court will not normally grant an application to extend time in relation to the remaining issues.

Respondent need not take any action when served with an appellant's notice

19. Unless the court directs otherwise, a respondent need not take any action when served with an appellant's notice until notified that permission to appeal has been granted.

Respondent's costs of permission applications

20. (1) In most cases an application for permission to appeal will be determined without the need for the respondent to file submissions or attend a hearing. In such circumstances an order for costs will not normally be made in favour of a respondent who voluntarily makes submissions or attends a hearing.

(2) If the court directs the respondent to file submissions or attend a hearing, it will normally award costs to the respondent if permission is refused.

SECTION V – TIMETABLE

21. The timetable for the conduct of an appeal after the date of the listing window notification is set out below:

Timetable Part 1 – Listing window notification to lodging bundle		
Period within which step is to be taken	**Action**	**Cross reference to relevant provisions in this Practice Direction**
Within 14 days of service of: i. the appellant's notice if permission has been given by the lower court or is not needed; ii. notification that permission has been granted by the Court of Appeal; or iii. notification that the permission application will be listed with the appeal to follow	**Respondent's notice** (if any) must be filed and served	Paragraph 8 (respondent's notice)
Within 14 days of filing a respondent's notice	**If respondent has filed a respondent's notice,** respondent must lodge and serve a skeleton argument on every other party	Paragraph 9 (skeleton argument to be lodged with the respondent's notice or within 14 days of filing respondent's notice)
7 days after date of listing window notification	Appellant must serve **proposed bundle index** on every respondent	Paragraph 27 (bundle of documents)
14 days after date of listing window notification	**Appeal questionnaire** must be filed and served on every respondent	Paragraph 1 (listing window notification defined) Paragraph 23 (Appeal questionnaire)
7 days after service of Appellant's Appeal Questionnaire	**If a respondent disagrees with appellant's time estimate**, that respondent must file and serve on every other party its own time estimate	Paragraph 24 (time estimate)
21 days after listing window notification	**Appeal skeleton:** appellant must serve on every respondent an appeal skeleton (without bundle cross references)	Paragraph 31 (skeleton argument)

Timetable Part 1 – Listing window notification to lodging bundle		
Period within which step is to be taken	Action	Cross reference to relevant provisions in this Practice Direction
21 days after date of the listing window notification	**Agree bundle**: the respondent must either agree the contents of the appeal bundle or notify the appellant of the documents that the respondent considers should be included in, or removed from, the appeal bundle by sending a revised index. If there is no agreement in relation to inclusion of a particular document, it must be placed in a supplemental bundle prepared by the party who has proposed its inclusion.	Paragraph 27 (bundle of documents)
		Paragraph 28 (bundle: Appeals from Upper Tribunal Immigration and Asylum Chamber)
42 days after date of listing window notification	**Where Respondent has not filed a respondent's notice**, respondent must lodge skeleton argument and serve on every other party	Paragraph 13 (respondent's skeleton argument (where no Respondent's Notice filed))
		Paragraph 31 (skeleton argument)

Timetable Part 2 – Steps to be taken once hearing date fixed: lodging bundles, supplemental skeletons and bundles of authorities		
Time before hearing date when step is to be taken	Action	Cross reference to relevant provisions in this Practice Direction
No later than 42 days before the appeal hearing	Lodge, as directed by the court, the appropriate number of appeal bundles and serve a copy on all other parties to the	Paragraph 27 (bundle of documents)
		Paragraph 28 (bundle: Appeals from Upper Tribunal Immigration and Asylum Chamber)
No later than14 days before date of appeal hearing	Appellant must lodge and serve replacement skeleton argument	Paragraph 1 (replacement skeleton argument defined)
		Paragraph 31 (skeleton argument content, length and format)
		Paragraph 32 (supplementary skeleton argument)
No later than 7 days before the date of the hearing	Respondent must lodge and serve replacement skeleton argument	Paragraph 1 (replacement skeleton argument defined)
		Paragraph 32 (supplementary skeleton argument)
No later than 7 days before date of appeal hearing	Bundles of authorities must be lodged	Paragraph 29 (bundle of authorities)
No later than 7 days before the date of the hearing	Every document needed for the appeal hearing (if not already lodged or filed) must be lodged or filed	

SECTION VI – MANAGEMENT OF THE APPEAL

Listing and hear-by dates

22. The hear-by date is the last day of the listing window.

Appeal Questionnaire

23. The appellant must complete and file the Appeal Questionnaire and serve it on the respondent within 14 days after the date of the listing window notification.

Time estimates

24. If the respondent disagrees with the appellant's time estimate, the respondent must inform the court within 7 days of service of the Appeal Questionnaire.

In the absence of such notification the respondent will be deemed to have accepted the appellant's time estimate.

Multiple appeals

25. (1) If two or more appeals are pending in the same or related proceedings, the parties must seek directions as to whether they should be heard together or consecutively by the same judges.

(2) Whether appeals are heard together or consecutively, the parties must attempt to agree a single appeal bundle or set of bundles for all the appeals and seek directions if they are unable to do so.

Expedition

26. (1) The court may direct that the hearing of an appeal be expedited.

(2) The court will deal with requests for expedition without a hearing. Requests for expedition must be made by letter setting out succinctly the grounds on which expedition is sought. The letter (or, if time is particularly short, email) must be marked for the immediate attention of the court and copied to the other parties to the appeal.

(3) If an expedited appeal hearing is required as a matter of extreme urgency, the Civil Appeals Office must be informed as soon as possible. If necessary, parties or their legal representatives should call the Royal Courts of Justice switchboard on 020 7947 6000 and ask a member of the security staff to contact the Duty Judge.

(4) An expedited hearing will be listed at the convenience of the court and not according to the availability of counsel.

SECTION VII – BUNDLES, AMENDMENT AND SKELETON ARGUMENTS

Bundle of documents

27. (1) The appellant must lodge an appeal bundle which must contain only those documents relevant to the appeal. The bundle must –

(a) be paginated and in chronological order;

(b) contain an index at the front.

(2) **Documents relevant to the appeal:** Subject to any order made by the court, the following documents must be included in the appeal bundle –

(a) a copy of the appellant's notice;

(b) a copy of any respondent's notice;

(c) a copy of any appellant's or respondent's skeleton argument;

(d) a copy of the order under appeal;

(e) a copy of the order of the lower court granting or refusing permission to appeal together with a copy of the judge's reasons, if any, for granting or refusing permission;

(f) a copy of any order allocating the case to a track;

(g) the approved transcript of the judgment of the lower court (except in appeals in cases which were allocated to the small claims track but subject to any order of the court).

(3) **Documents which may be included:** The following documents should also be considered for inclusion in the appeal bundle but should be included only where relevant to the appeal –

(a) statements of case;

(b) application notices;

(c) other orders made in the case;

(d) a chronology of relevant events;

(e) witness statements made in support of any application made in the appellant's notice;

(f) other witness statements;

(g) other documents which the appellant or respondent consider relevant to the appeal.

(4) **Bundles not to include originals:** Unless otherwise directed, the appeal bundle should not include original material such as original documents, photographs and recorded media. Such material should be provided to the court, if necessary, at the hearing.

(5) **Destruction of bundles:** Bundles lodged with the court will not be returned to the parties but will be destroyed in the confidential waste system at the conclusion of the proceedings and without further notification.

Appeals from the Upper Tribunal Immigration and Asylum Chamber

28. (1) In an appeal from the Immigration and Asylum Chamber of the Upper Tribunal (other than an appeal relating to a claim for judicial review) –

(a) the Immigration and Asylum Chamber of the Upper Tribunal, upon request, shall send to the Civil Appeals Office copies of the documents which were before the relevant Tribunal when it considered the appeal;

(b) the appellant is not required to file an appeal bundle;

(c) the appellant must file with the appellant's notice the documents specified in paragraph 4(3)(a) to (e) and (g) of this Practice Direction.

Bundle of authorities

29. (1) After consultation with any opposing advocate, the appellant's advocate must file a bundle containing photocopies of the authorities upon which each party will rely at the hearing.

(2) The most authoritative report of each authority must be used in accordance with the Practice Direction on Citation of Authorities (2012) and must have the relevant passages marked by a vertical line in the margin.

(3) Photocopies of authorities should not be in landscape format and the type should not be reduced in size.

(4) The bundle should not–

(a) include authorities for propositions not in dispute; or

(b) contain more than 10 authorities unless the issues in the appeal justify more extensive citation.

(5) A bundle of authorities must bear a certificate by the advocates responsible for arguing the case that the requirements of sub-paragraphs (2) to (4) of this paragraph have been complied with in respect of each authority included.

Amendment of appeal notice: rule 52.8

30. (1) An appeal notice may not be amended without the permission of the court.

(2) An application for permission to amend made before permission to appeal has been considered will normally be determined without a hearing.

(3) An application for permission to amend (after permission to appeal has been granted) and any submissions in opposition will normally be dealt with at the hearing unless that would cause unnecessary expense or delay, in which case a request should be made for the application to amend to be heard in advance.

(4) Legal representatives must–
  (a) inform the court at the time they make the application if the existing time estimate is affected by the proposed amendment; and
  (b) attempt to agree any revised time estimate no later than 7 days after service of the application.

Skeleton Argument

31. (1) Any skeleton argument must comply with the provisions of Section 5 of Practice Direction 52A and must–
  (a) not normally exceed 25 pages (excluding front sheets and back sheets);
  (b) be printed on A4 paper in not less than 12 point font and 1.5 line spacing.

  (2) Where an appellant has filed a skeleton argument in support of an application for permission to appeal, the same skeleton argument may be relied upon in the appeal or the appellant may file an appeal skeleton argument (Timetable Section 5, Part 1).

  (3) At the hearing the court may refuse to hear argument on a point not included in a skeleton argument filed within the prescribed time.

  (4) The court may disallow the cost of preparing an appeal skeleton argument which does not comply with these requirements or was not filed within the prescribed time.

Supplementary skeleton arguments

32. (1) A party may file a supplementary skeleton argument only where strictly necessary and only with the permission of the court.

  (2) If a party wishes to rely on a supplementary skeleton argument, it must be lodged and served as soon as practicable. It must be accompanied by a request for permission setting out the reasons why a supplementary skeleton argument is necessary and why it could not reasonably have been lodged earlier.

  (3) Only exceptionally will the court allow the use of a supplementary skeleton argument if lodged later than 7 days before the hearing.

PART 54: JUDICIAL REVIEW AND STATUTORY REVIEW

Contents of this part

I JUDICIAL REVIEW

Scope and interpretation

54.1 (1) This Section of this Part contains rules about judicial review.

(2) In this Section –

   (a) a 'claim for judicial review' means a claim to review the lawfulness of–

   (i) an enactment; or

   (ii) a decision, action or failure to act in relation to the exercise of a public function.

   (b) an order of mandamus is called a 'mandatory order';

   (c) an order of prohibition is called a 'prohibiting order';

   (d) an order of certiorari is called a 'quashing order';

   (e) 'the judicial review procedure' means the Part 8 procedure as modified by this Section;

   (f) 'interested party' means any person (other than the claimant and defendant) who is directly affected by the claim; and

   (g) 'court' means the High Court, unless otherwise stated.

(Rule 8.1(6)(b) provides that a rule or practice direction may, in relation to a specified type of proceedings, disapply or modify any of the rules set out in Part 8 as they apply to those proceedings)

Who may exercise the powers of the High Court

54.1A (1) A court officer assigned to the Administrative Court office who is –

   (a) a barrister; or

(b) a solicitor,

may exercise the jurisdiction of the High Court with regard to the matters set out in paragraph (2) with the consent of the President of the Queen's Bench Division.

(2) The matters referred to in paragraph (1) are –
   (a) any matter incidental to any proceedings in the High Court;
   (b) any other matter where there is no substantial dispute between the parties; and
   (c) the dismissal of an appeal or application where a party has failed to comply with any order, rule or practice direction.

(3) A court officer may not decide an application for –
   (a) permission to bring judicial review proceedings;
   (b) an injunction;
   (c) a stay of any proceedings, other than a temporary stay of any order or decision of the lower court over a period when the High Court is not sitting or cannot conveniently be convened, unless the parties seek a stay by consent.

(4) Decisions of a court officer may be made without a hearing.

(5) A party may request any decision of a court officer to be reviewed by a judge of the High Court.

(6) At the request of a party, a hearing will be held to reconsider a decision of a court officer, made without a hearing.

(7) A request under paragraph (5) or (6) must be filed within 7 days after the party is served with notice of the decision.

When this section must be used

54.2 The judicial review procedure must be used in a claim for judicial review where the claimant is seeking–

(a) a mandatory order;

(b) a prohibiting order;

(c) a quashing order; or

(d) an injunction under section 30 of the Supreme Court Act 1981 (restraining a person from acting in any office in which he is not entitled to act).

When this section may be used

54.3 (1) The judicial review procedure may be used in a claim for judicial review where the claimant is seeking–

   (a) a declaration; or

   (b) an injunction

(Section 31(2) of the Supreme Court Act 1981 sets out the circumstances in which the court may grant a declaration or injunction in a claim for judicial review)

(Where the claimant is seeking a declaration or injunction in addition to one of the remedies listed in rule 54.2, the judicial review procedure must be used)

(2) A claim for judicial review may include a claim for damages but may not seek damages alone.

(Section 31(4) of the Supreme Court Act sets out the circumstances in which the court may award damages on a claim for judicial review)

Permission required

54.4 The court's permission to proceed is required in a claim for judicial review whether started under this Section or transferred to the Administrative Court.

Time limit for filing claim form

54.5 (1) The claim form must be filed–

(a) promptly; and

(b) in any event not later than 3 months after the grounds to make the claim first arose.

(2) The time limit in this rule may not be extended by agreement between the parties.

(3) This rule does not apply when any other enactment specifies a shorter time limit for making the claim for judicial review.

Claim form

54.6 (1) In addition to the matters set out in rule 8.2 (contents of the claim form) the claimant must also state–

(a) the name and address of any person he considers to be an interested party;

(b) that he is requesting permission to proceed with a claim for judicial review; and

(c) any remedy (including any interim remedy) he is claiming; and

(d) where appropriate, the grounds on which it is contended that the claim is an Aarhus Convention claim.

(Rules 45.41 to 45.44 make provision about costs in the Aarhus Convention claim).

(Part 25 sets out how to apply for an interim remedy)

(2) The claim form must be accompanied by the documents required by the relevant practice direction.

Service of claim form

54.7 The claim form must be served on–

(a) the defendant; and

(b) unless the court otherwise directs, any person the claimant considers to be an interested party,

within 7 days after the date of issue.

Judicial review of decisions of the Upper Tribunal

54.7A (1) This rule applies where an application is made, following refusal by the Upper Tribunal of permission to appeal against a decision of the First Tier Tribunal, for judicial review–

(a) of the decision of the Upper Tribunal refusing permission to appeal; or

(b) which relates to the decision of the First Tier Tribunal which was the subject of the application for permission to appeal.

(2) Where this rule applies –

(a) the application may not include any other claim, whether against the Upper Tribunal or not; and

(b) any such other claim must be the subject of a separate application.

(3) The claim form and the supporting documents required by paragraph (4) must be filed no later than 16 days after the date on which notice of the Upper Tribunal's decision was sent to the applicant.

(4) The supporting documents are–
   (a) the decision of the Upper Tribunal to which the application relates, and any document giving reasons for the decision;
   (b) the grounds of appeal to the Upper Tribunal and any documents which were sent with them;
   (c) the decision of the First Tier Tribunal, the application to that Tribunal for permission to appeal and its reasons for refusing permission; and
   (d) any other documents essential to the claim.

(5) The claim form and supporting documents must be served on the Upper Tribunal and any other interested party no later than 7 days after the date of issue.

(6) The Upper Tribunal and any person served with the claim form who wishes to take part in the proceedings for judicial review must, no later than 21 days after service of the claim form, file and serve on the applicant and any other party an acknowledgment of service in the relevant practice form.

(7) The court will give permission to proceed only if it considers –
   (a) that there is an arguable case, which has a reasonable prospect of success, that both the decision of the Upper Tribunal refusing permission to appeal and the decision of the First Tier Tribunal against which permission to appeal was sought are wrong in law; and
   (b) that either –
      (i) the claim raises an important point of principle or practice; or
      (ii) there is some other compelling reason to hear it.

(8) If the application for permission is refused on paper without an oral hearing, rule 54.12(3) (request for reconsideration at a hearing) does not apply.

(9) If permission to apply for judicial review is granted –
   (a) if the Upper Tribunal or any interested party wishes there to be a hearing of the substantive application, it must make its request for such a hearing no later than 14 days after service of the order granting permission; and
   (b) if no request for a hearing is made within that period, the court will make a final order quashing the refusal of permission without a further hearing.

(10) The power to make a final order under paragraph (9)(b) may be exercised by the Master of the Crown Office or a Master of the Administrative Court.

Acknowledgment of service

54.8 (1) Any person served with the claim form who wishes to take part in the judicial review must file an acknowledgment of service in the relevant practice form in accordance with the following provisions of this rule.

(2) Any acknowledgment of service must be–
   (a) filed not more than 21 days after service of the claim form; and
   (b) served on–
      (i) the claimant; and

(ii) subject to any direction under rule 54.7(b), any other person named in the claim form,

as soon as practicable and, in any event, not later than 7 days after it is filed.

(3) The time limits under this rule may not be extended by agreement between the parties.

(4) The acknowledgment of service–
   (a) must–
      (i) where the person filing it intends to contest the claim, set out a summary of his grounds for doing so; and
      (ii) state the name and address of any person the person filing it considers to be an interested party; and
   (b) may include or be accompanied by an application for directions.

(5) Rule 10.3(2) does not apply.

Failure to file acknowledgment of service

54.9 (1) Where a person served with the claim form has failed to file an acknowledgment of service in accordance with rule 54.8, he–
   (a) may not take part in a hearing to decide whether permission should be given unless the court allows him to do so; but
   (b) provided he complies with rule 54.14 or any other direction of the court regarding the filing and service of–
      (i) detailed grounds for contesting the claim or supporting it on additional grounds; and
      (ii) any written evidence,
   may take part in the hearing of the judicial review.

(2) Where that person takes part in the hearing of the judicial review, the court may take his failure to file an acknowledgment of service into account when deciding what order to make about costs.

(3) Rule 8.4 does not apply.

Permission given

54.10 (1) Where permission to proceed is given the court may also give directions.

(2) Directions under paragraph (1) may include a stay of proceedings to which the claim relates.

(Rule 3.7 provides a sanction for the non-payment of the fee payable when permission to proceed has been given)

Service of order giving or refusing permission

54.11 The court will serve–
   (a) the order giving or refusing permission; and
   (b) any directions,
on –
   (i) the claimant;
   (ii) the defendant; and
   (iii) any other person who filed an acknowledgment of service.

Permission decision without a hearing

54.12 (1) This rule applies where the court, without a hearing–
   (a) refuses permission to proceed; or
   (b) gives permission to proceed–

(i) subject to conditions; or

(ii) on certain grounds only.

(2) The court will serve its reasons for making the decision when it serves the order giving or refusing permission in accordance with rule 54.11.

(3) The claimant may not appeal but may request the decision to be reconsidered at a hearing.

(4) A request under paragraph (3) must be filed within 7 days after service of the reasons under paragraph (2).

(5) The claimant, defendant and any other person who has filed an acknowledgment of service will be given at least 2 days' notice of the hearing date.

(6) The court may give directions requiring the proceedings be heard by a Divisional Court.

Defendant, etc, may not apply to set aside

54.13 Neither the defendant nor any other person served with the claim form may apply to set aside an order giving permission to proceed.

Response

54.14 (1) A defendant and any other person served with the claim form who wishes to contest the claim or support it on additional grounds must file and serve–

(a) detailed grounds for contesting the claim or supporting it on additional grounds; and

(b) any written evidence,

within 35 days after service of the order giving permission.

(2) The following rules do not apply–

(a) rule 8.5(3) and 8.5(4)(defendant to file and serve written evidence at the same time as acknowledgment of service); and

(b) rule 8.5 (5) and 8.5(6) (claimant to file and serve any reply within 14 days).

Where claimant seeks to rely on additional grounds

54.15 The court's permission is required if a claimant seeks to rely on grounds other than those for which he has been given permission to proceed.

Evidence

54.16 (1) Rule 8.6(1) does not apply.

(2) No written evidence may be relied on unless–

(a) it has been served in accordance with any–

(i) rule under this Section; or

(ii) direction of the court; or

(b) the court gives permission.

Court's powers to hear any person

54.17 (1) Any person may apply for permission–

(a) to file evidence; or

(b) make representations at the hearing of the judicial review.

(2) An application under paragraph (1) should be made promptly.

Judicial review may be decided without a hearing

54.18 The court may decide the claim for judicial review without a hearing where all the parties agree.

Court's powers in respect of quashing orders

54.19 (1) This rule applies where the court makes a quashing order in respect of the decision to which the claim relates.

(2) The court may–

    (a) (i)   remit the matter to the decision-maker; and

        (ii) direct it to reconsider the matter and reach a decision in accordance with the judgment of the court; or

    (b) in so far as any enactment permits, substitute its own decision for the decision to which the claim relates.

(Section 31 of the Supreme Court Act 1981[23] enables the High Court, subject to certain conditions, to substitute its own decision for the decision in question.)

Transfer

54.20 The court may

    (a) order a claim to continue as if it had not been started under this Section; and

    (b) where it does so, give directions about the future management of the claim.

(Part 30 (transfer) applies to transfers to and from the Administrative Court)

---

23 Section 31 is amended by section 141 of the Tribunals, Courts and Enforcement Act 2007.

PRACTICE DIRECTION 54A – JUDICIAL REVIEW

THIS PRACTICE DIRECTION SUPPLEMENTS PART 54

SECTION I – GENERAL PROVISIONS RELATING TO JUDICIAL REVIEW

1.1 In addition to Part 54 and this practice direction attention is drawn to:
- section 31 of the Senior Courts Act 1981; and
- the Human Rights Act 1998

The Court

2.1 Part 54 claims for judicial review are dealt with in the Administrative Court. (Practice Direction 54D) contains provisions about where a claim for judicial review may be started, administered and heard.)

2.2 Omitted

2.3 Omitted

2.4 Omitted

3.1 Omitted

3.2 Omitted

Rule 54.5 – Time limit for filing claim form

4.1 Where the claim is for a quashing order in respect of a judgment, order or conviction, the date when the grounds to make the claim first arose, for the purposes of rule 54.5(1)(b), is the date of that judgment, order or conviction.

Rule 54.6 – Claim form
Interested parties

5.1 Where the claim for judicial review relates to proceedings in a court or tribunal, any other parties to those proceedings must be named in the claim form as interested parties under rule 54.6(1)(a) (and therefore served with the claim form under rule 54.7(b)).

5.2 For example, in a claim by a defendant in a criminal case in the Magistrates or Crown Court for judicial review of a decision in that case, the prosecution must always be named as an interested party.

Human rights

5.3 Where the claimant is seeking to raise any issue under the Human Rights Act 1998, or seeks a remedy available under that Act, the claim form must include the information required by paragraph 15 of Practice Direction 16.

Devolution issues

5.4 Where the claimant intends to raise a devolution issue, the claim form must:
(1) specify that the applicant wishes to raise a devolution issue and identify the relevant provisions of the Government of Wales Act 2006, the Northern Ireland Act 1998 or the Scotland Act 1998; and
(2) contain a summary of the facts, circumstances and points of law on the basis of which it is alleged that a devolution issue arises.

5.5 In this practice direction 'devolution issue' has the same meaning as in paragraph 1, Schedule 9 to the Government of Wales Act 2006, paragraph 1, Schedule 10 to the Northern Ireland Act 1998; and paragraph 1, Schedule 6 to the Scotland Act 1998.

Claim form

5.6 The claim form must include or be accompanied by –

(1) a detailed statement of the claimant's grounds for bringing the claim for judicial review;

(2) a statement of the facts relied on;

(3) any application to extend the time limit for filing the claim form;

(4) any application for directions.

5.7 In addition, the claim form must be accompanied by

(1) any written evidence in support of the claim or application to extend time;

(2) a copy of any order that the claimant seeks to have quashed;

(3) where the claim for judicial review relates to a decision of a court or tribunal, an approved copy of the reasons for reaching that decision;

(4) copies of any documents on which the claimant proposes to rely;

(5) copies of any relevant statutory material; and

(6) a list of essential documents for advance reading by the court (with page references to the passages relied on).

5.8 Where it is not possible to file all the above documents, the claimant must indicate which documents have not been filed and the reasons why they are not currently available.

Bundle of documents

5.9 The claimant must file two copies of a paginated and indexed bundle containing all the documents referred to in paragraphs 5.6 and 5.7.

5.10 Attention is drawn to rules 8.5(1) and 8.5(7).

Rule 54.7 – Service of claim form

6.1 Except as required by rules 54.11 or 54.12(2), the Administrative Court will not serve documents and service must be effected by the parties.

6.2 Where the defendant or interested party to the claim for judicial review is –

(a) the Immigration and Asylum Chamber of the First-tier Tribunal, the address for service of the claim form is Official Correspondence Unit, PO Box 6987, Leicester, LE1 6ZX or fax number 0116 249 4240;

(b) the Crown, service of the claim form must be effected on the solicitor acting for the relevant government department as if the proceedings were civil proceedings as defined in the Crown Proceedings Act 1947.

(Practice Direction 66 gives the list published under section 17 of the Crown Proceedings Act 1947 of the solicitors acting in civil proceedings (as defined in that Act) for the different government departments on whom service is to be effected, and of their addresses.)

(Part 6 contains provisions about the service of claim forms.)

Rule 54.8 – Acknowledgment of service

7.1 Attention is drawn to rule 8.3(2) and the relevant practice direction and to rule 10.5.

Rule 54.10 – Permission given
Directions

8.1 Case management directions under rule 54.10(1) may include directions about serving the claim form and any evidence on other persons.

8.2 Where a claim is made under the Human Rights Act 1998, a direction may be made for giving notice to the Crown or joining the Crown as a party. Attention is drawn to rule 19.4A and paragraph 6 of Practice Direction 19A.

8.3 Omitted

Permission without a hearing

8.4 The court will generally, in the first instance, consider the question of permission without a hearing.

Permission hearing

8.5 Neither the defendant nor any other interested party need attend a hearing on the question of permission unless the court directs otherwise.

8.6 Where the defendant or any party does attend a hearing, the court will not generally make an order for costs against the claimant.

Rule 54.11 – Service of order giving or refusing permission

9.1 An order refusing permission or giving it subject to conditions or on certain grounds only must set out or be accompanied by the court's reasons for coming to that decision.

Rule 54.14 – Response

10.1 Where the party filing the detailed grounds intends to rely on documents not already filed, he must file a paginated bundle of those documents when he files the detailed grounds.

Rule 54.15 – Where claimant seeks to rely on additional grounds

11.1 Where the claimant intends to apply to rely on additional grounds at the hearing of the claim for judicial review, he must give notice to the court and to any other person served with the claim form no later than 7 clear days before the hearing (or the warned date where appropriate).

Rule 54.16 – Evidence

12.1 Disclosure is not required unless the court orders otherwise.

Rule 54.17 – Court's powers to hear any person

13.1 Where all the parties consent, the court may deal with an application under rule 54.17 without a hearing.

13.2 Where the court gives permission for a person to file evidence or make representations at the hearing of the claim for judicial review, it may do so on conditions and may give case management directions.

13.3 An application for permission should be made by letter to the Administrative Court office, identifying the claim, explaining who the applicant is and indicating why and in what form the applicant wants to participate in the hearing.

13.4 If the applicant is seeking a prospective order as to costs, the letter should say what kind of order and on what grounds.

13.5 Applications to intervene must be made at the earliest reasonable opportunity, since it will usually be essential not to delay the hearing.

Rule 54.20 – Transfer

14.1 Attention is drawn to rule 30.5.

14.2 In deciding whether a claim is suitable for transfer to the Administrative

Court, the court will consider whether it raises issues of public law to which Part 54 should apply.

Skeleton arguments

15.1 The claimant must file and serve a skeleton argument not less than 21 working days before the date of the hearing of the judicial review (or the warned date).

15.2 The defendant and any other party wishing to make representations at the hearing of the judicial review must file and serve a skeleton argument not less than 14 working days before the date of the hearing of the judicial review (or the warned date).

15.3 Skeleton arguments must contain:
   (1) a time estimate for the complete hearing, including delivery of judgment;
   (2) a list of issues;
   (3) a list of the legal points to be taken (together with any relevant authorities with page references to the passages relied on);
   (4) a chronology of events (with page references to the bundle of documents (see paragraph 16.1);
   (5) a list of essential documents for the advance reading of the court (with page references to the passages relied on) (if different from that filed with the claim form) and a time estimate for that reading; and
   (6) a list of persons referred to.

Bundle of documents to be filed

16.1 The claimant must file a paginated and indexed bundle of all relevant documents required for the hearing of the judicial review when he files his skeleton argument.

16.2 The bundle must also include those documents required by the defendant and any other party who is to make representations at the hearing.

Agreed final order

17.1 If the parties agree about the final order to be made in a claim for judicial review, the claimant must file at the court a document (with 2 copies) signed by all the parties setting out the terms of the proposed agreed order together with a short statement of the matters relied on as justifying the proposed agreed order and copies of any authorities or statutory provisions relied on.

17.2 The court will consider the documents referred to in paragraph 17.1 and will make the order if satisfied that the order should be made.

17.3 If the court is not satisfied that the order should be made, a hearing date will be set.

17.4 Where the agreement relates to an order for costs only, the parties need only file a document signed by all the parties setting out the terms of the proposed order.

SECTION II – APPLICATIONS FOR PERMISSION TO APPLY FOR JUDICIAL REVIEW IN IMMIGRATION AND ASYLUM CASES – CHALLENGING REMOVAL

18.1 (1) This Section applies where –
      (a) a person has been served with a copy of directions for his removal from the United Kingdom by the UK Border Agency of the Home Office and notified that this Section applies; and

(b) that person makes an application for permission to apply for judicial review before his removal takes effect.

(2) This Section does not prevent a person from applying for judicial review after he has been removed.

(3) The requirements contained in this Section of this Practice Direction are additional to those contained elsewhere in the Practice Direction.

18.2 (1) A person who makes an application for permission to apply for judicial review must file a claim form and a copy at court, and the claim form must –

(a) indicate on its face that this Section of the Practice Direction applies; and

(b) be accompanied by –

   (i) a copy of the removal directions and the decision to which the application relates; and

   (ii) any document served with the removal directions including any document which contains the UK Border Agency's factual summary of the case; and

(c) contain or be accompanied by the detailed statement of the claimant's grounds for bringing the claim for judicial review; or

(d) if the claimant is unable to comply with paragraph (b) or (c), contain or be accompanied by a statement of the reasons why.

(2) The claimant must, immediately upon issue of the claim, send copies of the issued claim form and accompanying documents to the address specified by the UK Border Agency.

(Rule 54.7 also requires the defendant to be served with the claim form within 7 days of the date of issue. Rule 6.10 provides that service on a Government Department must be effected on the solicitor acting for that Department, which in the case of the UK Border Agency is the Treasury Solicitor. The address for the Treasury Solicitor may be found in the Annex to Part 66 of these Rules.)

18.3 Where the claimant has not complied with paragraph 18.2(1)(b) or (c) and has provided reasons why he is unable to comply, and the court has issued the claim form, the Administrative Court –

(a) will refer the matter to a Judge for consideration as soon as practicable; and

(b) will notify the parties that it has done so.

18.4 If, upon a refusal to grant permission to apply for judicial review, the Court indicates that the application is clearly without merit, that indication will be included in the order refusing permission.

SECTION III – APPLICATIONS FOR PERMISSION TO APPLY FOR JUDICIAL REVIEW OF DECISIONS OF THE UPPER TRIBUNAL

19.1 A person who makes an application for permission to apply for judicial review of the decision of the Upper Tribunal refusing permission to appeal must file a claim form which must –

(a) state on its face that the application is made under Rule 54. 7A;

(b) set out succinctly the grounds on which it is argued that the criteria in Rule 54.7A(7) are met; and

(c) be accompanied by the supporting documents required under Rule 54.7A(4).

19.2 If the Upper Tribunal or any interested party wishes there to be a hearing of the substantive application under Rule 54.7A(9), it must make its request in writing (by letter copied to the claimant) for such a hearing no later than 14 days after service of the order granting permission.

PRACTICE DIRECTION 54C – REFERENCES BY THE LEGAL SERVICES COMMISSION

References by the Legal Services Commission

1.1 This Practice Direction applies where the Legal Services Commission ('the Commission') refers to the High Court a question that arises on a review of a decision about an individual's financial eligibility for a representation order in criminal proceedings under the Criminal Defence Service (Financial Eligibility) Regulations 2006.

1.2 A reference of a question by the Legal Services Commission must be made to the Administrative Court.

1.3 Part 52 does not apply to a review under this paragraph.

1.4 The Commission must –
(a) file at the court –
  (i) the individual's applications for a representation order and for a review, and any supporting documents;
  (ii) a copy of the question on which the court's decision is sought; and
  (iii) a statement of the Commission's observations on the question; and
(b) serve a copy of the question and the statement on the individual.

1.5 The individual may file representations on the question at the court within 7 days after service on him of the copy of the question and the statement.

1.6 The question will be decided without a hearing unless the court directs otherwise.

PRACTICE DIRECTION 54D – ADMINISTRATIVE COURT (VENUE)

THIS PRACTICE DIRECTION SUPPLEMENTS PART 54

Scope and purpose

1.1 This Practice Direction concerns the place in which a claim before the Administrative Court should be started and administered and the venue at which it will be determined.

1.2 This Practice Direction is intended to facilitate access to justice by enabling cases to be administered and determined in the most appropriate location. To achieve this purpose it provides flexibility in relation to where claims are to be administered and enables claims to be transferred to different venues.

Venue – general provisions

2.1 The claim form in proceedings in the Administrative Court may be issued at the Administrative Court Office of the High Court at –

(1) the Royal Courts of Justice in London; or

(2) at the District Registry of the High Court at Birmingham, Cardiff, Leeds, or Manchester unless the claim is one of the excepted classes of claim set out in paragraph 3 of this Practice Direction which may only be started and determined at the Royal Courts of Justice in London.

2.2 Any claim started in Birmingham will normally be determined at a court in the Midland region (geographically covering the area of the Midland Circuit); in Cardiff in Wales; in Leeds in the North-Eastern Region (geographically covering the area of the North Eastern Circuit); in London at the Royal Courts of Justice; and in Manchester, in the North-Western Region (geographically covering the Northern Circuit).

Excepted classes of claim

3.1 The excepted classes of claim referred to in paragraph 2.1(2) are –

(1) proceedings to which Part 76 or Part 79 applies, and for the avoidance of doubt –

(a) proceedings relating to control orders (within the meaning of Part 76);

(b) financial restrictions proceedings (within the meaning of Part 79);

(c) proceedings relating to terrorism or alleged terrorists (where that is a relevant feature of the claim); and

(d) proceedings in which a special advocate is or is to be instructed;

(2) proceedings to which RSC Order 115 applies;

(3) proceedings under the Proceeds of Crime Act 2002;

(4) appeals to the Administrative Court under the Extradition Act 2003;

(5) proceedings which must be heard by a Divisional Court; and

(6) proceedings relating to the discipline of solicitors.

3.2 If a claim form is issued at an Administrative Court office other than in London and includes one of the excepted classes of claim, the proceedings will be transferred to London.

Urgent applications

4.1 During the hours when the court is open, where an urgent application needs to be made to the Administrative Court outside London, the application must be made to the judge designated to deal with such applications in the relevant District Registry.

4.2 Any urgent application to the Administrative Court during the hours when the court is closed, must be made to the duty out of hours High Court judge by telephoning 020 7947 6000.

Assignment to another venue

5.1 The proceedings may be transferred from the office at which the claim form was issued to another office. Such transfer is a judicial act.

5.2 The general expectation is that proceedings will be administered and determined in the region with which the claimant has the closest connection, subject to the following considerations as applicable –

(1) any reason expressed by any party for preferring a particular venue;

(2) the region in which the defendant, or any relevant office or department of the defendant, is based;

(3) the region in which the claimant's legal representatives are based;

(4) the ease and cost of travel to a hearing;

(5) the availability and suitability of alternative means of attending a hearing (for example, by videolink);

(6) the extent and nature of media interest in the proceedings in any particular locality;

(7) the time within which it is appropriate for the proceedings to be determined;

(8) whether it is desirable to administer or determine the claim in another region in the light of the volume of claims issued at, and the capacity, resources and workload of, the court at which it is issued;

(9) whether the claim raises issues sufficiently similar to those in another outstanding claim to make it desirable that it should be determined together with, or immediately following, that other claim; and

(10) whether the claim raises devolution issues and for that reason whether it should more appropriately be determined in London or Cardiff.

5.3 (1) When an urgent application is made under paragraph 4.1 or 4.2, this will not by itself decide the venue for the further administration or determination of the claim.

(2) The court dealing with the urgent application may direct that the case be assigned to a particular venue.

(3) When an urgent application is made under paragraph 4.2, and the court does not make a direction under sub-paragraph (2), the claim will be assigned in the first place to London but may be reassigned to another venue at a later date.

5.4 The court may on an application by a party or of its own initiative direct that the claim be determined in a region other than that of the venue in which the claim is currently assigned. The considerations in paragraph 5.2 apply.

5.5 Once assigned to a venue, the proceedings will be both administered from that venue and determined by a judge of the Administrative Court at a suitable court within that region, or, if the venue is in London, at the Royal Courts of Justice. The choice of which court (of those within the region which are identified by the Presiding Judge of the circuit suitable for such hearing) will be decided, subject to availability, by the considerations in paragraph 5.2.

5.6 When giving directions under rule 54.10, the court may direct that proceedings be reassigned to another region for hearing (applying the considerations in paragraph 5.2). If no such direction is given, the claim will be heard in the same region as that in which the permission application was determined (whether on paper or at a hearing).

PART 66: CROWN PROCEEDINGS

Scope of this Part and interpretation

66.1 (1) This Part contains rules for civil proceedings by or against the Crown, and other civil proceedings to which the Crown is a party.

(2) In this Part –

(a) 'the Act' means the Crown Proceedings Act 1947;

(b) 'civil proceedings by the Crown' means the civil proceedings described in section 23(1) of the Act, but excluding the proceedings described in section 23(3);

(c) 'civil proceedings against the Crown' means the civil proceedings described in section 23(2) of the Act, but excluding the proceedings described in section 23(3);

(d) 'civil proceedings to which the Crown is a party' has the same meaning as it has for the purposes of Parts III and IV of the Act by virtue of section 38(4).

Application of the Civil Procedure Rules

66.2 These Rules and their practice directions apply to civil proceedings by or against the Crown and to other civil proceedings to which the Crown is a party unless this Part, a practice direction or any other enactment provides otherwise.

Action on behalf of the Crown

66.3 (1) Where by reason of a rule, practice direction or court order the Crown is permitted or required –

(a) to make a witness statement,

(b) to swear an affidavit,

(c) to verify a document by a statement of truth;

(d) to make a disclosure statement; or

(e) to discharge any other procedural obligation,

that function shall be performed by an appropriate officer acting on behalf of the Crown.

(2) The court may if necessary nominate an appropriate officer.

Counterclaims, other Part 20 claims, and set-off

66.4 (1) In a claim by the Crown for taxes, duties or penalties, the defendant cannot make a counterclaim or other Part 20 claim or raise a defence of set-off.

(2) In any other claim by the Crown, the defendant cannot make a counterclaim or other Part 20 claim or raise a defence of set-off which is based on a claim for repayment of taxes, duties or penalties.

(3) In proceedings by or against the Crown in the name of the Attorney-General, no counterclaim or other Part 20 claim can be made or defence of set-off raised without the permission of the court.

(4) In proceedings by or against the Crown in the name of a government department, no counterclaim or other Part 20 claim can be made or defence of set-off raised without the permission of the court unless the subject-matter relates to that government department.

Applications in revenue matters

66.5 (1) This rule sets out the procedure under section 14 of the Act, which allows the Crown to make summary applications in the High Court in certain revenue matters.

(2) The application must be made in the High Court using the Part 8 procedure.

(3) The title of the claim form must clearly identify the matters which give rise to the application.

Enforcement against the Crown

66.6 (1) The following rules do not apply to any order against the Crown –
    (a) Parts 69 to 73;
    (b) RSC Orders 45 to 47 and 52; and
    (c) CCR Orders 25 to 29.

(2) In paragraph (1), 'order against the Crown' means any judgment or order against the Crown, a government department, or an officer of the Crown as such, made –
    (a) in civil proceedings by or against the Crown;
    (b) in proceedings in the Administrative Court;
    (c) in connection with an arbitration to which the Crown is a party; or
    (d) in other civil proceedings to which the Crown is a party.

(3) An application under section 25(1) of the Act for a separate certificate of costs payable to the applicant may be made without notice.

Money due from the Crown

66.7 (1) None of the following orders –
    (a) a third party debt order under Part 72;
    (b) an order for the appointment of a receiver under Part 69; or
    (c) an order for the appointment of a sequestrator under RSC Order 45,
may be made or have effect in respect of any money due from the Crown.

(2) In paragraph (1), 'money due from the Crown' includes money accruing due, and money alleged to be due or accruing due.

(3) An application for an order under section 27 of the Act –
    (a) restraining a person from receiving money payable to him by the Crown; and
    (b) directing payment of the money to the applicant or another person,
may be made under Part 23.

(4) The application must be supported by written evidence setting out the facts on which it is based, and in particular identifying the debt from the Crown.

(5) Where the debt from the Crown is money in a National Savings Bank account, the witness must if possible identify the number of the account and the name and address of the branch where it is held.

(6) Notice of the application, with a copy of the written evidence, must be served –
    (a) on the Crown, and
    (b) on the person to be restrained,
at least 7 days before the hearing.

(7) Rule 72.8 applies to an application under this rule as it applies to an application under rule 72.2 for a third party debt order, except that the court will not have the power to order enforcement to issue against the Crown.

PRACTICE DIRECTION 66 – CROWN PROCEEDINGS

THIS PRACTICE DIRECTION SUPPLEMENTS CPR PART 66

Transfer

1.1 Rule 30.3(2) sets out the circumstances to which the court must have regard when considering whether to make an order under section 40(2), 41(1) or 42(2) of the County Courts Act 1984 (transfer between the High Court and County Court), rule 30.2(1) (transfer between county courts) or rule 30.2(4) (transfer between the Royal Courts of Justice and the district registries).

1.2 From time to time the Attorney General will publish a note concerning the organisation of the Government Legal Service and matters relevant to the venue of Crown proceedings, for the assistance of practitioners and judges. When considering questions of venue under rule 30.3(2), the court should have regard to the Attorney General's note in addition to all the other circumstances of the case.

Service of Documents

2.1 In civil proceedings by or against the Crown, documents required to be served on the Crown must be served in accordance with rule 6.10 or 6.23(7). (The list published under section 17 of the Crown Proceedings Act 1947 of the solicitors acting for the different government departments on whom service is to be effected, and of their addresses is annexed to this Practice Direction).

ANNEX 1: DISPUTES AS TO VENUE – FACTORS TO BE TAKEN INTO CONSIDERATION

Attorney General's Note to Supplement the Practice Direction

Introduction

Until the recent rule changes, the Crown was entitled in High Court matters to insist that venue was the Royal Courts of Justice in London (RCJ) (RSC O77, rule 2). This rule has now been revoked. A new rule 30.3(2)(h) provides that in cases involving civil proceedings by or against the Crown, when considering whether to order a transfer of those proceedings, the court must have regard to, 'the location of the relevant government department or officers of the Crown and, where appropriate, any relevant public interest that the matter should be tried in London.'

The Practice Direction to Part 66, at paragraph 2, provides that the Attorney-General will publish a note concerning the organisation of the Government Legal Service and matters relevant to the venue of Crown Proceedings, for the assistance of practitioners and judges. When considering questions of venue under rule 30.3(2), the court should have regard to the Attorney-General's note in addition to all the other circumstances of the case.

This note sets out the further factors to be taken into consideration where there is a dispute as to venue between a claimant and a government department. Where there is such a dispute, it should be dealt with at a case management conference.

Organisation of the Government Legal Service

The Government Legal Service (GLS) has the responsibility for advising the Government about its legal affairs and has the conduct of civil litigation on its behalf. The Treasury Solicitor conducts this litigation for the majority of

Government Departments but lawyers in HM Revenue and Customs, the Department for the Environment, Food and Rural Affairs and the Department for Work and Pensions (which also acts for the Department of Health and the Food Standards Agency) have the conduct of litigation for their Departments. All Government litigation lawyers are based in the London with the exception of HM Revenue and Customs, whose personal injury lawyers are in Manchester. A full list of addresses for service is annexed to the Practice Direction accompanying Part 66 of the CPR.

Factors be taken into account generally
Location
Whilst a number of government departments have offices outside London, central government bodies are based in London and the GLS is geared towards processing claims in the RCJ (see above). Where there is a High Court claim, many witnesses as well as lawyers and officials are London based and there may be a disproportionate cost in transferring them to a venue outside London. That is not to say, bearing in mind the overriding objective, that the Crown would oppose transfer away from the RCJ where it was appropriate, for example in personal injury disputes.

Precedent value
Some cases have important precedent value or are of general importance to the public, which may make them more suitable for being heard in the RCJ.

Special considerations in relation to HM Revenue and Customs
HM Revenue and Customs has no lawyers outside London, except for those personal injury lawyers based in Manchester.

The work of HM Revenue and Customs is very specialised, needing in many cases to be dealt with by specialist judges in the Chancery Division familiar, for example, with tax work.

There is also the public interest to consider. All revenue cases (including those of HM Revenue and Customs) have important precedent value that applies across the entire tax system, with implications for the Exchequer.

ANNEX 2: LIST OF AUTHORISED GOVERNMENT DEPARTMENTS

AUTHORISED GOVERNMENT DEPARTMENTS	SOLICITOR AND ADDRESSES FOR SERVICE
Advisory, Conciliation and Arbitration Service Board of Trade Cabinet Office Central Office of Information Commissioners for the Reduction of National Debt (see Note (3)) Crown Prosecution Service Department for Business, Innovation and Skills Department for Children, Schools and Families)	The Treasury Solicitor One Kemble Street London WC2B 4TS

AUTHORISED GOVERNMENT DEPARTMENTS	SOLICITOR AND ADDRESSES FOR SERVICE
Department for Culture, Media and Sport Department for Communities and Local Government Department of Energy and Climate Change Department for International Development Department for Transport Food Standards Agency Foreign and Commonwealth Office Government Actuary's Department Government Equalities Office Health and Safety Executive Office for Standards in Education, Children's Services and Skills Her Majesty's Chief Inspector of Schools in Wales Her Majesty's Treasury Home Office Ministry of Defence Ministry of Justice National Savings and Investments National School of Government Northern Ireland Office Ordnance Survey Privy Council Office Public Works Loan Board Royal Mint Serious Fraud Office The National Archives Wales Office (Office of the Secretary of State for Wales) (see Note (5))	The Treasury Solicitor One Kemble Street London WC2B 4TS
Child Maintenance and Enforcement Commission Department of Health Department for Work and Pensions UK Statistics Authority	The Solicitor to the Department for Work and Pensions and the Department of Health The Adelphi 1–11 John Adam Street London WC2N 6HT
Crown Estate Commissioners	Legal Director The Crown Estate 16 New Burlington Place London W1S 2HX

AUTHORISED GOVERNMENT DEPARTMENTS	SOLICITOR AND ADDRESSES FOR SERVICE
Department for Environment, Food and Rural Affairs Forestry Commissioners	The Solicitor to the Department for Environment, Food and Rural Affairs Nobel House 17 Smith Square London SW1P 3JR
Export Credits Guarantee Department	The General Counsel, Export Credits Guarantee Department, P.O. Box 2200, 2 Exchange Tower, Harbour Exchange Square, London E14 9GS
Gas and Electricity Markets Authority	Senior Legal Director Office of Gas and Electricity Markets 9 Millbank London SW1P 3GE
Her Majesty's Revenue and Customs	General Counsel and Solicitor to Her Majesty's Revenue and Customs HM Revenue and Customs South West Wing Bush House, Strand London, WC2B 4RD
Office of Fair Trading	General Counsel Fleetbank House 2–6 Salisbury Square London EC4Y 8JX
Office of Rail Regulation	Director of Legal Services ORR One Kemble Street London WC2B 4AN
Postal Services Commission	The Chief Legal Adviser Postal Services Commission Hercules House 6 Hercules Road London SE1 7DB
Revenue and Customs Prosecutions Office (RCPO)	The Director Revenue and Customs Prosecutions Office New King's Beam House 22 Upper Ground London SE1 9BT

AUTHORISED GOVERNMENT DEPARTMENTS	SOLICITOR AND ADDRESSES FOR SERVICE
Water Services Regulation Authority (OFWAT)	Director of Legal Services and Board Secretary Water Services Regulation Authority (OFWAT) Centre City Tower 7 Hill Street Birmingham B5 4UA
Welsh Assembly Government	The Director of Legal Services to the Welsh Assembly Government Cathays Park Cardiff CF10 3NQ

PRE-ACTION PROTOCOL FOR JUDICIAL REVIEW

Contents

Introduction

A   Letter before claim

B   Response to a letter before claim

C   Notes on public funding for legal costs in judicial review

INTRODUCTION

This protocol applies to proceedings within England and Wales only. It does not affect the time limit specified by Rule 54.5(1) of the Civil Procedure Rules which requires that any claim form in an application for judicial review must be filed promptly and in any event not later than 3 months after the grounds to make the claim first arose.[24]

1   Judicial review allows people with a sufficient interest in a decision or action by a public body to ask a judge to review the lawfulness of:

* an enactment; or
* a decision, action or failure to act in relation to the exercise of a public function.[25]

2   Judicial review may be used where there is no right of appeal or where all avenues of appeal have been exhausted.

Alternative Dispute Resolution

3.1   The parties should consider whether some form of alternative dispute resolution procedure would be more suitable than litigation, and if so, endeavour to agree which form to adopt. Both the Claimant and Defendant may be required by the Court to provide evidence that alternative means of resolving their dispute were considered. The Courts take the view that litigation should be a last resort, and that claims should not be issued prematurely when a settlement is still actively being explored. Parties are warned that if the protocol is not followed (including this paragraph) then the Court must have regard to such conduct when determining costs. However, parties should also note that a claim for judicial review 'must be filed promptly and in any event not later than 3 months after the grounds to make the claim first arose'.

3.2   It is not practicable in this protocol to address in detail how the parties might decide which method to adopt to resolve their particular dispute. However, summarised below are some of the options for resolving disputes without litigation:

* Discussion and negotiation.
* Ombudsmen – the Parliamentary and Health Service and the Local Government Ombudsmen have discretion to deal with complaints relating to maladministration. The British and Irish Ombudsman Association provide information about Ombudsman schemes and other complaint handling bodies and this is available from their website at www.bioa.org.uk .

---

24   While the court does have the discretion under Rule 3.1(2)(a) of the Civil Procedure Rules to allow a late claim, this is only used in exceptional circumstances. Compliance with the protocol alone is unlikely to persuade the court to allow a late claim.

25   Civil Procedure Rule 54.1(2).

Parties may wish to note that the Ombudsmen are not able to look into a complaint once court action has been commenced.

• Early neutral evaluation by an independent third party (for example, a lawyer experienced in the field of administrative law or an individual experienced in the subject matter of the claim).

• Mediation – a form of facilitated negotiation assisted by an independent neutral party.

3.3 The Legal Services Commission has published a booklet on 'Alternatives to Court', CLS Direct Information Leaflet 23 (www.clsdirect.org.uk), which lists a number of organisations that provide alternative dispute resolution services.

3.4 It is expressly recognised that no party can or should be forced to mediate or enter into any form of ADR.

4 Judicial review may not be appropriate in every instance.

Claimants are strongly advised to seek appropriate legal advice when considering such proceedings and, in particular, before adopting this protocol or making a claim. Although the Legal Services Commission will not normally grant full representation before a letter before claim has been sent and the proposed defendant given a reasonable time to respond, initial funding may be available, for eligible claimants, to cover the work necessary to write this. (See Annex C for more information.)

5 This protocol sets out a code of good practice and contains the steps which parties should generally follow before making a claim for judicial review.

6 This protocol does not impose a greater obligation on a public body to disclose documents or give reasons for its decision than that already provided for in statute or common law. However, where the court considers that a public body should have provided relevant documents and/or information, particularly where this failure is a breach of a statutory or common law requirement, it may impose sanctions.

This protocol will not be appropriate where the defendant does not have the legal power to change the decision being challenged, for example decisions issued by tribunals such as Asylum and Immigration Tribunal.

This protocol will not be appropriate in urgent cases, for example, when directions have been set, or are in force, for the claimant's removal from the UK, or where there is an urgent need for an interim order to compel a public body to act where it has unlawfully refused to do so (for example, the failure of a local housing authority to secure interim accommodation for a homeless claimant) a claim should be made immediately. A letter before claim will not stop the implementation of a disputed decision in all instances.

7 All claimants will need to satisfy themselves whether they should follow the protocol, depending upon the circumstances of his or her case. Where the use of the protocol is appropriate, the court will normally expect all parties to have complied with it and will take into account compliance or non-compliance when giving directions for case management of proceedings or when making orders for costs.26 However, even in emergency cases, it is good practice to fax to the defendant the draft Claim Form which the claimant intends to issue.

26 Civil Procedure Rules Costs Practice Direction.

A claimant is also normally required to notify a defendant when an interim mandatory order is being sought.

The letter before claim

8   Before making a claim, the claimant should send a letter to the defendant. The purpose of this letter is to identify the issues in dispute and establish whether litigation can be avoided.

9   Claimants should normally use the suggested *standard format* for the letter outlined at Annex A.

10 The letter should contain *the date and details of the decision, act or omission being challenged and a clear summary of the facts* on which the claim is based. It should also contain the *details of any relevant information* that the claimant is seeking and an explanation of why this is considered relevant.

11 The letter should normally contain the *details of any interested parties*[27] known to the claimant. They should be sent a *copy* of the letter before claim *for information. Claimants are strongly advised to seek appropriate legal advice when considering such proceedings and, in particular, before sending the letter before claim to other interested parties or making a claim.*

12 A claim should not normally be made until the proposed reply date given in the letter before claim has passed, unless the circumstances of the case require more immediate action to be taken.

The letter of response

13 Defendants should normally respond within 14 days using the *standard format* at Annex B. Failure to do so will be taken into account by the court and sanctions may be imposed unless there are good reasons.[28]

14 Where it is not possible to reply within the proposed time limit the defendant should send an interim reply and propose a reasonable extension. Where an extension is sought, reasons should be given and, where required, additional information requested. *This will not affect the time limit for making a claim for judicial review*[29] nor will it bind the claimant where he or she considers this to be unreasonable. However, where the court considers that a subsequent claim is made prematurely it may impose sanctions.

15 If the *claim is being conceded in full,* the reply should say so in clear and unambiguous terms.

16 If the *claim is being conceded in part or not being conceded at all,* the reply should say so in clear and unambiguous terms, and:

(a) where appropriate, contain a new decision, clearly identifying what aspects of the claim are being conceded and what are not, or, give a clear timescale within which the new decision will be issued;

(b) provide a fuller explanation for the decision, if considered appropriate to do so;

(c) address any points of dispute, or explain why they cannot be addressed;

(d) enclose any *relevant* documentation requested by the claimant, or explain why the documents are not being enclosed; and

---

27 See Civil Procedure Rules Rule 54.1(2)(f).
28 See Civil Procedure Rules Pre-action Protocol Practice Direction paragraphs 2–3.
29 Civil Procedure Rule 54.5(1).

(e) where appropriate, confirm whether or not they will oppose any application for an interim remedy.

If the letter before claim has stated that the claim is an Aarhus Convention claim but the defendant does not accept this, the reply should state this clearly and explain the reasons.

17 The response should be sent to all interested parties[30] identified by the claimant and contain details of any other parties who the defendant considers also have an interest.

ANNEX A – LETTER BEFORE CLAIM

SECTION 1. INFORMATION REQUIRED IN A LETTER BEFORE CLAIM

Proposed claim for judicial review

1 **To**
(Insert the name and address of the proposed defendant – see details in section 2)

2 **The claimant**
(Insert the title, first and last name and the address of the claimant)

3 **Reference details**
(When dealing with large organisations it is important to understand that the information relating to any particular individual's previous dealings with it may not be immediately available, therefore it is important to set out the relevant reference numbers for the matter in dispute and/or the identity of those within the public body who have been handling the particular matter in dispute – see details in section 3)

4 **The details of the matter being challenged**
(Set out clearly the matter being challenged, particularly if there has been more than one decision)

5 **The issue**
(Set out the date and details of the decision, or act or omission being challenged, a brief summary of the facts and why it is contented to be wrong)

6 **The details of the action that the defendant is expected to take**
(Set out the details of the remedy sought, including whether a review or any interim remedy are being requested)

7 **The details of the legal advisers, if any, dealing with this claim**
(Set out the name, address and reference details of any legal advisers dealing with the claim)

8 **The details of any interested parties**
(Set out the details of any interested parties and confirm that they have been sent a copy of this letter)

9 **The details of any information sought**
(Set out the details of any information that is sought. This may include a request for a fuller explanation of the reasons for the decision that is being challenged)

30 Civil Procedure Rule 54.1(2)(f).

10 The details of any documents that are considered relevant and necessary
(Set out the details of any documentation or policy in respect of which the disclosure is sought and explain why these are relevant. If you rely on a statutory duty to disclose, this should be specified)

11 The address for reply and service of court documents
(Insert the address for the reply)

12 Proposed reply date
(The precise time will depend upon the circumstances of the individual case. However, although a shorter or longer time may be appropriate in a particular case, 14 days is a reasonable time to allow in most circumstances)

SECTION 2. ADDRESS FOR SENDING THE LETTER BEFORE CLAIM

Public bodies have requested that, for certain types of cases, in order to ensure a prompt response, letters before claim should be sent to specific addresses.

Where the claim concerns a decision in an Immigration, Asylum or Nationality case:
—The claim may be sent electronically to the following UK Border Agency email address: UKBAPAP@UKBA.gsi.gov.uk
—Alternatively the claim may be sent by post to the following UK Border Agency postal address:
> Judicial Review Unit
> UK Border Agency
> Lunar House
> 40 Wellesley Rd
> Croydon CR9 2BY

Where the claim concerns a decision by the Legal Services Commission:
The address on the decision letter/notification; and
> Legal Director
> Corporate Legal Team
> Legal Services Commission
> 102 Petty France
> London SW1H 9AJ

Where the claim concerns a decision by a local authority:
The address on the decision letter/notification; and
Their legal department[31]

Where the claim concerns a decision by a department or body for whom Treasury Solicitor acts *and Treasury Solicitor has already been involved in the case* a copy should also be sent, quoting the Treasury Solicitor's reference, to:
> Treasury Solicitor
> 1 Kemble Street
> London WC2B 4TS

In all other circumstances, the letter should be sent to the address on the letter notifying the decision.

---

31 The relevant address should be available from a range of sources such as the Phone Book, Business and Services Directory, Thomson's Local Directory, CAB, etc.

SECTION 3. SPECIFIC REFERENCE DETAILS REQUIRED

Public bodies have requested that the following information should be provided in order to ensure prompt response.

Where the claim concerns an Immigration, Asylum or Nationality case, dependent upon the nature of the case:
- The Home Office reference number
- The Port reference number
- The Immigration Appellate Authority reference number
- The National Asylum Support Service reference number

Or, if these are unavailable:
- The full name, nationality and date of birth of the claimant.

Where the claim concerns a decision by the Legal Services Commission:
- The certificate reference number.

ANNEX B – RESPONSE TO A LETTER BEFORE CLAIM

INFORMATION REQUIRED IN A RESPONSE TO A LETTER BEFORE CLAIM

Proposed claim for judicial review

1. **The claimant**
   (Insert the title, first and last names and the address to which any reply should be sent)

2. **From**
   (Insert the name and address of the defendant)

3. **Reference details**
   (Set out the relevant reference numbers for the matter in dispute and the identity of those within the public body who have been handling the issue)

4. **The details of the matter being challenged**
   (Set out details of the matter being challenged, providing a fuller explanation of the decision, where this is considered appropriate)

5. **Response to the proposed claim**
   (Set out whether the issue in question is conceded in part, or in full, or will be contested. Where it is not proposed to disclose any information that has been requested, explain the reason for this. Where an interim reply is being sent and there is a realistic prospect of settlement, details should be included)

6. **Details of any other interested parties**
   (Identify any other parties who you consider have an interest who have not already been sent a letter by the claimant)

7. **Address for further correspondence and service of court documents**
   (Set out the address for any future correspondence on this matter)

ANNEX C – NOTES ON PUBLIC FUNDING FOR LEGAL COSTS IN JUDICIAL REVIEW

Public funding for legal costs in judicial review is available from legal professionals and advice agencies which have contracts with the Legal Services Commission as part of the Community Legal Service. Funding may be provided for:

- *Legal Help* to provide initial advice and assistance with any legal problem; or
- *Legal Representation* to allow you to be represented in court if you are taking or defending court proceedings. This is available in two forms:

    - *Investigative Help* is limited to funding to investigate the strength of the proposed claim. It includes the issue and conduct of proceedings only so far as is necessary to obtain disclosure of relevant information or to protect the client's position in relation to any urgent hearing or time limit for the issue of proceedings. This includes the work necessary to write a **letter before claim** to the body potentially under challenge, setting out the grounds of challenge, and giving that body a reasonable opportunity, typically 14 days, in which to respond.

    - *Full Representation* is provided to represent you in legal proceedings and includes litigation services, advocacy services, and all such help as is usually given by a person providing representation in proceedings, including steps preliminary or incidental to proceedings, and/or arriving at or giving effect to a compromise to avoid or bring to an end any proceedings. Except in emergency cases, a proper **letter before claim** must be sent and the other side must be given an opportunity to respond before Full Representation is granted.

Further information on the type(s) of help available and the criteria for receiving that help may be found in the Legal Service Manual Volume 3: *The Funding Code*. This may be found on the Legal Services Commission website at: www.legalservices.gov.uk

A list of contracted firms and Advice Agencies may be found on the Community Legal Services website at: www.justask.org.uk

PRACTICE DIRECTION: FRESH CLAIM JUDICIAL REVIEW IN THE IMMIGRATION AND ASYLUM CHAMBER OF THE UPPER TRIBUNAL

PART 1: PRELIMINARY

1. Interpretation

1.1 In these Practice Directions:

'applicant' has the same meaning as in the UT Rules;

'the application' means the written application under rule 28 for permission to bring judicial review proceedings;

'fresh claim proceedings' has the same meaning as in the UT Rules;

'party' has the same meaning as in the UT Rules;

'respondent' has the same meaning as in the UT Rules;

'the Tribunal' means the Immigration and Asylum Chamber of the Upper Tribunal;

'UKBA' means the UK Border Agency of the Home Office;

'UT Rules' means the Tribunal Procedure (Upper Tribunal) Rules 2008 and 'rule', followed by a number, means the rule bearing that number in the UT Rules.

PART 2: SCOPE

2. Scope

2.1 Parts 3 and 4 of these Practice Directions apply to fresh claim proceedings.

2.2 Part 5 of these Practice Directions applies to proceedings to which Part 3 applies, where:

(a) a person has been served with a copy of directions for that person's removal from the United Kingdom by UKBA and notified that Part 5 applies; and

(b) that person makes an application to the Tribunal or a court for permission to bring judicial review proceedings or to apply for judicial review, before the removal takes effect.

2.3 In the case of proceedings transferred to the Tribunal by a court, the Tribunal will expect the applicant to have complied with all relevant Practice Directions of that court that applied up to the point of transfer. In the event of non-compliance, the Tribunal will make such directions pursuant to rule 27(1)(b) as are necessary and which may, in particular, include applying provisions of these Practice Directions.

PART 3: GENERAL PROVISIONS

THE APPLICATION TO BRING JUDICIAL REVIEW PROCEEDINGS

3. Form of application

3.1 The application must be made using the form displayed on the Upper Tribunal's website at the time the application is made.

4. Additional materials to be filed with the application

4.1 Without prejudice to rule 28, the application must be accompanied by:

(a) any written evidence on which it is intended to rely (but see paragraph 4.2 below);

(b) copies of any relevant statutory material; and

(c) a list of essential documents for advance reading by the Tribunal (with page references to the passages relied on).

4.2 The applicant may rely on the matters set out in the application as evidence under this Practice Direction if the application is verified by a statement of truth.

5. Bundle of documents to be sent etc. with the application

5.1 The applicant must file two copies of a paginated and indexed bundle containing all the documents required by rule 28 and these Practice Directions to be sent or delivered with the application.

6. Permission without a hearing

6.1 The Tribunal will generally, in the first instance, consider the question of permission without a hearing.

THE SUBSTANTIVE HEARING

7. Additional grounds at the substantive hearing

7.1 Where an applicant who has been given permission to bring judicial review proceedings intends to apply under rule 32 to rely on additional grounds at the substantive hearing, the applicant must give written notice to the Tribunal and to any other person served with the application, not later than 7 working days before that hearing.

8. Skeleton arguments for the substantive hearing

8.1 The applicant must serve a skeleton argument on the Tribunal and on any other person served with the application, not later than 21 days before the substantive hearing.

8.2 The respondent and any other party wishing to make representations at the hearing must serve a skeleton argument on the Tribunal and on the applicant, not later than 14 days before the hearing.

8.3 Skeleton arguments must contain:

(a) a time estimate for the complete hearing, including the giving of the decision by the Tribunal;

(b) a list of issues;

(c) a list of the legal points to be taken (together with any relevant authorities with page references to the passages relied on);

(d) a chronology of events (with page references to the bundle of documents (see Practice Direction 9 below);

(e) a list of essential documents for the advance reading of the Tribunal (with page references to the passages relied on) (if different from that served with the application) and a time estimate for that reading; and

(f) a list of persons referred to.

9. Bundle of documents for the substantive hearing

9.1 The applicant must serve on the Tribunal and any other person served with the application a paginated and indexed bundle of all relevant documents required for the substantive hearing, when the applicant's skeleton argument is served.

9.2 The bundle must also include those documents required by the respondent and any other person who is expected to make representations at the hearing.

10. Agreed final order

10.1 If the parties agree about the final order to be made, the applicant must file at the Tribunal a document (with 2 copies) signed by all the parties setting out the terms of the proposed agreed order, together with a short statement of the matters relied on as justifying the proposed agreed order and copies of any authorities or statutory provisions relied on.

10.2 The Tribunal will consider the documents referred to in paragraph 10.1 above and will make the order if satisfied that the order should be made.

10.3 If the Tribunal is not satisfied that the order should be made, a hearing date will be set.

PART 4: URGENT APPLICATIONS FOR PERMISSION TO BRING JUDICIAL REVIEW PROCEEDINGS

11. Request for Urgent Consideration

11.1 Where it is intended to request the Tribunal to deal urgently with the application or where an interim injunction is sought, the applicant must serve with the application a written 'Request for Urgent Consideration', in the form displayed on the Upper Tribunal's website at the time the application is made, which states:

(a) the need for urgency;

(b) the timescale sought for the consideration of the application (eg. within 72 hours or sooner if necessary); and

(c) the date by which the substantive hearing should take place.

11.2 Where an interim injunction is sought, the applicant must, in addition, provide:

(a) the draft order; and

(b) the grounds for the injunction.

12. Notifying the other parties

12.1 The applicant must serve (by fax and post) the application form and the Request for Urgent Consideration on the respondent and interested parties, advising them of the application and that they may make representations.

12.2 Where an interim injunction is sought, the applicant must serve (by fax and post) the draft order and grounds for the injunction on the respondent and interested parties, advising them of the application and that they may make representations.

13. Consideration by Tribunal

13.1 The Tribunal will consider the application within the time requested and may make such order as it considers appropriate.

13.2 If the Tribunal specifies that a hearing shall take place within a specified time, the representatives of the parties must liaise with the Tribunal and each other to fix a hearing of the application within that time.

PART 5: APPLICATIONS WHICH CHALLENGE REMOVAL

14. General

14.1 The requirements contained in this Part are additional to those contained in Part 3 and (where applicable) Part 4 of these Practice Directions.

14.2 Nothing in these Practice Directions prevents a person from making the application after that person has been removed from the United Kingdom.

15 Special requirements regarding the application

15.1 Without prejudice to rule 28, the application must:

(a) indicate on its face that this Part of these Practice Directions applies; and

(b) be accompanied by:

(i) a copy of the removal directions and the decisions to which the application relates; and

(ii) any document served with the removal directions including any document which contains UKBA's factual summary of the case; and

(c) contain or be accompanied by the detailed statement of the applicant's grounds for making the application.

15.2 If the applicant is unable to comply with paragraph 15.1(b) or (c) above, the application must contain or be accompanied by a statement of the reasons why.

15.3 Notwithstanding rule 28A, immediately upon issue of the application, the applicant must send copies of the issued application form and accompanying documents to the address specified by the United Kingdom Border Agency.

16. Referral in case of non-compliance

16.1 Where the applicant has not complied with Practice Direction 15.1(b) or (c) above and has provided reasons for not complying, and the Tribunal has issued the application form, the Tribunal's staff will:

(a) refer the matter to a Judge for consideration as soon as practicable; and

(b) notify the parties that they have done so.

17. Application clearly without merit

17.1 If, upon a refusal to grant permission to bring judicial review proceedings, the Tribunal indicates that the application is clearly without merit, that indication will be included in the order refusing permission.

These Practice Directions are made by the Senior President of Tribunals with the agreement of the Lord Chancellor. They are made in the exercise of powers conferred by the Tribunals, Courts and Enforcement Act 2007.

LORD JUSTICE CARNWATH
SENIOR PRESIDENT OF TRIBUNALS

17 October 2011

FIRST-TIER TRIBUNAL: CRIMINAL INJURIES COMPENSATION PRACTICE AND GUIDANCE STATEMENT

Criminal Injuries Compensation Schemes 1996, 2001 & 2008 (the tariff based Schemes)
Tribunal Procedure (First-tier Tribunal) (Social Entitlement Chamber) Rules 2008 (the Rules)

Appeals on error of law against final decision of the Tribunal

None of the tariff based Schemes and the Rules applicable to decisions made by the First-tier Tribunal in this jurisdiction provide for a final decision of the Tribunal to be reviewed, appealed, amended or otherwise interfered with, *apart from*

(i)   the right to apply for re-instatement (a) where proceedings, or part of them, have been struck out (Rule 8(5)–(7)) or (b) where proceedings or part of them have been withdrawn (Rule 17(4));

(ii) the right to apply for a decision to be reconsidered at a hearing where the Tribunal makes a decision which disposes of proceedings without a hearing, other than decisions to which Rule 27(5) apply (Rule 27(4));

(iii) the right to apply for a rehearing where the tribunal proceeded with a hearing in a party's absence (Rule 31);

(iv) the correction of a clerical or other accidental slip or omission in a decision (Rule 36);

(v)   the right to apply for a decision, or part of a decision, to be set aside subject to certain conditions (Rule 37).

Other than these above-mentioned specific exceptions, the only legal remedy open to an appellant who wishes to challenge the final decision of the Tribunal in this jurisdiction is to apply to bring judicial review proceedings of the decision:

- (in respect of incidents occurring and decisions made in England & Wales) to the Upper Tribunal,32 or

- (in respect of incidents and decisions made in Scotland) to the Outer House of the Court of Session

on the grounds that the decision was '**erroneous in law**'.

---

32 Pursuant to Order of Lord Chief Justice of England & Wales – classes of cases specified under section 18(6) of the Tribunals & Courts & Enforcement Act 2007 (the 2007 Act) – direction in relation to an application made to the High Court of Upper Tribunal on or after 3 November 2008 that seeks relief of a kind mentioned in section 15(1) of the 2007 Act; direction that the following classes of case are specified for the purposes of section 18(6) of the 2007 Act:

(a) any decision of the First-Tier Tribunal on an appeal made in exercise of a right conferred by the Criminal Injuries Compensation Scheme in compliance with section 5 of the Criminal Injuries Compensation Act 1995 (appeals against decisions on review);

(b) any decision of the First-Tier Tribunal made under Tribunal Procedure Rules or section 9 of the 2007 Act where there is no right of appeal to the Upper Tribunal and that decision is not an excluded decision within paragraph (b), (c) , or (f) of section 11(5) of the 2007 Act.

Parties who are contemplating making application to bring judicial review proceedings should follow the guidance below.

1. (Unless the Tribunal has already provided a full written statement of reasons for the decision), as soon as possible and in any event no later than 1 month after notification of the final decision, a party must make a written request for a full statement of reasons for the decision complained about, addressed to **The Tribunals Service – Criminal Injuries, Wellington House, 134–136 Wellington Street, Glasgow G2 2XL.** The request must quote the name of the appellant and the Tribunal's full case reference.

2. A party contemplating making an application to bring judicial review proceedings is requested without delay to provide to the First-tier Tribunal at the address above, written details of the alleged error of law, and all facts and matters relied on in support of the alleged error. The First-tier Tribunal's Principal Judge or nominated Tribunal Judge will scrutinise the allegation and, where satisfied that it is appropriate to do so in accordance with the paragraphs 36 or 37 of the Tribunal Procedure (First-tier Tribunal)(Social Entitlement Chamber) Rules 2008, will consider correcting or setting aside the decision or part of it.

3. Without prejudice to the above two paragraphs, the burden is on the dissatisfied party to make application to bring judicial review proceedings in accordance with applicable Upper Tribunal or Court of Session Rules.

Where incident occurred in Scotland and any hearing took place in Scotland

4. Application for judicial review must be made to the Outer House of the Court of Session, Court of Session, Parliament House, Parliament Square, Edinburgh EH1 1RQ in accordance with Chapter 58 of the Rules of the Court of Session. Note that whilst there is no prescribed time limit for lodging an application for judicial review in Scotland, objections may be taken if there is undue delay in lodging a petition.

Where the claimant lives in England or Wales, the incident occurred in England or Wales and any hearing took place in England or Wales

5. Any application for judicial review must be made in accordance with Rule 27 of the Tribunal Procedure (Upper Tribunal) Rules 2008 SI No 2698) on a prescribed claim form JR1. The time limit is 3 months after the date of the decision complained of, or 1 month after the date written reasons were given or the applicant was notified that an application for the setting aside of the decision had been unsuccessful, whichever period ends latest. The applicant may apply for an extension of time to the Upper Tribunal but must give reasons. The address of the Upper Tribunal is: The Upper Tribunal (Administrative Appeals Chamber), 5th floor Chichester Rents, 81 Chancery Lane, London WC2A 1DD. If the claimant lives in Wales or any hearing was in Wales, the application may be sent or delivered to: The Upper Tribunal (Wales), Columbus House, Langstone Business Park, Chepstow Road, Newport NP18 2LX. The application form JR1 may be obtained from the London Office or on its website: www.administrativeappeals.tribunals.gov.uk.

Where the case has connections with both Scotland and England & Wales

6. An application to bring judicial review proceedings may be made to whichever of the Court of Session or the Upper Tribunal is more appropriate in the circumstances of the case, having particular regard to the convenience of the parties and the issues arising on the application for judicial review. The other party or parties may object to the choice made by the applicant but it should be borne in mind that the Upper Tribunal may sit in Scotland as well as in England and Wales and that the Court of Session may refer a case to the Upper Tribunal who would then be able to hear it in either Scotland or England & Wales.

Correct Defendant and address for service

7. The Defendant in all judicial review proceedings in tariff based Scheme cases is **First-tier Tribunal**; the address for service is **The Tribunals Service, Criminal Injuries, Wellington House, 134–136 Wellington Street, Glasgow G2 2XL.** Applications for judicial review in tariff based Scheme cases served at any other address will not be accepted. An appellant should consider joining the Criminal Injuries Compensation Authority as a Defendant or Interested Party. Where there is a challenge to a tariff based Scheme itself, the appellant will need to consider whether to add as Defendant the Secretary of State for the Ministry of Justice.

8 August 2010

Anthony Summers
Principal Judge
Social Entitlement Chamber – criminal injuries compensation.

PRACTICE DIRECTION: CLASSES OF CASES SPECIFIED UNDER SECTION 18(6) OF THE TRIBUNALS, COURTS AND ENFORCEMENT ACT 2007

IN THE SUPREME COURT OF ENGLAND AND WALES

It is ordered as follows:

1. The following direction takes effect in relation to an application made to the High Court or Upper Tribunal on or after 3 November 2008 that seeks relief of a kind mentioned in section 15(1) of the Tribunals, Courts and Enforcement Act 2007 ('the 2007 Act').
2. The Lord Chief Justice hereby directs that the following classes of case are specified for the purposes of section 18(6) of the 2007 Act:
   (a) Any decision of the First-Tier Tribunal on an appeal made in the exercise of a right conferred by the Criminal Injuries Compensation Scheme in compliance with section 5(1) of the Criminal Injuries Compensation Act 1995 (appeals against decisions on review); and
   (b) Any decision of the First-Tier Tribunal made under Tribunal Procedure Rules or section 9 of the 2007 Act where there is no right of appeal to the Upper Tribunal and that decision is not an excluded decision within paragraph (b), (c), or (f) of section 11(5) of the 2007 Act.
3. This direction does not have effect where an application seeks (whether or not alone) a declaration of incompatibility under section 4 of the Human Rights Act 1998.
4. This Direction is made by the Lord Chief Justice with the agreement of the Lord Chancellor. It is made in the exercise of powers conferred by section 18(6) of the 2007 Act and in accordance with Part 1 of Schedule 2 to the Constitutional Reform Act 2005.

THE RIGHT HONOURABLE LORD JUDGE
LORD CHIEF JUSTICE OF ENGLAND AND WALES

PRACTICE DIRECTION: CLASSES OF CASES SPECIFIED FOR THE PURPOSES OF SECTION 18(6) OF THE TRIBUNALS, COURTS AND ENFORCEMENT ACT 2007

IN THE SENIOR COURTS OF ENGLAND AND WALES

1. The Lord Chief Justice hereby specifies that the following class of case for the purposes of section 18(6) of the Tribunals, Courts and Enforcement Act 2007 ('the 2007 Act'):

   Applications calling into question a decision of the Secretary of State not to treat submissions as an asylum claim or a human rights claim within the meaning of Part 5 of the Nationality, Immigration and Asylum Act 2002 wholly or partly on the basis that they are not significantly different from material that has previously been considered.

2. An application also falls within the class specified in paragraph 1 if, in addition to calling into question a decision of the sort there described, it challenges

   i) A decision or decision to remove (or direct the removal of) the applicant from the United Kingdom; or

   ii) A failure or failures by the Secretary of State to make a decision on submissions said to support an asylum or human rights claim;

   Or both (i) and (ii); but not if it challenges any other decision.

3. This Direction takes effect on 17/10/11 in relation to applications made on or after that date to the High Court or Upper Tribunal for judicial review or for permission to apply for judicial review that seek relief of a kind mentioned in section 15(1) of the 2007 Act.

4. For avoidance of doubt:

   i) a case which has been transferred under this direction continues to fall within the specified class of case and the Upper Tribunal has the function of deciding the application, where, after transfer, additional material is submitted to the Secretary of State for decision but no decision has been made upon that material.

   ii) This direction does not have effect where an application seeks a declaration of incompatibility under section 4 of the Human Rights Act 1998, or where the applicant seeks to challenge detention.

5. This Direction is made by the Lord Chief Justice with the agreement of the Lord Chancellor. It is made in the exercise of powers conferred by section 18(6) and (7) of the 2007 Act and in accordance with Part 1 of Schedule 2 to the Constitutional Reform Act 2005.

THE RIGHT HONOURABLE LORD JUDGE
LORD CHIEF JUSTICE OF ENGLAND AND WALES

Guidance and forms

ADMINISTRATIVE COURT GUIDANCE: NOTES FOR GUIDANCE ON APPLYING FOR JUDICIAL REVIEW[1]

Section 1: general introduction

1. These notes are not intended to be exhaustive but are designed to offer an outline of the procedure to be followed when seeking to make an application for judicial review in the Administrative Court. For further details of the procedure to be followed you and your representatives/legal advisers should consult Part 54 of the Civil Procedure Rules (CPR) and the Practice Directions accompanying Part 54.

Section 2: what is judicial review?

2.1 Judicial review is the procedure by which you can seek to challenge the decision, action or failure to act of a public body such as a government department or a local authority or other body exercising a public law function. If you are challenging the decision of a court, the jurisdiction of judicial review extends only to decisions of inferior courts. It does not extend to decisions of the High Court or Court of Appeal. Judicial review must be used where you are seeking:

- a mandatory order (i.e. an order requiring the public body to do something and formerly known as an order of mandamus);
- a prohibiting order (i.e. an order preventing the public body from doing something and formerly known as an order of prohibition); or
- a quashing order (i.e. an order quashing the public body's decision and formerly known as an order of certiorari)
- a declaration
- HRA Damages

2.2 Claims can either be heard by a single Judge or a Divisional Court (a court of two judges). The Administrative Court sits at the following locations, although in appropriate cases arrangements may be made for sittings at alternative locations:

- The Royal Courts of Justice in London – (address for correspondence: Room C315, Royal Courts of Justice, Strand, London, WC2A 2LL);
- Birmingham Civil Justice Centre – (address for correspondence: Priory Courts, 33 Bull Street, Birmingham, B4 6DS);
- Cardiff Civil Justice Centre – (address for correspondence:2 Park Street, Cardiff, CF10 1ET);
- Leeds Combined Court Centre – (address for correspondence:1 Oxford Row, Leeds, LS1 3BG);
- Manchester Civil Justice Centre – (address for correspondence:1 Bridge Street West, Manchester, M3 3FX)

Section 3: what is the pre-action protocol?

3.1 The protocol sets out a code of good practice and contains the steps which parties should generally follow before making a claim for judicial review. The objective of the pre-action protocol is to avoid unnecessary litigation.

3.2 Before making your claim for judicial review, you should send a letter to the defendant. The purpose of this letter is to identify the issues in dispute and

---

1   Updated April 2011.

establish whether litigation can be avoided. The letter should contain the date and details of the decision, act or omission being challenged and a clear summary of the facts on which the claim is based. It should also contain the details of any relevant information that the claimant is seeking and an explanation of why this is considered relevant. A claim should not normally be made until the proposed reply date given in the letter before claim has passed, unless the circumstances of the case require more immediate action to be taken.

3.3 Defendants should normally respond to that letter within 14 days and sanctions may be imposed unless there are good reasons for not responding within that period.

NB: The protocol does not affect the time limit specified by CPR Part 54.5(1) namely that an application for permission to apply for judicial review must be made promptly and in any event not later than 3 months after the grounds upon which the claim is based first arose.

NB: You should seek advice as to whether the protocol is appropriate in the circumstances of your case. Use of the protocol will not be appropriate where the defendant does not have the legal power to change the decision being challenged. It also may not be appropriate in circumstances where the application is urgent.

NB: A letter before claim will not automatically stop the implementation of a disputed decision.

NB: Even in emergency cases, it is good practice to fax the draft claim form that you are intending to issue to the defendant. You will also normally be required to notify a defendant when you are seeking an interim order; i.e. an order giving some form of relief pending the final determination of the claim.

3.4 Any claim for judicial review must indicate whether or not the protocol has been complied with. If the protocol has not been complied with, the reasons for failing to do so should be set out in the claim form.

Section 4: where should I commence proceedings?

4.1 Claims for judicial review under CPR Part 54 are dealt with in the Administrative Court.

4.2 Claims may be issued at the District Registry of the High Court at Birmingham, Cardiff, Leeds or Manchester as well as at the Royal Courts of Justice in London. Cases started in Birmingham will normally be determined at a court in the Midland region; in Cardiff in Wales; in Leeds in the North-Eastern Region; in London at the Royal Courts of Justice and in Manchester, in the North-Western Region.

4.3 The general expectation is that proceedings will be administered and determined in the region with which the claimant has the closest connection, subject to the following considerations as applicable:

(1) any reason expressed by any party for preferring a particular venue;

(2) the region in which the defendant, or any relevant office or department of the defendant, is based;

(3) the region in which the claimant's legal representatives are based;

(4) the ease and cost of travel to a hearing;

(5) the availability and suitability of alternative means of attending a hearing (for example, by videolink);

(6) the extent and nature of media interest in the proceedings in any particular locality;

(7) the time within which it is appropriate for the proceedings to be determined;

(8) whether it is desirable to administer or determine the claim in another region in the light of the volume of claims issued at, and the capacity, resources and workload of, the court at which it is issued;

(9) whether the claim raises issues sufficiently similar to those in another outstanding claim to make it desirable that it should be determined together with, or immediately following, that other claim; and

(10) whether the claim raises devolution issues and for that reason whether it should more appropriately be determined in London or Cardiff.

Can I get Legal Services Commission[2] funding (legal aid) for my application?

4.4 Neither the Court nor the Administrative Court Offices have power to grant funding (previously legal aid). The responsibility for the provision of public funding is held by the Legal Services Commission.[3]

4.5 Further information on the type(s) of help available and the criteria for receiving that help may be found on the Legal Services Commission website at www.legalservices.gov.uk/.[4]

4.6 A list of contracted firms and Advice Agencies may be found on the Community Legal Services website at www.communitylegaladvice.org.uk/. Community Legal Advice can also provide you with a list of solicitors in your area if you telephone them on 0845 345 4 345.

Section 5: when should I lodge my application for permission to apply for judicial review?

5.1 The claim form must be filed promptly and in any event not later than three months after the grounds upon which the claim is based first arose (CPR Part 54.5).

5.2 The court has the power to extend the period for the lodging of an application for permission to apply for judicial review but will only do so where it is satisfied there are very good reasons for doing so.

NB: The time for the lodging of the application may not be extended by agreement between the parties.

NB: If you are seeking an extension of time for the lodging of your application, you must make the application in the claim form, setting out the grounds in support of that application to extend time (CPR Part 54.5).

Section 6: is there a fee to pay and if so, when should I pay it?

6.1 A fee of £60.00 is payable when you lodge your application for permission to apply for Judicial Review. A further £215.00 is payable if you wish to pursue

---

2 Now Legal Aid Agency.

3 Now Legal Aid Agency.

4 Now www.justice.gov.uk/legal-aid.

the claim if permission is granted (Civil Proceedings Fees (Amendment) Order 2011).

NB: If you are in receipt of certain types of benefits you may be entitled to remission of any fee due as part of judicial review proceedings. If you believe you may be entitled to fee remission you should apply to the relevant Administrative Court Office using Form EX160 (Application for a Fee Remission) and lodge the application with your claim form.

NB: Cheques should be made payable to HMCTS. If you lodge your claim form at the court office in person, personal cheques must be supported by a cheque guarantee card presented at the time the claim form is lodged.

Fees may be paid by credit or debit card in London when presented in person to the Royal Courts of Justice Fees Office. The Administrative Court Office in Cardiff will accept payment by debit card only when presented in person at their office, and the Birmingham and Manchester offices accept payment by both credit and debit cards at their counters and over the telephone.

At the present time, the Administrative Court Office in Leeds does not accept payment of fees by credit or debit card.

Section 7: how do I apply for judicial review?

7.1 An application for permission to apply for judicial review must be made by claim form (Form N461).

7.2 The claim form must include or be accompanied by:
- a detailed statement of the claimant's grounds for bringing the claim for judicial review;
- a statement of the facts relied on;
- any application to extend the time limit for filing the claim form; and
- any application for directions.

7.3 Where you are seeking to raise any issue under the Human Rights Act 1998, or a remedy available under that Act, the claim form must include the information required by paragraph 16 of the Practice Direction supplementing Part 16 of the Civil Procedure Rules.

7.4 Where you intend to raise a devolution issue, the claim form must specify that you (a) wish to raise a devolution issue (b) identify the relevant provisions of the Government of Wales Act 1998, and (c) contain a summary of the facts, circumstances and points of law on the basis of which it is alleged that a devolution issue arises. Cases involving Welsh devolution issues are expected to be lodged at the Administrative Court Office in Wales.

7.5 The claim form must also be accompanied by
- any written evidence in support of the claim or application to extend time;
- a copy of any order that you are seeking to have quashed;
- where the claim for judicial review relates to a decision of a court or tribunal, an approved copy of the reasons for reaching that decision;
- copies of any documents upon which you propose to rely;
- copies of any relevant statutory material;
- a list of essential documents for advance reading by the court (with page references to the passages relied upon). Where only part of a page needs to be read, that part should be indicated, by side-lining or in some other way, but not by highlighting.

NB: Where it is not possible for you to file all the above documents, you must indicate which documents have not been filed and the reasons why they are not currently available. The defendant and/or the interested party may seek an extension of time for the lodging of its acknowledgement of service pending receipt of the missing documents.

What documents do I need to lodge?

7.6 You must file the original claim form and witness statement, together with a set of paginated and indexed copy documents for the courts use containing the documents referred to in paragraph 7.5 above (CPR Part 54.6 and Practice Direction 54). You should also file a complete set of copy documents (including a copy claim form and witness statement) in a paginated and indexed set for the courts use. Please ensure you paginate in consecutive page number order throughout your bundle. Also ensure that each page has a page number on it and provide an index, which lists the description of documents contained in your bundle together with their page reference numbers.

7.7 Please note that if your case is of a criminal nature then the Court will require you to lodge two paginated and indexed bundles of copy documents.

7.8 You must also lodge sufficient additional copies of the claim form for the court to seal them (i.e. stamp them with the court seal) so that you can serve them on the defendant and any interested parties. The sealed copies will be returned to you so that you can serve them on the defendant and any interested parties.

7.9 If you are represented by solicitors they must also provide a paginated, indexed bundle of the relevant legislative provisions and statutory instruments required for the proper consideration of the application. If you are acting in person you should comply with this requirement if possible.

NB: Applications that do not comply with the requirements of CPR Part 54 and Practice Direction 54 will not be accepted, save in exceptional circumstances. In this context a matter will be regarded as exceptional where a decision is sought from the Court within 14 days of the lodging of the application. In such circumstances an undertaking will be required to provide compliance with the requirements of the CPR within a specified period.

NB: If the only reason given in support of urgency is the imminent expiry of the three month time limit for lodging an application, the papers will nonetheless be returned for compliance with Part 54 and Practice Direction 54. In those circumstances you must seek an extension of time and provide reasons for the delay in lodging the papers in proper form.

Whom should I serve my application on?

7.10 The sealed copy claim form (and accompanying documents) must be served on the defendant and any person that you consider to be an interested party (unless the court directs otherwise) within 7 days of the date of issue (i.e. the date shown on the court seal). The Administrative Court Office will not serve your claim on the defendant or any interested party.

NB: An interested party is a person who is likely to be directly affected by your judicial review application.

NB: Please note that under the provisions of the Crown Proceedings Act 1947 service must be upon the Department responsible for the Defendant.

NB: Where the claim for judicial review relates to proceedings in a court or tribunal, any other parties to those proceedings must be named in the claim form as interested parties and served with the claim form (CPR 54 PD.5). For example, in a claim by a defendant in a criminal case in the Magistrates' or Crown Court for judicial review of a decision in that case, the prosecution must always be named as an interested party.

7.11 You should lodge a Certificate of Service in Form N215 in the relevant Administrative Court Office within 7 days of serving the defendant and other interested parties.

7.12 The date of deemed service is calculated in accordance with CPR part 6.14 (see methods of service below).

Method	Deemed date of service
First class post, Document Exchange (DX) or other service which provides for delivery on the next business day	The second business day after it was posted, left with, delivered to or collected by the relevant service provider provided that day is a business day; or if not, the next business day after that.
	Posted *Deemed served*
	Monday Wednesday
	Tuesday Thursday
	Wednesday Friday
	Thursday Monday
	Friday Monday
	Please note: If the service date falls on a Public Holiday the deemed service date is the first working day following the Public Holiday.
Method Delivering the document to or leaving it at the relevant place.	**Deemed date of service** Where it is delivered to or left at the relevant place before 12.00 midnight, on the second business day after that day
Method Fax	**Deemed date of service** The second business day after the transmission of the fax (eg if the fax is sent at 10.30pm on Monday, it will be deemed served on Wednesday.
Method Other electronic method eg, e-mail	**Deemed date of service** The second business day after sending the email or other electronic transmission.
Method Personal Service	**Deemed date of service** The second business day after completing the relevant step required by CPR 6.5 (3).

NB: The time for a Defendant and any Interested Party to lodge an acknowledgement of service (21 days) commences from the date that the claim is deemed served upon them.

Section 8: what do I do if my application is urgent?

8.1 If you want to make an application for your application for permission to be heard/considered by a Judge as a matter of urgency and/or to seek an interim injunction, you must complete a Request for Urgent Consideration, Form N463, which can be obtained from the HMCTS website or the relevant Administrative Court Office. The form sets out the reasons for urgency and the timescale sought for the consideration of the permission application, eg within 72 hours or sooner if necessary, and the date by which the substantive hearing should take place.

8.2 Where you are seeking an interim injunction, you must, in addition, provide a draft order; and the grounds for the injunction. You must serve the claim form, the draft order and the application for urgency on the defendant and interested parties (by fax and by post), advising them of the application and informing them that they may make representations directly to the Court in respect of your application.

8.3 A judge will consider the application within the time requested and may make such order as he/she considers appropriate.

NB: The judge may refuse your application for permission at this stage if he/she considers it appropriate, in the circumstances, to do so.

8.4 If the Judge directs that an oral hearing must take place within a specified time the Administrative Court Office will liaise with you and the representatives of the other parties to fix a permission hearing within the time period directed.

8.5 Where a manifestly inappropriate urgency application is made, consideration may, in appropriate cases, be given to making a wasted costs order.

Section 9: what is an acknowledgement of service?

9.1 Any person who has been served with the claim form and who wishes to take part in the judicial review should file an acknowledgment of service (Form N462) in the Administrative Court Office, within 21 days of the proceedings being served upon them.

NB: Whilst there is no requirement upon you to serve the defendant and any interested party with a Form N462 for completion by them, it is good practice to do so.

9.2 The acknowledgement of service must set out the summary of grounds for contesting the claim and the name and address of any person considered to be an interested party (who has not previously been identified and served as an interested party).

9.3 The acknowledgement of service must be served upon you and the interested parties no later than 7 days after it is filed with the court.

NB: Failure to file an acknowledgement of service renders it necessary for the party concerned to obtain the permission of the court to take part in any oral hearing of the application for permission.

Section 10: what happens after the defendant and/or the interested party has lodged an acknowledgement of service, or the time for lodging such has expired?

10.1 Applications for permission to proceed with the claim for judicial review are considered by a single judge on the papers. The purpose of this procedure is to ensure that applications are dealt with speedily and without unnecessary expense.

10.2 The papers will be forwarded to the judge by the Administrative Court Office upon receipt of the Acknowledgement of Service or at the expiry of the time limit for lodging such acknowledgement – whichever is earlier.

10.3 The judge's decision and the reasons for it (Form JRJ) will be served upon you, the defendant and any other person served with the claim form.

10.4 If the judge grants permission and you wish to pursue the claim, you must lodge a further fee of £215.00 (or a further Application for Remission of Fee (Form EX160) with the relevant Administrative Court Office within 7 days of service of the judge's decision upon you.

NB: If you do not lodge the additional fee, your file will be closed.

Section 11: what happens if my application for permission is refused, or if permission is granted subject to conditions or in part only?

11.1 If permission is refused, or is granted subject to conditions or on certain grounds only, you may request a reconsideration of that decision at an oral hearing.

11.2 Request for an oral hearing must be made on the Notice of Renewal, Form 86b, (a copy of which will be sent to you at the same time as the judge's decision) and must be filed within 7 days after service of the notification of the judge's decision upon you (CPR Part 54.11 & 54.12).

11.3 Where the judge directs an oral hearing or you renew your application after refusal following consideration on paper, you may appear in person or be represented by an advocate (if you are legally represented). If you are not legally represented you may seek the court's permission to have someone speak on your behalf at the hearing.

NB: Any application for permission to have someone speak on your behalf should be made to the judge hearing the application who will make such decision as he considers appropriate in all of the circumstances.

11.4 Notice of the hearing is given to you, the defendant and any interested party by the Administrative Court List Office. An oral hearing is allocated a total of 30 minutes of court time. If it is considered that 30 minutes of court time is insufficient, you may provide a written estimate of the time required for the hearing and request a special fixture.

11.5 Neither the defendant nor any other interested party need attend a hearing on the question of permission unless the court directs otherwise.

Section 12: what happens if my application for permission is granted?

12.1 On granting permission the court may make case management directions under CPR 54.10(1) for the progression of the case. Case management directions may include directions as to venue, as to the service of the claim form and any evidence on other persons and as to expedition.

12.2 Where a claim is made under the Human Rights Act 1998, a direction may be made for the giving of notice to the Crown or joining the Crown as a party. In that regard you attention is drawn to the requirements of Civil Procedure rule 19.4A and paragraph 6 of the Practice Direction supplementing Section I of Part 19.

When should the defendant/interested party lodge its evidence following the grant of permission?

12.3 A party upon whom a claim form has been served and who wishes to contest the claim (or support it on additional grounds) must, within 35 days of service of the order granting permission, file and serve on the Court and all of the other parties
   • Detailed grounds for contesting the claim or supporting it on additional grounds and
   • Any written evidence relied upon.

12.4 Any party who has done so may be represented at the hearing.

12.5 Where the party filing the detailed grounds intends to rely on documents not already filed, a paginated bundle of those documents must be filed at the Court when the detailed grounds are filed.

12.6 The Court has power to extend or abridge the time for lodging evidence.

Section 13: what happens when my case is ready for hearing?

13.1 When the time for lodging of evidence by the parties has expired, the case enters a warned list and all parties are informed of this by letter.

13.2 Where a direction has been given for expedition, the case will take priority over other cases waiting to be fixed and enters an expedited warned list.

What is the procedure for the listing of a case for hearing?
NB: The procedure is the same whether you act in person or are legally represented.

13.3 Where advocate's details have been placed on the court record, the parties will be contacted by the relevant Administrative Court List Office in order to seek to agree a date for the hearing. You and advocate's clerks will be offered a range of dates and will have 48 hours to take up one of the dates offered. If the parties fail to contact the List Office within 48 hours, the List Office will fix the hearing on one of the dates offered without further notice and the parties will be notified of that fixture by letter. Where a hearing is listed in this way the hearing will only be vacated by the Administrative Court Office if both parties consent and good reason is provided for the need to vacate the fixture, using the adjournment form available from Administrative Court Listing Offices.

13.4 There may be circumstances where you are unable to attend at court on the date fixed to hear your application, i.e. as a result of illness or accident. If you are unlikely to be able to attend court on the hearing date you must notify the relevant List Office immediately. You should contact the other parties to seek their consent to the adjournment using the adjournment form. If illness is the cause of your inability to attend, a medical certificate should also be provided. Your application for an adjournment will be considered by the Appropriate Officer of the relevant Administrative Court Office. Please note there is a fee payable for any application to adjourn unless the application is made with the consent of all parties and lodged with the court no later than 14 days before the date of the hearing. If you are entitled to fee remission, you must lodge an Application for a Fee Remission (Form Ex160) with your adjournment form.

13.5 Where agreement to an adjournment cannot be reached, a formal application for adjournment must be made to the Court (on notice to all parties) using Form PF244 - Administrative Court Office. Please note that there is a fee payable (£80.00) for any application to adjourn made without the consent of all parties, notwithstanding when it is lodged, unless you are entitled to fee remission, in which case you must lodge an Application for a Fee Remission (Form Ex160) with your application. Where all parties consent to an adjournment within 14 days of the date of the hearing, a fee of £45.00 is payable.

13.6 There are occasions when circumstances, outside the control of the List Office, may necessitate them having to vacate a hearing at very short notice. Sometimes this can be as late as 4.30pm the day before the case is listed. This could be as a result of a case unexpectedly overrunning, a judge becoming unavailable, or other reasons. The List Office will endeavour to re-fix the case on the next available date convenient to the parties.

What is the short warned list?

13.7 Whilst the Administrative Court usually gives fixed dates for hearings, there is also a need to short warn a number of cases to cover the large number of settlements that occur in the list. Parties in cases that are selected to be short warned will be notified that their case is likely to be listed from a specified date, and that they may be called into the list at less than a day's notice from that date. If the case does not get on during that period, a date as soon as possible after that period will be fixed in consultation with the parties.

What is a Skeleton Argument and do I need to lodge one?

13.8 A skeleton argument is a document lodged with the court by a party prior to the substantive hearing of any application for judicial review.

13.9 Whilst there is no requirement for a litigant in person to lodge a skeleton argument there is nothing to prevent you from doing so if you wish and if you consider that it would assist the Court.

13.10 If you wish to lodge a skeleton argument you must file it with the Court and serve it on the other parties not less than 21 working days before the date of the hearing of the judicial review or the short warned date, where a case has been 'short warned'.

13.11 The defendant and any other party wishing to make representations at the hearing of the judicial review must file and serve a skeleton argument not less than 14 working days before the date of the hearing of the judicial review (or the short warned date).

13.12 The skeleton argument must contain:

- A time estimate for the complete hearing, including delivery of judgment;
- A list of issues;
- A list of the legal points to be taken (together with any relevant authorities with page references to the passages relied on);
- A chronology of events (with page references to the bundle of documents);
- A list of essential documents for the advance reading of the court (with

page references to the passages relied on) (if different from that filed with the claim form) and a time estimate for that reading; and
• A list of persons referred to.

What is a trial bundle and when should I lodge it?

13.13 You must file a paginated and indexed bundle of all relevant documents required for the hearing of the judicial review whether or not you file a skeleton argument. The bundle must be filed with the court and served on the other parties not less than 21 working days before the hearing.

NB: Two copies of the bundle are required by the Court when the application is to be heard by a Divisional Court.

NB: The bundle must also include those documents required by the defendant and any other party who is to make representations at the hearing.

Section 14: what if I need to make an application to the court for further orders/directions after the grant of permission?

14.1 Where case management decisions or directions are sought after permission has been granted, application should be made by way of an application under CPR Part 23, using Form PF244 – Administrative Court Office. You will be required to pay a fee for such application (currently £80.00, or £45.00 if all parties provide their written consent to the order being made), unless you are entitled to fee remission (in which case you should complete and submit a form EX160 with you application).

Section 15: can my substantive application be determined without the need for a hearing?

15.1 The court may decide a claim for judicial review without a hearing where all parties agree (CPR Part 54.18).

Section 16: what do I need to do if the proceedings settle by consent prior to the substantive hearing of the application?

16.1 If you reach agreement with the other parties as to the terms of the final order to be made in your claim, you must file at the court a document (with 2 copies) signed by all the parties setting out the terms of the proposed agreed order.

NB: There is a fee of £45.00 payable on lodging the consent order, unless you are entitled to fee remission, in which case you must complete and submit a Form EX 160 (Application for a Fee Remission) with your application.

NB: If you agree with the other parties that a mandatory order etc. is required, the draft order should be accompanied by a statement of reasons (i.e. a short statement of the matters relied on as justifying the proposed agreed order) and copies of any authorities or statutory provisions relied on. If settlement is reached before permission is considered, the draft consent order must include provision for permission to be granted.

NB: Such a statement is not required where the agreement as to disposal (usually by way of withdrawal of the application) requires an order for costs or a detailed assessment of the Claimant's Legal Services Commission costs - in those circumstances the parties should file a draft consent order setting out the terms of settlement signed by all parties.

16.2 The court will consider the documents submitted and will make the order if it is satisfied that the order should be made. If the court is not satisfied that the order should be made, the court will give directions and may direct that a hearing date be set for the matter to be considered further. Section 17

What if I want to discontinue the proceedings at any stage?

Before service of the claim form etc, on the other parties,

17.1 If you have not yet served any of the parties with the sealed claim form and accompanying documents you may discontinue the proceedings by notifying the Court in writing of your intention to do so. The Court will accept a letter of withdrawal provided that you confirm in writing that you have not effected service on the parties.

After service of the claim form etc. on the other parties,

17.2 Discontinuance of a claim is governed by CPR Part 38. Discontinuance renders you liable for the costs incurred by the other parties until the date of discontinuance.

17.3 There is a right to discontinue a claim at any time, except where:

- An interim injunction has been granted or an undertaking has been given – in those circumstances the permission of the court is required to discontinue the proceedings (an example of this would be where bail had been granted pending determination of the application for judicial review)
- Interim payment has been made by defendant - in those circumstances the consent of the defendant or the permission of the court is required to discontinue the proceedings
- There is more than one claimant - in those circumstances the consent of every other claimant or the permission of the court is required to discontinue the proceedings.

17.4 If you wish to discontinue the proceedings at any stage after the service of those proceedings upon the other parties you must file a Notice of Discontinuance in the requisite form (N279) at the relevant Administrative Court Office and serve a copy on every other party.

17.5 A defendant may apply to set aside the Notice of Discontinuance, within 28 days of being served with it (CPR Part 38.4).

NB: If the parties require any order for costs, then a draft order setting out the terms of the order sought is required. A Notice of Discontinuance would not be appropriate in those circumstances.

Section 18: will I be responsible for the costs of the defendant and/or the interested parties if my application is unsuccessful?

18.1 The general rule is that the party losing a substantive claim for judicial review will be ordered to pay the costs of the other parties. However, the Judge considering the matter has discretion to deal with the issue of costs as he/she considers appropriate in all of the circumstances.

NB: Costs may be awarded in respect of an unsuccessful paper application. Any application by the defendant/interested party for costs will normally be made in the Acknowledgment of Service.

Section 19: What can I do if I am unhappy with the Judge's decision?
Civil matters
Appeal after refusal of permission
19.1 If you are unhappy with the Court's decision in a civil matter you can appeal to the Court of Appeal Civil Division (with permission of the Court of Appeal (CPR Part 52.15)). Application to the Court of Appeal for permission to Appeal must be made within 7 days of the refusal by the Administrative Court of permission to apply for judicial review.

Appeal after substantive hearing
19.2 In substantive applications, permission to appeal may be sought from the Administrative Court when it determines the claim for judicial review. If an application for permission to appeal is not made at the conclusion of the case, the application for permission to appeal must be made to the Court of Appeal Civil Division within 21 days (CPR Part 52.3 & 52.4).

19.3 Guidance as to procedure should be sought from the Civil Appeals Office, Royal Courts of Justice, Strand, London, WC2A 2LL.

Criminal matters
Appeal after refusal of permission
19.4 There is no further remedy in the domestic courts after a refusal of permission by the Administrative Court.

Appeal after substantive hearing
19.5 If you are unhappy with the Court's decision in a substantive claim for judicial review in a criminal matter, you can appeal to the Supreme Court but only with the leave of the Administrative Court or the Supreme Court and such leave may only be granted if:
(a) The Administrative Court certifies that a point of law of general public importance is involved in its decision; and
(b) It appears to the Administrative Court or the Supreme Court that the point is one which ought to be considered by the Supreme Court. (see The Administration of Justice Act 1960 s1).

Section 20: where can I get advice about procedural matters?
20.1 If in doubt about any procedural matter you can contact the relevant Administrative Court Office, telephone numbers below. Court staff cannot give legal advice as to the merits of a case.
- Birmingham Civil Justice Centre – 0121 250 6319;
- Cardiff Civil Justice Centre – 029 2037 6460;
- Leeds Combined Court Centre – 0113 306 2578;
- Manchester Civil Justice Centre – 0161 240 5313;
- The Royal Courts of Justice in London – 020 7947 6655.

20.2 The forms referred to in this guidance can be downloaded from the Justice website (www.justice.gov.uk).

GUIDANCE NOTES ON COMPLETING THE JUDICIAL REVIEW CLAIM FORM (N461)[5]

Set out overleaf are notes to help you complete the form. You should read the notes to each section carefully before you begin to complete that particular section.

Use a separate sheet if you need more space for your answers, marking clearly which section the information refers to.

If you do not have all the documents or information you need for your claim, you must not allow this to delay sending or taking the form to the Administrative Court Office within the correct time. Complete the form as fully as possible and provide what documents you have. The notes to section 9 will explain more about what you have to do in these circumstances.

The Court and venue

- CPR part 54 – claims for Judicial Review are dealt with by the Administrative Court.
- Subject to the considerations in Practice Direction 54D 5.2, the general expectation is that proceedings will be administered and determined in the region in which the claimant has closest connection.
- Where the claim is proceeding in the Administrative Court in **London**, documents must be filed in the Administrative Court Office, Room C315, Royal Courts of Justice, Strand, London, WC2A 2LL.
- Where the claim is proceeding in the Administrative Court in **Birmingham**, documents must be filed in the Administrative Court Office, Birmingham Civil Justice Centre, Priory Courts, 33 Bull Street, Birmingham B4 6DS.
- Where the claim is proceeding in the Administrative Court in **Wales**, documents must be filed in the Administrative Court Office, Cardiff Civil Justice Centre, 2 Park Street, Cardiff, CF10 1ET.
- Where the claim is proceeding in the Administrative Court in **Leeds**, documents must be filed in the Administrative Court Office, Leeds Combined Court Centre, 1 Oxford Row, Leeds, LS1 3BG.
- Where the claim is proceeding in the Administrative Court in **Manchester**, documents must be filed in the Administrative Court Office, Manchester Civil Justice Centre, 1 Bridge Street West, Manchester, M3 3FX.

Time limit for filing a claim

- Unless Section 18 Practice Direction 54 applies in relation to the deferral of removal, the claim must be filed promptly and in any event no later than three months after the grounds to make the claim first arose.

Note: Section 18 Practice Direction 54 and Practice Direction 54D are set out on our website (www.justice.gov.uk). Should you need a hard copies of these Practice Directions, please contact the Administrative Court office or your local Citizen's Advice Bureau.

If you need help to complete the form you should consult a solicitor or your local Citizen's Advice Bureau.

Section 1: details of the claimants and defendants
Give full name(s) and address(es) to which all documents relating to the judicial review are to be sent. Include contact information e.g. telephone numbers and any other reference numbers.

Section 2: details of other interested parties
Where the claim for judicial review relates to proceedings in a court or tribunal, any other parties to those proceedings must be named in the claim form as interested parties. Full details of interested parties must be included in the claim form.

For example, if you were a defendant in a criminal case in the Magistrates or Crown Court and are making a claim for judicial review of a decision in that case, the prosecution must be named as an interested party.

In a claim which does not relate to a decision of a court or tribunal, you should give details of any persons directly affected by the decision you wish to challenge.

Section 3: details of the decision to be judicially reviewed
Give details of the decision you seek to have judicially reviewed. Give the name of the court, tribunal, person or body whose decision you are seeking to judicially review, and the date on which the decision was made.

Section 4: permission to proceed with a claim for judicial review
This section must be completed. You must answer all the questions and give further details where required.

Section 5: detailed statement of grounds
Set out, in detail, the grounds on which you contend the decision should be set aside or varied.

Section 6: Aarhus Convention Claim
Indicate whether you contend that this is a claim to which the Aarhus Convention applies. If so, then unless you indicate that you do not wish the costs limits in

CPR 45.43 to apply, those limits will apply. If you indicate that the claim is an Aarhus Convention claim then you should set out the grounds for contention.

Section 7: details of remedy
Complete this section stating what remedy you are seeking:
(a) a mandatory order;
(b) a prohibiting order;
(c) a quashing order; or
(d) an injunction restraining a person from acting in any office in which he is not entitled to act.

A claim for damages may be included but only if you are seeking one of the orders set out above.

Section 8: other applications
You may wish to make additional applications to the Administrative Court in connection with your claim for Judicial Review. Any other applications may

be made either in the claim form or in a separate application (Form PF244). This form can be obtained from any of the Administrative Court Offices listed overleaf or from our website at www.justice.gov.uk.

Section 9: statement of facts relied on

The facts on which you are basing your claim should be set out in this section of the form, or in a separate document attached to the form. It should contain a numbered list of the points that you intend to rely on at the hearing. Refer at each point to any documents you are filing in support of your claim

Section 10: supporting documents

Do not delay filing your claim for judicial review. If you have not been able to obtain any of the documents listed in this section within the time limits referred to on the previous page, complete the notice as best you can and ensure the claim is filed on time. Set out the reasons why you have not been able to obtain any of the information or documents and give the date when you expect them to be available.

FORM N461

| Click here to reset form | Click here to print form |

Judicial Review
Claim Form

In the High Court of Justice
Administrative Court

Notes for guidance are available which explain
how to complete the judicial review claim
form. Please read them carefully before you
complete the form.

For Court use only	
Administrative Court Reference No.	
Date filed	

Seal

SECTION 1 Details of the claimant(s) and defendant(s)

Claimant(s) name and address(es)

┌name─────────
│
└─────────────

┌address──────
│
│
└─────────────

┌Telephone no.─── ┌Fax no.───
│ │
└─────────── └───────

┌E-mail address───
│
└─────────────

Claimant's or claimant's solicitors' address to which
documents should be sent.

┌name─────────
│
└─────────────

┌address──────
│
│
└─────────────

┌Telephone no.─── ┌Fax no.───
│ │
└─────────── └───────

┌E-mail address───
│
└─────────────

Claimant's Counsel's details

┌name─────────
│
└─────────────

┌address──────
│
│
└─────────────

┌Telephone no.─── ┌Fax no.───
│ │
└─────────── └───────

┌E-mail address───
│
└─────────────

1st Defendant

┌name─────────
│
└─────────────

Defendant's or (where known) Defendant's solicitors'
address to which documents should be sent.

┌name─────────
│
└─────────────

┌address──────
│
│
└─────────────

┌Telephone no.─── ┌Fax no.───
│ │
└─────────── └───────

┌E-mail address───
│
└─────────────

2nd Defendant

┌name─────────
│
└─────────────

Defendant's or (where known) Defendant's solicitors'
address to which documents should be sent.

┌name─────────
│
└─────────────

┌address──────
│
│
└─────────────

┌Telephone no.─── ┌Fax no.───
│ │
└─────────── └───────

┌E-mail address───
│
└─────────────

N461 Judicial review claim form (04.13)   1 of 6   © Crown copyright 2013

SECTION 2 Details of other interested parties

Include name and address and, if appropriate, details of DX, telephone or fax numbers and e-mail

name

name

address

address

Telephone no.

Fax no.

Telephone no.

Fax no.

E-mail address

E-mail address

SECTION 3 Details of the decision to be judicially reviewed

Decision:

Date of decision:

Name and address of the court, tribunal, person or body who made the decision to be reviewed.

name

address

SECTION 4 Permission to proceed with a claim for judicial review

I am seeking permission to proceed with my claim for Judicial Review.

Is this application being made under the terms of Section 18 Practice Direction 54 (Challenging removal)?   ☐ Yes ☐ No

Are you making any other applications? If Yes, complete Section 8.   ☐ Yes ☐ No

Is the claimant in receipt of a Community Legal Service Fund (CLSF) certificate?   ☐ Yes ☐ No

Are you claiming exceptional urgency, or do you need this application determined within a certain time scale? If Yes, complete Form N463 and file this with your application.   ☐ Yes ☐ No

Have you complied with the pre-action protocol? If No, give reasons for non-compliance in the box below.   ☐ Yes ☐ No

Have you issued this claim in the region with which you have the closest connection? (Give any additional reasons for wanting it to be dealt with in this region in the box below). If No, give reasons in the box below.   ☐ Yes ☐ No

Does the claim include any issues arising from the Human Rights Act 1998?
If Yes, state the articles which you contend have been breached in the box below. ☐ Yes ☐ No

SECTION 5 Detailed statement of grounds

☐ set out below ☐ attached

SECTION 6 Aarhus Convention claim

I contend that this claim is an Aarhus Convention claim ☐ Yes ☐ No

If Yes, indicate in the following box if you do not wish the costs limits
under CPR 45.43 to apply.

If you have indicated that the claim is an Aarhus claim set out the grounds below

SECTION 7 Details of remedy (including any interim remedy) being sought

SECTION 8 Other applications

I wish to make an application for:-

SECTION 9 Statement of facts relied on

Statement of Truth

I believe (The claimant believes) that the facts stated in this claim form are true.

Full name_____

Name of claimant's solicitor's firm _____

Signed_____ Position or office held_____

      Claimant ('s solicitor)   (if signing on behalf of firm or company)

SECTION 10 Supporting documents

If you do not have a document that you intend to use to support your claim, identify it, give the date when you expect it to be available and give reasons why it is not currently available in the box below.

Please tick the papers you are filing with this claim form and any you will be filing later.

☐ Statement of grounds   ☐ included   ☐ attached

☐ Statement of the facts relied on   ☐ included   ☐ attached

☐ Application to extend the time limit for filing the claim form   ☐ included   ☐ attached

☐ Application for directions   ☐ included   ☐ attached

☐ Any written evidence in support of the claim or
  application to extend time

☐ Where the claim for judicial review relates to a decision of
  a court or tribunal, an approved copy of the reasons for
  reaching that decision

☐ Copies of any documents on which the claimant
  proposes to rely

☐ A copy of the legal aid or CSLF certificate *(if legally represented)*

☐ Copies of any relevant statutory material

☐ A list of essential documents for advance reading by
  the court *(with page references to the passages relied upon)*

If Section 18 Practice Direction 54 applies, please tick the relevant box(es) below to indicate which papers you are filing with this claim form:

☐ a copy of the removal directions and the decision to which   ☐ included   ☐ attached
  the application relates

☐ a copy of the documents served with the removal directions
  including any documents which contains the Immigration and   ☐ included   ☐ attached
  Nationality Directorate's factual summary of the case

☐ a detailed statement of the grounds   ☐ included   ☐ attached

Reasons why you have not supplied a document and date when you expect it to be available:-

Signed _____ Claimant ('s Solicitor)_____

Click here to print form

PRACTICE STATEMENT (ADMINISTRATIVE COURT: LISTING AND URGENT CASES)

Scott Baker J
February 2002

Scott Baker J, the lead judge of the Administrative Court, delivered the annual statement of the Administrative Court at the sitting of the court.

1. Nominated judges

There are presently 25 judges nominated by Lord Woolf CJ to sit in the Administrative Court. They include two judges of the Chancery Division and two of the Family Division who act as additional judges of the Queen's Bench Division when dealing with Administrative Court cases. A list of those currently nominated is attached at Annex A. The Administrative Court now has regular use of six courtrooms – courts 1, 2, 3, 10, 27 and 28. Routinely there are approximately eight judges allocated to single judge sittings and one or two Divisional Courts sit.

2. Modern judicial review

October 2000 saw the introduction of the Administrative Court and two fundamental changes to the work of the former Crown Office List – the introduction of CPR Part 54 and the coming into force of the Human Rights Act 1998. There has now been time to assess the impact of those changes.

Part 54 CPR followed the recommendations of the Bowman Review and has reformed the judicial review process. There are two particular areas of note. First, the requirement to serve the defendant and interested parties with the claim form and the ability of those parties to put summary grounds of defence before the Court prior to the Court considering whether permission should be granted to proceed. This change has enabled the Court to dispose at the paper stage of many cases that are bound to fail. Secondly, the introduction of consideration of all applications for permission on paper in the first instance has meant a more structured allocation of cases to judges. Court time is now allocated for consideration of paper applications. The rate of renewal after refusal – an unknown factor in the Bowman recommendations –has stabilised at around 50%. Paper consideration has been a major contributor to the reductions in waiting times achieved over the past year. I shall return to the subject of waiting times.

Of the cases received from 2 October 2000 to 31 December 2001 some 19% were identified as raising HRA issues. The Act does not, however, appear to have generated a large increase in the receipts. Receipts for 2001 showed an overall increase of 11% on 2000. The increase was attributable to an increase in civil judicial review, in particular in asylum cases (2159 compared to 1876 – an increase of 15%). There have been a number of high profile cases raising human rights issues such as *Alconbury* – the issue of the planning appeal system and *Kebilene* – the issue of pre HRA prosecutions.

3. Performance of the court in 2001

During 2001 there were 274 Divisional Court sitting days, 1447 Single Judge sitting days and 102 Deputy High Court judge sitting days.

The statistics for 2001 show an increase in receipts but an improvement in waiting times

Receipts: 5298 (4407 civil judicial review)
Disposals: 5398 cases were determined in 2001

Adjourned Generally	85
Determined By Court	2564
Discontinuance	372
No Motion after grant of permission (pre Bowman cases)	28
Not Renewed	828
Withdrawn	1521
Grand total	5398

Waiting times during 2001
The average waiting time for a decision on an application for *permission to apply for judicial review was eight weeks* (from lodging to decision). The average waiting time for a *substantive determination (of all types of case) was 20 weeks* (from lodging to decision). Expedited cases are being listed in a matter of weeks.

Legal representatives should bear these figures in mind when preparing cases.

In the light of the performance of the court a short warned list has been reintroduced to ensure the court is fully listed and time is not wasted when cases settle at the last minute. Parties in cases which are short warned will be notified that their case is likely to be listed from a specified date, and that they may be called into the list at less than a day's notice from that date. Approximately six cases are short warned for each week. If the case does not get on during that period, a date as soon as possible after that period will be fixed in consultation with the parties.

For the benefit of users the current listing policy of the Administrative Court is annexed to this statement (Annex C).

4. Users group

The Administrative Court Users Group provides a useful forum for discussion between the court users, the court staff and the nominated judges. Some of the forthcoming initiatives I am about to announce resulted from those discussions.

I intend for the group to continue to meet each term. I welcome suggestions for the agenda and the feedback which court users are uniquely placed to give.

5. Use of alternative means of resolution

I draw the attention of litigants and legal advisers to the decision of the Court of Appeal in *R (Cowl) v Plymouth City Council (Practice Note)* [2001] EWCA Civ 1935, [2002] 1 WLR 803. The nominated judges are fully committed to resolving disputes by alternative means where appropriate and are exploring ways of promoting this.

6. Forthcoming initiatives
Pre-action protocol for judicial review
The protocol was published in December 2001 and comes into force on 4 March 2002. Any claims for judicial review lodged on or after that date must indicate that the protocol has been complied with. Reasons for noncompliance must be given in the claim form. The form is currently being reconsidered in the light of the experience of the past 16 months and the comments of users. The revised form will be available on the Court Service website shortly.

Urgent cases procedure
CPR Pt 54 makes no express provision for urgent applications for permission to apply for judicial review to be made orally. As the result of users' concerns I now issue guidance on the procedure to be applied for urgent applications and for interim injunctions. Advocates must comply with this guidance; and where a manifestly inappropriate application is made, consideration will be given to a wasted costs order. The full terms of the guidance and the form for use in this procedure are annexed to this statement (Annex B).

1. The Administrative Court currently allocates paper applications for judicial review on a daily basis and one judge also act as the 'urgent judge'.
2. Where a claimant makes an application for the permission application C to be heard as a matter of urgency and/or seeks an interim injunction, he must complete a prescribed form which states:
   (a) the need for urgency;
   (b) the timescale sought for the consideration of the permission application, eg within 72 hours or sooner if necessary; and
   (c) the date by which the substantive hearing should take place.
3. Where an interim injunction is sought, a claimant must, in addition, provide
   (a) a draft order; and
   (b) the grounds for the injunction.
4. The claimant must serve (by fax and post) the claim form and application for urgency on the defendant and interested parties, advising them of the application and that they may make representations.
5. Where an interim injunction is sought, the claimant must serve (by fax and post) the draft order and grounds for the application on the defendant and interested parties, advising them of the application and that they may A make representations.
6. A judge will consider the application within the time requested and may make such order as he considers appropriate.
7. If the judge directs that an oral hearing take place within a specified time the representatives of the parties and the Administrative Court will liaise to fix a permission hearing within the time period directed.

E-mail addresses for use for urgent post
The Administrative Court Office now has e-mail addresses for *urgent post.* The addresses are not available for formal filing of documents. When using these addresses the office opening hours must be borne in mind and it cannot be assumed that mail sent after 4.30 p m will be opened before 9am on the following day. The e-mail addresses are:

For mail relating to paper applications: Administrativecourtoffice.generaloffice@courtservice.gsi.gov.uk

For mail relating to listed cases: Administrativecourtoffice.listoffice@courtservice.gsi.gov.uk

For mail relating to court orders: Administrativecourtoffice.courtclerks@courtservice.gsi.gov.uk

Revised renewal form – judicial review
With immediate effect, when completing the form used for renewing applications for permission to apply for judicial review, claimants must set out the grounds for renewal in the light of the reasons given by the single judge when refusing permission on the papers.

Annex A: The Administrative Court
The Hon Mr Justice Turner
The Hon Mr Justice Scott Baker
The Hon Mr Justice Hidden
The Hon Mr Justice Forbes
The Hon Mr Justice Mitchell
The Hon Mr Justice Evans Lombe
The Hon Mr Justice Harrison
The Hon Mr Justice Lightman
The Hon Mr Justice Collins
The Hon Mr Justice Maurice Kay
The Hon Mr Justice Hooper
The Hon Mr Justice Newman
The Hon Mr Justice Moses
The Hon Mr Justice Sullivan
The Hon Mr Justice Richards
The Hon Mr Justice Burton
The Hon Mr Justice Jackson
The Hon Mr Justice Elias
The Hon Mr Justice Silber
The Hon Mr Justice Munby
The Hon Mr Justice Stanley Burnton
The Hon Mr Justice Ouseley
The Hon Mr Justice Wilson
The Hon Mr Justice Crane
The Hon Mr Justice Keith

Annex B: The procedure for urgent applications to the Administrative Court[6]

3. In October 2000 CPR Part 54 was introduced which makes no express provision for urgent applications for permission to apply for judicial review to be made orally.

4. The Administrative Court is now issuing the following guidance on the procedure to be applied for urgent applications and for interim injunctions. It is

---

6 Note numbering in Annex B is inconsistent. This is taken from the original document.

the duty of the advocate to comply with this guidance; and where a manifestly inappropriate application is made, consideration will be given to a wasted costs order.

5. The Administrative Court currently allocates paper applications for judicial review on a daily basis and one Judge also act as the 'Urgent Judge'.
6. Where a claimant makes an application for the permission application to be heard as a matter of urgency and/or seeks an interim injunction, he must complete a prescribed form which states:
   (d) the need for urgency;
   (e) the timescale sought for the consideration of the permission application, e.g. within 72 hours or sooner if necessary (see paragraph 8 below); and
   (f) the date by which the substantive hearing should take place.
5. Where an interim injunction is sought, a claimant must, in addition, provide:
   (c) a draft order; and
   (d) the grounds for the injunction.
10. The claimant must serve (by FAX and post) the claim form and application for urgency on the defendant and interested parties, advising them of the application and that they may make representations.
11. Where an interim injunction is sought, the claimant must serve (by FAX and post) the draft order and grounds for the application on the defendant and interested parties, advising them of the application and that they may make representations.
12. A Judge will consider the application within the time requested and may make such order as he considers appropriate.
13. If the Judge directs that an oral hearing take place within a specified time the representatives of the parties and the Administrative Court will liaise to fix a permission hearing within the time period directed.

Administrative Court Office Reference Number: CO/

REQUEST FOR URGENT CONSIDERATION THIS FORM MUST BE COMPLETED BY THE ADVOCATE FOR THE CLAIMANT

THIS FORM AND THE CLAIM FORM MUST BE SERVED BY THE CLAIMANT'S SOLICITORS, BY FAX AND POST, ON THE DEFENDANT AND INTERESTED PARTIES

NAME OF CLAIMANT:
Name, address and fax number of solicitor acting for the claimant
Name of counsel/advocate acting for the claimant

NAME OF DEFENDANT:
Date of service of this form and claim form Fax number served

NAME OF INTERESTED PARTY(IES):
Date of service of this form and claim form
Fax number served

1. REASONS FOR URGENCY

2. PROPOSED TIMETABLE
(a) The application for permission should be considered within hours/days

(b) Abridgement of time is sought for the lodging of acknowledgments of service

(c) If permission is granted, a substantive hearing is sought by (date)

3. INTERIM RELIEF

Interim relief is sought in terms of the attached draft order on the following grounds:

SIGNED:

ADVOCATE FOR THE CLAIMANT

DATE

NOTE TO THE DEFENDANT AND INTERESTED PARTIES

Representations as to the urgency of the claim may be made to the Administrative Court Office by fax: 020 7947 6802.

Annex C: Listing Policy in the Administrative Court February 2002

Fixing substantive hearings

Where a case is ready to be heard substantively, it enters a warned list and all parties are informed of this by letter. Some cases require an early hearing date and take priority over other cases waiting to be fixed – these enter the expedited warned list.

Where counsel has been placed on the court record, their chambers are contacted by the Administrative Court list office in order to agree a convenient date for the hearing. Counsel's clerks are offered a range of dates and have 48 hours to take up one of the dates offered. If counsel's clerk fails to contact the list office within 48 hours, the list office will fix the hearing on one of the dates that was offered, without further notice and the parties will be notified of that fixture by letter. Where a hearing is listed in this way the hearing will only be vacated by the Administrative Court Office if both parties consent. Failing that, a formal application for adjournment must be made (on notice to all parties) to the court. The same procedure is followed where a claimant is in person.

Short warned list

Whilst the Administrative Court usually gives fixed dates for hearings, there is also a need to short warn a number of cases to cover the large number of settlements that occur in the list. Parties in cases that are selected to be short warned will be notified that their case is likely to be listed from a specified date, and that they may be called into the list at less than a days notice from that date. Approximately six cases are short warned for any specified week. If the case does not get on during that period, a date as soon as possible after that period will be fixed in consultation with the parties.

Vacating fixtures

There are occasions when circumstances, outside the control of the list office, may necessitate them having to vacate a hearing at very short notice. Sometimes this can be as late as 4.30 p m the day before the case is listed. This could be as a result of a case unexpectedly overrunning, a judge becoming unavailable, or other reasons. In deciding which hearing has to be vacated, the list office will assess the cases listed for the following day and take the following factors into consideration:

- Which case(s), if removed, will cause the least disruption to the list (the aim is to adjourn as few cases as possible, ideally one)
- How many cases need to be adjourned given the reduced listing time available
- Have any matters previously been adjourned by the court
- The urgency and age(s) of the matter(s) listed
- Where the parties and/or their representatives are based (this is relevant as in some cases the parties travel to London the day before the hearing)
- Whether it is appropriate to "float" the case in the event of another listed matter going short (cases will not be floated without the consent of the parties)
- The likelihood of a judge becoming available to hear a floated case

After taking these factors into account, the list office decide upon the case(s) which will have to be refixed and will inform the parties concerned that their hearing has been vacated. The case record will be noted that the matter is not to be adjourned by the court again. The court will also endeavour to refix the case on the next available date convenient to the parties.

Index